THE BIBLICAL CANON

Its Origin, Transmission, and Authority

Lee Martin McDonald

The Biblical Canon: Its Origin, Transmission, and Authority

P. O. Box 3473
Peabody, Massachusetts 01961-3473

ISBN 978-1-56563-925-6

The Biblical Canon: Its Origin, Transmission, and Authority is revised from *The Formation of the Christian Biblical Canon,* Revised and Expanded Edition, © 1995.

Printed in the United States of America

First Printing — January 2007

Library of Congress Cataloging-in-Publication Data

McDonald, Lee Martin, 1942–
The biblical canon : its origin, transmission, and authority / Lee Martin McDonald. — [Updated & rev. 3rd ed.].
p. cm.
Rev. ed. of: Formation of the Christian biblical canon. c1988.
Includes bibliographical references and indexes.
ISBN-13: 978-1-56563-925-6 (alk. paper)
1. Bible—Canon. I. McDonald, Lee Martin, 1942– Formation of the Christian biblical canon. II. Title.
BS465.M38 2006
220.1'2—dc22

2006021312

THE BIBLICAL CANON

To Mary
My lifetime companion, best friend,
and the most patient and caring person I have ever met!

Table of Contents

Part 2: Hebrew Bible/Old Testament Canon

Part 3: New Testament Canon

Preface to the Third Edition

MUCH HAS COME TO LIGHT THROUGH NEW RESEARCH SINCE THE SECOND EDItion of this volume was published. Many contributions to canon formation have been published, and more information on the primary ancient literature has come to my attention since 1995. Similarly, a few earlier conclusions espoused both by me and others whose work informed mine are no longer tenable. As a result, this third edition is overdue, even though many of the most important conclusions reached in previous editions remain the same. I believe that the conclusions about canon formation have been strengthened considerably with this new edition. It reflects a fresh attempt to understand some of the many perplexing questions related to the origins and canonicity of the Bible. The vast majority of this volume has been completely rewritten, and many new sources consulted. I am hopeful that its readers will appreciate the additional resources that have been brought to bear on the highly complex issues that still elude final resolution.

This volume had its origin in a term paper written while I was a student at Harvard University in 1982. I subsequently expanded the paper into a thesis that was read and approved by Helmut Koester and George MacRae. Interestingly, I did not approach the subject with a thesis in mind that I wanted to prove so much as with a natural curiosity about the truth of canon formation. Most of what I had learned earlier about the origins and stabilization or canonization of the Bible simply did not square with new information I had learned. I became intrigued with the subject when a layperson at a church I pastored asked me some straightforward questions about books that did not make it into our Bible. My inability to answer these questions involved me in a study that took me to Harvard and has involved me in research on the topic for the last twenty-four years.

Since I began this journey of inquiry, I have been guided by a basic premise that has served me well, namely, I have been willing to challenge unsubstantiated claims about the origins of the Bible. I have appreciated Jacob Neusner's dictum that says unambiguously: "What we cannot show, we do not know."[1] In what follows, I have been careful not to make assumptions that I could not back from the primary evidence. Too many scholars are willing to accept untested or unsupported conclusions that lead them to make anachronistic statements about what did and did not take place in the time of Jesus. I am not convinced that scholarship advances significantly if we do not force ourselves to root our conclusions in the primary literature of antiquity. We cannot advance our understanding of this or any complex subject with our untested assumptions cluttering the way.

In terms of the OT biblical canon, many new studies on the Dead Sea Scrolls have emerged in the last fifteen years that have helped build a stronger case that the move toward fixing or stabilizing the contents of the Hebrew Bible, the OT, came near the end of the first century C.E. for the Jewish community and much later for the Christians since the Jewish influence on the Christians was largely over after 62 C.E., when the Christians left Jerusalem for Pella on the east side of the Jordan). The canonizing process *began* in the Jewish community, perhaps influenced by other canons of literature established in the famous library of Alexandria, Egypt, and was largely settled for some Jews at the end of the first century, but for the majority of them not until the third and fourth centuries C.E. The process of determining which books are Scripture and belong in the OT canon was roughly completed by the mid-fourth century. In what follows, I strengthen the case that the first followers of Jesus never received from him either the notion of a closed biblical canon or any listing of the books that belonged to it. I continue to argue that the process of canonization was not complete until the fourth and fifth centuries for most of Christendom.

Since the publication of the second edition, I have learned much from James A. Sanders, James VanderKam, Marty Abegg, Peter Flint, J. J. Collins, Julio Trebolle Barrera, Florentino García Martínez, Eugene Ulrich, Emanuel Tov, and several others about the scope of the Bible at Qumran during the first century C.E. In terms of the Jewish and Greco-Roman context of early Christianity, I have also benefited significantly from the research of Bruce Chilton, Helmut Koester, Anthony J. Saldarini, E. P. Sanders, Martin Hengel, and my colleague Craig A. Evans.

I am also more familiar now with the rabbinic tradition than I was when I first investigated the origins of the biblical canon. Earlier I was largely dependent upon the work of Emil Shürer, George Foot Moore, Sid Leiman, and others of an earlier generation for knowledge of the Jewish context of early Christianity, but much more is now known in the scholarly community about the context of early Christianity, and this edition reflects some of that newly available research. This new data has a significant bear-

---

[1] This phrase is the subtitle of Neusner's *Rabbinic Literature and the New Testament*. See also idem, "Mishna in Philosophical Context," 302–3.

ing on our understanding of the biblical canon and its formation. For example, we are finally beyond the age of speaking about a "normative Judaism" in the first century and we can now focus our attention instead on the common or shared characteristics of the various Judaisms of the first century, of which two—Pharisaic Judaism and Christianity—are the primary survivors.

The significant role that the rabbinic teachers of the second through the fifth centuries played in the final shape of the Hebrew Scriptures was not as clear earlier as it is now. It is finally possible to do electronic searches of the early church fathers, Dead Sea Scrolls, Josephus, Mishnah, Tosefta, and other Jewish writings, as well as most noncanonical Jewish and Christian writings such as the apocryphal and pseudepigraphal writings that informed both Judaism and early Christianity in their respective formative stages.

As a result of increased familiarity with these writings, more reliable information is available, and our knowledge of the context of early Christianity and the formative stages of the Bible is greater. Much of what we know in these areas today is due in large measure to the efforts of Jacob Neusner, James Charlesworth, J. K. Elliott, Jack Lightstone, David Kraemer, Louis Feldman, Joseph Fitzmyer, and others who opened some previously closed doors. We are all in their debt.

Likewise, the church fathers in the second to fourth centuries authoritatively cited many ancient texts that are now identified as apocryphal or pseudepigraphal (both Jewish and Christian). Much of this literature has been known for a long time, but its meaning and influence are better known to us today as a result of R. H. Charles's *Apocrypha and Pseudepigrapha of the Old Testament,* J. H. Charlesworth's *Old Testament Pseudepigrapha,* J. K. Elliott's *The Apocryphal New Testament,* and Wilhelm Schneemelcher's *New Testament Apocrypha.*

There is also a better understanding today of the importance of the Septuagint than was previously acknowledged. Both Martin Hengel and Emanuel Tov make clear the importance of this information for understanding the origins and text of the OT. Nevertheless, few Christian scholars appear to appreciate that the first Christian Bible was the Septuagint (LXX), the Greek translation of the Hebrew Scriptures. Even in the NT writings themselves, more than 90 percent of the quotations from the OT come from the Greek Bible! That has clear implications for canon formation. Remarkably few seminaries have classes on the LXX, and they prefer instead to focus exclusively on the Hebrew OT for ministry preparation. Septuagint scholars have recently provided fresh translations and critical appraisals of several ancient texts of the LXX and apocryphal and pseudepigraphal literature. Without their important contributions, no serious advances can be made in our understanding of the formation of the biblical canon. The more familiar we are with these works, the more obvious it becomes that we have to revisit the important canonical questions that this area of inquiry raises.

A significant change in canonical thinking took place following Albert Sundberg's foundational research in the canons of both Testaments. Since then (the mid-1960s), much more information has come to light that might not have surfaced had Sundberg not spurred the scholarly community into rethinking many of its earlier "assured" conclusions about the origins of the biblical canon. He essentially dismantled the familiar old Alexandrian canon hypothesis that tried to account for the larger Christian canon of OT books adopted and used by the early Christians. Because of Sundberg, that view has now been retired.

While many scholars accepted Sundberg's views on the myth of a so-called Alexandrian canon, many initially rejected his views on the fourth-century dating of the Muratorian Fragment with an eastern provenance. Nevertheless, he rightly challenged the centrality of this Latin text, which was poorly translated from an earlier Greek text. A shift in thinking has taken place, however, and several other scholars have gravitated toward his position and reinforced his basic arguments. Geoffrey Hahneman and Harry Y. Gamble are among the most notable to support Sundberg's basic views. Sundberg saw that the Muratorian Fragment had become central to an indefensible position that dated the NT canon at the end of the second century C.E. No one before Sundberg challenged so forcefully the scholarly consensus in these matters, and for that reason we are all in his debt.

Likewise, scholars like B. M. Metzger, Kurt Aland, Barbara Aland, E. J. Epp, J. K. Elliott, and Bart Ehrman have added greatly to our understanding of the importance of textual criticism as an invaluable resource on the canonization of the Bible. They are asking significant questions about the text and translation of the Bible. Textual scholars no longer have as much hope in recovering *the* original text (or the autographs), though that aim is not necessarily abandoned. Instead they are looking more for a history of the textual tradition behind individual books as well as more clarity on the most likely text of the Bible. In the past, biblical scholars frequently ignored text-critical work, but now textual scholars are making their work both more accessible and also more compelling. The results of their research have considerable importance for canon research, as we will see below.

Historically, canon discussions have been concerned almost exclusively with the books that made it into the biblical canon and those that did not. There has not been much interest in the text of those books or even their translation. The early church largely opted for the Greek Bible, with a later attempt to prepare an authoritative biblical translation of the Bible (Jerome's Latin Vulgate), nevertheless historically the church has never agreed on one single textual tradition on which to base all subsequent texts and translations of the Bible. It addressed primarily the question of which *books* belonged and which did not, but not which text or translation was authoritative for the church.

On a related note, why is it that very few manuscripts of the church contain all of the books of the Bible *and no others*? Those manuscripts that do have all of the books of the Bible often have *more* books in them than we find in the current Bible. Why? There is also a growing awareness of the lack of an authoritative text in the church, namely, which text is canonical and which ones are not? For example, we now know that the concluding verses of Mark's Gospel (16:9–20) are not original to it and that the original ending was probably lost (a majority of scholars today hold this view) or that Mark never finished it,[2] but what should we conclude about a book whose ending (and perhaps beginning also) might have been lost? Further, which translation(s) of the Bible today should be affirmed and read in the churches? The first two editions of this book did not focus much on these questions, and yet such inquiry is critical to a careful understanding of the biblical canon.

In terms of the NT, the trend in recent years has been away from saying that the NT was pretty well formed by the end of the second century. This is because there is a greater recognition that a lot of canonical activity took place during the second through fourth centuries, and it was largely in the fourth to sixth centuries that significant canon formation activity took place. For example, fewer scholars today think that Marcion constructed the first NT canon (the well-known thesis of Adolf von Harnack) and that the second century church simply corrected him by adding more books to his small collection. The challenges of the second century, including local persecution of Christians and the growth of heresy (Gnosticism, Marcion, and the Montanists), were not responded to by the establishment of a biblical canon in the second century, but rather by setting forth a "canon of faith" (*regula fidei*), namely, a creed that stated what was generally believed to be the true teaching of the church at that time. There was no firmly fixed biblical canon at the end of the second century, but rather several books of the NT—primarily the Gospels and several of Paul's Letters—were beginning to be called "Scripture."

For centuries, early church leaders cited a variety of noncanonical Jewish and Christian texts in an authoritative manner, some of which were initially welcomed by Christians as Scriptures but subsequently rejected. We see evidence of this in the writings of the church fathers and in the surviving biblical manuscripts from the fourth to sixth centuries.

More recently Harry Gamble has put us in his debt by showing the relevance of the development and use of the book (or codex) for an understanding of the origins of the Bible.[3] He asks whether the development of the codex or book affected the parameters of the biblical canon. As I will attempt to show, the valuable information that Gamble presents has considerable significance for our understanding of the canonization of the Bible.

---

[2] See Croy, *Mutilation of Mark's Gospel,* 174–77, for a helpful listing of scholars who hold this position.

[3] Gamble, *Books and Readers in the Early Church*.

It is also encouraging to see in recent years a growing interest in the processes of canonization and a significant amount of literature emerge arguing various positions on the origins and stabilization of the Bible. Because of the increase of research on this topic, some of the views that I expressed in earlier editions are no longer tenable, but others have been strengthened. For these reasons, I am grateful for the opportunity to advance my research on the origins and formation of the Bible to address these issues more carefully.

In the first and second editions of this book, I included a short section on the issue of canonical criticism, namely, the perspective that the believing communities attach to the biblical text. While several scholars suggest that I misunderstood Brevard Childs, others told me that I accurately reflected his position on the issues that I discussed, namely, which biblical text is canonical for the church today.[4] I argued against Childs's position on the earliest forms of the biblical text, which he appears to have largely rejected in favor of a later canonical text that became the authoritative text of the church. Discussion of this subject is no longer as relevant to what I hope to accomplish in this volume, and my attention is better focused on the biblical text and its historical development rather than on Childs's work. I might say, however, that while I disagree with some of Childs's conclusions, I find myself in substantial agreement with his understanding that the Bible is the church's book and not the academy's. Further, I agree with him that the Bible is best studied and lived out in the context of the community of faith from which it emerged and for whom it was written.

In terms of my responsibility in this project, I am reminded of a quip made by Ralph Martin a few years ago when a copy of his Word Biblical Commentary on 2 Corinthians was presented to him: "I have milked many cows to produce this volume, but the butter is all mine!" I could easily say that while I am indebted to many individuals who have been helpful in my understanding of the biblical canon, what you see in the pages that follow is mine—errors, misstatements, and all! Nevertheless, I would be remiss if I failed to mention those whose guidance over the years has helped me formulate questions, investigate matters, and draw conclusions that I may not have been able to draw without their counsel.

In terms of canon studies, I owe much to my mentor and friend, Helmut Koester of Harvard University, for his early guidance in my research on this project and for his continual encouragement over the years as I expanded my contributions to this subject. He graciously agreed to provide the foreword to the first two editions of this volume, and I con-

---

[4]One of the strongest criticisms of my work came from one of Childs's former doctoral students, Stephen B. Chapman, in some less-than-flattering comments in *Law and the Prophets,* 68–70, 108. I should note, however, that we have subsequently met and had a very good and amicable exchange over our different views on this subject.

tinue to learn from him, not only in terms of his scholarship but also his commitment to the church. I have also been greatly enriched by the many contributions that James A. Sanders has made to this subject. He raised questions that no one else was asking about how both Judaism and the early church got their Bibles, and he has mentored me in more ways than he can imagine. I have grown to appreciate him on two important levels. First, of course, he is an impeccable scholar who has helped me avoid many serious blunders in my own research, and for his help in this regard I am deeply grateful. More than this, however, I have found him to be a gentle spirit with a great deal of the grace that we read about in the Bible, and we have become friends. His grace comes out in his personal demeanor as well as in his preaching, one of his special passions. I was honored a few years ago when he invited me to speak to his students on the formation of the biblical canon. I kept saying to myself that it was strange to have "Mr. Canon" himself introduce me to talk about the canon! I was also privileged to have the opportunity to contribute a chapter to a Festschrift in his honor[5] and to share the editorial responsibilities with him for *The Canon Debate*. I greatly appreciate his friendship and wise counsel.

I would be remiss if I failed to mention the many courtesies extended to me by Hendrickson Publishers. They agreed to publish the second edition of the *Formation of the Christian Biblical Canon* in 1995, and once again they allow me the opportunity to improve on that earlier work, which this volume represents and replaces. Patrick Alexander and Shirley Decker-Lucke were most helpful in getting the second edition published, and now Shirley Decker-Lucke as chief academic editor for Hendrickson has offered many useful comments on how to improve this volume. I have often said to others that editors were invented by publishers to deal with people like me! I have needed the aid of the folks at Hendrickson, and they have been gracious, professional, and expert in their many comments and suggestions that have made this volume much better than I thought originally possible.

Finally, I offer a special word of appreciation to my wife, Mary, who has been a true friend and companion for more than forty years. She has continually been my greatest source of encouragement and an inspiration in my life's work. Mary has sacrificed more than was fair or could be expected of her to enable me to pursue my career as a minister, educator, and writer. I cannot imagine much good ever happening in my life without her. This edition, as was true of the first, is affectionately and appreciatively dedicated to her.

---

[5] McDonald, "First Testament."

Foreword to the First and Second Editions

THE BIBLE OF THE CHRISTIANS' RELIGIOUS TRADITION INCLUDES TWO BOOKS, the Old Testament and the New Testament. The first of these two books has always been a substantial part of the Christian scriptural authority. However, the exact definition of the writings that should be a part of the Old Testament canon never played a decisive role in the discussions about the Christian canon of Holy Scripture and its authority. While the so-called "Old Testament Apocrypha" are an undisputed part of the canon of the Greek church and a smaller corpus of apocryphal writings is included in the Bible of the Roman Catholic Church, most Protestant churches have ascribed authority only to a smaller Old Testament canon, corresponding to the Hebrew Bible, from which the Apocrypha are excluded. But these differences are rarely considered to be divisive.

In contrast, the question of the exact extent of the New Testament canon has often been hotly debated among Christians. In recent decades, this issue has taken on new dimensions through the discovery of an increasing number of ancient Christian gospels, epistles, and books of revelation under apostolic names such as Peter, Thomas, Philip, and even Mary. At the same time, critical scholarship has questioned the "apostolic" authorship of writings of the New Testament canon itself. Matthew and John may not be the authors of the Gospels transmitted under their names, the apostle Paul was not the author of all the letters of the Pauline corpus, and both Epistles of Peter were probably written half a century after Peter's death. Should we, therefore, revise the canon of the New Testament? Should we exclude the Second Epistle of Peter? Should we include the newly discovered *Gospel of Thomas?*

It is understandable that many Christians are disturbed by critical questions regarding the authority of writings of the New Testament canon, while others are excited about the discovery of new and hitherto unknown gospels, which claim to have been written by apostles. But what is happening to canonical authority, when there are apostolic writings outside of the canon and when the apostolic authorship of writings of the New Testament is questioned? The New Testament no longer seems to be the one and only collection of inspired writings from the hands of genuine apostles and disciples of Jesus. Its authority as Holy Scripture appears to be seriously questioned.

If there is an answer to this question, it will not come through abstract theological controversy but only through a reconsideration of the history that once created the canon of the New Testament. What did the Christians who established the canon mean when they spoke of "scripture," "inspiration," "tradition," and "apostolic authorship"? Why were these twenty-seven writings included and others excluded? How did these writings function in nourishing and building Christian communities, and why were other writings found lacking? What were the competing forces in the formation of the early Christian churches, and what roles did various writings claiming "apostolicity" play in these controversies?

Early Christianity appears to have been much less united and much more diversified than we have thought. The writings of the New Testament were not necessarily the only early Christian apostolic witnesses. Rather, from the beginning they had to compete with other books, produced by other followers of Jesus who were later considered to be heretics. The collection of the twenty-seven writings now comprising the New Testament canon was a long and arduous process, extending over many centuries. In order to understand this process, several generations of scholars have done most of the groundwork, have investigated the Greek and Latin sources from early Christian times, have tested, approved, and rejected various hypotheses, and have thus come to a much better understanding of the process. The literature on this topic is immense, often very technical and learned, and not always easily understood. But it is also very exciting, and it has opened up a much better understanding of the story of the formation of the canon. Holy books do not fall from heaven; rather, they are created in the historical experiences of religious communities. Scholars have learned much about this in an intense international debate.

But this story must also be told so that everyone can be informed by a better understanding of the developments that took place in the early centuries of the Christian communities. It is an exciting and enriching story, filled with the experiences and thoughts of Christian believers from the time of the apostles to the consolidation of the church three centuries later. The story must be told in terms easily comprehended by every reader, the interested layperson as well as the student in a theological school. The story must be told in such a way that everyone in the divided Christian churches of our day may share it and learn from it, evangelical Christians as well as those of a more liberal persuasion. The story must be told without apology and without zeal so that all may enter into the discourse with the history that created the foundations through which all Christians belong to the one church universal and are bound to the same God whose word and witness are preserved in the book we call the New Testament.

I have spent countless hours with the author of this book, and I have been deeply impressed by his scholarship, his learning, his faith, and his commitment to Christian education. This book, the result of many years of research, has accomplished what few have ever achieved: telling a difficult story well. There are no shortcuts, no facile solutions, no easy reconciliations of problems. All the materials are there. All the relevant texts are quoted and interpreted. Everyone is treated fairly and judiciously. All scholarly hypotheses are presented and discussed. All that is required of the reader is the same fairness and the same patience that are evident in the author's effort of presenting both the ancient sources and the modern scholarly debate.

Helmut Koester
John H. Morison Research Professor of Divinity
and Winn Research Professor of Ecclesiastical History
Harvard University, The Divinity School

Preface to the Second Edition

THE RESPONSE TO THE FIRST EDITION OF THIS BOOK WAS IN GENERAL QUITE positive, and it seems to have stimulated several thoughtful responses that I have tried to keep in mind in writing the second edition. Several reviewers have, in fact, encouraged me to write the second edition with the hope that it will be an improved guide through the highly complex question of the formation of the biblical canon.

Several mistakes, omissions, and weaknesses of argument in the first edition have come to my attention through the reviewers, and I am pleased that they have taken the time to inform me of these. My friend, Everett Kalin, whose competence in the area of canonical studies is well-known, has graciously taken the time to list some of the "bloopers" of the first edition and also to make other suggestions for improving the second. I appreciate his significant correspondence on the matter, and I am deeply grateful for his and others' observations and recommendations, which I have tried to incorporate. The most important changes include the following corrections and additions.

First, some significant works had eluded me in the first edition. These were brought to my attention, especially with regard to my treatment of the OT canon, and I have reflected on most of them in this revision and have noted them in the expanded select bibliography. It seems impossible these days to include everything in a bibliography and especially in a discussion, but I think that the most important works have been cited.

Second, I did not reproduce many canonical lists in the first edition because they are found in so many easily accessible places, but I have included a few more significant ones in the second edition. I agree that many students will not have the time to look them up elsewhere and some laypersons do not have access to a theological library where they can find these "lists." I have received the kind permission to use some of these from collections published elsewhere. Also, in a couple of instances, and especially in the case of the more important Muratorian Fragment, I have replaced Hennecke's translation with Metzger's more recent and smoother translation. He has made better sense out of some very clumsy Latin phrases in the Muratorian Fragment than I was able to. I have also improved on a few awkward translations from the church fathers that were in the first edition.

Third, and more importantly, several reviewers were disappointed that I had treated so briefly the highly complex development of the OT canon (Hebrew Bible). I had included the one brief chapter on the formation of the OT canon in order to make it a more useful tool for beginning students and also for the sake of completeness. It was not intended for scholars, but rather to summarize for students and laypersons some of the recent developments in the formation of the OT of the early Christian church. Several colleagues have encouraged me to treat more equitably the complex issues related to the formation of the Hebrew biblical canon (the OT), and I have tried to be more responsive.

I have further aimed at supplying for the reader the most important ancient sources that are employed in drawing conclusions about the formation of the OT canon. With this I have also strengthened, I believe, the case for a late development of the notion of a closed or fixed OT canon. I do not believe that Jesus was born with a "closed biblical canon in his hands" as so many have argued. I have used Jacob Neusner's well-known and reasonable dictum—"what you can't show, you don't know!"—to reinforce some of my conclusions at this point. It is difficult to find a wide acceptance of a fixed Hebrew biblical canon of twenty-two or twenty-four books among the adherents of Judaism before the end of the second century C.E. at the earliest. And even if there is some agreement, this does not necessarily mean that a biblical canon of twenty-two or twenty-four books was universally adopted by all Jews either in Palestine or in the Dispersion.

Most scholars examine the same ancient sources and secondary literature but come to significantly different conclusions about their meaning that often have more to do with the value judgments we all bring to our sources than with a fair assessment of the data itself. E. Earle Ellis, for instance, has made an important contribution to the study of the origins of the Hebrew Bible, *The Old Testament in Early Christianity* (1992), that has helpful critical notations. His knowledge of the field is impressive, and he has helped me to look more carefully at a number of issues, not to mention sources, but we disagree significantly on whether the OT canon was fixed before the time of Jesus. I simply do not see from the evidence he has mustered that the matter was completely settled or even discussed before the first century C.E..

In that same regard, F. F. Bruce's excellent work, *The Canon of Scripture* (1988) has also informed many of my comments, but he was not very helpful with respect to my conclusions about the time of the formation of the Christian biblical canon. In terms of the NT canon, I am deeply indebted to the very capable work of Bruce M. Metzger, though again I cannot follow his conclusions on the dating of the Muratorian Fragment or the context of its origins. I am only sorry that his and Bruce's work did not appear earlier so I could have made use of their scholarship in my first edition and saved considerable time in my own research! Roger Beckwith's monumental work, *The Old Testament Canon of the New Testament Church* (1985), draws similar conclusions as those found in Ellis' and Bruce's work, with the exception that he seems to have an axe to grind, which has led him to conclusions beyond those that are called for by his very extensive homework. A case in point is his dealing with the exceptions to his proposals, especially the pseudepigraphal book *1 Enoch* appealed to in Jude 14. That example will be discussed in more detail below.

As I began rewriting the section on the OT canon I realized that I would have to get more into the nitty gritty problem of the formation of the Hebrew biblical canon *for Judaism* before I could draw any conclusions about the church's OT canon. Some of the notable sources from Judaism were previously unknown to me. There are many Jewish sources that could and perhaps should have been included, but this would have expanded this book beyond what seems reasonable. I have, therefore, dealt with a number of issues in summary form once again with the hope that the reviewer will understand that the book is primarily intended for the student and not for the more technical and critical scholarly community. In regard to the formation of Judaism and its various canons of authority, I have relied quite heavily on the work of Jacob Neusner. I have also spent time re-working through Sid V. Leiman's foundational work on the Hebrew biblical canon, *The Canonization of the Hebrew Scripture: The Talmudic and Midrashic Evidence* (1976), along with the many primary sources he cites. We are all in his debt for this significant contribution, but, as Jack Lightstone has ably shown (see chs. 3 and 4), Leiman's work is not without its awkward assumptions about what was true in first-century Judaism. Geoffrey Hahneman's formidable dissertation on the date and provenance of the Muratorian Fragment, *The Muratorian Fragment and the Development of the Canon* (1992), should be the foundational work for all subsequent studies on this important source for NT canonical research. His helpful discussion of the OT formation supports Albert Sundberg's conclusions.

I believe my new work on the OT canon has strengthened the case I presented in the first edition: the formation of the Hebrew biblical canon was a long and slow process in both Judaism and the early church, culminating in the second through the fifth centuries and becoming more focused for the Christian community in the fourth through the sixth centuries. I deeply appreciate those who encouraged me to make the book more complete by adding the focus on the OT canon. I hope the additional comments will prove valuable.

Fourth, several of the reviewers appreciated the many questions that I put at the end of the book, but they were disappointed that I did not take the time to answer them. The reason for that has to do in part with the incomplete state of the research on the biblical canon. I do not believe that firm conclusions about the formation of the biblical canon or its expansion or contraction can be drawn at the moment. The canon did not emerge overnight, and any changes in our views about it ought to be tempered with caution, not to mention a practical hesitation for those whose constituencies follow closely their innovative notions! Moreover, to answer the questions based on the scarce available evidence would surely have limited the audience for the book and taken away some of the challenge for the student.

Although some members of the Westar Institute's Jesus Seminar have decided to open the question of the continuing viability of the current biblical canon, most scholars, for practical considerations (safety?) and/or because the evidence does not yet warrant such a move, have wisely chosen not to draw such conclusions at this time. There appears to be no doubt, however, that in the future many will question the continuing viability of the current biblical canon. Such dialog is almost in vogue now. For some of us, however, the matter has to do with whether what is offered as candidate for future inclusion could in fact improve our current picture of Jesus. Would, for example, the inclusion of the *Gospel of Peter* and the *Gospel of Thomas* in our biblical canons be an advantage or disadvantage? Do they significantly add to our understanding of who Jesus was, what he did, and what he asked from his followers? I can only surmise what the church's response might be from the responses that I have received from women in my classes when they read for the first time (or second and third!) the closing comments of the *Gospel of Thomas*.[1] What would the members of the congregation do with that passage if it were read in a church worship service on a Sunday morning! Are many of the comments attributed to Jesus in both of those works actually worthy of the Jesus we have grown accustomed to? I, for one, have serious doubts.

Nevertheless, with the publication of the Dead Sea Scrolls, and especially with the recent publication of the previously guarded Qumran material, there are a number of canonical questions as well as historical and theological issues that need to be addressed and debated among the scholars before we can draw final conclusions about some of the questions I raise in the book. If we add to that the recent interest in the Nag Hammadi documents from early Gnostic Christianity and the several (some 266) "agrapha," or isolated sayings of Jesus that circulated in the writings of the church fathers, the apocryphal NT writings, and in some of the biblical manuscripts of the early church, then we have a lot of work to do before we can draw final and responsible conclusions on the viability of changing our current biblical canon.

---

[1]The passage in question reads:

> Simon Peter said to them, "Let Mary leave us, for women are not worthy of life." Jesus said, "I myself shall lead her in order to make her male, so that she too may become a living spirit resembling you males. For every woman who will make herself male will enter the kingdom of heaven." (*Gos. Thom.* 114, NHLE)

In regard to the OT, it has become clear that there was no normative Judaism that defined for all Jews the scope of their Bibles. That notion is a product of later rabbinic Judaism.

I will be surprised if there are not several attempts to change the biblical canon in the next few years or even to downplay the significance of the current biblical canon. There may also be more attempts to define the "canon within the canon" for the twentieth-century church as we reflect on the books that made it into the Bible and those that did not. I do not yet see in the extracanonical sources currently available, however, anything that warrants inclusion or serious consideration as a "data base" of authority for the church today (one of the meanings of "canon" that we will explore presently). I am, rather, more of the opinion that these other extracanonical sources should at the least inform our understanding of the growth, development, and theology of early Christianity. Indeed, since we know that much of the apocryphal and pseudepigraphal literature did inform, and in some cases support, the theology of some of the writers of the NT literature, and since we have traditionally and rightly called upon the model of Jesus and the apostolic community for guidance in such matters, I think that we would be well-served to allow the extracanonical sources to inform our theological inquiry as well. This is a far cry, however, from saying that we should include them into our biblical canon.

Further, although I have questioned the viability of certain works like Ecclesiastes, Esther, Job, Song of Songs, 2 Peter, and others in our biblical canon, I am not doing anything here that was not done in the early church and in Judaism, as I will show. Why should the church of today have less freedom in evaluating the Scriptures that inform its beliefs and practices than did the churches of the fourth to the sixth centuries? Each of the noncanonical writings has a theological statement to make if understood in a "diachronic" fashion, that is, within the collection of theological works in which they are currently found, and from within the theological perspective of the developing believing communities that included such works in their sacred collections. I incorporate these writings in the current discussion, not in support of canonical inclusion, but to aid serious inquiry, knowing that they informed a significant part of early Christianity. I acknowledge that they do not represent the core of what the biblical canon is all about and that they are generally more on the *fringe* or marginal side of the "mainstream" of the biblical literature. Is it yet permissible to reflect on these matters and their significance in the churches where we serve and in the theological schools where we teach?

Fifth, I have moved the comments about canonical criticism to the *end* of the book. I believe that several of the points that Childs and Sanders make about the interpretation of the biblical text "canonically" are important, but I want at the same time to distance myself from Childs' position on accepting as canon the final "frozen" form of the biblical text. Childs' enterprise is far more encompassing than what can be deduced from my brief observations. I have restricted myself to those issues that I think are most important for our discussion of the formation of the biblical canon, namely, which text is canonical or authoritative for the church.

Sixth, as a result of the comments and conclusions of the first edition, my own theological perspective was questioned by a few. Therefore, I thought that I should share a little of my "theological baggage" with those who have such questions. I have come from a very narrow conservative theological background that is still very important to me. I use the name "evangelical" freely and with full conviction in regard to my views. I believe in the Gospel, the Good News of God in Christ, which, when shared with love and conviction, continues to draw men and women into a new and wonderful relationship with God. I delight in leading men and women to a new understanding of their relationship with God through the message of and about Jesus the Christ. I have seen many persons changed and given the hope and peace of God through the sharing of that simple and yet profound message of Christ. There is Good News to share in the story of Jesus! I refuse, however, to equate the raising of probing questions in the church with a denial of the faith. We do not advance our cause as evangelicals by refusing to question.

The following study reflects what I believe are reasonable conclusions about the matter of the biblical canon drawn from an examination of the ancient sources. The focus in both editions of this book has been predominantly historical with the knowledge that historical issues can also raise a lot of theological questions. I have not hesitated to question well-accepted positions such as the traditional dating of the Muratorian Fragment and the view that the NT canonical process was essentially finished at the end of the second century. Above all, I have tried to do careful inquiry without foregone conclusions. The success of that attempt will, of course, be measured by the reviewers.

Seventh, several students have asked me to add indexes to make the book more of a resource for them. I did not think that the length of the first edition warranted indexes, but they have been added to this edition. I hope they are useful.

Eighth, I want to say that my interest in this topic began, not in the academic setting at Harvard as was supposed by some, but rather in the setting of a rural community church, the First Baptist Church of Fremont, Nebraska, which I was privileged to pastor some years ago. During a Bible study at the church, several informed laypersons asked me probing questions about the books that did and did not get into the biblical canon. I wanted to answer their questions as well and as honestly as I could. Fortunately, I have served in churches that have allowed me the freedom to do that.

The *canonical authority* of the biblical message will be discovered not in the academy, but in its loving and humble proclamation in the communities where people live. The biblical canon, which has never garnered full agreement in the church, is not the focus of Christian faith. The focus is the

Christ who brings life and peace to those who have found a way to make the message of the biblical canon adaptable and renewable in ever changing circumstances.

In preparation for the publication of the second edition, my special thanks are in order for Patrick Alexander, the editorial director for Hendrickson Publishers, who graciously extended to me the opportunity to make important revisions and expansions for this edition. I also want to thank Rex Matthews, senior academic editor of Abingdon, who was most instrumental in the publication of the first edition and also of the second. I want to thank Helmut Koester again for his fine comments in the Foreword. I am also deeply indebted to James Sanders, whose own work on the biblical canon and the many canonical issues has informed my work throughout. In this edition he has offered several helpful suggestions and pointed me toward sources that had escaped my attention. The willingness of both Helmut Koester and James Sanders to share their favorable responses about the book on its cover and to use it with their students is both an encouragement to me and a great honor. Both scholars have added considerably to the credibility of the conclusions drawn in the book, though I am under no false illusion that they share in or agree with all of the conclusions I have made. This again speaks of their stature and generosity.

Finally, the greatest joy in this project has come from those parishioners, colleagues in ministry, and students who have said that they have read, understood, and appreciated what I have written. It was for the inquisitive minds in the church that this project was started in the first place. The churches that I have served over the years have kindly provided me with large enough pastoral and administrative staffs to allow me time to write. Those churches have also been very patient with me when I could not always be there for them, when the requirements for research and writing demanded more of my time than seemed fair to them. All pastors should have such understanding and forgiving congregations! It is to them that this second edition is affectionately dedicated.

Preface to the First Edition

INTEREST IN THE FORMATION OF THE CHRISTIAN BIBLICAL CANON OF SCRIPTURES has been growing over the last few years. Whatever the causes, several important new questions have been raised about the normative status of the Scriptures of both the Old and the New Testaments. Numerous articles, essays, and books on this subject have appeared in the last few years, which are challenging many of the traditional views about the biblical canon. Likewise, the growing interest in ancient nonbiblical religious literature, both "orthodox" and "heretical," has led many scholars to raise some very perplexing questions about what is referred to as "canonical criteria"—that is, the factors that led the church to recognize the biblical literature and no other as sacred and authoritative. How do we know that these biblical books and no others are inspired and authoritative for the church? What were the criteria that the early church used to distinguish its sacred literature from the other ancient Christian literature? Why did it take the church so long (centuries in fact) to recognize its canon of normative Scriptures? Finally, why are a growing number of scholars asking whether the notion of a biblical canon is in fact Christian?

Although I will address these and other questions in the following study, my primary concern in this book is to provide a helpful guide to the origins of the Christian biblical canon for students, pastors, and informed laypersons who want to explore the often elusive historical processes of how we got our Bible.

Many of the standard introductions to OT and NT literature offer but a few pages of information on the origin of the Christian biblical canon and frequently only repeat older and no longer tenable positions. On the other hand, some authors refer their readers to some of the more technical works on the subject, such as Hans von Campenhausen's masterful, but highly technical (and consequently often neglected), opus on the canon. That work and a few others like it were written especially for the advanced scholar, and, unfortunately, not many students will take the time to work through it. For that reason, I have sought to provide a more readable and not too technical historical guide to the origins of the biblical canon as well as offer some understanding of the major issues involved in canonical research today. Although a number of Greek and Latin words are found in this book, all of them have been translated for the reader, using at times my own translations but most often some of the better known standard translations with a few of my own "modernizations" of those texts. Most of the canonical studies with which I am familiar have either presented ancient material in the original languages (which has great merit for critical scholarship, but not for most students in college or seminary) or worse, have only listed references to it in footnotes, which most readers would not have access to unless they were close to a theological library. As one who has taught for several years, I know the struggles professors have in trying to motivate their students to look up ancient references even when such resources are available in libraries! With that in mind, I have tended to add more of these primary sources in the body of the text so that the reader can see some of the context in which the more popular quotations are found. I have often been frustrated by writers who have included in their work only one or two lines of a crucial ancient text, a practice that allows the passage to be understood in more than one way. The sometimes lengthy quotations given here will, I hope, prove more helpful than burdensome to the reader. Also, numerous notes are provided throughout the book, especially for the reader who is interested in a more critical perspective and/or in knowing the sources that have informed my conclusions.

The book begins with a brief look at the recent focus on "canon criticism" and the problem of the Bible as canon. The essential study of the origins of the biblical canon, however, begins in chapter 2 with an understanding of the notion of "Scripture" and its place in a religious community. It becomes clear that though there is an important overlap in meaning, one must distinguish between the notion of "Scripture" and that of "canon." From there the focus is on the emergence of the notion of Scripture and canon as they relate to both the OT and the NT.

A look at the table of contents will quickly show that the OT does not receive equal treatment with the NT in the discussions. This is certainly not because the development of the OT canon is easier to understand or that there is less controversy with it, but because many of the issues and arguments related to the study of the NT canon are equally applicable to the OT. I should also hasten to add that I am less knowledgeable in the OT than in the NT, and it is best that I do not extend myself further than the scope of my competence. In terms of the purpose of this study—to provide a readable text for students who wish to examine the formation of the Christian biblical canon—the chapter on the OT canon, though brief, has been added for the sake of completeness and is, therefore, more general both in detail and in scope. It is hoped, however, that it will offer very important information, which will help the student's understanding of how we arrived at our present Christian OT canon of Scriptures.

It is unfortunate that the recent publication of Bruce M. Metzger's significant new work *The Canon of the New Testament: Its Origins, Development, and Significance* (Oxford: The Clarendon Press, 1987) arrived in the States only as I was about to send the final form of this manuscript to Abingdon Press. Although I have made several references to Metzger's work, I did not have adequate time to review it completely. I have noticed that several of our conclusions are different, but I am impressed with the wealth of information as well as the helpful approach to the NT canon provided by Metzger.

This book is in part the product of a long theological pilgrimage that began years ago in a fairly narrow conservative context. Many individuals have been pivotal in the transitions of my pilgrimage, and it is only fitting that a few of their names be mentioned here. I have learned significantly from each of them, not only in the classroom but also by the way each has tried in his own way to make faith and thought compatible and, indeed, complimentary. None of them is alike either in personality or in theological persuasion, but all have played important roles in my personal development and in the theological stance I have taken in the following pages. Each has been for me a gifted professor and a friend in my time of need. They include James Rosscup, whose biblical scholarship has always been beautifully combined with his love for Christ, his humility, and a strong dedication to Christian service. The late George Eldon Ladd, whose sometimes painfully honest inquiry into biblical literature was paralleled by his challenging his students to be prophetic witnesses in the church, was the most instrumental person in challenging me to pursue my interest in theological education and in showing me that it was indeed a ministry. Hugh Anderson, my "doctor father," shared with me an invaluable historical-critical perspective as well as a genuine sense of responsible Christian mission and charity toward those who differ in theological stance. Douglas A. Templeton graciously offered many of his insightful observations about history, faith and the resurrection as well as generous amounts of his time not only as my tutor but also as my friend. Finally, I must mention Helmut Koester, whose example of dedicated scholarship, as well as his love for the church and its students of theology, is one from which I have personally profited greatly. His prophetic-like concern for truth both in his classes and in his writings has been a most significant challenge to me, and his many kindnesses both during and after my studies at Harvard have been especially meaningful. I am deeply grateful to God for all of these individuals, and I offer my heartfelt thanks for their time, patience, understanding, and guidance extended to me in my theological pilgrimage.

In terms of this book, I owe special thanks again to Professor Helmut Koester of the Harvard Divinity School for his guidance and encouragement throughout the various stages of my research on the biblical canon. There is no adequate way to express to him my sincere appreciation for all of his help. I would also like to offer my gratitude for the late Professor George MacRae, also of the Harvard Divinity School, for his many insightful suggestions, relevant observations that I had over-looked, and words of encouragement regarding the publication of this book. He and Helmut Koester were the original readers of my thesis on the canon, out of which this book has developed. Brian Daley of the Weston School of Theology was also encouraging to me in the initial stages of my research on this project and offered a number of helpful suggestions and corrections, which I have tried to incorporate.

I would be remiss if I did not mention several other persons by name who have given me their encouragement and practical help in bringing this manuscript to publication. My long time friend Craig Evans, whose many calls and letters of encouragement kept me from leaving this book in manuscript form on the top of a shelf, has drawn to my attention some important concerns that I have tried to address in the manuscript. My thanks are also in order to James A. Sanders, who not only expressed his pleasure with this work but also graciously took time out of a busy trip to the Graduate Theological Union at Berkeley to discuss with me the Christian biblical canon. He brought to my attention a number of significant essays and articles on the canon that I had overlooked, and I have sincerely appreciated his advice. In terms of practical help and astute observations, I must also mention Dr. Rex Matthews of Abingdon Press, whose numerous suggestions have not only improved the quality of this book but have also saved me some embarrassment! He has been most helpful and encouraging. Charles Hotchkiss, a computer engineer, a good friend, and a faithful member of the church I pastor was the first to introduce me to the world of computers and donated his valuable time putting this manuscript on the computer, which made its revising infinitely easier. He also found a number of mistakes and inconsistencies. His was a labor of love for which I am deeply grateful. Finally, I want to say how much I have appreciated the invaluable typing and editorial assistance of my wife, Mary, whose love, patience, and understanding have been constant throughout the years of our marriage. Without her ministry in *word and deed* this book could not have been written. She has been an outstanding companion and source of strength during my career, and it is to her that this book is affectionately dedicated.

I approach the publication of this book in the spirit and equal fear of Rufinus (ca. 401–404 C.E.) who introduced his *Expositio Symboli* with the words, "I am neither much inclined nor am I well-equipped for writing . . . for I know well the danger of exposing my poor talents to the criticism of the many." The following study is offered, however, in the hope that it will add to our understanding not only of the origins of the Bible but also of the authority and role of the Scriptures in the church. At the very least, I sincerely hope that this book will promote an honest inquiry into how the church got its Bible and what the implications of that inquiry might be for the church today.

Fall 1987

Abbreviations

1 Apol.	Justin Martyr, *First Apology*
2 Apol.	Justin Martyr, *Second Apology*
Ag. Ap.	Josephus, *Against Apion*
ANF	*Ante-Nicene Fathers*
Ant.	Josephus, *Jewish Antiquities*
Autol.	Theophilus, *To Autolycus*
b.	Babylonian Talmud
B	Codex Vaticanus
Bar	Baruch
Barn.	*Letter of Barnabas*
B.C.E.	Before the Common Era
1 Clem.	*1 Clement*
2 Clem.	*2 Clement*
c.	century
C	Codex Ephraemi
ca.	around, approximately
C.E.	In the Common Era
cf.	confer, compare
Contempl. Life	Philo, *On the Contemplative Life*
Dial.	Justin Martyr, *Dialogue with Trypho*
Did.	*Didache*
Diogn.	*Letter of Diognetus*
1 En.	*1 Enoch (Ethiopic Apocalypse)*
1 Esd	1 Esdras
2 Esd	2 Esdras
4 Ezra	*4 Ezra* (= 2 Esdras)
Ecclus	Ecclesiasticus (Sirach)
ed.	editor, edited by
Ep. fest.	Athanasius, *Festal Letters*
Ep Jer	Epistle of Jeremiah
esp.	especially
f(f).	following page(s)

Gk.	Greek
Gos. Thom.	*Gospel of Thomas*
Haer.	Irenaeus, *Against Heresies*
HB	Hebrew Bible
Herm. Mand.	*Shepherd of Hermas, Mandate*
Herm. Sim.	*Shepherd of Hermas, Similitude*
Herm. Vis.	*Shepherd of Hermas, Vision*
Hist. eccl.	Eusebius, *Ecclesiastical History*
Ign. *Eph.*	Ignatius, *To the Ephesians*
Ign. *Magn.*	Ignatius, *To the Magnesians*
Ign. *Phld.*	Ignatius, *To the Philadelphians*
Ign. *Pol.*	Ignatius, *To Polycarp*
Ign. *Rom.*	Ignatius, *To the Romans*
Ign. *Smyrn.*	Ignatius, *To the Smyrnaens*
Ign. *Trall.*	Ignatius, *To the Trallians*
Jdt	Judith
Jub.	*Jubilees*
J.W.	Josephus, *Jewish War*
Lam Jer	Lamentations of Jeremiah
LCL	Loeb Classical Library
Let. Aris.	*Letter of Aristeas*
Life	Josephus, *The Life*
LXX	Septuagint
1 Macc	1 Maccabees
2 Macc	2 Maccabees
3 Macc	3 Maccabees
4 Macc	4 Maccabees
m.	Mishnah
Marc.	Tertullian, *Against Marcion*
Mart. Pol.	*Martyrdom of Polycarp*
Moses	Philo, *On the Life of Moses*
MT	Masoretic Text
n(n).	note(s)
NPNF	*Nicene and Post-Nicene Fathers*
NRSV	New Revised Standard Version
NT	New Testament
OT	Old Testament
OTP	*Old Testament Pseudepigrapha.* Edited by J. H. Charlesworth. 2 vols. New York, 1983
Pan.	Epiphanius, *Refutation of All Heresies*
Pol. *Phil.*	Polycarp, *To the Philippians*
Praescr.	Tertullian, *Prescription Against Heretics*
Prax.	Tertullian, *Against Praxeus*
Pss. Sol.	*Psalms of Solomon*
1Q, 2Q, etc.	Qumran numbered caves

4QMMT	*Miqsat Ma'aseh ha-Torah* from Qumran Cave 4
Q	source (German *Quelle*)
Sir	Sirach
Strom.	Clement of Alexandria, *Stromata* or *Miscellanies*
t.	Tosefta
TDNT	*Theological Dictionary of the New Testament*. Edited by G. Kittel and G. Friedrich. Translated by G. W. Bromiley. 10 vols. Grand Rapids, 1964–1976
Tob	Tobit
v(v).	verse, verses
Wis	Wisdom of Solomon
y.	Jerusalem Talmud (Talmud of the Land of Israel)

Part One

Scripture and Canon

CHAPTER ONE

Introduction

I. Some Tough Questions about the Bible

Some years ago while I was conducting a Bible study in a church, a layperson asked me a fairly straightforward question that caught me off guard: Why did some ancient books make it into our Bibles, and others did not? He also asked how important this question is for Christians today. The simple answer to the first question is that the Bible is one of the great resources of the church, without which we would be at a great loss to know who God is, who we are as the people of God, and what the will of God is for us. But what if someone asked us why some books in antiquity were added to our Bible and others were not? Further, what books *should* be in the Bible? When current Bibles do not contain the same books, which collection of books should we be reading?

One might also ask, why do Catholics have a different collection of books in their Bible than do Protestants? Or, why do Greek Orthodox Christians have an even larger number of books in their Bible than do Catholics or Protestants? Why are the OT books of Protestants the same as those of Jews, but they are not in the same order? Who is right and how can we know? Not only is it important to know something about books that "made the cut" and were included in our Bibles, but what about books that were excluded? Who made those decisions and what criteria did they use? Do all of these books reflect the will of God for the church, or would the Christian faith be considerably different if other books were added and others deleted from the Bible?

All of these questions are essentially *canon* questions and they ask about the books that make up the current Bibles in churches. These questions are easier to formulate than to answer; they are, nevertheless, important for religious communities of faith that order their lives and ministries by a collection of sacred writings they call the Bible. To answer these questions, we have to go behind the scenes and learn something of the origins of the Bible, as well as how, when, by whom, and why the writings in it came to be acknowledged as authoritative Scripture. Answering these questions will not be easy, however, because no surviving documents either in the church or in Judaism offer clear answers to these questions. The available evidence is very sketchy and inferential in nature, and Bible scholars with impeccable academic and ecclesiastical credentials have difficulty agreeing on these matters.

To carry this discussion a step further, most Bible students know that until the invention of the printing press, the church employed scribes to make individual copies of their sacred Scriptures. Until the invention of the printing press no two biblical manuscripts were exactly alike, and yet each manuscript that the scribes produced functioned as Scripture for the communities for which they were copied and preserved. The copiers had differing abilities, and some copies were better than others and some were worse, but each copy functioned as Scripture in the community that authorized or was responsible for their production.

Many mistakes and even deliberate changes were made in the production of these manuscripts, and, as a result, a new craft called "textual criticism" emerged in the church to determine the original wording of the biblical text. Textual critics want to know what the original author of a manuscript wrote, and many have spent their lives trying to decipher and discover as best they can what the original writers put down on parchment or papyrus. Those engaged in this activity often compare thousands of manuscripts, but at the end of the day few claim to have discovered either the original text or even precise criteria for uncovering the original text in the surviving manuscripts.[1] Indeed, some text-critical scholars have abandoned that pursuit as an unattainable goal. Those who study biblical Greek soon learn that the original wording of many passages in the Bible is uncertain, and questions continue to emerge from biblical scholars not only on the meaning of ancient texts, but also on their original wording as well.

The work of text-critical scholars forms the basis for all modern translations of the Bible, and, with the continual discovery of ancient biblical manuscripts that often predate the manuscripts used to translate the King James Bible and other older translations, we must ask which ancient text(s) should be employed in the translation of the Bible. The church has not universally adopted any particular text of the Bible even when text-critical scholars agree on the wording of a particular biblical text. Similarly, of the many translations of the Bible available in the English language and in more

---

[1] Schnabel, "Textual Criticism," 73–75, observes that because of the many variables in the history of the transmission of the text and the oral history that lies behind much of it many textual critics have given up on finding the original wording of the biblical text, even if that continues to be the underlying goal of some textual critics.

than two thousand other languages,[2] which translation is appropriate for the church today? Biblical translations are not all the same, so which translation is the best for church use today? Since many Christians hinge their faith on specific words and phrases of the biblical text, this subject continues to be important. We could well ask, what might the churches' beliefs look like and what changes would take place if they all began to use the same Bible with the same text and the same translation? Again, all of these questions highlight the importance of canonical issues facing the church today.

No credible person today seriously believes that the Bible fell out of heaven fully bound in its current state with guilded edges and with a highly precise interpretation from God in it. The human dimension of the origin and production of the Bible, as well as how the divine message is conveyed through human words and ideas, cannot be ignored. Human beings were involved in the origins and production of the Bible, and all of the words and ideas in the Bible are also reflective of human involvement. How the Bible is the word of God and yet comes to us in human form continues to be a mystery to Christians of every generation. This is not only an important part of the church's understanding about the Bible, but also about God's involvement in the human activity of Jesus, whom the church continues to confess as Lord and Christ.

Some of us were taught in seminary that the early church received from Jesus a closed biblical canon, our present OT, that was later expanded by the Catholics to include noncanonical (and thereby uninspired) apocryphal writings.[3] In regard to the Hebrew Scriptures (or the OT), we were often taught that Jesus, the church's final authority, cited or referred to a closed canon of Hebrew Scriptures and that his authentication of them (he cited verses from the three major parts of the OT: Law, Prophets, and Writings) was the church's mandate for accepting them as authoritative Scripture. In other words, the church simply adopted the canon of Jesus. In regard to the NT writings, many of us were taught that the early church simply *recognized* (as opposed to *determined*) its own inspired NT Scriptures that were believed to be *apostolic,* that is either written by or authorized by an apostle within general proximity to the time of Jesus and the apostles or at least written in the first century. We were further taught that these NT writings were *unified in their teaching* (i.e., they were orthodox),

---

[2] According to Metzger, as of 2000, the complete Bible was available in 371 languages, and portions of it were translated into 1,862 other languages and dialects. See his *Bible in Translation,* 9.

[3] The books that Protestants call "apocryphal" (meaning "hidden" or "unrecognized") are what Roman Catholics call "deuterocanonical," which form a part of the Catholic OT Scriptures. Major doctrine is not built upon the apocryphal writings, but they are valued for edifying reading and provide many historical details that are important for understanding the context of early Christianity. The books that Protestants refer to as "pseudepigraphal" the Roman Catholics frequently call "apocryphal." This literature will be discussed in chapter 5 §V.

and for these reasons they were recognized by the majority of the churches to be inspired by God.

This traditional view has been slowly eroding over the years, largely as a result of several important studies on the formation of the biblical canon, especially those by Adolf von Harnack, Robert M. Grant, Hans von Campenhausen, James A. Sanders, A. C. Sundberg, James Barr, John Barton, and G. M. Hahneman (see bibliography). Their efforts caused many scholars to reexamine the historical data related to the formation of the Christian biblical canon. Until recently most (but not all) introductions to both the OT and NT devoted only a few pages to this discussion, but more recent introductions give more serious attention to the major questions involved in canon and by doing so stimulate further research. Of course, not all discussions on the formation of the Bible are of equal value. Some of them offer few advances in our understanding and often simply repeat unjustified assumptions.[4]

Other important questions are under consideration as well:

1. Why were discussions about the scope of the OT biblical canon still going on in the church well into the fourth through sixth centuries (and even later) if the matter had been largely settled before the time of Jesus?

2. Why did it take the church three hundred to four hundred years to establish its twenty-seven-book NT canon?

3. What precisely is a biblical canon, and how sure are we that such notions flourished in the time before, during, or immediately after the first century C.E.?

4. Do biblical canons exist whenever a NT writer or early church father cites a source from an earlier ancient text? In other words, should a cited text automatically become part of an ancient writer's biblical canon?[5] More recently, one rabbinic scholar has questioned whether

---

[4]The most disappointing aspect of Farmer and Farkasfalvy's otherwise excellent work on the canon, *Formation of the New Testament Canon,* is that the authors continue to employ the traditional assumptions of canonical research: (1) if ancient authors cited a NT writing, they must have considered it Scripture; (2) if one author called a text "Scripture," then everyone in that writer's time and provenance did the same; and (3) the compilation of all of the citations, quotations, or allusions to biblical literature by an ancient author constitute that writer's biblical canon. These assumptions should have been laid to rest with the publication of von Campenhausen's *Formation of the Christian Bible,* but they continue to persist as unfounded assumptions of canonical inquiry.

[5]Beckwith, "Formation of the Hebrew Bible," 46, 48–49, suggests this without explicitly stating it when he simply adds the references a writer made to earlier sources and calls that collection of references or citations that writer's biblical canon. Interestingly, however, when he deals with Jude 14's citing of *1 En.* 1:9, he equivocates on this understanding and asks more of Jude than he asks of other NT

the issue of a closed biblical canon was ever discussed among the sages of late antiquity.[6]

5. What sources more accurately reflect the earliest strands of Christian faith? Some scholars today are considering other ancient sources that they believe relate more faithfully the earliest Jesus traditions than those we find in the canonical Gospels. It is not uncommon to hear current discussions about the enlargement of the traditional database for knowledge about the historical Jesus, for example, to include the *Gospel of Thomas,* the "Unknown Gospel" discovered in the Egerton Papyri, and other noncanonical writings.

6. What of the so-called agrapha, that is, the sayings of Jesus not found in the canonical Gospels? Some scholars suggest that the agrapha, or portions of these sayings at least, ought to be added to the database of reliable information about the historical Jesus. This is not a new proposal, of course, and it continues to surface.[7] The legitimacy of the question stems from these agrapha serving as a scriptural (or authoritative) resource for the Christians who cited them. If we can with some assurance determine which of the more than two hundred sayings are authentic, should those sayings of Jesus be added to the database of information about Jesus, or even to the church's Scriptures

---

writers when they cite or quote sacred texts. The very criteria he uses with other texts to establish a canon, namely, citing it in an authoritative manner, is rejected for the NT writers when they cite texts other than the OT literature. Beckwith acknowledges that the later writer of *Barnabas* cited *1 Enoch* as Scripture (*Barn.* 4.3; 16.5), but he claims that this had no effect on Jude's conclusions about *1 Enoch.* See his *Old Testament Canon,* 401–3, where he claims that Jude is referring to *1 Enoch* and the *Assumption of Moses* only because they were edifying literature but not canonical! VanderKam, in his *Revelation to Canon,* 17–28, observes Beckwith's inconsistencies in this example and elsewhere and argues cogently that *1 Enoch* was more highly regarded among Jews and Christians than Beckwith is willing to concede. Despite Beckwith's inconsistency here, such references often provide little evidence for the notion of a biblical canon in the time of Jesus. What evidence do we have that the notion of a fixed biblical canon was even present during these times? There is considerable value in simply delaying the presence of a closed or fixed scriptural canon until we see it clearly discussed in the ancient literature. Was the notion of an *unclosed* biblical canon present, even though the early church did not yet have a term available to describe it?

[6] Neusner, *Judaism and Christianity in the Age of Constantine,* 128–45. See also idem, *Midrash in Context,* 1–22. In the formative years of Judaism, Neusner claims, the notion of Torah was expanded to include the Mishnah, Tosefta, the two Talmuds, and the various *Midrashim.* A canon was constructed by defining Torah in a new way that encompassed all the literature that followed it. It was tied together through exegesis. The notion of a biblical canon, however, is not a *prominent* feature in second-century rabbinic Judaism or even later.

[7] Metzger, *Canon of the New Testament,* 272 n. 11, notes just such a proposal from E. Platzhoff-Lejeune as long ago as 1949.

and used in worship, catechetical studies, and the church's mission?[8] Early texts circulated in the churches apart from the Gospels, but were eventually added to them, and those early agrapha continue to function scripturally in churches to the present day, for example, Mark 16:9–20.

7. Finally, what about the appropriate canonical text for the church today? Childs asks which text of Scripture should be the focus of authority for the church: the text in its original and earliest form or the later canonical form of the text? The latter admittedly has received many textual additions, some of which were intentional and others accidental. For instance, is the canonical or authoritative text of the church the original form of Philippians or the one that currently exists in our NT?[9] Does it make a difference if the two parts are separated for both study and preaching? Is the Gospel of John best read as it was written, namely, as a single gospel, or as the *Fourth* Gospel? Is the final form of Isaiah the authoritative base for preaching and teaching or do we look for an earlier 1, 2, and even 3 Isaiah? Should we receive into our biblical canon Mark 16:9–20, John 21, Acts 8:37, and other texts with questionable textual support, even though most scholars agree that they were later additions to the text? In the same line of thinking, should we accept as our Scriptures only the earliest texts available to us today, that is, those that most closely reflect the original hand of the author? We have a clue on how to answer this question from the way that the early church sought to root its theology in the witness from the apostolic community.[10]

---

[8]Jeremias, *Unknown Sayings of Jesus,* claims that of the 266 extant agrapha only 18 are likely to be genuine and none of them significantly affects our understanding of Jesus presented in the canonical Gospels. What should be done with such sayings, however, if they are genuine? The agrapha are introduced, listed, and discussed in several works. Stroker, *Extracanonical Sayings of Jesus,* offers the text of these sayings without sufficiently evaluating their contents or attributing authenticity or inauthenticity to them. They have been discussed more recently in detail in Hofius, "Isolated Sayings of Jesus." The agrapha are also conveniently listed and discussed in Charlesworth and Evans, "Jesus in the Agrapha and Apocryphal Gospels," where Evans contends that there is essentially nothing new in the agrapha that should cause concern or that would alter the understanding of Jesus found in the canonical Gospels. See also Hofius, "Unknown Sayings of Jesus."

[9]It is likely that the Letter to the Philippians is a composite of Paul's writings from at least two separate occasions, namely, 1:1–3:1 and 3:2–4:23.

[10]Notice, for example, that Eusebius, *Hist. eccl.* 3.25.7 emphasizes both "apostolic style" and "orthodoxy" as criteria for genuiness, and even the Muratorian Fragment lines 73–80 (see chapter 13 §I.D) excluded a work from consideration (*Shepherd of Hermas*) because it did not stem from the time of apostolic community. The rise of NT pseudepigraphy also demonstrates a desire to ground theology in the witness of the apostolic community. The early church anchored its life and

These questions, and others as well, have given rise to the recent interest in the formation of the biblical canon and related issues. Before any new advances can be made in our understanding of the formation of the Bible, however, much more inquiry than has emerged thus far needs to take place. I think that we are on the threshold of new advances in canonical studies that will change our perceptions of the canonical process. As a result, we will probably see more attempts at redefining the biblical canon, even though the current shape of the Christian Bible will probably not change much as a result. Some Christians will probably continue to find clever ways to marginalize those parts of the biblical canon that no longer appear relevant or that offend their sensibilities rather than explore new ways of changing the canon or interpreting it in fresh and more applicable ways![11] On the other hand, it is refreshing to find more references to noncanonical literature in evangelical writings, primarily as reference points to understand the meaning of the biblical text.[12]

What has contributed to the growing interest in the origins and formation of the Bible? In the last fifty years there have been several significant inquiries into the viability of the current biblical canon. With little or no change in the biblical canon for hundreds of years, why is there such vigorous inquiry now into the formation and authority of the Bible, and why are some scholars making recommendations about changing the contents of the Bible? Aland, for example, raises the question of reducing the biblical canon to take out those portions of the Bible that he believes are an embarrassment to the majority of Christians with the

---

faith in God's activity in Jesus. Those writings believed to be closer in time to Jesus (namely, from the apostles) that also reflected the early tradition about him that was passed on in the church were those writings that survived and became the Bible of the church.

[11] It is amazing what some will do to make an embarrassing text say something different from what is obvious in the text, whether it is about women's roles in the church or home (1 Cor 11:7–10; Eph 5:22–33; 1 Tim 2:9–15), the immediacy of the return of Jesus (1 Thess 4:13–17; Rev 3:20), justification for killing innocent victims in the OT (1 Sam 15:3), praying for the demise of one's enemies (Pss 58, 109, etc.), or early Christianity's apparent acceptance of the practice of slavery (1 Cor 7:21–24; Eph 6:5–9; Col 3:22–4:1).

[12] I am especially impressed in this regard with Arnold's *Zondervan Illustrated Bible Background Commentary* and Evans's *Bible Knowledge Background Commentary*. Both of these works show that evangelical scholarship has acquired a keen interest in the value of noncanonical writings for assisting in our interpretation of the biblical text. An earlier and useful resource on the socio-historical context of the Bible is Keener's *IVP Bible Background Commentary*. Keener makes generous use of noncanonical literature in his commentary, but unfortunately he does not provide adequate references to most of the specific resources that he cites, and it is difficult to inquire further into his research unless one is quite familiar with the ancient sources. Again, however, it is a good sign that conservative scholarship has begun to make use of this literature as a means of understanding the Bible in its historical context.

goal of promoting church unity.[13] Similarly, Käsemann also asks whether there should be some way to recognize a "canon within the canon"—in essence, a selective use of the Bible and a reduction of the biblical text—in order to alleviate the concern over the diversity within the Bible.[14] Some members of the well-known and often controversial Jesus Seminar promote the notion of both reducing the current biblical canon (eliminating especially Revelation and other apocalyptic literature in the Bible such as Mark 13, Matt 24, etc.) and expanding it to include the *Gospel of Thomas* and the "Unknown Gospel" of the Egerton Papyri.[15] One can well imagine the response of dispensational and Adventist churches to the proposed rejection of the book of Revelation by the Jesus Seminar in their projected Scholars' Canon!

I agree with Metzger, who contends that although the Bible canon may in principle be changed, in all practicality that can no longer be done.[16] It is complete and finished, but that does not mean that there are no important issues to resolve about the contents of the Bible or its future within the Christian communities. I am aware that any changes in the present Christian Bible will undoubtedly adversely affect many segments of the Christian community and cause more divisions and disputes than may be wise. Although some scholars suggest that changing the shape of the biblical canon was a part of my original aim in writing the two previous editions of this book, that was never my intention, nor did I suggest that noncanonical writings be included or that certain writings of the NT

---

[13] Aland, *Problem of the New Testament Canon,* 28–33.

[14] Käsemann, "Canon of the New Testament." Dunn, *Living Word,* 141–42, 161–74, also discusses the notion of a canon within the canon, albeit in a different sense, and, after describing four levels of canonical activity or four ways to view the canon, he asks what is the most important level of authority for exegesis and faith. He answers that it is the level of "final composition" (172).

[15] Sheler, "Cutting Loose the Holy Canon." Some members of the Jesus Seminar, under the leading of Karen King of Harvard University, have initiated a "Canon Seminar" that hopes to create what its members call a "Scholars' Canon." They hope that they will be able to agree on what books or passages to withdraw from their new Bible and what new material to include. For example, some members want to include the *Gospel of Thomas* and the *Gospel of Mary* as part of a new biblical canon. See also Perkes, "Scripture Revision Won't Be a Bible," who interacts with Robert Funk, founder and director of the Jesus Seminar and its parent organization, the Westar Institute, along with its publishing agency, Polebridge. Interestingly, Milgrom, "Amputated Bible," notes that the publisher Simon & Schuster eliminated from the Bible what they thought was either boring or irrelevant. Milgrom disagrees with their decisions and tries to show the relevance of those very sections that were eliminated from the Hebrew Scriptures. Several years ago, I was invited both to speak to members of the seminar and to interact with its members on a paper I prepared for them on questions about the origins of the biblical canon. I was well treated by them and appreciated the interaction, but clearly there was little about the subject of canon formation on which all of them could agree.

[16] Metzger, *Canon of the New Testament,* 275.

be excluded.[17] It is fair to say, however, that I do think that the church would be well served if it were at least informed by the same literature that informed the earliest Christians, including what we now call the apocryphal and pseudepigraphal literature. Indeed, some allusions to several examples of that literature can be seen in the NT itself and especially in the early church writings, as we will see below.

Although the biblical canon has received periodic scholarly attention over the last one hundred years or so,[18] the current interest in its formation seems out of proportion to the attention it received earlier. Recent scholarly research has challenged some of the most widely held views on the origins and formation of the Bible, including the following: (1) the Hebrew Scriptures reached their canonical acceptance among the Jews in a three-stage development beginning around 400 B.C.E. for the Pentateuch, around 200 B.C.E. for the Prophets, and around 90–100 C.E. for the Writings; (2) the early Christians received from Jesus a closed or fixed collection of OT Scriptures; (3) most of the collection of NT Scriptures was fixed by the end of the second century C.E.; and (4) evidence of the latter is provided by a late-second-century canonical list called the Muratorian Fragment. All of these views are well-known assumptions and others have been significantly questioned in recent years, and there is currently no scholarly consensus on any of them. It is widely acknowledged that scholarly conclusions on these matters are changing.

In what follows, I will address these and many other questions about the origins, stabilization, and authority of the Bible. This story begins with an ancient community's belief that God is interested in the human condition and has acted in significant saving or redemptive ways that have affected humanity's present and will influence humanity's future. That belief also acknowledges that God revealed the correct interpretation of that activity to prophets who not only spoke this message, but also wrote down that story of God's activity. What they wrote has become known as the sacred Scriptures for both Jews and Christians.

This story is at the heart of biblical faith and also lies at the root of the origins of Scripture. As we will see below, it influenced the limits that were placed on the scope of both the Jewish and Christian Scriptures. The NT, for example, tells the story that gave rise to its production, namely, the story about what God has done in the life, ministry, death, and resurrection of

---

[17] See, for example, Klein, Blomberg, and Hubbard, *Introduction to Biblical Interpretation,* 53 and n. 1.

[18] Much of this interest began with the research of H. E. Ryle, Alexander Souter, Heinrich H. Graetz, Moses Stuart, Edward Reuss, Theodore Zahn, and Caspar R. Gregory and has been carried on more recently by Kurt Aland, Hans von Campenhausen, James A. Sanders, Brevard Childs, Harry Gamble, Robert Grant, Bruce M. Metzger, Sid Leiman, Albert Sundberg, F. F. Bruce, Roger Beckwith, E. Earle Ellis, John Barton, J. Trebolle Barrera, Eugene Ulrich, and James VanderKam. See bibliography for a list of works by these scholars.

Jesus, which has great significance for those who trust in him. This story gave identity to a "new Israel" and gave rise to the call to be faithful witnesses of Jesus the Christ. This story was first shared orally, but within some thirty years began to be written down, shared widely among Christians, and used in Christian proclamation and apologies throughout the Greco-Roman world. What was written down initially was not transcribed in formal or literary writings, but was transmitted rather on ancient notepads, sometimes using shortcuts or abbreviations. In time, more formal literary transmissions of the same biblical story began to use these same literary structures. As we will see, the transmission of the biblical story in writing is also a part of the larger puzzle that we call the canonization of the Scriptures.

II. An Adaptable Bible

Sanders contends that the Jews were able to adapt their authoritative Scriptures to new and changing circumstances, and the very adaptability of those Scriptures allowed them to continue to serve as authoritative texts within the Jewish community.[19] Over many centuries of use, the biblical writings proved to be adaptable to the changing life of the believing community, and that is undoubtedly the reason why our current Bible continues to function as it does in churches, namely, the books within it continue to be relevant to the church's needs. The ancient collections of sacred writings changed generally by expansion, but occasionally by reduction, as, for example, when the *Shepherd of Hermas* and the *Letter of Barnabas* eventually dropped out of canonical lists. As the Jewish community developed, a time came when they recognized more than the Law of Moses as their sacred Scriptures, that is, they included the Prophets, a group of writings that at one time likely contained a larger number of books than those that were finally accepted into that division of the HB. For example, Job, Psalms, and Daniel were initially placed among the Prophets before they found their current place in the third part of the HB, the Writings.

From the church's beginning, early Christians accepted the words of and about Jesus as their final norm for faith and conduct. As the church developed, however, it became obvious that the written Gospels and soon thereafter the Letters of Paul benefited the ongoing life of the Christian community. Many other writings were also added to this growing collection, but when some writings that had been included in the sacred collections ceased to be relevant to the religious needs of the Christian community, they also ceased being "canonical" to that community. The neglect of those texts led to their disappearance in the church (e.g., the *Shep-*

---

[19] J. A. Sanders, *From Sacred Story,* 9–39, especially 23–30.

herd of Hermas, 1 Clement, and *Eldad and Modad*). Some writings were firmly established as a part of the NT Scriptures in the early church, while others were set aside from neglect and, later when a fixed collection was established, were not included. And some writings firmly entrenched as a part of the church's Scriptures became no longer relevant to the church's needs and were radically reinterpreted for the church. Paul, for example, "decanonized" much of the OT's emphasis on the law, especially its focus on clean and unclean foods or ritualistic cleansings, because such things were deemed no longer relevant to Christian faith.[20] Dunn makes the point that the OT can never function as canon for Christians in the same way that it does for the Jews. For the Christian, the NT always functions to some extent as *the* canon within the biblical canon.[21]

The issue in all of the above questions, of course, has to do with the viability and integrity of our current biblical canon. Can there be a theological integrity to our Bibles in light of all of the recent historical inquiry into its origins and formation? Carr asks a similar question that stems from his examination of the history of use of the Song of Songs. After observing the lack of knowledge on how that book was produced, its author's original intent, and the variety of interpretations of the book, Carr rather pessimistically concludes: "For these reasons the Song of Songs is merely a clear example of the extent to which the triumph of a critical approach can divest a text of its canonical function"![22] Does it follow that a critical analysis of the literature that makes up our Bible will lead to its decanonization? While Carr shows how a careful understanding of the origins of a text may cause doubts about its continued use in a manner foreign to its original intent, it does not necessarily follow that this is true for all of the sacred texts that comprise the Bible.

Because of their background in Judaism, the early Christians were accustomed to recognizing the authority of written documents as Scripture—that is, the Christians believed that the revelation and will of God were located in a deposit of written materials that served both the cultic and moral needs of the community of faith. The earliest Christian community did not doubt the notion of authority residing in what was later called the OT, even though many Christians questioned the normative status of the law in those Scriptures in the first and second centuries (Heb 8:5–8a). Jewish recognition of its own divinely inspired (and therefore authoritative) writings was a model for the church to recognize some of its own literature as authoritative, that is, as prophetic, inspired, and sacred writings that

[20] Dunn, *Living Word,* 156, uses the term *decanonize,* and it appears in the title of an important volume on the origins and function of biblical canons: Kooij and Toorn's *Canonization and Decanonization.* It is also used among literary critics as well; see for example, Guillory, "Canon," 246.

[21] Dunn, *Living Word,* 156.

[22] Carr, "Song of Songs as a Microcosm," 186.

were guidelines for faith and conduct. This happened especially when it became clear to many Christians that parts of the OT, especially its legal codes and rites, were no longer relevant to their developing communities. The specific factors that led to this recognition, however, are somewhat obscure due to the lack of clear historical references that make the transition from written text to Scripture more understandable. This change in the church's understanding of the continuing relevance of the law is recognizable in the NT, however, in the writings of Paul (Rom 4–8; Gal 3–4). And in the second century, Justin Martyr was the first teacher in the church after Paul to make the case for Christians not abiding by some laws of Moses, namely, the purification and other ceremonial laws.

III. Emergence of the Old Testament and New Testament

The terms *Old Testament* and *New Testament*[23] were not originally identical to the OT and NT canons, but focused more on the notion of the "new covenant" referred to in both the OT (Jer 31:31; cf. Ezek 37:26) and

[23] I do not care much for the terms *Hebrew Bible, Hebrew Scriptures,* or *Hebrew biblical canon* because they all send the wrong message; there is nothing particularly special or divine about the Hebrew language. Nevertheless, they are familiar terms, and I use them throughout this book simply because they communicate to the reader that we are talking about the Scriptures of the Jews that the early Christians also acknowledged as sacred Scripture. There is nothing special, however, about the Scriptures existing in Hebrew as opposed to Aramaic or Greek or any other language. While I occasionally use these terms so not to offend and to make sure that the reader understands what I am trying to say, I find myself more and more in favor of using what James A. Sanders calls "First Testament" and "Second Testament" when we are in conversation with the Jewish community or when biblical scholars try to be respective of the religious diversity of the various communities of faith that acknowledge the biblical literature as sacred Scripture. Not only is "Hebrew Bible" imprecise since portions of the OT Scriptures are in Aramaic, for the most part, early Christians and many Jews made use of the Greek translation of these Scriptures (often referred to as the Septuagint (LXX), even though this term originally applied only to the Pentateuch). While in a mixed theological community of Jews and Christians, the terms *First Testament* for the OT and *Second Testament* for the NT may be preferable to other terms since the reference to *Old* Testament suggests something passé or outdated. In antiquity *old* was a mark of authenticity and high value. In Western culture today, *old* seems equivalent to "out of touch," "out of date," or even "irrelevant." That was never the understanding of those who first heard and used these terms to designate the two parts of the Christian Bible. Had the early Christians viewed the OT writings that way, they would not have kept them in their Bibles. Perhaps in time something like the designations *First Testament* and *Second Testament* will obtain in the church and synagogue when the two are in dialogue. I believe that their use will provide more opportunity for free and respectful dialogue between Jewish and Christian scholars. If using more neutral designations enables a greater dialogue and promotes mutual respect, then

the NT (Luke 22:20; 1 Cor 11:25; Heb 8:8, 13; 9:15; 12:24) and the "first" or "old covenant" (Heb 9:1). "Old Testament" as a reference to the Scriptures of the Jews and of the earliest church is a thoroughly Christian invention and is found in neither Jewish or Christian Scriptures—or in the rabbinic writings of the second century C.E. and later. The origins of these terms may be rooted in Paul's writings when he speaks of those Jews who "hear the reading of the old covenant" but cannot grasp its meaning (2 Cor 3:14). He clarifies that this is in regard to the reading of "Moses" (3:15). The NT writings do not use the term *New Testament* (or *covenant*) in reference to its writings, but rather in regard to the new covenant or agreement between God and his people that has roots in Jer 31:31–34 (see 1 Cor 11:25; 2 Cor 3:6; also Matt 26:28; Mark 14:24; Luke 22:20). The Jewish notion of covenant (Heb. *berit*) may reflect an early use of the term to denote a sacred book, as in Exod 24:7: "He [Moses] took the book of the covenant, and read it in the hearing of the people" (see also 2 Kgs 23:2, 21). The "book of the covenant" (Heb. *sefer haberit*) may be an extension of God's written law. Early on, Jeremiah used the terms *torah* ("law") and *covenant* interchangeably (Jer 31:31–32; cf. 2 Kgs 22:8, 10; 23:2, 21). Later, Sir 24:23 used "book of the covenant" (Gk. = *biblos diathēkēs*) to speak of the Torah (Gk. *nomos*) or law of Moses. This practice is also found later in 1 Macc 1:56–57: "The books of the law that they [the Seleucids] found they tore to pieces and burned with fire. Anyone found possessing the book of the covenant, or anyone who adhered to the law, was condemned to death by decree of the king [Antiochus Epiphanes]."

Because the terms *law* and *covenant* were often interchanged well before the time of Jesus, it is not difficult to understand how "old" and "new" covenant were eventually applied to the Christian Scriptures. The terms *Old Testament* and *New Testament* were introduced in the second century C.E. to refer to these two bodies of literature, but they were not *regularly* used in the church for a body of sacred Scriptures until the fourth century C.E. To distinguish the Jewish writings that we *now* call the OT from the more recent Christian Scriptures, the designations *Old Testament* and *New Testament* first began to appear in the writings of Irenaeus (ca. 170–180), but it is not certain that he invented these categories.

> Inasmuch, then, as in both Testaments there is the same righteousness of God [displayed] when God takes vengeance, in the one case indeed typically, temporarily, and more moderately; but in the other, really, enduringly, and more rigidly. . . .

---

we have paid a small price that will have a good return for both communities of faith. I will, however, for the sake of clarity continue to use both "Hebrew Bible" for the Scriptures of Judaism and "Old Testament" and "New Testament" for the Scriptures of the church, despite the differences in the order and content of books with the Protestant, Catholic, and Orthodox collections.

> For as, in the New Testament, that faith of men [to be placed] in God has been increased, receiving in addition [to what was already revealed] the Son of God, that man too might be a partaker of God. (*Haer.* 4.28.1–2, *ANF*)

At roughly the same time, Melito of Sardis speaks of "the books of the old covenant [testament]" [*ta tēs palaias diathēkēs biblia*] in a quotation preserved by Eusebius around 325–30 (*Hist. eccl.* 4.26.14). We do not know if Melito was the first to use these terms, but he is the first to identify specific books that comprise this "Old Testament" (see the full quotation in chapter 8 §IV.A.1). We also find similar references in Clement of Alexandria (ca. 170; *Strom.* 15.5.85). Later, Tertullian (ca. 200) similarly writes:

> If I fail in resolving this article (of our faith) by passages which may admit of dispute out of the Old Testament, I will take out of the New Testament a confirmation of our view, that you may not straightway attribute to the Father every possible (relation and condition) which I ascribe to the Son. (*Prax.* 15, *ANF*)

Around 220 C.E. in Alexandria, Origen, criticizing the gnostics, wrote:

> It appears to me, therefore, to be necessary that one who is able to represent in a genuine manner the doctrine of the Church, and to refute those dealers in knowledge, falsely so-called, should take his stand against historical fictions, and oppose to them the true and lofty evangelical message in which the agreement of the doctrines, found both in the *so-called* Old Testament and in the *so-called* New, appears so plainly and fully. (*Commentary on John* 5.4, *ANF*, emphasis added; see also 10.28 and *Princ.* 4.11)

Origen's use of "so-called" suggests a lack of familiarity of these terms to his readers. Likewise, Eusebius, while describing Josephus's canon of Scripture, writes, "In the first of these he gives the number of the canonical scriptures of the *so-called* Old Testament, and showed as follows which are undisputed among the Hebrews as belonging to ancient tradition" (*Hist. eccl.* 3.9.5, LCL, emphasis added). Later, however, while speaking of the NT he says, "At this point it seems reasonable to summarize the writings of the New Testament which have been quoted" (*Hist. eccl.* 3.25.1, LCL). From this, I conclude that these terms originated in the second century but were not generally used in the churches until the fourth century.

In any case, what comprised the collections of Scriptures so designated by these terms were not the same among all churches (see appendixes B–D). In canon 59 of the Synod of Laodicea (ca. 360 C.E.), for instance, we read, "[It is decreed] that private psalms should not be read in the church, *neither uncanonized books, but only the canonical [books] of the New and Old Testament* [*oude akononista biblia, alla mona ta kanonika tēs kainēs kai palais*]."[24] It is interesting that here the NT is listed before the Old and

[24] Theron, *Evidence of Tradition,* 125, emphasis added.

there is acknowledgment that other books were being read in the churches! This kind of ordering of the biblical books led to the criticism by some Jews that since the Christians had abandoned the law, it was no longer a priority in their Bibles. Schwarz, for instance, writes concerning the order and collections of books in the Christian OT:

> This generic grouping fails to keep the Torah in a class by itself and identifies prophecy as the climax of the Bible. These two features may account for the acceptance of this division [i.e., "historical books" that include Genesis through Chronicles, Ezra-Nehemiah, and Esther] in the Christian world, since Christianity abrogated Torah law and saw its own gospel as the fulfillment of Old Testament messianic prophecies.[25]

For Christians, the God of the OT was indeed the God of the NT, and the continuity between these two Testaments was only occasionally questioned in the church. When that happened, as in the case of Marcion in the second century who abandoned the OT and even spoke against it, the church quickly condemned his attempt to sever its relations with its inherited past in the Jewish Scriptures.

We should note in passing that what the Christians call the OT the Jews commonly refer to as Tanak. This term is an acronym made up of the first letters of the words *Torah* (Law), *Nebiim* (Prophets), and *Ketubim* (Writings). Since the Middle Ages, the term has been regularly used by Jews to refer to their sacred Scriptures. They also make frequent use of the Hebrew term *Mikra* ("that which is read aloud"), which emphasizes the importance of the Scriptures of the Jews not only being written down, but also passed on orally both in the synagogue and in the study house. Christians use the more familiar term *Bible* (derived from Gk. *biblos,* "book") to designate their sacred Scriptures. They also call these writings "Holy Scriptures" (Latin *biblia sacra*), which is similar to the Hebrew *kitvei haqodesh* ("holy books"). The Latin and Hebrew terms suggest that Christians have Scriptures (plural) rather than a single book called the Bible. In Christian Bibles, the OT ends with the Prophets rather than the Writings, as in the HB.

Rabbinic Jews (second to the sixth centuries C.E.) not only adopted a fixed collection of Scriptures, but also a fixed text because of their methods of interpretation (known as "midrash") in which special laws and teachings were derived from the textual details of their biblical books. A fixed text aided in interpretation and application. Later, vowel points and musical notations were added to the text to preserve its textual authenticity, and this gave way to the production of the Masoretic Text (MT) of the HB, the standard text appealed to by both Jews and Christians today. Christians apparently had no interest in a fixed text and did not attempt to produce one until much later in church history.

---

[25] Schwartz, "Bible," 121.

IV. Process(es) of Canonization

An examination of the origins and development of the Bible for both Judaism and Christianity is essentially about the processes of canonization that led to the stabilizing of fixed collections of writings that undergird the core beliefs and religious practices of Jewish and Christian communities of faith. The corollary to canon formation is the belief that the writings that make up those collections have their origin in God, that is, that they are inspired by God and are consequently sacred and authoritative for worship and contain instruction in core beliefs, mission activity, and religious conduct. As we will observe in the next chapter, while the definition of a biblical canon has more to do with the end of a process, that is, with a fixed list of sacred Scriptures, the authority attributed to those writings was recognized much earlier, when they were in a fluid state of development and more adaptable or open to change to meet the emerging needs of the religious community. Many factors played a role in the complex history of the formation of the Bible, including the origin of the notion of sacred literature itself, the processes that led to the recognition of that literature, and the final fixing of a closed collection of sacred literature.

As we will see presently, there is little agreement among scholars on *when* this canonical activity began and especially when it ended. The problem is made more difficult by there being no discussion of the origins, development, and eventual recognition of the Bible in antiquity. By all appearances, canonization was an unconscious process throughout most of its development. Most of the ancient sources on this subject are tenuous and are generally drawn from an investigation of the collection of ancient sources. There is no evidence from the time of Jesus or before that either the Jews or the followers of Jesus were even remotely interested in the notion of a closed collection of sacred Scriptures, and this is what makes any investigation of such notions in the time of Jesus so challenging.

Our first focus in what follows will deal first with the difficult issue of defining the terms *Scripture* and *canon* (part 1). It is often surprising to students to find out that there is little agreement on the meaning of these important terms and that scholars often use them inconsistently, an accusation noted of this present writer that probably has merit![26] After a careful investigation of these two important terms, we will examine the origins and development of the OT Scriptures as a tripartite collection of sacred books among the Jews and then focus on the Christian collection of OT Scriptures (part 2). We will then examine the origin and stabilization

[26] Ulrich, "Notion and Definition of Canon," brings my own inconsistency in this matter to my attention, and hopefully this will be corrected in this edition.

of the NT Scriptures and the various influences that led to their inclusion in the Christian Bible (part 3). This book concludes with several useful appendixes for those who want to "dig deeper." Many of the most relevant ancient sources are conveniently listed there to facilitate research on canon formation.

CHAPTER TWO

The Notion and Use of Scripture

Among the world's religious traditions, Judaism, Christianity, and Islam have defined themselves in terms of a sacred written text. The development of a collection of Scriptures in these traditions appears to have come from a common belief in the notion of a "heavenly book" that contains both divine knowledge and decrees from God. This heavenly book generally contains wisdom, destinies (or laws), a book of works, and a book of life—a notion that goes back to ancient Mesopotamia and Egypt, where the heavenly book not only indicated the future plans of God, but also the destinies of human beings.[1] This is similar to what we find in the OT, where Moses pleads with God to forgive the Israelites for their sin and offers himself on their behalf: " 'But now, if you will only forgive their sin—but if not, blot me out of the book that you have written.' But the LORD said to Moses, 'Whoever has sinned against me I will blot out of my book' " (Exod 32:32–33). Likewise, the psalmist writes about the future plans of God:

> My frame was not hidden from you,
> when I was being made in secret,
> intricately woven in the depths of the earth.
> Your eyes beheld my unformed substance.
> In your book were written
> all the days that were formed for me,
> when none of them as yet existed. (Ps 139:15–16)

In the NT, this notion of God having a "book of life" is found in Phil 4:3, where Paul speaks of Clement and the rest of his colleagues in ministry "whose names are in the book of life." The notion of judgment based upon this book of life is found in the book of Revelation, when at the end of the ages people stand before the great white throne of God and books were opened: "Another book was opened, the book of life. And the dead were judged according to their works, as recorded in the books. . . . And anyone

---

[1] Graham, *Beyond the Written Word,* 49–50.

whose name was not found written in the book of life was thrown into the lake of fire" (Rev 20:12,15).

According to Graham, this belief in a divine book or books gave rise to the notion that the repository of divine knowledge and heavenly decrees is a divine book that is symbolized in written Scriptures.[2] The Qur'an also speaks of a divine book of destinies in which "no misfortune strikes on earth or in yourselves without its being [written] in a Book before we cause it to be" (*Surah* 57.22).[3] Among the ancient Israelites, and long before the notion of a Bible existed, the law was believed to have come directly from God. The Jews believed that Moses proclaimed the words and ordinances of God (Exod 24:3) and that he was commissioned by God to write them down (Exod 34:4, 27). They believed that God himself was the writer of the Decalogue, or Ten Commandments (Exod 34:1; Deut 4:13; 10:4). In time the Jews came to believe that the laws of God were written and preserved in sacred writings, and this belief played a pivotal role in the development of their notion of a revealed and authoritative Scripture.

I. Scribes and Scriptures in the Ancient World

In antiquity, scribes (Heb. *soferim*) were highly esteemed and almost given a divine status, especially in the Jewish community. Whatever they wrote—much of which was simply copying what others had said—was considered important, and it often had a divine authority attached to it.[4] Literary writings were highly valued, and if the words *it is written* were attached to a document, they reflected the divine authority of the document. Special virtue was attached to almost anything that was written because it was now "fixed." The importance of writing things down can be seen in Rev 1:19, in which solemn words were inscribed or written in books (see also Rev 2:17; 14:13; 19:16). The Scriptures were considered sacred because they revealed the very word of God, and consequently they were preserved and revered both among Jews and later among Christians. For example, when the Jews objected to the inscription that was placed over Jesus' cross indicating the charge against him, namely, "King of the Jews," Pilate responded, "What I have written I have written" (John 19:22).[5]

According to Farley, the basic properties of Scriptures include for both ancient Judaism and early Christianity at least four essential ingredients: (1) they are written, (2) have divine origin, (3) communicate the will and truth of God, and (4) function as an enduring source of regulations

[2] Ibid., 50–51.
[3] Ibid.
[4] Bar-Ilan, "Writing in Ancient Israel and Early Judaism."
[5] Davies, "Jewish Scriptural Canon," 42–44.

for the corporate and individual life of the people.[6] Layton adds that when a particular writing was recognized by a group of Christians to contain the presence of inspired authority it was elevated to the status of Scripture.[7] He correctly observes the limited agreement in the early church on such matters and finds only sporadic affirmation of the scriptural status of Christian writings in the first three centuries. For him, Scripture is a body of written religious literature that members of a religious group consider authoritative in matters of belief, conduct, rhetoric, or the running of practical affairs.[8]

These descriptions of Scripture form only a part of an overall understanding of the matter in the early church. For many early Christians, Scripture was also eschatological at its core, that is, they believed that the Scriptures had their primary fulfillment in Jesus (e.g., Matt 2:5, 17, 23; 3:3; 4:14; Mark 14:49; 15:28; Luke 4:21; Acts 1:16; John 17:12; 19:24, 28). Although Paul adds that this fulfillment is also found in the Christian community (see Rom 4:23; 15:4; 16:26; 1 Cor 9:10; 10:11), Jesus was the primary norm for the understanding and use of the OT Scriptures by the early church (see especially 2 Cor 3:12–16). This, however, does not negate the church's acknowledging the unimpeachable authority of the OT Scriptures (John 10:35; Matt 5:18). Schrenk notes that for primitive Christianity Scripture is "the authoritative declaration of the divine will," but it is "not valid apart from the 'I say unto you,'" of Jesus—that is, its christological fulfillment.[9] Childs observes that Christians understood Scripture in a theologically different way than the Jews did. The church adopted its notion of Scripture as an authoritative collection of sacred writings from the Jews, along with the largely undefined collection of Scriptures current among the Jews when Christianity separated from Judaism, but Christianity's basic stance toward those Scriptures was shaped by its Christology. Childs correctly states that for the early church "the Old Testament functioned as Christian Scripture because it bore witness to Christ. The Scriptures of the

---

[6] Farley, *Ecclesial Reflection,* 58. See also Kelsey, *Uses of Scripture,* 89–94, for a similar definition.

[7] Layton, *Gnostic Scriptures,* xviii.

[8] Ibid. Layton's understanding of the term *canon* is not clear, however, and he suggests the presence of several early closed canons of Christian literature before 200 (xix–xxi). If, however, we can speak at all of a completed biblical canon at that time, it was only in Judaism, but what evidence is there that such notions were even being discussed at that time? In chapter 8 §IV.A.1 we will show that Melito's canon or list of sacred Old Testament Scriptures was derived from his contact with the Jews on a visit to Palestine at the end of the second century C.E. Besides that, only Irenaeus's fourfold gospel canon is in existence at that time. Whether Marcion (ca. 140) had a biblical canon as such is highly debatable (see discussion in chapter 11 §I). Layton provides no evidence, however, for the existence of multiple Scripture canons at that time.

[9] Schrenk, "γραφή," *TDNT* 1.759–61. See also Barr, *Holy Scripture,* 14–15; and Kümmel, *Introduction to the New Testament,* 335.

Old and New Testament were authoritative in so far as they pointed to God's redemptive intervention for the world in Jesus Christ."[10]

The book of Acts claims that the community life of the early church was focused primarily on "the apostles' teaching" (Acts 2:42). The regular daily activities do not appear to have involved study of the OT Scriptures (2:46–47). Although the book of Acts is sprinkled throughout with OT references that were employed as sacred texts for preaching about Jesus (e.g., 2:17–21, 25–28, 34–35; 4:25–26; 8:32–33), one does not find any particular devotion to a study of the OT Scriptures in most of the NT. Second Timothy 2:15 and 3:14–15 may not be reflective of the usual practices of the earliest church.

The OT Scriptures (the limits of which in the time of Jesus were not yet precisely defined) were viewed as authoritative in the early Christian churches (e.g., Matt 21:42; 22:29; 26:56; Luke 24:32, 44; John 5:39; 1 Cor 15:3–4), but the matter of when the NT literature began to be given the same status as the OT writings in the ancient churches is difficult to determine and will be a subject of our discussion in part 3 below. However, it can be said in advance that when the early churches began to place Christian writings alongside the OT Scriptures as authoritative religious documents of the church, the transition to their recognition as sacred Scripture had begun.

When the word *fulfill,* as well as *fulfilled* or *as it is fulfilled,* is used of ancient literature, this implies its authority and sacredness. Likewise, all revelatory material was given special consideration in antiquity. When prophets spoke about a revealed word from God, they were thought to convey the very word and will of God. If they wrote down a prophecy, it took on divine significance in the religious community. If one believed that a prophecy given earlier had been fulfilled in subsequent event(s), the divine origin of the prophecy was validated and affirmed. Prophecy-fulfillment motifs appear frequently in biblical literature and were received as authoritative sacred writings among Jews and Christians. In the NT, as well as in the early Christian communities, various designations were used to emphasize the sacredness of the body of literature that we now call the OT: "it is written," "the writings say," "the Scripture says," or "as the Scripture says."[11]

When a particular writing was acknowledged by a religious community to be divinely inspired and authoritative, it was elevated to the status of Scripture, even if the writing was not yet called "Scripture" and even if that status was only temporary. For example, the noncanonical writings *Eldad and Modad,*[12] *Barnabas, Shepherd of Hermas, 1 Clement,* and the

---

[10] Childs, *Biblical Theology of the Old and New Testaments,* 64.

[11] Schrenk, "γραφῆ," *TDNT* 1.742–61.

[12] The ancient source *Eldad and Modad* is an apocryphal fictional book forged in the names of the prophets mentioned in Num 11:26–30 and cited as inspired literature in the second century by Christians. It is cited in *Herm. Vis.* 2.3 and possibly also in *1 Clem.* 23.3–4 and *2 Clem.* 11.2–4. The name *Modad* is sometimes spelled Medad or Modat.

letters of Ignatius were initially given this status in the church, but in time that practice ceased. There was limited discussion or agreement in the early church on such matters, and in the first two centuries only selective agreement on books acknowledged as Scripture took place.

When was the term *Scripture* actually transferred to a body of Jewish and Christian literature? The earliest known source that uses the term *writing* (Gk. *graphē*) in its absolute sense, that is, as a reference to sacred Scripture, appears to be the legendary *Letter of Aristeas* (second century B.C.E.):[13] "We are exhorted through scripture also by the one who says thus, 'Thou shalt remember the Lord, who did great and wonderful deeds in thee' " (*Let. Aris.* 155, *OTP* 2.23). The author later clarifies the importance of the law of God (the Pentateuch), claiming that all of the laws have been made with righteousness in view and "that no ordinances have been made in scripture without purpose or fancifully, but to the intent that through the whole of our lives we may also practice justice to all mankind in our acts, remembering the all-sovereign God" (*Let. Aris.* 168, *OPT* 2:24). These two examples do not try to defend the term *Scripture,* but simply use it and assume that the readers will understand it in the absolute sense of sacred and inspired writing. This, of course, suggests that this meaning obtained currency prior to the writing of the *Letter of Aristeas.* Writing something down was a mark of revelation, as in the case where God wrote the law (Exod 24:12; 31:18; 32:15, 32; 34:1; Deut 4:13; 9:10). Moses wrote down the commandments of God (Exod 24:4; 34:27), and later the king of the nation was instructed to preserve the law by having it copied or reproduced (Deut 17:18). The act of writing down or copying the law of God was viewed as an act that declares the will of God.

The origin of this notion of Scripture among the Jews, of course, is traced to the biblical writers who spoke of the divine status of the words of God that were to be read and etched on doorposts (Deut 6:6–9). There are no references to the technical term *Scriptures* (Heb. *ketubim;* Gk. *graphai*) in the OT itself, even though the notion of sacred writings certainly existed from the penning of Deuteronomy.[14]

Paul also reflects the view that the Scriptures were written for our benefit. Citing the story of Abraham's faith and God's promise, he writes: "Therefore his faith 'was reckoned to him as righteousness.' Now the

---

[13] It is difficult to establish the date of the *Letter of Aristeas* with any precision, but it is likely to have been written sometime around or shortly after 130 B.C.E. The termination date is 35 C.E., since Philo's *Moses* 2.26–44 is clearly dependent upon it.

[14] Although the notion of sacred Scripture is infrequent before the reforms of Josiah in 621 B.C.E., subsequent literature frequently cites the failure of the Jews to keep the law of Moses or the law of God or speaks of them in a scriptural or authoritative manner: 1 Kgs 2:3; 2 Kgs 10:31; 14:6; 17:13; 21:8; 22:3–13, 23:24–25; 1 Chr 16:40; 22:12; 2 Chr 6:16; 12:1; 23:18; 30:16; 35:26; Ezra 3:2; 7:6; Neh 8:1; Jer 2:8; 5:4–5; 44:10; Dan 9:11, 13. Before then, however, there are only a few references to observing the law of God (Hos 4:6; Amos 2:4).

words, 'it was reckoned to him,' were written not for his sake alone, but for ours also" (Rom 4:22–24a). He adds to this the purpose of the Scriptures: "Whatever was written in former days was written for our instruction" (15:4). After citing Deut 25:4, Paul claims that "it was indeed written for our sake, for whoever plows should plow in hope and whoever threshes should thresh in hope of a share in the crop" (1 Cor 9:10). Finally, after citing the fate of those mentioned in Scripture who grumbled and were destroyed, he writes: "These things happened to them to serve as an example, and they were written down to instruct us, on whom the ends of the ages have come" (10:11). In these examples, Paul contends that the Scripture was not only for past generations, but for the current one as well. Scriptures are relevant and authoritative without respect of time.

The closest parallel to sacred writings outside of the biblical literature is probably Homer's *Iliad* and *Odyssey*. Heraclitus, philosopher from Ephorus, ca. 500 B.C.E., (around the turn of the era), for instance, observes that children were trained in the writings of Homer and that they were to occupy their life to the end of their days (Heraclitus Stoicus, *Allegorae: Questiones Homericae* 1.2).

The rabbis of the second century C.E. and following assume that Scripture is not only authoritative and permanent, but also "holy" and given by God. The notion of "holy Scripture" or "holy Scriptures" (Heb. *kitbey haqodesh;* Gk. *hai hierai graphai*) is widespread in the rabbinic writings from the third century C.E. onward. For example, in the Tosefta (mid-third century C.E.) we read, "Even though they have said, 'They do not read in Holy Scriptures [on the Sabbath]' they do review [what they have read] in them, and they do expound [what is in them]" (*t. Shabbat* 13.1.A–B, Neusner, *Tosefta,* 404). The roots of this notion, however, are earlier and possibly come from Philo (early first century C.E.), who frequently speaks of "holy Scriptures" (Gk. *hai hierai graphai*).[15] The Maccabean writer (ca. 135 B.C.E.), who originally wrote in Hebrew but whose text remains only in Greek, spoke of "the holy books [*ta biblia ta hagia*] that are in our hands" (1 Macc 12:9). Similarly, the author of 2 Macc 8:23 (ca. 104–63 B.C.E.) spoke of Judas Maccabeus appointing Eleazar "to read aloud from the holy book [*hieran biblon*]."

The NT writers seldom speak of *holy* Scripture, though the message that the disciples preach is called "holy" (Matt 7:6). In Rom 1:2, Paul uses the word *holy* in reference to the Scriptures, but here he uses *hagios* instead of the more usual *hieros.* In Rom 7:12, Paul says that the law is holy (*hagios*), and in 2 Tim 3:15 the Scriptures are called "sacred writings" (Gk. *hiera grammata*). The notion of "holy Scripture" is found more often in the early church fathers, however, than in first-century Christian thought.

---

[15] For example, see *On the Life of Abraham* 61; *On the Preliminary Studies* 34; 90; *On the Decalogue* 8; 37; *On the Special Laws* 1.214; 2.104, 134.

Clement of Rome, for instance tells his readers in Corinth that "you have gazed into the holy and true Scriptures that were given through the Holy Spirit" (*1 Clem.* 45.2, LCL) and later "you know the sacred Scriptures" (53.1, LCL), but this notion is largely absent from the NT.

The use of the term *holy Scripture* appears to have emerged among the Jews before the first century C.E. and in time was adopted by the Christians, but the notion of reverence for things that are written down and believed to have come from God is rooted in the OT itself, namely, in those texts that speak of God or Moses writing down God's laws (especially Exod 24:3–4, 12).

Occasionally, the Scriptures are personified as God speaking. In Jas 2:23, "the Scripture" is a personification of God speaking through the Scripture (see also Gal 3:8, 22), and sometimes the word *Scripture* refers to a single passage (Gal 4:30; Rom 4:3; 9:17; 10:11; 11:2). Christians believed that their Scriptures expressed the will of God and that the divine Spirit spoke through them (Matt 22:43; Mark 12:36; Acts 1:16; Heb 3:7; 9:8; 10:15). The early Christians also believed that the Scriptures had their fulfillment in Jesus (Luke 24:27, 32, 45) and that the gospel of and about Jesus was revealed in the Scriptures (Rom 16:26). The Scriptures were also considered "prophetic writings," which is another way of saying that they are inspired by God and reveal the will of God.

The terms for Scripture vary in antiquity, but there are some common themes. One of the early titles given to the sacred writings of the Jews was simply "the books" (Heb. *hasefarim*). Daniel appears to use this term in reference to the writing prophets of Israel (Dan 9:2; cf. Jer 25:11–12; 29:10). This is not unlike the way that Tannaitic literature refers to books (see *m. Megillah* 1:8; *m. Mo'ed Qatan* 3:4; *m. Gittin* 4:6; *m. Kelim* 15:6).[16] Greek-speaking Jews, following the Hebrew and Aramaic practice, called the sacred Scriptures simply "the books" (Gk. *ta biblia*). The English word *Bible* has its roots in the Latin version of this Greek term. By the Middle Ages, the Jews were referring to their sacred books as "the holy books" (*sifre haqodesh*).

Eventually the Scriptures of the Jews were called "holy books" (Josephus, *Ant.* 20.261) and those of the Christians were called "sacred books [*hierais biblois*]" (*1 Clem.* 43.1). In early rabbinic writings, "holy writings" (Heb. *kitvei haqodesh*) referred to the Jewish Scriptures (*m. Shabbat* 16:1; *m. Eruvin* 10:3; *m. Yadayim.* 3:2, 5; 4:6; *m. Bava Batra* 1:6; *m. Parah* 10:3). The Hebrew word *ktb* ("writing") in the plural is *ktbm* or *ketubim* ("writings")

[16]Tannaitic literature is Jewish rabbinic literature written following the times of Hillel and Shammai (30 B.C.E.–10 C.E.), namely between 10 C.E. and 220 C.E. The term comes from Aramaic *tanna,* meaning "one who studies/teaches/repeats" traditions. Some of the best known *Tannaim* (rabbinic teachers) of this period lived after the destruction of Jerusalem in 70 C.E. The last of them, Rabbi Judah the Prince, collected the rabbinic oral teachings of this period and placed them in the sixty-three tractates known as the Mishnah.

and is similar to Greek *graphē* ("writing") or *graphai* ("writings"). The Greek term was translated into Latin as *script* or *scriptum,* and in English Bibles the terms are most often transliterated "Scripture" or "Scriptures."

The Greek noun *graphē* ("writing") is used some forty-nine times in the NT to refer to sacred Scriptures.[17] The Greek verb *graphō* ("I write") is often used of the simple act of writing with no special connotations, but it is also used in the absolute sense of sacred writings. In the passive voice, the Greek verb *gegraptai* ("it is written") is used some sixty-five times in the NT to refer to Israel's and the church's sacred Scriptures (e.g., Matt 4:4–10; Luke 4:8; 19:46; 1 Cor 9:9). This practice underscores the belief that God speaks through the words of Scripture. Frequently the words *it is written* (*for it is written* [Gk. *gar gegraptai*] or *just as it is written* [Gk. *kathōs gegraptai*]) precede the quoting of a Scripture passage.[18] While it is not always clear which Scriptures are in view, there is little question that the Scriptures were believed to have divine origins and were authoritative for the life and mission of the church and the synagogue. Sometimes unknown Scriptures are cited as in John 7:38 and Jas 4:5 (see also 1 Cor 2:9; 9:10; Eph 5:14; and Luke 11:49), which reflects the uncertainty in the first century about the scope of the collection of Scriptures.

Among the Jews the word *Torah* ("Law"), which refers specifically to the Pentateuch, was a frequent designation for all of the Scriptures of the Bible—regardless of their place in the sacred collection. For example, *b. Mo'ed Qatan* 5a calls Ezek 39:15 *Torah,* and *b. Sanhedrin* 91b calls Ps 82:6 *Torah* (cf. Matt 22:36). In rabbinic literature, eventually the word *Torah* included not only all of the written Scriptures, but also the oral traditions that interpreted the Scriptures, namely, the Mishnah, Tosefta, and the two Talmuds; among the rabbinic Jews these traditions became known as "oral Torah." The emergence of this oral torah can be seen in several rabbinic texts: "The Torah in writing is made up of general rules; the Torah by word of mouth is made up of specific details";[19] "thy cheeks are comely with circlets (*torim*)—with two Torahs, the one in writing and the one by word of mouth."[20] The following is even more explicit:

---

[17] The singular *graphē* ("writing" or "Scripture") occurs in Mark 12:10; Luke 4:21; John 2:22; 7:38; 7:42; 10:35; 13:18; 17:12; 19:24, 28, 36, 37; 20:9; Acts 1:16; 8:32, 35; Rom 4:3; 9:17; 10:11; 11:2; Gal 3:8, 22; 4:30; 1 Tim 5:18; 2 Tim 3:16; Jas 2:8, 23; 4:5; 1 Pet 2:6; 2 Pet 1:20. The plural *Scriptures* (*hai graphai*) is found in Matt 21:42; 22:29; 26:54, 56; Mark 12:24; 14:49; Luke 24:27, 32, 45; John 5:39; Acts 17:2, 11; 18:24, 28; Rom 1:2; 15:4; 1 Cor 15:3, 4; 2 Pet 3:16.

[18] For example, Mark 1:2 (cf. 2 Chr 32:32); Luke 2:23; Acts 7:42; and 15:15. The phrase *just as it is written* occurs some sixteen times in Romans alone (1:17; 2:24; 3:4, 10; 4:17; 8:36; 9:13, 33; 10:15; 11:8, 26; 12:19; 14:11; 15:3, 9, 21). Whether *it is written* or *just as it is written* is used, both refer to the sacred Scriptures recognized by Israel and by the church.

[19] *Tanhuma, Noah* 3, Bialik and Ravnitzky, *Book of Legends,* 442.

[20] *Song Rabbah* 1:10 §1, Bialik and Ravnitzky, *Book of Legends,* 442.

> The Holy One foresaw that the nations of the world would get to translate the Torah and, reading it in Greek, would declare, "We are Israel." And to this day the scales appear to be evenly balanced between both claims. But then the Holy One will say to the nations of the world, "You claim you are My children? I have no way of knowing other than that My children are those who possess My secret lore." What secret lore? Mishnah, which was given by word of mouth.
>
> "And the Lord said to Moses: 'Write thou these words' " [Exod 34:27]. When the Holy one came to give the Torah to Israel, he uttered it to Moses in its order, Scripture and Mishnah, Talmud and *Aggadah,*[21] as is said, "the Lord spoke all these words" [Exod 20:1]. Even what a faithful student was someday to ask his teacher, the Holy One uttered to Moses at that time. . . . Therefore give them Scripture in writing and Mishnah by word of mouth. "Write thou these words"—Scripture. Then: "By these words uttered with the mouth I have made a covenant with thee"—these words being Mishnah and Talmud, which make it possible to tell Israel and the nations of the world apart. (*Tanhuma B, Ki Tissa,* §17, *Tanhuma, Ki Tissa* §60; *Exod Rabb.* 47:1, Bialik and Ravnitzky, *Book of Legends,* 441).

For the rabbinic schools, eventually the whole of their oral tradition became Torah and was treated as sacred, even if the written Scriptures were given priority. In regard to the HB, the Torah always had priority over the Prophets and Writings, and in the rabbinic tradition, the written Torah had priority over the oral Torah, even though both are sacred to the Jews and in practice talmudic law became as important as biblical law.[22]

Another Hebrew term that the Jews used for the Bible is *Mikra* ("reading"). This term emphasizes the public reading of the Scriptures in Jewish worship and is first found in the Tannaitic literature of the Mishnah (*m. Nedarim* 4:3; *m. Avot* 5:21; see *m. Ta'anit* 4:2, 68a). It became a popular designation for the HB among Jews in the Middle Ages.

Although the acceptance of and belief in divinely inspired writings was widespread in Israel of late antiquity and also in early Christianity, what each acknowledged as Scripture is not always clear. Simply because an an-

---

[21]The Hebrew word *haggadah* ("narrative" or "telling") has to do with prerabbinic interpretation of the HB in narrative form. The writers of haggadah interpret sacred texts by telling a story that makes the point about the texts' interpretation. This kind of story is also found in the New Testament when Matthew tells the story of Jesus' infancy in a way that mirrors the antagonism between Moses and Pharaoh (cf. Matt 2:20 and Exod 4:19; Matt 2:15 and Hos 11:1). On the other hand, the term *halakah* ("to go") refers to the legal aspects of Judaism. Halakoth (the plural of *halakah*) are legal prescriptions and proscriptions, such as the tractates that make up the Mishnah. There is very little haggadah in the Mishnah, but almost a third of the Jerusalem Talmud and a fourth of the Babylonian Talmud are made up of haggadah, narrative stories that illustrate the meaning of the sacred text.

[22]Interestingly, in a recent interview, Elie Wiesel noted that even today this equal priority given to the talmudic law is still quite common among the Jews. See Shanks, "Contrasting Insights of Biblical Giants," 32–33.

cient writer cited a written text, it does not necessarily mean that it was viewed as sacred and inviolable Scripture. Each reference must be considered on its own merit within its own context to determine how it was used by the author or how it was received in the community to which the author wrote. Likewise, when an ancient source cites a particular text *as Scripture,* one cannot conclude that all teachers of that time and place drew the same conclusions about the writing. For example, Paul is reported to have cited several nonbiblical sources in his speaking and writing (Epimenides and Aratus in Acts 17:28; Epimenides in Titus 1:12) but one cannot conclude that he cited them as Scripture. Also, even though Irenaeus argued for a fourfold gospel collection, those four and no more, after him Bishop Serapion of Antioch initially allowed the *Gospel of Peter* to be read in the churches, but after examining its theological contents he later reversed himself on the matter (see chapter 10 §II.A). The bishop's reversal was not because he discovered that the book was not a part of a widely accepted fixed collection of gospels or other sacred Scriptures, but rather because of its contents. For him, the criterion for acceptance or rejection was orthodoxy, not a fixed list of what books were acceptable. As late as the mid-fourth century, Athanasius published his twenty-seven-book list of the writings of the NT in his *Thirty-ninth Festal Letter,* but it was not universally accepted in the rest of the Roman Empire or even in Egypt itself in his lifetime. Widespread approval took much longer. Just because a text was cited by a well-known church father, one cannot assume that the writing was a part of either his or others' biblical canon. This was often misunderstood even in antiquity. Every citation or quote must be evaluated on its own merit before being added to someone's biblical canon.

The church inherited its collection of OT Scriptures from first-century Judaism before its separation from the synagogue. The writings that the mostly Pharisaic Jews believed were sacred before this parting of the ways are the same ones that the early Christians also acknowledged as Scripture. This collection was largely, but not completely, formed before the time of Jesus, and it included the Law, the Prophets, and an imprecise collection of other writings. Whether these other writings were fewer than, the same as, or more than those in the current Hebrew Scriptures (i.e., the twenty-four books of the HB or the thirty-nine books of the Protestant OT) cannot yet be determined with precision. Many early Christians also accepted several apocryphal writings as Scripture—or at least cited them as Scripture with the typical scriptural introductions ("it is written," "the Scripture says," etc.)—from the second century onward, and several of these writings appear in biblical manuscripts and canonical lists in the fourth and fifth centuries (see appendixes B–D). The variety of books represented in those collections diminished in time, but some diversity existed for several centuries, indeed throughout most of church history. Had there been any understanding in the early church that Jesus himself had received and passed on to his disciples a fixed collection of Scriptures, it is unthinkable that the early church would have produced another "Testament" of sacred writings or received any books as sacred that Jesus had rejected. Even more unimaginable is the view that once they had received a closed collection of Scriptures from Jesus, the disciples somehow lost it.

Barr observes that generally in the OT "the writers do not reckon with a written 'Scripture' as a totally dominant, known, and acknowledged factor and force in the life of Israel."[23] He goes on to argue that even the prophets who say, "Thus says the Lord," are not speaking on the basis of an already existing text. Very little in the OT suggests that there were sacred Scriptures to turn to when guidance was needed.[24] Indeed, David, Solomon, and Hezekiah never spoke of sacred books current and normative in the life of Israel. Rather, as Barr notes, the OT individuals related to God more through persons (priests, prophets) and institutions (tabernacle, temple) than through sacred writings.[25] This does not suggest that Israel was without traditions that functioned in an authoritative manner among its people. No religious community exists without such traditions (or rules), whether they are expressed in oral traditions, creeds, liturgies, or written Scriptures.

There are some hints that a few in the community of Israel were aware of the laws of God given earlier in Israel's history (Hos 4:6; Amos 2:4), and there are several references to the laws and commandments or statutes of God following the reforms of Josiah, but little attention is given to the law of God or the laws of Moses before the seventh century B.C.E. Barr's point is well taken. The influence of the law among the Jews was probably not significant before the reforms of Josiah (621 B.C.E.) and certainly no later than the reforms of Ezra (Neh 8:1–8; 9:1–3). The Deuteronomic movement in Israel in the eighth and seventh centuries B.C.E. no doubt played a major role in instituting that change, especially its admonition to obey the commandments of Yahweh and not to add to them or take away from them (Deut 4:2). When that which was written down in Israel began to be translated and explained to the people as having normative value in the life of their community (Neh 8:9–11), the notion of Scripture was clearly present in Judaism.

The earliest Christian communities also shared the earlier Jewish belief that the revelation and will of God were preserved in written documents, and they also believed that God had acted decisively in the life, death, and resurrection of Jesus and that this activity had also been foretold as a revelation from God in the normative literature of Judaism—the Hebrew Scrip-

---

[23] Barr, *Holy Scripture,* 5.

[24] Many of the Psalms, especially 19 and 119, which focus on the meditation on the word, law, precepts, and statutes of God, are almost certainly preexilic in origin, but most of these do not date before the time of Josiah's finding of the book of the Law (probably Deuteronomy) around 622–621 B.C.E. (compare 2 Kgs 18:20a with 22:3–13).

[25] Barr, *Holy Scripture,* 5.

tures (whatever they consisted of at that time). This proclamation of and about Jesus was passed on at first through the oral traditions of the church, much of which was written down within a few decades of the time when Jesus lived and died. Because these traditions focused on the life and fate of Jesus, they clearly had normative value in the life of the congregations for whom they were preserved in writing. Around 170–80 C.E. several of these writings were called "Scripture," and their divinely inspired status was recognized by many churches at the end of the second century C.E. While the new Christian writings clearly functioned in the capacity of Scripture much sooner, they were not generally called "Scripture" by large segments of the church until the end of the second and the beginning of the third century.

The recognition of several NT writings as Scripture can only be described as a growing process that was neither unanimously nor simultaneously acknowledged in the ancient churches. The churches did not initially accept all of the same books as their Scriptures, and even where there was eventually some agreement, it seldom occurred at the same time and was never representative of all of the churches at that time. This variation can be seen in the differences among the lists of early Christian literature recommended or tabulated for church use in the fourth century and later.[26]

It is not possible to date with any precision how soon the *recognition* of the inspiration and authority of the NT literature took place—that is, the recognition of its scriptural status—but with one possible exception no part of that body of literature was so recognized in the first century. Only the book of Revelation (ca. 90–95) claims for itself such a lofty position that would come close to the notion of inspiration and Scripture:

> I warn everyone who hears the words of the prophecy of this book: if anyone adds to them, God will add to that person the plagues described in this book; if anyone takes away from the words of the book of this prophecy, God will take away that person's share in the tree of life and in the holy city, which are described in this book. (Rev 22:18–19; cf. Deut 4:2 and Rev 1:3, 10–11; 22:7–9)

Stendahl correctly observes that this is the only book in the NT that claims to be a revelation from God.[27] The author of 2 Pet 3:15–16 (written ca. 120–150 C.E. and perhaps as late as 180 C.E.) apparently recognized Paul's Letters as "Scripture," but nowhere does Paul or any other author of the NT claim this special and unambiguous recognition for his own writings. Even the Gospels, which tell the story of Jesus, do not in themselves claim final authority. Such divine authority appears to be reserved for Jesus

---

[26] See appendix C for lists that compare and contrast several important collections of New Testament books in the Christian community in the fourth and fifth centuries.

[27] Stendahl, "Apocalypse of John," 240.

alone (Matt 28:19–20), even though the many OT citations and allusions in the Gospels are evidence of their authoritative status in the life and ministry of the early Christian communities.

Although Paul was mindful that he was communicating the authoritative words of Jesus on occasion (1 Cor 7:10–11; 9:14; 11:23–26), he apparently was unaware of the divinely inspired status of his own advice (7:12, 25). He never wrote as if he himself were setting forth Scripture, although he did acknowledge the superior authority of the words of Jesus in settling matters of Christian ethics and did emphasize his own apostolic authority in resolving disputes in the churches that he founded (e.g., 1 Cor 4:14–5:5; 7:12–16; 2 Cor 13:10) and is the first NT writer to make a qualified claim to inspiration by the Spirit regarding what he said. Nevertheless, he does not write "scripturally," that is, as if he was consciously writing from a divinely inspired and therefore scripturally authoritative perspective. Even though his counsel to the Christians at Corinth about marriage is joined by the words "and I think that I too have the Spirit of God" (1 Cor 7:40), this is a far cry from an acknowledgment by Paul of the scriptural status of his letter to the Corinthian community. Apparently, Paul was aware that he was speaking by the power of the Spirit and writing what he believed was the will of God on issues related to marriage, but was unaware that he was actually writing Scripture.

What makes it difficult to believe that the Gospels were initially acknowledged or received as Scripture is the liberty that the Evangelists took in changing or adapting their sources to fit their own aims. Matthew and Luke evidently felt free to adapt, change, and smooth out the Gospel of Mark[28] and the so-called Q source,[29] which both Matthew and Luke used in their own way. At any rate, the warning given in Rev 22:18–19 was certainly not heeded in reference to Mark. Furthermore, as late as the last half of the second century, Tatian, who had a special interest in the Gospels, was evidently concerned enough with the differences between the Gospels to change or harmonize them in order to set forth a unified gospel commonly called the *Diatessaron*. Would he have taken such liberties with the Gospels had he considered them to be sacred Scripture and therefore inviolable? Even at the end of the second century, Christian writings were not yet generally called "covenant" or "Scriptures." Although Christian writings existed almost from the beginning of the church[30] and functioned au-

[28] For example, both Matt 3:3 and Luke 3:4 drop the first part of the quotation in Mark 1:2, which was attributed to Isaiah but originated with Mal 3:1. The subject changes are also quite striking; for example, compare Matt 3:16 to Mark 1:10 and Matt 14:1 to Mark 6:14, where Matthew smoothes out the more embarrassing title of Antipas.

[29] Q is an abbreviation for the German word *Quelle* meaning "source." This is a convenient way to designate a source containing sayings of Jesus common to both Matthew and Luke and not found in Mark.

[30] For example, Q, but see also Luke 1:1–4.

thoritatively in the early church, being frequently cited by the Apostolic Fathers, the early Christians did not seem to have an interest in writing or adopting new Scriptures. Von Campenhausen rightly concludes that early Christianity was not a "religion of the Book," but rather "the religion of the Spirit and the living Christ."[31] The church had an oral tradition concerning Jesus that was taught and proclaimed in the early communities of faith (Acts 2:42; 4:33; 6:4), as well as the Scriptures of Judaism, which they searched diligently in order to find a witness (prophetic announcement) to the event of Jesus that they had experienced.[32]

II. The Scriptures of Ancient Israel

As we noted above, many places in the OT have an admonition from a prophet about keeping the Law of Moses or simply the Law, but most of them are toward the end of the OT era, namely, after the time of the reforms of Josiah (2 Kgs 23:1–3; cf. 2 Chr 34:1–7).[33] Before those reforms, there are only a few references to observing the law of God (Hos 4:6; Amos 2:4), and it appears that the laws of God given through Moses are largely ignored. For example, there are numerous places in the OT writings where a prophet spoke a word of admonition to ancient Israel but could have strengthened his case considerably by citing a text from the Law. Amos, for instance, could easily have enlisted texts from the law to support his accusations against Israel (see Amos 2:6–16; 5:1–6:14; 7:1–9:15) had they been circulating in some canonical (authoritative) fashion in the eighth century, but he did not. Although Hosea warns the people of Israel that they had "forgotten the law of your God" (Hos 4:6), in several locations he could have cited specific texts from the Decalogue about having other gods (Exod 20:4–6) and thus considerably strengthened his case, but he did not. He referred to the Jews' unfaithfulness to Yahweh (Hos 2:11–13 and 4:1–11), but it is not clear that the Decalogue was in mind. No specific part of the law is invoked here, even though the first commandment could have been used with significant effect. In Hos 6:7 and 8:1 an "agreement" is mentioned, but is this the same as the Decalogue in Exod 20?

Nathan the prophet could also have strengthened his case against David's adultery and murder and charged him with a violation of the law of God had he quoted "you shall not kill" or "you shall not commit adultery"

---

[31] Von Campenhausen, *Formation of the Christian Bible,* 62–66. A similar stance could be argued for the ancient Jewish community of faith, as Barr, *Holy Scripture,* 2–7, shows.

[32] A. R. C. Leaney, "Theophany, Resurrection, and History," *StEv* 103.5.112, correctly observes that the early Christians were concerned to find a Scripture "to fit a fact, and were far from inventing a fact to fit the Scripture."

[33] See references listed in n. 14 above.

from the Decalogue (Exod 20:13–14; 2 Sam 12:1–15). He does say that David has broken the word of the Lord (12:9), but does not say what that word is. Was this Nathan's own perceived will of God? It is difficult to read into this passage a reference to a codified law that prohibited such conduct, but even if it did stand behind the prophet's message, the citing of a specific violation of a sacred Scripture or code that was well recognized by the people would have greatly added to the impact of this writer's message. Joshua appeals to the keeping of the "book of the law" (Josh 1:8), but this kind of reference is rare and not as obvious in Judg 6:8–10, for example, which refers to a prophet, without any clear recollection of a sacred text.

What inferences may be reasonably drawn from this absence of citations of the Law in the earlier parts of the OT era, namely, during the time of the judges and kings of Israel? At the least, the role of a fixed textual scriptural authority was apparently not an important part of the authoritative structure of the people of Israel before the time of Josiah and especially after the time of Ezra. If the Torah had been formed in its present condition before Josiah's reforms, the laws themselves apparently did not have a significant impact on the movers and shapers of Israel's preexilic traditions. If the Law had been received and functioned as canon or absolute authority in the nation of Israel earlier, why does it not function as canon more prominently before the reforms of Josiah in 621 B.C.E. (2 Chr 34:14–33)?[34] Only at the end of the First Temple period is there a concerted effort to show the relevance of the laws of Moses to the people and the importance of observing those laws (Ezra 10:2–3; Neh 8:1–8). With the reforms of Ezra there is a clear call to obey and observe the laws of Moses, but even here we are not certain whether the "law of Moses" in Neh 8:1 refers to the Pentateuch, the book of Deuteronomy, or simply the laws themselves.

The Former Prophets were probably also a recognized authority in the time of Ezra, especially when the people of Israel believed that God had judged them because they had failed to listen to the prophets who witnessed to or proclaimed the message of the Law (Ezra 9:10–15).[35] In the time of Ezra, however, only the Mosaic codes were given a fixed-canon recognition, and the prophets themselves were not yet brought into that

---

[34] Barr, *Holy Scripture,* 6–8, argues the point that in the earlier stages of Israel its religion was not yet the scriptural religion that it later became. It may be probable that only the Deuteronomic code is behind the reforms of Josiah, as most Old Testament scholars suggest. Only in the later stages of the religion of Israel do we find a concern for the interpretation of former prophetic writings, as in the case of Dan 9:2 focusing on the meaning of the seventy weeks of Jer 29:10.

[35] The prophets witnessed to or reminded the people of the law of Moses in regard to intermarriage (cf. Exod 34:15–16; Deut 7:1–5). The judgment came as a result of failure to listen to the message from Moses, which was viewed as inviolable, but it is not clear that other writings were so viewed at this time.

arena, even though they were mentioned occasionally. All references to the prophets in the postexilic writings of Ezra-Nehemiah have to do with the prophets' public proclamation and to their work on the temple, but nothing is said about their literary productions (Ezra 5:1–2 [Haggai and Zechariah]; 9:11; Neh 6:7, 14; 9:26, 30, 32). If the Prophets, as a fixed collection of books had existed in the days of Ezra, this would have been a perfect place to introduce them to the people, but only the books (or laws) of Moses are mentioned in Ezra and Nehemiah.

If a book or collection of books became a permanent part of a sacred collection, this does not always mean that it had an inviolable text. In the Qumran community, for instance, it was not uncommon during Hellenistic times for scribes to make changes in spelling and orthography and even delete sentences from the Torah and other scrolls found at Qumran. These changes suggest that the Law, Prophets, and Psalms carried a lot of authority in the pre-rabbinic times, but they had not yet graduated to the rank of inviolable Scripture that we see in later rabbinic times in which every word and every letter had to be presented accurately and copied faithfully.[36] Even though the Psalter was widely accepted as Scripture, in the first centuries B.C.E. and C.E., the scribes at Qumran felt free to make significant additions to the text, provide elaborations, and even revise it.[37] This suggests that for those at Qumran the Scriptures, including the Torah, had not yet become fixed or inviolable. The apparent inviolability of Scripture that we see in Matt 5:18 in the last quarter of the first century C.E. cannot be found in practice among the scribes at Qumran, or at the least, they did not believe as the later rabbis did that one could not make textual changes to the Scripture collection.

Evidence that the Prophets had not yet moved into a fixed-canon category by the late third century B.C.E. is seen in the translation of the LXX (ca. 280–250 B.C.E.), when the Law *alone* was translated into Greek. Had other OT writings been accepted as inviolable Scripture at that time, it seems likely that they too would have been part of that translation project. Later (ca. 150–130 B.C.E.), the Prophets circulated in a somewhat loose collection of Scriptures, as the prologue to Sirach suggests; and the Writings were circulating in a looser form until sometime later in the second or first century B.C.E., when they and other religious texts were translated into Greek and added to the LXX.

It is difficult to know the precise contents of the LXX at the turn of the era, since no copies exist from that period, but that the LXX eventually expanded to include the Prophets and the Writings is obvious. The NT writers, for instance, use the LXX in more than 90 percent of their references to the OT, and these came from all three sections of the Hebrew Scriptures: Law,

---

[36] Silver, *Story of Scripture,* 141.

[37] J. A. Sanders, "Cave 11 Surprises."

Prophets, and Writings. This does not imply that these categories were complete or that the NT writers were not informed by other sacred texts as well. In fact, Luke 24:44 implies that the third division of the HB was not a well-known category in the middle of the first century C.E. The canonical categories were not complete at the time of the writing of Luke.

The authority attributed to the LXX in antiquity is obvious from the sensational description of its translation in the legendary *Letter of Aristeas* (ca. 130 B.C.E.–35 C.E.). For the author of this letter, the Law of Moses was unquestionably accepted as fixed canon, and the translation was based upon some standard text from Jerusalem. Again, if the Prophets and Writings had already obtained this same status when the LXX translation was produced, it is puzzling why they were not also included in the translation.

By the fifth century C.E., if not sooner, a high priority was given to the accurate translation of the Law of Moses and to the actual handling of the sacred scrolls themselves. Jews were not allowed to divide or separate the Torah scrolls, and they reserved a special place in the synagogues for keeping the Torah (the *tevah*). Whatever the scriptural status of the Prophets and the Writings at the time, the priority of the Torah was indisputable, and it has remained in the place of priority historically. Only the books of the Law were and are completely read annually as an essential part of the Jewish Sabbath liturgy. Whatever else this means, equal priority was not given to all of the literature of the Tanak. Priority was always given to the Law (Pentateuch).

Some canon scholars interpret pre-Christian Jewish texts such as the prologue to Sirach, Philo's *Contemplative Life,* 4QMMT, and other writings of the first century anachronistically; that is, the perspective of second-century rabbinic sages and/or church fathers from the fourth and fifth centuries is claimed to be everywhere present in both the first and second centuries. For instance, some scholars cite the late-second-century *baraita*[38] *b. Bava Batra* 14b as evidence for a widespread understanding of the state of the biblical canon in the land of Israel in the first century C.E. There is no evidence that this tradition was widely held *even in second-century* Jewish communities, whether inside or outside the land of Israel. It was not included in the Mishnah in the early third century and does not represent any second-century community so far as the current evidence shows. Unfortunately, some scholars do not restrict themselves to what they can show, and they frequently draw unwarranted conclusions about what was obtained in the first century from this passage.

---

[38] A *baraita* ("external") is a Hebrew term referring to a tradition from the Tannaitic teachers (roughly 10–210 C.E.) that was not included in the Mishnah but is looked upon as authoritative. That *b. Bava Batra* 14b was not included in the Mishnah suggests that it was not a strong tradition or a well-known tradition when the Mishnah was produced at the end of the second and early third centuries C.E

Those traditions that eventually became canon for ancient Israel also empowered that community for life, that is, they gave hope even in hopeless situations (the exile) and brought life to the remnant of the nation of Israel. The survivability, or endurance, of the ancient writings had much to do with their ability to be interpreted afresh to new communities and in new circumstances. The new interpretations were the product of hermeneutics that searched for the relevance and meaning of this literature in the new and changing circumstances. The adaptability of the writings that did survive ultimately led to their canonicity. This feature has become a primary characteristic of canonical writings. The stabilization of the biblical canon was a later development in the canonical processes, though the church as a whole has never officially opted for any particular text of the biblical Scriptures.

C H A P T E R   T H R E E

The Notion and Use of Canon

THE WORD *CANON* IS SOMETIMES USED IN LITERARY SCHOLARSHIP TO SPEAK OF the "classics" or the standards of literary productions that became models for subsequent writers. When it is used in the Christian community, it often refers to those writings or Scriptures that comprise the Bible. The term was first used in this capacity in the latter half of the fourth century to refer to those theological books that Christians believed came from God, that is, divinely inspired books that clarify both who God is and what the will of God is for the people of God in the world. Because of their beliefs about the importance of Scripture, both Jews and Christians became known as "people of the Book." In its popular use today, canon speaks primarily of a closed collection of sacred Scriptures that Jews and Christians believe had their origins in God and are divinely inspired. The terminology for the notion of canon differs considerably in the Jewish and Christian communities, and in some instances different books are included in each sacred collection, but the notion that lies behind these collections—namely, that God has spoken through a specific collection of sacred literature—is the same. Protestant, Catholic, and Greek Orthodox churches all use the word *canon* for the fixed collection of their sacred Scriptures, but all three collections of Scriptures differ. In what follows we will explore the notion of canon in the Greco-Roman world and in the Jewish and Christian communities.

The roots of the term *canon* are obscure; it likely came from a Semitic language of Sumerian origin and may have some parallel with the Babylonian/Assyrian word *kannu*.[1] The word *canon* itself comes from a form of the Greek word *kanōn* and is derived from *kanē,* a loanword that has a parallel in the Semitic term *kaneh* that initially referred to a "measuring

[1]Hermann Wolfgang Beyer, "Κανών," *TDNT* 3.596. See also Funk, *Parables and Presence,* 151–53. Achtemeier, *Inspiration of Scripture,* 118–23, offers a brief but useful theological and historical description of the use of the term. Metzger, *Canon of the New Testament,* 289–93, offers a more recent and more detailed discussion of the term.

rod" or "measuring stick" (see Ezek 40:5). Among the Greeks, the word came to refer to a standard or norm by which all things are judged or evaluated, whether the perfect form to follow in architecture or sculpture or the infallible criterion (*kritērion*) by which things are to be measured. The notion of canon also appears in music, where the monochord was the canon that controls all other tonal relationships.

Knowing something of the history and development of the term helps explain how it came to be used of biblical literature and clarifies a great deal of the debate among scholars over canon formation today. It is rare among scholars to find a clear definition of the biblical canon that deals adequately with the surviving sources from antiquity and with the biblical text itself. Much of the controversy surrounding canon formation has to do with the lack of agreement on the meaning of canon and when we begin to see signs of it in Israel and early Christianity. We will begin with an examination of the origin of the term and how it was used first in the ancient world and then focus on how it came to be used in the church. As we will see in §V below, the Jews did not use the word *canon* to speak of a fixed collection of their Scriptures, but they had other ways of describing the same phenomenon.

I. Canons in the Ancient World

The ancient world was filled with canons (guides, models, regulations) for almost every sphere of art or activity. The Egyptians had canons of art by which the artisans were guided in their craft. The cartouche, for example, a rectangular closed circle containing the pharaoh's name in hieroglyphics, is uniform in almost all paintings and statuary of the ancient dynasties in Egypt. Other canons of art from the Old Kingdom (ca. 2700–2160 B.C.E.)[2] and the Middle Kingdom (2106–1786 B.C.E.) include the uniform shape of human figures, skin color (women were uniformly given a lighter skin color than men), arms crossed over the chest to indicate the death of the person portrayed, a foot extended forward with the hands at the side or extended to indicate that the person portrayed by the painter or sculptor was still alive, and symbols of the cobra and/or the falcon-god Horus (a deity that became associated with kingship) on the headdress of the king or within the design of art objects related to kingship.[3]

The same conformity to a canon of art appears on grave stelae from ancient Greece. These stelae, from around 600 B.C.E. to roughly 300 B.C.E.,

[2] Egyptian dates taken from *Anchor Bible Dictionary* 2.328.

[3] Only in the New Kingdom (1550 B.C.E. and following) was there a temporary loosening of some of the more rigid patterns of art to allow for more realistic depictions of the torsos of the pharaohs with larger stomachs and weaker or even odd-looking torsos.

are quite uniform in style, progressing from one-dimensional to two-dimensional and finally three-dimensional stelae. The same figures are represented on the stone carvings, and the stelae are topped first by a sphinx and finally by a palmette finial,[4] with widespread uniform relief decoration on the shaft.

Several other examples of standards or canons are found in antiquity. For example, the notion of a standard was also employed in philosophy as the criterion or canon by which one discovers what is true and false. Beyer shows that Epicurus himself argued that logic and method in thought stemmed from a canon (*kanōn*) or basis by which one could know what was true or false and thus whether it was worth investigating.[5] Epicurean philosopher Diogenes Laertius (200–250 C.E.) identifies one of the writings of Epicurus (341–270 B.C.E.) as "Of the Standard, a Work Entitled Canon" (*Peri Kritēriou ē Kanōn*), calling it "canonic" (*kanonikon*) (*Lives of Eminent Philosophers* 10.27, 30). He later explains the substance of this work: "Now in *The Canon* Epicurus affirms that our sensations and preconceptions and our feelings are the standards of truth; the Epicureans generally make perceptions of mental presentations to be also standards" (*Lives of Eminent Philosophers* 10.31, LCL).[6] This use is similar to the way that the term *canon* came to be used as the standard of truth applied to the early Christian faith.

Epictetus (ca. 50–130 C.E.) argued that the goal of philosophy is to determine a "standard of judgment" and that whatever subject needs to be investigated, one needs to "subject it to the standard [*hypage autēn tō kanoni*]" (*Dissertationes* 2.11.13, 20; cf. 2.23.21). Aeschines of Athens (ca. 397–322 B.C.E.) says essentially the same thing:

> In carpentry, when we want to know whether something is straight, we use a ruler [*kanōn*] designed for the purpose. So also in the case of indictments for illegal proposals, the guide [*kanōn*] for justice is this public posting of the proposal with accompanying statement of the laws that it violates. (*Against Ctesiphon* 199–200, quoted in Danker, *II Corinthians,* 160)

Both Homer and Hesiod were widely revered among the Greeks and used as standards or models for literary writings. Alexander the Great, under the influence of Aristotle, actually worshipped Homer and founded a cult in his name at Alexandria.[7] The gods mentioned in Homer's *Iliad* and *Odyssey* are the ones that became canon for the Greeks, that is, became recognized and honored deities. Homer functioned canonically or authoritatively among the Greeks and in a very real sense became canon par excellence for them. This included a special religious significance. Unlike

---

[4]The palmette finial is an ornament with divisions resembling a palm leaf. This symbol completes the artwork and appears on the apex, top, or corner of the stela.

[5]Beyer, "Κανών," 596–98.

[6]For similar examples, see also Seneca, *Epistles* 89.11–12.

[7]Graham, *Beyond the Written Word,* 52.

other ancient Greek writings, both of Homer's works were divided into twenty-four parts (books or chapters), and each part was identified by a letter of the Greek alphabet.

The use of the alphabet as a sign of the divine origin and importance of something (whether writings or persons) is helpful for understanding the New Testament references to God and Jesus as "Alpha and Omega," the first and last letters of the Greek alphabet (Rev 1:8; 21:6; 22:13), and for understanding the Jewish practice of dividing some psalms into twenty-two verses (e.g., Pss 25, 33, 34, 103) or twenty-two sections (e.g., Ps 119), apparently on the basis of the twenty-two-letter Hebrew alphabet (Pss 25 and 34 are also acrostics). Like those who revered Homer and used the Greek alphabet to designate chapters in his works, the Jews at first identified the number of books in their sacred collection with the number of letters in the Hebrew alphabet (twenty-two), but later adopted the number of the Greek alphabet (twenty-four) to identify the number of books in their Scriptures.

By about 25 B.C.E., many Roman grammarians were following the model of Vergil's *Aeneid,* Cicero, or Sallust. Even Tacitus (78–115 C.E.), perhaps "the most individualistic and most psychological of ancient historians,"[8] was still guided by the model of Vergil's *Aeneid.* Among the Greeks, Plato especially and later also Aristotle were the canons or models for subsequent philosophers.

Latin grammarians, in the tradition of the Greeks, deemed it very important to follow certain models in their writing. According to Suetonius, they were also actively involved in training the rhetoricians of the day in the best principles of grammar. The importance of strict adherence to these rules of grammar can be illustrated with three examples from Suetonius's *Lives of Illustrious Men.* One writer by the name of Marcus Pompilius Andronicus was more interested in his Epicurean sect than in giving special attention to matters of grammar in his writing. The resulting grammatical criticisms of his work by his colleagues, however, forced him to leave Rome:

> Marcus Pompilius Andronicus, a native of Syria, . . . was considered somewhat indolent in his work as a grammarian and not qualified to conduct a school. Therefore, realizing that he was held in less esteem at Rome, not only than Antonius Gnipho, but than others of even less ability, he moved to Cumae, where he led a quiet life and wrote many books. (Suetonius, *Lives of Illustrious Men: On Grammarians* 8, LCL)

Similarly, one of the worst insults of the day was to be accused of ignorance of proper grammar. For example, Lenaeus, the freedman of Pompey, criticized Sallust (who had criticized Pompey) with biting satire and several debasing adjectives, concluding with this final salvo: "And who was

[8] C. Moore, *Tacitus,* 2: xiii.

besides an ignorant pilferer of the language of the ancients" (Suetonius, *Lives of Illustrious Men: On Grammarians* 15, LCL)!

The significant authority attributed to the canons or standards of grammar around the time of the birth of Jesus can be seen in the well-known account of Marcellus's attack on the grammar of leading Roman officials, including an attack on Caesar Tiberius:

> Marcus Pomponius Marcellus, a most pedantic critic of the Latin language, in one of his cases (for he sometimes acted as an advocate) was so persistent in criticizing an error in diction made by his opponent, that Cassius Severus appealed to the judges and asked for a postponement, to enable his client to employ a grammarian in his stead: "For," said he, "he thinks that the contest with his opponent will not be on points of law, but of diction." When this same Marcellus had criticized a word in one of Tiberius's speeches, and Ateius Capito declared that it was good Latin, or if not, that it would surely be so from that time on, Marcellus answered: "Capito lies; for you, Caesar, can confer citizenship upon men, but not upon a word." (Suetonius, *Lives of Illustrious Men: On Grammarians* 22, LCL)

The notion of a written canon was practiced by the Alexandrians in Egypt both in reference to grammar and the literary models for all writers to follow. They did not use the term *canon* to describe their activity, but rather the Greek term *pinakes*.[9] However, the very selectivity used in compiling their famous lists of works to include in the Alexandrian library showed the high standards that were employed in the selectivity. The grammarians serving at the great library of Alexandria sought to preserve an accurate and faithful text of the classics in literature and thus produced a canon of writers whose Greek was used as a model for other writers. Among the most commonly recognized ancient classics were the works of Homer, Euripides, Menander, Demosthenes, Hesiod, Pindar, Sappho, Aeschylus, Sophocles, Plato, Aristotle, Aristophanes, Herodotus, Thucydides, and Aesop. In antiquity, those who wrote literary works did not move far from these models in subject matter, style, or grammar. Those who departed from these standards were soon criticized and often ignored.

These classic writers (and a few others) became the standards in the Alexandrian library. Not everything written in the ancient world was selected to be placed in that collection in the library, but those that were included were copied with great care by people trained to preserve the

---

[9] *Pinax* (plural *pinakes*) originally referred to a board or plank or tablet, often used to create a list, catalogue, or index. Eventually, the term was widely used in reference to the list or catalogue itself. *Pinakes* is similar in meaning to Cicero's Latin term *classici* ("classes") and Quintilian's Latin term *ordo* ("series, order"). Indeed the very word *classic,* when applied to the ancient writers, suggests that these writers were among those who had reached certain standards of excellence and thought that others should and did imitate (see Rudolf Pfeiffer, *History of Classical Scholarship,* 206–7). While Greek *kanōn* did not originally have the sense of a finished or complete repertory as did the word *pinakes,* it eventually came to be used in this fashion.

accuracy of their texts and order them for identification and location. For example, the list of poets among the old Greek classics is undeniably selective. The Greek grammarians at Alexandria selected Homer, author of the *Iliad* and *Odyssey,* along with Hesiod, author of *Theogony* and *Erga,* as the standards of epic poetry. Likewise, Pindar, Bacchylides, Sappho, Anacreon, Stesichorus, Simonides, Ibycus, Alcaeus, and Alcman became the nine standard lyric poets and were sometimes referred to as "the Nine." Although the order differs in the various epigrams that list these works, the names were all the same; it was a standard list. These names, as well as those of the ten great orators, circulated widely not only in Alexandria, but also in Pergamum, Rhodes, Athens, and Rome, the other important learning centers and locations of major libraries in the ancient world. After listing the orators and writers with the best skills, Quintilian (born ca. 35 C.E.) explains the value of imitating them:

> It is from these and other authors worth reading that we must draw our stock of words, the variety of our Figures, and our system of composition, and also guide our minds by the patterns they provide of all the virtues. It cannot be doubted that a large part of art consists of imitation. Invention of course came first and is the main thing, but good inventions are profitable to follow. Moreover, it is a principle of life in general that we want to do for ourselves what we approve in others. Children follow the outlines of letters so as to become accustomed to writing. Singers find their model in their teacher's voice, painters in the works of their predecessors, and farmers in methods of cultivation which have been tested by experience. In a word, we see the rudiments of every branch of learning shaped by standards prescribed for it. We obviously cannot help being either like the good or unlike them. Nature rarely makes us like them; imitation often does. (*Orator's Education* 10.2.1–3, LCL)

In other Greco-Roman literature, the word *canon* was employed as a means of determining the quality of something, of whether it "measured up."[10] This is similar to the term *canon of faith,* which refers to the religious beliefs that were the standards of faith and practice in the early church. Unlike the Christian and Jewish understanding of their biblical canons, however, Quintilian urges caution when reading the best authors. They were merely human, he stresses, and could make mistakes. That should be held in mind when reading the best orators and writers:

> The reader must not let himself be automatically convinced that everything which the best authors said is necessarily perfect. They do sometimes slip, stagger under the load, and indulge in the pleasures of their own ingenuity. They do not always concentrate, and they get tired from time to time. Cicero thinks Demosthenes sometimes drops off to sleep, and Horace thinks the

[10]For example, see Euripides, *Hecuba* 602; Demosthenes 18.18, 296; Aeschines *Against Ctesiphon* 88; Sextus Empiricus, *Pros Logikous* 2.3; Epictetus, *Discourses* 1.28.28.

> same even of Homer. Great men they are, but they are only human, and it can happen that people who make everything they find in them into a law of oratory come to imitate their less good features (which is easier) and fancy themselves sufficiently like them if they attain to the great men's faults. However, we should be modest and circumspect in pronouncing judgement on men of such stature, and avoid the common mistake of condemning what we do not understand. If we must err on one side or the other, I should prefer readers to approve of everything in the masters than to find many things to disapprove. (*Orator's Education* 10.1.24–26, LCL)

To the contrary, those who followed a biblical canon believed that their writings came from God, and they were not likely to criticize them or stand in judgment on them.

Upon request from Alexander the Great, Aristotle set forth the standard "rules" or guidelines for the practice of rhetoric in the political arena. He called his enterprise "principles of political oratory" and purposed to present them "with a degree of accuracy that has not yet been attained by any other of the authors dealing with it" (Aristotle, *Rhetoric to Alexander,* 1420a, LCL).

Alexandrian grammarians, who set forth a canon of writers whose Greek was used as a model, may well have influenced both Jews and Christians who sought to identify the books that established the standard guidelines of their faith and practice. The gathering together of an authoritative collection of classical writings in the great library at Alexandria, Egypt, has some parallels with the canonical processes of the Jews and Christians.[11] John Van Seters argues more forcefully that the act of gathering and copying the classical texts in the library at Alexandria was the direct ancestor of the biblical canons of both Judaism and early Christianity:

> The scholarly tradition of the Alexandrian library was likewise concerned with the listing and classification of its works. In this regard it established tables, i.e. lists (*pinakes*) of writers and classical works from the past, and excluded spurious works whose creation was very common in the Hellenistic period. These tables are the ancestors of the "canons of writers" that one encounters in the Roman and Byzantine periods. I think it is obvious that the concern to establish a canon of scripture in Judaism and Christianity draws directly upon this scholarly tradition.[12]

The legendary story about the origins of the Greek translation of the Law presented in the *Letter of Aristeas* is in harmony with this theory. Its author gives a reasonable account of how the library began and how the Jewish sacred scriptures were added to it:

> On his appointment as keeper of the king's [Ptolemy II Philadelphus, 285–247 B.C.E.] library, Demetrius of Phalerum undertook many different negotiations aimed at collecting, if possible, all the books in the world. By purchase and

---

[11]VanderKam, *Revelation to Canon,* 29–30, also suggests this influence.

[12]Quoted in ibid., 30.

> translation he brought to successful conclusion, as far as lay in his power, the king's plan. We were present when the question was put to him, "How many thousand books are there (in the royal library)?" His reply was, "Over two hundred thousand, O King. I shall take urgent steps to increase in a short time the total to five hundred thousand. Information has reached me that the lawbooks of the Jews are worth translation and inclusion in your royal library." (*Let. Aris.* 9–10, *OTP* 2.12)

The *Letter of Aristeas,* though generally acknowledged as Jewish fictional propaganda, is nonetheless probably reliable in several aspects, such as the claim that individuals in Alexandria sought to collect important literary productions.[13] It is also likely, as the *Letter of Aristeas* states, that that the translators of the Law of Moses from Hebrew into Greek came from Jerusalem to Egypt, which assumes a standard text of Jewish Scriptures in Jerusalem, and it also assumes some relationship between the Jews in the land of Israel and those in Alexandria.

The notion that this tradition of collecting the standard or classical writings in one library collection was a model for the Jews is enhanced by the reference that the Jewish "lawbooks" are worthy of translation and inclusion in the royal library. Obviously, not everything written was considered worthy of inclusion, and the selectivity on the part of the librarians at the Alexandrian library, witnessed to by the *Letter of Aristeas,* may well give the context or background necessary to understand why both Jews and Christians adopted the notion of a fixed standard of sacred writings.

Those connected with the famous Alexandrian library commissioned the famous writer Callimachus[14] to compile a catalogue (*pinakes*) of the ancient authors and works housed in the library at Alexandria. Again, it is possible that both Jews and Christians derived their understanding of the notion of a biblical canon as a fixed collection of authoritative writings from this example.[15] There were certainly large numbers of Jews in Alexandria both

---

[13] Rudolf Pfeiffer, *History of Classical Scholarship,* 99–104, discusses the importance of the *Letter of Aristeas* with its other ancient parallel, Tzetzes' *Prolegomena to Aristophanes,* and while acknowledging the fictitious nature of the former, he nevertheless accepts many of its features as reflective of the origins and development of the library at Alexandria.

[14] Callimachus was born in Cyrene around 300 B.C.E. and educated in Athens. After teaching for a while near Alexandria, he was commissioned to produce a catalogue of the library, with notes on all of its estimated 500,000 volumes in order to make them more accessible. A poet and a prolific writer (supposedly producing more than 800 volumes)—but never head librarian at Alexandria—Callimachus's most valuable contribution is his 120-volume catalogue, which he entitled *Pinakes.* See Lesky, *History of Greek Literature,* 5, 700–717; Rudolf Pfeiffer, *History of Classical Scholarship,* 123–51; and Zetzel, "Re-creating the Canon," 122–25.

[15] Davies, *Scribes and Schools,* 6–8, 15–36, offers a useful discussion of how the term *canon* was used in antiquity and also suggests that the Christians only later adopted a well-used term in the Greco-Roman world for their own biblical canon. See also VanderKam, *Revelation to Canon,* 29–30.

before and during the time when the Hebrew Scriptures were translated into Greek, and they may well have gained their understanding of a fixed biblical canon from the model close at hand, namely, the canon of literary texts in the library at Alexandria. Likewise, many Christians were living in Alexandria in the latter part of the first century C.E. and thereafter, well before the time when they discussed canon formation. Did the Alexandrian literary canon influence the Christian biblical canon? It is not yet possible to draw clear lines of dependence, but both the proximity and influence of Alexandria on the land of Israel in the third century B.C.E. and thereafter suggests this possibility. Indeed, the Egyptian Ptolemies controlled the land of Israel until the battle at Pan (called Caesarea Philippi in the New Testament and more recently Banias) in 198 B.C.E. It may be significant that there is no record of a fixed or stabilized collection of Scriptures in Judaism before Alexandria. It is not a great leap in logic to see how the librarians at Alexandria might well have influenced the Jews, especially when their sacred writings were translated, given to the king, and placed in the Alexandrian library.

Notions of canon were widespread in the Greco-Roman world well before Jews and Christians began to talk about fixed collections of sacred Scriptures, and those notions may have had some influence on both communities' understanding of canon. Literary canons were widespread in the ancient world and continue to this day, but what appears to be unique to Judaism, and was subsequently adopted by the Christian community, is the notion of a *fixed* collection of sacred or theological books that defines the will of God, sets forth the identity of God and the people of God, and are considered inviolable (Deut 4:2; Rev 22:18–19). Nothing else quite parallels this focus in antiquity, although special religious significance was given to Homer, as we observed above.

The processes of canonization have striking parallels in the Greco-Roman world and in modern times, including the selective decanonization that canons often undergo when the times, culture, and needs of a community change. For example, over time the formal literary styles of language that were once dominant in a culture inevitably change, and the former standards of literary activity are no longer the same as those in the emerging culture. In times of change and transition, educational institutions become the primary custodians of the classical literature of the past. Through a variety of interpretive measures that regularly introduce the past standard to the contemporary culture, the educational institutions seek ways of enabling the classical literature to remain relevant to the emerging communities.[16]

In the case of Judaism and Christianity, the institutions are the synagogue and the church respectively, and they use a variety of hermeneutical

---

[16]Guillory, "Canon," offers an excellent summary of how literary canons emerged in the ancient world and how they were maintained in both antiquity and the modern world.

skills to bring the past into the present and to show the relevance of the standards of church and synagogue for the contemporary communities of faith. Historically, the oldest hermeneutical skill that sought to bridge the gap between the old and sacred standards was allegory. Both Judaism and early Christianity utilized allegory to show the continuing relevance of their Scriptures. Because ancient literary canons spoke differently than contemporary canons, contemporary educators—both Jewish and Christian—contemporized the classical literature so that those canons could address the people of their day. Changing times always pose a problem for literary and biblical canons. How can that which has become canon for one generation remain such for the next? Just as the ancient teachers of the literary canons developed interpretive processes that allowed their established canons to remain relevant to the present generation, historically the educators or teachers of Judaism and Christianity have done the same. They sought to engage and interpret their sacred traditions in order to make them more relevant to the emerging communities of faith, though periodically, the canons of one generation ceased being relevant to the needs of the next and at times selected literature became decanonized.

These overlaps cannot be inconsequential for a study of canon formation, despite the considerable differences between the ancient literary canons and biblical canons, namely, the former did not have permanently closed boundaries, and the leaders of the next generation of literary writers did not hesitate to criticize the canons of the previous generations. In the case of biblical canons, however, Jews and Christians believed that their biblical canons came from God, reflected the will of God for all times, and were therefore perfect as well as sacred. They did not need changing, but only interpreting. As this view took root in the synagogue and in the church, decanonization was harder to accomplish, and more creative ways—that is, hermeneutics—were introduced to make the biblical literature more relevant to contemporary generations. These similarities, as well as the differences, between the Jewish and Christian biblical canons and the ancient literary canons are the subject of several significant works on literary canons, and future advances in canon formation will of necessity need to be informed by them.[17]

Canons (i.e., laws, regulations, patterns, models) were quite common in many spheres of life in the ancient world long before Jews and Christians began to focus on closed Scripture canons. The extent to which these and similar cultural influences had an effect on the decisions that Jews and Christians made regarding their own biblical canons requires

[17] For a more thorough examination of the social context of literary canons, see Guillory's *Cultural Capital* and Von Hallberg's *Canons,* a collection of essays on the wide range of canon formation, including the formation of the HB. A standard and still relevant discussion that deals with the origin and perpetuation of literary canons is Fiedler and Baker, *English Literature.*

further exploration.[18] As we will see below, a push for unity and conformity was a hallmark of Roman emperors, and this was especially prominent during the reign of Constantine in the fourth century when various Christian teachers began to produce lists of Scriptures that they believed were inspired by God and formed the Christian Bible.

II. Biblical and Faith Canons

The early church used the term *canon* primarily in reference to a "canon of faith," or *regula fidei,* that formed the essence of Christian belief. The Jewish community did not use this term, but the notion of a standard of sacred literature was known among the Jews, who used other means to refer to their sacred collection of writings (see §V below).

Ulrich recognizes how confusing it is to use the word *canon* for writings that were used authoritatively (as Scripture) in Israel, but had not yet been placed into a fixed collection of sacred texts. Authoritative Scriptures were discovered at Qumran, but it is difficult to determine from them a *fixed* collection of Scriptures, that is, a biblical canon. To identify that canon with any level of certainty, Ulrich says, requires several kinds of evidence: (1) the clear mention of the title of a canon or its individual parts, such as a list of books that make up a biblical canon; (2) multiple copies of the books, which indicate the popularity of the text or book in that community; (3) formulas such as "it is written" or "the Scripture says" used to introduce quotations of Scripture as well as books specifically quoted as Scripture; (4) commentaries produced on biblical books; and (5) books translated into the vernacular languages, either Greek or Aramaic.[19] Regardless of whether all of these criteria are operative, the very act of copying and preserving ancient documents, as scribes did at Qumran, suggests this significance or usefulness to some segments of that community. The problem with the Qumran example is that we do not know the full extent of the collection that the Jews of Qumran tried to preserve. Eleven caves have been discovered, but no one

---

[18] It is disappointing that almost every significant investigation of the Christian canon today omits discussion of the Greco-Roman influence on the notion of canon in the ancient Christian community. Clearly there are differences between literary canons and biblical canons, but there are also considerable overlaps in concept, some of which may have influenced the church at various junctures in the canonical processes. Georgi's *Opponents of Paul,* 427–45, includes a most welcomed epilogue on the question of canon in the ancient Greco-Roman world. He raises questions, makes observations about the social context of canon formation, and offers helpful bibliography and footnotes to pursue the question. A doctoral seminar that Georgi directed at the Harvard Divinity School in the fall of 1979 produced many important papers on the topic, but unfortunately the papers are still on the closed shelves of the Andover Library and remain unpublished.

[19] Ulrich, "Qumran and the Canon."

can be sure that another cave does not exist somewhere and is waiting to be discovered. Likewise, had there been fewer worms in some of the caves, much more might have been discovered there!

Smith notes that translating a book or copying it into the same language was quite tedious and time consuming. As a result, he contends that neither activity would have been carried out without some strong motivation regarding the value of the document. The same is true for those who took the time to produce, edit, and correct the various documents discovered in and around Qumran.[20] Using his criteria, Ulrich agrees that the Qumran community recognized many books as the word of God, that is, as divine Scripture, and that at times this literature was referred to as "Torah and Prophets," but he cautiously concludes that no evidence enables the interpreter to determine precisely which books were part of those authoritative collections.[21] In a similar note of caution, Sanders points out that "we simply do not know if we have everything they [the residents at Qumran] had in their library, probably indeed not."[22]

We will return later to the important issues raised by the discovery of the Dead Sea Scrolls, but in the meantime, I conclude that the term *Scripture* is covered by the notion of canon, namely, something written down that became normative for a believing community. Both terms are often interchangeable, but they are also distinguishable, and it is important to keep them that way.[23] On the other hand, there can be no doubt that the individual documents that comprise a biblical canon functioned authoritatively as inspired sacred writings within a believing community *before* they were incorporated into a canonized or fixed corpus.[24] If a biblical canon is a *fixed*

---

[20] M. Smith, *Palestinian Parties and Politics,* 7.

[21] Ulrich, "Qumran and the Canon," 77. In a paper delivered at the 2003 annual convention of the Society of Biblical Literature in Atlanta, Georgia, entitled "Canon," Ulrich suggests that based on the criteria listed above we may now know the parameters of the biblical canon at Qumran, but he had difficulty when asked to account for the noncanonical literature discovered there that apparently functioned canonically for the Essenes, namely, the *Temple Scroll.* Rather confusingly, he says in his unpublished paper that "there is strong evidence to demonstrate that the writings in the library at Qumran—just as the NT and the majority of Judaism—recognized a number of books as containing the word of God, thus as authoritative Scripture, and that they were at times referred to as the Torah and the Prophets. There is no conclusive evidence, however, to determine what the exact contents of the collection were that the community considered the authoritative books of Scripture. Thus, there were recognized books of authoritative Scripture, but there is no clear evidence for a canon of Scripture." He lists *1 Enoch, Jubilees,* Tobit, Sirach, and the Epistle of Jeremiah as candidates, but ignores several other possible candidates such as 4QMMT and the *Temple Scroll.*

[22] J. A. Sanders, "Canon: Hebrew Bible," 842.

[23] For further discussion of this topic, see Ulrich, "Notion and Definition of Canon."

[24] This distinction is noted by Sarna, "Canon, Text, and Editions," 822. Whatever else we call the writings that were appealed to as divinely inspired and

list of Scriptures, what do we call a book or piece of literature that functioned authoritatively as a sacred writing *before* it became part of a fixed list of sacred Scriptures?

The word *canon* is present in Jewish writings, though it was not used in reference to a fixed collection of sacred Scriptures. For example, Josephus (ca. 90 C.E.) refers to Josiah's ascension to the throne (2 Kgs 22:1; 2 Chr 34:1) and says that King David was a model "whom he [Josiah] made the pattern and rule [*kanoni*] of his whole manner of life" (*Ant.* 10.49, LCL).[25]

In the New Testament, the Greek word *kanōn* is found only in Paul's Letters, where it speaks of guidelines established by God, the limits of Paul's ministry, or the boundaries of another's ministry (2 Cor 10:13, 15, 16) and once as the standard or norm of true Christianity (Gal 6:16). Later, Clement of Rome (ca. 90 C.E.) used "canon" in reference to the church's revealed truth when he encourages the Christians at Corinth to "put aside empty and vain cares, and let us come to the glorious and venerable *rule* of our tradition [*tēs paradoseōs hēmon kanona*]" (*1 Clem.* 7.2, LCL).[26] In second-century Christianity, *kanōn* was used in the church to describe a "rule of faith" (Latin *regula fidei;* Gk. *ho kanōn tēs pisteōs*) or a "rule of truth" (Latin *regula veritatis;* Gk. *ho kanōn tēs alētheias*). It designated a core of beliefs that identified the Christian community, its understanding of the will of God, and its mission.[27]

At the end of the second century C.E., Irenaeus used the term *canon* in reference to the rule of faith that governed orthodox Christianity in Rome. He also used the term to refer to the essence or core of Christian doctrine, saying that a true believer retains "unchangeable in his heart the *rule of the truth* which he received by means of baptism" (*Haer.* 1.9.4, *ANF*). This usage is similar to Latin *norma* ("standard"). Eusebius (ca. 320–330) says that Clement of Alexandria (ca. 170–180) spoke of an "ecclesiastical canon" or "body of truth" (Gk. *kanōn ekklēsiastikos*) (*Hist. eccl.* 6.13.3). Clement also spoke of the "rule" (*kanōn*) of faith that was the truth of the church, even though he did not apply the term specifically to the biblical literature.[28] From approximately the middle of the fourth century C.E., *kanōn*

---

authoritative *before* they were included in a biblical canon, because they functioned canonically or authoritatively as sacred literature, there needs to be some means of identifying them as such (see §IV below).

[25] See other examples in Josephus, *Ag. Ap.* 2.174; Philo, *Allegorical Interpretation* 3.233; *Testament of Naphtali.* 2:3; 4 Macc 7:21; and *Let. Aris.* 2.

[26] The precise meaning of this phrase is difficult to determine. It could refer to the Christian message and its implications that were passed on in the church, to a common code of church ethics, or to the *Christian* use of the Old Testament Scriptures. Probably the first of these is intended.

[27] Metzger, *Canon of the New Testament,* 251–52.

[28] See Clement of Alexandria, *Strom.* 6.15.125, where *kanōn* is the harmony between the Law and the Prophets on the one side and the *covenant* instituted by the incarnation of the Lord on the other.

was increasingly used of the collection of sacred writings of both the Old and New Testaments.[29]

Eusebius is sometimes credited with being the first person to use the term *kanōn* in reference to a collection of Christian Scriptures (see *Hist. eccl.* 6.25.3), but careful study of Eusebius's references to the Scriptures of the church indicates that his favorite terms for this literature was *homologoumenon* ("recognized") and *endiathēkos* ("covenanted") or more accurately "encovenanted" (*Hist. eccl.* 3.25.3 and 3.25.6 respectively; see also 3.24.2).[30] His usual term for describing a list of sacred Scriptures is *katalogos* ("catalogue"; *Hist. eccl.* 3.25.6; 4.26.12). When he uses the term *kanōn,* he is generally referring to the church's traditions or its rule of faith. Of the ten times Eusebius uses the term, only two are possible (but unlikely) candidates for an exclusive list of sacred Scriptures (*Hist. eccl.* 5.28.13; 6.25.3). Although he provides the first *datable* list of the New Testament canonical books of the church (*Hist. eccl.* 3.25.1–7), he does not use the term *kanōn* to refer to it. He apparently did use *kanona,* however, in reference to a list of the four Gospels (*Hist. eccl.* 6.25.3).

Setting forth what he claimed was Origen's canon of Scriptures, Eusebius writes: "In the first of his [commentaries] on the Gospel according to Matthew, defending the *canon* of the Church [*ton ekklēsiastikon phylattōn kanona*], he gives his testimony that he knows only four Gospels" (*Hist. eccl.* 6.25.3, LCL, emphasis added). The question here is whether "canon of the church" refers to the rule of faith or to a body of sacred Christian literature, that is, a list of Scriptures. While the context deals with a collection of writings, Eusebius is clearly speaking here about a rule of faith presented in a collection of sacred writings (see also *Hist. eccl.* 6.25.1, where he cites Origen's "encovenanted books" [*endiathēkous biblous*]).

In an annual Easter letter of 367 C.E., commonly referred to as his *Thirty-ninth Festal Letter,* Athanasius made use of the verbal form of *kanonizomenōn* ("canonized") in reference to a collection of sacred literature that he wanted to distinguish from a collection of apocryphal writings commonly read in the churches in Egypt and elsewhere.[31] This is the earliest use of *kanōn* for a collection or listing of the church's Scriptures.

The word *canon* was not regularly used in reference to a closed collection of writings until David Ruhnken used it this way in 1768. In his treatise entitled *Historia critica oratorum Graecorum,* he employed the term *canon* for a selective list of literary writings. According to Pfeiffer, "his

---

[29] Several scholars make this point. See, for example, Beyer, "κανών," *TDNT* 3.600–601; Schneemelcher, "General Introduction," 22–24; and Lampe, "Early Church," 24–26.

[30] Metzger, *Canon of the New Testament,* 292, translates *endiathēkos* as "contained in the covenant" (i.e., not apocryphal).

[31] See chapter 13 §I.E for a list of the writings that formed Athanasius's New Testament canon.

coinage met with worldwide and lasting success, as the term was found to be so convenient." Pfeiffer further suggests that this unusual use of the word *canon* for a Scripture collection came from the biblical tradition, even though the biblical canons consist of a list of writers rather than books that are accepted as genuine and inspired.[32] Pfeiffer concludes that Ruhnken's use of the term *canon* to identify literary lists is closer to the biblical tradition than it is to how the ancients used the term, who did not use it in reference to a standard list. Pfeiffer suggests that Ruhnken likely discovered this use in the biblical tradition and not in antiquity, where *pinakes* is more commonly used of catalogues or lists. Pfeiffer concedes that while he avoids the language, it is nevertheless appropriate to speak of an "Alexandrian canon" of the nine lyric poets: "The expression is sanctioned by its age and convenience, and will, I am afraid, never disappear. But if one calls such lists 'canons,' one should be aware that this is not the proper significance of the Greek κανών but a modern catachresis that originated in the eighteenth century."[33]

While it is tempting to think that what has become commonplace in modern religious jargon was also true in antiquity, that is simply not the case.[34] One is hard pressed to say that the ancient term *pinakes* was used to identify standard or classical writings of antiquity, which are significantly different from the collections of Scriptures that identified the Jewish and Christian communities.

Some object to any connections between *pinakes* and the way that *kanōn* eventually came to be used. They sometimes appeal to *Pinakes,* the famous 120-volume catalogue of the books in the Alexandria library compiled by Callimachus in the third century B.C.E. Callimachus listed not only the author and subject, but also made comments about the authors and their work, including the quality of their work. Aristarchus later criticized Callimachus for placing *Cassandra* among the *paeans,*[35] which suggests that Callimachus also analyzed and classified the writings in the library. While he produced a *complete* listing of the holdings in the library and entitled his work *Pinakes,* this does not contradict the fact that the library housed the standard literary texts of the ancient world. Also, the word *pinakes* was used by others as a standard collection of standard literary

---

[32] Rudolf Pfeiffer, *History of Classical Scholarship,* 207.

[33] Ibid.

[34] For a helpful discussion of the background on the use of the term *kanōn* for a collection of Scriptures, see Robbins, "Eusebius' Lexicon of 'Canonicity,'" who argues cogently that Eusebius never used the word *canon* as it is employed in modern times in reference to a fixed collection of sacred Scriptures. He also agrees that the list of Origen's OT canon is Eusebius's invention. In fact, Origen spoke of the number twenty-two only in reference to the books of the *Jewish* Scriptures, but not his own (see 140).

[35] A *paean* was a Greek hymn of praise or thanksgiving in honor of Apollo or other divine beings.

writers, even though there were standards that writers followed. Archilochus was *the* iambic poet, Homer *the* epic writer, and Pindar *the* standard for lyric poets. Further, as Pfeiffer cautions, to deny the existence of selective lists alongside the complete *Pinakes* produced by Callimachus is to miss the importance of a select number of books that did exist as standards. He claims that this list of the nine poets "became authoritative in the same way as his [Aristophanes'] terminology, classification, and colometry. The order might differ, but the actual names were the same in all the Hellenistic epigrams and prose lists until the latest Byzantine times."[36]

At the end of the canonical process, the writings that made up those collections were looked upon as inviolable and placed into sacred collections called the holy Scriptures. In the early and fluid stages of development, however, some of the writings were often changed, and in some instances churches and synagogues ceased making use of some of them. Those books that still had favor among the believing communities, even if for a short time, nevertheless impacted the life, worship, conduct, and mission of these communities of faith. Eventually, by the early to middle second century C.E., some Jews began to arrange their Scriptures in three parts, namely, Law, Prophets, and Writings, but the Christians separated the same books into four parts in their Bible, namely, Law, History, Poetry, and Prophets.

The distinctions between Scripture and the various processes or stages of canonical development are variously expressed and often confused in contemporary scholarship. At the beginning of the process, one can speak of a biblical canon only anachronistically, but it is difficult to find the appropriate vocabulary to identify and describe the processes of canonization at that time, since the ancient religious communities showed little interest in telling the story that led to the final fixing of their biblical canons. It is not unusual for scholars today to speak of canon in reference to the early recognition of the authority and value of some of the biblical writings, but such uses of the term did not exist in the ancient church until the fourth century C.E. While it is probably better to speak of a "canonical process" or "canonical processes" at these early stages, we are still left without precise language to describe the canonical formation of the Bible. Sacred writings initially circulated alone in various communities, but were eventually collected and placed into larger collections to form a biblical canon. The gathering of such writings in the first place suggests a respect for and recognition of their authority in the religious communities that possessed and copied them. In some cases, this recognition took place almost from the time they were produced, as in the case of the Gospels.

Canonizing, as Davies rightly argues, involves all of the stages of composing, editing, archiving (or combining two or more writings on a single

---

[36] Rudolf Pfeiffer, *History of Classical Scholarship*, 205.

scroll), then collecting and placing those writings into larger scrolls.[37] These are canonical processes, but none of these actions would have happened had not the value of the writings become apparent to those involved in these various processes of preservation and circulation.

The eventual end of the canonization process is a fixed text and a fixed collection of books, but that was not the goal in the initial stages so much as a recognition of the value of these books. We know the end result of the process, namely, the production of a biblical canon, more than we know the processes that led up to its formation because the steps taken in "getting there" are never explained in Judaism or the church. The steps are therefore more difficult to identify and describe, and the evidence is largely inferential. Further, the processes that led to canonization are not uniform for each book, since some writings that seemed to be heading for canonization and were initially welcomed as sacred literature were not finally included into the fixed canon of the Jews (Sirach and Wisdom of Solomon) or the Christians (*1 Enoch, 1 Clement, Barnabas, Didache*).

The meaning of "canon" is not equal to that of "Scripture" even though there is considerable overlap in definition. Scripture has to do with the divine status of a written document that is accepted as authoritative in the life, mission, worship, and teaching of a community of faith. The term *Scripture* can be, and often is, used in the most general sense of a document that functions authoritatively in a religious community, that is, it is believed to have its origins in God. The word *canon* primarily refers to a fixed standard or collection of Scriptures that defines the faith and identity of a particular religious community. In a sense, all Scripture is canon, but a biblical canon is more specifically a fixed or selected collection of Scriptures that comprise the authoritative Scriptures for a religious body.

To what extent was the Hellenistic idea of following a perfect guide taken over into the religious thought of Judaism, Christianity, and Islam (the three major ancient religions with a canon of sacred Scriptures)? In the historical climate of the developing churches of the second century and later, the church's many interactions with so-called heretical teachings and other factors led it to propose a standard by which it could define authentic Christianity. This standard at first was called a "rule of faith," which appears to have embodied the oral tradition about Jesus, but eventually also included certain writings that were believed to transmit faithfully the tradition of Jesus. Only in the latter example is a fixed collection of writings enlisted to address such matters in the church, but that is a later development (mostly in the fourth and fifth centuries).

The notion of a standard or rule eventually led to the formation of a *closed* canon of authoritative writings (Scriptures) which, as Sundberg argues, was unique for the church since it had not received a closed canon of

[37] Davies, *Scribes and Schools,* 57–58.

Scriptures from Judaism.[38] The church, then, inherited from Judaism the *notion* of sacred Scripture, but not a closed *canon* of Scriptures (see chapter 8). Several factors led the church to establish its biblical canon, and there are two distinct ways of describing this canonical process.

III. Canon 1 and Canon 2

Part of what complicates inquiry into the origins of the biblical canon is the lack of agreement among scholars on what precisely constitutes a biblical canon. Do biblical canons exist whenever an ancient book is cited in another source? Should we infer that cited texts comprised an ancient writer's biblical canon, as Beckwith and other scholars appear to do (see chapter 1 §I). There are no such discussions in antiquity, and Neusner questions whether the issue of a closed biblical canon was ever discussed among the sages of late antiquity.[39] Because of the scarcity of information about these matters, and also for fear of drawing conclusions that cannot be substantiated, some Bible scholars are beginning to make more cautious comments about the formation of the biblical canon.

Sheppard, influenced by Sanders, recognizes two realities of canon formation among Jews and Christians, and he offers two terms to identify those realities. The first reality was an authoritative voice in written or oral form that was read and received as having the authority of God in it. Sheppard calls this reality "canon 1." In a very real sense, Israel had a canon when the tradition about Moses receiving the Torah on Sinai was received into the community. Whatever functioned in the community of Israel as an authoritative guide was canon in the sense of Sheppard's canon 1. On the other hand, the term *canon* came to refer to a perpetual fixation or standardization, namely, when the books of the Bible were fixed or stabilized. Sheppard calls this "canon 2."[40] These distinctions recognize that a variety of literature and even persons (e.g., Moses and Jesus) were often recognized as authorities (canon 1) in the ancient religious communities long before they were placed into fixed or standardized norms (canon 2). Many writings at one time or another became canon 1 in the early church

---

[38] Sundberg, "Making of the New Testament Canon," 1216.

[39] Neusner, *Judaism and Christianity in the Age of Constantine,* 128–45; idem, *Midrash in Context,* 1–22.

[40] Sheppard, "Canon," 64–67, where he cites many examples of both kinds of canon. Barr, *Holy Scripture,* 75–79, describes three forms of canon that he designates "canon 1," "canon 2," and "canon 3," but in a quite different sense than what we find in Sheppard. For Barr, canon 1 refers to the list of books that comprise the biblical Scriptures; canon 2 has to do with the final stages of each book as opposed to the original form of the book; and canon 3 is "the principle of attraction, value, and satisfaction that makes everything about canons and canonicity beautiful" (76–77).

without becoming canon 2.[41] Even some Christian writings were deemed inspired and authoritative in the early Christian community but later were no longer considered a part of its authoritative body Scriptures. It is no wonder that writings such as Sirach and Wisdom of Solomon were a part of an authoritative and respected canon 1 of the early church, and yet at the end of the process they did not achieve the status of canon 2 or a fixation in the tradition of the church or in Judaism. Sanders stresses the need to make this distinction between the two meanings of canon:

> Keeping in mind the two meanings of the word *canon,* authority and invariability, one should be careful to distinguish between the near stability of the Genesis-to-Kings complex at the end of the sixth century B.C. and the dynamic character of a nascent collection of prophets. A canon begins to *take shape* first and foremost because a question of identity or authority has arisen, and a canon begins to *become unchangeable* or invariable somewhat later, after the question of identity has for the most part been settled.[42]

Elsewhere Sanders identifies these two functions of canon as *norma normans* (i.e., texts or stories in a believing community that *function* canonically or authoritatively) and *norma normata* (i.e., sacred texts with a fixed shape, that is, unchangeable).[43] This is similar to Sheppard's canon 1 and canon 2 and the two kinds of canon argued earlier by Sanders.[44] Biblical canons are by their nature a human response to what is believed to be the revelation of God. In the case of canon 1, the authority is not fixed, and keeping this in mind will resolve many of the difficulties in canon formation. Why did the residents of Qumran feel free to change the biblical text, even the Law of Moses, and why is there so much discussion among rabbis of the second through the fifth centuries C.E. about whether books like Ezekiel, Ruth, Esther, Ecclesiastes, and Sirach "defile the hands" (see §IV)? Perhaps because the literature had not yet reached canon 2 status, but was nevertheless recognized as sacred Scripture by many if not most of the Jews from the first century or sooner.

In the broadest definition of the term *canon,* neither the Israelites nor the Christians were ever without a canon or authoritative guide, that is to say, they always had a *story* that enabled them to establish their identity and give life to their community, even though they did not have a stabilized text of Scriptures in their earliest development. While it may be better to follow Ulrich's line of reasoning to not use the term *canon* at all until

---

[41] For example, *1 Clement* was called a "recognized" letter by Eusebius in *Hist. eccl.* 3.16.1 and 3.29.1, but it was not included in the final stabilized canon of the church.

[42] J. A. Sanders, *Torah and Canon,* 91. This notion is also found in Dunn, *Living Word,* 145–53, who follows Sanders's main theses.

[43] J. A. Sanders, "Canon: Hebrew Bible," 847. See also idem, "Scrolls and the Canonical Process"; "Stabilization of the Tanak"; and "From Prophecy to Testament."

[44] J. A. Sanders, *Torah and Canon,* 1–9.

there is a final fixing of the limits of the books that make up the biblical canon,[45] it is difficult not to acknowledge the functional authority of several biblical texts among the Jews and the early Christians well before the fixing of their biblical canons. When Scriptures function the way they always do, they function canonically, that is, authoritatively, and the appropriate response to canonical literature is always the same, namely, obedience to and reverence for the text. To describe this phenomenon simply as a process, or even as a canonical process, does not quite fit the reality of the normativity or authority of the text, and for that reason, some scholars continue to use the word *canon* to describe the reality it suggests. It is true that some writings that functioned as canon at one time no longer did so at a later date, but during the time that they were received in a community of faith as sacred and inspired of God, they were therefore authoritative, and that is also a definition of canon.

Virtually all who use the term *canon* in reference to biblical literature say essentially that the literature was used in an authoritative-scriptural manner among the Jews and the Christians. There is little difference of opinion on this issue; the primary debate is over *when* this literature took on that status, when it formed a fixed collection of sacred writings, and what writings were included or excluded by the believing communities.

The distinctions between canon 1 and canon 2 are useful and convenient precisely because they are understandable and speak of two realities surrounding sacred and authoritative writings in the Jewish and Christian communities of faith. The first of these realities came before there was a fixed list of sacred books, and the other came when a fixed list of authoritative Scriptures was constructed in both Jewish and Christian communities. Ulrich is correct in saying that canon as such was not a reality or fact until there was a fixed collection of books and that prior to the end of the first century C.E. there were no fixed biblical canons in either Judaism or Christianity.[46] These two realities—namely, a canon that is not fixed but in process, and a canon that is fixed and can no longer be changed—are at the heart of many confusions within the scholarly community today. It is not uncommon for scholars to talk past one another by saying one thing and meaning another. For example, Ulrich prefers to speak of "canonical process" rather than "canon" when describing the reality of books being "on the way." And he is quite right to say that fixed or closed collections of sacred writings are a late development in the believing communities and are never discussed before the turn of the era in Judaism (and then only vaguely) and until the fourth century in the Christian community.

I am not saying that believing communities suddenly came upon writings that they believed were sacred or inspired of God and then declared

[45] See Ulrich, "Canonical Process," 272. See also idem, *Dead Sea Scrolls,* 51–61, 73–78.

[46] Ulrich, *Dead Sea Scrolls,* 53–61; idem, "Notion and Definition of Canon."

them to be canonical. Rather, during a long and complex process believing communities, both Jewish and Christian, acknowledged certain sacred writings that defined for them the will of God, their own identity, and their mission in the world. This recognition was often present almost from the beginning of the composition of the writings, as in the case of the Gospels. The essential feature is that the text or tradition was accepted as an authority, even though it was also flexible or fluid in a given community often for a long time and often modified or adapted to meet the needs of the community.[47]

The other understanding of canon, Sheppard's canon 2, comes when a canon 1 authority has become so well established that its text becomes stabilized or fixed in a community, that is, nothing can be added to or taken away from it (Deut 4:2; Rev 22:7–9, 18–19). Canon scholars often attribute to an ancient writer a canon 2 understanding when in fact only a canon 1 notion is in view, that is, its authority is fluid and open to change even though it is functioning as authority in a believing community. In the case of the New Testament, only a few books were generally accepted in a canon 2 fashion by the end of the second century C.E., namely, the Gospels and the Letters of Paul. Even then, however, it is doubtful that these texts were deemed inviolable, since there are many second-century textual changes in these writings (especially in the Gospels).

Throughout this book I use the terms *canon 1* and *canon 2* with full awareness of Ulrich's concerns over likely confusion in the use of the term *canon*. By canon 1 I mean nothing more than what Ulrich does when he speaks of a canonical process, but Sheppard's terms and Sanders's *norma normans* and *norma normata* are more helpful than the word *process,* since they speak more clearly about the authoritative functionality of the Scriptures before they were placed in a fixed collection.[48]

IV. Defiling the Hands: A Jewish Notion of Canon

Judaism of late antiquity did not use the word *canon* to speak of its sacred literature. Rather, it used a strange and somewhat surprising expression to identify its sacred literature: books that "defile the hands" or "make the hands unclean." These designations are commonly used in the Mishnah, Tosefta, and talmudic literature to identify literature that is deemed inspired of God and sacred to the Jews.

---

[47] An example of this modification may be seen in the use of Ps 68:18 in Eph 4:8, where the original text is changed from "received" to "gave" gifts.

[48] My use of Sheppard's terms, and also those employed by Folkert, "'Canons' of Scripture," are noted and discussed in J. Smith, "Canons, Catalogues, and Classics."

According to Lewis, the first person to use these words as a designation for books in the HB was Rabbi Johanan ben Zakkai (ca. 40–80 C.E.), who escaped Jerusalem during its siege in 70 C.E. and, with permission from the Romans, established an academy and the Jewish Sanhedrin at Jamnia.[49] Around 50 C.E. the famous rabbi apparently used the phrase in a debate with the Sadducees over whether certain revered texts "defile the hands," but the phrase did not become standard terminology in Judaism to distinguish its sacred literature until the second century C.E. An important mishnaic text from that time addresses the meaning of this phrase:

> The Sadducees say: We have a quarrel to pick with you, O Pharisees, for according to you the Holy Scriptures defile the hands whereas the writings of Homer would not defile the hands. Rabban Johanan ben Zakkai (40–80) replied: Have we naught against the Pharisees save this: According to them the bones of an ass are clean while the bones of Johanan the High Priest are unclean? They answered him: Their uncleanness corresponds to their preciousness, so that no man would make spoons out of the bones of his father and mother. He said to them: So too the Holy Scriptures, their uncleanness corresponds to their preciousness. The writings of Homer, which are not precious, do not defile the hands. (*m. Yadayim* 4.6, Leiman, *Canonization of the Hebrew Scripture,* 107–8)

Later, in the Tosefta we read: "Said to them Rabban Yoḥanan b. Zakkai, 'The preciousness of Holy Scriptures accounts for their uncleanness, so that a man should not make them into bedding for his cattle'" (*t. Yadayim* 2:19, Neusner, *Tosefta,* 1909). Another explanation for the origin of the phrase comes from around 350–375 C.E. from Babylon:

> And why did the rabbis impose uncleanness upon a Book? Said R. Mesharshiya: Because originally food of *terumah* was stored near the Scroll of the Law, with the argument, "This is holy and that is holy." But when it was seen that they [the holy books] came to harm, the Rabbis imposed uncleanness on them. "And the hands"? Because hands are fidgety. It was taught: Also hands which came into contact with a Book [of Scripture] disqualify *terumah* (*b. Sanhedrin* 100a, Soncino Talmud)

It seems that the Jews were following the ancient practice of storing sacred writings in the temple with the heave offerings to the Lord (the *terumah*), and both were considered holy items. When they did this, however, mice ate not only the *terumah,* but also the holy writings. As a result, the sages declared that these writings made the hands unclean, with perhaps the hope that this conclusion would make Jews change the place where they stored them (away from the *terumah*), and the writings would thus be saved from destruction.

---

[49] Lewis, "Some Aspects of the Problem," 170, 172–76; idem, "What Do We Mean by Jabneh?"; idem, "Jamnia Revisited."

The words *defile the hands* are regularly employed in the second century C.E. and later as a designation for sacred literature.[50] *M. Yadayim* 3.2–5, for instance, uses these words to describe the holiness of a text and also informs us of a late-second-century C.E. debate whether Song of Songs and Ecclesiastes were inspired literature. The whole text is useful to understand the meaning of the notion of delfiling the hands and imparting uncleanness, but the most relevant portion is *m. Yadayim* 3:5:

> All the Holy Scriptures defile the hands. The Song of Songs and Ecclesiastes defile the hands. R. Judah (135–70) says: The Song of Songs defiles the hands but there is a dispute concerning Ecclesiastes. R. Jose (135–70) says: Ecclesiastes does not defile the hands but there is a dispute concerning the Song of Songs. R. Simeon (135–170) says: Ecclesiastes is among the lenient decisions of the School of Shammai and among the stringent decisions of the School of Hillel. R. Simeon b. Azzai (110–135) said: I have heard a tradition from the seventy-two elders on the day that R. Eleazar ben Azariah (110–135) was appointed head of the academy, that the Song of Songs and Ecclesiastes defile the hands. R. Akiba (110–135) said: God forbid: No man in Israel ever disputed the status of the Song of Songs saying that it does not defile the hands, for the whole world is not worth the day on which the Song of Songs was given to Israel; for all the writings are holy, the Song of Songs is the holiest of the holy. If there was a dispute, it concerned Ecclesiastes. R. Johanan (135–170) b. Joshua, the son of R. Akiba's father-in-law, said: Ben Azzai's version of what they disputed and decided is the correct one. (*m. Yadayin* 3:5, Leiman, *Canonization of the Hebrew Scripture,* 103–4)

The relationship between holiness and defilement (i.e., the contagious nature of holiness), probably lies behind the notion of "defiling the hands," and this idea likely relies on a rabbinic understanding of several Old Testament passages, especially Hag 2:11–13: "Thus says the LORD of hosts: Ask the priests for a ruling: If one carries consecrated meat in the fold of one's garment, and with the fold touches bread, or stew, or wine, or oil, or any kind of food, does it become holy? The priests answered, 'No.' Then Haggai said, 'If one who is unclean by contact with a dead body touches any of these, does it become unclean?' The priests answered, 'Yes, it becomes unclean' " (similar concepts are found in Lev 6:20–30; Deut 22:9; Isa 65:5; and Ezek 44:19).

The defilement or holiness that comes from touching the sacred altar may also lie behind this notion (Exod 29:37; 30:29). Later rabbinic literature

---

[50] Rabbinic texts that use these words in reference to the Scriptures of the Jews are *b. Shabbat* 14a–b; *b. Yoma* 29a; *b. Megillah* 7a; *b. Sanhedrin* 100a; *m. Eduyyot* 5.3; *m. Kelim* 15.6; *m. Yadayim* 3.2–5; 4.6; *t. Kelim Bava Metzi'a* 5.8; *t. Yadayim* 2.14, 19. Rabbinic literature that discusses the status of noncanonical literature is *m. Yadayim* 4.5; *t. Yadayim* 2.12–13; *y. Sotah* 18a. These rabbinic texts and others are listed, discussed, and translated in Leiman, *Canonization of the Hebrew Scripture,* 104–20, and several of them are discussed in chapter 6 below.

cites several of these passages to explain the holiness or defilement transferred from the holy to the hands. This notion of defilement from the holy can also be seen in the famous story of David bringing the sacred ark of God to Jerusalem from Philistia when Uzzah reached out his hand to steady the ark when the cart stumbled and he was struck dead, perhaps because he was not ritually clean and touched the holy object (2 Sam 6:16–17; cf. 1 Sam 5).

In the Babylonian Talmud, when Esther was being discussed, affirmed, and challenged as a sacred book, we read:

> R. Assi said: Why was Esther compared to the dawn? To tell you that just as the dawn is the end of the whole night, so is the story of Esther the end of all the miracles. But there is Hanukkah?—We refer to those included in Scripture. That will be right according to the opinion that Esther was meant to be written, but what can be said according to him who held that it was not meant to be written? (*b. Yoma* 29a, Soncino Talmud)[51]

Leiman suggests that part of the problem in distinguishing within the rabbinic literature between canonical and noncanonical literature has to do with the distinction between the words *canonical* and *inspired.* He reserves the term *defile the hands* for inspired literature and allows that some literature, such as Sirach and Ecclesiastes, was uninspired yet canonical for the Jews. Noncanonical literature, he claims, was not only viewed as uninspired but was also deemed inappropriate for reading.[52] He cites in support of this the following condemnation from the rabbis: "The Gospels and heretical books do not defile the hands. The books of Ben Sira [Sirach] and all other books written from then on, do not defile the hands" (*t. Yadayin* 2:13, Leiman, *Canonization of the Hebrew Scripture,* 109).

Leiman recognizes the variability in the rabbinic tradition regarding which writings were sacred Scripture and canon, but he answered the problem with an indefensible conclusion that some literature was considered canonical but not inspired. An inspired book, believed to have been written under divine inspiration and thus canonical, was "considered authoritative for religious practice and doctrine."[53] But in his attempt to make sense of the variable positions on the sacredness of the biblical books among the rabbis, Leiman introduces this rather strange conclusion:

> By definition, then, a canonical book need not be inspired; an inspired book need not be canonical; and a book can be at once canonical and inspired. In tannaitic times, all books considered inspired were canonical, but not all canonical books were considered inspired. Megillath Taanith was treated as a canonical but uninspired book; similarly, we have seen that Ecclesiastes was considered canonical even by those who denied its inspired status. It is therefore crucial to trace the history of the notion of canonicity (as opposed to the

[51] Whether Esther "defiles the hands" is the subject of debate in *b. Megillah* 7a.
[52] Leiman, *Canonization of the Hebrew Scripture,* 14–16, 128–31.
[53] Ibid., 127.

> notion of inspiration), and to determine the dates when all uninspired books (such as Ben Sira and Megillath Taanith) attained canonical status. For when a book attained canonical status it became an authoritative guide for religious practice and doctrine, and was expounded publicly and privately. Is not this precisely what the historian of the canon is after?[54]

Leiman's rather novel views on the distinction between canon and inspiration are somewhat confused, but might have been clearer if he had followed Sheppard's distinctions between canon 1 and canon 2. Kraemer agrees that Leiman's position on the distinction between canon and inspiration is troublesome and "at least in the context of the community that finally defined that canon—not tenable."[55] He goes on to show from the Tannaitic literature and also from comments by Leiman that the final definition of the biblical canon was not yet made in the first three centuries of the common era.[56] Kraemer, contra Leiman, concludes that "while it may be so that early rabbinic documents were considered both uninspired and canonical (= authoritative to a certain degree), the community apparently found this status to be intolerable. In a society where canon/authority was equated with Torah, the claim had finally to be made that all religiously authoritative works were Torah, and therefore inspired."[57]

Kraemer also observes that as later rabbinic writings were gradually received into the authoritative base of Judaism, the boundaries of the earlier canons became less secure. Ultimately, he says, all rabbinic teachings became Torah and "the canons that were once closed were forced to admit a wealth of new traditions and documents."[58] Kraemer is, of course, correct in these comments, even if some of the difficulties remain unresolved with his explanation. The distinction between two kinds of canon existing side by side in both the Jewish and Christian communities helps explain the recognition of the authority of certain writings (canon 1) that did not attain to the later fixed traditions (canon 2) of both Judaism and early Christianity.

In the early church fathers it is clear that some writings had attained the place of canon 1 but were not included in the later fixed canonical traditions. Tertullian, for example, cites *1 En.* 8:1 as Scripture and calls it such (*On the Apparel of Women* 1.3), and later he included references to the authority of the *Sibylline Oracles* (200 B.C.E.–250 C.E.), both Jewish and Christian.[59] In the first few centuries of the church many writings obtained canon 1 status but were later excluded from canon 2 status.

Leiman's distinction between uninspired canonical literature and inspired canonical literature is unconvincing and cannot be sustained with

---

[54] Ibid.

[55] Kraemer, "Formation of Rabbinic Canon," 616.

[56] Ibid., 628.

[57] Ibid., 628–29.

[58] Ibid., 629.

[59] I owe this observation to F. F. Bruce, *Canon of Scripture,* 85–86.

an appeal to the biblical or rabbinic tradition. The problem comes from his attempt to have a closed biblical canon long before the matter was in fact settled among the Jews. If we start with the premise that the biblical canon begins to emerge only at the end of the first century C.E. and that its full contents were not determined before the end of the second century C.E. at the earliest for most of the rabbis, we then have a better grasp of the situation that prevailed and a better understanding of the rabbinic tradition that follows. Leiman's conclusions are anachronistic and do not settle the problem of the silence in the first century C.E. on which books made up the sacred collection. The difficulty we find here helps us better understand rabbinic Judaism's conflicting comments about which books are sacred among them. The long-standing traditions about the closure of the Jewish biblical canon and, in particular, the problems in recognizing the Scriptures that made up the Hebrew Scriptures[60] may be illustrated by a talmudic tradition about continued doubt about the book of Esther: "Levi ben Samuel and R. Huna ben Hiyya were repairing the mantles of the scrolls of R. Judah's college. On coming to the Scroll of Esther, they remarked, 'O, this Scroll of Esther does not require a mantle.'[61] Thereupon he reproved them, 'This too smacks of irreverence' " (*b. Sanhedrin* 100a, Soncino Talmud).

While the term *canon* was not used by the Jews to describe their sacred collection, the notion of canon is clearly present in their understanding of a limited number of sacred books that defile the hands. There is not much difference here between Jews and Christians on the notion of sacred inspired literature that had its origins in God, nor eventually in the notion that a limited collection of books qualified for this status.

The Jews did not use the word *uncanonical* in reference to writings, but they did have an expression that reflected the same idea: "external books" (Heb. *sefarim hizonim*), a term translated in the Mishnah as "heretical books." After asking who will have no share in the world to come, several kinds of persons are identified, and then Rabbi Akiba says: "Also he that reads the *heretical books*" (*m. Sanhedrin* 10:1; Danby, *Mishnah*, 397, emphasis added).

V. Canon Characteristics: Adaptability and Life

For more than a hundred years scholars have seriously examined the scope of the biblical canon in its final stages, but Sanders was one of the first to focus on its origins and prehistory in ancient Israel. In a perceptive

[60] For further reading on this subject, see Friedman, "Holy Scriptures Defile the Hands"; and Broyde, "Defilement of the Hands." See chapter 7 §III for more examples of rabbinic disputes about the status of biblical books.

[61] The point is that its sanctity is of a lower grade, so it would not defile the hands; cf. *b. Shabbat* 14a.

essay, he asks some penetrating and enduring questions about the nature and chief characteristics of the notion of canon, which have become foundational for all subsequent canon inquiry.[62] He contends that the nature of canon has much to do with its repetition in believing communities and its ability to change in order to meet the variable circumstances of the community of faith (adaptability). The primary function of canon, he observes, is to aid the community of faith in its own self-definition (who we are) and to offer guidelines for living (what we are to do). He knows that adaptability alone, however, is not sufficient for a writing to be recognized as canon and contends that those traditions that eventually became canon for ancient Israel also had to empower that community for life, that is, they had to give hope even in hopeless situations (the exile) and bring life to the nation.

The literature that may have spoken to the needs of one generation but was unable to be interpreted or adapted to meet the needs of later generations simply did not survive in either Judaism or Christianity. The survivability, or endurance, of sacred literature has to do with its ability to be interpreted afresh to new communities and in new circumstances. That the biblical writings have had the ability to be reinterpreted in both Judaism and Christianity underscores their adaptability and ultimately their canonicity. Sanders carefully argues that "the major characteristic of canonical material is its adaptability—not its rigidity."[63] He acknowledges the eventual stabilization of the biblical text, but also observes that the need for such a fixed tradition in the believing community comes much later in the canonical process.[64]

This is similar to Burns's contention that the distinction between canonical and noncanonical is not the same as the distinction between authentic and inauthentic or between true and false, but rather, "it is the distinction between texts that are forceful in a given situation and those which are not. From a hermeneutical standpoint, in which the relation of a text to a situation is always of primary interest, the theme of canonization is *power*."[65] He adds that the canonization or significance of the Law lies "not only in what it contains or means but also in its power over those who stand within its jurisdiction. It is precisely within such a textual jurisdiction that the true meaning of canonicity begins to emerge."[66] The power of a text is not intrinsic to it, but rather the text draws its power from the situation in which it makes its "unexpected appearance" and speaks to the situation at hand.[67] Burns rightly argues that the authority of a text is related

---

[62] J. A. Sanders, "Adaptable for Life."

[63] J. A. Sanders, *From Sacred Story,* 22; see also idem, "Stabilization of the Tanak."

[64] J. A. Sanders, *From Sacred Story,* 22.

[65] Burns, "Canon and Power," 65.

[66] Ibid., 67.

[67] Ibid., 69.

directly to the circumstances that the people who hear it and obey it are facing. Canon in antiquity was always a relevant issue in which the force or power of a given text was released in specific contexts.

Sanders claims that at the heart of the earliest Scripture canon of the Jews was a story (or *mythos*) about a people who migrated from Egypt to Canaan under the guidance and protection of Yahweh, even though other elements were later added to the beginning and the ending of that story, for example, the Genesis story of beginnings, the prophetic tradition, and the history of the fall of the nation. The earliest development of the story, he contends, did not include a Decalogue or other lists of divine commandments. Rather, it consisted of telling about God's calling of a people to a hope and promise in a new land and the preservation of those people through divine mighty acts. The response of the people to these acts of preservation or salvation was the monotheizing move to recognize the one true God and to obey God's call. There are many examples of this story in the Old Testament Scriptures, especially in the Prophets.[68]

In the New Testament that same story is also preserved in several key passages (Acts 7:2–53; 1 Cor 10:1–11; Heb 3:5–19). That story was clearly expandable, and after the exile of Israel to Babylon the Jews reconsidered their circumstances from the perspective of the classic prophets whose witness to God's activity among them gave them life and hope. In the message from Ezekiel, for example, the people could, through the faithfulness of Yahweh, look forward to the resurrection of the nation following its death (Ezek 36–37). In the exilic sojourn, Ezekiel began to echo the vision of Jeremiah, who also spoke of the reforming of the nation (Jer 18:1–11).[69]

After Israel had lost everything in terms of its national identity—especially its temple and cultus—in the terrible destruction of 586 B.C.E., what was it that enabled the Jewish people to continue their identity? Why not like many other nations before them and after them simply merge with other nations and become extinct as a people with a separate identity who served Yahweh? Merger with and assimilation into other nations and cultures, with the consequent loss of separate national identity, would have been the most natural course of action and has many parallels in the ancient world, but instead the nation of Israel was reborn. What was it that kept them alive as a nation when all of the things that identified them as a nation had been taken away—their land, sovereignty/rulership, temple, cultus, and language? Sanders argues that only something indestructible, commonly available, adaptable, and portable could keep this people from extinction. The only thing that fits this description, he claims, was a *story* that could be transported to Babylon and adapted to

[68] J. A. Sanders, *From Sacred Story,* 18–19. See examples of the story about God's people in Amos 2:9–11; 3:1–2; 4:10–11; 5:25; 9:7, 11. Other early summations of the story are Deut 26:5–9 and Josh 24.

[69] Ibid., 15–29.

the new circumstances of the nation in captivity.[70] He adds that during the exile a remnant remembered the witness of the prophets who had predicted accurately what would happen to the nation. As these individuals realized that the prophets had told the truth regarding the fate and story of Israel, they realized that the message of the judgmental prophets before the exile also had a story that could offer them hope and allow them to survive the terrible judgments currently inflicted upon them.

Unlike other nations that saw in their defeat in battle also the defeat of their gods, the Jews accepted the message of the prophets and took responsibility for their failure as a nation and accepted their captivity and destruction as a judgment from Yahweh for their own misdeeds. It was in this context that the prophets were remembered and their story was repeated. When the prophets had earlier proclaimed this story, warning the people of the consequences of their behavior, they were accused of being "madmen, unpatriotic, blasphemous, seditious, and traitorous" (Jer 29:26),[71] but now they were remembered precisely because what they had said actually came to pass. The exiles concluded that the core of the prophetic message was also a story that was reflected and contained in the Torah. This notion was eventually expanded to include the Former Prophets and then the Latter Prophets and finally the Writings, but the Law was always at the core of the story that gave life (John 5:39) and identity to the nation. As the Jews returned from Babylon, the canon of the community of Israel—that which gave it an identity and purpose with guidelines to follow—was the laws of Moses.

In the repetition of this story (a feature of canon), the remnant found life and hope. The fluidity of the transmission of this story continued well into the time of Jesus, when the lack of a fixed or stabilized tradition was a contributing factor to the existence of the variety of Jewish sects (or "Judaisms") that flourished in the first century C.E., namely, the Sadducees, Pharisees, Essenes, Samaritans, and Christians. After the destruction of the temple and its cultus in 70 C.E. and following the failure of the messianic movement in the Bar Kokhba rebellion of 132–35 C.E., the two most important Judaisms that survived these traumatic events were rabbinic Judaism, which was born out of the remnants of first-century Pharisaism, and early Christianity. The First Testament thus developed over a long period, beginning with a fluid and adaptable story in preexilic times and becoming fixed in the second to fourth centuries C.E. for the Jews.

A similar story can also be told about the emergence of the New Testament canon. What first gathered the Christian community together and gave it its identity and reason for being (i.e., its mission) was a story about God's activity in Jesus of Nazareth. The story was first told in preaching

---

[70] Ibid., 18–19.
[71] Ibid., 28.

(Acts 2:17–36) and teaching (1 Cor 15:3–8). In time, the story of God's activity in Jesus, along with its implications for humanity, was expanded and expressed in a variety of literary forms (gospel, letter, history, sermon, and apocalypse). The movement toward stabilizing these writings began in the second century, but was not finalized until the late third or early fourth centuries, after the canonical (i.e., stabilized or fixed) status of the NT writings was widely accepted.

Almost at the same time, the First Testament was also moving toward the final stage of its stabilization in the Christian community. The adaptability of the Jewish Scriptures to new circumstances was due in part to the creative genius of the surviving community that reinterpreted and applied this story of Yahweh's activity to the new circumstances in which God's people found themselves. This genius is what Sanders calls the employed hermeneutics that grew out of a need "to keep a stabilized tradition adaptable"[72] and the ability to see in the literature something that was not only adaptable, but also highly relevant and useful for the community of faith.

Since canons are by their nature adaptable to the ever-changing life of a believing community, the continuing usefulness of the current biblical canon gives witness to its ability to be relevant in specific and changing circumstances of the synagogue and the church. Canons often change, however, most typically by expansion, though sometimes by reduction. For example, the *Shepherd of Hermas* and the *Letter of Barnabas* eventually dropped away from the church's sacred Scriptures after having been included by some Christians for centuries. Codex Sinaiticus (א), which dates from the last half of the fourth century, included these two books in its collection. Later, Codex Constantinoplitanus (C) included *1–2 Clement, Barnabas, Didache,* and the letters of Ignatius. On the Jewish side, some rabbis accepted Sirach and the Wisdom of Solomon as Scripture. As the church grew and developed, the early Christians at first accepted the words of and about Jesus as their final norm, even though they clearly acknowledged the authority of the Old Testament Scriptures. The OT was employed by the church primarily as a predictive witness to the Christ event, but also as an authority on Christian conduct, as seen in *1 Clement*'s generous collection of references to OT verses. As the church developed, however, it became obvious that the written Gospels and eventually the Letters of Paul were also advantageous in the ongoing life of the Christian community.

Other books were temporarily added to the NT. For example, the *Shepherd of Hermas* and *1 Clement* were commonly welcomed but eventually rejected by the majority of Christians. When some writings ceased being relevant to the religious needs of the Christian community, that is, when their relevance for the life and hope of the church in its new and changing circumstances ceased, then they also ceased being canon to that community.

---

[72] Ibid., 25.

Similarly, Paul "decanonized"[73] much of the OT emphasis on law, especially its focus on clean and unclean foods, ritual cleansings, and sabbath laws because such things were deemed by him to be no longer relevant to faith. Dunn makes the point that the Old Testament can never function as canon for Christians in the same way that it does for the Jews. For the Christian, the New Testament always functions to some extent as *the* canon *within* the biblical canon.[74] Paul (Gal 3:15–22) and Justin (*Dial.* 16.2; 27.2–4; 46.5) were the first to deal with the problem of accepting the law as a part of their authoritative Scriptures while at the same time rejecting its prescriptions for conduct. For Paul, promise and faith preceded the law, but Justin claims that the regulations of the law were given because of the hardness of heart and rebellion among the Jews and that such prescriptions are no longer needed by the church.

The solution to this problem for many Christians was the later adoption of an allegorical hermeneutic or spiritual interpretation of the law. Marcion (ca. 140 C.E.) rejected this spiritual interpretation and subsequently rejected the Law and other books of the OT. The church condemned this option and taught that the OT revealed the truth and will of God and was also the church's Scripture.

The literature that survived in the biblical canon was precisely that which was perceived to have continuing viability for Judaism and Christianity. The law's ability to be adapted and reinterpreted for a new era and in new circumstances gave to it a canonical identity. The remnant of Jews in the Diaspora defined their identity in terms of the law, but adapted it to their needs, thereby surviving assimilation into the cultures and societies of their neighbors. As the law was adapted to the new life of the community (Neh 8:1–8), it also brought new life and hope to the people. The viability of the current biblical canon has much to do with its power to address the needs and hopes of modern communities of faith, and this ability is aided through the genius of its contemporary interpreters. Scripture interpretation and application continues unimpeded in both Jewish and Christian communities, and, as the production of many new commentary series demonstrates, there is no sign of ending the adaptation of the ancient Scriptures to new circumstances.

VI. Summary

Jews and Christians regularly make use of terms that identify their sacred literature. While it is not clear precisely what literature that they had in

---

[73] This is Dunn's expression in *Living Word,* 156. See also Kooij and Toorn, *Canonization and Decanonization,* which deals with this phenomenon in the development of the biblical canon.

[74] Dunn, *Living Word,* 156.

view in the first century C.E. for either religious community, there is no doubt that the Law and most if not all of the Prophets formed the heart of the Scriptures that were accepted by Jews and Christians. Those writings are regularly cited in an authoritative manner. One of the important challenges in the early church had to do with determining which books comprised their biblical canon. That no discussions of these matters exist in the known literature of Jews or Christians until late in the process complicates matters for those who want to inquire into the such issues. Although there was wide recognition of the fact of Scripture, there is no discussion of the meaning of canon in the first century C.E. or before or on the number of sacred books that comprised the Bible for Judaism or the early church.

Today there is renewed interest in the subject of canon formation, and because of it we have the potential for new advances in canonical studies that will change our perceptions of the canonical process, if not the way in which we define the notion of canon and the books included in it. Christians are not likely to wait for new discoveries and future scholarly investigations, but will likely go on using those portions of the Bible that are relevant to their community needs and that offer hope to them during critical crises and challenges that come to everyone. This need not deter capable scholars from continuing the inquiry, however, or put a damper on the hope that the results of their labors will eventually bear fruit in their own communities of faith.

Sanders's challenge to reexamine the origins of the biblical canon yielded several valuable results, including a better understanding of the nature of canon itself and its chief characteristics. When this is known, the origins of the biblical canon and the move toward its stabilization are more comprehensible than before. He is certainly correct, therefore, when he concludes that "we cannot deal adequately with the question of the structure of canon, or what is in and what is out, until we have explored seriously and extensively the question of the function of canon. It is time to attempt to write a history of the early canonical process."[75] Sanders's challenge will be taken up in the remainder of this volume.

[75] J. A. Sanders, *From Sacred Story,* 11.

Part Two

Hebrew Bible/ Old Testament Canon

CHAPTER FOUR

Origins of the Hebrew Bible

BEFORE WE CAN UNDERSTAND THE ORIGINS OF THE CHRISTIAN OT CANON, IT IS essential that we first explore the origins and development of the HB. The reason for this is quite simple: at the time when the early Christians were mostly Jewish and worshipped regularly at the Jewish temple in Jerusalem or in the synagogues, they received both their understanding of sacred Scripture and their OT Scriptures from their Jewish traditions.

I. THE LAW AS SACRED SCRIPTURE

It is generally agreed that Israel had acknowledged the authoritative and sacred nature of some writings at least by the time of the Josiah reforms (621 B.C.E.) following the discovery and reading of the "book of the law" (probably the book of Deuteronomy) in the temple (2 Kgs 22:8–13). Many OT scholars acknowledge that the Law (Torah) was in existence well before the time of Josiah and that parts of it may have preceded Moses,[1] but it is not certain that the Law was the moving force behind the religion of Israel in its early formative period. Bruce correctly observes that when Moses read the commandments of God to the people (Exod 24:3–7), he was most certainly reading to them what he understood to be the very word of God, and when "the law-code of Deuteronomy was put 'beside the ark of the covenant of Yahweh' (Deut 31:26), this was to be a token of its sanctity and a reminder to the people of the solemnity of their obligation to continue in the way which God had commanded them."[2] There was a time when the people of Israel were significantly influenced by sacred writings, but exactly when this started is not clear.

According to Barr, the Deuteronomic movement, which began in the eighth and seventh centuries B.C.E., initiated "something like a 'scripture'"

[1] Barr, *Holy Scripture,* 6–7. See also Davies, *Scribes and Schools,* 89–106, on the origins of the Mosaic canon.

[2] F. F. Bruce, *Canon of Scripture,* 36–37.

having a central role in the life of the nation of Israel.[3] He contends that only with this development and the reforms of Josiah did the religion of Israel *begin* to be built around a book (or sacred Scripture). Following the return of Israel from exile in Babylon during the reign of Artaxerxes I (roughly 465–423 B.C.E.), and as a result of the religious reforms of Ezra and Nehemiah (Neh 8:1–9:5), a significant move led the religion of Israel to recognize or adopt a body of sacred Scriptures.

It is widely acknowledged that the Law was recognized as sacred Scripture in Israel *no later* than approximately 400 B.C.E. (the latest time for dating the reforms of Nehemiah), and most scholars agree that it probably started sooner during the reforms of Josiah (2 Kgs 22–23), but then became more substantial following the reforms of Ezra and Nehemiah. The Law, or "law of Moses," as Ezra called it, may not, however, be the same as the Pentateuch, which contains far more than laws or regulations, including the Genesis stories of beginnings. In those days, there was no notion of a *closed* canon of Scriptures, but the Law was undoubtedly recognized as Scripture for these postexilic Jews, even if their sacred writings were not yet called "Scripture."

When the Jews began to identify their sacred literature, it was quite common to speak of the *book* of the Law rather than the *books* of Moses. The Chronicler, for instance, invokes the "law of Moses" during the reign of Jehoiada (2 Chr 23:18), and in the reign of Amaziah he speaks of the "book of Moses" (2 Chr 25:4). In the reign of Josiah, the high priest Hilkiah reports to the king that he has found the "book of the law" in the temple (2 Kgs 22:8). Later, we see that Josiah "established the words of the law that were written in the book that the priest Hilkiah had found" (2 Kgs 23:24; cf. 2 Chr 34:14–16, 24), with "book" in the singular.[4] What was found in the temple and functioned as sacred Scripture for the Jews in Josiah's day is generally acknowledged to have been the book of Deuteronomy. Davies observes that Deuteronomy is the only book of the Law that calls itself a "torah book" (Deut 4:1–2; cf. 6:1–9; 8:1, 11; 10:13; 11:1, 8, 13; 12:1; etc.) and some scholars argue that Deuteronomy was the original "book of the Law" and that the other books of the Law were added later.[5] The Pentateuch was still in the process of development and likely expanded during the reforms of Ezra and Nehemiah.

In the largely legendary *Letter of Aristeas* (second century B.C.E.), the books of Moses, perhaps for the first time, are specifically called "Scripture": "So we are exhorted through scripture also by the one who says thus, 'Thou shalt remember the Lord, who did great and wonderful deeds in thee'" (*Let. Aris.* 155, *OTP* 2.23). This letter had a very important influ-

[3] Barr, *Holy Scripture*, 7.

[4] I owe this observation to Davies, *Scribes and Schools*, 99.

[5] Ibid., 93; and Lightstone, *Society, the Sacred, and Scripture*, 21–43.

ence on Second Temple[6] Judaism and early Christianity, and it tells in legendary fashion of the creation of the Greek translation of the Law in Egypt. According to the *Letter of Aristeas,* an earlier attempt at translation was deemed unworthy, and so a more accurate translation was needed:

> Scrolls of the Law of the Jews, together with a few others, are missing (from the library), for these (works) are written in Hebrew characters and language. *But they have been transcribed somewhat carelessly and not as they should be,* according to the report of the experts, because they have not received royal patronage. These (books) also must be in your library in an accurate version because this legislation, as could be expected from its divine nature, is very philosophical and genuine. (*Let. Aris.* 30–31, *OTP* 2.14–15, emphasis added)

After the new translation of the "whole Law" had been prepared, the writer says that a curse was put "on anyone who should alter the version by any addition or change to any part of the written text, or any deletion either" (*Let. Aris.* 311, *OTP* 2.33). This is not unlike Deut 4:2 (cf. Deut 12:32 and Rev 22:18–19), which reminded the Jews of the sacredness of that inspired text. Several terms used to describe the writings of Moses in the *Letter of Aristeas* suggest that the books translated were indeed acknowledged as sacred Scripture. For example, the writings are called "divine Law" (*Let. Aris.* 3), "sacred law" (5, 45), "Law" (142, 176, 310), "scrolls of the Law of the Jews" (30), and "Bible" (316). In the latter case, this word is used in the story of a poet named Theodectus, who was about to include a passage from the Law in his play, but was afflicted with cataract of the eyes because he had tried to add "what is written in the Bible." This is the first known time that the word *Bible* is used of the Jewish Scriptures.

In his influential *Canon of the Old Testament* (1909), Ryle argued that the OT developed in a three-tiered fashion. This roughly approximated the recognition of the Law (Heb. *torah*) by no later than 400 B.C.E., the Prophets (Heb. *nebi'im*) possibly by the late third century B.C.E. but no later than around 200 B.C.E., and the Writings (Heb. *ketubim;* Gk. *hagiographa*), which included the rest of the sacred writings, by no later than the Council of Jamnia in 90 C.E. Although this view is hypothetical and cannot be substantiated on the basis of specific primary textual evidence—this is

[6]The term *Second Temple* refers to the temple of Herod the Great, begun in 37 B.C.E. and destroyed by the Romans in 70 C.E. The First Temple was destroyed in 587/586 B.C.E. (2 Kgs 25:8–17), and following the decree of Cyrus (538 B.C.E.) to free the Jews and allow them to rebuild their temple, Zerubbabel attempted to rebuild the temple between 520 B.C.E. and 515 B.C.E. (Ezra 1:1–4; 5:2–6:18; see also Hag 1:1–4, 12; 2:1–4; Zech 4:9; 6:15), but local opposition prevented him from rebuilding anything on the scale of the former temple built by Solomon. The structure begun by Zerubbabel had many additions and changes and was finally replaced by Herod the Great in 37 B.C.E. The phrase *Second Temple period* usually refers to the time between the rebuilding of Zerubbabel's temple and the destruction of the Second Temple of Herod in 70 C.E.

especially true in regard to the closing of the third part of the HB—still, in its broadest terms the notion of a threefold development of the biblical canon is not as unreasonable as some recent scholars suppose.[7] The dates for this development are clearly beyond demonstration, but the gradual expansion of the scriptural collection that eventuated in a three-part scriptural collection is reasonable, and is supported by the development of literary canons.[8]

The collective summation of the whole of the Hebrew Scriptures by the term *Torah* continued well into the NT era and suggests the historical priority of the acceptance of the Law. With the acceptance of the Prophets as a part of the Jewish sacred collection of Scriptures, the term *Law and Prophets* became a frequent designation of the Scriptures of the Jews, even if the latter category was fluid for a time. When a third collection of Scriptures began to be distinguished from the Prophets, initially only the Psalms was included in it (Luke 24:44), but by the second century C.E. some of the writings that were earlier called Prophets were included in this third category by the Jews. The first two categories of the Hebrew Scriptures (Law and Prophets) were established well before the birth of Christianity, but the third category (the Writings) was not settled for some time after the separation of the church from the synagogue.

The Christians took longer to determine the boundaries of their OT Scriptures and also placed them in four divisions (Law, History, Poetry, Prophets) rather than the three divisions of the Jews. When that began to occur, some writings that are now classified as apocryphal literature were included in the Christian collection and welcomed in the Jewish community as well. Sundberg contends that the early church inherited a collection of Scriptures from the Jews that was more extensive than the one eventually adopted by the rabbinic sages at the end of the first century. He argues that the Christians simply adopted the sacred writings in use within Pharisaic Judaism prior to the separation of Christians from the Jews.[9] Lightstone, however, rightly cautions: "One may not assume that books known and respected in one circle will have soon come even to the attention of other groups—let alone to be revered."[10]

Sundberg's position assumes that at the supposed Council of Jamnia the Jews made a decision about which books were or were not sacred. Although this view can no longer be reasonably defended, his main point

---

[7]See, for instance, Leiman, *Canonization of the Hebrew Scripture,* 120–24; Lightstone, "Formation of the Biblical Canon"; Ellis, *Old Testament in Early Christianity,* 125–26; Beckwith, *Old Testament Canon,* 276–77; and Bruce, *Canon as Scripture,* 34–36.

[8]See Guillory, *Cultural Capital;* idem, "Canon"; Zetzel, "Re-creating the Canon"; and Burns, "Canon and Power."

[9]Sundberg, *Old Testament of the Early Church.*

[10]Lightstone, "Formation of the Biblical Canon" 141.

is valid, namely, that the views of what literature was held to be sacred and authoritative by the early Christians was the same as that which existed in pre-70 C.E. Pharisaic Judaism in Palestine. In addition, this particular collection of Scriptures at the end of the first century C.E. was still in a fluid state (canon 1), that is, it was not yet fixed as in the later collections (canon 2).

Ellis disagrees with Sundberg and claims that the Pentateuch and the Prophets were a part of the biblical canon of the Jews in the early postexilic times,[11] but his position is difficult to prove from the available data. If the Prophets were accepted as part of the canon of the Jews by the time of Ezra, why are they not mentioned in Ezra or Nehemiah, and why was only the Law of Moses read to the people? For example, mention of a written law or sacred writings in Ezra and Nehemiah refers only to the Pentateuch, and the references to the law or commandments of God or Moses cite particular admonitions found in the Pentateuch (Ezra 3:2; 7:6, 10, 12; 9:10; 10:3; Neh 1:5–9; 8:9–15, 18; 9:3, 13–14, 16, 29, 34; 10:28–29, 34; 12:44; 13:1). Although the prophets are mentioned in Nehemiah, this refers to the verbal warnings that God gave through the prophets to the people and not to a collection of Scriptures (Neh 9:26, 30).

The evidence suggests that the scriptural support for the reforms of Josiah and Ezra-Nehemiah were rooted in the Law alone and not in the Prophets. There is no reference to a study of the Prophets, nor are they given the same reverence or devotion that was attributed to the laws of Moses. The identity of the Prophets as sacred literature and the holiness of their collected writings are not in view in Ezra-Nehemiah.

It may be, as some argue, that the Former (or Early) Prophets (Joshua, Judges, 1–2 Samuel, and 1–2 Kings) were collected by and circulated among the Jews in the late sixth century to early fifth century B.C.E., but it is quite another matter to say that they were recognized as sacred Scripture on par with the Law of Moses.[12] No ancient source suggests this, and it is even less likely that the Latter Prophets (Isaiah, Jeremiah, Ezekiel, and the Minor Prophets) had obtained such a position among the Jews by that time. Sanders rightly calls on scholars to distinguish on the one hand between the stability of the "Genesis to Kings complex," which was most likely circulating among the Jewish people at the end of the sixth century B.C.E., and the "dynamic character of a nascent collection of prophets."[13] In the case of the former collection, he concludes that the Law and the Former Prophets began to acquire a primitive form of canonical authority, or canonization, for the Jews who survived the traumatic experience of exile

---

[11] Ellis, OT *in Early Christianity,* 37–38, especially n. 115.

[12] Davies, *Scribes and Schools,* 104, argues against this position from Hecataeus of Abdera (ca. 300 B.C.E.), who tells the story of the Jews and shows awareness of the Law of Moses, but shows no knowledge of the Former Prophets.

[13] J. A. Sanders, *Torah and Canon,* 91.

in Babylon.[14] The literature of the Torah, which was shaped in a context of exile, spoke with authority to the Jews who survived exile. Sanders also claims that the language of the Latter Prophets was remembered after the exile and the rebuilding of the nation precisely because those prophets who had once spoken a message to them now seemed all the more credible and relevant. The scenario for such acceptance and the eventual canonization of that literature, according to Sanders, is as follows:

> Little by little some of us [the Jews following the exile] began to recall that back in the old country from time to time there had been loners we had called madmen who had precisely said that this is what would happen. Where were they now? Ezekiel, by all means. But did we not see around here just the other day that fellow who was always talking about Amos? A disciple, he called himself. Let us get him to recite all that Amos said and listen to it for what it says to us *now*. And there was one called Hosea, others called Micah, Isaiah, Jeremiah, and so on. Perhaps they were right and all the rest of us wrong. Let's hear *now* what they said.[15]

In this kind of a context, a prophetic canon likely emerged and developed within a nation that had need of hope, stability, and an authoritative guide in very troubled times. The final invariable and fixed form of a biblical canon, however, was still in process. How much later is difficult to say with precision, but there are some clues. For instance, the author of the book of Malachi concludes his message with a call to "remember the teaching of my servant Moses, the statutes and ordinances that I commanded him at Horeb for all Israel" (4:4). There is no reference to the Prophets as a collection of sacred writers or to any other sacred literature in this admonition. Since Malachi is one of the latest books of the OT Scriptures, if a collection of prophetic sacred writings, whether the Former Prophets or Latter Prophets, had acquired by Malachi's time the status of sacred Scripture on par with the Law, it is remarkable that nothing is said about it in his admonition. There is no evidence that the Prophets were widely acknowledged as Scripture in the postexilic community of Ezra or Nehemiah. Sirach (ca. 180 B.C.E.) is one of the earliest writers to refer to several of the prophets by name and to the Minor Prophets in his praise of the great men of the faith (Sirach 49:9–10, discussed in §III.A below; see also Dan 9:2 referring to Jeremiah and 2 Chr 32:32 referring to Isaiah).

II. Recognition of the Prophets as Scripture

There seems to be little doubt among biblical scholars that around 200 B.C.E. at the latest, and quite possibly earlier, *some* of the Prophets had received some recognition as a collection of sacred writings. The bulk of the

[14] Ibid.

[15] Ibid., 93.

Prophets no doubt *existed* earlier than 400 B.C.E., but the collection of those writings had not yet been generally acknowledged as Scripture in Israel. Indeed, reference to the biblical writings as Scripture appears to be a rather late development. While the terms *Scripture* (*graphē*) and *Scriptures* (*graphai*) are commonly used in the NT in reference to OT writings, they are nevertheless not used in the Septuagint, which uses the terms *decree, word, statute, precept, testimony, way, ordinance, commandment,* and *law,* to identify the later OT writings.[16] These terms are probably synonymous with Scripture at that time, even if Scripture was not yet called Scripture.

Some of the latest writings in the book of the Twelve (the so-called Minor Prophets),[17] namely, Haggai, Zechariah, and Malachi, had probably not yet been written when earlier prophetic writings began gaining influence among the Jews. Pfeiffer argues that the Former Prophets and *some* of the Latter Prophets were adopted into Israel's sacred collection not only because of growing public interest in them, but also because of their recognized value "for enhancing the national pride and the hopes for a better future."[18] I would add three more reasons why they were welcomed: (1) they extended Israel's story of God's activity among the Jews; (2) they were recognized as having intrinsic worth in the worship and religious instruction of the Jewish people; and (3) they gave to Israel an identity and knowledge of the will of God that enabled them to renew themselves as a people of God and to rebuild their nation.

It is not known precisely when this prophetic tradition was added to Israel's sacred Scripture collection, but it is likely that by the beginning of the second century B.C.E. at the latest they were highly esteemed and valued by many if not most Jews in Israel. This does not mean that the Jews viewed the Law and the Prophets and no others as Scripture, but only that these writings and probably others were included. There is no talk about a closed collection of Scriptures at this time. The earliest specific references to the term *the Law and the Prophets* comes to us in the prologue to Sirach in the late second century B.C.E. (see §III.B below) and in 2 Macc 15:9 (ca. first century B.C.E.), which describes Judas Maccabeus in battle with the forces of Nicanor. After exhorting his troops not to fear attack from the Gentiles, Judas began "encouraging them from the law and the prophets, and reminding them also of the struggles they had won."

According to Blenkinsopp, involving the prophets in communicating history was a way of commending the prophets, and he notes that most of

---

[16]See, for example, the variety of terms used in Ps 19:7–10 and Ps 119.

[17]They are called Minor Prophets because of their shorter length, not because their message was less important. Most often in antiquity these writings are referred to as the "Twelve." For a helpful discussion of their formation as a single collection, see Jones, *Formation of the Book of the Twelve.*

[18]Robert Pfeiffer, "Canon of the Old Testament," 507.

the sources cited by the Chronicler were seers and prophets.[19] Interestingly, Josephus (ca. 95–100 C.E.) argued that only prophets could write the history of Israel since they alone had access to information through divine inspiration: "From the death of Moses until Artaxerxes, who succeeded Xerxes as king of Persia, the prophets subsequent to Moses wrote the history of the events of their own times in thirteen books" (*Ag. Ap.* 1.40, LCL).

Freedman posits that the prophetic collection was recognized as Scripture in the sixth century B.C.E.,[20] but we cannot substantiate from any ancient sources that the prophetic writings were acknowledged as sacred Scripture at that time. Freedman's conclusions are based both on the arbitrary early dating of the prophetic corpus and the rather early addition of the postexilic prophets to that collection. On the other hand, although Blenkinsopp agrees that the Former Prophets were collected early on, possibly in the sixth century B.C.E., he concludes that this process took considerably longer for the Latter Prophets.[21] For example, the book of Isaiah undoubtedly went through a long period of revision in which the "Apocalypse of Isaiah" (Isa 24–27) and the additional writings of chapters of 40–66 were edited and connected with the original text of Isaiah (probably chapters 1–33, with the subsequent addition of chapters 34–39). There is also considerable debate over the dating of Zech 9–14, since the two supplementary oracles of Zech 9–11 and Zech 12–14 were likely added later to the original text of Zech 1–8. The terms *Former Prophets* and *Latter Prophets* did not exist at the time of Ben Sirach (200–180 B.C.E.), but both collections were circulating in the land of Israel and were evidently venerated by many Jews at that time.

III. The Writings and a Three-Part Canon

Along with the Prophets, a body of literature, some of which was written well before 200 B.C.E. and some perhaps even later (e.g., Daniel), circulated widely among the Jews. These writings circulated in Palestine and were later translated from Hebrew into Greek—probably by Sirach's grandson—not only for the Jews in Egypt, but also for the other Jews in the Diaspora. The name given to this group of writings was simply the "Writings."[22]

---

[19] Blenkinsopp, *Prophecy and Canon,* 98.

[20] Freedman, "Symmetry of the Hebrew Bible," 102–5.

[21] Blenkinsopp, *Prophecy and Canon,* 99–101.

[22] The Hebrew term for the third part of the HB is *Ketubim* ("things written down"). The equivalent Greek term for the third part of the Hebrew Scriptures is *Hagiographa* ("sacred writings" or "holy writings"). "Writings" is represented in Latin by "Scripture," and "holy Scripture" became the common reference among Christians for all of their sacred writings.

Some texts have been widely cited as evidence for a three-part biblical canon before the time of Jesus. Before examining them, however, it is important to recall that the HB was not defined until some time *after* the Jamnia council,[23] when the Writings also became a more precisely defined and ordered fixed canon of authoritative Scriptures for the surviving elements of Judaism (primarily Pharisaic Jews). Sarna agrees with this and contends that the name *Writings* was indeterminate initially and not made clear until the second century C.E. Before that time, all of the sacred writings of the Jews were referred to as the Law and the Prophets.[24] There is evidence, however, for an expanding prophetic collection before the time of Jesus, which points to an expanding collection of sacred writings among the Jews both before and contemporary with early Christianity.

A. SIRACH 49:8–10

The book of Sirach (also known as Ecclesiasticus) was written in the early decades of the second century B.C.E. (ca. 180). In it Jesus ben Sirach speaks of the Scriptures of the Jews as "the law of the Most High" and identifies several genres in that collection:

> How different the one who devotes himself
> to the study of the law of the Most High!
> He seeks out the wisdom of all the ancients,
> and is concerned with prophecies;
> he preserves the sayings of the famous
> and penetrates the subtleties of parables;
> he seeks out the hidden meanings of proverbs
> and is at home with the obscurities of parables. (Sir 38:34b–39:3)

Sirach praised those who study wisdom and quotes the personification Lady Wisdom: "I will again pour out teaching like prophecy, and leave it to all future generations" (24:33). Later Sirach says that he himself has poured forth wisdom out of his heart (50:27) and that he himself is filled with the "spirit of understanding" (39:6).[25] This apparently led Sirach's grandson, who translated his work into Greek, to conclude that Sirach's work was

---

[23] Barr, *Holy Scripture,* 56–57, does not believe that an actual council at Jamnia empowered Jewish leaders to determine which books would be included in the third part of the Jewish canon of Scriptures. So also Lewis, "What Do We Mean by Jabneh?" Lightstone, "Formation of the Biblical Canon," argues similarly and calls into question whether much of anything was really settled at Jamnia regarding the Jewish canon. I return to this issue in chapter 7 §II, but note in advance the growing consensus among scholars that no council decisions were made about the biblical canon at Jamnia.

[24] Sarna, "Canon, Text, and Editions," 824.

[25] VanderKam, *Revelation to Canon,* 21.

inspired and worthy of being placed alongside the other sacred books among the Jews:

> So my grandfather Jesus, who had devoted himself especially to the reading of the Law and the Prophets and the other books of our ancestors, and had acquired considerable proficiency in them, *was himself also led to write* something pertaining to instruction and wisdom, so that by becoming familiar also with his book those who love learning might make even *greater progress in living according to the law.* (Sir Prologue, emphasis added)

The instruction and wisdom that he attributes to his grandfather are also attributed to the "Law and the Prophets and the others," and he brings his grandfather's work together with these writings when he acknowledges the difficulty in translating them into Greek: "Not only this book, but even the Law itself, the Prophecies, and the rest of the books differ not a little when read in the original" (Sir Prologue). We will return to the prologue later, but it is sufficient here to observe that Sirach was received as sacred wisdom writings among the Jews before the final definition of their Scriptures. In fact, both Sirach and the Wisdom of Solomon are cited much more frequently by Christians than even the books of Samuel and the Kings.[26]

In the well-known Sir 49:8–10, Sirach shows familiarity with some of the prophetic writings since he refers to the exilic prophet Ezekiel, Job, and the Twelve Prophets, as if the latter were circulating as a collection:

> It was Ezekiel who saw the vision of glory,
> which God showed him above the chariot of the cherubim.
> For God also mentioned Job
> who held fast to all the ways of justice.
> May the bones of the Twelve Prophets
> send forth new life from where they lie,
> for they comforted the people of Jacob
> and delivered them with confident hope. (Sir 49:8–10)

This passage is in the heart of Sirach's celebrated "history of famous men," which illustrates significant familiarity with the Law and Prophets and which begins in Sir 44:1 with the words, "Let us now sing the praises of famous men, our ancestors in their generations." Sirach shows an awareness of the books of Joshua (46:1–6), Samuel (46:13–47:11), and Kings (47:12–49:3) as well as several other well-known names in the OT writings: Isaiah (48:20–25), Jeremiah (49:6–7), Ezekiel (49:8), and the Twelve Prophets (49:10). His reference to the "Twelve Prophets" suggests that by the time that Sirach wrote (180 B.C.E.), all of the Minor Prophets were collected in one scroll.[27]

---

[26] Barton, *Holy Writings, Sacred Text,* 146, makes this observation.

[27] Sirach cites Mal 4:5–6 in Sir 48:10, suggesting the completion of the Twelve sometime around 250 B.C.E.. For more information on this, see Jones, *Formation of the Book of the Twelve,* 7–42.

The entire passage, Sir 44:1–49:10, suggests that the heroes described in these prophetic writings were familiar to the Jews, that they probably were widely acknowledged in a scriptural or authoritative manner, and that their authors were viewed as spokespersons for God. Sirach does not introduce these famous persons (except for Elijah [48:10]), but assumes widespread knowledge of them. His purpose was not to celebrate their writings, but to celebrate their lives. Whether their writings were identified as Scripture is not obvious, but Sirach's knowledge of them is at least suggestive of their authoritative role in the Judaism of his day.

B. PROLOGUE TO SIRACH

The grandson of Sirach, who translated his grandfather's work into Greek, added a very important prologue to this work, possibly as early as 130 B.C.E., but more likely around 116–110 B.C.E.,[28] which acknowledges the presence of three categories of sacred writings: Law, Prophets, and a rather vague category called "the other books of our ancestors." The entire prologue emphasizes the purpose of Sirach and its relationship to other sacred writings:

> Many great teachings have been given to us through *the Law and the Prophets and the others that followed them,* and for these we should praise Israel for instruction and wisdom. Now, those who read the scriptures must not only themselves understand them, but must also as lovers of learning be able through the spoken and written word to help the outsiders. So my grandfather Jesus, who had devoted himself especially to the reading of *the Law and the Prophets and the other books of our ancestors,* and had acquired considerable proficiency in them, was himself also led to write something pertaining to instruction and wisdom, so that by becoming familiar also with his book those who love learning might make even greater progress in living according to the law.
>
> You are invited therefore to read it with goodwill and attention, and to be indulgent in cases where, despite our diligent labor in translating, we may seem to have rendered some phrases imperfectly. For what was originally expressed in Hebrew does not have exactly the same sense when translated into another language. Not only this book, but even *the Law itself, the Prophecies, and the rest of the books* differ not a little when read in the original.

---

[28] So argues Kahle, *Cairo Geniza,* 216. Not all scholars agree that the prologue to Sirach is genuine, that is, that it was written by the grandson, since it is not found in the Old Latin translation of the OT writings, and it is missing in several Greek cursive manuscripts. Also, a different prologue is found in some Greek manuscripts. If Sirach's grandson did not write the prologue—and it is by no means certain that he did—there may be, as Kahle argues, no *clear* examples of a three-part division of the Hebrew Scriptures before 70 C.E. G. Kilpatrick also denies that the grandson of Sirach wrote this introduction; cited by Kahle, *Cairo Geniza,* 217.

> When I came to Egypt in the thirty-eighth year of the reign of Euergetes and stayed for some time, I found opportunity for no little instruction. *It seemed highly necessary that I should myself devote some diligence and labor to the translation of this book.* During that time I have applied my skill day and night to complete and publish the book for those living abroad who wished to gain learning and are disposed to live according to the law. (Sir Prologue, emphasis added)

Although we are not certain how the grandson viewed his grandfather's work, that is, whether he included Sirach among the "other books" or even among the "Prophecies," we start from the obvious: the book was valued enough to be translated into Greek for religious or pious use in the Jewish community of Alexandria. For example, the grandson wrote: "By becoming familiar also with his book [Sirach] those who love learning might make even greater progress in living according to the law." Those who read this book would be "disposed to live according to the law." He translated Sirach's work so that it might be used for edifying reading, and like his grandfather, he also believed that the writing was from the Lord. Sirach, for instance, wrote: "All wisdom is from the Lord, and with him it remains forever" (Sir 1:1) and then he proceeded to write such wisdom as if he believed that it came from God. The book was used in a canonical fashion (canon 1), being cited as "Scripture" or as an authoritative book over the following several hundred years in Jewish writings and also in the early church fathers.

According to the Babylonian Talmud, Sirach was capable of being cited for the good teachings that it contained, but it was not considered inspired at that time, even if it was widely cited among the rabbis. For example: "R. Akiba said: Also he who reads uncanonical books, etc. A. Tanna taught: [This means], the books of the Sadducees. (6) R. Joseph said: it is also forbidden to read the book of Ben Sira" (*t. Sanhedrin* 100b, Epstein, trans.). On the other hand, several texts, even in the same tractate cites with approval the writings of Sirach as in the following: "R. Joseph said: [Yet] we may expound to them (17) the good things it [Sirach] contains. (18) E.g., 'a good woman is a precious gift, who shall be given to the God-fearing man'." Likewise in the same passage, "All the days of the poor (24) are evil. (25) Ben Sira said: His nights too. The lowest roof is his roof, and on the highest mountain is his vineyard. The rain of [other] roofs [drip] on to his, whilst the earth of his vineyard is [borne] on [to other] vineyards (26)." The popularity of Sirach among the rabbis is illustrated by several references where various passages in Sirach are cited with approval, for example, in *b. Aboth* 4:4; *b. Pesahim* (or *b. Pesachim*) 113b; *b. Bava Metzi'a* 112a; *Tanhuma, Mikketz* 10; *Exodus Rabbah* 21:7; *Tanhuma, Va-Yishlah* 8; *Genesis Rabbah* 73:12; *b. Bava Batra* 98b and *Tanhuma, Hukkath* 1.[29]

[29] These references were supplied by Sid Leiman, *Canonization of Hebrew Scripture,* 93–97, plus fnn. 442–52 on p. 185.

Sirach was introduced with scriptural introductions ("as it is written") to support positions or argue points. Sirach, however, has a mixed tradition in the Talmudic literature. On the one hand it was eventually rejected as a part of the Jewish canon, especially by Rabbi Akiba in the late first century C.E.,[30] but it is sometimes cited as a part of Scripture in other texts, especially in *b. Bava Qamma* 92b.

After the writing of the two Talmuds, it appears that the common use of Sirach ceased from widespread use in Judaism, but it continued in the Christian community.

C. 2 MACCABEES 2:13–15

One of the more controversial texts related to canon formation is 2 Macc 2:13–15, and scholars cannot agree on its merits for canon purposes. It was written sometime between 104 B.C.E. and 63 B.C.E. (see 2 Macc 15:37) and reflects a time following the Jewish rebellion that brought them back into full control of their own land for a brief period of time.[31] We should note that both Leiman and Beckwith appeal to this passage to justify their view that a three-part biblical canon existed in the second century B.C.E. It reads as follows:

> The same things are reported in the records and in the memoirs of Nehemiah, and also that he founded a library and collected the books about the kings and prophets, and the writings of David, and letters of kings about votive offerings. In the same way Judas [Maccabeus] also collected all the books that had been lost on account of the war that had come upon us, and they are in our possession. So if you have need of them, send people to get them for you. (2 Macc 2:13–15)

This tradition claims that Nehemiah collected books for a library comprising the books of the "kings" (1–2 Samuel and 1–2 Kings?), the "prophets," and the "writings of David" (the psalms?). It is not clear what "letters of kings about votive offerings" refers to. Quite likely there was a historical tradition about the gathering of the prophetic books following the exile since other indications suggest that postexilic prophets were referring to a prophetic tradition (e.g., Dan 9:2).

Leiman argues that 2 Macc 2:14–15 supports his view that Judas Maccabeus collected the sacred books and was himself instrumental in closing the third category of Hebrew canonical books, the Writings: "The literary activity ascribed here to Judah Maccabee may, in fact, be a description of the closing of the Hagiographa, and with it the entire biblical canon."[32] Although

---

[30] See *b. Sanhedrin* 100b and *t. Yadayim* 2:13.

[31] Namely, before 63 B.C.E., when Pompey invaded Palestine and the Jews were subsequently subjected to the will and control of Rome.

[32] Leiman, *Canonization of the Hebrew Scripture,* 29.

he acknowledges that no clear literary activity leading to a canonical collection of Scriptures is mentioned in the traditions that survive this period, he nevertheless states that a canonization process was begun by Judas Maccabeus's response to Antiochus Epiphanes' attempt to destroy the Hebrew Scriptures. According to 1 Macc 1:54–57, the Seleucid (Syrian) king Antiochus IV Epiphanes plundered the temple in Jerusalem in 167 B.C.E. and directed his troops to destroy the sacred books of the law:

> Now on the fifteenth day of Chislev, in the one hundred forty-fifth year, they erected a desolating sacrilege on the altar of burnt offering. They also built altars in the surrounding towns of Judah, and offered incense at the doors of the houses and in the streets. *The books of the law* that they found they tore to pieces and burned with fire. Anyone found possessing *the book of the covenant,* or anyone who adhered to the law, was condemned to death by decree of the king. (1 Macc 1:54–57, emphasis added)

Leiman insists that "law" in this passage is a general reference to all of the Jewish Scriptures, not just the Pentateuch, and that Judas Maccabeus was involved in the canonization process.[33] He acknowledges that other Jewish groups did not adopt the same collection of Scriptures, but nevertheless declares that the canonical activity started by Nehemiah (according to 2 Macc 2:13–15) was completed by Judas Maccabeus. Whatever the sacred literature of the Jews was at that time, however, would surely have been targeted by the Seleucid troops when they stormed the temple.[34]

The basic problem with Leiman's argument is the lack of corroborating evidence for a canonization process during the second or first century B.C.E. in the land of Israel, and nothing in 2 Macc 2:13–15 or other texts suggests anything close to a fixation of canonical books in the biblical canon. Leiman offers only an unfounded assumption that the books that Judas Maccabeus collected are identical with a later closed collection of Scriptures identified in the second-century C.E. *baraita* known as *b. Bava Batra* 14a–15b (see chapter 6 §II.B) and that he ordered them in three collections, namely, Law, Prophets, and Writings. Leiman is even more speculative when he suggests that Judas may have canonized the books in the Hebrew

---

[33] Ibid., 151 n. 138.

[34] The burning of the books by the Syrian army in 1 Macc 1:56–57 and the burning of the "law" in *4 Ezra* (= 2 Esdras) 14:21 may be the same event, or the latter text may be a response to the report in 2 Macc 2:13 about Nehemiah's activity in gathering the lost books of the law. If so, it is interesting that the author of *4 Ezra* says, "Your law has been burned, and so no one knows the things which have been done or will be done by you" (14:21). Following this, Ezra requests that God "send the holy spirit into me and I will write everything that has happened in the world from the beginning, the things that were written in your law" (14:22). Here "law" evidently refers to "twenty-four books" that can be read publicly and the other "seventy [books] that were written . . . [for] the wise" (14:45–46). It is therefore quite likely that the author of 2 Maccabees believed that all of the sacred books in the temple—not just the Pentateuch—were destroyed.

or Jewish Scriptures: "The literary activity ascribed here to Judah Maccabee may, in fact, be a description of the closing of the Hagiographa, and with it, the entire biblical canon."[35]

How can Leiman be so certain about what was in the collection of books that Judas saved, especially when the first specific identification of any Jewish collection of sacred Scriptures comes considerably later? Since the contents of the twenty-two-book or twenty-four-book collections differed in many respects, it seems appropriate to conclude that precise decisions about lists of books in the biblical canon were simply not made at this time. No extant evidence shows that such decisions were made during the time that Leiman supposes. It is also anachronistic to claim that the twenty-two-book canon of Josephus and the twenty-four-book canon of the talmudic period are the same as the books collected by Judas Maccabeus. It is especially difficult to identify any of the books in the lists at this time (first century B.C.E. and first century C.E.), especially when we know that the fringe areas of the canon were still imprecise and continued to be so for another hundred years or more.

D. PHILO, *ON THE CONTEMPLATIVE LIFE* 25–29

In his treatise entitled *On the Contemplative Life,* Philo of Alexandria (ca. 20 B.C.E.–40 C.E.) admiringly describes the life of a Jewish sect known as the Theraputae, who are in some ways similar to the Essenes, but also distinct from them. The Theraputae lived near Alexandria on the shores of Lake Mareotis. We know practically nothing about them apart from what we read in Philo, but in the following description, he describes the books that these individuals used for reading during their devotional time. This collection of books, as with 2 Macc 2:13–15, is the source of controversy, since there appear to be three or four categories, but the specific identity of the books in these categories is not clear. We may be able to make some educated guesses about which books were involved, but there is still considerable doubt about their identity:

> In each house [of the Theraputae] there is a consecrated room which is called a sanctuary or closet [*monastērion*] and closeted in this they are initiated into the mysteries of the sanctified life. They take nothing into it, either drink or food or any other of the things necessary for the needs of the body, but *laws and oracles delivered through the mouth of prophets, and psalms and anything else* [*ta alla,* lit., "the others" (perhaps "other books")] which fosters and perfects knowledge and piety. (*Contempl. Life* 25, LCL, emphasis added)

Here we have an important statement about the sacred Scriptures of a group of Jewish sectarians living in Egypt in the early first century C.E. Of special interest is Philo's reference to the kinds of writings that comprise

[35] Leiman, *Canonization of the Hebrew Scripture,* 29.

the sacred literature of this group of Jewish ascetics: "Laws and oracles delivered through the mouth of prophets, and psalms and anything else." Unfortunately, Philo does not identify the sacred books that make up the categories listed in the above statement. He does, however, indicate that these Theraputae had a fairly large and unrestricted collection of writings.

In his own practice of referring to the Scriptures, Philo strongly favors the Law, as we can see from some eleven hundred references to the Torah in his writings, but only about fifty references to other books in the HB.[36] In practice, the books that he acknowledges as sacred seems to be rather conservative, compared, for example, to the Mishnah, where the rabbis cite the books of Moses only twice as often as they cite the rest of the books in the HB.[37] Leiman concedes that Philo's scriptural exegesis is largely confined to the Torah, but he strangely argues that Philo's practice was simply characteristic of Jewish exegesis in the first century and has no bearing on the shape of his canonical collection.[38] An obvious priority was given to the Torah, with all other books taking a lesser role in the canonical or authoritative status of ancient Judaism, even in talmudic literature. Philo seems to distinguish between the history of the kings and "oracles delivered through the mouth of prophets." Are they the same? If not, were 1–2 Samuel and 1–2 Kings as well as 1–2 Chronicles included? What about Ezra and Nehemiah? Ruth and Esther? It is possible to put them in the "other" category, but to do so is an argument from silence.

Ellis translates this passage as follows: "[They take into their study rooms nothing] but the laws, the oracles uttered by the prophets, and hymns and the other [books] . . . that foster and perfect knowledge and purity."[39] However, because of a connective *kai* ("and") after the word *laws,* the passage is more accurately translated "laws *and* oracles uttered by the prophets." The difference here is more than mere semantics. Ellis's translation isolates the law from the oracles by the prophets, but a more accurate translation makes clear that the Theraputae use nothing but "laws and oracles uttered by the prophets and hymns and the others." We cannot, however, establish from this vague reference precisely what books Philo had in mind. Nor can we even determine how many categories he indicates: two, three, or four: laws, prophetic oracles, psalms, and other books. We simply do not have enough information to go on, and nothing in the text clearly identifies the threefold division of the Hebrew Scriptures that emerges in the second century C.E. (Law, Prophets, Writings). We know nothing specific about the contours of Philo's or the Theraputaes' biblical

---

[36] See Hengel, *Septuagint as Christian Scripture,* 78–79.

[37] Leiman, *Canonization of the Hebrew Scripture,* 31, 151 n. 146.

[38] Ibid., 31.

[39] Ellis, *Old Testament in Early Christianity,* 8 (words in brackets are provided by Ellis).

canon from this passage. Of related interest is Philo's continued description of the Theraputaes' reading activity:

> They read the Holy Scriptures [*hierois grammasi*] and seek wisdom from their ancestral philosophy by taking it as an allegory, since they think that the words of the literal text are symbols of something whose hidden nature is revealed by studying the underlying meaning. They have also *writings of men of old* [*syngrammata palaiōn andrōn*], the founders of their way of thinking, who left many memorials of the form used in allegorical interpretation and these they take as kind of archetype and imitate the method in which this principle is carried out. And so they do not confine themselves to contemplation but also compose hymns and psalms to God in all sorts of metres and melodies which they write down with the rhythms necessarily made more solemn [or, "which they write down in solemn rhythms as best they can"]. (*Contempl. Life* 28–29, LCL, emphasis added)

The reference to the "writings of men of old" alongside the "Holy Scriptures" suggests something like the noncanonical writings found at Qumran, such as the *Damascus Document, Community Rule,* 4QMMT, and others. Could such writings have been taken into their closets for meditations? We cannot tell from the description provided, and we cannot tell if they distinguished these other books from what were later called "biblical books." How they related to these other "writings of men of old" is not clear in the text, but from the context it appears as if these writings were also highly prized as sacred or inspired literature.

In addition to Philo giving high priority to the Law of Moses and citing it extensively in his large body of writings, all of his scriptural commentaries were on the Law of Moses, an indication that he either had "a canon within a canon" or that at the core of his sacred tradition was the Law of Moses and everything else was second to that. It may also mean that only the Law was canon for Philo. All other writings could have been canon 1, but probably not canon 2.

Much has been made of Philo's not citing any apocryphal (deuterocanonical) literature, but does this restriction of his exegesis to the Torah mean that he rejected the scriptural status of all non-Torah literature? This issue takes us beyond the evidence available, but Leiman himself cites examples in Philo where he calls the Torah "Scripture" and calls the Prophets and the Writings "sacred word" and "divine." Leiman suggests that Philo had a different attitude toward the non-Torah literature that he knew.[40] In addition, even though Philo does not cite apocryphal or pseudepigraphal books, he also does not make much use of the rest of the books of the HB either.

Is it possible, then, to know what Philo's Scripture canon was? It may be an overstatement, as Leiman notes, to argue that Philo limited his biblical canon only to the Law of Moses, but at least it is clear from his practice

---

[40] Leiman, *Canonization of the Hebrew Scripture,* p. 151, n. 147.

that he placed the Law at the apex of what he considered sacred and authoritative. Leiman acknowledges that this argument from silence about the shape of Philo's biblical canon and which books he employed is not strong.[41] Since Philo does not cite all of the canonical literature, can we conclude that he rejected what he did not cite? This inference takes us beyond the available evidence. Were it true, however, Philo would have a significantly smaller biblical canon than both his predecessors and most of his contemporaries.

E. 4QMMT

4QMMT, a fragmented text (4Q394–99) discovered among the Dead Sea Scrolls at Qumran, is frequently cited as evidence for a three-tiered biblical canon in the century before the time of Jesus. Also called 4QHalakic Letter, "A Sectarian Manifesto," *Miqsat Ma'aseh ha-Torah* ("some works of the law"), or "The Second Letter on Works Reckoned as Righteousness," this recently published text is dated by some scholars as early as 150 B.C.E. The primary subject matter of this text, which possibly though not necessarily comes from the famed Teacher of Righteousness who led the Qumran community, is one of three ancient documents that speak about works-righteousness (Paul's letters to the Galatians and Romans are the other two). Translating this heavily reconstructed text is educated guesswork, and the variety of translations underscore the difficulty in drawing strong conclusions about the text:[42]

> [Indeed,] we [have written] to you so that you might understand the book of Moses, the book[s of the Pr]ophets, and Davi[d . . .] [. . . all] the generations. In the book of Moses it is written [. . .] not [to] you and days of old [. . .] It is also written that you ["will turn] from the pa[t]h and evil will befall you" (Deut 31:29). And it is writ[ten] "that when [al]l these things[s happ]en to you in the Last Days, the blessing [and] the curse, [that you call them] to m[ind] and return to Him with all your heart and with [al]l [your] soul" (Deut 31:1–2, [. . .] at the end of [the age,] they [you] shall l[ive . . .]
>
> [It is also written in the book of] Moses and in the [books of the prophet]s that [the blessings and curses] shall come [upon you . . . some of] [the bles]sin[gs] came on [. . . and] in the days of Solomon the son of David. (4QMMT 86–103, Wise, Abegg, and Cook, *Dead Sea Scrolls,* 363–64)

---

[41] Ibid., 31.

[42] The brackets and ellipses in both translations show the many gaps or blurred words in the original text and also illustrate how difficult it is to translate the text accurately. The gaps in the original text have been filled by the translators with words of the same approximate length that appear to fit the context of the passage. The supplied material is consistent in both translations, but not the same, and some of the supplied texts are merely educated guesses.

The difficulty of making sense of this text is seen in the translation of the same passage by García Martínez:[43]

> [. . . and further] to you we have wr[itten] that you must understand the book of Moses [and the words of the] prophets and of David [and the annals] [of eac]h generation. And in the book it is written [. . .] . . . [. . . not to] [. . .] . . . And further it is written that [you shall stray] from the path and you will undergo [evil. And it is written that a]ll [these] things [shall happen to you at the e]nd of days, [the blessing] [and the curse . . . and you shall ass]ent in your heart [and will turn to me with all your. . . . (4QMMT 86–103, García Martínez, *Dead Sea Scrolls Translated,* 84)

This text shows a threefold or fourfold division of the Hebrew collection of Scriptures, but it is not clear what was in each of these groupings. The references are not precise enough, and thus Schiffman's overly optimistic confidence that this is an "explicit reference to the tripartite canon" cannot be sustained.[44] The focus of the passage is rather on looking at the biblical history for a proper understanding of the error of one's ways,[45] and more important, it emphasizes the consequences of one's obedience to the Law of Moses. Obedience to the Law of Moses is at the heart of the whole letter, and, consequently, failure to observe the Law of Moses is at the heart of God's judgment. Deuteronomy is cited twice in the passage quoted above, and only occasionally are the "prophets" mentioned in the entire letter (e.g., 4QMMT 103), but not specific texts. Citations of or allusions to Scripture in 4QMMT are to passages from Leviticus, Numbers, and Deuteronomy, and no other part of the OT Scriptures is mentioned that one should obey. No blessings or curses are related to any other part of the OT Scriptures except the Law.

The mention of David may be a reference to the Psalms, not unlike that in Luke 24:44. Although the author had a high regard for David (he is mentioned in 4QMMT 95, 104, 111), elsewhere only Moses and the Prophets (4QMMT 103) or Moses alone (4QMMT 91, 107) is mentioned. While 4QMMT may indicate a threefold division of the Hebrew Scriptures in its initial stages, the canon had not yet reached its final form by the time of this writing.

Only in a very broad sense are the people asked to remember the history of the kings of Israel (4QMMT 109–111), and the whole focus of this letter is on keeping of the Law. The history of Israel preserved in the

---

[43]García Martínez's translation is based on Qimron and Strugnell, *Miqsat Ma'ase ha-Torah*. Other English translations include Dombrowski, *Annotated Translation of Miqsat Ma'aseh ha-Torah,* 14–15; and Eisenman and Wise, *Dead Sea Scrolls Uncovered,* 196–200. For an evaluation of these translations, see Harrington and Strugnell, "Qumran Cave 4 Texts," 494–96.

[44]Schiffman, "Place of 4QMMT," 95.

[45]Bernstein, "Employment and Interpretation of Scripture," 49.

Former Prophets (lines 109–113) is mentioned, but only in regard to whether the Jews kept the Law:

> Remember the kings of Israel and reflect on their deeds, how whoever of them who respected [the Torah] was freed from his afflictions; those who sought the Torah . . . [were forgiven] their sins. Remember David, one of the "pious" and he, too, was freed from his many afflictions and was forgiven. And also we have written to you some of the works of the Torah which we think are good for you and for your people, for [we saw] in you intellect and knowledge of Torah. (4QMMT 109–114, García Martínez, *Dead Sea Scrolls Translated,* 84)

It is clear throughout this passage that the Law of Moses is central to the life of the community and must be kept. The "explicit reference to the tripartite canon" that Schiffman refers to is not explicit at all. Only this isolated text suggests that more writings exist, but blessing or discipline came only from keeping or failing to keep the law of Moses (Torah). Also, one cannot argue from this reference that "law" refers to all of the Scriptures of the HB, since every specific biblical citation in 4QMMT is from the Pentateuch.

Apart from this text having several letters and words missing that make all conclusions about it arbitrary—even if the reconstruction that refers to three or four parts of a biblical canon is correct—the text still lacks clarity on the scope of the categories in the Hebrew Scriptures. At best, and in the context of the whole letter, the text is ambiguous and not as clear as the testimony of Luke 24:44 where we clearly see "the law of Moses, the prophets, and the psalms." Ellis acknowledges that there is no identification of the specific books that make up the categories mentioned in 4QMMT, but he attributes this lack of precision to the conjecture that everyone knew the contents of these categories when 4QMMT was written and that only in the second century C.E., "when uncertainty existed about their number or order, are the books of the OT listed by name."[46] That is, of course, speculation and does not take into account the context of 4QMMT.

While the majority of scholars seem to be moving toward a mid-second-century B.C.E. dating of 4QMMT, this is not yet certain. Dombrowski argues that it comes from the second century C.E. as a forerunner to the Amora literature, perhaps around 150 C.E.[47] He asserts that in style, vocabulary, and grammar 4QMMT is closer to *b. Bava Batra* 14b–15a than it is to anything earlier.[48] Dombrowski reasons that although 4QMMT is a "genuine piece of the Jewish Writings," it is nevertheless distinct from other literature at Qumran because it has no references to communal living. While

---

[46] Ellis, *Old Testament in Early Christianity,* 10.

[47] Dombrowski, *Annotated Translation of Miqsat Ma'aseh ha-Torah,* 15–17. I am inclined to accept the 150 B.C.E. date, but this is difficult to prove.

[48] Dombrowski (ibid., 17, 42–43 n. 222) gives examples of the similarity of 4QMMT with mishnaic style, grammar, and vocabulary.

this may be due to its late origin, it could, of course, also be an indication of an earlier date.[49] Certainty is not yet possible, but again, the majority opinion seems to date 4QMMT to around 150–100 B.C.E.

F. LUKE 24:44

Israel's tripartite canon was only *beginning* to close when the Evangelists were writing their Gospels, that is, when Christianity had essentially ceased being another Jewish sect heavily influenced by Judaism. Even then, however, the boundaries of the third part of the OT canon were not yet firmly fixed. This seems clear in Luke 24:44, where the risen Jesus, after eating with his disciples, says to them: "These are my words that I spoke to you while I was still with you—that everything written about me in the *law of Moses, the prophets, and the psalms* must be fulfilled" (emphasis added).

This is the only reference in the NT to a tripartite canon of the Hebrew Scriptures, but the problem is that it does not include all of the literature that eventually made up the third part of the HB, especially Ezra-Nehemiah, Chronicles, Daniel, and the rest of the Wisdom literature. Leiman, Ellis, Beckwith, and Bruce, however, insist that "psalms" in this passage refers to the first book of the Writings and that it is representative of that whole collection.[50] There is considerable doubt about this position, for there is no evidence for a three-part canon at Qumran or elsewhere with the Writings led by the Psalms. These scholars try to impose a later notion that cannot easily be substantiated even in the rabbinic tradition of the second century C.E. on the first century. Also, the Psalms were quite important in their own right and would easily be given their own place of prominence in a collection of Scriptures, but on what basis can we say that they had first place in the third part of the HB? What we have in Luke is an early beginning of a three-part biblical canon that had not yet developed. In it, a special place is given to the Psalms, following the already widely recognized two-part biblical collection called the Law and the Prophets.

More copies of the Psalms (thirty-seven) were discovered at Qumran than any other book of the HB. That both the MT and the LXX translation of the Psalms follow the same order suggests that there was some fixing of the text of the Psalms quite early, but there is no indication that this included the rest of the Writings. This also does not imply that the Psalms at Qumran

---

[49] Ibid., 16.

[50] Leiman, *Canonization of the Hebrew Scripture,* 40; Ellis, *Old Testament in Early Christianity,* 9 n. 30, contends that since the Psalms stand in the first place in some Hebrew manuscripts, they may "represent the third division of the Old Testament canon in Luke." See also Beckwith, *Old Testament Canon,* 111–15. F. F. Bruce, *Canon of Scripture,* 32, argues that " 'psalms' may refer to the whole of the Writings since the psalms were simply the first book of that collection, but we cannot be sure of this."

were fixed and that nothing could be added or deleted. In fact, several additions to the Psalms took place in the first century. According to Davies: "Some of the psalms contain additional material and a different sequence from the Masoretic [text], including the Cave 11 scroll, the most extensively preserved, which includes 'David's Last Words' (2 Sam. 23:1–7), Psalms 154–55 of the Syriac canon, the Greek Psalm 151, and ben Sira 51:13–30."[51]

Kümmel correctly concludes that it is unlikely that Luke intended this reference to the Psalms to include all of the documents later designated as the Writings.[52] Rather, this passage further supports my view that the third part of the Jewish biblical canon had not yet been clearly defined in the time of Jesus—or even later when Luke was writing his gospel. Since there is no clear evidence for the precise threefold division of the Hebrew Scriptures before the middle of the second century C.E., one should be cautious about declaring its presence before we have solid evidence of its existence. This is also true even later in the talmudic period when we find frequent references to this division of the Jewish Scriptures. It is best, therefore, not to argue dogmatically about those divisions and especially their contents at a time prior to or during the ministry of Jesus in the first century C.E. There is little evidence that the Psalter itself was complete before the fall of Jerusalem in 70 C.E., even though major sections of it were fairly stable in the Jewish communities from the Persian period.[53]

The later rabbinic period has many references to the Writings. For instance: "The Torah and prophets may be written on one scroll; this is the ruling of R. Meier (135–170). The Sages, however, say that the Torah and Prophets may not be written on one scroll, but that the Prophets and the Hagiographa may be written on one scroll" (*y. Megillah* 73d–74a, Leiman, *Canonization of the Hebrew Scripture,* 60). In this case, the Prophets and Writings do not yet rise to the level of the Torah. In fact, they never do. We also see the three parts of the Jewish Scriptures mentioned in a text that, though written at a later time, may reflect a time around 80–110 C.E.: "Sectarians asked Rabban Gamaliel: Whence do we know that the Holy One, blessed be He, will resurrect the dead? He answered them from the Torah, Prophets, and Hagiographa, yet they were not convinced" (*b. Sanhedrin* 90b, Leiman, *Canonization of the Hebrew Scripture,* 67).[54]

Even though "psalms" in Luke 24:44 cannot be shown to refer to the Writings in any first century C.E. source, Beckwith argues from talmudic references that the term *Fifths* (Heb. *homashim* or *homashin*) sometimes re-

[51] Davies, *Scribes and Schools,* 162.

[52] Kümmel, *Introduction to the New Testament,* 335.

[53] J. A. Sanders, *Torah and Canon,* 97.

[54] Other examples are *b. Bava Batra* 13b; *y. Hagigah* 72b (reporting the teachings of Elisha b. Abuyah [110–135 C.E.] and Rabbi Joshua [80–110 C.E.]); and *Leviticus Rabbah* 16.4 (reporting the tradition of Ben Azzai [110–135 C.E.]). See Leiman, *Canonization of the Hebrew Scripture,* 61–62, 66–67.

fers to the five parts of the book of Psalms (this term usually indicates the Pentateuch). Beckwith asserts that "psalms" refers to the third part of the Hebrew biblical canon in the talmudic literature:

> In a scroll of the Law, the space of the two finger-breadths must be left (between columns), but in scrolls of the Prophets and in scrolls of the Fifths the space of one thumb-breadth. In the lower margin of a scroll of the Law the space of a hand-breadth is left, and in the upper margin two thirds of a hand-breadth, but in scrolls of the Prophets and the Fifths three finger-breadths in the lower margin and two finger-breadths in the upper.[55]

Beckwith also claims that all of the Writings are referred to as the "Fifths" in a Tosefta text: "The Scroll of Ezra which went forth outside [the court] renders the hands unclean. And not only of the Scroll of Ezra alone did they speak, but even the Prophets and the Pentateuch. And another scroll which entered there renders the hands clean" (*t. Kelim Bava Metzi'a* 5.8, Neusner, *Tosefta,* 1617).

Beckwith's point is that both "Scroll of Ezra" here and "psalms" in Luke 24:44 refer to the Writings as a whole. Again, however, the text he cites does not demonstrate this even for a later period, let alone for the first century. Also, it is not clear what books the "Scroll of Ezra" contained. Beckwith projects a slim possibility from the middle to late third century C.E. as a certainty back on the time of Jesus and before. He reasons that since Jesus also cites the book of Daniel (e.g., Dan 4:26 in Matt 4:17 and 9:27; 11:31; 12:11 in Matt 14:15 and Dan 7:13 in Mark 14:62), which was a part of the Writings, he surely must have intended the whole of the Writings when he mentioned the "psalms" in Luke 24:44.[56] This argument is based on the assumption that the Writings were fixed before the time of Jesus—and Beckwith then cites as evidence a text that he assumes reflects this view! Leiman and Beckwith acknowledge that the meaning of the term *Fifths* is not uniform in rabbinic tradition, but this does not deter their willingness to use it as a defense of their interpretation of Luke 24:44.[57]

At any rate, we again must exercise caution not to impose on a first-century text the meaning of a term that may have obtained several different meanings in the late second and third centuries C.E. Likewise, it is difficult under any reckoning to assume that the books of Ezra-Nehemiah or the Chronicles can be implied in Jesus' reference to the "psalms."[58] Because there were considerably more books in the Writings than just psalmic literature, and because there is such a wide range of meanings of

---

[55] Beckwith, *Old Testament Canon,* 438 (citing *Sepher Torah* 2.3–4 and *Sopherim* 2.4); see also 111–14.

[56] Ibid., 111–12.

[57] Leiman, *Canonization of the Hebrew Scripture,* 61–63; and Beckwith, *Old Testament Canon,* 438–47.

[58] Reuss, *History of the Canon,* 10, agrees with this conclusion.

the term *Fifths* in the later rabbinic traditions, one must conclude that the third division had not yet come to its final form at the time of the writing of Luke's Gospel (ca. 65–70 C.E.) and that it is not useful to employ later meanings that have no parallels in the first century to interpret what a first-century writer (Luke) says.[59]

G. LUKE 11:48–51 AND MATTHEW 23:34–35

Two passages from the Gospels are sometimes cited by canon scholars as evidence of a biblical canon complete and closed before the time of Jesus:

> So you are witnesses and approve of the deeds of your ancestors; for they killed them [prophets], and you build their tombs. Therefore also the Wisdom of God said, "I will send them prophets and apostles, some of whom they will kill and persecute," so that this generation may be charged with the blood of all the prophets shed since the foundation of the world, from the blood of Abel to the blood of Zechariah, who perished between the altar and the sanctuary. Yes, I tell you, it will be charged against this generation. (Luke 11:48–51)

> Therefore I send you prophets, sages, and scribes, some of whom you will kill and crucify, and some you will flog in your synagogues and pursue from town to town, so that upon you may come all the righteous blood shed on earth, from the blood of righteous Abel to the blood of Zechariah son of Barachiah, whom you murdered between the sanctuary and the altar. (Matt 23:34–35)

In recent discussions these texts have become arguments for an early canonical development. The claim made by some scholars is that Jesus—by mentioning Abel, whose death is the first recorded in Scripture (Gen 4:8), and Zechariah, who was the last martyr mentioned in supposedly the last book of the HB (2 Chr 24:20–22)—was referring to a complete biblical canon or to a collection of Scriptures that extended from Genesis to 2 Chronicles, the complete Hebrew canon later designated in the three-part collection of Law, Prophets, and Writings. Bruce concludes from this that the third part of the canon (the Writings) began with Psalms and ended with 2 Chronicles.[60] However, does this passage really show that Jesus accepted a closed biblical canon made up of the twenty-two (or twenty-four) books of the Hebrew biblical canon that extended from Genesis (the reference to Abel) to 2 Chronicles (the reference to Zechariah)? Bruce states that since *canonically* Zechariah the son of Jehoiada[61]

---

[59] Stuhlmacher, "Significance of the Old Testament Apocrypha," 2, agrees with this conclusion and adds that "nowhere in the New Testament writings can any special interest in the canonical delimitation and fixing of the Holy Scriptures be detected."

[60] F. F. Bruce, *Canon of Scripture,* 29.

[61] The problematical parallel in Matt 23:35 appears to have the wrong family tree for Zechariah. It is possible that Matthew and Luke may be referring to the murder of Zechariah the son of Baris in Jerusalem during the first Jewish revolt (see Josephus, *J.W.* 4.335).

was the last *mentioned* prophet martyred in the Hebrew canon, then these texts suggest the completeness of the Hebrew biblical canon by the time of Jesus.[62] This explanation assumes, of course, that there was a clearly identifiable order of the HB by the time of Jesus and that the reference in Luke 24:44 to "the law of Moses, prophets, and the psalms" does not interfere with that order. If the order of the Writings was already set by the time of Luke's writing (ca. 65–70 C.E.), it is strange that Josephus (ca. 95–100 C.E.) does not have such an ordering in his writing (*Ag. Ap.* 1.37–41). Also, it is strange (see chap. 7, A.1) that none of the early Christians picked up on this three-part biblical canon, and it is not found in any of the church fathers. The best explanation for this, of course, is that the three-part biblical canon of the Jews was developed in the second century C.E., long after the Jews ceased having an influence on the scope of the Christian Scriptures.

Rather than Chronicles being the last book in the Hebrew biblical canon, however, Freedman argues convincingly that Chronicles stands in *first* place in the Writings, and he supports this by references to the major medieval manuscripts, including the standard Masoretic Aleppo Codex and Leningrad Codex. Rather than concluding with 1–2 Chronicles, the Writings end with Ezra-Nehemiah.[63] A further argument against Bruce's position is Freedman's assertion that because 2 Chr 36:22–23 and Ezra 1:1–4 are identical, the books were separated spatially since, had they been consecutive, there would have been no need for the repetition.[64] By contrast, the primary historical books that are consecutive (i.e., 1–2 Samuel and 1–2 Kings), have no repetitive texts connecting them.

There is also some question whether Josephus included 1–2 Chronicles in his collection of prophets since his final section has only "four books [which] contain hymns to God and precepts for the conduct of human life" (*Ag. Ap.* 1.40, LCL), which is similar to the reference in Luke 24:44 to "psalms." It is only in the second century C.E., however, that we first read of the specific groups, contents, and order of the three parts of the Hebrew Scriptures in *b. Bava Batra* 14b–15a.

Evans argues that the words *righteous* ("innocent" in some translations), *son of Barachiah,* and *whom you murdered* in Matt 23:35 are probably Matthean additions to the tradition cited in Luke, and they are designed to intensify and clarify the meaning of the utterance. Evans adds that the Matthean evangelist either

---

[62] F. F. Bruce, *Canon of Scripture,* 31.

[63] Freedman, "Symmetry of the Hebrew Bible," 95–96. The order of books in the Aleppo Codex is as follows: Genesis to Judges (same as usual), 1–2 Samuel, 1–2 Kings, Isaiah, Jeremiah, Ezekiel, the Twelve (in the standard sequence), 1–2 Chronicles, Psalms, Job, Proverbs, Ruth, Ecclesiastes, Lamentations, Esther, Daniel, Ezra. (Ezra includes Nehemiah. He does not mention Song of Songs.)

[64] Ibid., 96.

> added "son of Barachiah," thus identifying the martyr with the prophet Zechariah, or the Lukan evangelist deleted the familial epithet, because he realized that the person murdered "between the sanctuary and the altar" was another Zechariah. On balance, it is more likely that Matthew added the epithet to the Q tradition, for Jesus more typically refers simply to the given name, e.g., "Jonah" not "Jonah son of Amittai," or "Isaiah" not "Isaiah the son of Amoz."[65]

Evans concludes that the argument put forth by Bruce and others assumes not only that 2 Chronicles was considered canonical in the time of Jesus but that it had already been assigned the last place in the Jewish scriptural collection. He rightly concludes that in context, Jesus' reference to Abel and Zechariah was "probably meant to sum up Israel's history, not Israel's sacred Scripture."[66] Further, Jesus did not believe as some Pharisaic Jews of his generation did that prophecy had ceased and that the age of the prophets was over. Indeed, he claimed that John the Baptist was a prophet of God (Matt 11:7–15). How could prophecy have ceased and the canon begun for the early church if Jesus believed that the age of the Spirit was present?[67] A three-part biblical canon assumes that the age of prophecy was over, but this concept is not found anywhere in the teaching of Jesus or the early church. On the contrary, the early Christians believed that the age of the Spirit had come in full measure (Acts 1:8; 2:1–21). There was no such discussion of a closed canon of Scriptures because the age of the Spirit that manifested itself in prophecy was among them (Rom 12:6; 1 Cor 12:4–11; Eph 4:8–13).

Clearly there was development in the notion of what was sacred in the Jewish collections of Scriptures, but in the early stages, as we see in Luke 24:44, no evidence indicates that specific notions were held about the contents of the third part of the Hebrew Scriptures—or even what was in the second part! The following examples are instructive of the views about various parts of Scripture in the early rabbinic literature (second century C.E.). In *m. Rosh HaShannah* 4:6 we read: "He begins with [verses from] the Torah and ends with [verses from] the Prophets. R. Jose (ca. 135–170 C.E.) says: If a man ended with [verses from] the Torah he has fulfilled his obligation."[68] There is no reference here to the Writings, nor is there in *m. Megillah* 4:1: "On Mondays and Thursdays and on Sabbath afternoons three people read the Torah, no more and no less. They do not

---

[65] Evans, "Scriptures of Jesus," 90 n. 17.

[66] Ibid., 190.

[67] Before moving on, we should probably note that the reference to Wisdom in Luke 11:49 is often cited as a reference to the Wisdom of Solomon, an apocryphal book. Although this is a good possibility, there is no way to argue the point dogmatically. This may be an allusion or simply common language circulating among Jews in the first century and earlier.

[68] All translations of rabbinic texts in this paragraph from Leiman, *Canonization of the Hebrew Scripture,* 58, 63.

close with a reading from the Prophets." But in the later Tosefta text *t. Rosh HaShannah* 2.12G, the Writings are added to what is read: "The reciter opens with verses from the Torah, and closes with verses from the Torah, and recites from the Prophets and Hagiographa in between." Leiman acknowledges that the earlier *m. Megillah* 4:1 and 4:4 do not mention the Writings as a part of the Hebrew sacred collection, but the later *t. Rosh HaShannah* 2:12G includes the Prophets and the Writings after the Torah. This suggests, of course, a development in the recognition of the authority of the Writings somewhere between the writing of those two texts. Or, perhaps it more likely suggests that the emergence of the third part of the HB into which went several writings that were earlier acknowledged as Prophets in the time of Jesus.

Although Leiman disagrees with this conclusion and prefers to say that this was simply a liturgical expansion rather than a canonical one,[69] I nevertheless conclude that this is a sound inference taken from an expanding tradition in rabbinic Judaism. I also find it is difficult to distinguish the authority attributed to Scriptures in a so-called canonical context from those writings used in a liturgical context.

With the exception of Luke 24:44, which is an unusual (indeed, unique) reference in the NT to a three-part collection of Scriptures, only the Law or the Law and the Prophets are mentioned in the NT in reference to the Jewish Scriptures (e.g., Matt 5:17; 7:12; Luke 24:27; and Acts 28:23, where "the law and the prophets" appear to comprise all of the sacred Scriptures). Sometimes the whole of the sacred writings is referred to simply as "law" (e.g., John 10:34 cites Ps 82:6 as "law," and 1 Cor 14:21 introduces Isa 28:11–12 with "in the law it is written"). Other designations for the Jewish Scriptures include "scripture" (John 13:18; Gal 3:8), "old covenant" (2 Cor 3:14), and "Moses and all the prophets" (Luke 24:27; John 1:45).[70] Barr concludes from these and other NT references that perhaps the Prophets as a collection were much wider in scope than we have previously thought. He concludes that all authoritative sacred writings, not just the Former Prophets and Latter Prophets, were called "prophets." Even these terms are a late development in Judaism and found nowhere in the early church before the second century C.E. Barr claims that the presence of such references "strongly suggests that the category of 'Prophet' was not a closed one: any non-Torah book that was holy Scripture was a 'Prophet.'"[71] This is further supported by Melito's reference to the Jewish Scriptures in 170–180 C.E. as simply "the Law and the Prophets" (Eusebius, *Hist. eccl.* 4.26.13–14; see chapter 9 §IV.A.1). Melito lists books that are later placed in the Writings, but he does not have these categories, and his list concludes with Daniel, Ezekiel, and Ezra. The Writings are included earlier

---

[69] Ibid., 63–64.

[70] These terms are discussed in Ellis, *Old Testament in Early Christianity,* 3.

[71] Barr, *Holy Scripture,* 55.

in his collection and intermingled with the Former Prophets and Latter Prophets, similar to the historic order of the Christian OT (he also includes the Wisdom of Solomon in his list of books). Barr agrees that the Law was a separate and distinct part of the Jewish canon, but maintains that the boundaries between the Prophets and the other books were still imprecise in the first century C.E.[72] This imprecision is reflected in early Christian collections of OT Scriptures.

In summary, Luke 11:48–51 and Matt 23:34–35 give evidence for an emerging tripartite biblical canon in the first century B.C.E. and first century C.E., but its precise boundaries and contents cannot be discerned from the available evidence. That suggests, of course, that the full development of these three categories was simply not present in the first century. They become a reality for Judaism in the second century C.E. and even later for the church.

IV. The Myth of an Alexandrian Canon

The presence of additional literature in the Greek translation of the OT has led many scholars to conclude that the earliest Christian churches adopted an *Alexandrian* canon of Jewish Scriptures that contained a larger number of writings than did the Hebrew canon of Scriptures. Pfeiffer, for example, argues for the existence of an Alexandrian Jewish canon and distinguishes it from the canon of Palestinian Jews, which he claims was a conservative group who "made a sharp distinction between inspired Scripture and human writings."[73] The Alexandrians, on the other hand, "tended to accept as Scripture any writing in Hebrew or Aramaic which came from Palestine."[74] Pfeiffer holds that the same was true of the rest of the Diaspora Jews, who, unlike the Palestinian Jews, did *not* believe that prophecy had ceased with Ezra, but instead had continued.

A comparison of the LXX used in the early church to the HB shows significant differences in the text, the order of the books, and even the books that comprise it. The LXX[75] contains more books than does the HB. An important question here is whether the LXX contained those books before the birth of Christianity or if the Christians were responsible for including

[72] Ibid., 55–56.

[73] Robert Pfeiffer, "Canon of the OT," 510.

[74] Ibid.

[75] Using the term Septuagint (LXX) as an abbreviation for the whole Greek translation of the OT Scriptures is, of course, imprecise. It is more appropriate to speak of the Old Greek, but because the term *Septuagint* is so firmly entrenched in the language that scholars use to identify the Greek translation of the Hebrew Scriptures, I will use it here, but encourage the reader to keep the distinctions in mind. Technically, the term *Septuagint* refers to only the Greek translation of the Pentateuch.

them. It is likely that the additions to Daniel (Song of the Three Children, Susanna, and Bel and the Dragon), the extended portions of Esdras that were added to Ezra, and the Epistle of Jeremiah (sometimes included as the last chapter of 1 Baruch) were added by the Jews in the first century B.C.E. or before and were a part of a popular Jewish collection of sacred writings before the church separated from Judaism. This larger collection reflects the Scriptures of many Jews before there was a fixed biblical canon, and this more open collection of Scriptures is what stands behind the Christians' larger biblical canon in the first three centuries. With the exception of some of the Christian editing of *4 Ezra* (also called 2 Esdras), it is unlikely that the Christians added these writings to an earlier more firmly fixed Jewish biblical canon. It is more likely that they were considered holy or sacred by some Jews well before the time of Jesus,[76] and because they circulated widely among the Jews in Israel, they were adopted by the Christians.

The grandson of Ben Sirach states that in addition to the Law, the Prophets, and "the other books" that he was translating for the Jews in Alexandria, his grandfather's work also deserved special attention. Why else, of course, would he take the time to translate it into Greek? Noncanonical Jewish books such as Sirach probably had their origin in the land of Israel and were transported and translated from Israel to Alexandria wherever Jews lived in significant numbers in the Roman Empire. The NT allusions to some of the noncanonical literature found in the LXX indicates that the earliest Christian collections of the OT Scriptures contain much of that literature.[77]

The biggest problem with the theory of an Alexandrian canon is that there are no extant Alexandrian canons that one can point to and say that these books and no others comprised it. Pfeiffer himself acknowledges that no one knows what the Scriptures of the Alexandrian Jews and other Diaspora Jews were before the LXX was condemned about 130 C.E. in Palestine. Long ago (1909) Reuss concluded that we in fact know nothing about the Septuagint before the time when the church made extensive use of it.[78] This lack of knowledge includes the condition of the text and its form as well as the extent of this canon. What is more, there is no evidence that the Alexandrian Jews, or the other Jews of the Diaspora, were any more likely to adopt additional writings into their sacred Scriptures than were the Jews of Palestine in the last two centuries B.C.E. and the first century C.E. Further, no evidence shows the existence of a biblical canon in Alexandria in the second century B.C.E. or up to the second century C.E. that differs from the one in Palestine.[79]

---

[76] *4 Ezra* is an exception, of course, because of the lateness of its composition.

[77] See appendix B for some ancient lists of OT Scriptures.

[78] Reuss, *History of the Canon,* 7.

[79] A strong refutation of Robert Pfeiffer's position is found in Sundberg, *Old Testament of the Early Church,* 51–79.

Although there are many differences between Philo and the second-century C.E. rabbis in Palestine in terms of their interpretation of the Scriptures, most of Philo's references to Scripture are from the Law, and only a few to other books. Philo of Alexandria appears, therefore, to have had an *even smaller* Scripture collection than did the Jews of Palestine. Moreover, since the communications between Jerusalem and Alexandria were quite good during the first century B.C.E. and first century C.E., it is unlikely that either the notion or extent of divine Scripture varied significantly between the two locations during the period before 70 C.E. This does not necessarily mean, of course, that there were no differences between the Jews in the Diaspora and those in Palestine. Since there were several differences between the Jewish sects in Palestine (e.g., Sadducees, Essenes, and Pharisees) regarding what was acknowledged as Scripture, were there also such differences among the Jews who lived outside the land of Israel? The Jews of the Diaspora were more affected by Hellenism than were the Jews of Palestine, but there is no evidence to suggest that these differences also affected their notion of Scripture or the boundaries of their Scriptures. The additional writings that found their way into the Christian Bible were, for the most part, first written in Palestine in Hebrew and were more likely to be revered by Jews there than elsewhere. On the other hand, Jewish writings acknowledged as Scripture in Babylon, unlike in Palestine, were restricted to those written before Artaxerxes.

The significant influence of the Greek language and culture in Palestine in the time of Jesus is becoming more widely acknowledged now than in the past. There is little question anymore over whether Jesus could speak Greek.[80] Jewish funerary boxes recently discovered in Israel with Greek inscriptions that date from the first century C.E. strongly suggest the influence of both the Greek language and the Greek culture in Israel before, during, and after the time of Jesus. Likewise, Greek documents found at Qumran (mostly Cave 7) and at Naḥal Ḥever raise questions about who wrote them and who read them. For most early Christians, the Greek Bible was their only Bible from the very beginning of the Christian movement.

The likely explanation for the larger number of writings in the LXX is that the process of limiting the Scriptures began in Palestine after the time when Judaism ceased having a significant influence upon the Christian community and also at a time when the Christians were producing copies of the Greek Scriptures that they inherited from the Jews. Christian Scriptures were larger because the Jews at an earlier time included more writings than they did later under the influence of rabbinic Judaism. When the Christians left Jerusalem in 62–66 C.E. following the death of James the brother of Jesus, they moved to Pella on the east side of the Jordan river and the influence of Judaism upon the Christians, and especially its under-

[80] See Porter, *Language of the New Testament,* for a history of this discussion.

standing and limits of authoritative Scriptures, significantly diminished. When the last Christians were finally and completely excluded from the synagogue in 132–35 C.E. because they did not support the Bar Kokhba rebellion, there was no more Jewish influence on the scope of the Christian OT Scriptures.

V. The Biblical Canon in the First Century C.E.

Many biblical scholars claim that the earliest Christians received from Judaism a *closed* canon of Scriptures, that is, a biblical canon that is essentially the same as the HB and the Protestant Christian OT canon. Some Jewish and Christian scholars contend that the HB was essentially complete around 150 B.C.E. or slightly earlier (165 B.C.E.). Some conservative scholars insist that *Jesus* endorsed the current OT canon made up of Law, Prophets and Writings. LaSor, Hubbard, and Bush, for instance, claim that "the Christian church was born with a canon in its hands" and that "the New Testament authors never cite apocryphal writings directly, and it is probably safe to assume that the OT they used was identical with that known today."[81]

Freedman contends that the major components of the Hebrew Scriptures, the "Primary History" made up of the Pentateuch and the books Joshua through 2 Kings, were completed in Babylon before the return from exile in 538 B.C.E.[82] The rest of the HB, he argues, was complete by the time of Ezra and Nehemiah, with the exception of the book of Daniel, which he places in the second century B.C.E. (165).[83]

A. The Emerging Scriptural Canon

In his detailed discussion of the origins of the OT canon, Beckwith argues that the OT reached its final form in the time of Judas Maccabeus around 164 B.C.E.[84] He oddly claims that there were no essential differences in the biblical canons of the Pharisees, Sadducees, Essenes, and early Christians. Beckwith acknowledges that at a later time a distinction can be found between the Christian OT canon and that of Judaism, but this took place only after the breach between the church and the synagogue when

---

[81] LaSor, Hubbard, and Bush, *Old Testament Survey,* 17, 21. See also F. F. Bruce, *Books and the Parchments,* 128; idem, *Canon of Scripture,* 28–32; Harrison, *Introduction to the Old Testament,* 287, says the OT canon in all of its essentials was complete by 300 B.C.E.; Ewert, *From Ancient Tablets to Modern Translations,* 71; Leiman, *The Canonization of Hebrew Scripture;* Beckwith, *Old Testament Canon;* Trebolle Barrera, *Jewish and the Christian Bible.*

[82] Freedman, "Earliest Bible," 29. See also idem, "Symmetry of the Hebrew Bible."

[83] Freedman, "Symmetry of the Hebrew Bible," 86.

[84] Beckwith, *Old Testament Canon,* 406.

Christians expanded the OT canon because "their knowledge of the original Christian canon was becoming blurred."[85] The evidence that he presents to support this claim, however, lacks precision at critical points, and the likelihood that the biblical canon of the early Christians became "blurred" and that they somehow forgot the boundaries of their own holy Scripture, if it were known, is unthinkable and without support. Given the high regard that the early church had for its Scriptures, the thought of the scope of those Scriptures, had the church known it, becoming blurred is highly unlikely. Would the earliest disciples forget a biblical canon that Jesus passed on to them, as Beckwith supposes? It is most unlikely that any generation of Christians would forget the teaching of Jesus on so weighty an issue, and there are no traces of Jesus' position on such a fixed collection either in the NT Scriptures or in the writings of the early church fathers. Clearly, the burden of proof lies with those who say that Jesus left behind or endorsed a biblical canon and that the early Christians forgot it or lost it. No source in early Christianity supports this conclusion.

Reflecting on early Christianity having a wider biblical canon than the one later adopted in rabbinic Judaism and Protestant Christianity, Childs suggests that the early church's loss of the scope of their sacred Scriptures came when the church became more and more Gentile in its composition. When the early church began using the Greek translation of the HB, it lost sight of the original contents of its Bible.[86] This loss must have taken place rather early, since the NT writers overwhelmingly cite the Greek translation of their Scriptures. Indeed, their (OT) Bible was the Greek Bible, and the assumption also follows that the Greek Bible was much larger than the HB. At present, however, there is no way of knowing precisely what was in the Greek Scriptures at that time.

A better explanation for the wider biblical canon in the early church is that the earliest Christians remained loyal to the loosely defined collection that they inherited from Judaism in the first century before their separation from the synagogue. It was instead the rabbis—not the Christians—who later narrowed their collection of sacred books to the books now in the HB. The biblical canon in the time of Jesus and before was not sharply defined, even though the Law and the Prophets were widely received as authoritative Scriptures in the early Christian churches along with a less well-defined category that included the Psalter, other Wisdom literature, and perhaps writings such as Daniel. Other writings likely to have been received among the early Christians probably include some of the noncanonical writings discovered at Qumran and the "seventy" other sacred books referred to by the author of *4 Ezra* 14:44–48. The collection of sacred writings among the Jews in the land of Israel was much larger than it

[85] Ibid. See his reasoning on 339–408.

[86] Childs, *Biblical Theology of the Old and New Testaments,* 63.

eventually became after the end of the first century C.E. Only later, when there was a move toward defining sacred literature more narrowly, did discussions and debates about the scope of the biblical canon emerge within Judaism. There is no evidence that Jews or early Christians were concerned with the limits of their scriptural collections in the first century C.E., and Christians seem to have taken longer to finalize the scope of their OT. Is this because such matters had already been settled long before, or could it be that such matters were simply not anyone's concern earlier?

All Jewish literature that helped the church to effectively communicate its faith in Jesus as the Christ was received and used in the churches in its formative stages. Some of those writings were initially in a canon 1 stage of development and capacity, but later they were rejected by the greater church at large (e.g., *1 Enoch, Testaments of the Twelve Patriarchs,* Wisdom of Solomon, and Sirach). Some of those writings were also highly valued by several segments of the Jews in the first century and were only later rejected (Sirach, Wisdom of Solomon, *Testaments of the Twelve Patriarchs,* etc.) when the contents of their Scriptures became more narrowly defined in the second and later centuries of the common era.

Von Harnack, von Campenhausen, and Metzger argue that Marcion (ca. 140), the most prominent second-century heretic in the church, rejected the OT Scriptures of the Jews and the early church, which precipitated a concerted effort in the church to come to grips with the scope of its Scriptures. It is not clear, however, how or whether Marcion's views affected the church's OT collection, and the case has not been made that as a result of Marcion the early church determined either its own Old or New Testament (see chapter 11 § I).

B. *1 ENOCH:* A TROUBLING EXCEPTION

Beckwith's fairly detailed discussion of the closure of the canon fails to demonstrate convincingly that Judaism between the first century B.C.E. and the second century C.E. distinguished in practice or theory between the OT canonical books and those that were later known as the apocryphal and pseudepigraphal books. He insists that only the canonical OT Scriptures were believed by the various Jewish sects of that day—including Jesus and his earliest followers—to be inspired by God. He maintains that the apocryphal and pseudepigraphal writings were not accepted as inspired Scripture by either the Jews or the Christians. He does not establish any clear separation in how these noncanonical writings were used, but he acknowledges that they are sometimes cited in the same manner as the canonical literature is cited, that is, as Scripture.[87] Beckwith is least convincing when

[87] Beckwith, *Old Testament Canon,* 16–19, and especially 389–400, where he acknowledges the "authoritative" use of this noncanonical literature in the early church fathers.

he discusses the use of or reference to apocryphal and pseudepigraphal literature in the developing Christian communities. For example, in his discussion of the pseudonymous writing(s) in Jude 14–15 (*1 Enoch* and probably the *Assumption of Moses*), Beckwith argues that Jude saw this literature merely as edifying but not as sacred Scripture.[88] His reasoning, however, does not show an awareness of how prophetic literature was understood in antiquity or how Jude appealed to *1 Enoch* as one who has "prophesied." Jude bases his warning of judgment on the reliability and inspiration of *1 Enoch*. Is there any example of a writing classified as prophetic but considered not true and not inspired by God? By definition, that is what Scripture is![89] Beckwith concludes that "if Jude had selected two such edifying stories from books which he may even have regarded as otherwise unedifying, this would neither have impugned his own authority nor have conferred authority upon the pseudonymous apocalypses from which he drew."[90] On the contrary, when Jude claims that Enoch prophesied, he at the same time also conferred authority (or recognized the authority) on a pseudonymous document, namely, *1 Enoch*. Beckwith, along with many others, has a reluctance to acknowledge that the NT writers appealed to or used pseudonymous writings (i.e., the Pseudepigrapha) to understand and present their case about the Christian faith, but the fact remains that Jude used *1 Enoch* to argue his case for right living.

Beckwith's view that Jude was not appealing to *1 Enoch* as sacred Scripture is confusing since it is especially in Jude's appeal to and use of such literature that one can see how the author understood the book.[91] Jude cites the passage as a prophetic text, that is, as a Spirit-led text. By most definitions of Scripture, this is a reference to sacred Scripture. If Jude thought that the passage was spoken through prophecy, then he clearly saw it as inspired and equal to the status of Scripture.

If there was a widely accepted closed biblical canon of Scriptures among the Jews of the first century, namely, a fixed twenty-two-book or twenty-four-book Hebrew biblical canon, as Beckwith contends, then one would hardly expect to find the diversity that we see in the Jewish canon. Further, Tertullian cited *1 Enoch* as Scripture at the end of the second century—and based his doing so on Jude's acceptance of the book as Scripture:

---

[88] Ibid., 401–5.

[89] Davies, *Scribes and Schools,* 164–65, acknowledges the sacred status of *1 Enoch* and concludes, "The Enoch writings are a distinct, continually evolving corpus which would readily define on my terms as a canon. The final fivefold structure has been suggested as an imitation of the Mosaic canon. . . . Like an early collection of Daniel stories, Enoch is an Aramaic canon."

[90] Beckwith, *Old Testament Canon,* 405.

[91] Childs, *Biblical Theology of the Old and New Testaments,* 62, similarly dismisses this reference and categorically states: "The New Testament does not cite as Scripture any book of the Apocrypha or Pseudepigrapha. (The reference to *Enoch* in Jude 14–15 is not an exception.)"

> I am aware that the Scripture of Enoch, which has assigned this order (of action) to angels, is not received by some, because it is not admitted into the Jewish canon either. I suppose they did not think that, having been published before the deluge, it could have safely survived that world wide calamity [the flood], the abolisher of all things. If that is the reason (for rejecting it), let them recall to their memory that Noah, the survivor of the deluge, was the great-grandson of Enoch himself. . . .
>
> But since Noah in the same Scripture has preached likewise concerning the Lord, nothing at all must be rejected *by* us that pertains *to* us; and we read that "every Scripture suitable for edification is divinely inspired [2 Tim 3:16]." By the Jews it may now seem to have been rejected for that (very) reason, just like all the other (portions) nearly which tell of Christ. Nor, of course, is this fact wonderful, that they did not receive some Scriptures that spoke of Him whom even in person, speaking in their presence, they were not to receive. To these considerations is added the fact that Enoch possesses a testimony in the Apostle Jude. (*On the Apparel of Women* 1.3, adapted from *ANF*)

Jerome in the early fifth century C.E. also speaks of the problem that some had in accepting Jude because he cited *1 Enoch,* but eventually the problem was overcome in the church:

> Jude, the brother of James, left a short epistle which is reckoned among the seven catholic epistles, and because in it he quotes from the apocryphal book of Enoch it is rejected by many. Nevertheless by age and use it has gained authority and is reckoned among the Holy Scriptures. (*Lives of Illustrious Men* 4, *ANF*)

The issue is not whether Jude cited *1 Enoch,* of course, but how he cited it. And from the early church fathers, it appears that he cited it as Scripture.

The Enoch tradition was also quite strong at Qumran and was accepted in a canonical manner (i.e., as sacred Scripture). VanderKam shows that in each of the five sections of *1 Enoch* Enoch saw visions, dreams, heavenly visions, heavenly tablets, and various other heavenly phenomena and that all such activity had divine origins. God is the source of the revelations given to Enoch (*1 En.* 10:1–11:2; 14:1, 24; 15:1–16:3; 37:4; 39:2; 45:3–6; 55:1–2; 62:1; 63:12; 67:1; 90:22; 105:1–2; 106:19) and the source for the heavenly tablets (*1 En.* 81:1–2; 93:1; 103:2; 106:19; 107:1). VanderKam concludes that the Enochic compositions "were presented as the true record of divine or celestial disclosures made to the antediluvian sage" and that *1 Enoch* is a regular member of the canonical lists of the Abyssinian church.[92] It is likely that the opinions about *1 Enoch* at Qumran were also shared by others in the early church, and this suggests a wider recognition of the work than what one isolated text in the NT might suggest.

---

[92] VanderKam, *Revelation to Canon,* 24–26.

Along with what we now call the OT, the various segments of the Judaisms of the first century made selective use of a variety of books now known as a loosely defined collection of apocryphal (or deuterocanonical) and pseudepigraphal literature. All of these writings were deemed both inspired and authoritative by several of the Jewish sects of the first century C.E. The final fixing of the canon of Scriptures in Judaism, or in the surviving Jewish sects, is a rather late development that did not take place before the end of the first century C.E. in its beginning stages and no later than the end of the second century C.E. for most Jews.

Leiman and Beckwith produced fairly detailed and impressive discussions of the OT biblical canon and include a significant body of relevant data for their investigations.[93] Both scholars are well informed and provide useful information on the origins of the biblical canon of Judaism and the earliest Christian community. However, they have not given an adequate acknowledgment of how and why the Jews and the early Christians made use of a larger body of noncanonical literature in their worship, apologetic, and instruction. Further, they offer no convincing evidence that there was anything like a fixed biblical canon prior to the time of Jesus. The arguments, though plentiful and multifaceted, are frequently based on no more than arguments from silence or a collection of references and allusions to what is *now* (but was not then) called canonical. Beckwith in particular largely ignores the many references in early Christian literature to the noncanonical literature and especially its significant place among the Dead Sea Scrolls. For example, in Beckwith's treatment of the seventy other books described in *4 Ezra* 14:45–47, he ignores that the author of this work places the "seventy [books] that were written last" alongside the "twenty-four books" and at an even higher spiritual place than the twenty-four, claiming that both collections were inspired by God.

VanderKam makes four specific criticisms of Beckwith's and Leiman's handling of canon issues: (1) their questionable use of sources, especially their interpretation of Nehemiah's founding a library and Judas Maccabeus's collecting sacred books in 2 Macc 2:13–15; (2) Leiman's view that the prophetic canon was closed in the fifth century B.C.E. and that 1–2 Chronicles was placed in the Writings because the prophetic canon was closed then; (3) Beckwith's view that the number of sacred books was already fixed in the second century B.C.E.; and (4) Beckwith's method of explaining away impressive evidence that at least some Jewish writers considered more than twenty-two books to be canonical. Essentially, VanderKam argues that Beckwith and sometimes Leiman tend to read their texts anachronistically and try to make what later obtained in Judaism and later Protestant Christianity a reality before the time of Jesus.[94]

---

[93] Leiman, *Canonization of the Hebrew Scripture;* Beckwith, *Old Testament Canon*.

[94] VanderKam, *Revelation to Canon,* 19–27.

Even though there is evidence that many, if not all, of the books that became a part of the rabbinic Bible were long recognized in the Jewish and Christian communities of faith, their canons were still imprecise, and there was no fixed tripartite canon among the Jews in the time of Jesus and before. It is likely that what later obtained canon status in Judaism and in Protestant Christianity was a pared down version of what was in place earlier than the time of Jesus. It does appear that many other books were present and appealed to by both Jews and the early Christians, but in time that collection was reduced in size rather than expanded.

Beckwith claims that the noncanonical writings at Qumran were merely interpretations of or commentary on the canonical literature and not a part of the fixed Scriptures of Judaism at that time: "It is probably no coincidence that the revelations to which the Qumran community laid claim were revelations of the *true meaning* of the Mosaic Law."[95] There is no evidence from the Dead Sea Scrolls to support this view, and it ignores what we do find at Qumran.

Davies identifies four important factors that were common among the books accepted as sacred at Qumran: the presence of multiple copies, the citation of the contents of a writing as authoritative, the extent to which a text has been fixed (or not fixed), and the extent to which a writing generated interpretive literature (commentaries and interpretations of particular texts).[96]

On the other hand, manuscripts of noncanonical writings often outnumber some of the canonical literature found at Qumran: *1 Enoch* (twelve copies), *Jubilees* (fourteen), Tobit (five), Sirach (two), and Epistle of Jeremiah (one) versus Joshua (three), Judges (four), 1–2 Samuel (four), 1–2 Kings (three), Proverbs (one), Ezra (partial manuscript), Nehemiah (none), Ecclesiastes (two), Esther (none), and 1–2 Chronicles (one).

What Beckwith needs in order to substantiate his claims for an early biblical canon—but what we do not have from the surviving biblical and noncanonical ancient sources—is a clear statement from Jesus or the early Christians on the contents of their collection of sacred literature. The ancient Christian sources never discuss the question of a *closed* biblical canon before the fourth century at the earliest. Further, the Jews do not show any interest in cataloging or archiving their own sacred Scriptures before the end of the first century at the earliest.[97] The arguments and sources that some scholars produce for a fixed collection of Scriptures at an earlier date are inferential in nature and without adequate specificity.

---

[95] Beckwith, *Old Testament Canon,* 360 (emphasis original), in his fuller discussion of the noncanonical literature at Qumran as merely "interpretation" of the canonical literature (360–66).

[96] Davies, *Scribes and Schools,* 154.

[97] The two earliest texts that reflect this interest are Josephus, *Ag. Ap.* 1.37–43 and *4 Ezra* 14:22–48, both dating to the end of the first century C.E. See chapter 6 §I.A and §II.A.

Beckwith's argument from silence that there is no reference to the OT canon because it was already settled is unconvincing and flies in the face of the many allusions to and citations of noncanonical literature in Jewish and early Christian writings. Since there are no Christian references to a biblical canon in the time of Jesus or before, it seems clear that such matters were simply not of special concern at that time. One may reasonably think that if the issue of discerning which books were sacred was settled long before the birth of Jesus, and if Jesus had given to his disciples, or endorsed, a fixed collection or list of sacred Scriptures, that some tradition or information from that time would state that such a collection existed and what its contents were. To the contrary, there is no such evidence.

The biggest problem with many of the inferences that scholars make about the biblical canon from the limited primary literature that has survived antiquity is that they are anachronistic. They assume that the notion of canon that developed later (in the second to fourth centuries C.E.) in the Jewish and Christian communities was present in the first century, and they transpose such notions to that earlier period.

In an old but still important contribution to canonical studies, Reuss (1891) claims correctly that the question of the biblical canon depends on a theory of inspiration that simply was not present or even an issue for the apostles and their immediate disciples.[98] By the middle of the second century C.E., some Jews began to make three fairly common divisions of sacred Scriptures (Law, Prophets, and Writings), but the contents of the Writings was still vague, and most of these writings were simply acknowledged as "prophets." Only later were some of them moved into the third category. In other words, any literature that was deemed sacred and inspired was also acknowledged as prophetic Scripture and therefore was identified as Law, Prophets, or Writings. There is evidence that writings eventually placed in the third division of the HB (e.g., Job, Daniel, and Psalms) were sometimes referred to as prophetic literature. The book of Acts, for example, attributes prophetic literature to David (1:16; 2:25–31, 34–36). Qumran exhibits a similar sentiment:

> And David, son of Jesse, was wise, a luminary like the light of the sun, learned, knowledgeable, and perfect in all his paths before God and men. And to him YHWH gave a wise and enlightened spirit. And he wrote psalms: . . . The total was four thousand and fifty. He composed them all through *the spirit of prophecy* which had been given to him from before the Most High. (11QPs[a] 27.2–4, 10–11, García Martínez, *Dead Sea Scrolls Translated,* 309, emphasis added)

In a later rabbinic text, Job is called a prophet, and the text identifies both who Job was and the time that he lived:

---

[98] Reuss, *History of the Canon,* 9.

> Seven prophets prophesied to the heathen, namely Balaam and his father, Job, Eliphaz the Temanite, Bildad the Shuhite, Zophar the Naamathite, and Elihu the son of Barachel the Buzite. . . . So too Job [is included because] he prophesied to the heathen. But did not all the prophets prophesy to the heathen?—Their prophecies were addressed primarily to Israel, but these addressed themselves primarily to the heathen. (*b. Bava Batra* 15b, Soncino Talmud)

This ties in with 1 Chr 25:1, which acknowledges that David prophesied through music. The collection of Prophets was still vague in the first century and seems to have included all sacred literature except for the Law. In the second century C.E., the term *Prophets* was used occasionally for all of the OT Scriptures. Justin, for example, describes early Christian worship when the people are gathered: "The memoirs of the apostles or the writings of the prophets are read, as long as time permits" (*1 Apol.* 67, *ANF*).

Since both Jews and Christians believed that God had inspired all Scripture, all of it was prophetic. We should not, therefore, be surprised to see that books eventually placed in the third part of the HB were earlier referred to as *prophetic* books and listed among the Prophets. The Writings were essentially a broad collection of literature believed to be inspired of God, and most, if not all of them, were earlier included in this open collection of Prophets. Eventually, however, they found their place in the third part of the tripartite Jewish biblical canon.[99]

C. SONG OF SONGS: HERMENEUTICS AND CANON

Many scholars, especially those who practice ministry, observe that several biblical texts are either ignored altogether in the lectionaries of the church or spiritualized beyond any relationship to their original intent. For example, it would be difficult to find a minister today who preaches on a woman's menstrual cycle from the book of Leviticus (see Lev 15:19–30; cf. 12:1–8; 15:16–18). Such laws about the natural discharges of the body as signs of impurity and uncleanness are irrelevant to modern society unless one can find a way to allegorize them. Hermeneutical handstands have been done to show the relevance of a variety of texts over the years (e.g., finding Jesus and the church symbolized in the Jewish tabernacle or the Christian gospel in the book of Esther), but with the ever-growing assumption of biblical inquiry that the meaning of a text must be rooted in its historical context, problems are posed for believing communities.

A good example is the traditional interpretation of the Song of Songs by allegory versus its current interpretation by biblical scholars and the church or synagogue. Most biblical scholars today hold that the book was originally produced as a nontheological volume that closely parallels Near

---

[99] Jones, *Formation of the Book of the Twelve,* 64–68, also makes this argument about the prophetic nature of all sacred literature.

Eastern poetry celebrating human love. This (re)discovery of knowledge about the book, which caused it considerable trouble in being accepted into the Jewish and Christian biblical canons, has led to its demise in the communities of faith today. It is not referred to or cited in the NT or in Josephus's writings at the end of the first century C.E. It is rare that any preacher uses this book as the basis for a sermon or Bible study, though some illustrate from it occasionally in premarriage and marriage counseling. When the sexual aspects of the book (e.g., 7:7–9) are no longer spiritualized to represent the love between Yahweh and Israel or between Christ and the church,[100] ministers have discomfort in addressing its literal message. The Jews were prone to allegorize the book early on and make the female of the book represent either the house of Torah study, Moses, Joshua, an individual woman, a local court, the Sanhedrin, a group of righteous Jews, the Jewish community in the Diaspora in Syria, or more commonly the community of Israel as a whole. According to the Mishnah, during a celebration on the Day of Atonement the daughters of Jerusalem wore white raiments that had been immersed (i.e., to make them ceremonially clean), and they went forth to dance in the vineyards. The rabbis cited Song of Songs 3:11 on this occasion:

> Likewise it saith, *Go forth ye daughters of Sion, and behold king Solomon with the crown wherewith his mother hath crowned him in the day of his espousals and in the day of the gladness of his heart: In the day of his espousals*—this is the giving of the Law; *and in the day of the gladness of his heart*—this is the building of the Temple. May it be built speedily, in our days! Amen. (*m. Ta'anit* 4:8, Danby, *Mishnah,* 201, emphasis original)

Likewise, in the *Tosefta* we find a similar interpretation of Song of Songs:[101]

> Similarly you say: *Under the apple tree I awakened you* (Song 8:5), said the Holy Spirit. *Set me as a seal upon your heart* (Song 8:6), said the congregation of Israel. *For love is strong as death, jealousy is cruel as the grave* (Song 8:6), said the nations of the world. (*t. Sotah* 9:8, Neusner, *Tosefta,* 875, emphasis original)

Early church fathers Hippolytus and Origen reinterpreted Song of Songs to refer to the love between Christ and the church and also the love between God and an individual person. For example, in Origen's commentary on Song of Songs 2:5, we read:

---

[100] Rabbi Akiba in the second century C.E. is reportedly the first to spiritualize the message of the Song of Songs, based on a talmudic interpretation (*y. Sheqalim* 6:1) of perhaps *m. Yadayim* 3:5. Hananiah nephew of Joshua is said to relate the praise of the man's body in Song 5:14 to the Ten Commandments and their interpretation in rabbinic discussion; see Carr, "Song of Songs as a Microcosm," 175 n. 5.

[101] Other Jewish examples of this allegorizing of the Song of Songs include *b. Shabbat* 88; *b. Yoma* 75a; *b. Sukkah* 49b; and *b. Ta'anit* 4a. See a complete list in ibid., 175–76.

> If there is anyone anywhere who has at some time burned with this faithful love of the Word of God; if there is anyone who has at some time received the sweet wound of him who is the chosen dart, as the prophet says: if there is anyone who has been pierced with the love-worthy spear of his knowledge, so that he yearns and longs for him by day and night, can speak of naught but him, would hear of naught but him, can think of nothing else, and is disposed to no desire nor longing nor yet hope, except for him alone, if such there be, that soul then says in truth: "I have been wounded by charity."[102]

This allegorizing of the book allowed for its acceptance in both the church and the synagogue, but the emergence of historical-critical approaches to the Bible has led to its obscurity in both communities of faith since any discussion of sexuality, which a literal rendering of the text suggests, is often viewed as out of place by Jewish and Christian ministers. *Functionally,* as Carr observes, both the church and the synagogue have decanonized the Song of Songs and seldom refer to it.[103]

The church's use of the Scriptures that it inherited from its Jewish roots was marked by the spiritualizing of the biblical text to allow it to speak to the relevant issues facing the church in its day. One of the signs of the recognition of the scriptural status of a biblical writing is the hermeneutics used to interpret it. If relevance and adaptability are reference points of all sacred literature, then a study of biblical hermeneutics is essential in discovering its meaning in both the Jewish and Christian communities of faith.

In summary, early Christian collections of Scriptures more closely resembled those found at Qumran than those of the rabbinic tradition that eventually won the day. If Christianity emerged out of Judaism, one would think that there would be more consistency between the two traditions. Instead the considerable discrepancy in the contents of the two collections of Scripture came about because the early Christians departed from the influence of Judaism quite early (62–66 C.E.) when the Christians moved from Jerusalem to Pella on the east side of the Jordan River, just south of the Sea of Galilee. Although some Christians remained in the Jewish synagogues, that ceased during the Bar Kokhba rebellion of 132–135 C.E. During the period of roughly 70–135 C.E., sharper definition of the scope of the HB became a matter of concern among the Jews, and during this same time Hillel, who came from Babylon, took prominence among the Jews as a faithful teacher of the law. The books that he recognized were fewer in number than those recognized by the Essenes and perhaps more than those recognized by the Pharisees of the land of Israel.[104]

---

[102]Translation from Lawson, *Song of Songs,* 198; cited by Carr, "Song of Songs as a Microcosm," 178.

[103]Carr, "Song of Songs as a Microcosm," 184–85. He goes on (185–88) to speak of the "recanonization" of the book in the postmodern and postcritical world in which each interpreter reads the text for himself or herself, and the stigma formerly attached to discussions of sexuality no longer exist.

[104]F. M. Cross, *From Epic to Canon,* 217–18.

CHAPTER FIVE

Early Jewish Scriptures

IT IS REGULARLY ACKNOWLEDGED TODAY THAT THERE WAS NO NORMATIVE JUDAISM to which all Jews subscribed in the first century C.E., even if there were several shared "Judaisms," that is, religious activities and beliefs, common among most Jews in the land of Israel and in the Greco-Roman world at that time. Most Jewish sects seem to have held in common Sabbath keeping, circumcision, worship in the temple when possible, acceptance of the sacrificial cultus in the temple along with its priesthood, and care for the temple though a temple tax. The residents at Qumran had a different understanding of who should be in leadership in the temple and priestly structures, and they had strict rules regarding diet, poverty, and marriage. Also, participation in local religious activities in synagogues, including worship and teaching, especially for Jews living far from the temple in Jerusalem, seems to have been widespread in the first century C.E.[1]

Synagogues were scattered around the Greco-Roman world both in the land of Palestine, especially Jerusalem, and in the Diaspora. Local languages were used in the synagogues, and most Jews outside the land of Israel spoke Greek. Jews frequently disagreed with each other on a variety of issues, including the nature and mode of life after death, whether there

[1] In antiquity, a synagogue was sometimes called *proseuchē* ("prayer" or "place of prayer"; cf. Acts 16:13, 16), but the origin of synagogues is somewhat obscure. The earliest evidence for the existence of synagogues comes from Egypt in the third century B.C.E., but they probably antedate that time and likely have roots either in the reforms of Josiah (621 B.C.E.), in the exile in Babylon, or shortly after that during the reforms of Ezra and Nehemiah and the reconstruction of Jerusalem and the temple. Whenever and wherever the synagogue began and whatever it was called, by the first century B.C.E. synagogues were known throughout the Greco-Roman world and in Palestine as well. They were a common feature among the various sects of Judaism in the Mediterranean world in the time of Jesus and following and were typically used for Jewish gatherings for prayer, the reading of Scriptures, and liturgical purposes. The standard work on the origin of the synagogue is Levine's *Ancient Synagogue,* 19–41.

was life after death, and the books that they acknowledged as Scripture. Jewish apocalypticism was common among some Jews, but such notions about the rapidly approaching end of the ages, the impending judgment of God, and the establishment of God's kingdom on earth by a messianic figure were not universally held by all Jews in the time of Jesus. There were also several Jewish messianic claimants both before and after the time of Jesus in the land of Israel. Judaism in the first century was a mixed variety of expressions of piety. This is especially true in terms of the Scriptures that they acknowledged. So far as current knowledge is aware, all Jewish sects in the first century, including Christianity, acknowledged the authority and inspiration of the books of Moses (the Pentateuch), even if the Samaritans had their own edition of the Pentateuch that differed in several respects from the Jewish Pentateuch acknowledged by both Jews and Christians today.

In the early to mid-third century B.C.E., a Greek translation of the Hebrew Scriptures was produced near Alexandria, Egypt. It was originally only of the Pentateuch, but gradually expanded to include the rest of the OT writings and even many apocryphal writings. This translation, called the Septuagint (LXX), had an enormous impact upon the early church, and it is not inappropriate to say that the Greek Bible was the Bible of the early church.

During the first century B.C.E. and following, several collections of Scriptures circulated among the Jews both inside and outside the land of Israel. There is little clarity on the contents of these collections, but they are nonetheless highly instructive for our understanding of the scope and development of the Jewish biblical canon in this formative era of early Christianity. These collections and questions related to them will be the primary focus of our inquiry in this chapter, but because of the growing relevance of the Dead Sea Scrolls for our understanding of the biblical canon in its formative stages, we will also focus on the Essenes at Qumran before looking briefly at other collections of Jewish Scriptures. They tell us a great deal about the development of the HB and also have considerable importance in our understanding of the formation of the Christian OT.

I. The Greek Bible

When the Law was translated into Greek in Alexandria, the Prophets were in the process of being recognized as sacred literature by the Jews. The Greek translation of the Jewish Scriptures is important in our understanding of the development of the biblical canon since that very act recognizes the religious value of the Scriptures for the Jews who could no longer speak Hebrew. This translation affected not only the Jews living in the Diaspora but also the Christians at a later date. The Greek Bible was the Bible of the early Christians, and its contents vary considerably in content and order from the HB. Many scholars argue at length that the early Christians adopted a longer Alexandrian biblical canon that included some of the apocryphal and pseudepigraphal writings, but this view was sufficiently dismantled by Sundberg, who shows conclusively that the Bible at Alexandria was probably *smaller* than the one adopted by the Jews in the land of Israel and that no Alexandrian canon ever existed.

A. GREEK LANGUAGE AND CULTURE AMONG JEWS

Following the decree of King Cyrus of Persia to allow the Jews who were taken captive to Babylon in 587–586 B.C.E. to resettle in their homeland (Ezra 1:1–4), many chose to return to the land of Israel, but many did not. A large number of Jews either remained in Babylon or resettled in large numbers in major cities around the Mediterranean world. As the book of Acts readily shows (Acts 2:5–11), many Jews were living in major cities and regions throughout the Greco-Roman world. Jews who made their homes outside Palestine were referred to as "Diaspora Jews," or "Jews of the Dispersion" (e.g., Jas 1:1; 1 Pet 1:1). After taking up residence in the Diaspora, it was not long before many of the Jews had forgotten their native Hebrew tongue and could communicate only in the language of the lands where they had migrated.

In the fourth century B.C.E., a leader from Greece emerged whose actions had a later impact upon the future of the Jews of the Diaspora, Jews in Palestine, and the Christian community. When Alexander the Great came to power, it was his plan to create a universal empire dominated by the Greek culture and Greek language. Following his conquest of a people, he immediately instituted the reforms that made the Greek language and Greek culture a dominant influence on the peoples that he conquered. The author of 1 Maccabees provides a succinct history of this period of time:

> After Alexander son of Philip, the Macedonian, who came from the land of Kittim, had defeated King Darius of the Persians and the Medes, he succeeded him as king. (He had previously become king of Greece.) He fought many battles, conquered strongholds, and put to death the kings of the earth. He advanced to the ends of the earth, and plundered many nations. When the earth became quiet before him, he was exalted, and his heart was lifted up. He gathered a very strong army and ruled over countries, nations, and princes, and they became tributary to him. (1 Macc 1:1–4)

The Hellenization of the ancient world was quite successful in spite of great resistance offered by some Jews in the land of Israel and others in different parts of Alexander's empire. This Hellenization program included learning the Greek language, religion, literature, art, architecture, government, and administration. This was accomplished chiefly through the use of the ancient gymnasiums, which were centers for physical exercise and the dissemination of the language and culture. In a short period of time, many people throughout the Mediterranean world, including many of the leaders in the land of Israel, learned both the language and the culture of the Greeks. Although this process began during Alexander's lifetime and was carried on with various degrees of intensity and success by his generals, the *Diadochi* ("successors") who ruled after him, Hellenization was such a complex notion that it took several generations before it became the dominant socialization program in the Greco-Roman world. Indeed, this influence carried on for centuries after the demise of the Greek Empire.

Hellenization, which also amalgamated Greek culture, language, and religious heritage with other languages and cultures, eventually led to a universal language and shared culture throughout the Mediterranean world and beyond. While many Jews resisted this activity, some freely embraced it. The Jewish books 1–2 Maccabees tell how this process was imposed in the land of Israel and how many Jews resisted, even to the death. Eventually, because of greater threats elsewhere and the growing resistance of the Maccabees, the Seleucid Dynasty withdrew from the Jewish homeland and the Jewish Hasmonean Dynasty began. The departure of the Greeks, however, did not mean that the Greek language was no longer spoken in the land of Israel. Hellenization continued to impact the whole of the East and many parts of the West even during the Roman Empire.

Many Diaspora Jews were receptive to the Hellenistic influence, but they continued to be loyal to their own Jewish religious heritage from the land of Israel. Philo (ca. 15 B.C.E.–45 C.E.), for example, was both a Hellenistic Jew who spoke and wrote in Greek and embraced much of the culture that came with it. He also tried to influence the Hellenistic community of Alexandria by showing the relevance and superiority of the Law of Moses over other philosophies, and he interpreted the Jewish Scriptures allegorically, as the Greeks interpreted their own sacred literature, in order to make it more relevant to the Hellenistic community. In the late first century C.E., Josephus, a Jewish general during the 66–70 C.E. rebellion against Rome, moved to Rome and wrote numerous volumes in Greek on the history of the Jews. Many Jews in Israel in the first century spoke Greek, perhaps even including Jesus. As the early Christians began proclaiming their good news about Jesus, they did so in the Greek language, and all of their Scriptures were written in Greek. The importance of the Hellenization program is obviously considerable, not only upon the early Christians, but also the Jews in the Diaspora or in the land of Israel.

B. ORIGIN AND USE OF THE GREEK SCRIPTURES

Because most Diaspora Jews could communicate only in Greek, their religious heritage was becoming more distant to them, and they were in need of having their sacred books translated into Greek. A major project to translate the Law of Moses took place in Alexandria, Egypt, sometime during or shortly after the reign of Ptolemy II Philadelphus (ruled 285–246 B.C.E.). According to the author of the *Letter of Aristeas* (ca. 140–100 B.C.E.), who offers a legendary account of this process (which still has some historical value), Ptolemy II wanted to develop the largest library in the world, and he took considerable measures to acquire the classic writers and copies of all of the volumes that he could. By the mid-to-late-third century B.C.E., his library at Alexandria may well have exceeded half a million volumes.

The author of the *Letter of Aristeas* claims that the king wanted to have a copy of the Law of Moses in Greek for his library and took remarkable steps to insure the quality and integrity of the translation. The king contacted the high priest in Jerusalem and requested that he send six skilled translators from each of the twelve tribes of Jews to translate the Hebrew Scriptures into Greek. These seventy-two translators came to Egypt and reportedly finished their task in seventy-two days—with each translator's work being exactly like that of the others! The *Letter of Aristeas* is unquestionably an apologetic for the inspiration and reliability of the Greek translation of the Pentateuch. Its claim that this translation was miraculously accomplished with the help of God is an ancient way of acknowledging its inspired status. The *Letter of Aristeas,* a fictitious account probably written by a Jew for propaganda purposes, commends the work of translation thusly:

> When the work was completed, Demetrius collected together the Jewish population in the place where the translation had been made, and read it over to all, in the presence of the translators, who met with a great reception also from the people, because of the great benefits which they had conferred upon them. They bestowed warm praise upon Demetrius too, and urged him to have the whole law transcribed and present a copy to their leaders.
>
> After the books had been read, the priests and the elders of the translators and the Jewish community and the leaders of the people stood up and said, that since so excellent and sacred and accurate a translation had been made, it was only right that it should remain as it was and no alteration should be made in it. And when the whole company expressed their approval, they bade them pronounce a curse in accordance with their custom upon any one who should make any alteration either by adding anything or changing in any way whatever any of the words which had been written or making any omission. This was a very wise precaution to ensure that the book might be preserved for all the future time unchanged. (*Let. Aris.* 308–311, Charles, *Apocrypha and Pseudepigrapha,* 2.121)

Eventually this translation became known as the Septuagint.[2] The original translation was of only the Pentateuch,[3] but this changed in time, certainly before the first century C.E., as the prologue to Sirach shows.

Kahle notes that the reference to the inviolability of the Greek translation mentioned in *Let. Aris.* 310–11 was a way of speaking about its inspired status.[4] The *Letter of Aristeas* shows the centrality of the Torah in Jewish life, which also suggests that the Prophets and Writings had not yet attained the status of sacred Scripture. In other words, when the *Letter of Aristeas* was written, what was included in the translation is what constituted the sacred and inviolable writings of the Jews. This does not preclude the Prophets, Writings, or other texts from being cited and used in the Jewish community of faith at that time, but clearly the Law had special prominence for the Jews, and it alone was translated into Greek initially.

In the second century C.E., many Jews believed that the Septuagint translation had theological problems, and indeed, various sections of the LXX are at significant odds with the text of the HB. The difficulty of translating the Hebrew Scriptures into Greek was noticed by the grandson of Sirach in his prologue: "What was originally expressed in Hebrew does not have exactly the same sense when translated into another language. Not only this book, but even the Law itself, the Prophecies, and the rest of the books differ not a little when read in the original." Corrective measures were taken at various times to bring the Greek translation into line with the Hebrew text (e.g., Origen's Hexapla and Jerome's Vulgate).

Although no one today seriously believes *everything* in the *Letter of Aristeas's* composite and anachronistic story of the translation of the

---

[2]The traditional name given to the Greek translation of the Jewish sacred Scriptures is the Septuagint (LXX), which should technically be applied to only the Pentateuch and not to the rest of the OT Scriptures, but it is commonly used as a reference to the whole Greek Bible. The term supposedly derives from the tradition in the *Letter of Aristeas* that seventy-two translators worked on the translation. Lohse, *New Testament Environment,* 129, suggests that the number seventy-two was simply rounded off to seventy, but it is also quite possible that the number derives from the tradition of the seventy elders (Exod 24:1, 9) who accompanied Moses to Mount Sinai when he received the law from Yahweh on tablets of stone; see Koester, *Introduction to the New Testament,* 1.252; Wevers, "Septuagint," 273; and Leaney, *Jewish and Christian World,* 153. If this is the case, then the use of the term *Septuagint* could well be an acknowledgment of the early belief in the divinely inspired status of the translation, that is, it authentically and faithfully conveyed the full intent of the law given to Moses.

[3]The term *Pentateuch* (Gk. *pentateuchos,* "five-volume [book]") appears for the first time in the early church in the gnostic *Letter to Flora,* when Ptolemy admonishes Flora (possibly a reference to the Roman church) that "you must learn that the Pentateuch of Moses was not ordained by one legislator—I mean, not by God alone; some commandments are Moses', and some were given by men" (Barnstone, *Other Bible,* 622).

[4]Kahle, *Cairo Geniza,* 211–12.

Hebrew Scriptures,[5] it is fair to say that it probably accurately reports that the translation began when Palestine was under the rule of the Egyptian Ptolemies, that it was produced in Egypt by bilingual Jews during the expansion of the Alexandrian library, and that it initially included only the Law of Moses. During this time, good relations between Alexandria and Jerusalem were common, and quality Hebrew manuscripts from the Jewish temple in Jerusalem, as well as capable Jewish scholarship to help with the project, were obtainable from Jerusalem.[6]

The *Letter of Aristeas* suggests a unity of translation that scholars have long recognized is simply not there. The text of the LXX is generally faithful to the Hebrew text, but that probably came as a result of many later attempts to bring the LXX into line with the Hebrew. Some time after the translation of the Pentateuch into Greek, other OT writings were translated, and by the end of the second or early third century C.E., the term LXX was transferred to all of the literature that comprised the Greek Bible.[7] The translation is uneven in quality (best in the Pentateuch and worst in Isaiah), but it helped to meet the religious needs of the Jews in Alexandria and of Diaspora Jews. The LXX also circulated throughout Palestine in the first century C.E.[8]

The apologetic tone of the *Letter of Aristeas* also suggests that the translation needed a defense against its opponents. The *Letter of Aristeas* was passed on and cited by Jews (e.g., Philo and Josephus), and also by Christian writers like Justin, Irenaeus, Tertullian, Clement of Alexandria, Origen, and Eusebius. Philo, for example, writes:

> Sitting here (on the island of Pharos [the traditional site of the translation work]) in seclusion . . . they became as it were possessed, and, under inspira-

---

[5]Scholars have rejected the authenticity of the account of Septuagint origins given in the *Letter of Aristeas* for more than four hundred years, and no one today seriously believes that it is an eyewitness account of the events it describes. On the other hand, while many of its fictitious stories are intended to argue for the inspired status of the Greek Old Testament, most scholars agree that some of its features are probably genuine (listed in the text above). The *Letter of Aristeas* has been dated as early as 200 B.C.E., but the majority of scholars place it between 130 B.C.E. and 70 B.C.E., with a few suggesting as late as 35 B.C.E., the terminus ad quem since it is referred to by Philo. For discussion, see Herbert Andrews in Charles's *Apocrypha and Pseudepigrapha,* 2.83–93; Zuntz, "Aristeas"; R. J. H. Shutt in *OTP* 2.7–11; Fernández Marcos, *Septuagint in Context,* 18–51; Hengel, *Septuagint as Christian Scripture,* 19–56; McLay, *Use of the Septuagint,* 100–136; and Jobes and Silva, *Invitation to the Septuagint,* 19–44.

[6]The Greek translation of the Law was undoubtedly an Alexandrian project, but the writer of the *Letter of Aristeas* may be correct in stating that help for the project came from Palestine. It also suggests that a standard text in Jerusalem was used in the project.

[7]Fernández Marcos, *Septuagint in Context,* 48–51.

[8]Some Greek fragments discovered in Cave 7 at Qumran may be sections of the LXX. They are, however, quite small, and it is difficult to speak with certainty.

> tion, wrote, not each several scribe something different, but the same word for word, as though dictated to each by an invisible prompter. . . . The clearest proof of this is that, if Chaldeans have learned Greek, or Greeks Chaldean, and read both versions, the Chaldean and the translation, they regard them with awe and reverence as sisters, or rather one and the same, both in matter and words, and speak of the authors not as translators but as prophets and priests of the mysteries, whose sincerity and singleness of thought have enabled them to go hand in hand with the purest of spirits, the spirit of Moses. (Philo, *Moses* 2.37–40, Kahle, *Cairo Geniza,* 215)

Kahle observes that Philo did not know sufficient Hebrew (which Philo calls Chaldean) to be able to make such claims about the similarities or differences in the Hebrew and Greek texts of Scripture, but the LXX had become widely accepted as an inspired translation long before Philo, and his euphoric comments reflect the elevated status of the translation among Jews in the first century C.E. Kahle also observes what scholars of the Greek Bible and the HB know well: there are numerous differences between the two texts.[9]

Similarly, Eusebius claims to report a tradition from Irenaeus regarding the origins and recognition of the inspired status of the LXX. He dates the translation at a slightly later time than does the *Letter of Aristeas,* but shares much the same story and is clearly dependent upon it:

> For before the Romans established their government, while the Macedonians still possessed Asia, Ptolemy, the son of Lagus, being very anxious to adorn the library, which he had founded in Alexandria, with all the best extant writings of all men, asked from the inhabitants of Jerusalem to have their Scriptures translated into Greek. They, for they were at that time still subject to the Macedonians, sent to Ptolemy seventy elders, the most experienced they had in the Scriptures and in both languages, and God thus wrought what he willed. But Ptolemy, wishing to make trial of them in his own way, and being afraid lest they should have made some agreement to conceal by their translation the truth in the Scriptures, separated them from one another and commanded them all to write the same translation. And this he did in the case of all the books. But when they came together to Ptolemy, and compared each his own translation, God was glorified and the Scriptures were recognized as truly divine, for they all rendered the same things in the same words and the same names, from beginning to end, so that even the heathen who were present knew that the Scriptures had been translated by the inspiration of God. (*Hist. eccl.* 5.8.11–14, LCL)

For canon inquiry, one of the most amazing facts about the LXX is the rapidity of its adoption within the Christian community as the Bible of the Christian church. This was true even in Palestine where the Hebrew Scriptures were also in circulation. Because it was in Greek, the language of the

[9] Kahle, *Cairo Geniza,* 215.

majority of the Greco-Roman world, it was an especially useful tool in the Christian evangelization of the Roman world.

This near-universal use of the LXX by the Christian community contributed to the Jewish reaction against it at the end of the first century C.E. and eventually their rejection of it altogether in the second century C.E., calling for the production of other Greek translations of their Scriptures. The Jewish rejection of the LXX could have stemmed from legitimate claims that some Christians based some of their criticisms of Judaism upon faulty LXX texts.[10] In the second century C.E., the LXX became identified as the Bible of the Christians, and another version was deemed necessary for the Jewish community. The responsibility for producing another Greek translation of the OT was given to Aquila, a Jewish proselyte from Pontus, who produced in 128 C.E. a literal translation that was slavishly loyal to the Hebrew text. However, his translation was generally not understandable to those unfamiliar with the Hebrew text, and it soon fell into disuse and neglect.[11] Two other Greek translations of the Hebrew Scriptures were produced in the second century (probably), one by Theodotion, of whom little is known, and the second by Symmachus, an Ebionite (or "semi-Christian").

Other Greek versions of the OT Scriptures emerged in the third century C.E., including one by Origen, who set out to amend the LXX in his Hexapla and/or Tetrapla.[12] Eusebius preserves some interesting background about the work of Origen:

> And so accurate was the examination that Origen brought to bear upon the divine books, that he even made a thorough study of the Hebrew tongue, and got into his own possession the original writings in the actual Hebrew characters, which were extant among the Jews. Thus, too, he traced the editions of the other translators of the sacred writings besides the Seventy; and besides the beaten track of translations, that of Aquila and Symmachus and Theodotion, he discovered certain others, which were used in turn, which, after lying hidden for a long time, he traced and brought to light, I know not from what recesses. With regard to these, on account of their obscurity (not knowing whose in the world they were) he merely indicated this: that the one he found at Nicopolis, near Actium, and the other in such another place. At any rate, in the Hexapla of the Psalms, after the four well-known editions, he placed beside them not only a fifth but also a sixth and a seventh translation; and in the case of one of these he has indicated again that it was found at Jeri-

---

[10] These texts were most likely tampered with by Christians.

[11] Wevers, "Septuagint," 275.

[12] The Hexapla is a six-column text of the OT produced by Origen in order to establish a reliable text of the Bible by eradicating errors through comparison of the current Greek translations (LXX, Aquila, Symmachus, and Theodotion) and the Hebrew texts available to him. Fernández Marcos, *Septuagint in Context,* 204–22, has a very useful discussion of the origins of the Hexapla and notes that it may be the same as the Tetrapla (an eight-column text).

> cho in a jar in the time of Antoninus the son of Severus. All these he brought together, dividing them into clauses and placing them one over against the other, together with the actual Hebrew text; and so he has left us the copies of the Hexapla, as it is called. He made a further separate arrangement of the edition of Aquila and Symmachus and Theodotion together with that of the Seventy, in the Tetrapla. (*Hist. eccl.* 6.16.1–4, LCL)

The value attributed to the LXX in the early church cannot be overestimated. It was the *Christian* Bible. There was a strong belief in the early church that the LXX was an inspired translation that was superior to the Hebrew. Indeed, when the Hebrew and the LXX differed, the latter was preferred because the LXX translators who changed the Hebrew text were inspired by God to do so, which the apostles recognized by citing the LXX. In the fifth century, Augustine likewise expresses the opinion that the Greek translation of the Scriptures is inspired and therefore may be trusted in the Christian community:

> But, if scribal error is not involved, it must be believed that, where the sense corresponds to the truth and proclaims the truth, they [i.e., the seventy translators], moved by the divine Spirit, wished to deviate [from the Hebrew original], not in the manner of interpreters [translators], but in the freedom of those prophesying. Consequently, the apostles, in *their* authority, when they appealed to the Scriptures, quite rightly utilized not only the Hebrew, but also their own—the witness of the Seventy. (*City of God* 15.14, Hengel, *Septuagint as Christian Scripture,* 17, emphasis original)

Fernández Marcos notes the irony of the early church's use of the LXX, and the concomitant support that this gives to the *Letter of Aristeas:* "A Jewish propaganda document which recommends the Greek translation of the Pentateuch has become the principal witness for the defending [of] the whole LXX, now adopted by Christianity as its official Bible."[13]

The importance of the LXX from a canonical perspective is not only that it was *the* Bible of the early Christian church and cited more than 90 percent of the time by the NT writers when quoting the OT, but that it also differs considerably from the Hebrew text in several important passages, the best known, of course, being Isa 7:14—a fact that was not missed in the early church. According to Irenaeus (ca. 170 C.E.), as reported by Eusebius, the differences with the Jews that arose over this matter were settled by appealing to the inspiration of the Septuagint:

> Hear also, word for word, what he [Irenaeus] writes about the interpretation of the inspired Scriptures according to the Septuagint. "So God became a man and the Lord himself saved us, giving us the sign of the virgin, but not as some say, who at the present time venture to translate the Scriptures, 'behold a young woman shall conceive and bear a son,' as Theodotion the Ephesian

[13] Fernández Marcos, *Septuagint in Context,* 49.

translated it and Aquila from Pontus, both of them Jewish proselytes, whom the Ebionites follow and aver that he was begotten by Joseph." (*Hist. eccl.* 5.8.10, LCL)

The MT of Isa 7:14 reads: "The Lord himself will give you a sign. Look, the young woman [*almah*] is with child and shall bear a son, and shall name him Immanuel." The LXX has: "Therefore the Lord himself shall give you a sign; behold, a virgin [*parthenos*] shall conceive in the womb, and shall bring forth a son, and thou shalt call his name Emmanuel."[14] The question, of course, is whether the Hebrew term *almah* ("young woman, girl, maiden") may mean "virgin" (the usual Hebrew word for virgin is *bethulah*). The translators of the LXX used the Greek term *parthenos* ("virgin"), and Matt 1:23 follows the LXX: "The virgin shall conceive and bear a son."[15] One can easily understand the Christian preference for a translation that advances belief in the virgin birth of Jesus—and also why the Jews authorized production of a different Greek translation of the Scriptures.[16]

It is no wonder that in earlier years there was a tendency to marginalize, and even ignore, the Greek text of the LXX in favor of the MT of the HB. In some conservative Christian seminaries, students preparing for Christian ministry hear of the LXX only as a secondary source that is of not much use to the Bible student since the inspiration of the OT was rooted in its original (Hebrew) text. The Greek translation, so the argument often goes, is a mere translation of the authentic originals.

More recently, however, following the discovery and examination of biblical texts found at Qumran, some scholars speak of the value of the Greek translation of the Bible and suggest that at times it may even be superior to the Hebrew text.[17] There is a growing preference today among textual scholars to rely on an eclectic text[18] that appeals to the LXX, Vulgate, Dead Sea Scrolls, and MT to recover the most reliable and earliest text of the HB.

---

[14] Brenton, *Septuagint Version of the Old Testament,* 689.

[15] Shires, *Finding the Old Testament,* 82–84, lists several other examples of the NT writers' preference for the LXX.

[16] For further discussion of this point, see Hengel, *Septuagint as Christian Scripture,* 25–42.

[17] Cook, "Septuagint Proverbs," 80, observes that in some instances the LXX was translated from a parent text that differed from the MT. Tov, "Status of the Masoretic Text," questions his former position of seeking an *Urtext* ("original text") that was believed to be roughly identifiable with the MT and instead, like many NT textual critics, prefers an eclectic system to determine a more reliable biblical text since, as he says, we are no longer able to call "a single source, extant or reconstructed, '*the* text of the Bible' " (251). See also idem, "Recensional Differences" and *Textual Criticism of the Hebrew Bible.*

[18] Eclecticism in textual criticism is the process of selecting from various sources—rather than relying on a single source—to determine the original reading of a given text. In this case, all of the ancient versions and manuscripts of the OT are used to try to arrive at the most reliable biblical text.

II. Essenes and Their Sacred Scriptures

Among the various renewal movements in Palestine in the time of Jesus, a group of Jews lived on the northwest shores of the Dead Sea in a place today called Khirbet Qumran.[19] These Jews are not identified by name in the NT, but they are almost certainly those identified by both Philo and Josephus as the Essenes. This group copied, transmitted, and produced literature that sheds considerable light on Jewish beliefs around the turn of the era. This literature, commonly known as the Dead Sea Scrolls, was discovered in eleven caves near the ruins of the Qumran community.[20] The literary activity of the Essenes tells us a great deal about the books that many Jews in the first century C.E. acknowledged as sacred and authoritative for their communities of faith. The parallels between the scrolls and the NT help us understand many difficult passages in the NT.[21] They also help us understand Judaism in the first century and the books that many Jews believed were normative for faith at that time.

The first caves were discovered near Khirbet Qumran in the winter of 1946–47, and the remaining scrolls were found in other caves throughout the early 1950s. The scrolls are most likely the literary products of the Essene religious sect and date from approximately 150 B.C.E. to 68 C.E. The scrolls contain thousands of small and large fragments and complete books from about nine hundred documents. Some of the documents have multiple copies, and some represent only a small portion of a larger writing. Many of the manuscripts at Qumran were likely wrapped in linen and placed in jars by the Jews prior to their impending Roman capture in 68 C.E. Alternatively, the documents may have been stored or hidden over a period of time much like worn out and unusable copies of the Scriptures were placed in a genizah.[22]

---

[19] For useful summaries of the Qumran inhabitants, see Magness, *Archaeology of Qumran,* 32–46; Vermes, *Dead Sea Scrolls,* 87–136; E. P. Sanders, "Dead Sea Sect and Other Jews"; and Patte, *Communities of the Last Days,* 53–84.

[20] Not all of the so-called Dead Sea Scrolls came from Qumran. The majority of them were found in the caves at Qumran, but several others were found in the general vicinity of Qumran and at Massada and Naḥal Ḥever. For a helpful summary of the scrolls, see Cross, *Ancient Library at Qumran,* 19–53; and Abegg, Flint, and Ulrich, *Dead Sea Scrolls Bible,* xiv–xv.

[21] For examples of Qumran texts that clarify the meaning of NT passages, see Evans, "Jesus and the Dead Sea Scrolls"; Fitzmyer, "Paul and the Dead Sea Scrolls"; and Aune, "Qumran and the Book of Revelation."

[22] *Genizah* ("to hide, store up") is an Aramaic loanword for a storeroom in a synagogue. Such places emerged from a need to retire old sacred manuscripts. The most famous genizah is the one discovered in an old synagogue in Fustat in Cairo, Egypt, and is commonly known as the Cairo Genizah, an amazing collection of ancient texts with thousands of manuscripts and fragments of manuscripts that have yielded significant resources for both textual and canonical research. Genizahs are quite valuable since they can tell us what books functioned as Scripture in various Jewish synagogues or communities. See an early discussion of genizahs in *b. Shabbat* 16:1.

A third explanation why the Essenes placed these documents in caves is that the community was on the verge of dying and so they hid their most precious and sacred documents to preserve them as long as they possibly could. The caves have been numbered 1 through 11, and the manuscripts are usually identified by cave number plus the number or name assigned to the manuscripts or fragments found in each cave.[23]

A. BACKGROUND OF THE ESSENE COMMUNITY

Although the Essenes are not mentioned by name in the NT, their presence was certainly known in Palestine in the time of Jesus. They were also known in Asia Minor between Colossae and Ephesus during Paul's and John's ministries and in Egypt. During the early life of Jesus, Philo of Alexandria summarized their virtues as follows: (1) they do not sacrifice animals; (2) they live in villages; (3) they work industriously at a variety of occupations that are neither military nor commercial positions; (4) they keep no slaves; (5) they study morals and religion, especially the allegorical interpretation of their Scriptures; (6) they pursue and practice virtue; (7) they refuse to swear oaths and reject ceremonial purity; (8) they hold all goods and clothing in common; (9) they care for the sick and elderly; (10) they admit only adults to their order; and (11) they reject marriage and have low opinions of women.[24] At the end of the first century C.E., Josephus produced a lengthy and generally positive description of the Essenes, observing that there were several orders of Essenes and offering descriptions of their daily activities and how they practiced their religious piety (*J.W.* 2.119–161). Philo and Josephus have considerable overlap in their descriptions of this religious sect, but Josephus adds more detail than does Philo:

> The doctrine of the Essenes is wont to leave everything in the hands of God. They regard the soul as immortal and believe that they ought to strive especially to draw near to righteousness. They send votive offerings to the temple, but perform their sacrifices employing a different ritual of purification. For this reason they are barred from those precincts of the temple that are frequented by all the people and perform their rites by themselves. Otherwise they are of the highest character, devoting themselves solely to agricultural labour. They deserve admiration in contrast to all others who claim their share of virtue because such qualities as theirs were never found before among any Greek or

---

[23] One of the common difficulties that beginning students have when investigating the now translated Dead Sea Scrolls is that they are not consistently identified by the scholars who examine and refer to them. Perhaps in the future, scholars will find a more consistent set of identification tags to facilitate easier access to these important texts.

[24] This summary of Essene characteristics comes from Colson, *Philo,* 9.514–15. For Philo's description of the Essenes, see his *That Every Good Person Is Free,* 75–87, and *Hypothetica* 11.

> barbarian people, nay, not even briefly, but have been among them in constant practice and never interrupted since they adopted them from of old. Moreover, they hold their possessions in common, and the wealthy man receives no more enjoyment from his property than the man who possesses nothing. The men who practise this way of life number more than four thousand [the same number mentioned by Philo]. They neither bring wives into the community nor do they own slaves, since they believe that the latter practice contributes to injustice and that the former opens the way to a source of dissension. Instead they live by themselves and perform menial tasks for one another. They elect by show of hands good men to receive their revenues and the produce of the earth and priests to prepare bread and other food. (*Ant.* 18.18–22, LCL)

The Dead Sea Scrolls exhibit similarities with the New Testament writings, the most important being the Apostle Paul's notion of works righteousness (Rom 4; Gal 3–4; 2 Cor 6:14–7:1) and 4QMMT (see chapter 4 §III.E). Other Essene parallels with Paul's terminology include "mystery," "flesh and spirit," "perfect," "truth," and "justification." Qumran parallels with the Gospel of John include "sons of light" and "the spirit of truth." It may also be possible that the heresy mentioned in Paul's Letter to the Colossians was an Essene-type theology, but that is not certain. These similarities do not suggest any dependence of Christians upon the Essenes, but rather reflect the shared characteristics of first-century Jewish sects.

B. SCRIPTURES AT QUMRAN

Although other Essene communities existed in Palestine, Egypt, and elsewhere, the primary Essene literature available to us today comes from the Qumran community. Some Essene writings were discovered in the Cairo Genizah in Egypt, but the large number of the documents discovered at or near Qumran have considerable significance for the Jewish and Christian biblical canons.[25]

The biblical manuscripts[26] found at Qumran are mostly in Hebrew and are fully one thousand years earlier than the Leningrad Codex (ca. 1008/9

---

[25] Recent works on the relevance of the Qumran literature for understanding Judaism in the time of Jesus and the biblical canon at that time include Abegg, Flint, and Ulrich, *Dead Sea Scrolls Bible;* Fitzmyer, *Dead Sea Scrolls and Christian Origins;* Flint and VanderKam, *Dead Sea Scrolls after Fifty Years;* García Martínez, *Dead Sea Scrolls Translated;* Schiffman, *Reclaiming the Dead Sea Scrolls;* Tov, see articles in select bibliography; Trebolle Barrera, *Jewish Bible and the Christian Bible;* Ulrich, *Dead Sea Scrolls;* and VanderKam, *Dead Sea Scrolls Today.*

[26] The terms *biblical* and *nonbiblical* are, of course, modern terms that are included here to clarify our discussion. To some extent, the Essenes valued everything found in the caves at Qumran. Whether it was valued in the same sense that sacred Scripture is understood today is not always easy to answer, but that the literature discovered there—biblical and nonbiblical alike—was not only copied but also stored in the caves without any distinguishing features regarding its canonicity

C.E.) and the Aleppo Codex (ca. 925 C.E.), which are the chief witnesses of the MT of the HB. Most of the scrolls are in Hebrew, but a hundred of them are in Aramaic, and several from Qumran Cave 7 and Naḥal Ḥever (south of Qumran) are in Greek. Some 40 percent of the Hebrew biblical manuscripts are of the Pentateuch, which suggests where the primary scriptural authority of the Essenes was placed. Of the rest, thirty-six manuscripts (or thirty-seven) are of the Psalms and thirty-three from the major prophets (Isaiah has either nineteen or twenty-one, Jeremiah and Ezekiel have six each).[27] If Daniel is figured into the major prophets, then eight more are added to this list.[28]

Some 650 nonbiblical scrolls or manuscripts were also discovered at Qumran and elsewhere in the Judean desert. The noncanonical writings have been conveniently classified as (1) rules and regulations, (2) poetic and wisdom texts, (3) rewritten Scriptures (e.g., *Genesis Apocryphon*), (4) commentaries (e.g., *Pesher on Habakkuk*), and (5) a miscellaneous section that includes a variety of other writings that do not fit the above categories.[29]

The full range of Qumran literature includes the following texts:[30]

1. Old Testament Texts

Although some argue that a small fragment of a manuscript discovered at Qumran is from the Gospel of Mark, this view is largely discredited, and scholars generally agree that no NT texts were found at Qumran.[31] All of the OT books, except perhaps Esther and Nehemiah,[32] have been found at

---

indicates the value that the community attached to it. While much of this literature was probably considered sacred Scripture, it is difficult to makes such claims about all of the Qumran literature, including some of the so-called biblical literature.

[27] It is not always easy to determine the precise number of manuscripts found at Qumran due to their fragmentation. Because of this, various numbers are set forth by scholars.

[28] These figures come from Abegg, "Hebrew of the Dead Sea Scrolls"; and Greenspoon, "Dead Sea Scrolls and the Greek Bible." For a more complete list of the Qumran writings, see García Martínez, *Dead Sea Scrolls Translated,* 466–519; Vermes, *Complete Dead Sea Scrolls in English,* 602–18; Reed et al., *Dead Sea Scrolls Catalogue;* and Tov and Pfann, *Companion Volume to the Dead Sea Scrolls.*

[29] Abegg, Flint, and Ulrich, *Dead Sea Scrolls Bible,* xv.

[30] This list of the main Qumran documents is based in part on Milik's *Ten Years of Discovery,* chapter 2, supplemented from later sources. For discussion of recently released documents, see García Martínez, *Dead Sea Scrolls Translated.*

[31] For a discussion of whether 7Q5 is a fragment of Mark 6:52–53, see Stanton, *Gospel Truth?* 20–32, who concludes that it is not.

[32] Several biblical scholars argue that Esther was not found at Qumran and was omitted because of calendar conflicts. While no part of the biblical book of Esther has been found to date at Qumran, several fragments of a loosely parallel work called proto-Esther were discovered and should cause some hesitation in concluding that the Qumran community did not know Esther: 4Q550, 4Q550a, 4Q550b, 4Q550c, 4Q550d, and perhaps 4Q550e (see García Martínez and Tigchelaar, *Dead Sea Scrolls Study Edition,* 1096–1103; and Wise, Abegg, and Cook, *Dead Sea Scrolls,*

Qumran, but this is not the same thing as saying that the canon of Qumran is equal to the biblical canon of later rabbinic Judaism or the Protestant OT canon. For example, the psalmic texts at Qumran exhibit significant variation from the later MT, which became the fixed text of the HB.[33]

2. Sectarian Literature

The following writings are generally recognized as peculiarly Essene literature.

1. *Damascus Document* (abbreviated CD), was found in Cairo in 1895. The Qumran manuscripts appear to be later versions of the *Community Rule.*
2. *Community Rule* or *Manual of Discipline* (1QS or *Serekh*) consists of rules of life for the community: (a) aims and ideals; (b) annual census instructions, including moral outlook (humility); (c) treatise on the spirits of good and evil; (d) regulations regarding obedience; (e) oath of allegiance; and (f) a hymn with reference to calendar details and secrecy of doctrine.
3. *Rule Annex* or *Messianic Rule* (1QSa) consists of supplementary provisions for instruction that describe the treatment of the aged and mentally ill, plus offering more council rules.

437–39). In these texts, Bagasraw (or Bagasro) seems to play the role of Haman. Mordecai and Esther are not mentioned, but the story, as best as can be discerned from the fragments, seems to resemble the story of the book of Esther (C. A. Evans, personal correspondence). It is difficult to know what to make of such discoveries, but one cannot leap from these texts to say that Esther was a part of a biblical canon at Qumran. The argument to include Nehemiah among the books found at Qumran stems from a later development in Judaism when Ezra and Nehemiah were often coupled together in one scroll; since, therefore, Ezra was found at Qumran, Nehemiah must have been at Qumran as well. This argument is anachronistically flawed and is not well supported. See arguments against the presence of Nehemiah at Qumran in Davies, *Scribes and Schools,* 154, 197; and VanderKam, "Ezra-Nehemiah."

[33] Most English translations of the OT are based on a single manuscript, the Leningrad Codex, which was copied in 1009/8 and is the oldest and most complete manuscript of the MT of the HB. An earlier manuscript, the Aleppo Codex, was produced in 925 C.E., but it is not complete and must be augmented by the Leningrad Codex. The Masoretic scribes produced many biblical manuscripts that exist now largely in fragmentary condition, but the Bible they produced is essentially the same as what is available today, though the books are not always in the same order. This rabbinic Bible is based on a meticulous amount of painstaking work to maintain textual consistency in the biblical text. The final stages of this process were carried out by a group of scribes known as the Masoretes, who added vowel points to the consonantal text to insure that it could be properly pronounced and carefully interpreted. The standardized form of the text that resulted is found in both the Leningrad and Aleppo texts. See Abegg, Flint, and Ulrich, *Dead Sea Scrolls Bible,* x–xi.

4. *Book of Blessings* (1QSb) is a handbook of benedictions for members and officials.

5. *War Scroll* (4QM or *Milhama*), a nineteen-column document, contains instructions on the preparations for the great eschatological battle when the universal dominion of God's holy race will be established (cf. Ezek 38–39 and Daniel).

6. *Hymn Scroll* (1QH or Hodayot) contains some thirty hymns, many of which are thanksgivings for salvation and knowledge. It is somewhat parallel to the canonical Psalms, but more individualistic.

7. *Halakic Letter* (4QMMT or *Miqsat Ma'aseh ha-Torah* ["some works of the law"]), is a collection of rules for behavior or law codes derived from a particular interpretation of the scriptural law codes (similar to the *Temple Scroll* and *Jubilees*). It has considerable relevance for the study of the canonical process in that it speaks of the kinds of literature that the community was especially concerned, namely, the law of Moses (see chapter 4 §III.E).

8. *Liturgical and astrological fragments.*

9. *Florilegia* (or testimony books) include three fragments from Cave 4 with assembled selections from OT passages.

10. *Genesis Apocryphon* (1QapGen or Lamech Scroll) is similar to *Jubilees* and contains a rewritten and "modernized" version of parts of Genesis in Aramaic.

11. *Temple Scroll* (11QTemple), a scroll of over thirty feet long, was highly influential in the Qumran community.

3. Biblical Commentaries

The commentaries found at Qumran consist of passages from the OT accompanied by *pesherim,* literalistic and eschatological interpretations of the scriptural books in the light of the life and history of the community at Qumran. These constituted for the residents of Qumran the true meaning of the OT.

4. Late Jewish Apocryphal and Pseudepigraphal Works

Several apocryphal and pseudepigraphal writings were found at Qumran, including a Hebrew version of Sirach, Tobit, an Aramaic version of Tobit, a Greek version of the Epistle of Jeremiah, *Jubilees,* an Aramaic version of *1 Enoch,* and the *Testaments of the Twelve Patriarchs*—all of which are of special interest because they indicate the theological outlook in Palestine in the time of early Christianity. Several of these works were also welcomed and cited as authoritative documents in early Christianity.

What is the significance of these finds? The absence of Esther and Nehemiah in the Qumran collection may not be as important as earlier thought, for only one small fragment of the larger book of Chronicles was found at Qumran.[34] What was discovered in and around Qumran cannot be affirmed to be a complete library of what was actually stored there, for the residents made no list of what they stored, and we do not know if one day another cave will be discovered with many more ancient manuscripts. Therefore, a certain amount of caution is necessary before making strong statements about the contents of the Qumran library. And because of this uncertainty, it is wise to soften conclusions about what was *not* found there.

Even though all but two biblical books were found at Qumran, this does *not* mean that the Qumran community had the same biblical canon as the Pharisees and the later rabbis in the second century C.E. who were responsible for fixing the number and contents of the biblical books in the current HB. Bruce incorrectly argues that "it is probable, indeed, that by the beginning of the Christian era the Essenes (including the Qumran community) were in substantial agreement with the Pharisees and Sadducees about the limits of Hebrew scripture."[35] Beckwith similarly argues that the presence of all of the OT canonical books at Qumran, save Esther (he does not mention Nehemiah's absence), points to the acceptance in that community essentially of the same biblical canon as the one found in Pharisaic Judaism and later identified and promoted in rabbinic Judaism.[36] However, the discovery of parallels with Pharisaic Judaism in *some* of the books found at Qumran does not support the conclusion that they utilized the same biblical canon. The Qumran texts include considerably more than the OT canonical books, and this suggests that their collection of sacred texts was considerably broader than the current OT biblical canon. In fact, more nonbiblical writings were discovered at Qumran than biblical ones.[37]

Beckwith concludes that the Qumran community accepted as Scripture only the canonical writings of the OT, though he concedes that the Essenes excluded Esther for reasons related to the Jewish calendar. Oddly, however, he claims that essentially all of the other books found at Qumran, whether books dealing with legal matters or prophetic texts, were simply commentary or interpretations of Scriptures—and even "revealed interpretation" of

---

[34] Cross, *From Epic to Canon,* 225. Cross adds, "an additional worm, and Chronicles, too, would have been missing."

[35] Bruce, *Canon of Scripture,* 40.

[36] Beckwith, *Old Testament Canon,* 291–94, 312–13, and especially 358–366.

[37] For example, *Jubilees* is found in 14 or 15 manuscripts, and *1 Enoch* in 12; by contrast, if the biblical books were considered more valuable at Qumran, why do Genesis and Exodus have only 15 manuscripts each, with similar counts for Deuteronomy (25), Isaiah (19), and Psalms (30)? See VanderKam, *Revelation to Canon,* 25–26; Davies, *Scribes and Schools,* 154–57.

the biblical books.[38] VanderKam challenges Beckwith's view that *Jubilees* and *1 Enoch* were simply commentary or interpretation and argues that they presented as *new* revelations. For example, *1 En.* 72:1 states that the contents of *1 En.* 72–82 (the so-called Astronomical Book or Book of Heavenly Luminaries) were revealed to the writer by the angel Uriel, and in *Jub.* 6:29–35 a special calendar is traced to "heavenly tablets":[39]

> And they set them upon the heavenly tablets. Each one of them in thirteen weeks from one to another of the remembrances, from the first to the second, and from the second to the third, and from the third to the fourth. And all of the days which will be commanded will be fifty-two weeks of days, and all of them are a complete year. Thus it is engraved and ordained on the heavenly tablets, and there is no transgressing in a single year, from year to year. (*Jub.* 6:29–31, *OTP* 2:68)

VanderKam appropriately asks of Beckwith which OT texts the author of *Jubilees* or *1 Enoch* is citing or alluding to in these passages.[40] While there are some allusions to the OT Scriptures in these books, the majority of their contents have no discernible reference to biblical books. This leads VanderKam to ask: "What is the writer of the Astronomical Book interpreting?"[41] Again, we must underscore that at Qumran nonbiblical texts were discovered right beside the biblical books with no discernible way to distinguish between them.

A recent publication, that in all other ways is an excellent piece of work, illustrates my point about misleading information about the Dead Sea Scrolls. Abegg, Flint, and Ulrich's *Dead Sea Scrolls Bible* contains a useful translation of a select number of writings found at Qumran, but it is not exhaustive of the Qumran literature found there, nor does it offer an adequate rationale for the literature that it selected—or that it omitted. The title of the book is misleading and simply hype since the volume in no way represents a "Bible" at Qumran.[42] The term *Bible* suggests both a selected and limited collection of books that were placed side by side to form the stabilized Scriptures of a religious community. The title of this volume suggests, however, that contrary to all of the evidence that the authors themselves supply—somehow a "Bible" was discovered at Qumran, namely, the books

---

[38] Beckwith, *Old Testament Canon,* 362; cf. 359–60. See also Davies, *Scribes and Schools,* 163–65.

[39] VanderKam, *Revelation to Canon,* 27–28.

[40] Ibid.

[41] Ibid., 27.

[42] When I questioned one of the authors of this volume about its title, he admitted to me that it was unfortunate and that it was the publisher's choice because it was believed that "Bible" in the title would make the volume more marketable! Knowing all three authors of the volume, their views on the biblical canon, and their excellent contributions to Dead Sea Scrolls scholarship, I can accept this explanation, but the title nevertheless still confuses readers.

identified in their volume and no others. That is not the case, however, for though Abegg, Flint, and Ulrich do include *Jubilees, 1 Enoch,* some noncanonical Psalms, Sirach, Epistle of Jeremiah, and Tobit, they omit without explanation *Temple Scroll, Rule of the Community, Damascus Document, Book of the Giants, 4 Enoch, Book of Noah, Books of the Patriarchs,* and many others. The authors are rightly more comfortable with the term *Scriptures* than with *Bible,* but the reader may overlook the brief comments in their introduction.[43] In any case, the title is misleading, for it ignores that little or nothing distinguishes the books that eventually became a part of the HB from the books that did not. No evidence of canonical activity at Qumran justifies the word *Bible* in their title.

Elsewhere, Ulrich clarifies his views on the Bible at Qumran, which clearly reflects what scholars have found there. I am in full agreement with his position on the status of the biblical canon during the time of the Qumran community's existence:

> I do not think that "The Bible" in our modern sense (whether Jewish, Protestant, or Catholic, or any other) existed as such in the Second Temple period, if by "Bible" we mean a complete, fixed, and closed collection of books of Scripture. There is sufficient and sufficiently broad reference to "the Scriptures" or "the Law and the Prophets" to ensure that certainly there were Sacred Scriptures at the end of the Second Temple period, but the point would have to be demonstrated that "The Bible" as such was an identifiable reality at the end of the Second Temple period.[44]

Further, Ulrich raises important questions that must be answered before any conclusions can be made about the fixing or stabilizing of the Bible in its modern canonical sense. While he focuses on the standardizing of the biblical text, his questions are also suitable for the standardized books as well:

1. What are the available data for determining the nature and characteristics of the scriptural texts in the first century B.C.E. and first century C.E.?

---

[43] Abegg, Flint, and Ulrich acknowledge that the term *Bible* is historically anachronistic to represent the works found at Qumran and that "there is little evidence that people were seriously asking the question yet about the extent or the limits of the collection—the crucial question for a 'Bible' or 'canon'—which books are *in* and which books are *outside* this most sacred collection. Thus, *The Dead Sea Scrolls Scriptures* may be a more historically accurate title for this volume. At any rate, it presents the remains of the books for which there is good evidence that Jews at that time viewed them as Sacred Scripture" (vii). I accept this explanation if they drop the definite article *the,* which also obscures the actual finds at Qumran, but it still does not address the question of what is omitted in their book. Entitling their work *Dead Sea Scrolls Scriptures* would be more accurate than the current title.

[44] Ulrich, "Qumran Biblical Scrolls," 69–70.

2. Even if we have the proper data, are we looking at them through the correct interpretive lenses?

3. Since "standard biblical text" normally refers to the MT, what was the MT? What would be an adequate description of it? Was there such a thing as "a/the standard text"? If so, was the MT the standard text?

4. Was there an identifiable group of leaders in the first century B.C.E. and the first century C.E. that knew of the variety of texts, was concerned about the diversity of textual forms, selected a single form, had the authority to declare a single form to be the standard text, and succeeded in having that standard text acknowledged by a majority of Jews? At the turn of the era, was there sufficient cohesion in Judaism and sufficiently acknowledged leadership to make it conceivable that a majority of Jews recognized and used a standard text?[45]

Yadin argues convincingly that the *Temple Scroll* was venerated as the Essene Torah and held to be equal in importance to the traditional Torah.[46] He observes that the so-called Tetragrammaton, the four letters *y-h-w-h* that form the unpronounced name of God (Yahweh) in the Hebrew Scriptures, is replaced in the *Temple Scroll* with the personal pronouns *I* or *me*. For example, Num 30:3 in the *Temple Scroll* states: "When a woman vows a vow to *me*," which replaces the traditional Torah: "When a woman vows a vow to *the LORD*."[47] Yadin's point is that the author presents the law as if it came directly from God himself rather than through Moses. Yadin also notes that the square Aramaic script is used in the *Temple Scroll* to write the name of God, just as it is in the other biblical books, which is a further indication that the people at Qumran viewed this scroll as sacred literature. Again, Yadin notes that this lengthy scroll was copied several times at Qumran, more times in fact than Isaiah. This leads him to the conclusion that "the Temple Scroll was, for the Essenes, a holy canonical book on par, for them, with the other books of the Bible."[48]

There also existed at Qumran a common practice of altering and changing the biblical text, which did not seem to violate their understanding of the sacredness of the texts that they were examining, copying, or editing. A command in Deut 4:2 forbids adding to or taking from the text, and this became a standard for how Jews (cf. *Let. Aris.* 311) and Christians (cf. Rev 22:18–19) dealt with their sacred literature to maintain its inviolability: "You must neither add anything to what I command you nor take away anything from it, but keep the commandments of the LORD your God with which I am charging you." The command is repeated in Deut 12:32: "You

[45] Ibid., 70.
[46] Yadin, "The Temple Scroll—longest"; and idem, *Temple Scroll*.
[47] Yadin, "Temple Scroll," 168.
[48] Ibid., 172.

must diligently observe everything that I command you; do not add to it or take anything from it." The Essene community, however, frequently changed or altered sacred texts.

Silver calls attention to how the scribes at Qumran felt free to alter the order and wording of the Psalms, even to the point of adding the refrain "Praised be the LORD and praised be his name forever and ever" after each verse of Ps 145, and they also changed the script, spelling, grammar, and content of the two scrolls of Isaiah found in Cave 1. At the time of the writing of the Qumran scrolls, there were no agreed formal methods for the presentation of sacred writings, and so the practice of changing the text extended to books that eventually were not accepted into the biblical canon and to the Torah, Prophets, and Writings. The Essenes at Qumran deleted or added sentences and words within the texts and made other changes as well. Matters such as word division, syntax, and spelling appear to have been of little concern to the scribes at Qumran.

Silver concludes that in pre-rabbinic times the Law, Prophets, and Psalms carried a large degree of authority in the Qumran community, but they had not yet attained the status given to Scripture by the later rabbinic schools, which copied every letter and word as accurately as possible.[49] This supports the idea that the concept of Scripture as inviolable was not uniformly understood or followed by at least the Essenes in the first century C.E. There is no evidence, however, that they handled their sacred texts differently than other Jewish sects and Christians in the first century C.E.

Tov, whose work supports Silver's conclusions, observes that the scribes at Qumran often incorporated their thoughts on the biblical text into the new version of the text that they produced: "In the newly created text scribes and readers inserted sundry changes, which are recognizable because the limitations of the ancient materials and the rigid form of the manuscript did not allow them to hide the intervention."[50] He further adds that notations and changes in the various texts had little to do with whether they were biblical or nonbiblical texts:

> Very little distinction, if any, was made between the writing of biblical and nonbiblical texts. For example, the scribe who wrote 1QS, 1QSa and 1QSb, as well as the biblical 4Qsam[c] and some of the corrections in 1QIsa[a] (e.g., at col. 33:7), employed the same system and notations throughout all five texts (including the use of four dots for the tetragrammaton). In addition, 1QS and 1QIsa[a] also share three unusual marginal signs, which were probably inserted by the same scribe.[51]

Tov goes on to say that in a few cases, however, some scribes did distinguish the biblical texts from the nonbiblical texts by writing on only one

---

[49] Silver, *Story of Scripture,* 136–41.
[50] Tov, "Scribal Practices" (1998), 424.
[51] Ibid., 425.

side of the parchment for biblical texts and on both sides for nonbiblical texts. Also, he notes that the biblical texts were almost exclusively written on parchment and only a few on papyrus, probably for personal use. Finally, Tov notes that a special arrangement was devised for writing poetical sections in only the biblical books—and this included Sirach.[52]

Neusner also claims that the Essene community had a much wider collection of sacred Scriptures than did other Jews in the land of Israel. He acknowledges that the Essenes' library at Qumran encompassed a diverse group of writings, surely received as authoritative and holy, that "other Jews did not know within their canon":

> We have no evidence that the relation to the canon of Scripture of the Manual of Discipline, the Hymns, the War Scroll, or the Damascus Covenant perplexed the teacher of righteousness and the other holy priests of the Essene community. To the contrary, these documents at Qumran appear side by side with the ones we now know as canonical Scripture.[53]

The above comments and observations argue for various notions of Scripture and canon in the Judaism sects of the first century C.E. that differed from those that existed in later rabbinic and Christian traditions. There is no direct evidence that Christianity borrowed any Essene view, but some Essene influence may be detected in Jesus' understanding of poverty and divorce.[54]

III. Samaritan Bible

Many of the Jews who survived the 721 B.C.E. Assyrian invasion of the northern tribes of Israel and the capture of its capital, Samaria, subsequently intermarried with the Assyrians and became known as "Samaritans." They were generally despised by the Jews, who tended to view them as despised "half-breeds" and rejected their participation in the life of the nation and its temple cultus. After the devastation of the nation that began in 596/595 B.C.E. and concluded with the subsequent destruction of the temple and deportation of the people in 587/586 B.C.E., the only thing that remained for the Jews who returned to Palestine after more than fifty years of exile was a story about their heritage, including their experience with Yahweh.[55] They had concluded that the destruction of their homeland and

---

[52] Ibid., 426. See also idem, "Scribal Practices" (1996).

[53] Neusner, *Talmud: A Close Encounter,* 174.

[54] Broshi argues this point in "What Jesus Learned from the Essenes." He makes a very good case and also acknowledges that this influence may have come directly from John the Baptist, who may have grown up in such a community.

[55] J. A. Sanders, *From Sacred Story,* 127–47, 175–90, explains that it was not the cultus or the monarchy or anything else other than a *story* of Israel's life and heri-

temple was due to their own failure to keep their covenant with Yahweh. The school of interpretation that began with Ezra added a new focus on the Law and its practical implications in the lives of the Jewish people. After renewing their covenant with God (Ezra 10:1–5; Neh 7:73–9:38), they rebuilt the temple under Zerubbabel by around 515 B.C.E. (Hag 1–2; Zech 1–8) and then rebuilt the walls around the city no later than approximately 445–443 B.C.E. During the rebuilding of the walls, the Jews met with opposition from Sanballat, the governor of Samaria (Neh 4:2).[56] This is the first time the Samaritans are mentioned by name.

Later, by the first century B.C.E., the Jews generally viewed the Samaritans with disdain (John 4:4–12, 19) and as natural enemies of the Jews. The point of Jesus' parable of the Good Samaritan (Luke 10:25–37)—that his disciples are to be good neighbors even to their natural enemies—is emphasized by long-standing Samaritan-Jewish antagonism. The Samaritans built their own temple on Mount Gerizim around 330 B.C.E., but John Hyrcanus, the Hasmonean king (ca. 128–125 B.C.E.), destroyed it, although not the Samaritans' devotion to Mount Gerizim. The period of Persian domination of Palestine (ca. 532–330 B.C.E.) was often turbulent for the Samaritans, but in comparison with the time of the Seleucid domination (198–142 B.C.E.) it was relatively peaceful. Evidence for the upheaval during this period may be recorded in Zech 9–14, which some scholars place between 330 B.C.E. and 150 B.C.E. since in 9:13 the rise of the Greeks had already occurred.

What is most important for our purposes is that the Samaritans adopted as their Scripture what became known as the Samaritan Pentateuch, which has many variations not found in the MT. There is no specific information that they ever adopted as Scripture any of the other books of the HB. It is likely that the limited biblical canon of the Samaritans was adopted in the fifth–fourth century B.C.E., when the Jews themselves acknowledged as Scripture only the Pentateuch. Immediately after the reforms of Ezra and Nehemiah, only the Law of Moses functioned as Scripture among the Jews, and the Samaritans received a version of the Pentateuch when they separated from the Jews. This is not to suggest that the Samaritans copied and modified the Jews' Scriptures. On the contrary, it is likely that they had an earlier version of the Law than what was eventually accepted by the Jews in their Scripture collection. Ulrich observes how the discoveries at Qumran show remarkable parallels between several texts in the Dead Sea Scrolls Pentateuch and the Samaritan Pentateuch against the MT, and this, he claims, argues for an earlier and separate text of the Pentateuch.[57]

---

tage, wrapped up in the call of Yahweh, that gave Israel its identity and the incentive to continue its existence in the face of overwhelming odds.

[56] The dating of these events and the conflict that ensued is summarized in Cross, *From Epic to Canon,* 188–89.

[57] Ulrich, "Qumran Biblical Scrolls," 75–76.

While these two forms of the Pentateuch have much that overlaps, several textual variations may indicate two literary editions of an earlier Pentateuch. Certainly, the Samaritans considered their Pentateuch to be the authoritative form of the text. For example, the MT of Deut 27:4–5 says that after the Jews cross the Jordan River, they are to build an altar to the Lord on Mount Ebal, but the Samaritan Pentateuch of the same passage, which may well be the earlier text, says that it is to be built on Mount Gerizim.[58] On the other hand, the Samaritan Pentateuch adds to the Decalogue a command to build an altar on Mount Gerizim. The Samaritans did not see themselves as a sect of Judaism, but rather as the community that interpreted the Mosaic tradition more accurately, unlike the other Jewish sects that wrongly promoted Jerusalem as the religious center of God. According to Purvis, the Samaritans may be understood as a "variety of Judaism," since both the Samaritans and the Jews saw themselves as the faithful "carriers of Israel's sacred traditions."[59]

The division between Jews and Samaritans so well known in the NT was discussed later among the rabbinic sages, who saw the Samaritans as ritually unclean (*b. Niddah* 4:1), and asserted that they made unacceptable offerings to God (*b. Bekhorot* 7:1), did not observe the holy days properly (*b. Rosh HaShanah* 22b), and could not be relied on to give a reliable witness (*b. Gittin* 1:5). A question about when the Samaritans would be acceptable to the Jews is answered in the Babylonian Talmud: "When they renounce Mount Gerizim, and confess Jerusalem and the resurrection of the Dead," which is the conclusion of the *Masseket Kutim*.[60]

Although other writings are found in the Samaritan collection of ancient literature, only the Pentateuch is canonized and read in all services of worship. Waltke says that one of the important features of the Samaritan Pentateuch for canonical criticism is that it bears witness to texts being adapted to meet the needs of the living community and "assisted the Samaritans in preserving themselves as a unified community for over two millennia."[61]

IV. Scriptures of the Sadducees

The Sadducees were a wealthy priestly group made up mostly of aristocratic families. They were responsible for public order and cooperated with the Romans in order to insure that the Jewish sacrifices would not be interrupted. They have a poor reputation in the NT, as well as in much other ancient Jewish literature, especially that of rabbinic Judaism. After

---

[58] R. Anderson, "Samaritans," 946.

[59] Purvis, "Samaritans and Judaism," 90–92. See also idem, *Samaritan Pentateuch*.

[60] Cited by R. Anderson, "Samaritan Literature," 1053.

[61] Waltke, "Samaritan Pentateuch," 938–39.

the destruction of Jerusalem and its temple in 66–70 C.E., the Sadducees did not survive long in the religious life of Israel, and not much from their past survives.

A. BACKGROUND

The origins of the Sadducees are somewhat obscure in Israel's traditions, in part because we have no extant literature from them (apart from the possible exception of Ecclesiastes). There are three possibilities for their origins. First, it is possible, but unlikely, that their name is derived from the OT Zadok (from the line of Aaron), whose sons were recognized as the legitimate priests of Israel (Ezek 40:46). Both Ezra (Ezra 7:2) and the high priests of the postexilic and pre-Maccabean period (1 Chr 24:3; Hag 1:1; Sir 51:12 addition) founded their reigns as priests after the order of Zadok. No evidence supports this view, and there is sufficient reason to reject it since the Sadducees themselves reportedly supported the non-Zadokite priesthood of Annus (Acts 4:1; 5:17). Only the Essenes claimed to be the spiritual sons of Zadok (1QS 5.2; *Damascus Document* 4.1–5). Second, it is possible that the Sadducees' name is derived from the Hebrew term *tsaddiq* ("righteous"), but many religious groups used this designation of themselves, and therefore this view is difficult to substantiate. Third, and most likely, the name *Sadducee* came from the term *tsadduqim,* which is a Hebraization of the Greek word *syndikoi* ("members of the council"). This is more in keeping with the role assigned to the Sadducees in the NT, but it is difficult to make a strong case for any of these options.

Religiously, the Sadducees were both conservative and traditional. They cooperated with the Romans for pragmatic reasons because by doing so they were allowed to keep the sacrificial system going in Israel; but they, like most other Jews, despised the Romans for occupying their homeland. What is known about their religious beliefs is rather brief, but it is generally understood that they recognized only the Law of Moses as authoritative Scripture. Since a belief in the resurrection from the dead is not clearly supported in the Torah, the Sadducees rejected this popular belief, as well as the messianic beliefs of many Jews in the first century C.E. The debate between the Pharisees and the Sadducees when Paul was arrested in the temple area (Acts 23:6–10) is understandable in this light.

B. SCRIPTURES OF THE SADDUCEES

The most important question for our purposes has to do with whether the collection of Scriptures acknowledged by the Sadducees was different from the recognized Scriptures of other first-century sects of Judaism. For some time it has been understood that the Sadducees appealed only to the Torah or Laws of Moses and rejected all other Jewish Scriptures. More recently, some scholars questioned whether there was any essential difference between the Sadducees and the Pharisees and even the Essenes in regard to their Scriptures. Bruce, for instance, argues that the notion of a limited Sadducee biblical canon comes from a common misunderstanding of Josephus's references to the Sadducees:

> The Sadducees hold that the soul perishes along with the body. They own no observance of any sort apart from the laws; in fact, they reckon it a virtue to dispute with the teachers of the path of wisdom that they pursue. There are but few men to whom this doctrine has been made known, but these are men of the highest standing. They accomplish practically nothing, however. For whenever they assume some office, though they submit unwillingly and perforce, yet submit they do to the formulas of the Pharisees, since otherwise the masses would not tolerate them. (Josephus, *Ant.* 18.16–17, LCL)

This passage is usually taken to mean that only the Law of Moses was sacred to the Sadducees and that they excluded all other authoritative writings accepted by the Pharisees. Bruce claims instead that this passage refers only to their rejection of the oral traditions of the Jews, not their rejection of the Prophets and Writings.[62]

Bruce cites another passage from Josephus that he claims makes clear that *Ant.* 18.16–17 refers to only the oral traditions of the Pharisees and not the Prophets and the Writings:

> For the present I wish merely to explain that the Pharisees had passed on to the people certain regulations handed down by former generations and not recorded in the Laws of Moses, for which reasons they are rejected by the Sadducaean group, who hold that only those regulations should be considered valid which were written down (in Scripture) and that those which had been handed down by former generations need not be observed. (*Ant.* 13.297, LCL)

Based on these texts alone, we cannot tell conclusively if the Sadducees rejected the Prophets, the Writings, *and* the oral traditions of the Jews, but this is a reasonable conclusion, especially in light their rejection of belief in the resurrection of the dead, which is well established in Josephus and the book of Acts. Further, it is difficult to argue that the Sadducees could affirm the scriptural status of passages like Isa 25:7; 26:19–21; Ezek 37:1–14; and Dan 12:2, which speak clearly about the resurrection of the dead, and then deny this doctrine.[63] More important, Jesus' argument against the Sadducees' denial of the resurrection in Matt 22:23–33 (see also Mark 12:18–27) is not based on the clearer texts in Isaiah, Ezekiel, and Daniel, but rather on an inference taken from the Law (Exod 3:6), which

---

[62] F. F. Bruce, *Canon of Scripture,* 40–41.

[63] Beckwith recognizes the force of this argument but rejects it, claiming that the Sadducees also rejected a belief in angels, which *is* taught in the Torah (e.g., Gen 19:1, 15; 28:12; 32:1), and that this line of reasoning would imply that the Sadducees also rejected the law of Moses. See Beckwith, *Old Testament Canon,* 87–88 and 30–39 (his discussion of the Sadducees).

the Sadducees clearly affirmed. Had the Sadducees accepted the Prophets, Jesus' case would have been stronger if he cited Isaiah, Ezekiel, and Daniel. Jesus' response also fits the obvious assertions of Acts 23:6–10 that the Sadducees denied the resurrection from the dead:

> When Paul noticed that some were Sadducees and others were Pharisees, he called out in the council, "Brothers, I am a Pharisee, a son of Pharisees. I am on trial concerning the hope of the resurrection of the dead." When he said this, a dissension began between the Pharisees and the Sadducees, and the assembly was divided. (The Sadducees say that there is no resurrection, or angel, or spirit; but the Pharisees acknowledge all three.) Then a great clamor arose, and certain scribes of the Pharisees' group stood up and contended, "We find nothing wrong with this man. What if a spirit or an angel has spoken to him?" When the dissension became violent, the tribune, fearing that they would tear Paul to pieces, ordered the soldiers to go down, take him by force, and bring him into the barracks.[64]

Origen and Jerome, who lived in the land of Israel and had access to Jewish thought in their day, also conclude that the Sadducees limited their scriptural collection to the Pentateuch. Origen, for instance, makes this statement: "But although the Samaritans and Sadducees, *who receive the books of Moses alone,* would say that there were contained in them predictions regarding Christ, yet certainly not in Jerusalem, which is not even mentioned in the times of Moses, was the prophecy uttered" (*Against Celsus* 1.49, *ANF,* emphasis added).[65] Both Origen and Jerome agree that the Sadducees accepted only the Law of Moses as Scripture, and it is possible, as Bruce suggests, that both depended on the Josephus texts for this information,[66] but this is neither obvious nor stated in either of these authors. Both writers had independent access to informed Jews in their own respective communities.

Saldarini acknowledges that scholars differ over the meaning of Josephus's *Ant.* 18 and concludes that "Josephus does not say explicitly that the Pharisees follow oral law, nor does he say that the Sadducees only follow the laws written in the Bible, contrary to the claims made in many descriptions of these groups. This passage says that their traditions differed, but not how."[67] He is correct, of course, but given what Josephus does say about

---

[64]The difference in the biblical canons of the Pharisees and the Sadducees is unclear in the NT, but it is obvious that there was a lack of belief in the resurrection by the Sadducees. The differences between the Sadducees and the Pharisees in the Mishnah (see *m. Yadayim* 4:6) are primarily over matters of purity, and this distinction is carried over to the Tosefta (*t. Parah* 3.7). For additional references to the Sadducees in the Mishnah, Tosefta, and Talmuds, see Porton, "Sadducees," 892–93.

[65]See also Jerome's *Commentary on Matthew* 22.31–32 for the same understanding of the Sadducees.

[66]F. F. Bruce, *Canon of Scripture,* 40–41 and n. 41.

[67]Saldarini, *Pharisees, Scribes, and Sadducees,* 113.

the Sadducees' rejection of notions of life after death, including the perishing of the soul and the body, and given what we read about them in the NT and the early church fathers, this leads us to conclude that their Scriptures were different from those adopted by the Pharisees or the Essenes.

V. Jewish Apocryphal and Pseudepigraphal Writings: Literature That Did Not Make the Cut

At some point between the first century B.C.E. and the fourth century C.E., several religious writings were excluded first from the Jewish sacred collection and later from the Christian sacred collection because their usefulness, adaptability to the communities, and even suitability for worship and instruction were no longer recognized. The rejected literature is often called apocryphal and pseudepigraphal writings, and it was variously spurned or welcomed by various Jewish and Christian communities.

The term *Apocrypha* (Gk. *apokrypha,* "hidden") refers to a collection of Jewish writings dating from roughly 300 B.C.E. to 70 C.E. that are incorporated into the Roman Catholic and Orthodox Old Testaments. These writings are generally referred to in the Roman Catholic community as "deuterocanonical" and include fifteen writings or portions of writings: Tobit, Judith, Additions to the Book of Esther, Wisdom of Solomon, Sirach, Baruch, Epistle of Jeremiah, Prayer of Azariah and Song of the Three Jews, Susanna, Bel and the Dragon, 1–2 Maccabees, 1 Esdras, the Prayer of Manasseh, and 2 Esdras. Sometimes these books are scattered throughout the OT, and sometimes they are grouped together, but the order is not always consistent. All of these books are present in the LXX version of the OT. The term *Apocrypha* is also applied to many Christian writings, known collectively as "New Testament Apocrypha," that is, Christian books that were rejected by the ancient church.

Sirach was one of the more popular writings discussed in the rabbinic literature. Sarna indicates that the need of the rabbis to emphasize that this book did not "defile the hands," that is, it was not canonical, shows that the Ketubim was still fluid in the second century and that Sirach had already acquired a "measure of sanctity in the popular conscience." He further notes that even after its ban by the rabbis (*t. Yadayim* 2:13), some of the Amoraim continued to quote it.[68]

From the beginning, the word *Apocrypha* referred to writings that were not to be read in public worship, but rather to be used in private, generally by the more mature believers. Oepke concludes that the Greek term

---

[68] Sarna, "Canon, Text, and Editions," 826. See, for example, *y. Sanhedrin* 28a and *m. Sanhedrin* 10:1. He adds that a third-generation *amora* cited Sirach and placed it in the Writings (*b. Bava Qamma* 92b).

apokryphos is essentially a translation of the Hebrew verb *gnz* (participial form *genuzim*), though he acknowledges that in time the term took on various meanings, including a reference to rejected books of the biblical canon.[69] In the *Avot of Rabbi Nathan* 1:3, Proverbs, the Song of Songs, and Ecclesiastes are "hidden" (*genuzim*) because of the fictitious and symbolic language in them. The preservation of the apocryphal books was not the work of the rabbinic sages, but rather of the church fathers, and it was done in some cases with considerable modifications to the text.[70]

The term *Pseudepigrapha* (Greek *pseudo* ["false"] plus *epigraphos* ["superscription"] yields "false superscription"), on the other hand, refers to an open and undetermined number of books that are only a very loose collection at best. These noncanonical writings are generally pseudonymous Jewish and Christian documents dating from 300 B.C.E. to around 200 C.E. (perhaps as late as 325 C.E.). They are religious documents written in the name of a well-known biblical personality, for example, Enoch, Abraham, Moses, the sons of Jacob, or others, hence "Pseudepigrapha" and "pseudepigraphal." At times, there is very little distinction between the apocryphal and pseudepigraphal writings in terms of pseudonymous authorship.

The pseudepigraphal literature initially enjoyed a fair amount of respect and popularity in Judaism and early Christianity. Some of this literature was preserved in the Cairo Geniza and some by the Essenes at Qumran. Much of this literature was preserved in Christian translations in Ethiopic, Syriac, Armenian, Slavonic, and Greek.[71]

Both terms, Apocrypha and Pseudepigrapha, refer to writings that did not make it into the Bible. Many issues that are important in our understanding of the intertestamental period (i.e., Second Temple Judaism), the NT writings, and the early church are discussed or have frequent parallels in this literature. By the fourth century C.E., several pieces of literature that had been initially welcomed in various churches were rejected as spurious. There was widespread neglect of it for centuries, but in modern times there has been a resurgence of interest in these writings because they help us interpret difficult texts of the NT and illuminate the context of early Christianity. They also add greatly to our understanding of the notions of Scripture and canon in antiquity.[72]

It is difficult to know precisely why the Jewish Pseudepigrapha and some of the Apocrypha fell into disrepute in the Christian communities[73]

---

[69] Oepke, "κρύπτω," *TDNT* 3:997–1000.

[70] Ibid., 995.

[71] See discussion in Vermes, *Dead Sea Scrolls,* 209–11; and G. Anderson, "Canonical and Non-canonical," 155–59.

[72] See Suter, "Apocrypha, Old Testament"; Metzger, *Introduction to the Apocrypha;* and Kee, *Cambridge Annotated Study Apocrypha.*

[73] Adler, "Pseudepigrapha in the Early Church," has an excellent discussion of the mixed reception of this literature in early Christianity.

and why these writings were rejected altogether by rabbinic Judaism in the third century C.E. and later. The textual tradition in the Christian communities was far more fluid in the second through fifth centuries. After that, the church used hermeneutics—instead of a fluid textual tradition—to adapt its sacred Scriptures to its ever-changing circumstances. This fluidity in the canonical tradition was also present in rabbinic Judaism in roughly the same period. Some Amoraim were discussing the authority of the Wisdom of Solomon and Sirach well into the fourth and fifth centuries C.E. Since reading a text in worship and teaching it in a religious community implies recognition of its sacredness and authority by a believing community, forbidding a congregation to read a document in public worship conversely suggests that it was not yet or no longer viewed as Scripture. The exception to this may be *4 Ezra* 14:43–47, where readers are permitted to read twenty-four books in public, but seventy other books are to be read only by the spiritually wise. A few books that were eventually received as a part of the HB were earlier excluded by the rabbis from public reading: Song of Songs (*m. Yadayim* 3.5; *b. Megillah* 7a), Ecclesiastes (*m. Yadayim* 3.5; *b. Shabbat* 100a; see also Jerome on Eccl 12:14), Ruth (*b. Megillah* 7a), Esther (*b. Sanhedrin* 100a; *b. Megillah* 7a), Proverbs (*b. Shabbat* 30b), and Ezekiel (*b. Shabbat* 13b; *b. Hagigah* 13a; *b. Menahot* 45a).

Charlesworth cautions that not all of the pseudepigraphal literature is cut from the same cloth, in that it does not originate from the same sources or have the same motives (i.e., deception). Charlesworth identifies five loosely defined categories of pseudepigraphal writings:[74]

1. Apocalyptic literature and related works
   - *1 (Ethiopic Apocalypse of) Enoch* (Jewish, ca. 200 B.C.E.–50 C.E.)
   - *2 (Slavonic Apocalypse of) Enoch* (Jewish, ca. 75–100 C.E.)
   - *3 (Hebrew Apocalypse of) Enoch* (Jewish, present form ca. fifth–sixth century C.E.)
   - *Sibylline Oracles* (Jewish and Christian, second century B.C.E.–seventh century C.E.)
   - *Treatise of Shem* (ca. end of first century B.C.E.)
   - *Apocryphon of Ezekiel* (mostly lost, original form ca. late first century B.C.E.)
   - *Apocalypse of Zephaniah* (mostly lost, original form ca. late first century B.C.E.)
   - *4 Ezra* (Jewish, after 70 C.E., with final Christian additions later)
   - *Greek Apocalypse of Ezra* (present form is Christian, ca. ninth century C.E., with Jewish and Christian sources)
   - *Vision of Ezra* (Christian, fourth–seventh century C.E.)
   - *Questions of Ezra* (Christian, date imprecise)

[74] Charlesworth, "Pseudepigrapha," 836–40.

Revelation of Ezra (Christian, sometime before ninth century C.E.)
Apocalypse of Sedrach (present form is Christian, ca. fifth century C.E., with earlier sources)
2 (Syriac Apocalypse of) Baruch (Jewish, ca. 100 C.E.)
3 (Greek Apocalypse of) Baruch (Christian, ca. first–second century C.E., with Jewish sources)
Apocalypse of Abraham (primarily Jewish, ca. 70–150 C.E.)
Apocalypse of Adam (gnostic, ca. first century C.E., with Jewish sources)
Apocalypse of Elijah (Jewish and Christian, ca. 150–275 C.E.)
Apocalypse of Daniel (present form ca. ninth century C.E., with Jewish sources from ca. fourth century C.E.)

2. Testaments
Testaments of the Twelve Patriarchs (present form is Christian, ca. 150–200 C.E., but Levi, Judah, and Naphtali are Jewish, before 70 C.E. and probably second–first century B.C.E.)
Testament of Job (Jewish, ca. late first century B.C.E.)
Testaments of the Three Patriarchs (Jewish versions of Abraham, Isaac, and Jacob, ca. 100 C.E., linked with Christian versions of Isaac and Jacob)
Testament of Moses (Jewish, ca. early first century C.E.)
Testament of Solomon (Jewish, present form ca. third century C.E., but earliest form ca. 100 C.E.)
Testament of Adam (present form is Christian, ca. late third century C.E., with Jewish sources from ca. 150–200 C.E.)

3. Expansions of the OT and other legends
Letter of Aristeas (Jewish, ca. 200–150 B.C.E.)
Jubilees (Jewish, ca. 130–100 C.E.)
Martyrdom and Ascension of Isaiah (first section is Jewish from ca. 100 B.C.E.; second section is Christian from ca. second century C.E.; and third section, the *Testament of Hezekiah,* is Christian from ca. 90–100 C.E.)
Joseph and Asenath (Jewish, ca. 100 C.E.)
Life of Adam and Eve (Jewish, ca. early to middle first century C.E.)
Pseudo-Philo (Jewish, ca. 66–135 C.E.)
Lives of the Prophets (Jewish, ca. early first century C.E., with later Christian additions)
Ladder of Jacob (Jewish, late first century C.E.; one chapter is Christian)
4 Baruch (Jewish original edited by a Christian, ca. 100–110 C.E.)
Jannes and Jambres (present form is Christian, ca. first century B.C.E., with Jewish sources)
History of the Rechabites (present form is Christian, ca. sixth century C.E., with some pre-100 C.E. Jewish sources)

Eldad and Modad (now lost, before first century C.E.; quoted in *Shepherd of Hermas,* ca. 140 C.E.)
History of Joseph (Jewish, difficult to date)

4. Wisdom and philosophical literature
   Ahiqar (Jewish, late seventh or six century B.C.E.; quoted in Tobit)
   3 Maccabees (Jewish, ca. first century B.C.E.)
   4 Maccabees (Jewish, ca. before 70 C.E.)
   Pseudo-Phocylides (Jewish maxims attributed to sixth-century B.C.E. Ionic poet, ca. 50 B.C.E.–100 C.E.)
   Sentences of the Syriac Menander (Jewish, ca. third century C.E.)

5. Prayers, psalms, and odes
   More Psalms of David (Jewish, ca. third century B.C.E.–100 C.E.)
   Prayer of Manasseh (Jewish, ca. early first century C.E.; sometimes listed in Apocrypha)
   Psalms of Solomon (Jewish, ca. 55–50 B.C.E.)
   Hellenistic Synagogal Prayers (Jewish, ca. second–third century C.E.)
   Prayer of Joseph (Jewish, ca. 70–135 C.E.)
   Prayer of Jacob (Jewish, mostly lost, ca. fourth century C.E.)
   Odes of Solomon (Christian, ca. 100 C.E., influenced by Judaism and Qumran)

Some of this literature influenced early Christianity and in some cases was also acknowledged as Scripture. Whether one acknowledges this literature as sacred Scripture, it is important that the church have some understanding of it. Besides witnessing frequently to the authority of the OT books, their use indicates the early church's interest in the major OT figures (e.g., Adam, Enoch, Moses, and Elijah) and also the continuity of faith between the Testaments. De Jonge is certainly correct when he claims that "because Christians were convinced of the continuity in God's revelation through the great figures of the 'Old Testament' and through Jesus Christ and his apostles, the distinction between 'Jewish' and 'Christian' was for them only of relative importance."[75]

VI. Decanonization: Subtracting Sacred Books

Before concluding our discussion, the reader should be aware that many books involved in the selection process were rejected either formally or more commonly by gradual lack of use in the Jewish communities of faith. Not everything that was written in the early history of the Jewish nation, even those acknowledged as sacred writing, survived in the Scripture

---

[75] De Jonge, "Old Testament in the Pseudepigrapha," 478.

collections of the Jews or Christians. Besides the growing collection of books that reflected the faith and hope of the Jews and Christians, an active "decanonization"[76] process was also going on. For example, many books mentioned in the OT no longer exist and evidently played little or no role in the final canonization process. Those books are not mentioned in either the NT or contemporary Jewish writings (Philo, Dead Sea Scrolls, and Josephus), and we have no idea about their contents other than what we can ascertain from their titles. Listed in a handful of OT passages that reflect their existence in an earlier stage in the history of the Jewish people, these writings evidently played a significant role among the Jewish people at one time, but for whatever reasons(s) they did not continue to do so.

The following list of written materials,[77] some of which may have functioned authoritatively in the Jewish community at one time, are referred to in the OT at a fairly early stage in the development of the notion of Scripture and canon. Unfortunately, they are now lost and essentially unknown to modern scholarship. It is difficult to tell how much the ancient community of Jewish believers accepted them as scriptural writings, but occasionally, they appear to have been acknowledged as sacred writings:

1. In the Torah
   Book of the Wars of the LORD (Num 21:14)

2. In the Former Prophets (Joshua, Judges, Samuel, Kings)
   Book of Jashar (Josh 10:12–13; 2 Sam 1:18–27; 1 Kgs 8:12–13 in LXX)
   Book of the Annals of the Kings of Judah (1 Kgs 14:29; 15:7, 23; 22:45; 2 Kgs 8:23; 12:19; 14:18; 15:6, 36; 16:19; 20:20; 21:17, 25; 23:28; 24:5)
   Book of the Annals of the Kings of Israel (1 Kgs 14:19; 15:31; 16:5, 14, 20, 27; 22:39; 2 Kgs 1:18; 10:34; 13:8, 12; 14:15, 28; 15:11, 15, 21, 26, 31)
   Book of the Acts of Solomon (1 Kgs 11:41)

3. In Chronicles, Ezra, and Nehemiah
   Book of the Kings of Israel (1 Chr 9:1; 2 Chr 20:34)
   Book of the Kings of Judah and Israel (2 Chr 16:11)
   Book of the Kings of Israel and Judah (2 Chr 27:7)
   Annals of the Kings of Israel (2 Chr 33:18)
   Records of the seer Samuel (1 Chr 29:29)
   Records of the seer Gad (1 Chr 29:29)
   Records of the seer Nathan (1 Chr 29:29)
   History of the prophet Nathan (2 Chr 9:29)

---

[76] I acknowledge the awkwardness of using the term *decanonization* in an anachronistic fashion. Here it refers to books that once had a significant impact on the religious life of the Jews, but later lost their influence and relevance.

[77] This list is adapted and expanded from Christensen, "Lost Books of the Bible."

Prophecy of Ahijah the Shilonite (2 Chr 9:29)
Visions of the seer Iddo (2 Chr 9:29)
Records of the prophet Shemaiah and of the seer Iddo (2 Chr 12:15)
Annals of Jehu son of Hanani ("which are recorded in the Book of the Kings of Israel"; 2 Chr 20:34)
Records of the seers (2 Chr 33:19)
Story of the prophet Iddo (2 Chr 13:22)
Commentary on the Book of the Kings (2 Chr 24:27)
A book written by the prophet Isaiah son of Amoz containing the history of Uzziah (2 Chr 26:22)
A vision of the prophet Isaiah son of Amoz in the Book of the Kings of Judah and Israel (2 Chr 32:32; cf. Isa 1:1)
Annals of King David (1 Chr 27:24)
Annals of your ancestors (Ezra 4:15)
Book of the Annals (Neh 12:23)

The frequent references to writings that did not survive the canonization processes in antiquity suggest their importance in the nation of Israel. Some of these lost books were important enough to require written commentary, as seen in the reference to "the Commentary on the Book of the Kings" (2 Chr 24:27). That a commentary was written on a now-lost book suggests the sacredness, or at least the high significance and influence, of this document, since commentaries were made only on such documents. The "Laments" mentioned in 2 Chr 35:25 is not a reference to the biblical book of Lamentations, but rather to a book produced by or for Josiah. Undoubtedly other ancient texts have been lost, and it is impossible to determine how much authority the Jewish community attributed to them. Since at one time the "book of the law" (Deuteronomy) was lost (2 Kgs 22–23), it is also likely that other sacred books not mentioned in the Bible were also lost. When they no longer functioned authoritatively in a religious community, their decanonization was set in motion.

What do we make of books that once functioned in the religious community of Israel but no longer do? Not much is said about them in most canonical studies, and yet their origin and significance is a legitimate question that should not be ignored. This matter refocuses on the question of decanonization. When writings no longer served the life and worship needs of the community of faith, they were neglected and eventually no longer mentioned or cited in communities of faith. Although scholars would love to have such books to help their historical understanding of the growth and development of the Jewish religion, the historic religious communities no longer needed these books, or they no longer reflected adequately the religious needs of the community, and so they were lost. Speaking about these lost books, Sarna offers several explanations for the disproportionate number of literary productions in the ancient world and the few that remain. He explains the primary factor involved in literary canonization:

> The absence of mass literacy, the labor of hand copying, and the perishability of writing materials in an inhospitable climate all combined to limit circulation, restrict availability, and reduce the chances of a work becoming standard. In addition, the land of Israel was more frequently plundered and more thoroughly devastated than any other in the ancient Near East. . . . The change in script that occurred in the course of Persian hegemony doubtless drove out of circulation many books, while the mere existence of canonized corpora almost inevitably consigned excluded compositions to oblivion.[78]

This, of course, suggests textual fluidity among the Jewish scribes and later among the rabbis. The many duplicates in the HB also suggest textual fluidity prior to its stabilization.

Duplicates in the Hebrew Bible include the following:

2 Sam 22 = Ps 18
2 Kgs 18:13–20:19 = Isa 36–39
2 Kgs 24:18–25:30 = Jer 52
Isa 2:2–4 = Mic 4:1–3
Ps 14 = Ps 53
Ps 40:13–17 = Ps 70
Ps 57:7–11 = Ps 108:1–5
Ps 60:6–12 = Ps 108:7–13
Ps 96:1–13a = 1 Chr 16:23–33
Ps 105:1–15 = 1 Chr 16:8-22
Ps 106:1, 47–48 = 1 Chr 16:34–36[79]

According to Sarna, the very notion of canonicity carries with it an expectation of reverence for the text and care in handling the text, but the above examples suggest to him that canonicity was not yet in view in Jewish thought when these writings began circulating in Israel.

The NT also mentions books that we no longer have and somehow were not preserved in the churches: for example, a letter that Paul wrote to the Laodiceans (Col 4:16), or the "first" letter that Paul wrote to the Corinthians, that is, the one that he wrote prior to writing what is now called 1 Corinthians (see 1 Cor 5:9). In addition, Luke refers to other books on the life of Jesus (Luke 1:1–4) prior to his gospel, and he says that "many" made such attempts, which might have included Mark, Matthew, and perhaps a document now called Q. Again, scholars would greatly appreciate having access to this lost written material, and perhaps it will one day show up in an archaeological find or ancient library. In the mean time, we know that such writings were once useful in a religious community and enabled it to establish its identity and practice its religious activities.

---

[78] Sarna, "Canon, Text, and Editions," 817.

[79] Besides these, there are many parallels between Samuel/Kings and Chronicles, even if there is some textual variance; see Sarna, "Canon, Text, and Editions," 832.

C H A P T E R   S I X

Stabilization of the Hebrew Bible

BY THE END OF THE FIRST CENTURY C.E., TWO SEPARATE TRADITIONS SPOKE of a limited collection of sacred writings. The number of books in each collection is close enough (twenty-two and twenty-four), and both are tied to the number of letters in the Hebrew and the Greek alphabets. It appears that for both traditions the number of books is settled, even though the sources do not identify which books are in the collections. In addition to these two ancient traditions, another view on the fixing of the Hebrew biblical canon is proposed by David Noel Freedman, who analyzes the symmetry in the HB for its relevance to the closing of the canon.

The esteem that the Greeks had for Homer's *Iliad* and *Odyssey* can be seen in all of the gods mentioned in these works becoming part of the Greek pantheon. Both works are divided into twenty-four chapters or books, and each chapter is identified by a successive letter of the twenty-four-letter Greek alphabet. The use of the Greek alphabet in antiquity signified completeness and divine origin or inspiration. A Christian example of this notion is the reference to God and Jesus as "alpha and omega" (Rev 1:8; 21:6; 22:13). A Jewish example of using the alphabet in sacred literature is the division of certain psalms into twenty-two sections, each beginning with a different letter of the Hebrew alphabet (Pss 25, 34, 119). Using the alphabet in this way demonstrated both the completion and the divine origin of the sacred writings.

I. The Twenty-two-Book Canon

Not surprisingly, Jews used the twenty-two letters of the Hebrew alphabet to enumerate the books of their OT canon, although various combinations of books were used at various times to achieve this number. A few Christians acknowledged twenty-two books in the Hebrew Bible,[1] but the primary proponents of this number were Josephus and *Jubilees.*

A. JOSEPHUS

Josephus is best known as a Jewish historian and advocate of Judaism at the end of the first century C.E. He was born Joseph ben Matthias in 37 C.E., was well educated in Jewish law and Greek literature, and was knowledgeable about the three major sects of Judaism in the first century (Sadducees, Pharisees, and Essenes), and Samaritan and Jewish history. He became a priest at age twenty-nine, but also identified himself with the Pharisees. Soon thereafter he became a general in the Jewish army in the Galilee region during the 66–70 C.E. war against Rome. After surrendering to the Romans, Josephus prophesied that Vespasian, the Roman general, would one day become the Roman emperor. At first Josephus was disbelieved, but when his prophecy came true, both Vespasian and his son Titus, who also became emperor, treated Josephus with respect and gave him many privileges. Where Josephus got this prophecy is not known, but stories circulating in the Greco-Roman world in the first century stated that someone from Judea would rule the world:

> There had spread over all the Orient an old and established belief, that it was fated at that time for men coming from Judaea to rule the world. This prediction, referring to the emperor of Rome, as afterwards appeared from the event, the people of Judaea took to themselves. (Suetonius, *Lives of the Caesars: Vespasian* 4.5, LCL)

> Few interpreted these omens as fearful; the majority firmly believed that their ancient priestly writings contained the prophecy that this was the very time when the East should grow strong and that men starting from Judaea should possess the world. This mysterious prophecy had in reality pointed to Vespasian and Titus, but the common people, as is the way of human ambition, interpreted these great destinies in their own favour, and could not be turned to the truth even by adversity. (Tacitus, *Histories* 5.13, LCL)

Whether Josephus knew these stories and simply shared them with Vespasian is not known, but when the prophecy came true in 69 C.E., Josephus was favored by Vespasian and Titus and eventually taken to Rome.

More important for our purposes, when the city of Jerusalem lay in ruins in 70 C.E., Josephus reports that Titus told him that he could have anything he wanted from the city. Josephus asked to have some of his family

---

[1] For example, Hilary of Poitiers (died 367 C.E.) mentions the twenty-two books of the Old Testament based on the Hebrew alphabet (*Instructio Psalmorum* 15), but then adds Judith and Tobit because the Greek alphabet has twenty-four letters! See Hengel, *Septuagint as Christian Scripture,* 62 n. 13.

and friends freed from captivity and also for some of the sacred books stored in the temple. Being a priest, Josephus was "not ignorant of the prophecies in the sacred books" (*J.W.* 3.352, LCL), which may have prompted him to take some from the temple in Jerusalem to Rome, where he began his career as a writer of Jewish history. Josephus tells the story of his interest in taking these sacred volumes:

> And after the city of Jerusalem was being held by force, he [Titus] tried to persuade me to take anything I might like from the ruin of my native place. He insisted that he gave his consent. Having nothing of greater value in the fall of my native place that I might take and cherish as a consolation for my circumstances, I put the request to Titus for the freedom of persons, and for some sacred volumes . . . I received as an expression of Titus' favor. A little later, in fact, when I requested [freedom for] my brother along with fifty friends, I was not disappointed. (*Life,* 418–19, Mason, *Life of Josephus,* 165–66)

After his departure to Rome, Josephus took the name Flavius, the family name of Domitian, the Roman emperor. Toward the end of the first century, after completing his *Jewish War* and *Jewish Antiquities,* he wrote *Against Apion* as an apology for the Jewish religion and against anti-Semitism. In this work, Josephus became the earliest person to describe a specific number of sacred books in the Hebrew Scriptures. Because of his unique role at the time of the destruction of Jerusalem and because of his access to sacred literature kept in Jerusalem, Josephus is an important figure in our understanding of the Jewish Scripture collection at the end of the first century.

In *Against Apion,* written shortly before his death around 100 C.E., Josephus defends the Jewish people against attacks by Apion from Egypt, who represented the Greek citizens of Alexandria against the Jews in a case argued before Caligula, the Roman Emperor, in Rome. Apion made many unsubstantiated charges against the Jews, including their hiding a Greek in the temple for later sacrifice by the Jews. During his defense of the Jews, Josephus claims that the Jews' sacred Scriptures contained twenty-two books,[2] which he identifies by classification or grouping, not by name. He further claims that these books were "justly accredited" by the Jews and that the matter had been settled for all Jews for a long time:[3]

> It therefore naturally, or rather necessarily, follows (seeing that with us it is not open to everybody to write the records, and that there is no discrepancy in what is written; seeing that, on the contrary, the prophets alone had this privilege, obtaining their knowledge of the most remote and ancient history

---

[2]Sarna ("Canon, Text, and Editions," 828) suggests that Josephus may not have included Song of Songs and Ecclesiastes in his collection, which is why he has only twenty-two books rather than the more usual twenty-four.

[3]See Mason, "Josephus and His Twenty-two Book Canon," 110 n. 2, critical literature on *Ag. Ap.* 1:37–43.

> through the inspiration which they owed to God, and committing to writing a clear account of the events of their own time just as they occurred)—it follows, I say, that we do not possess myriads of inconsistent books, conflicting with each other. *Our books, those which are justly accredited, are but two and twenty,* and contain the record of all time.
>
> Of these, *five are the books of Moses,* comprising the laws and the traditional history from the birth of man down to the death of the lawgiver. This period falls only a little short of three thousand years. From the death of Moses until Artaxerxes, who succeeded Xerxes as king of Persia, *the prophets subsequent to Moses wrote* the history of the events of their own times *in thirteen books. The remaining four books* contain hymns to God and precepts for the conduct of human life.
>
> From Artaxerxes to our own time the complete history has been written, but has not been deemed worthy of equal credit with the earlier records, because of the failure of the exact succession of the prophets.
>
> We have given practical proof of our reverence for our own Scriptures. For, although such long ages have now passed, *no one has ventured either to add, or to remove, or to alter a syllable;* and it is an instinct with every Jew, from the day of his birth, to regard them as the decrees of God, to abide by them, and, if need be, cheerfully to die for them. Time and again ere now the sight has been witnessed of prisoners enduring tortures and death in every form in the theatres, rather than utter a single word against the laws and the allied documents. (*Ag. Ap.* 1.37–43, LCL, emphasis added)

Although Josephus does not specify which books comprise his three-division canon, some of the books may be assumed: Genesis to Deuteronomy, Joshua to Kings, and at least part of the Psalms. One wonders, however, on what basis Leiman boldly asserts that Josephus included the precise books of the Hebrew biblical canon found later in the Talmud.[4] Nothing here justifies Leiman's identification of the books in Josephus's list with the books that finally obtained in the Jewish Bible. Leiman clearly works backward in anachronistic fashion from the closed collection first identified in the second century. His conclusions are not based on Josephus's writings, but are drawn from later witnesses to the biblical canon, when such matters were of more interest to both Judaism and the early Christian church. In addition, Josephus's divisions of the twenty-two books differ considerably from the threefold division that obtained in later Judaism, especially in regard to the contents of the Writings.

Zevit acknowledges the difficulty of finding room in Josephus's list for Song of Songs and Lamentations. Observing the difficulty of identifying the books in Josephus's list, he states:

---

[4]Leiman, *Canonization of the Hebrew Scripture,* 32–33.

> Scholars usually try to squeeze all books of the extant canon into these numerical references [in *Ag. Ap.* 1.39–40]. It appears to me, however, that since most of the essay *Against Apion* is concerned with the issue of whether or not the Jews possess authentic, accurate historical records written in terms that a contemporary historian may appreciate, Josephus is referring to historical compositions exclusively. The 13 books were Joshua, Judges, Ruth, 1 and 2 Samuel, 1 and 2 Kings, 1 and 2 Chronicles, Daniel, Ezra, Nehemiah, and Esther. The four books tacked on at the end were Psalms, Proverbs, Job, Ecclesiastes. Prophetic books, i.e., Isaiah, Jeremiah, Ezekiel, the Twelve, would have contributed nothing to his argument at this stage of its development in the essay and were not implicit in his enumeration. So too, Canticles and Lamentations were ignored.[5]

How reliable are Josephus's comments about the scope of the Jewish biblical canon at the end of the first century C.E.? Since he claims that "the exact succession of prophets" ceased with Artaxerxes son of Xerxes, whom he elsewhere identifies as Ahasuerus from the book of Esther (*Ant.* 11.184), it is understandable why he concludes his biblical canon as early as he did, namely, in the time of Artaxerxes.[6] Does Josephus's accounting of these matters reflect what was believed among most Jews at the end of the first century or an emerging view that had not yet gained widespread acceptance among the Jews? One factor in this issue is the obvious apologetic tone of the passage as a rebuttal of not only Apion, but all who deny the antiquity of the Jews and their sacred literature. Leiman argues, therefore, that Josephus was contending for the accuracy of the Bible as reliable history and not as sacred Scripture.[7] In fact, Josephus's comment that "no one has ventured either to add, or to remove, or to alter a syllable" is simply without justification since "it is inconceivable that Josephus was unaware of the wide range of textual divergency that characterized the Hebrew, Greek, and Aramaic versions of Scripture current in first century Palestine."[8]

How do we account, then, for such exclusive language about the contents and inviolability of the Hebrew Scriptures in Josephus? Leiman observes that this rhetoric has parallels in classical historiography and that Josephus need not be taken literally.[9] And in a later period, Maimonides (died 1204) and Joseph Albo (fifteenth century) made similar statements in an apologetic context.[10] Feldman is even more critical of Josephus's reliability than Leiman, noting examples of Josephus's exaggerations and his bent toward propaganda, especially in the defense of Judaism.[11] After reviewing the prejudices and inaccuracies of Josephus, Feldman concludes

---

[5] Zevit, "Second–Third Century Canonization," 140 n. 20.

[6] This point is made by Leiman, "Josephus and the Canon of the Bible," 51.

[7] Ibid., 51–52.

[8] Ibid., 52.

[9] Ibid., 52–53.

[10] Ibid., 53.

[11] Feldman, "Introduction," gives several examples from Josephus to substantiate this point.

that "he is far from infallible."[12] Josephus is quite reliable in matters of topography and geography of the land of Israel and in matters of economics, but he is nonetheless a propagandist in regard to the defense of Judaism against the pagan intellectuals of his day.[13] Silver also concludes that this passage reveals Josephus's wish rather than the actual state of affairs regarding the biblical canon current in his day.[14]

Barr raises the question of whether Josephus actually acknowledged a tripartite biblical canon. Even if the number of books found in Josephus's list is the same as in the present Jewish canon, the division of books in the Prophets and Writings clearly differs, possibly indicating that Josephus did *not* have a tripartite canon, but rather a two-part canon.[15] If this is so, we are led to the conclusion that various sects of Judaism at the turn of the era were not uniform in their understanding of which writings were considered sacred. Apparently many views circulated both inside and outside the land of Israel at that time about which writings were sacred among the Jews.

Cross likewise acknowledges that Josephus "not infrequently overstated his case in propagandizing a Greek-speaking audience," but grants that Josephus believed that the scope of the HB was a fixed entity in his day.[16] Leiman, however, incorrectly argues that Josephus faithfully reported a standardized biblical canon that could be verified by any Roman reader of his time. Acknowledging Josephus's propensity for exaggeration, Leiman nevertheless claims: "Even if one allows for exaggeration on Josephus's part, he could hardly lie about the extent or antiquity of the canon; any Roman reader could inquire of the nearest Jew and test the veracity of Josephus's statement."[17] This test of veracity sounds plausible enough, but it assumes that the "nearest Jew" would know the contents of the biblical canon and that all Jews would all agree on the matter. What evidence exists that all Jews accepted the same books in their collection of sacred Scriptures?

If it were true that all Jews everywhere agreed on the precise number and identity of the books that made up their Scriptures, one can only wonder why at the end of the second century C.E., Bishop Melito of Sardis could not find sufficient awareness of that collection in his own community at Sardis, which had a very large synagogue, in fact, one of the largest ever found in the Greco-Roman world in the second to third century C.E. (see fuller discussion of Melito in chapter 8 §IV.A.1). When he investigated which books were included in the Jewish Scriptures, it is odd that he made

[12] Ibid., 46–47.
[13] Ibid., 47.
[14] Silver, *Story of Scripture,* 134.
[15] Barr, *Holy Scripture,* 55.
[16] Cross, *From Epic to Canon,* 205.
[17] Leiman, *Canonization of the Hebrew Scripture,* 34.

a lengthy journey to the East (Jerusalem probably), when he could have simply crossed the street and asked the "nearest Jew." If, therefore, the number were settled for all Jews everywhere, and if the early Christians had received a biblical canon endorsed by Jesus, why would a well-known and distinguished bishop at the end of the second century not know the number or the specific books that were in it? And if Melito did not know the contents of the Jewish canon, how certain can we be that any Roman citizen could have verified Josephus's comments about the extent of the HB by asking the nearest Jew?

I am not suggesting that the books comprising the Law of Moses were unknown, or even that the Prophets and many Writings were not cited as Scripture at the end of the first century. Most of these books were highly treasured and valued in the religious life of most Jewish communities in the time of Jesus, and many are cited or alluded to in the NT. We do not, however, know that these books alone were in those categories that Josephus names. Books from all three categories were revered for their sacredness, inspiration, and authority in both Jewish and Christian religious communities, but we cannot conclude from the surviving evidence that *only* these books, or even that *all* of the books that now comprise the HB, were intended by Josephus and later formed the Hebrew Scriptures for Jews and Christians. If such a biblical canon was in existence at the end of the first century, it materialized after the separation of the church from Judaism, since the early Christians continued to use and cite several other books as Scripture in the second century and later.

So what are we to make of Josephus's statement at the end of the first century C.E. about the scope and contents of the Jewish Scriptures? Mason acknowledges the many inconsistencies in Josephus's writings, but nevertheless concludes that Josephus limited the number of sacred books to twenty-two. Mason also notes that Josephus's statement that prophecy had ceased in Israel ("because of the failure of the exact succession of the prophets") is the only way that we know that *Ag. Ap.* 1.37–43 refers to a fixed biblical canon, especially since Josephus cites the *Letter of Aristeas* and 1 Maccabees in the same manner that he cites the biblical material.[18] It is clear that Josephus is out of step with other Jewish open-ended or fluid canons of the first century, for example, those at Qumran, which made no distinction between writers before and writers after Artaxerxes (i.e., the Ezra tradition), and of early Christianity.

The freedom of the Jews at Qumran to add to or subtract from the biblical text suggests that there was no *universally* accepted closed biblical canon in the first century C.E. Further, Mason suggests that Josephus's fixed collection was "an inner-Pharisaic view that could only have gradually come to prominence with the emergence of the rabbinic coalition after

---

[18] Mason, "Josephus and His Twenty-two Book Canon," 126.

70 [C.E.]; it cannot reflect a common first-century Jewish view."[19] Since he elsewhere also refers to thirteen prophets,[20] it is clear that Josephus himself limited the number of prophets who were authoritative among the Jews:

> As for the prophet [Isaiah], he was acknowledged to be a man of God and marvellously possessed of truth, and, as he was confident of never having spoken what was false, *he wrote down in books all that he had prophesied* and left them to be recognized as true from the event by men of future ages. And *not alone this prophet, but also others, twelve in number,* did the same, and whatever happens to us whether for good or ill comes about in accordance with their prophecies. (*Ant.* 10.35, LCL, emphasis added)

Josephus appears to be ahead of his time in terms of limiting the books in the Jewish sacred collection to twenty-two books. Since there are no other clear parallels to this position, where did he get this view?

Cross posits a possible Babylonian origin for Josephus's view on the scope for the Hebrew Bible at the end of the first century.[21] During Maccabean times, many Diaspora Jews began coming back to their homeland from Syria, Babylon, and Egypt, bringing with them to Palestine a variety of textual traditions of the Hebrew Scriptures. Hillel, the most creative and influential teacher of his day, immigrated from Babylon to Israel in the first century B.C.E., and successive generations of his students developed the proto-rabbinic text (first century C.E.) and rabbinic recension (second century C.E.) of the Hebrew Bible.[22]

To quell the confusion resulting from multiple textual traditions, the Tannaitic schools of Hillel and Shammai developed rules of interpretation and discussed a fixed text of Scriptures. This emphasis on fixing the text perhaps also prompted the rabbis—sometime between the Jewish revolts (i.e., between 66 C.E. and 132 C.E.)—to prefer the common Aramaic script (sometimes called "Assyrian" in ancient sources) over the Paleo-Hebrew script.[23]

---

[19] Ibid, 126.

[20] Josephus mentions at least fifteen prophets in his writings, so he may be coupling some of them together when he says "thirteen."

[21] Cross, *From Epic to Canon,* 213–18.

[22] This so-called Pharisaic-Hillelite recension became the parent of the ninth-century C.E. Masoretic Text.

[23] The Paleo-Hebrew script had survived from preexilic times and was revived during the Maccabean revolt against the Seleucid Empire and subsequently used on official Jewish seals and coins. It continued to be used at Qumran and is found today in the manuscript tradition behind the Septuagint, in the name of God in manuscripts written in the Aramaic script, and in inscriptions found in the temple area in Jerusalem. The Mishnah contains a proscription against using a script other than Aramaic: "The [Aramaic] version that is in Ezra [4:8–7:18] and Daniel [2:4–6:28] renders the hands unclean. If an [Aramaic] version [contained in the Scriptures] was written in Hebrew, or if [Scripture that is in] Hebrew was written in an [Aramaic] version, or in Hebrew script, it does not render the hands unclean. [The Holy

Unlike other Jewish sects of the day (e.g., Essenes, Hellenistic-Jewish communities in Alexandria and Palestine, Samaritans, and Jewish-Christians), the Pharisaic tradition of Hillel was interested in a fixed text and canon of Scriptures,[24] and Josephus's Pharisaic tradition led him to adopt this tradition.[25] Josephus's understanding of the scope or contours of the Hebrew Scriptures thus had a Babylonian origin.[26]

If Cross's argument is correct, the Pharisaic biblical canon—Josephus's biblical canon—may be dated between the destruction of Jerusalem in 70 C.E. and the end of the first century when Josephus wrote *Against Apion* and *Jewish Antiquities*. Contra Josephus, however, this "canon and text did not immediately supplant other traditions or receive uniform acceptance even in Pharisaic circles."[27]

In fact, early Christians and Jews in Israel were open to books produced in Israel after Ezra's time (including the Apocrypha and Pseudepigrapha), but these books had little effect on Jews in Babylon during the last two centuries before Jesus. The result is that Jews at Qumran and early Christians—who had more in common with the Pharisees—had a longer list of sacred writings that originated on Palestinian soil and not in the Diaspora. The influence of Babylonian Jews, on the other hand, played a significant role in the shorter list of Scriptures adopted by rabbinic Judaism in the second century.

B. *JUBILEES* 2:23–24

The book of *Jubilees* refers to a twenty-two-book collection of Scriptures and to several other important twenty-two number groupings in the Jewish traditions.[28] Although the earliest known manuscript of *Jub.*

Scriptures] render the hands unclean only if they are written in the Assyrian character, on leather, and in ink" (*m. Yadayim* 4.5, quoted from Danby, *Mishnah,* 784).

[24] Cross (*From Epic to Canon,* 215) argues that the fixation of the biblical text and the stabilization of the biblical canon were bound together in the canonical process.

[25] Ibid., 221–25.

[26] A Babylonian origin for the rabbinic recension of the Hebrew Bible makes sense given Hillel's homeland and his significant influence on Pharisaism in first-century Palestine. This origin is supported by the Babylonian Talmud: "When the Torah was forgotten in Israel, Ezra came up from Babylon and established it; and when it was once again forgotten, Hillel the Babylonian came up and reestablished it" (*b. Sukkah* 20a, quoted from Cross, *From Epic to Canon,* 217). Even though Hillel and the Babylonian Talmud (e.g., *b. Bava Batra* 14b–15a) are the two prime examples of Babylonian influence on Israel, the Jewish community in Babylon repeatedly "developed spiritual and intellectual leaders who reshaped the direction of Palestinian Judaism and defined its norms" (218).

[27] Ibid., 225.

[28] According to O. S. Wintermute in *OTP* 2.43–44, the earliest possible date for this book is around 161–140 B.C.E.

2:23–24, discovered at Qumran, does not mention the sacred writings, a later form of the text refers to twenty-two books comprising the Jewish sacred Scriptures. This reference may lie behind Josephus's twenty-two-book collection. The Qumran manuscript reads as follows:

> There were twenty-two chief men from Adam until Jacob, and twenty-two kinds of works were made before the seventh day. The former is blessed and sanctified, and the latter is also blessed and sanctified. One was like the other with respect to sanctification and blessing. And it was granted to the former that they should always be the blessed and sanctified ones of the testimony and the first law just as he had sanctified and blessed sabbath day on the seventh day. (*Jub.* 2:23–24, *OTP* 2.57)

A portion of this text is believed to have been recovered by Charles, who bases this addition on *On Weights and Measures* by Bishop Epiphanius of Salamis (ca. 315–403 C.E.), who apparently drew directly on an early form of *Jubilees* to justify the twenty-two-book canon of the OT.[29] The additional words from Epiphanius make the first sentence of this passage read: "As there were twenty-two letters and twenty-two books and twenty-two chief men from Adam until Jacob, so twenty-two kinds of works were made before the seventh day." Beckwith believes that the twenty-two-book tradition referred to by Epiphanius was also cited by Origen (as reported by Eusebius, *Hist. eccl.* 6.25.1–2), who identifies all of the books in the canon. He reasons that it is "hard to believe that so learned a man as Origen was ignorant of the book [of *Jubilees*]."[30] VanderKam challenges Beckwith by noting that the earliest text of *Jubilees* says nothing about twenty-two books. In addition, there is no space in the Qumran text for these words, which are also lacking in the earliest Ethiopic manuscripts. VanderKam concludes: "The simple fact is that no text of Jubilees—whether Hebrew, Syriac, or Ethiopic—contains these words."[31]

Similar wording is found in two late sources: Symeon Logothetes (a tenth-century C.E. manuscript in Constantinople) and George Syncellus (ca. 800 C.E.).[32] These three textual traditions could be dated as early as the first century B.C.E., or even C.E., and if so they might well suggest that there may have been a twenty-two-book canon in the second century B.C.E. While possible, however, this scenario is highly unlikely and too many "ifs" have to fall into place for it to be taken seriously. If this addition is a part of the earliest form of the text, it would be the earliest reference to a precise number of sacred books that is also without parallel for another 250 years! Although it is possible that Josephus used such a source for numbering his

---

[29] Ibid., 57 n. *y;* Beckwith, *Old Testament Canon,* 237–40, and Charles, *Book of Jubilees,* lxxvii–lxxx.

[30] Beckwith, *Old Testament Canon,* 263 n. 9.

[31] VanderKam, *Revelation to Canon,* 18–19.

[32] Beckwith, *Old Testament Canon,* 236–37.

twenty-two-book biblical canon, one certainly cannot prove this on the basis of a textual variant in *Jubilees* recovered from Epiphanius in the late fourth or early fifth century C.E.

It seems more reasonable to assume an imprecise understanding in both Judaism and early Christianity about the scope of their biblical canons at the end of the first century C.E. Canon consciousness appears to have emerged first in Judaism in the late first century, but this emergence is not a fully developed biblical canon like we see later in more developed Judaism and in fourth-century Christianity. This view also accounts for the diversity in the collections later identified in early Christianity and Judaism. The final biblical canon for both religious communities was determined not by a council so much as by widespread use of sacred literature in the communities of faith. Councils typically confirm widespread practice, and that was the case when decisions about canon were made by councils in the fourth and fifth centuries and later: they simply endorsed choices made earlier by majorities or by consensus and convenience rather than by conscious council decisions. Bruce correctly states: "It is probable that, when the canon was 'closed' in due course by competent authority, this simply meant that official recognition was given to the situation already obtaining in the practice of the worshipping community."[33]

II. The Twenty-four-Book Canon

Both Christians and Jews showed a preference for a twenty-four-book canon in antiquity. In addition to *4 Ezra* 14:22–48 and *b. Bava Batra* 14b–15a (discussed below), a few other sources deserve brief mention:[34]

1. The Amoraim (third–sixth centuries C.E.) preferred the number twenty-four (*b. Ta'anit* 8a; *Numbers Rabbah* 13:16; 14:4, 18; 18:21; *Song Rabbah* 4:11; *Ecclesiastes Rabbah* 12:11–12).

2. The *Gospel of Thomas* 52 (ca. 100–140 C.E.) says that "twenty-four prophets spoke in Israel, and they have all spoken of you [Jesus]" (quoted from Schneemelcher, *New Testament Apocrypha,* 125). If this refers to the books of Scripture acknowledged among early Christians, it is the earliest Christian document that identifies a limited number of books in the Christian Old Testament. A recent argument that the *Gospel of Thomas* depends on Tatian's Diatessaron (ca. 170 C.E.) would, if correct, modify the date of this document.[35]

---

[33] F. F. Bruce, *Canon of Scripture,* 42.

[34] See Hengel, *Septuagint as Christian Scripture,* 57–74, for other examples.

[35] Perrin, *Thomas and Tatian.*

3. Victorinus (ca. 280 C.E.) writes: "The twenty-four elders are the twenty-four books of the Law and the Prophets, which give testimonies of the Judgment. . . . The books of the Old Testament that are received are twenty-four, which you will find in the epitomes of Theodore" (*Commentary on Revelation* 4.7–10, quoted from *ANF* 7.348).

4. Jerome (early fifth century C.E.) compared the twenty-four books of the Hebrew Scriptures with the twenty-four elders of the book of Revelation (*Prologue to Kings* [= *Prologus Galestus*]). He acknowledged the same number of sacred books, but like other Christians of his time, he accepted a variety of additional materials into his canon.

A. *4 EZRA* 14:22–48

Fourth Ezra[36] is a pseudonymous Jewish writing that was highly regarded by the early Christians, who added material to the book and used it in worship and instruction in the second century C.E.[37] The book contains an important reference to a collection of sacred books among the Jews and deals with the question of why God delivered his people into the hands of their enemies.[38] The writer also explains how Ezra miraculously recovered the Scriptures of Israel following the return of the Jews from Babylon. The passage begins with Ezra's appeal to God for help in recovering the law of God, which included not only a collection of twenty-four books to be read by all Jews but an additional collection of seventy sacred writings reserved for those who were "wise." This passage gives a clear statement on the sacredness of both types of writings:

> "If then I have found favor with you, send the holy spirit into me, and I will write everything that has happened in the world from the beginning, the things that were written in your law, so that people may be able to find the path, and that those who want to live in the last days may do so."

---

[36]The identity of *4 Ezra* (also called 2 Esdras and "Apocalypse of Ezra") is quite confusing to biblical students and scholars alike. Bruce Metzger (in *OTP* 1.517) explains: "The treatise identified in Latin manuscripts as 4 Ezra (*Esdrae liber IV*) comprises chapters 3–14 of an expanded form of the book traditionally included among the Apocrypha of English Bibles under the title 2 Esdras." In addition, modern scholars frequently identify portions of *4 Ezra* as *5 Ezra* (= *4 Ezra* 1–2) and *6 Ezra* (= *4 Ezra* 15–16). The confusion becomes even more apparent when the titles given to these works in ancient versions (especially the Septuagint and Vulgate) are compared with those in modern English Bibles. For helpful tables that clarify the relationship of the ancient Ezra material, see F. F. Bruce, *Canon of Scripture,* 47 n. 11; and Alexander et al., *SBL Handbook of Style,* 167.

[37]*Fourth Ezra* must be interpreted carefully because of its mixture of Christian and Jewish writings: a Christian introduction (*4 Ezra* 1–2) and epilogue (*4 Ezra* 15–16) were added to an original Jewish core (*4 Ezra* 3–14), which was written around the end of the first century C.E. or the early part of the second century C.E.

[38]See Metzger in *OTP* 1.520–21.

> He [God] answered me and said, "Go and gather the people, and tell them not to seek you for forty days. But prepare for yourself many writing tablets, and take with you Sarea, Dabria, Selemia, Ethanus, and Asiel—these five, who are trained to write rapidly; and you shall come here, and I will light in your heart the lamp of understanding, which shall not be put out until what you are about to write is finished. And when you have finished, some things you shall make public, and some you shall deliver in secret to the wise; tomorrow at this hour you shall begin to write."
>
> Then I went as he commanded me, and I gathered all the people together, and said, "Hear these words, O Israel. At first our ancestors lived as aliens in Egypt, and they were liberated from there and received the law of life, which they did not keep, which you also have transgressed after them. Then land was given to you for a possession in the land of Zion; but you and your ancestors committed iniquity and did not keep the ways that the Most High commanded you. And since he is a righteous judge, in due time he took from you what he had given. And now you are here, and your people are farther in the interior. If you, then, will rule over your minds and discipline your hearts, you shall be kept alive, and after death you shall obtain mercy. For after death the judgment will come, when we shall live again; and then the names of the righteous shall become manifest, and the deeds of the ungodly shall be disclosed. But let no one come to me now, and let no one seek me for forty days."
>
> So I took the five men, as he commanded me, and we proceeded to the field, and remained there. And on the next day a voice called me, saying, "Ezra, open your mouth and drink what I give you to drink." So I opened my mouth, and a full cup was offered to me; it was full of something like water, but its color was like fire. I took it and drank; and when I had drunk it, my heart poured forth understanding, and wisdom increased in my breast, for my spirit retained its memory, and my mouth was opened and was no longer closed. Moreover, the Most High gave understanding to the five men, and by turns they wrote what was dictated, using characters that they did not know. They sat forty days; they wrote during the daytime, and ate their bread at night. But as for me, I spoke in the daytime and was not silent at night.
>
> So during the forty days, *ninety-four books were written*. And when the forty days were ended, the Most High spoke to me, saying, "Make public the *twenty-four books* that you wrote first, and let the worthy and the unworthy read them; but keep *the seventy* that were written last, in order to give them to the wise among your *people*. For in them is the spring of understanding, the fountain of wisdom, and the river of knowledge." And I did so.

There are interesting similarities between this passage and the *Letter of Aristeas*. Both focus on the miraculous origin of the Scriptures and the divine activity involved in their translation and preservation. And both show the presence and activity of God in the translation and copying of the Scriptures.

As with Josephus, *4 Ezra* does not specify which books were in the twenty-four-book collection (or in the additional seventy-book collection).

But both Josephus and *4 Ezra* speak of a limited collection of sacred books. It is highly probable that by the time when *4 Ezra* was written the twenty-four-book collection had the Law of Moses at its core (*4 Ezra* 14:22, 30). It is also quite possible that many, if not all, of the writings that currently make up the HB and the Protestant OT canon were either in the twenty-four-book collection or the seventy-book collection mentioned by this author. Again, however, since the specific books are not identified, we cannot be certain about their identity.

It is interesting that the author of *4 Ezra* distinguishes between the twenty-four books that everyone can read and the seventy books that are reserved for "the wise among your people." In these seventy books one may find "the spring of understanding, the fountain of wisdom, and the river of knowledge" (14:46–47). It is easy to conclude that the seventy books were held in equally high regard as the twenty-four books since all ninety-four books were received by Ezra through the presence of the Holy Spirit at the same time and place (14:22) over a forty-day period (14:23, 36, 42, 44, 45).[39] The division between the twenty-four books and the seventy books parallels the later distinction between canonical and apocryphal (or deuterocanonical) writings, which were read for catechetical and devotional purposes.

There is no way to know with certainty whether either collection in *4 Ezra* included Ruth, Lamentations, Ezekiel, Daniel, Ecclesiastes, or Song of Songs, the books more commonly disputed in the rabbinic tradition. Also, it is not certain that Wisdom of Solomon and Sirach were excluded. One should be very careful about attributing to *4 Ezra* a definition of canon that cannot be established. Nothing prior to the second century C.E. identifies which books made up the sacred writings in the various sects of Judaism at the turn of the era. It is possible to hazard a guess of the identity of some of the books in the emerging biblical canon by observing the way that various writings were cited at Qumran or by Josephus, but what specific books were in these categories is debatable.

B. BABYLONIAN TALMUD, TRACTATE *BAVA BATRA* 14B–15A

A tradition preserved in the Babylonian Talmud but not in the Mishnah is known as a *baraita*. One text (dated 70–200 C.E.),[40] *b. Bava Batra* 14b–15a, clearly identifies the twenty-four books that make up the Jewish

---

[39]The number forty in the Bible typically focuses on the presence and activity of God: forty days of flooding on the earth (Gen 7:17), Moses on Mount Sinai for forty days (Exod 24:18), the children of Israel in the wilderness for forty years (Exod 16:35), Elijah on Mount Horeb for forty days (1 Kgs 19:8), Jesus' temptation in the wilderness for forty days (Mark 1:13), and postresurrection appearances of Jesus for forty days (Acts 1:3).

[40]Childs, *Biblical Theology of the Old and New Testaments,* 58.

collection of sacred writings and also sets forth a threefold division of HB as Law, Prophets, and Writings (or Hagiographa):

> Our Rabbis taught: the order of the Prophets is, Joshua, Judges, Samuel, Kings, Jeremiah, Ezekiel, Isaiah, and the twelve Minor Prophets. Let us examine this. Hosea came first, as it is written (Hosea 1:2): *God spoke first to Hosea*. But did God speak first to Hosea? Were there not many prophets between Moses and Hosea? R. Johanan (250–290), however, has explained that [what it means is that] he was the first of the four prophets who prophesied at that period, namely, Hosea, Isaiah, Amos, and Micah. Should not then Hosea come first?—Since his prophecy is written along with those of Haggai, Zechariah and Malachi, and Haggai, Zechariah and Malachi came at the end of the prophets, he is reckoned with them. But why should he not be written separately and placed first?—Since his book is so small, it might be lost [if copied separately]. Let us see again. Isaiah was prior to Jeremiah and Ezekiel. Then why should not Isaiah be placed first?—Since his book is so small, it might be lost [if copied separately]. Because the book of Kings ends with a record of destruction and Jeremiah speaks throughout of destruction and Ezekiel commences with destruction and ends with consolation and Isaiah is full of consolation; therefore we put destruction next to destruction and consolation next to consolation. [Our Rabbis taught:] The order of the Hagiographa is Ruth, the book of Psalms, Job, Proverbs, Ecclesiastes, Song of Songs, Lamentations, Daniel and the Scroll of Esther, Ezra and Chronicles. Now on the view that Job lived in the days of Moses, should not the book of Job come first?—We do not begin with a record of suffering. But Ruth also is a record of suffering?—It is a suffering with a sequel [of happiness], as R. Johanan said: Why was her name called Ruth?—Because there issued from her David who replenished the Holy One, blessed be He, with hymns and praises.
>
> Who wrote the Scriptures?—Moses wrote his own book and the portion of Balaam and Job. Joshua wrote the book which bears his name and [the last] eight verses of the Pentateuch. Samuel wrote the book which bears his name and the book of Judges and Ruth. David wrote the book of Psalms, including in it the work of the ten elders, namely Adam, Melchizedek, Abraham, Moses, Heman, Yeduthun, Asaph, and the three sons of Korah. Jeremiah wrote the book which bears his name, the book of Kings, and Lamentations. Hezekiah and his colleagues wrote . . . Isaiah, Proverbs, the Song of Songs and Ecclesiastes. The Men of the Great Assembly wrote . . . Ezekiel, the Twelve Minor Prophets, Daniel and the scroll of Esther. Ezra wrote the book that bears his name and the genealogies of the book of Chronicles up to his own time. This confirms the opinion of Rab (220–250), since Rab Judah (250–290) has said in the name of Rab: Ezra did not leave Babylon to go up to Eretz Yisrael until he had written his own genealogy. Who then finished it [the book of Chronicles]?—Nehemiah the son of Hachaliah. (*b. Bava Batra* 14b–15a, Leiman, *Canonization of the Hebrew Scripture,* 52–53)

This collection of books is the biblical canon that finally obtained in rabbinic Judaism, but even after the writing of this text there was considerable debate and discussion over books on the fringes of the biblical canon.[41] That this tradition was classified as a *baraita* from the Tannaitic period and did not find a place in the Mishnah suggests that the text had not yet received widespread approval by the closure and codification of the Mishnah around 200 C.E. This time frame accords with the mid-second-century C.E. story of Rabbi Meier, who wrote from memory a copy of the Mishnah tractate *Megillah* (*b. Megillah* 18b), and the second-century story of Bishop Melito of Sardis, who traveled to the East to learn which books belonged in the OT.

Bava Batra is very important to canonical studies since it is the first listing of the twenty-four books that eventually formed the contents and groupings of the HB. That this tradition comes from Babylon fits with Cross's suggestion that Hillel, who came from Babylon, heavily influenced the scope of the biblical canon for Pharisaic Judaism. This biblical canon did not, however, have much influence on the early Christians, since they clearly depart from it and do not divide their Scriptures into the same groups. In addition, this text does not reflect the views of all Jews in the second century C.E., otherwise it probably would have been included in the Mishnah, which was codified around 200–220 C.E. And since it comes from Babylon, it does not necessarily reflect the debate still going on at a much later date in the land of Israel. But because it reflects the views that eventually obtained acceptance in rabbinic Judaism, this text cannot be easily dismissed.

III. The Twenty-three-Book Canon: D. N. Freedman

Freedman proposes that the original Hebrew biblical canon was a twenty-three-book collection (i.e., without the book of Daniel), that was consciously determined along symmetrical lines in the late fifth or early fourth century B.C.E. (he is not dogmatic about the date).[42] Because there is a rather evenly balanced symmetry in the two major parts of the HB, he concludes that the editor/collector put these parts together with such a

[41] The only exception is that 1–2 Chronicles comes at the end of the Jewish collection instead of preceding the book of Ezra, as in the Protestant Old Testament canon. The repetition of 2 Chr 36:22–23 = Ezra 1:1–4 is not really necessary since these two passages are sequential in Christian Bibles. If, however, 1–2 Chronicles originally fell at the end of the biblical canon, such repetition served to link these books with Ezra, which was some distance away. The current form of the Protestant biblical canon brought them together (cf. a similar link in Prov 25:1, which identifies those who copied and presumably circulated the proverbs of Solomon).

[42] Freedman, "Symmetry of the Hebrew Bible." I am grateful to David Noel Freedman for correspondence with me in which he clarified his position. I have yet to resolve some of the problems that his proposal presents, but his suggestions are bold, exciting, and worthwhile considering.

balance in mind. More specifically, the Torah (79,983 words) and Former Prophets (69,658 words) together have roughly 150,000 words compared to a similar number in the combined Latter Prophets (71,852 words) and Writings (78,085 words). Without the book of Daniel, Freedman claims that the two parts of the Hebrew Scriptures are quite balanced, which demonstrates for him that the specific intention of scribes in the time of Ezra-Nehemiah was to develop a well-balanced collection of Scriptures.[43]

Freedman acknowledges that certain other books may have been late (Esther and Ecclesiastes), but this does not alter his picture by much or his conclusions at all. He is convinced that "without Daniel, the rest of the Hebrew Bible as we have it reflects a symmetry that is astonishingly exact" and he goes on, "as exact as is likely in literary productions rather than mathematical ones."[44] He contends that "if we consider numerical symmetry an important factor, then there is really no choice: there was only one moment when the Bible and the alphabet coincided and all the editorial factors were present. It was precisely in this period (post-exilic, Babylonian and Persian)."[45]

The symmetry extends to various collections within the Bible as well. The five books of the Torah are balanced by the five major Writings (Chronicles [which comes first in the Writings in both Aleppo Codex and Leningrad Codex], Psalms, Job, Proverbs, and Ezra-Nehemiah) and by the five Megilloth (Ruth, Song of Songs, Ecclesiastes, Lamentations, and Esther). The four books of the Former Prophets (1–2 Samuel and 1–2 Kings) are balanced by the four books of the Latter Prophets (Isaiah, Jeremiah, Ezekiel, and the Twelve [the Minor Prophets were always considered a single book in antiquity]).

This symmetrical collection of twenty-three books, Freedman claims, was possible during only one period of Israel's history: the postexilic Persian era when the Hebrew alphabet was augmented to twenty-three characters because *sin* (שׂ) and *shin* (שׁ), two forms of the Hebrew letter (ש), were considered to be separate characters. Freedman claims support for his proposal from the somewhat mangled acrostics in Pss 25 and 34, which attempt to align their twenty-three lines with the twenty-two letters of the Hebrew alphabet. By contrast, each section of Ps 119 begins with a successive letter of the twenty-two-character Hebrew alphabet.

According to Freedman, the near-perfect symmetry of the twenty-three-book HB and the twenty-three-character alphabet coincided only between 450 B.C.E. and 350 B.C.E. Later attempts to establish a twenty-two-book canon based on the twenty-two-letter Hebrew alphabet resulted in Ruth being moved from the Writings to the Former Prophets and Lamen-

---

[43] Freedman believes that the final editors of the Hebrew biblical canon, without the addition of Daniel, were probably Ezra and Nehemiah; ibid., 105–6.

[44] Ibid., 94.

[45] Ibid., 104.

tations being moved from the Writings to the Latter Prophets. On the other hand, the HB contains twenty-four books only when the book of Daniel is included.[46]

Although Freedman offers a unique suggestion and supplies some helpful information on the development of the Hebrew alphabet, the difficulties with his proposals are several and obvious. First, it is interesting that this amazing symmetry, which Freedman found with the aid of a computer, was not noticed earlier within the rabbinic tradition. If the symmetry of the Bible was intended to teach something about the Bible, no tradition of antiquity tells of this remarkable feature. If it was important in the formation of the Bible, in categorizing its books, or in recognizing its sacredness, this never occurred to any Jewish rabbis or Christian teachers. Second, why is this twenty-three-book biblical canon *never* mentioned anywhere in antiquity? This silence is puzzling if this balanced symmetry was intended by the ancient scribes. Third, why did it take some 2,400 years to discover this phenomenon? Fourth, where is the evidence for the addition of the book of Daniel to an already fixed form of the HB in the second century B.C.E.? Fifth, how could Judaism in the first century C.E. lose sight of its already firmly fixed biblical canon if the matter had been settled earlier in the intertestamental period? Sixth, for those who contend that the church was born with a fixed biblical canon in its possession and that the early Christians either lost or disregarded it, why is there is no evidence for the existence of this Scripture canon anywhere in the time of Jesus? Seventh, if the books that comprised the OT/HB were fixed in the fifth or fourth century B.C.E., how is it that only the Torah was translated into Greek when the LXX was made in the third century B.C.E. in Egypt? Why did it take at least another hundred years to have a complete Greek translation that included the Prophets and Writings? Finally, why is there no obvious attempt to correlate the books of the HB with the alphabet until the end of the first century C.E. (as in Josephus and *Jubilees*) if that canon existed earlier?

Although Freedman's work is refreshingly new and intricately detailed in its argumentation, his proposal cannot be substantiated, and it draws little or no support among canon scholars. Freedman's unique approach to this subject is nevertheless valuable because it provokes critical thinking about the origins of the Bible, even if his overall thesis falls short of demonstration. If his dating of the emergence of such a collection were not so early, one might concede his point that an individual (or individuals) formed the Hebrew Scriptures into a finely tuned symmetrical pattern, but the date—no later than 350 B.C.E.—is a major part of his thesis. Although focus on the Hebrew alphabet is important in the early development of the HB canon, this interest is difficult to date before Josephus. Some Christians

[46] Ibid., 103–4.

in the East picked up on this association with the alphabet, but it is not clear how much it prevailed in Judaism of late antiquity or in the patristic era among the church fathers.

IV. Summary

All of this evidence suggests a considerable amount of fluidity throughout the process that resulted in the emergence of a biblical canon among Jews at the end of the first century C.E. On the other hand, the *Letter of Aristeas* implies a model text of the Scriptures in the Jerusalem temple:

> So they [the delegation of scribes from Eleazer, the high priest in Jerusalem] arrived [in Egypt] with the gifts which had been sent at their hands and with the fine skins on which the Law had been written in letters of gold in Jewish characters; the parchment had been excellently worked, and the joining together of the letters was imperceptible. (*Let. Aris.* 175, *OTP* 2.24)

That the Jerusalem priests had a text to send to Egypt aligns with rabbinic traditions that speak of "book correctors" (Heb. *maggihei sefarim*) attached to the temple in Jerusalem to correct scrolls (*b. Ketubbot* 106a; *y. Sheqalim* 4:3, 48a; *y. Ta'anit* 4:2, 68a; *Sifre Deuteronomy* 356; *Avot of Rabbi Nathan* 46, 65; *Soferim* 6:4). Their presence in the Temple suggests an authoritative text by which the accuracy of copies was measured. By the third century C.E., rabbis warned against using uncorrected biblical texts for more than thirty days (*b. Ketubbot* 19b), which fits with Josephus's note about Jews having a "permanent record of the past" (*Ag. Ap.* 1.8). Although the Hebrew biblical text was still in a state of fluidity, there was a move toward stabilization in the first century, as seen in the text-critical activity in Jerusalem in the first century (*m. Sotah* 5:1 reports that a temple priest based legal decisions on the presence of the conjunction *waw* ["and"]). To Rabbi Akiba "not a word of Torah, nor even a syllable or letter, was superfluous" (*b. Menahot* 29b). Akiba also warned against teaching from uncorrected books (*b. Pesahim* 112a) and emphasized the importance of protective devices or "fences" (*massoret*) around the Torah text (*m. Avot* 3:13 [3:14 in some editions]). Finally, one rabbi advised another rabbi to be "extraordinarily meticulous in his work of transcribing sacred texts lest he omit or add a single letter" (*b. Eruvin* 13a). Assuming that these talmudic reports reflect actual first-century practice, it is likely that some form of stabilization was taking place then, but the final fixing of the Hebrew biblical text occurred in the second century C.E.[47]

Christians were heavily influenced by Jewish teachings up until 62 C.E., when they left Jerusalem following the death of James. Because of this rup-

[47] Sarna, "Canon, Text, and Editions," 834–36.

ture, however, Christians did not become concerned about textual and canonical issues for several centuries. The vast majority of NT manuscripts attest to this lack of precision in preserving the text of biblical and other religious books that influenced early Christians.

After Josephus, the number twenty-two became a common tradition in the church fathers and was mentioned occasionally in rabbinic tradition, but none of the lists that contain twenty-two books are the same in either Jewish or Christian sources.[48] Since, however, there is constant witness to the twenty-two-book collection during 90–400 C.E., it is more likely that something special about the number twenty-two commended itself to the Jews, who admittedly followed the Greeks in recognizing in their alphabet something sacred. This identity of the number of OT Scriptures with the Hebrew alphabet was then taken over by the early Christians, and the number twenty-two is frequently mentioned in their writings.

[48] For details, see appendixes B–C. Helpful discussions may be found in F. F. Bruce, *Canon of Scripture,* 68–97; and Christensen, "Josephus and the Twenty-Two Book Canon."

CHAPTER SEVEN

Rabbinic Tradition (90–550 C.E.)

THERE WAS FAR LESS AMBIGUITY ABOUT THE SCOPE OF THE JEWISH BIBLICAL canon in the second through the sixth centuries C.E. than about the Christian OT canon. The relative silence about a well-defined collection of Scripture among the Pharisees, Essenes, and Sadducees in the first century strongly suggests an absence of concern with the idea of a closed biblical canon before the second century C.E. Some scholars, however, speak of rabbinic Judaism in the second century C.E. and later as if it were the same as the Judaisms of the first century C.E. and earlier. We would be well served again to heed Neusner's dictum: "What we cannot show, we do now know."

I. Cessation of Prophecy

Some Jews both before and during the time of Jesus believed that the age of prophecy and the concommitant production of inspired literature had ceased in Israel after the time of Ezra, although this was not a universal view.[1] For example, after Judas Maccabeus had retaken the temple from the Seleucids, who had defiled it, the author of 1 Maccabees (ca. 100 B.C.E.) says that the Jews "tore down the altar [of the temple], and stored the stones in a convenient place on the temple hill until a prophet should come to tell what to do with them" (1 Macc 4:45–46). Speaking about the chaos caused by the Syrian military in Israel, he says, "So there was great distress in Israel, such as had not been since the time that the prophets ceased to appear among them" (1 Macc 9:27). And he later describes the election of Simon Maccabeus as ruler and high priest this way: "The Jews and their priests have resolved that Simon should be their leader and high priest forever, until a trustworthy prophet should arise" (14:41).

---

[1] In addition to the biblical and rabbinic references noted in this and the next three paragraphs, see also *2 Baruch* 85.3; *Seder Olam Rabbah* 30; and *b. Sotah* 11a–b; 48b. For a more complete discussion and listing of texts that mention the cessation of prophecy in Israel, see Meyer, "προφήτης," *TDNT* 6.812–19.

For the author of these paragraphs, prophets were absent from Israel at least temporarily, but there was anticipation that the divine prophetic ministry would return. It is not known how or why this view emerged, but Joel 2:28–29; Ezek 13:9; 36:26–27; 37:14; 39:29; Ps 74:9; Zech 13:2–6; and Dan 9:24[2] likely played a role in the development of this view, which probably emerged during difficult times in the nation's history.

Much later, near the end of the first century C.E., Josephus echoes similar sentiments: "From Artaxerxes to our own time the complete history has been written, but has not been deemed worthy of equal credit with the earlier records, because of the failure of the exact succession of the prophets" (*Ag. Ap.* 1.41, LCL). This could mean, as some argue, that the production of inspired and authoritative literature by the prophets also ceased at this time.[3] However, in spite of these and other later Jewish writings indicating that the prophetic movement ceased in Israel following the time of Ezra,[4] some literature believed to be inspired by the Holy Spirit continued to be written long after this time and was highly regarded in Israel both before and after the time of Josephus.[5]

Aune challenges how widespread belief in the cessation of prophecy was in antiquity and offers evidences from the *t. Sotah* 13:2–4 (ca. 300 C.E.) that many later Jews were spiritually informed by oracles. Aune cites several examples from the first century B.C.E. and the first century C.E. that indicate an equally strong belief that prophecy and the presence of the Spirit had not ceased in Israel.[6]

Leiman, on the other hand, maintains that all of the primary Jewish literature of antiquity claims a cessation of prophecy in Israel by the close of the fifth century B.C.E.[7] Strangely, he argues that writings produced after

---

[2] Note the seventy weeks of 9:24 spoke of more divine activity coming.

[3] Blenkinsopp, "Formation of the Hebrew Bible Canon," 54 n. 3, notes two alternative rabbinic views for the date of the cessation of prophecy in Israel: the destruction of Solomon's Temple (*b. Baba Batra* 12a; *b. Yoma* 21b; *b. Sotah* 48a) and the death of the last biblical prophet (*b. Yoma* 9b; *b. Sanhedrin* 11a).

[4] Other post-70 C.E. references to the cessation of prophecy are noted by Sundberg, *Old Testament of the Early Church,* 113–19.

[5] When any religious movement considers that the authentic voice of divine authority (i.e., a prophet) is no longer present, then the writings produced in that community's past—when such religious authority was believed to be present—are set aside by that community as its sacred literature. This could well be one of the reasons why a closed collection of Scriptures emerged quite late in Israel's history and why the notion of a Christian biblical canon did not begin to develop until the second century C.E. In this period the role of prophecy and prophet diminished in the church, and there emerged a greater dependence upon authoritative voices of the past. This turn of events *may* have led some teachers to recognize various Christian documents as Scripture, and in fact the NT writings were not generally called "Scripture" until the end of the second century C.E. For further comment, see Jeffery, "Canon of the Old Testament," 33.

[6] Aune, *Prophecy in Early Christianity,* 103–54.

[7] Leiman, *Canonization of the Hebrew Scripture,* 130.

this time were viewed as canonical but *not* inspired. If such a view were prevalent in Israel before the time of Jesus, as Leiman contends, then a closed canon of Scriptures might well have prevailed among the people of the land of Israel.

Aune offers three reasons why the evidence set forth by Leiman and others should be received with caution and not as reflective of the actual state of affairs in Israel: (1) many of the postcanonical texts do not antedate the second century C.E.; (2) early Judaism had greater variety than many scholars previously thought; and (3) not all of the texts listed above claim that prophecy actually ceased in Israel.[8] Aune concludes that the rabbinic sages of the second century and later did not consider themselves as inspired but rather as traditionalists, and therefore they promoted the notion of the cessation of prophecy as a means of legitimating their own positions as the successors of the prophetic tradition.[9] In support of this view, Aune cites Sandmel's conclusion: "Outside the circle of the Rabbinic Sages the view that prophecy had ended simply did not exist."[10] This view that prophecy had *not* ceased also finds support at Qumran,[11] in Christian writings (1 Cor 12:4–11, 28; Rom 12:6; Eph 4:11), and in Philo (*Moses* 2.187) and even Josephus (*Ant.* 3.311–13; *J.W.* 6.286, 300–309).[12] In addition, the book of Sirach, obviously written after the time of Ezra, was accepted by some Jews as inspired Scripture and deemed worthy to be read by both the Hebrew- and Greek-speaking Jews. Its author wrote "instruction and wisdom," and his grandson does not hesitate to commend his grandfather's written work along with that of the Law and the Prophets (Sir Prologue).

The Jewish biblical canon was *not* fixed because of a view that prophecy had ceased in Israel. This implies that writings produced during the time when the Spirit was present were "scriptural" and those written after that time were not. The acceptance of a writing into Israel's sacred Scriptures did not have to do so much with a notion about the cessation of prophecy, but rather with Israel's use of such literature in its liturgy, instruction, and community over a long period of time. There is little question, however, that rabbinic discussion and decisions about this literature had an important influence on the Jewish community's acceptance of it into their sacred collection. There is simply no evidence, however, that Jews throughout the empire were of one mind regarding which books they acknowledged as Scripture. In conclusion, I agree with Barton that, if by

[8] Aune, *Prophecy in Early Christianity,* 103.

[9] Ibid., 104–6.

[10] Sandmel, *Judaism and Christian Beginnings,* 174.

[11] Ellis, *Old Testament in Early Christianity,* 50.

[12] Aune (*Prophecy in Early Christianity,* 106–52) offers other examples of the various types of prophecy known and practiced within the sects of Judaism during the first century B.C.E. and first century C.E. that show a strong belief that prophecy and the presence of the Spirit were still active in Israel.

prophecy one means the "phenomenon of inspiration such as existed in the 8th century," then there is little evidence that it ever died out in postexilic Israel, even though the forms of expression changed and the prophets then expressed their oracles as additions to existing collections of prophetic writings.[13]

II. Myth of the Council at Jamnia

Following the loss of the Jewish temple and its cultus, Rabbi Johanan ben Zakkai requested permission from the Romans to establish a religious academy at Jamnia. According to tradition (*b. Rosh HaShanah* 31a–b), this Sanhedrin met first at Jamnia, then (ca. 135 C.E.) moved to Usha, Shefara'am, Beth She'arim, Sepphoris (where the Mishnah was put into its final form under the direction of Judah the Prince), and finally Tiberias, where most of the Jerusalem Talmud was formed.

For more than a century, many scholars have taught that the Jews officially closed the third part of their biblical canon at the Council of Jamnia (also known as Javneh or Jabneh), a small town located about thirty miles west and slightly north of Jerusalem (2 Chr 26:6; 1 Macc 5:58; Josephus, *Ant.* 12.308). At Jamnia, so the argument goes, Jewish religious leaders determined the final shape of the HB. It is unlikely, however, that the Jewish religious leaders who gathered together (there was no council as such) at Jamnia around 90 C.E. made a *final* or binding decision about their biblical canon, for, as we have seen, the list of books acknowledged to be sacred (i.e., "to defile the hands") continued to vary within Judaism up through the fourth century C.E. Also, there does not appear to have been any recognized group of individuals speaking on behalf of all Jews both inside and outside the land of Israel regarding religious matters near the end of the first century C.E. Some scholars argue that decisions regarding which books would be included in the Jews' sacred collection of Scriptures had already been made long before the Jamnia meeting.[14] While I agree that Jamnia appears to have settled little or nothing regarding the third division of the Hebrew Scriptures, it is even less likely that such decisions took place *before* the time of Jesus.

The Jewish religious teachers met at Jamnia after the destruction of Jerusalem to clarify how a religious faith that was once based on a temple and sacrificial cult could survive without these institutions.[15] At this time, some Jews began to speak of the limits of the number of their sacred

---

[13] Barton, "Prophecy (Postexilic Hebrew)," 5:495.

[14] F. F. Bruce, *Canon of Scripture,* 34–35; Ellis, *Old Testament in Early Christianity,* 38–40; Beckwith, *Old Testament Canon,* 65–67, 80–86, 276–77; Leiman, *Canonization of the Hebrew Scripture,* 120–24.

[15] J. A. Sanders, *Canon and Community,* 9, states that this was one of Judaism's most important issues following the destruction of Jerusalem in 69–70 C.E.

books. In addition, the rapid growth within Judaism of the Christian movement, with its strong focus upon apocalyptic and messianic literature, may have influenced the Jewish religious community in Palestine to reject apocalyptic literature. In any case, such apocalyptic views coupled with messianic claimants, such as Bar Kokhba, probably had an impact on the literature that Jews focused on during the second century C.E. and following. With the devastating defeat of their uprising against Rome in 132–135 C.E., it is understandable why many Jews might well minimize messianic hopes for the nation.

A Jamnia council decision is attractive, since no other prior time can be identified when a significant decision was made about the scope of the Hebrew biblical canon by the rabbinic teachers. No evidence, however, supports any formal action taken at Jamnia, and this view is largely abandoned today.[16] The scope of the Hebrew biblical canon within Judaism was more likely settled in the second century C.E., and possibly even later than that.[17] This argument is supported by the discussion about the contents of the biblical canon still going on among the rabbis during the writing of the two Talmuds, some two hundred to four hundred years after the Jamnia meeting.

Who started this Jamnia hypothesis? Some suggest that it was the invention of Christian scholars, but Aune, denying that Jamnia was a "myth of Christian scholarship," shows how the idea emerged instead in Jewish scholarship. He traces this view to an 1871 publication by Jewish historian Heinrich Graetz, who probably depended on Baruch Spinoza's *Tractatus theologico-politicus* (1670). Both Spinoza and Graetz held that the Hebrew Scriptures were defined for the Jews late in the Second Temple period, that this definition was made by the Pharisees, and that they acted as a "council" making final decisions about their biblical canon.[18] It was then assumed, based on *m. Yadayim* 3:5 and other rabbinic texts (*t. Yadayim* 2:14; *b. Megillah* 7a; *b. Sanhedrin* 100a; and *b. Shabbat* 13b; 30a–b), that a gathering or college of the sages led by Rabbi Eleazar ben Azariah met at Jamnia and issued its decision about the canon. Again, this view is no longer viable, and the passages cited from rabbinic literature do not support it.

After the tragic events surrounding the destruction of the temple in Jerusalem (66–70 C.E.) and the Bar Kokhba rebellion (132–135 C.E.), the influence of messianic literature (i.e., literature that held out the hope of a coming messianic figure who would free Israel from oppression) rapidly

---

[16] For further discussion and refutation of the Jamnia hypothesis, see Leiman, *Canonization of the Hebrew Scripture,* 120–24; Lewis, "Jamnia Revisited," in 159–62; and idem, "Jamnia (Jabneh), Council of."

[17] Zevit, "Second–Third Century Canonization," 152, suggests that the canonization of the HB was not complete until after the Mishnah and Tosefta were accepted as closed texts by the followers of Judah the Prince (ca. 250–300 C.E.).

[18] Aune, "On the Origins."

declined.[19] During the period of self-definition and reassessment after 135 C.E., a more conservative canon of HB appears to have obtained recognition in the rabbinic community, with a minimal apocalyptic focus (e.g., the book of Daniel and Isa 24–26). The Bar Kokhba rebellion itself probably had a major impact on the kind of literature that the Jews later received as their sacred Scriptures. For instance, the messianic movement that led to the rebellion almost certainly was influenced by the apocryphal and pseudepigraphal literature current in Palestine in the first century C.E., but after 135 C.E., this literature was less likely to be viewed as inspired writings (see, for example, the relative absence of such literature or views in the Mishnah).[20] Many questions remain unanswered regarding why apocalyptic and messianic literature was not incorporated into the Jewish biblical canon, but the disaster of 132–135 C.E. that ended the Bar Kokhba rebellion seems to be the most likely reason.

That the so-called Council of Jamnia did not stabilize the canon of the HB/OT is also seen in the widespread debate throughout the rabbinic period (i.e., second to sixth centuries C.E.) whether certain writings "defiled the hands," a rabbinic designation for a canonical text (see list in §III.B below).[21]

III. The Bible in the Rabbinic Tradition

If, then, Jamnia did not result in a definitive stabilization of the Jewish canon, it is important to examine which books were (or were not) considered sacred by the rabbis.

A. TORAH

The Law had a central place in Philo, Qumran (4QMMT), and other writings. For example, more than 40 percent of the biblical texts discovered at Qumran were of various portions of the Torah. The rabbis of the second century and following also gave priority to the Torah, and it had

[19] For further discussion, and disagreement, about the influence of messianic notions on Second Temple and rabbinic Judaism, see Neusner, *Messiah in Context,* and Evans, "Mishna and Messiah."

[20] Christians were also heavily influenced by the apocalyptic and messianic fervor present in the land of Israel in the first century C.E. (see Mark 13; Matt 24; Acts 1:6–7; 1 Thess 4:13–5:11; and the book of Revelation), but Christians focused on Jesus as the long-expected Messiah and his soon return. For excellent discussions of the presence and influence of apocalyptic messianic notions in Judaism and early Christianity, see J. Collins, *Encyclopedia of Apocalypticism,* especially chapters by J. J. Collins (129–61), J. C. VanderKam (193–228), D. C. Allison (267–302), M. C. de Boer (345–83), and D. Frankfurter (415–53). See also VanderKam and Adler, *Jewish Apocalyptic Heritage;* and A. Collins, *Early Christian Apocalypticism.*

[21] See the use of this term in *m. Kelim* 15:6 and *t. Yadayim* 2.19–20.

the central place in their sacred Scriptures and was singled out for special recognition and authority. According to the Talmud, only Torah scrolls could not be divided for inheritance purposes, though scrolls of other holy books could be divided at an appropriate seam and under certain conditions.[22] Torah scrolls were kept separate from scrolls of the Prophets and Writings. Initially, they were placed in a *tevah* ("chest"),[23] but by the fifth century C.E. Torah scrolls were kept separately inside an ark in the prayer room behind a curtain (*parochet*), which recalled the curtain in front of the holy of holies in the temple.[24] A rabbi could not lay any other scroll on top of the Torah. Only the five scrolls of Moses were read through annually in the synagogue.[25] All of this suggests, of course, that there were distinctions among the Scriptures in the rabbinic tradition and that the Torah was at the core of sacred literature. Consequently, the Law was acknowledged as the most authoritative Scripture. All Scriptures after the Torah received their authority from the Torah and were always viewed in relation to it. Even the Mishnah was called the "oral Torah." The Torah prevails in all such discussions of authority within Judaism and, according to Sanders and Johnson,[26] also in early Christianity.

B. NONCANONICAL BOOKS

If the issue of canonicity was settled before time of Jesus, we must ask why debate about which books could be read in public (i.e., during worship) continued during the formation of the Talmud?[27] Since reading Scripture implies its sacredness and authority for a believing community, restricting the public reading of a document suggests that it is not sacred. The primary exception to this, of course, is the reference in *4 Ezra* 14:46–47 to the "seventy" books that were reserved for the wise and not read in public. Writings excluded by the rabbis from public reading are the following:[28]

Ecclesiastes (*m. Yadayim* 3:5; *b. Berakhot* 48a; *b. Shabbat* 100a; *Ecclesiastes Rabbah* 1:3; 11:9; *Leviticus Rabbah* 23; *Avot of Rabbi Nathan* 1; cf. Jerome on Eccl. 12:14)

Esther (*m. Megillah* 4:1; *b. Megillah* 7a; *b. Sanhedrin* 100a; cf. *t. Megillah* 2:1a; 2 Macc 15:36; Josephus, *Ant.* 11.184–296)

---

[22] Silver, *Story of Scripture,* 162.

[23] The *tevah* is also called a *bimah* ("platform or pulpit," derived from Gk. *bēma*), which sat in the center of the synagogue and had a desk for reading the Torah scroll. A platform for reading the Torah is mentioned in Neh 8:4.

[24] Silver, *Story of Scripture,* 162.

[25] Ibid., 160–72.

[26] J. A. Sanders, *Torah and Canon,* 121; and Johnson, *Writings of the New Testament,* 612–13.

[27] Oikonomos, "Significance of the Deuterocanonical Writings," 19.

[28] For other examples, see Lewis, "Jamnia Revisited," 154–57.

Ezekiel (Sir 49:8; *b. Shabbat* 13b; *b. Hagigah* 13a; *b. Menahot* 45a; cf. Jerome, *Epistle* 53.8)[29]
Proverbs (*b. Shabbat* 30b)
Ruth (*b. Megillah* 7a)
Song of Songs (*m. Yadayim* 3:5; *m. Eduyyot* 5:3; *t. Sanhedrin* 12:10; *t. Yadayim* 2:14; *b. Sanhedrin* 101a; *b. Megillah* 7a)

Interestingly, the difference between the biblical canons of Jews and Christians may be seen in their religious debates. When Christians were in dialogue with Jews, they used the Jewish Scriptures; but when involved in their own services and ministries, Christians used the presumably larger collection of OT Scriptures. Origen, for example, justified his use of deuterocanonical literature by appealing to NT figures who did the same: Jesus (Matt 23:29–36), Stephen (Acts 7:52), and Paul (whom Origen presumed to have written Heb 11:37). On the other hand, Origen followed the narrower Jewish biblical canon when in discussion with Jews: "We follow the practice of not ignoring the books which they [i.e., the Jews] accept as genuine. In discussion with the Jews, we do not bring forward what is not contained in their copies, but use in common with them the [books] which they recognize, even when they are not recognized in our books."[30]

Silver concludes that "even as late as the early Talmudic period, there were still debates about whether certain scrolls should be included or excluded from a collection that had not yet been named or defined."[31] The Qumran sect, for example, had no clearly defined Psalter, as seen in its many variations (e.g., the added refrain in Ps 145 and the addition of the well-known Ps 151).

It is not clear whether the majority of Jews in Palestine accepted the Scriptures (and theology) of the Pharisees. A Judaism "defined by holy texts" was only beginning to emerge during this period,[32] and the precise boundaries of that collection were not yet established. We cannot maintain, therefore, that the sacred writings at Qumran were the same as those of most other Jews in Palestine in the first century C.E. While such questions are of particular interest to scholars today, they were simply not discussed at that time.

C. SIRACH

A more concrete example is provided by Sirach, which is quoted or cited as Scripture several times in rabbinic literature (*b. Hagigah* 13a;

---

[29] The Jerome reference is found in ibid., 155.

[30] Quotation of Jerome from Oikonomos, "Significance of the Deuterocanonical Writings," 20.

[31] Silver, *Story of Scripture,* 135.

[32] Ibid., 136.

y. Hagigah 77c; *b. Yebamot* 63b; *Genesis Rabbah* 8:2b; *b. Bava Qamma* 92b).[33] What these examples suggest, of course, is that the Scripture canon of the rabbinic tradition was not as firmly settled as some argue.

Fragments of Sirach were found at Qumran (Sir 6:20–31; 51:13–19, 30) and at Masada (Sir 39:27–32; 40:10–44:17), which raises the question whether Sirach was a part of the biblical canon of these communities. It is difficult to draw any conclusions about its canonical status, and scholars disagree over whether it is simply a liturgical text used in worship or was actually included in a recognized canon of Scriptures.[34] Regardless of its canonical status, however, it is clear that Sirach functioned as Scripture in worship and that those who read it afforded it a special status. Leiman maintains that Sirach, though venerated among the Tannaim and the Amoraim, was not received by them as a canonical book. He adds that when sectarian groups of Jews (Christians?) included Sirach in their biblical canons, Rabbi Akiba banned the book from being read. Leiman acknowledges that the later Amoraim rabbis cited the book as Scripture, but this may be because Akiba gave only his own private opinion on the status of the book or because the portions of Sirach quoted as Scripture did not come from the book of Sirach, but are quotations cited from memory that were formulated before the Akiba ban.[35] Leiman acknowledges, however, that the book was cited as Scripture, and he gives twelve examples of this in rabbinic literature. For example: "Simeon b. Shetah from the (first century B.C.E.) answered him: *It is written* in the book of ben Sira" (see *y. Berakhot* 11b; *y. Nazir* 54b; *Genesis Rabbah* 91:3; *Ecclesiastes Rabbah* 7:11; and *b. Berakhot* 48a); and, "*As it is written* in the book of Ben Sira" (*Tanhuma,* tractate *Hukkat* 1).[36]

The book of Sirach thus points to some flexibility within the Jewish community well into the fourth century C.E. on which books were acknowledged as sacred Scripture.

D. THE MISHNAH'S USE OF SCRIPTURE

Only one tractate, *Avot,* of the Mishnah's sixty-three tractates has any reference to specific Scripture texts. This is quite remarkable since the NT writers make frequent use of Scripture texts, citing the OT frequently in support of various teachings and practices in the early church. The Jews at Qumran also cite the Law to support their various practices, and the same could be said of Philo and occasionally of Josephus. We are fairly confident that the Christians inherited this practice of "writing with

---

[33] Segal, *Sefer Ben-Sirah,* lists some eighty-five citations of Sirach in rabbinic literature through the tenth century C.E.

[34] See Gilbert, "The Book of Ben Sira," 85–87.

[35] Leiman, *Canonization of the Hebrew Scripture,* 92–102.

[36] Ibid., 96–97, 100. See 185 nn. 441–52 for the twelve examples and references.

Scripture"[37] from Judaism of the first century. If so, what does this say about a general understanding of the Scriptures during the production of the Mishnah?

The two Talmuds later support the claims of the Mishnah with Scripture references and in a manner more familiar to those who write *with* Scripture.[38] If the rabbis wrote prescriptions for living without the aid of or reference to the Scriptures, one cannot help but wonder about the notion of Scripture in the period of the Tannaim (i.e., the first two centuries C.E.). Lightstone raises the significant question of how the very circle of leaders supposedly responsible for fixing the final boundaries of the Hebrew biblical canon was also responsible for the Mishnah, which had very little to do with those Scriptures. He also observes that the Jewish biblical canon and the Mishnah reflect the social institutions and experiences of the second century C.E.[39] What was the cultural context that could not only define the Scriptures, but then largely ignore them when producing the writings that would be used for ordering daily living?

By contrast, the early Christian church had a clearly defined view of authority. If Jesus said it, that settled the matter (1 Cor 7:10, 25; 11:23; cf. 2 Thess 3:6, 12), and the goal in Christian living was to please the Lord (1 Cor 7:32; Col 3:15–17). They also supported or illustrated their beliefs and conduct with OT Scriptures (e.g., Matt 21:5, 16; 1 Cor 15:3–4, 54–55; 1 Pet 2:6–8; 3:6, 10–12). Given this context, how could there have been a time in Judaism when a rabbi could simply say, "Here is the way I see it"—with the obvious implication, "And so should you"? How could there be "writing *without* Scripture," as Neusner describes it?[40] I conclude from this that notions of Scripture and scriptural canons were not as clearly defined in the Tannaitic period as they were in the later Amoraic period, when the rabbis set out to support all of the Mishnah's teachings with scriptural references. As a result, both of the Talmuds add support from the recognized canon of Scripture for all of the teachings of the Mishnah.

E. OUTSIDE BOOKS

One cannot speak of "outside books" without first having some idea of what is acknowledged as Scripture and included in a fairly well-defined collection. The first reference to "outside books" appears in the 130s C.E.:

> But the following have no share in the world to come: he who maintains that the resurrection is not intimated in the Torah, or that the Torah was not

---

[37] This phrase comes from Neusner and Green, *Writing with Scripture,* 1–2, in which Neusner claims that the early Christians and Jews in the same period did not write *about* Scripture so much as they wrote *with* Scripture to express their thoughts.

[38] Neusner, "Rabbinic Judaism in Late Antiquity," 75–76.

[39] Lightstone, *Society, the Sacred, and Scripture,* 68.

[40] Neusner and Green, *Writing with Scripture,* 24–42.

> divinely revealed, and an Epicurean. R. Akiba (110–135) adds: one who reads the outside books, and one who whispers a charm over a wound and recites: I will not bring upon you any of the diseases that I brought upon the Egyptians, for I the Lord am your healer (Ex. 15:26). (*m. Sanhedrin* 10:1, Leiman, *Canonization of the Hebrew Scripture,* 86)[41]

This practice of excluding certain books from being read or brought into one's home for study assumes the notion of a closed collection of Scriptures, at least for the one who speaks of "outside books." What is not certain is whether all Jews at this same time acknowledged the same books for inclusion or exclusion. The practice merely suggests that there was no fixed canon of books in Judaism during the first century C.E.

F. CAIRO GENIZAH

In 882 C.E., King Ahmed Ibn Tulun of Egypt demanded from Michael, the 56th Coptic Patriarch, a large sum of money to pay for the king's military adventures. In order to raise the money, the patriarch had to sell some land and a church in Cairo. The church was sold to some Jews, who transformed it into a synagogue. Over the centuries, the Jews stored a great number of manuscripts and printed books in a back room of the synagogue, which were discovered by accident following a renovation in 1890.

The Jewish custom was to deposit literature containing the name of God into rooms called "genizahs"[42] for fear that the name of God would be profaned when these writings were discarded. From time to time, the Jews would consecrate a place and bury these documents in the ground. Fortunately for our sake, the documents in the Cairo Genizah were ignored and not discovered until the last century. The thousands of manuscripts found in this genizah are now in Leningrad, Oxford, Cambridge, and the Jewish Theological Seminary in New York. Along with versions of the Bible in Aramaic, Hebrew, and Arabic, were copies of apocryphal, pseudepigraphal, and talmudic writings. The total number of fragments found in the Cairo Genizah is estimated to be over two hundred thousand. They have yet to be fully edited and presented to the public, but significant work on them is progressing, even if slowly.

Among the more significant textual finds from the Cairo Genizah are fragments of the *Damascus Document* (sometimes also called the *Zadokite Document,* also discovered at Qumran), the Hebrew text of Sirach, and Aquila's Greek translation of the OT. We are not certain about the dating of most documents in the Cairo Genizah, because many of them could have been brought by the Jews into their newly acquired synagogue after having

---

[41] Leiman, *Canonization of the Hebrew Scripture,* 86, gives several other examples of this exclusion.

[42] The Hebrew word *genizah* refers to something "withdrawn" or "stored" and, by extension, to the place where sacred documents were stored.

been used in other synagogues prior to 882 C.E. We do know that many noncanonical writings were also placed in the Cairo Genizah, and this, of course, raises the question about the understanding of the Cairo Jews concerning the scope of their sacred Scriptures.

The Talmudic literature has many references to the withdrawal of canonical literature from synagogue usage, but a genizah could also contain noncanonical or heretical literature. For example, prior to disposing of heretical books (typically by burning), the rabbis cut the divine name or other sacred material from those documents and stored the scraps in a genizah. Because of the many fragments of obviously heretical literature found in the Cairo Genizah, we cannot be certain about the canonical status of other nonbiblical material (i.e., apocryphal and pseudepigraphal literature) found there.

In any case, the late dating of the material found in the Cairo Genizah makes it impossible to arrive at dogmatic conclusions about what the Jews of an earlier period thought of this literature. Certainly, sacred books were placed in the Cairo Genizah, but what was the scope of the biblical canon in Cairo? Much more study is needed here, but it is difficult to say that the Cairo Jews accepted only the sacred writings that were later canonized by the rabbis during the second to fourth centuries C.E.

IV. Writings of Rabbinic Judaism

A. MISHNAH AND RELATED WRITINGS

The primary schools of biblical interpretation that flourished in the time of Jesus were those of Hillel, a Jewish lawyer from Babylonia (ca. 50 B.C.E.–10 C.E.), and Shammai, his contemporary from Palestine. Shammai and his teachings were more popular in Israel before the destruction of Jerusalem in 70 C.E., but Hillel's interpretation prevailed and became foundational for surviving Judaism of the late first and second centuries C.E. Those of Shammai's teachings that remain tend to be strict and elitist, while Hillel's teachings are more liberal, patient, and popular with the people.[43] Many of the teachings of Hillel were passed on to his best-known pupil in the first century C.E., Rabban Gamaliel, who was the teacher of the Apostle Paul (Acts 22:3; cf. 5:34–35) and of whom it was said that when he died "the glory of the Law ceased and purity and abstinence died" (*m. Sotah* 9:15, Danby, *Mishnah,* 306).

After Gamaliel, and following the destruction of Jerusalem and the temple, Johanan ben Zakkai took the lead in the reorganization of Judaism. He had to deal with the problem of how Judaism, which had been so

[43] Koester, *Introduction to the New Testament,* 1.227–29, 383–85, 390.

directly tied to the temple cultus, could survive without its sacrificial system. He was instrumental in the reorganization of Israel's religious life through the rabbinic academy that met at Jamnia around 90 C.E. After him, rabbis Eliezer and Gamaliel II were prominent, but the latter had a less tolerant attitude toward the Christian community than did his grandfather. In the twelfth of his Eighteen Benedictions, Gamaliel II introduced a curse on all heretics, including Christians:

> For the apostates let there be no hope, and the dominion of arrogance [Rome] do Thou speedily root out in our days; and let the Nazarenes [Christians] and the heretics perish as in a moment, let them be blotted out of the book of the living and let them not be written with the righteous. Blessed art Thou, O Lord, who humblest the arrogant! (Ferguson, *Backgrounds of Early Christianity,* 543–44)[44]

Rabbi Akiba was the leading rabbinic figure around 120–140 C.E., and he recognized and supported the claims of Simeon ben Kosibah (also known as Simon bar-Kokhba) to be the king/messiah. Kosibah led an uprising against Rome in 132–135 C.E., seeking to make the Jewish state independent from Roman rule, but the result was an overwhelming defeat of the Jews and the death of Kosibah. After Hadrian evicted them from Jerusalem, which he renamed Aeolia Capitolina, the Jews saw Kosibah as a liar who had committed sins worthy of death. He was later called "ben Kozeba" ("lie"), a play on words speaking of his deceit of the people.[45]

After the death of Rabbi Akiba, Rabbi Meir (ca. 140 C.E.) began the process of codifying the oral traditions that were a "hedge" around the law (cf. *m. Avot* 1:1) and that guarded its proper implementation in the lives of the Jews in Palestine (it does not deal with Diaspora Jewry). That codification, which was completed under the direction of Judah the Prince around the end of the second century, was called the Mishnah. The Mishnah was essentially the codification of the Halakah (from Heb. *halak,* "to walk"), which focused on how to conduct oneself (i.e., walk), according to the law. It focused primarily upon the legal aspects of keeping the law. As the Christians needed another Testament to complete the sense of the OT, so also the Jews needed the Mishnah and its interpretations to complete their understanding of the Hebrew Scriptures. The Mishnah became the second canon of the Jews and was so important that whole traditions of interpreting it developed. When a rabbi commented on the Mishnah, his commen-

---

[44] Ferguson notes that the phrase *and let the Nazarenes* is contested as an original part of the Benedictions, but it is not out of keeping with the kinds of comments said about early Christians by the Jews on other occasions. See McDonald, "Anti-Judaism in the Early Church Fathers," 245–49.

[45] See *y. Ta'anit* 4:68d–69b; *Lamentations Rabbah* 2:4; and *b. Gittin* 57a–58a. Christian sources call Kosibah a bandit and murderer but also a worker of miracles. See Eusebius, *Hist. eccl.* 4.6.2.

tary was called "Gemara" (from Heb. *gemar,* "to complete"). Mishnah and Gemara were combined to create the two Talmuds: the Palestinian (for Jerusalem) Talmud and the Babylonian Talmud. The latter was more extensive and more conservative than the one produced in Galilee. Even though the Babylonian Talmud comments on fewer mishnaic tractates than does the Palestinian Talmud (361/2 versus 39), the Babylonian Talmud is almost four times as long as the Palestine version. Another major rabbinic document is the Tosefta ("supplement"), a collection of interpretations contemporary with the Mishnah but excluded from it; it is sometimes called *baraita* ("external") and does not have the status of the Mishnah. Finally, midrashim are rabbinic commentaries on Scripture.

This literature, which was produced well after the time of Jesus and the origins of early Christianity, has significance for understanding early Christianity and its sacred literature because the Mishnah is the codification of an oral tradition that partially overlapped the time of Jesus and in some cases came prior to his ministry. The Mishnah provides background material for understanding Jesus' teachings on, for example, the Sabbath (see tractate *Shabbat*), vows (*Nedarim*), and oaths (*Shevu'ot*). Other mishnaic parallels provide background on Jesus' teaching on marriage and divorce and the two greatest commandments.[46]

All of this literature dates in its current form between the end of the second century C.E. and the Middle Ages. It may, in many instances, reflect traditions from the time of Jesus and before, but caution must be exercised in using it. The reader could be easily mislead to conclude that the circumstances described in the Mishnah—and especially in the later Talmuds—had occurred much earlier.[47]

The Mishnah was written in Hebrew and has six orders (*sedarim*), which are made up of sixty-three tractates:[48]

1. *Zeraim* ("seeds")
    - Berakhot ("benedictions")
    - Pe'ah ("gleanings")
    - Demai ("produce not certainly tithed")
    - Kil'ayim ("diverse kinds")
    - Shevi'it ("seventh year")
    - Terumot ("heave offerings")
    - Ma'aserot ("tithes")

[46] See Ferguson, *Backgrounds of Early Christianity,* 461–69, for a more complete discussion of this topic.

[47] For helpful discussions of rabbinic literature, see Evans, *Noncanonical Writings,* 97–148; Neusner, *Rabbinic Tradition about the Pharisees;* idem, "Formation of Rabbinic Judaism."

[48] For helpful lists of abbreviations of this and other rabbinic writings, see Leaney, *Jewish and Christian World,* 230–36; and Alexander et al., *SBL Handbook of Style,* 79–81.

Ma'aser Sheni ("second tithe")
Hallah ("dough offering")
Orlah ("fruit of young trees")
Bikkurim ("firstfruits")

2. *Mo'ed* ("set feasts")
Shabbat ("Sabbath")
Eruvin ("Sabbath limits")
Pesahim ("Passover")
Sheqalim ("shekel dues")
Yoma ("Day of Atonement")
Sukkah ("tabernacles")
Yom Tov or Betzah ("festivals")
Rosh HaShanah ("new year")
Ta'anit ("days of fasting")
Megillah ("scroll of Esther")
Mo'ed Qatan ("midfestival days")
Hagigah ("festival offering")

3. *Nashim* ("women")
Yevamoth ("sisters-in-law")
Ketubbot ("marriage deeds")
Nedarim ("vows")
Nazir ("Nazirite vow")
Sotah ("suspected adulteress")
Gittin ("bills of divorce")
Qiddushin ("betrothals")

4. *Neziqin* ("damages")
Bava Qamma ("first gate")
Bava Metzi'a ("middle gate")
Bava Batra ("last gate")
Sanhedrin ("Sanhedrin")
Makkot ("stripes")
Shevu'ot ("oaths")
Eduyyot ("testimonies")
Avodah Zarah ("idolatry")
Avot ("fathers")
Horayot ("instructions")

5. *Qodashim* ("hallowed things")
Zevahim ("animal offerings")
Menahot ("meal offerings")
Hullin ("animals killed for food")
Bekhorot ("firstlings")
Arakhin ("vows of valuation")
Temurah ("substituted offering")

Keritot ("extirpation")
Me'ilah ("sacrilege")
Tamid ("daily whole offering")
Middot ("measurements")
Qinnim ("bird offerings")

6. *Teharot* ("cleanliness")
Kelim ("vessels")
Ohalot ("tents")
Nega'im ("leprosy signs")
Parah ("red heifer")
Teharot ("cleannesses")
Mikwa'ot ("immersion pools")
Niddah ("menstruant")
Makhshirin ("predisposers")
Zavim ("they that suffer a flux")
Tevul Yom ("he that immersed himself that day")
Yadayim ("hands")
Uqtzin ("stalks")

B. TARGUMS

An important source of information for establishing the Hebrew text of the OT Scriptures is the Targums (Heb. *targum* and Aramaic *targuma* both mean "translation"). These writings are translations or extended paraphrases of the Hebrew Scriptures into Aramaic, the language of the Jewish people following their return from exile in Babylon. Even though most Targums are paraphrastic (*Targum Onqelos* is the most literal), they provide valuable information about early Jewish understanding of the Scriptures and show remarkable parallels with the NT Gospels and some letters.[49] Neusner believes that the earliest Targums may be used to reconstruct the Aramaic dialect that Jesus spoke.[50]

The dating of the Targums is disputed, but Jewish tradition claims that they go back to the time of the Jews' return from Babylon under the leadership of Ezra (Neh 8:8, see *b. Megillah* 18b and *Genesis Rabbah* 36:8). Most of the known Targums date from the second to fifth centuries C.E. The tradition that they started with Ezra is probably legendary, but it is likely

[49]For example, both the Targums and the Gospels avoid anthropomorphic (i.e., representing God in human form) and anthropopathic (i.e., ascribing human emotions to God) language. They share similar views about this world and the world to come, resurrection, the Son of Man, a coming day of judgment, a Father in heaven, and heaven (paradise) itself. They frequently offer similar interpretations of the Hebrew Scriptures. As a result, scholars often use both to interpret each other.

[50]Nuesner, "Targums and the New Testament," 2.616.

that some Targums predate Christian times; in fact, three or four of them were found at Qumran and date to the first century B.C.E. or early first century C.E.[51]

There are Targums on all of the books of the HB except Daniel, Ezra, and Nehemiah. There are no Targums on noncanonical books, but since they date for the most part from the second century C.E. and later, when the Jews had fixed or stabilized their biblical text, this is understandable. Most of the Targums are of the Pentateuch (*Neofiti I, Pseudo-Jonathan, Onqelos, Fragmentary Targum,* Cairo Genizah Fragments, and the *Toseftot*), but there is one on the Prophets, traditionally called *Targum Jonathan*. There is no *official* Targum on the Writings, but Targums exist on all of these books except for Daniel, Ezra, and Nehemiah. These three books may have no Targum because all of them are written partially in Aramaic.

Since the Targums mostly date long after the establishment of the MT, their value for establishing the canon of the HB is marginal because by the time most of them were produced, a decision had already been made among the rabbis on the scope of the HB. On the other hand, the very lateness of the Targums on the Writings may indicate a late development in the universal acceptance of their sacredness or in the lateness of their being placed on an equal canonical footing with the Prophets. This is speculative, of course.

V. Conclusion

The notion of a biblical canon was not current in the time of Jesus or before. The primary evidence used to argue for a closed biblical canon of OT Scriptures among the Jews comes from the second century C.E. and afterward. One should be cautious, therefore, about attributing later conclusions to the first century B.C.E. and first century C.E. Jews generally were not concerned about canonical issues before the second century C.E. If the scope of canonical literature was a significant issue, then one would think that more evidence would have been left behind from that era.

In terms of how the biblical canon emerged for Judaism, I find Barton's citation of T. S. Eliot's analogy to English literature to be helpful. Eliot observes that a canon of English literature was acknowledged by all to "constitute the essential corpus of classics." However, as new books with a demonstrated stature were written, they were immediately placed in rela-

[51] More specifically, 4Q156 (= 4QtgLev) preserves Lev 16:12–15, 18–21; 4Q157 (= 4QtgJob) preserves Job 3:5–9(?); 4:16–5:4; and 11Q10 (= 11QtgJob) preserves Job 17:14–42:11. A fourth possible Targum is 6Q19 (= 6QtgGen?), which preserves Gen 10:20. These texts, which are completely independent of the later Targums and do not prove the antiquity of the later, were brought to my attention by C. A. Evans in personal correspondence.

tionship to the existing canon. Barton adds that if the new books were really classic pieces, they had the power to change the canon, "altering the relationships between the existing works and creating a new equilibrium in which every previous work takes on a new tinge of meaning."[52] This sort of ever-new inclusion seems to have occurred as the Prophetic collection was gradually recognized and added to the well-established "classics" of the Torah. Likewise for the early Christians, the writing of the NT literature caused a new sense of canon to emerge in which the older "classics" were no longer read in the same way; the earlier books were still canon, but viewed in a different manner. This parallel has certain limits, but what seems apparent is that Torah was always at the core, and everything else formed around it, either clarifying it or fulfilling it, but always in close proximity to it.

Whenever other literature was added to the canon, the older canonical books were looked at in a new way. As the Torah thus expanded beyond the Law of Moses to include the Prophetic writings and the Writings, each new expansion brought a redefinition of canon. Early Christianity emerged in the middle of the redefinition process in which certain books of the Writings were considered sacred and holy and some were simply not very useful in worship (e.g., Ecclesiastes, Song of Songs, and Esther). In time, some of these books were deemed unworthy to form part of the canon, while others were added to it. During this process of delimiting the biblical corpus, the church separated from Judaism and took with it some of the questions and ambiguity still prevalent in Judaism at the time of separation. The lack of interest in canon in the first century C.E., however, can be seen by the absence of Christian references to what went into its sacred Scriptures. If the early church was born with a canon in its hands, it nowhere identifies it. And it is an argument from silence to insist that the canon was so well known that it was not necessary to list its contents.[53]

It is better to say, on the basis of the available evidence, that the process of closing the Hebrew biblical canon began during the late first or second century C.E. The rabbis who shaped the Mishnah and put it into its final form are the same individuals who gave shape to the HB in its final form. These rabbis included in their sacred collection of Scriptures the books that they believed originated from the time of Ezra and Nehemiah and before. This literature, they believed, defined and reflected the meaning of being Israel. According to Lightstone, "the shape and character of the rabbinic canon bears a homological relationship with the shape and character of sacred space on earth, the 'Restored Jerusalem' of the returnees, and with sacred time, from Creation to 'Restoration.' So scripture begins with the

---

[52] Barton, *People of the Book?* 32.

[53] So argue Ellis, *Old Testament in Early Christianity,* 50, 125–38; and Beckwith, *Old Testament Canon,* 22–25.

'Torah of Moses' and ends with its realization under Ezra and Nehemiah."[54] This definition of a sacred Scripture is especially appropriate to the social context and experience of rabbinic Judaism during and after the late second century C.E.

If there was a clearly defined biblical canon in the third century B.C.E. or earlier, one would think that at least some statement saying so *from that period* would have survived. Perhaps the listing of such books in the late second century C.E. comes at that time because *only then* was there a special concern over the precise limits of Scripture in rabbinic Judaism. If a biblical canon existed before then, how could it have been lost or blurred in both Judaism and the early church? How could the two primary surviving religious sects of Judaism, Pharisaism (the forerunner of rabbinic Judaism) and early Christianity—both of which appealed to its sacred literature for support of the foundation of its life and ministries and all that it held sacred—have lost the contents of their sacred writings that at one time were clearly known and passed on in those communities?

Put another way, how is it that there is disagreement on the exact boundaries of the sacred Scriptures among both the rabbinic schools and early Christianity, if those boundaries were known by both faiths? If notions of scriptural canons were important to the Jews of the first century B.C.E., why are there no references to their contents in the literature that has survived? Why are no canonical lists available, such as those that begin to emerge at the end of the second century C.E. and later? Again, if we assume that lists of the canonical books were known in the time of Jesus and well before, we are at a loss to know what led to the disappearance of these lists within both Judaism and early Christianity. On the other hand, if such lists were available, what led to the circulation of lists of Scriptures that differed from one another in both Judaism and early Christianity? And even when Jews and Christians used a similar number of sacred texts, either twenty-two or twenty-four books, there was still variation in the lists regarding which books made up those collections. What processes of canonization could have allowed for such variance of opinion about the makeup of the sacred collection in the two Talmuds?

Scholars who want early closure of the Jewish biblical canon, and therefore the Christian OT canon, often have trouble dealing with rabbinic texts that cast doubt on certain books that became part of the fixed biblical collection of sacred books. The above questions are not easily answered if one assumes that a fixed biblical canon existed in the third or second century B.C.E. In fact, the later discussion among the rabbis is not understandable at all if the issue had clearly been settled earlier. How could such a

---

[54] Lightstone, *Society, the Sacred, and Scripture,* 63. Lightstone's larger discussion deals with the notion of Scripture in Judaism as a closed system (59–70), especially the social context in which Judaism defined its Scriptures (67–70). See also idem, "Formation of the Biblical Canon."

presumed collection be passed on generation after generation with no one specifying its contents—and only later have to be written down because the contents had been forgotten? No early traditions are appealed to by the rabbinic sages or the early church fathers when they listed the contents of the sacred collections in the second century C.E. and later. Again, if such a fixed collection had been established among the Jews of the first century C.E., one surely expects to find at least one early tradition that clearly enumerates the biblical books to which later authorities would appeal, but we look in vain for such a discussion or tradition in the Jewish writings before the second century C.E. or in any extant Christian writings.

In sum, evidence in support of a clearly defined biblical canon in the first two centuries C.E. is not substantial. The theory of an early Hebrew canon leaves many issues that are not easily resolved, namely, the Jewish debate about twenty-two or twenty-four books in its canon, the scope of the canon of Jesus, the influence of a larger Greek Bible in the early Christian community, and the relevance of the Dead Sea Scrolls.

CHAPTER EIGHT

The Scriptures of Jesus and Early Christianity

Some biblical scholars insist that Jesus and the apostles subscribed to a fixed biblical canon of the Hebrew Scriptures that was settled well before the first century C.E. Beckwith, for instance, argues that "the New Testament shows Jesus and his apostles endorsing a canon wider than that of the Samaritans and indistinguishable from that of the Pharisees, which now seems to have been the standard (if not, indeed, the only) Jewish canon."[1] It is strange, if not anachronistic, to say, however, that Jesus and or his apostles endorsed any biblical canon. It is not clear what evidence can be presented to substantiate such claims or even to show that such matters were of any concern in the time of Jesus or before. One can agree that most, if not all, of the literature that is now a part of the HB was recognized as Scripture by many Jews in Palestine in the time of Jesus, and perhaps even by Jesus, though we have no way to determine that since he never discusses the matter and does not cite or quote all of the books of the HB/ Protestant OT. The basic question, rather, is whether all of the books of the current HB were the *only* Scriptures acknowledged by Jesus or his contemporaries. The available evidence, which is minimal, indicates that there may well be more to this picture than the later collections suggest, and it raises doubts about whether only that literature was accepted as inspired Scripture. This chapter, then, will look at the Scriptures that Jesus used or cited in his teaching, the complex question of the NT use of the OT writings, and the sacred literature cited as Scripture in the early church fathers.

I. The Biblical Canon of Jesus

There is general agreement among scholars that quoting or citing a particular document does not mean that the writer considered what was

[1] Beckwith, "Canon of the Hebrew Bible," 102.

quoted or cited to be sacred and inspired. A familiar example of this is when Paul quotes Epimenides and the opening lines from Aratus's *Phaenomena* before the Areopagus on Mars Hill (Acts 17:28). No one seriously believes that these authors were part of Paul's (or Luke's) Scriptures so much as a reflection of his familiarity with classical writers and his employment of them to interest his hearers in Athens. On the other hand, it is seldom easy to distinguish one's high esteem for a source and one's views on its scriptural authority. If the source is cited in a scriptural or authoritative manner, introduced perhaps with the words *it is written* or *as the Scripture says* or some such designation, it then becomes easier to distinguish the writer's use, but that is not always the case. Beckwith speaks of the difficulty and inappropriateness of drawing conclusions about the scope of the biblical canon from simple references to other sources and lists five major methodological fallacies commonly followed by scholars:

1. failure to distinguish evidence that a book was known from evidence that a book was canonical
2. failure to distinguish disagreement about the canon between different parties from uncertainty about the canon within those parties
3. failure to distinguish between the adding of books to the canon and the removal of books from it
4. failure to distinguish between the canon which the community recognized and used, and the eccentric views of individuals about it
5. failure to make use of Jewish evidence about the canon transmitted through Christian hands, whether by denying its Jewish origins, or by ignoring the Christian medium through which it has come[2]

I am in agreement on each of these points and acknowledge the temptation of many scholars to say that what was quoted or used was necessarily also Scripture or canonical. Beckwith affirms that the NT writers did not quote any of the apocryphal or pseudepigraphal writings, as Scripture or canon, even though there is "an occasional correspondence of thought which suggests a knowledge of some of them."[3] There is far more to it, however, than an "occasional correspondence of thought," as we will presently see. The flip side of this argument is neither Jesus nor the NT writers cited or alluded to all of the OT Scriptures (does this mean that the OT books not cited are not "canonical"?). Conversely, there are many allusions or references to noncanonical writings in the NT (see Appendix A for a list). The presence or absence of references to or citations of the OT Scriptures and the apocryphal literature does not thereby include or exclude them

---

[2]Beckwith, *Old Testament Canon,* 7–8.
[3]Ibid., 387.

from consideration. What further complicates the issue is that we do not have a complete collection in our canonical Gospels of all that Jesus did or said (John acknowledges this in John 20:30); even if we include the so-called agrapha,[4] we possess only a brief outline of his ministry and teachings. Any conclusions drawn from this must be tempered by the limited sources that address the canonical issues.

It is essential that we examine carefully both the NT writings and the early church fathers on how each source is quoted, cited, or alluded to before drawing conclusions about the scope and identity of Jesus' sacred Scriptures. In other words, is the text in question referred to or cited as authoritative Scripture, as in the case of Jude 14 citing *1 En.* 1:9, or is it simply used as illustrative material, as in the case of Paul using well-known pagan sources: Epimenides and Aratus (Acts 17:28) and Epimenides (Titus 1:12)? Only after carefully examining each context can we draw responsible conclusions about how such ancient references were viewed by their users. For example, we must examine the OT texts that Jesus uses to determine if he was citing them in an authoritative manner. And even if he did cite them as sacred Scripture, that alone does not resolve the issue, for Jesus does not, for example, cite or quote from Judges, Proverbs, or Esther; should these books therefore be excluded from his canon? Also, can we not use the same argument to say that some of the apocryphal and pseudepigraphal documents should be included in the NT, since references to them are alluded to in the NT and sometimes even attributed to Jesus? Origen, for example, believed that Jesus used and recognized the Wisdom of Solomon (Luke 11:49; Matt 23:35).[5] Scholars have long acknowledged the significant parallels in word and thought with Paul's arguments in Rom 1:18–3:20 and the Wisdom of Solomon. Stuhlmacher also draws attention to the close parallels between the series of proverbs in Jesus' teachings in Matt 11:25–30 (see also Luke 10:21–22) to those found in Sir 24:19; 51:1, 23, 26).[6]

The book of Psalms was frequently cited by Jesus (e.g., Ps 22:1 in Mark 15:34),[7] or applied to him by his disciples (e.g., Ps 69:4–9 in John 2:17). In

---

[4]The agrapha are authentic or alleged sayings of Jesus recorded outside the canonical Gospels in other parts of the NT, in the early church fathers, in noncanonical writings, and in textual variations in the biblical manuscripts.

[5]These sources are supported in *Bibliotheke Ellenion Pateron kai Ekklesiastikon Syggrafeon* (Athens) 16:354–56.

[6]Stuhlmacher, "Significance of the Old Testament Apocrypha," 8–10, who also notes the close parallels in Jesus teaching in Matt 11:25–28 and the apocryphal 11Q Ps154 18.3–6.

[7]No one seriously doubts that Jesus made use of this psalm at his crucifixion. Because it appears to report Jesus' loss of faith, it is not the kind of text that the early church would have placed in the mouth of Jesus without some historical basis. For an interesting interpretation of the meaning of the passage see Dibelius, *From Tradition to Gospel,* 193–94, who claims that the reference to the first verse of Ps 22 was in fact a reference to the whole psalm.

fact, in the life and teaching of Jesus in the Gospels, the Psalms are cited more than any other book of the OT. But the issue is not whether most of the current Protestant OT canon was recognized as sacred Scripture by the earliest Christian community. The theology of the NT was without question firmly grounded in the theology (or theologies) of the OT, and the many references to OT texts believed to bolster the church's messianic claims about Jesus and to provide guidance for Christian conduct support this. That is beyond dispute. The issue is, which literature did Jesus actually appeal to or make use of?

Of the thirty-nine books in the OT (i.e., the twenty-four books of the HB), Jesus directly quotes or cites only twenty-three of them.[8] He alludes to or cites all five books of Moses (but prefers Deuteronomy); Isaiah, Jeremiah, Ezekiel, and Daniel (with Isaiah and Daniel taking priority); eight of the twelve Minor Prophets (not Obadiah, Nahum, Habakkuk, and Haggai); and Psalms, Proverbs, Job, and Chronicles (but omits Song of Songs, Ruth, Lamentations, Ecclesiastes, Esther, Ezra, and Nehemiah).

Evans compares the references that Jesus makes to the OT Scriptures with the quotation of biblical texts in noncanonical writings from Qumran.[9] In the Synoptic Gospels, Jesus quotes or alludes to Deuteronomy fifteen (or sixteen) times, Isaiah forty times, and Psalms thirteen times (Daniel and Zechariah are also frequently cited by Jesus). Evans's point is that Jesus' use of Scripture is similar to the practice of other Jews of his day. His frequent references to Isaiah, Deuteronomy, and Psalms are similar to references to this literature in the noncanonical writings at Qumran. Evans concludes that "Jesus' usage of scripture was pretty much in step with what we observe in similar circles, circles that took the Law very seriously, understood the Prophets eschatologically, and had some regard for the Writings, though this last division was very open-ended."[10] We cannot show that Jesus was particularly concerned about any form of a biblical text, but, as Evans observes, he "appealed to words, phrases, and sometimes whole passages—whatever their textual origin—in an ad hoc, experiential fashion."[11]

For our purposes here it is important to know whether Jesus (or the writers of the NT), also appealed to noncanonical literature in an authoritative manner. He did not write a book, of course, and the Scriptures that he appealed to were in the ad hoc context of his practice of ministry. He left no list of sacred books to follow, but his followers may hold a key to what Jesus himself taught. We do know that the early church was open to both noncanonical writings and those writings eventually placed in the Hebrew and Christian Bibles. Did the early Christians appeal to some of the apocryphal and pseudepigraphal literature in a scriptural manner? That seems to

---

[8] These are tabulated in France, *Jesus and the Old Testament*, 259–63.
[9] Evans, "Scriptures of Jesus," 185–86.
[10] Ibid., 186.
[11] Ibid., 195.

be beyond reasonable doubt, even though some scholars still deny it. Stuhlmacher is undoubtedly correct that "nowhere in the New Testament writings can any special interest in the canonical delimitation and fixing of the Holy Scriptures be detected."[12] In regard to Jesus, we simply do not know what his biblical canon was, though we can tell from the texts that he cited which books were more important to him: Psalms, Isaiah, and Deuteronomy.

II. The New Testament's Use of Scripture

We have much more information about which Scriptures the NT writers cited. The frequency with which they cited various OT books indicates which writings formed the core of the scriptural collections of the earliest Christians. NT citations of the Law and Prophets are considerable, while several OT books (Judges, Ruth, and Esther) are not mentioned in the NT, and others (Chronicles and Ecclesiastes) do not appear to have played much of a role in the formation and ministry of the early church.

The NT has numerous references to the Law and the Prophets (e.g., Matt 7:12; Rom 3:21; Luke 4:17; John 1:45; Acts 13:27; 28:23). The word *law,* however, sometimes refers to OT writings outside the Torah (e.g., Ps 82:6 in John 10:34, and a series of quotations from the Psalms in Rom 3:10–19 that Paul calls "law"). The Law and the Prophets were read regularly in the synagogue: "After the reading of the law and the prophets, the officials of the synagogue sent them [Paul and Barnabas] a message, saying, 'Brothers, if you have any word of exhortation for the people, give it'" (Acts 13:15).[13] On the other hand, the NT contains only one clear reference to a third division of the OT Scriptures: Luke 24:44. Jesus explains that everything written about him "in the law of Moses, the prophets, and the psalms must be fulfilled."

With numerous NT references, therefore, to a two-part collection of sacred writings (Law and Prophets) and only one text that mentions a book later placed in the Writings, we can only surmise that there was not at this time any widespread recognition of a tripartite biblical canon, but that all sacred literature was typically referred to as "the Law and the Prophets." This does not mean that the tripartite biblical canon was not emerging during the first century B.C.E. and first century C.E.; rather, references to the three parts in the Prologue to Sirach, 4QMMT, Philo, and Luke 24:44 may be looked upon as an early stage in its development. For most Jews in the first century, the two-part canon of Law and Prophets included all of their Scriptures, even though some of those writings were later assigned to the third part of the HB. Even Bishop Melito (ca. 170–180 C.E.) of Sardis, the ear-

[12] Stuhlmacher, "Significance of the Old Testament Apocrypha," 2.
[13] Leiman, *Canonization of the Hebrew Scripture,* 40.

liest Christian writer to identify the books that comprised the OT for the church, calls the collection "the Law and the Prophets," and he includes books now considered to be part of the Writings (Eusebius, *Hist. eccl.* 4.26.13). This cannot be unimportant at the time of his writing, especially in view of his consulting Jewish authorities in Palestine about the contents of the OT (see below §IV.A.1).

Some scholars argue that no apocryphal or pseudepigraphal books are quoted in the NT and that therefore they were not a part of the biblical canon of Jesus or the early Christians. Stuhlmacher, however, lists many parallels and allusions to this literature in the NT writings,[14] for example:

1. Mark 10:19 appears to make use of Sir 4:1 alongside the canonical Exod 20:12–16 and Deut 5:16–20.
2. Second Timothy 2:19–20 appears to cite Sir 17:26 alongside the canonical Num 16:5.
3. It is likely that Paul uses Wis 14:22–31 in Rom 1:24–32 and Wis 2:23–24 in Rom 5:12–21.[15]
4. In 1 Cor 2:9, Paul appears to cite as Scripture ("it is written") either the *Ascension of Isaiah* 11:34 or a lost *Elijah Apocalypse* derived from Isa 64:3.
5. Jude 14 expressly mentions Enoch who "prophesied" and refers explicitly to *1 En.* 1:9.
6. The author of 2 Pet 2:4 and 3:6 shows knowledge or awareness of *1 Enoch*.[16]
7. The author of Heb 1:3 makes clear reference to the Wis 7:25–26.
8. James 4:5 appears to cite an unknown Scripture.
9. The pseudepigraphal writings *Life of Adam and Eve* and *Apocalypse of Moses* have several parallels in the writings of the NT.[17]

---

[14] Stuhlmacher, "Significance of the Old Testament Apocrypha," 2–12. Harrington, "Old Testament Apocrypha," challenges the view that there was a lot of dependency on this literature in early Christianity, but he acknowledges the use of Tobit, 2 Maccabees, and Sirach. He questions how inclusive the early Christians were, but correctly recognizes a growing tendency in Judaism at the end of the first century C.E. toward a three-part Scripture canon and a growing acceptance of a wider and more inclusive OT canon among Christians in the fourth and fifth centuries.

[15] Barton, *People of the Book?* 25, 34, makes the observation that the canonicity of the Wisdom of Solomon does not appear to concern Paul, but only the theological arguments in it.

[16] Stuhlmacher, "Significance of the Old Testament Apocrypha," 2.

[17] *Life of Adam and Eve* and *Apocalypse of Moses* are the names given to somewhat different versions (respectively, Latin and Greek) of the same ancient book, which is also called *Life of Adam and Eve* (see *OTP* 2.249 for fuller explanation).

These and other parallels (see appendix A for a more complete list) do not necessarily reflect the NT writers' acknowledgement of noncanonical writings as Scripture or even their dependence upon them. The apparently parallel themes, words, and phrases may simply reflect a shared knowledge or perspective that was common among Jews in the first century C.E. Their cumulative effect shows the tenuous boundaries of sacred collections of Scriptures in the first century, even though the core of biblical literature—both then and later—was always the Law of Moses.

The Apostolic Fathers (ca. 90–150) are the closest writers chronologically to the NT writings, and they contain many parallels, quotations, and allusions to noncanonical literature.[18] The early church fathers do the same. Justin Martyr (ca. 160), in *Dial.* 120.5, appears to refer to the *Ascension of Isaiah* in an authoritative or scriptural manner and yet seems to base his argument on books accepted by the Jews. Justin refers to Genesis, Exodus, Leviticus, 1–2 Kings, 1–2 Samuel (possibly), Psalms, Proverbs, and Job. He names the prophets Isaiah, Jeremiah, Ezekiel, Daniel, the Minor Prophets, and 1 Esd 2:36–37 (see *Dial.* 72.1). He quotes (without referring to them by name) Numbers, Deuteronomy, and 2 Chronicles. These references to biblical literature do not imply Justin's biblical canon, since he is addressing specific situations in the *Dialogue with Trypho,* but it is reflective of the commonly accepted literature among Christians in the middle of the second century. Justin is surely on common ground in what he quotes, but he does not mention Ecclesiastes, Song of Songs, and Esther. This silence may reflect the doubts that existed about these books in the rabbinic community and possibly the Christian community in the second century.[19]

Several NT themes may be found in these two pseudepigraphal books: worship of God by angels (Heb 1:6; *Life of Adam and Eve* 13–14); God as light (Jas 1:17; *Life of Adam and Eve* 28:2; *Apocalypse of Moses* 36:3); tree of life (Rev 22:2; *Apocalypse of Moses* 9:3); Eve as the source of sin (2 Cor 11:3; 1 Tim 2:14; *Apocalypse of Moses* 14:2); death following the sin of Adam (Rom 5:12–21; *Apocalypse of Moses* 14:2); death as the separation of soul and body (2 Cor 5:1–5; *Apocalypse of Moses* 31); Satan as an angel of light (2 Cor 11:14; *Life of Adam and Eve* 9:1; *Apocalypse of Moses* 17:1); paradise located in the third heaven (2 Cor 12:2; *Apocalypse of Moses* 37:5); and covetousness as the root of all sin (Rom 7:7; *Apocalypse of Moses* 19:3). For additional NT themes drawn from apocryphal and pseudepigraphal literature, see Stuhlmacher, "Significance of the Old Testament Apocrypha."

[18]For example, Clement of Rome (ca. 90–95 C.E.) quotes Sir 2:11 (*1 Clem.* 60.1), Wis 12:10 (*1 Clem.* 7.5), and Wis 12:12 (*1 Clem.* 27.5, with allusions in 3.4 and 7.5), and he does not distinguish between the stories of biblical Esther and nonbiblical Judith (*1 Clem.* 55.4–6). The author of *2 Clement* (ca. 150 C.E.) has several quotations and references from unknown sources (*2 Clem.* 11.2–4, 7; 13.2). *Barnabas* has quotations from *1 En.* 89:56 (*Barn.* 16.5), *4 Ezra* 4:33 and 5:5 (*Barn.* 12.1). The *Didache* (ca. 70–90 C.E.), which itself was included in some fourth-century canonical lists (but excluded by Athanasius), makes use of Wis 12:5–7 and 15:11 (*Did.* 5.2) and Wis 1:14 (*Did.* 10.3), along with an unknown quotation (*Did.* 1.6). Lastly, Polycarp, *Phil.* 10.2 cites Tob 4:10 and 12:9.

[19]Grant, *Formation of the New Testament,* 38–41, makes this suggestion.

Grant proposes that later Christians may have avoided using most of the apocryphal and pseudepigraphal writings, unless they allegorized them, because they no longer addressed the special concerns of the Christian community.[20] Again, we must remember that the mere citing of canonical or noncanonical texts does not necessarily mean that they were at that time received as Scripture or as a fixed biblical canon. Each citation must be considered in context and on its own merits.

There is no question that the majority of references and quotations in Clement of Rome's *1 Clement* are from the OT, with a few references to some NT literature. This does not suggest, however, that the apocryphal and pseudepigraphal writings were only "fringe" literature that was not significantly used in early Christianity and had no impact on the early church's life, theology, and development. To the contrary, these books inspired homilies, meditations, and liturgical forms, and poets, dramatists, composers, and artists drew freely upon them for subject matter. And apparently even the discovery of the New World by Christopher Columbus came from the influence of 2 Esd 6:42. Columbus reasoned that if only one seventh of the earth's surface was covered with water, the distance between the coast of western Europe and the coast of eastern Asia could not be too far apart, and with a few good days of sailing, he could reach the eastern coast of Asia. Citing this text before Ferdinand and Isabella of Spain helped gain their financial support to begin his historic journey. This literature affected English literature, including Shakespeare and Henry Wadsworth Longfellow. In music, some of the words of the exalted hymn "Now Thank We All Our God" depends on Luther's translation of Sirach, and ideas included in "It Came upon the Midnight Clear" are derived from the OT Apocrypha (nothing is said in the NT writings about the exact time of Jesus' birth). Traces of the names of Susanna, Judas Maccabeus, and Alexander Balus are found in Handel's famous oratorios. Similarly, significant numbers of Renaissance paintings treat themes from the apocryphal writings.[21]

How passages from noncanonical books are cited in either the NT or in the second-century church fathers may be debated—that is, there is some question whether most of these documents were called Scripture—but Stuhlmacher argues that these references *at the least* demonstrate that at this time there was "no firm decision about the extent of the third part of the OT canon, the so-called Writings."[22] What all of this confirms, of course, is that the biblical canon of the early Christian community was still in a fluid state during the time of Jesus' ministry and later, when most of the canonical Christian literature was produced.

---

[20] Ibid., 41.

[21] The information in this paragraph comes from Metzger, "Introduction to Apocryphal/Deuterocanonical Books," viii–xi.

[22] Stuhlmacher, "Significance of the Old Testament Apocrypha," 3.

The additions to biblical books that appear in the LXX further demonstrate this point. For example, the various additions to Daniel—Song of the Three Young Men, Susanna, and Bel and the Dragon—became part of the LXX and were accepted by Clement of Alexandria, Irenaeus, Tertullian, and Origen. The additions to Esther, which are mentioned in Josephus, are referred to by Clement of Rome, Clement of Alexandria, and Origen. The Prayer of Manasseh is found in the Syriac *Didascalia* (third century C.E.), in *Apostolic Constitutions* 2.22.12–14 (second half of the fourth century C.E. in Syria), and in Codex Alexandrinus (fifth century C.E.).[23] According to Grant, examination of the Apostolic Fathers shows conclusively that they appealed to apocryphal and pseudepigraphal literature in much the same way that they appealed to the Scriptures of the HB. He adds: "We cannot deny, of course, that the Apostolic Fathers did make use of apocryphal documents. Indeed, the only explicit quotation in the *Shepherd of Hermas* comes from the lost *Book of Eldad and Modad* (*Herm. Vis.* 2–4; cf. Num 11:26)."[24]

III. The Inviolability of Scripture

With one exception (Rev 22:18–19), the notion of the inviolability of Scripture found in later discussions in the church is not present in the same way in the NT Scriptures themselves. The NT writers apparently do not view the OT Scriptures as inviolable in accordance with the command in Deut 4:2 and 12:32, *or* the admonition may more simply refer to that which is sacred and revealed from God. Several statements made by Jesus in the Sermon on the Mount (see Matt 5:21, 27, 31, 33, 38, 43) contrast his teachings with—and show their superiority to—those from the OT Scriptures, especially the Law of Moses (e.g., "you have heard that it was said . . . , but I say to you . . .").

Ellis objects to this suggestion,[25] but it seems to be the most natural way to understand the contrast with the Law in Matt 5. Although Jesus says that "not one letter, not one stroke of a letter, will pass from the law until all is accomplished" (5:18), this does not negate the clear contrast that Matthew says that Jesus made between the teaching of the Law of Moses and his own intensification of the Law. Jesus does not negate the Law in this passage, but radically intensifies its focus away from the externals to the internals. Nevertheless, his emphasis on loving unlovely persons in Matt 5:43–48 is a direct contrast with the OT focus on the punishment and hatred of one's enemies, seen in, for example, the imprecatory psalms (e.g., 69:21–29; 71:13; 109:6–25), and the instructions to kill the residents of the promised land (Deut 7:1–2; 13:12–15; 20:16–18).

---

[23] See Grant, *Formation of the New Testament,* 44.
[24] Ibid., 46.
[25] Ellis, *Old Testament in Early Christianity,* 128, 138.

How could Jesus have made such a series of comments in that context if the understanding of the Law was as inviolable as that later taught by the rabbinic Amoraim and the church fathers? Neusner says that when Jesus says, "You have heard that it was said . . . , but I say to you . . . ," he was saying "nothing less than the Torah, God himself speaking through his prophet Moses. Any observant Jew would immediately recognize that fact." Neusner goes on to say that Jesus is "not simply being assertive, in our modern parlance; he is claiming for himself the right to adapt, or modify, Divine Law." Neusner rightly asks of Jesus, "Who do you think you are—God?"[26]

The author of Hebrews, speaking to a Jewish-Christian community (probably Hellenistic), says that the old covenant made with Israel had fault and was surpassed by the new covenant initiated in the ministry of Jesus (Heb 8:7–12). And, if we are to suppose that the biblical writings had reached a final fixed form by the time of Jesus (i.e., canon 2), how could any Jew with this view of Scripture have taught that the Law, the very foundation of Judaism, was but a shadow of its "true form"? How could the author of Hebrews continue to show the superiority of the sacrifice of Jesus over the temple cultus and sacrifice made in the temple (Heb 10:1–14)?

What was the relationship of early Christianity to the canonical or the authoritative scriptural base that it had inherited from Judaism? How was that base understood? How could Paul, who was brought up in Judaism and became a "Pharisee of the Pharisees," have made the kinds of statements he did about the law and its abrogation because of what God did in Jesus (see Gal 2:21; 4:21–5:6; Rom 2:28–29)? Was Paul misunderstood, or did his opponents actually understand what he meant regarding the basis of their authority? Was James's concern over rumors about Paul's teaching about the law simply a case of misunderstanding Paul (Acts 21:18–25)? That the author of Acts felt obliged to mention this story undoubtedly reflects the many accusations against Paul's interpretation of the law. Further, if the NT writers were all that concerned with the text of the OT as the inviolable word of God (a view that we see in later Christianity and Judaism), then why does the author of Ephesians feel so free to change the text of Ps 68:18 from "receives" to "gives" in Eph 4:8?

A close parallel to this may be found in the contemporary Qumran community, where scribes did not hesitate to change the text to suit their needs: they made minor changes in spelling, deleted full sentences, and even wrote words into the text on top of other words when copying or transmitting the Torah. From this, Silver concludes that "the Law, the Prophets, and the Psalms carried a large and increasing measure of authority but, in these pre-rabbinic centuries, had not yet fully graduated to the rank of Scripture, in which it is crucial that every word and every letter be presented accurately and copied faithfully."[27]

---

[26] Quotations from Hutchinson, "What the Rabbi Taught Me," 28.

[27] Silver, *Story of Scripture,* 141.

In later centuries, this would have been most unusual and almost unthinkable, given the perceived holiness of the text. Irenaeus (ca. 130–200 C.E.), for instance, warns: "There shall be no light punishment [inflicted] upon him who either adds or subtracts anything from the Scripture, under that such a person must fall" (*Haer.* 3.30, *ANF*). Similarly, Tertullian (ca. 200 C.E.) writes: "If it is nowhere written, then let him [Hermogenes] fear the *woe* which impends on all who add to or take away from [the written word]" (*Against Hermogenes* 22). The same is true of rabbinic Judaism, which selected *maggihei sefarim* ("investigators of texts") to make sure that copies of Scriptures were free from error (*b. Ketubbot* 106a).

This view is not found at Qumran or in the NT because this later and more highly developed sense of Scripture and canon simply did not exist in the first century B.C.E. and first century C.E.[28] In other words, the way of looking at Scripture and canon in the first century C.E. (i.e., canon 1) is significantly different from the notion that developed later in both Judaism and early Christianity (i.e., canon 2).

IV. The Church Fathers and the Old Testament Canon

In exploring the early church's use of the OT and noncanonical writings, it is helpful to group the church fathers by geographical location, because their tendencies are linked to their locale. In this section we will examine some of the lists of Scriptures appealed to or listed by the church fathers in the second century and later.

A. EASTERN CHURCH FATHERS

Although the Eastern church fathers generally preferred the Jewish twenty-two-book or twenty-four-book biblical canon, they did not usually object to reading many of the deuterocanonical books in their churches.

1. Melito (ca. 180)

Because of some confusion in his region over the scope of the biblical canon, Bishop Melito of Sardis, upon the request of a fellow Christian, made a special trip to the East (Jerusalem?) in order to find out the number and names of the books in the Hebrew Scriptures. Melito describes his visit in a letter to Onesimus, as recorded by Eusebius:

---

[28] Levy's *Fixing God's Torah,* a useful description of the stabilizing of the text of the HB, includes a widely and carefully illustrated collection of primary texts from the talmudic literature. He also notes how unstable the text of the HB was prior to the production of the Masoretic Text.

> Melito to Onesimus his brother, greeting. Since you often desired, in your zeal for the true word, to have extracts from the Law and the Prophets concerning the Saviour, and concerning all our faith, and, moreover, since you wished to know the accurate facts about the ancient writings, how many they are in number, and what is their order, I have taken pains to do thus, for I know your zeal for the faith and interest in the word, and that in your struggle for eternal salvation you esteem these things more highly that all else in your love towards God. Accordingly when I came to the east and reached the place where these things were preached and done, and learnt accurately the books of the Old Testament, I set down the facts and sent them to you. These are their names: five books of Moses, Genesis, Exodus, Numbers, Leviticus, Deuteronomy, Joshua the son of Nun, Judges, Ruth, four books of Kingdoms, two books of Chronicles, the Psalms of David, the Proverbs of Solomon and his Wisdom, Ecclesiastes, the Songs of Songs, Job, the prophets Isaiah, Jeremiah, the Twelve in a single book, Daniel, Ezekiel, Ezra. From these I have made extracts and compiled them in six books. (*Hist. eccl.* 4.26.13–14, LCL)

Melito lists the books of the HB/OT (though not in their usual order),[29] omits Esther and Nehemiah but adds Wisdom of Solomon, and gives Greek titles for the books (though this may have come from Eusebius's editing). Even though he had to make such a trip (i.e., why did he not ask one of the many Jews at Sardis?),[30] his letter, at any rate, lets us know that others were confused about the canon at the end of the second century in the church and probably also in Judaism.

2. Origen (ca. 185–254)

Origen, who lived in two cities with large Jewish populations, Alexandria and Caesarea, reported the biblical canon of the Jews, as recorded by Eusebius:[31]

> Now while expounding the first Psalm he [Origen] set forth the catalogue [*katalogou*] of the sacred Scriptures of the Old Testament, writing somewhat as follows in these words: "But it should be known that there are twenty-two canonical books [*endiathēkous biblous*], according to the Hebrew tradition; the same as the number of the letters of their alphabet."
>
> Then further on he adds as follows: "These are the twenty-two books according to the Hebrews. . . ." (*Hist. eccl.* 6.25.1–2, LCL)

---

[29] Grant (*Formation of the New Testament,* 39) points out that variation in the sequence of even the books of the Law gives little confidence that the writings of David or Solomon or the Prophets could find a fixed sequence.

[30] See McDonald, "Anti-Judaism in the Early Church Fathers," for Melito's knowledge of the Jews in Sardis.

[31] Kalin ("Re-examining New Testament Canon History," 277) contends that Eusebius was not careful when he states that Origen is setting forth his own collection of Old Testament Scriptures. Rather, Kalin holds that Origen is offering a Jewish list, not his own views on what belonged in the Christian canon.

Origen did not, however, restrict himself to the biblical canon of the Jews or reject the use of deuterocanonical literature. In the list that Eusebius reports as being given in Origen's commentary on Ps 1, Origen includes in his canon the Epistle of Jeremiah (an apocryphal book allegedly written by the prophet Jeremiah to the captives at Babylon during the exile) and 1–2 Maccabees.[32] And in his *Homily on Numbers,* Origen recommends that a Christian's intellectual diet should begin with Esther, Judith, Tobit, and Wisdom of Solomon before proceeding to the Psalms and the Gospels. It was not good, he said, to set before the reader either Numbers or Leviticus![33]

When Julius Africanus, his contemporary, challenged him about the propriety of appealing to Susanna (one of the Septuagint additions to the book of Daniel), Origen replied that many things in the Greek Bible were not in the Hebrew Bible, and the church could not be expected to give them all up![34]

3. Athanasius (ca. 367)

Athanasius excluded some writings of the Apocrypha (Wisdom of Solomon, Sirach, Esther, Judith, Tobit, *Didache,* and *Shepherd of Hermas*), declaring that they were not canonical but nevertheless valuable for instructing new converts ("those who newly join us") in piety. On the other hand, he included in his list of canonical scriptures the Epistle of Jeremiah and Baruch:

> "Forasmuch as some have taken in hand," to reduce into order for themselves the books termed apocryphal, and to mix them up with the divinely inspired Scripture, concerning which we have been fully persuaded, as they who from the beginning were eyewitnesses and ministers of the Word, delivered to the fathers; it seemed good to me also, having been urged thereto by true brethren, and having learned from the beginning, to set before you the books included in the Canon, and handed down, and accredited as Divine; to the end that any one who has fallen into error may condemn those who have led him astray; and that he who has continued stedfast in purity may again rejoice, having these things brought to his remembrance.
>
> There are, then, of the Old Testament, twenty-two books in number; for, as I have heard, it is handed down that this is the number of the letters among the Hebrews; their respective order and names being as follows. The first is Genesis, then Exodus, then Leviticus, after that Numbers, and then Deuteronomy. Following these there is Joshua, the son of Nun, then Judges, then Ruth. And

---

[32] Aland, *Problem of the New Testament Canon,* 6–7.

[33] I owe this reference to Roberts, "Christian Book and the Greek Papyri," 164–65, who also shows how the Jews restricted the reading of Genesis and certain passages in Ezekiel and Song of Songs to the mature reader.

[34] I owe this reference to F. F. Bruce, *Canon of Scripture,* 76–77, who claims that Origen practiced a double standard by including apocryphal books in the canon because the Jews included them. Kalin ("Re-examining New Testament Canon History," 277–78.) rightly notes, however, that *Letter to Africanus* 13 states that the churches use Tobit and Judith even though the Jews do not.

> again, after these four books of Kings [i.e., 1–2 Samuel and 1–2 Kings], the first and second being reckoned as one book, and so likewise the third and fourth as one book. And again, the first and second of the Chronicles are reckoned as one book. Again Ezra, the first and second [Nehemiah] are similarly one book. After these there is the book of Psalms, then the Proverbs, next Ecclesiastes, and the Song of Songs. Job follows, then the Prophets, the twelve being reckoned as one book. Then Isaiah, one book, then Jeremiah with Baruch, Lamentations, and the epistle, one book; afterwards, Ezekiel and Daniel, each one book. Thus far constitutes the Old Testament. (*Ep. fest.* 39.3–4, *NPNF*)

4. Synopsis scripturae sacrae *(350–370)*

Similar to Athanasius is the anonymous *Synopsis scripturae sacrae,* which was reproduced in the works of Athanasius, but probably not written by him. The author lists in accordance with the Hebrew alphabet a twenty-two-book canon that separates Judges and Ruth and omits Esther. Esther is further specifically identified as "not canonical" along with the Wisdom of Solomon, Sirach, Judith, and Tobit.

5. Cyril of Jerusalem (ca. 350)

Like Origen and Athanasius, Cyril has a twenty-two-book canon in which he refers to the LXX Scriptures and the legend of their origin found in the *Letter of Aristeas* ("which were translated by the seventy-two interpreters"). He adds to Jeremiah both Baruch and the Letter of Jeremiah.

6. Gregory of Nazianzus (ca. 370)

In a list of canonical books that conforms to the twenty-two-letter Hebrew alphabet, Gregory of Nazianzus omits Esther. As a result, he divides Judges and Ruth in order to keep the same number of books.

7. Bryennios Canon

A strange list of twenty-seven canonical Old Testament books occurs in a Greek manuscript copied in 1056 and discovered in 1875. Known as the Bryennios Canon, it dates between the late second century C.E. and the fifth century C.E. (probably mid-fourth century, on the basis of its similarity to Epiphanius's list; see next section). Little is known of its background, but because it closely matches the contents (though not the order) of books in the second-century Hebrew Bible, some scholars believe that it has a Jewish origin. Oddly, the names in the list are in both Aramaic and Greek. Additionally, the Bryennios Canon provides a strange sequence of books:[35]

---

[35]This list is reproduced from Leiman, *Canonization of the Hebrew Scripture,* 43, who follows Audet, "Hebrew-Aramaic List of Books," 136. See also F. F. Bruce, *Canon of Scripture,* 71–72; and Beckwith, *Old Testament Canon,* 188–90.

Genesis	1–2 Chronicles
Exodus	Proverbs
Leviticus	Ecclesiastes
Joshua	Song of Songs
Deuteronomy	Jeremiah
Numbers	the Twelve
Ruth	Isaiah
Job	Ezekiel
Judges	Daniel
Psalms	1–2 Esdras (i.e., Ezra-Nehemiah)
1–2 Samuel	Esther
1–2 Kings	

8. Epiphanius (ca. 315–403)

Bishop Epiphanius of Salamis produced in his *On Weights and Measures* 23 a twenty-two-book catalogue of canonical writings that is similar to the list in the Bryennios Canon, although Epiphanius placed them in a more familiar order.[36] His list also parallels the current Protestant OT canon, and it depends on the twenty-two-letter Hebrew alphabet ("so twenty-two books are completed according to the number of the twenty-two letters of the Hebrews"). Elsewhere, Epiphanius clearly favors the Wisdom of Solomon and Sirach, which he calls "helpful and useful but are not included in the number of the recognized" (*Pan.* 8.6.1).[37]

B. WESTERN CHURCH FATHERS

Interest in the deuterocanonical writings was much more substantial in the Western churches, who acknowledged fifteen of the apocryphal writings as Scripture and added them to their biblical canon.

1. Hilary of Poitiers (ca. 315–367)

Hilary of Poitiers appears to follow Origen's example, but adds two extra books to his canon, namely, Tobit and Judith, in order to make a twenty-four-book biblical canon, which he wrongly believed followed the number of letters in the Hebrew alphabet! He, too, along with Cyprian and Ambrose, included the Epistle of Jeremiah with Jeremiah and Lamentations and cited all of them as having been written by Jeremiah.

---

[36] See Leiman, *Canonization of the Hebrew Scriptures,* 161 n. 28.

[37] Quoted from Leiman, ibid., 44–45, who also points out that in a third list Epiphanius included Baruch and the Epistle of Jeremiah. See n. 235 on Leiman, 159.

2. Jerome (342–420)

Jerome's canon of OT Scriptures follows the Hebrew biblical canon (represented by *b. Bava Batra* 14b–15a). Bruce notes that Jerome has three categories of writings: canonical, edifying but not canonical, and apocryphal.[38] The last category of books was to be avoided altogether. In the first category, Jerome put the Jewish biblical canon, consisting of twenty-four books, which he related to the twenty-four elders of Revelation, and he numbered them in the three Hebrew categories: Law (5), Prophets (8), and Writings (11).[39] Following his list, Jerome concludes:

> Whatever falls outside these must be set apart among the Apocrypha. Therefore Wisdom, which is commonly entitled Solomon's, with the book of Jesus the son of Sirach, Judith, Tobias, and the *Shepherd* are not in the canon. I have found the first book of Maccabees in Hebrew; the second is in Greek, as may be proved from the language itself. (*Prologue to Daniel,* Bruce, *Canon of Scripture,* 90)

Jerome omits the book of Esther from the canonical collection but includes it, along with Wisdom of Solomon, Sirach, Judith, Tobit, *Didache,* and *Shepherd of Hermas,* in the edifying category that could be read in the churches. Jerome cited Sirach over eighty times in the Greek translation, but he calls it "Proverbs" (*meshalim*), a title seen elsewhere in a commentary on the mishnaic tractate *Sanhedrin* found in the Cairo Genizah. Jerome refused to make a new Latin translation of Sirach, showing that he did not accept it as Scripture, but he nevertheless saw its value for Christian faith[40]

3. Augustine (354–430)

The most influential Western church father was unquestionably Bishop Augustine of Hippo in North Africa, who lists some forty-four books in his OT biblical canon. He identifies each of the twelve Minor Prophets, and also includes Wisdom of Solomon, Sirach, Tobit, Esther, Judith, 1–2 Maccabees,[41] the additions to the books of Daniel and Esther, Baruch, and the Epistle of Jeremiah.

---

[38] F. F. Bruce, *Canon of Scripture,* 90.

[39] Jerome placed Daniel in the Writings.

[40] Gilbert, "Book of Ben Sira," 85–87.

[41] Augustine was not the first Christian to appreciate the stories of 1–2 Maccabees. The story of the Maccabean brothers and their mother (2 Macc 7) was especially inspiring to Christians who were being persecuted because of their faith, as in the case of Cyprian and other Christians who suffered during the Decian persecution. Rutgers shows how the Maccabean literature endeared itself to persecuted Christians in his "Importance of Scripture."

4. Rufinus (ca. 345–410)

Rufinus tabulated a list of canonical books (*On the Creed,* 38), similar to that of Jerome, but adds to the "ecclesiastical" collection: Wisdom of Solomon, Sirach, Tobit, Judith, and 1–2 Maccabees.[42]

C. SUMMARY

From the beginning of the church, the LXX was the Christians' Bible, and the Jews never formally fixed what went into it.[43] Put another way, Stendebach writes: "the church Fathers did not treat as canonical what they found in the Septuagint; what they treated as canonical came into the Septuagint."[44] The contents of the LXX have always been elusive, but it is likely that the Greek Bible used by the Christians included writings that were a part of this collection from the earliest Christian community, before their separation from Judaism in the first century C.E. There is no evidence that their OT Scripture collection got bigger with time. Again, the LXX books were inherited from Judaism in Israel before the Christian community separated from Judaism, probably just prior to the destruction of Jerusalem in the first century (66 C.E.) , but no later than 132–135 C.E. following the Bar Kokhba rebellion.

Usually, the Eastern church fathers opted for the shorter OT canon, generally following either the twenty-two-book or twenty-four-book biblical canon that they believed were the sacred books of the Jews. The contents of these lists vary in the fringe areas (Baruch, Epistle of Jeremiah, and Esther especially), but they all have much in common. Generally speaking, the Western church followed the lead of Augustine and included many of the apocryphal writings. What is not clear from this examination of the church fathers is their preference for the apocryphal books alongside their simultaneous rejection of the pseudepigraphal writings.[45]

V. AUTHORITY OF THE OLD TESTAMENT IN EARLY CHRISTIANITY

Although acknowledgment of the OT literature as authoritative Scriptures in the early church was never seriously doubted before the time of Marcion, or even afterward, there is little evidence from the NT writers that they were interested in the original *contextual* message of the OT itself.

[42] F. F. Bruce, *Canon of Scripture,* 90–91.

[43] Stuhlmacher, "Significance of the Old Testament Apocrypha, " 3.

[44] Stendebach, "Old Testament Canon," 34, quoting H. Haag.

[45] Lewis examines the question why both the Greek and Latin church fathers rejected the Pseudepigrapha, but he does not find a suitable reason; see "Problems of Inclusion," 182.

Rather, as is clear from an examination of the NT references to the OT Scriptures, the early Christians were far more interested in finding prophecies of the life, death, and resurrection of Jesus in the Jewish Scriptures than in doing exegesis of scriptural texts for the purpose of discovering the meaning of these texts.[46] This suggests that the *primary* authority of the early church was not so much the message of the OT, but rather the proclaimed words and deeds of Jesus that the OT Scriptures, it was believed, foretold.[47] Greer claims that "while the Hebrew Scriptures were the Bible of the church, their authority was secondary to that of the Christian preaching."[48] He concludes that the Christian people as a whole "were less a 'people of the book' than the Jews, for the Christian revelation was located in Christ and only secondarily in the Scripture that bore witness to him."[49] This claim finds support in the fact that most Scripture references in the early church fathers are of the NT writings and not the OT writings! There are exceptions, of course (*1 Clement*), but until the fourth century, they are few. Barton brings this tension into full relief: "We see here a paradox. The early Church cited the Old Testament as 'Scripture,' but to begin with tended to possess it only in a fragmentary form. The New Testament, on the other hand, was widely available and was used much more heavily, but it was not yet cited as 'Scripture.' "[50] How could writings that were only beginning to be considered canonical so outstrip the earliest Scriptures of the church, namely, the writings of the OT?

The Christians believed that the whole story of God's plans and purposes for Israel developed in the OT Scriptures had reached its completion in the life and work of Jesus.[51] The NT writers saw continuity in what they were describing, presenting, or advocating with the ancient Jewish Scriptures. They fully accepted them as the authoritative word of God, but they also took many liberties in citing the OT, sometimes even altering the passages they cited (e.g., Ps 94:11 in 1 Cor 3:19–20; Ps 68:18 in Eph 4:8; and Ps 8:4–6 in Heb 2:6–8). A study of the NT use of the OT clearly shows that the driving force behind the NT writers was not an exacting interpretation or exegesis of the OT, but rather the word of and about the risen Lord.[52] Paul,

---

[46] Von Campenhausen, *Formation of the Christian Bible,* 21–102, especially 82–102.

[47] Williams, *Authority in the Apostolic Age,* 32–37.

[48] Kugel and Greer, *Early Biblical Interpretation,* 114. Greer claims that the Hebrew Scriptures played less of a role in the early Christian community than has been previously supposed. He supports this claim with many examples from the early church fathers (126–54). The church attempted to maintain both continuity and discontinuity with its Jewish heritage (113–17).

[49] Ibid., 202.

[50] Barton, *Holy Writings,* 65, citing Franz Stuhlhofer.

[51] Shires, *Finding the Old Testament,* 31–35.

[52] Numerous examples of this are listed in ibid., 183–84, a still useful work on this topic.

for example, in 2 Cor 3:12–18 set forth a commonly held view in the early church that the OT could be understood only through Jesus the Christ. Barr observes that the OT had the status of the word of God in the early church, but this "did not alter the fact that, for the men of the NT, the OT, though authoritative, was no longer the communicator of salvation. . . . Only the preaching of Jesus Christ as crucified and risen communicated salvation in the Christian sense."[53]

Barr adds that Jesus' teachings likewise do not result from an exegesis of OT texts; rather, Jesus uses the OT to support *his* claims, not so much to elucidate meanings of the OT texts.[54] Very seldom, Barr notes, do the NT writers interpret whole passages (e.g., Gen 1–3), mainly because the NT writers never set out to interpret the OT itself, but rather the new substance of the gospel.[55]

Christian use of the OT was highly selective and designed especially to clarify or confirm Christian beliefs. According to Shires, the real moving force of the NT, then, is not the OT but rather the experiences of Jesus.[56] The earliest Christian community most commonly appealed to the OT as a predictive book. The OT raised other difficulties for the Christian faith in the first and second centuries, primarily in conjunction with Marcion and Justin on issues related to keeping the law (see chapter 10 §I and chapter 11§I).

The above notwithstanding, there can be no question that the OT Scriptures were viewed by the earliest church as an authoritative source for Christian faith and life, even though the boundaries of the canon had not yet been fully decided. Almost every point of faith, order, and morals in *1 Clement* is driven home with the aid of OT citations or quotations. For Polycarp, the Prophets were inseparable from the authority of Jesus and the apostles: "So then 'let us serve him with fear and all reverence,' as he himself commanded us, and as did the Apostles, who brought us the Gospel, and the Prophets who foretold the coming of our Lord" (Pol. *Phil.* 6.3, LCL.). Tertullian also placed the NT writings on the same plane as the OT: "One Lord God does she [the church] acknowledge, the Creator of the universe, and Christ Jesus (born) of the Virgin Mary, the Son of God the Creator; and the Resurrection of the flesh; the law and the prophets she unites in one volume with the writings of evangelists and apostles, from which she drinks in her faith" (*Praescr.* 36, *ANF*).

In summary, the early church received from its Jewish heritage the notion of sacred Scriptures (though not a *closed* canon) that it believed

---

[53] Barr, *Holy Writings,* 14.

[54] Ibid., 68.

[55] Ibid., 68–70.

[56] Shires, *Finding the Old Testament,* 38–39. In his discussion of the OT predictions of Christ (43–51), Shires observes that Christians made the OT "their own special possession whose meaning relates directly to their situation" (51).

disclosed the revelation of God and predicted the Christ event. Even though this collection of Scriptures was used in the Christian communities to argue for church polity (e.g., Rom 14:10–13; 1 Cor 6:12–16; 9:7–10; 14:20–22; 1 Tim 5:17–18); mission (Rom 10:14–21), and many other functions relevant to the life of the early Christian community, the most important function of those Scriptures for the early church appears to have been their predictive witness to the Christ event (e.g., Luke 24:44; John 5:39; 2 Tim 3:15).

VI. Church Council Decisions

Some people think that church councils deliberated and determined what books should be included in the biblical canon, but a more accurate view is that the church councils of the fourth and fifth centuries acknowledged those books that had already obtained prominence from widespread usage among the various Christian churches in their areas. Church council decisions reflect what the communities *recognized,* and they subsequently authorized this recognition for the church. If any decisions were made by church councils in such matters, it was only in regard to books *on the fringe* of collections that had already obtained widespread recognition in the majority of churches. These decisions came only at the end of a long process of recognition in the churches, and they were not unilateral decisions issued from the top of an organization. In other words, *church councils did not create biblical canons,* but rather reflected the state of affairs in such matters in their geographical location. The Eastern churches appear to have been more conservative in such matters than those in the West.

Several important early church councils issued statements regarding the biblical canon. The Council of Laodicea (ca. 363) decided which psalms could be used in the churches (canon 59) and listed the books of the OT canon (canon 60). Since this list follows the canon of Athanasius's *Thirty-ninth Festal Letter* (except that Ruth is combined with Judges and Esther immediately follows), Bruce cautions that it may be corrupt.[57]

The Council of Hippo (393 C.E.) set forth a biblical canon similar to the one produced by Augustine. Although the deliberations of this council are now lost, they were summarized in the proceedings of the Third Council of Carthage (397 C.E.). This was apparently the first council to make a decision or, as Bruce puts it, a "formal pronouncement" on the biblical canon.[58]

---

[57] F. F. Bruce, *Canon of Scripture,* 80.
[58] Ibid., 97.

An important church council at the end of the process for the Roman Catholic Church is the Council of Trent, which, in its fourth session on April 8, 1546, set forth its decision regarding the limits of the OT canon. It included the books of Tobit, Judith, Wisdom of Solomon, Sirach, and 1–2 Maccabees and called them deuterocanonical (secondary) writings:

> The holy, ecumenical and general Council . . . , following . . . the examples of the orthodox Fathers, . . . receives and venerates with a feeling of piety and reverence all the books of the Old and New Testaments, since one God is the author of both; also the traditions, whether relating to faith or to morals, as having been dictated either orally by Christ or by the Holy Ghost, and preserved in the Catholic Church in unbroken succession. . . . If anyone does not accept as sacred and canonical the aforesaid books in their entirety and with all their parts, as they have been accustomed to be read in the Catholic Church . . . let him be anathema. (Stendebach, "Old Testament Canon," 35–36)[59]

This decision was reaffirmed by the First Vatican Council (1869–70).

The Reformed churches set forth in the 1559 Gallican Confession (arts. 3–4) and the 1561 Belgic Confession (arts. 4–5) a canon that excluded the apocryphal books. In England, the 1562/1571 Thirty-Nine Articles of the Church of England (art. 6) affirmed the use of the apocryphal books, but added that they were not to be used for the establishment of any doctrine: "And the other books (as Hierome [i.e., Jerome] saith) the Church doth read for example of life and instruction of manners, but yet doth it not apply them to establish any doctrine."[60]

As late as 1950 the Greek church authorized as its OT canon the entire Apocrypha, including 2 Esdras and 3 Maccabees (4 Maccabees was placed in an appendix). The 1956 Russian Bible has the same OT contents as the Greek Bible, but with 2 Esdras and 4 Maccabees omitted.[61]

The popularity of the Jewish biblical canon, that is, the twenty-four-book Hebrew Bible collection that obtained canonical status among early Christians, is undeniable. It is instructive, however, that all of the Christian lists of OT Scriptures in the fourth to sixth centuries differ slightly from the Jewish biblical canon.[62] And even when they attempt to reproduce the Jewish biblical canon, most of these lists still omit the book of Esther and add the Epistle of Jeremiah and Baruch.

---

[59] Stendebach, "Old Testament Canon," 36, observes that the legitimacy of the Council of Trent's declaration on canon is confirmed by the New Testament's use of the apocryphal literature; for example, the allusion to Sir 5:11 in Jas 1:19; the allusion to Wis 3:5–7 in 1 Pet 1:6–7; the parallel of or allusion to 2 Macc 7:9, 11, 14, 23, 29, 36 in Heb 11:35; the parallel of Wis 7:26 with Heb 1:3 and Col 1:15; and the parallel of Wis 13:1–9 with Rom 1:18–21.

[60] Chadwick, "Significance of the Deuterocanonical Writings," 117.

[61] Aland, *Problem of the New Testament Canon,* 5.

[62] Aland, ibid., 4–6, claims that no early church list exactly parallels the Jewish biblical canon.

VII. The Codices and the Biblical Canon

One of the peculiarities of the early Christian community is its preference by not much later than 100 C.E. for the codex, the ancient predecessor of the modern book format, over the use of the scroll.[63] The standard book in the ancient world was written and copied on rolls or scrolls, and this practice continued until the fourth century, when the codex began to overtake the scroll. There are many possible reasons for this change, but Roberts and Skeat conclude that none of the most obvious reasons answer the question why the Christians, more than anyone else, preferred the codex.[64] The practice probably began in Jerusalem when Christians wanted another means of transmitting their sacred literature than the one used by Jews (scrolls). The codex was developed by the Romans and used for nonliterary texts such as business documents, personal notes, memos, and billings; and when Paul began his ministry, he often wrote letters to churches in books (codices) made of papyrus sheets or parchments.[65] The standard format of transmitting the Scriptures of the HB was the scroll, generally made of animal skins. The Babylonian Talmud reports a long-standing tradition in the Jewish community:

> Books may not be thrown about from one place to another, nor may they be treated disrespectfully. A man is required to have a scroll of Torah written with good ink, a good quill, by competent scribes, on good sheets of parchment made out of hides of deer. He is then to wrap it in beautiful silks, in keeping with "this my god, I will glorify him" (Exod. 15:2). (*b. Soferim* 3, Bialik and Ravnitzky, *Book of Legends,* 448)

---

[63] The most up-to-date and informative standard text on this subject is Gamble, *Books and Readers in the Early Church*.

[64] Reasons for using the codex—economy, compactness, comprehensiveness, convenience of use, ease of reference—had to compete with the later medieval preference for scrolls and the effect of conservatism, that is, the tendency of scribes to continue using what they have always used; see Roberts and Skeat, *Birth of the Codex,* 45–61. Roberts and Skeat (57–61) combine this explanation with another Christian phenomenon: the use of *nomina sacra*. This activity in the Christian church developed at the same time as the outburst of activity among Jewish scholars in Israel that led to the standardization of the HB. The use of *nomina sacra* and the codex helped distinguish Christian writing from both Jewish and pagan writings. Gamble, however, challenges this notion of the distinctiveness of Christian writings and instead focuses on the portability of Christian writings and their being not considered Scripture initially, but rather handbooks for use in Christian worship and teaching; see *Books and Readers in the Early Church,* 42–81.

[65] In 2 Tim 4:13 Paul asks for the "books" (Gk. *ta biblia*) and "the parchments" (Gk. *tas membranas,* lit., "animal skins"). Gamble notes that *membranas* refers to a parchment codex, since had a scroll been intended, the more familiar term, *diphthera,* would have been used; see *Books and Readers in the Early Church,* 50. Parchment was preferred when available because it was higher quality material than papyrus sheets and was very durable if properly cared for.

Jews were not unaware of the codex and left room for it to be used in the transmission of sacred texts,[66] but they chose to use animal skins and the traditional scroll.

Gamble observes how unusual it was for the early Christians to adopt the use of the codex for their collection of Scriptures "since it was not recognized in antiquity as a proper book. It was regarded as a mere notebook, and its associations were strictly private and utilitarian." He goes on to add that the humble beginnings of the codex can be traced to the Latin term *caudex* ("a block of wood)."[67] The use of the codex cannot be accounted for on only economic reasons; even though the papyrus codex was about 25 percent less costly than the scroll, its larger margins offset the cost savings. While economy certainly dictated the production of ordinary writings, as may be seen in the many examples of cramped letters, unusually narrow margins, or frequent use of palimpsests,[68] we have no evidence that such economic measures were common or frequent in the early church when they transmitted their authoritative literature. Convenience of use and transportability made the codex valuable for a traveling missionary such as Paul.

The Roman poet Martial (ca. 80 C.E.) advises his readers to make use of the codex if they wanted to carry his poems on their journeys: "Those that parchment confines in small pages" (*Epigram* 1.2, LCL). Martial also indicates that even the great poets' works were transported in this fashion: Homer, Vergil, Cicero, Livy, and Ovid.[69] Gamble also notes that the codex was more comprehensive than the scroll and that one codex was able to hold the contents of several scrolls. What soon became apparent was the convenience of easy access and rapid referencing of material in teaching or debates with opponents. Because Paul made use of the codex, no doubt for convenience and portability, and because his writings were among the earliest to be acknowledged as Scripture in many churches (2 Pet 3:15–16), it is likely that he is the originator of the use of the codex in early Christianity. When his letters were collected at the end of the first century, it is likely that the use of the codex made it possible to circulate his writings in one volume. Gamble concludes that, although the codex may have been used in primitive Christianity for lists of *testimonia* (sayings of Jesus), "it was the religious authority of Paul's collected letters that set the standard for the transcription of subsequent Christian litera-

---

[66] "There are three kinds of writing-tablet: that of papyrus, which is susceptible to *midras*-uncleanness; that which has a receptacle for wax, which is susceptible to corpse-uncleanness; and that which is polished, which is not susceptible to any uncleanness" (*m. Kelim* 24:7, Danby, *Mishnah,* 639).

[67] Gamble, *Books and Readers in the Early Church,* 49–50.

[68] A palimpsest manuscript was one which was scraped and washed to remove the original writing so it could be reused. The term comes from Greek *palin* ("again") and *psaō* ("to scrape"). For a discussion of this practice, see ibid., 54–55.

[69] Ibid., 52, 269 n. 40.

ture in codices."[70] The codex became a standard among the Christians for practical reasons, namely, because "they were practical books for everyday use: the handbooks, as it were, of the Christian community."[71]

The initial stages of copying the NT writings, however, are often quite poor in quality because, as Gamble explains, the transcribers were not aware that they were transcribing sacred Scripture and as a result they were less careful in their work.[72] Evidence for this lack of awareness is the use of *nomina sacra* ("sacred names"), the practice of abbreviating divine names or sacred words. Because these abbreviations were not used in literary texts, but were common in secular documentary texts, they point to low-quality texts that were not generally valued as sacred.[73]

Roberts and Skeat claim that not until the fourth century were all the books of the OT and NT combined into a single codex.[74] Earlier in the second century, the most that could be circulated together in one codex was the four-gospel canon (some 220 pages or 110 leaves). By the fourth century, then, those writings that circulated in the same codex become very significant in the canonical discussions. With this in mind, three important codices from the fourth century, the century especially of canonical standardization of the Scriptures in the Christian church, deserve our attention: (1) Codex Sinaiticus (4th century) includes Tobit, Judith, Wisdom of Solomon, Sirach, 1 Maccabees, and 4 Maccabees; (2) Codex Vaticanus (fourth century) includes Baruch, Epistle of Jeremiah, Wisdom of Solomon, Sirach, Judith, and Tobit; (3) Codex Alexandrinus (fifth century) includes Baruch, Epistle of Jeremiah, Tobit, Judith, 1–4 Maccabees, Wisdom of Solomon, Sirach, and Psalms of Solomon; and (4) Codex Ephraemi Syri Rescriptus (fifth century) contains Sirach (including the Prologue) and Wisdom of Solomon.[75]

Based on the contents of codices, Roberts makes a cogent case for the late development of a fixed biblical canon in the church (after the fourth century). For example, many smaller pocket editions of the Scriptures on

---

[70] Ibid., 65; cf. 57–59.

[71] Ibid., 66.

[72] Ibid., 74–75.

[73] Ibid., 74–78. For fuller discussion of this phenomenon, see Tuckett, "Nomina Sacra"; Traube, *Nomina Sacra;* Hurtado, "Origins of the *Nomina Sacra*"; Paap, *Nomina Sacra in the Greek Papyri;* Metzger, *Text of the New Testament,* 13–14; and Roberts, *Manuscript, Society, and Belief,* 26–48. Several Greek manuscripts make extensive use of *nomina sacra*: 𝔓[45] (early third century), 𝔓[46] (late second century), and Codex Vaticanus (mid-fourth century).

[74] Roberts and Skeat, *Birth of the Codex,* 62–66.

[75] Aland (*Problem of the New Testament Canon,* 8) rightly observes that these additional books are included in the various codices "right among the other books of the OT," without any distinction being made. For the sequence of books in these fourth-century codices, see appendix C. For more information on these and other Septuagint manuscripts, see Swete, *Introduction to the Old Testament in Greek,* 122–70, 201–2.

vellum or papyrus, evidently designed as luxury books to attract pious women to the church, contain only apocryphal writings.[76] In addition, several late codices combine biblical books in strange groupings (e.g., Matthew and Acts), and some even combine canonical and noncanonical books (e.g., Song of Songs and *Apology of Aristides; Acta Pauli* in Greek and Song of Songs; and Lamentations in Coptic and Sirach in Greek and Coptic).[77] What does this say about the formation of the OT canon in the church before the fourth century? It suggests that the Christian communities were not yet clear on the contents of their biblical canon, and it also calls into question whether such discussions were in vogue in the various Christian communities before the fourth century. If, as many argue, the lack of discussion of such matters was because the churches had already decided which books went into their biblical canon, it is indeed strange to see so many references to the noncanonical writings in early Christianity. Instead of assuming that the early Christians paid little attention to what had been settled earlier, it is better to conclude that no such final decisions had been made in the church at this point.

VIII. Unsettled Questions

Our search for understanding the complex issues surrounding the origins and development of the HB and OT canon leaves several important questions unresolved.

A. CONCERN FOR AN OLD TESTAMENT CANON

The earliest Christian church was not canon conscious. The NT has no hint of a discussion of a closed biblical canon. Is it possible, therefore, that the canon of Scriptures that Jesus received and passed on to his disciples was lost in the church? That appears to be as unthinkable as it is unlikely. In the second century, Melito became the first church father to investigate which books comprise the OT Scriptures of the church, but our only source for this information is the fourth-century Eusebius, who *was* keenly interested in this question.

Despite the obviously large Jewish population at Sardis with whom the Christians had the opportunity to engage and Melito's evident preference for the Jewish biblical canon, the real issue is, why is Melito concerned in the first place with the notion of a biblical canon? It cannot be denied that the church fathers were considerably influenced by the Jewish canon of Scriptures, and because the Jews were beginning to define their Scriptures

[76] C. Roberts, "Christian Book and the Greek Papyri," 165.
[77] Ibid., 166.

in the second century C.E., it may be that such matters became a part of the discussion in his vicinity. In any case, this is the earliest example of a Christian community having interest in the subject of a biblical canon. The examples shown above demonstrate Jewish interest in identifying their canon with the number of letters in the Hebrew alphabet, but this influence—even in the cases of Jerome and Cyril of Jerusalem, who opted more for the Jewish biblical canon than did almost any other church fathers—was never able to overthrow the practice of the church.[78]

Further, why did the local Jewish community in Sardis not have the information that Melito wanted about the scope of the OT Scriptures? How universal or generally accepted could the Hebrew biblical canon have been at the end of the second century C.E. if the Jews in Sardis could not help Melito with the appropriate information? And why did the rest of the churches in Asia not have this information (if by some turn of events Melito did not know what they knew)? What Scriptures were the other churches using? Christians in Sardis (Rev 3:1–6) and Smyrna (Rev 2:9–10) had problems with their Jewish neighbors (who also are mentioned in Melito's *Paschal Letter* 72–99). Was Melito perhaps looking for a biblical canon that would not be despised in the very community where the church's survival was at stake? That Melito had to go outside the community for an answer suggests that even in the Jewish community there was doubt at that time about the scope of their biblical canon.

Those Christians who most strongly followed the Jewish biblical canon were themselves generally connected geographically with Judaism. Jerome, for example, concluded his career at Bethlehem and learned from the Jewish rabbis there. Origen moved from Alexandria to Caesarea, two places with large Jewish populations. Athanasius lived in Alexandria when some two hundred thousand Jews resided there. And Cyril of Jerusalem lived in the Jewish capital. What was it about the proximity of these persons to Jews that led them to adopt the Jewish biblical canon? Could it have been that Jews outnumbered Christians through the sixth or seventh century? At the turn of the first century C.E., by conservative estimates, Jews outnumbered Christians by approximately sixty to one.[79] Could this intimidation factor have contributed to these Christians' opting so strongly for the rabbinic biblical canon? We cannot be sure, but it is worth considering.

When we talk about the lack of precise definition in regard to the OT biblical canon of early Christianity, for the most part the discussion focuses on whether the early Christians made use of the apocryphal and pseudepigraphal literature in articulating their theology and faith (canon 1). This material, however, was almost always at the fringe of the Jews' sacred literature—not the core. What, then, was the canon of Jesus and the apostles?

---

[78] Aland, *Problem of the New Testament Canon,* 7, emphasizes this point.

[79] See discussion in McDonald, "Anti-Judaism in the Early Church Fathers," 242–45.

Were they in fact born with a canon in their hands? And why should the church accept the Jewish canon of Scriptures if it was not known in the first century or was loosely defined at the time of the break between Christianity and Judaism? These are important questions for canon scholars today and especially for the church.

Just as in Judaism of the first century B.C.E. and first century C.E., the early church had several different levels of authoritative literature that informed its faith. As the church was developing a canonical consciousness, which may have come from Judaism, they found that some of the literature was scriptural or sacred and important in their identity and practices; this literature reflected the core of what Christianity was all about. But the church also discovered that other Christian literature, including *1 Clement, Didache, Shepherd of Hermas,* and *Barnabas,* was also valuable for understanding the Christian faith. The church freely cited this literature in a scriptural manner, without discriminating between it and the canonical literature. All of this suggests that notions of Scripture, inspiration, and canon were differently understood in early developing Christianity than they came to be understood in the Reformation churches and later.

There is little doubt that the core of the biblical collection of authoritative books is essentially the same collection that we now have in the Protestant OT collection. What is in question in canonical studies are books on the fringe. These fringe books, that included both canonical and apocryphal books, were disputed among Jews and Christians for centuries, even though many leaders in the church and synagogue freely quoted these writings in an authoritative manner, sometimes even using the designations *Scripture* or *as it is written* to refer to them. Remarkably, these disputes took place for centuries after decisions were supposedly made about its canonicity. Yet in neither group—those who accepted and those who rejected the authority and inspiration of this literature—was there any noticeable change in theology.[80] Silver notes essentially the same thing in the Jewish communities earlier. Because the Jews read through the Torah once a year in the synagogue, there was never any doubt in the minds of the faithful what was at the core of Judaism—the Law:

> The ordinary Jew probably knew that the Exodus story was central, and the story of Samson and Delilah less so, since he rehearsed the Exodus deliverance every Passover, and heard about Samson only on the occasional visit of a wandering storyteller or professional reader. If he thought about it, as he probably did not, he might have sensed that there must be some gradations of authority among the scrolls. But he probably never saw all the scrolls finally included in the Hebrew scriptures, and certainly never in one place, bound together, and designated as scripture.[81]

---

[80] See Barton, *People of the Book?* 30–31.

[81] Silver, *Story of Scripture,* 132.

B. CONCERN ABOUT AN AMBIGUOUS BIBLICAL CANON

Many Christians, especially those in the more conservative evangelical traditions, are nervous about ambiguity in their theological base and often argue among themselves over issues that are not likely to be resolved anytime soon, for example, the time of Christ's return, the security of the believer, and the validity of speaking in tongues today. Because of a lack of clear and uniform biblical support, these controversial fringe topics are sometimes upsetting to various parts of the Christian family—but they do not affect the major areas of our agreement within the church: our unity and faith in Jesus the Christ.

The decision whether to accept or reject the deuterocanonical literature is not at the core of what Christianity is all about. As the Law of Moses formed the core of the OT, so also the Gospels and Paul have been at the heart of the NT biblical canon since the second century, even though there was a great deal of dispute over the deutero-Pauline epistles (especially the Pastorals), Hebrews, the Catholic (or General) Epistles, and Revelation. The Jews and later the Christians fully accepted the Law of Moses as the core of their sacred Scriptures. Soon thereafter, most if not all of the traditional Prophets and many of the Writings were accepted as canonical, but at a secondary level of scriptural authority among the Jews. Not everyone agreed on the contents of the Writings, especially not before the time of Jesus, but the division of opinion was not over the core, but over the fringe.[82]

It is important to acknowledge that the OT, the deuterocanonical or apocryphal writings, and much of the pseudepigraphal literature informed the theology of the NT writers. Whether this literature, and other noncanonical writings, should be included in the Protestant biblical canon is another matter that will not be solved here, but it should at least be read and considered for the valuable information that it gives about the meaning of much of the NT. Not only were many writers of the NT familiar with this literature, but Jesus probably was as well. That such literature was familiar to the writers of the NT and informed their theology at various points suggests that we should not remain ignorant of it. While I am not asking for its inclusion in the Bible, this literature merits more careful attention than has been paid to it in the past.

The authoritative writings of Judaism, prior to the separation of Christianity from Judaism, no doubt had a major impact on the first Christian community, which was born within the pale of Judaism and stayed there until it was forced to leave (no later than 135). The early church inherited from Judaism both the core and fringe elements in its collection of sacred writings. The later refinements and definitions of this collection in Judaism had little impact on the emerging church, except for Athanasius, Jerome,

---

[82] Barton speaks of this "fringe" in *People of the Book?* 30–31.

Cyril of Jerusalem, and a few others. The church at large did not allow Judaism to define its OT canon of Scriptures during the second through sixth centuries. Pious Christians decided these matters for themselves, and the later church councils affirmed them. It is no wonder, then, that the church would not allow Judaism to define its OT canon, for, as Childs correctly suggests, the Christian canon had to differ from that of Judaism:

> At the outset, it is crucial to recognize that the Christian understanding of canon functions theologically in a very different way from Judaism. Although the church adopted from the synagogue a concept of scripture as an authoritative collection of sacred writings, its basic stance toward its canon was shaped by its christology. The authority assigned to the apostolic witnesses derived from their unique testimony to the life, death, and resurrection of Jesus Christ. Similarly, the Old Testament functioned as Christian scripture because it bore witness to Jesus Christ.[83]

In any case, since we do not know for certain what criteria were employed in the canonization process of the Jewish sacred writings (see §VIII.C below), one wonders why some in the Christian community ever felt the need to adopt it, especially since the church followed a different "canon"—Jesus the Christ. Why was the number of books accepted into the Christian canon limited to the number of letters in the Hebrew alphabet? In this instance, the number twenty-two must have been linked to the Hebrew alphabet after the fact. Otherwise, it is a poor criterion to follow and does not explain the various combinations of books that some used to stay within the limits of a twenty-two-book canon. In sum, there is no good reason to say that the biblical canon of later Judaism ought to be the precise biblical canon of the Christian community.

Karl Rahner acknowledges that the OT canonical process was not completed in the pre-Christian times and says that it is therefore not surprising "that the Church also completed the definition of the OT canon, and did not take over from the synagogue a ready-made and as such binding canon."[84] This freedom is found throughout the Western church, in the Trullan Synod (692) held by Eastern bishops, and in later councils in both the East and the West. It is evident, therefore, that both Judaism and early Christianity used the deuterocanonical literature, and each made a later decision regarding its normative value in their respective communities.

C. CONCERN ABOUT CRITERIA FOR ESTABLISHING A CANON

What criteria were used to establish the Jewish canon of scriptures? It is not clear whether the matter was settled by date (i.e., no document written after the time of Ezra) or by language (i.e., no document not written first in

---

[83] Childs, *Biblical Theology of the Old and New Testaments,* 64.

[84] Quoted from Stendebach, "Old Testament Canon," 37.

Hebrew) or by location (i.e., no document not written in the land of Israel).[85] It is also possible that canonicity sometimes related to a writing's theological conformity to Torah, to its usefulness in the liturgy, or to its perceived moral content.[86]

In many cases, however, there appears to be no qualitative difference between books that made it into the Jewish biblical canon and those that did not. For example, based on content alone, a better case could be made for the inclusion of Sirach and the Wisdom of Solomon and the exclusion of Ecclesiastes. By similar reasoning, why was Esther, which never mentions the name of God, included, while *Jubilees* and various *Testaments of the Patriarchs* were excluded? In any case, the material finally included was found by the Jewish community of faith to be useful in defining and shaping its religious life and identity.

Unlike the contracting Jewish canon of Scriptures, the Christian OT canon was expanding to allow Christian writers to inform their faith and ministries. To some extent, this was also happening in Judaism as the oral traditions took shape in the Mishnah during the second century C.E. Almost as soon as the oral traditions reached their final written form in the Mishnah, there was widespread acceptance of them. Despite the ambiguity (and tension) caused by this expansion, the early Christian OT canon better represents the canon of Jesus and first-century Judaism than does the restricted canon of second-century Judaism and later. The biblical canon of early Judaism, that was largely followed in the early Christian community, was much broader and probably included various apocryphal and pseudepigraphal literature that the Jews later excluded. Unlike many of the adherents of Judaism at the end of the first century C.E., the Christians in the developing church did not believe that the age of prophecy was over, but indeed it had just begun. This belief made it easier for the Christians to acknowledge apocryphal and pseudepigraphal literature as inspired Scripture and at a later time Christian writings, too.

Another influence on the scope of the biblical canon for Judaism may have been the Jewish-Christian conflicts that resulted in the rabbis trying to keep Christian literature from being read by the Jews. Moore claims that a decision about the extent of the Jewish biblical canon was made in part due to the rise of "Christian heresy and the circulation of Christian writings" in the Jewish community in Palestine.[87] Jewish polemic against the Christians and their writings continued vigorously until around the mid-second

---

[85] See Leiman, "Inspiration and Canonicity," 61–63, for more detail.

[86] Silver, *Story of Scripture,* 134, is wrong to claim that "the decision to include or exclude [was] sometimes made for reasons as superficial as a scribe finding empty space available at the end of a scroll he had just copied, and filling it with something he liked."

[87] G. Moore, "Definition of the Jewish Canon," 101–102. See also Bloch, "Outside Books."

century, when Christianity became less of a threat to Judaism and rabbinic concern about the influence of the Gospels upon Jewish people subsided due to the effective separation of the Jewish-Christians from the synagogue.[88] Christian nonparticipation in the Bar Kokhba rebellion against Rome (132–135) was viewed as treason by many Jews, and the influence of the Jewish-Christians declined rapidly after that.

In the continuing quest to determine which books were sacred among the Jews, the Christians no longer had a voice. Moore boldly concludes from this that "the attempt authoritatively to define the Jewish canon of the *Hagiographa* begins with the exclusion by name of Christian Scriptures."[89] Two key Tosefta texts influenced Moore's conclusion on this matter: "The Gospels (GYLYWNYN)[90] and books of heretics do not impart uncleanness to hands. And the books of Ben Sira and all books written thenceforward do not impart uncleanness to hands" (*t. Yadayim* 2:13, Neusner, *Tosefta,* 1907); "the books of the Evangelists and the books of the *minim* [heretics] they do not save from the fire. But they are allowed to burn where they are, they and the references to the Divine Name which are in them" (*t. Shabbat* 13:5 A–B, Neusner, *Tosefta,* 405). There was an obvious difference of opinion about this matter among the rabbis:

> R. Yosé the Galilean says, "On ordinary days, one cuts out the references to the Divine Name which are in them and stores them away, and the rest burns." Said R. Ṭarfon, "May I bury my sons, if such things come into my hands and I do not burn them, and even the references to the Divine Name which are in them. And if someone was running after me, I should go into a temple of idolatry, but I should not go into their houses [of worship]. For idolators do not recognize the Divinity in denying him, but these [Christians] recognize the Divinity and deny him." (*t. Shabbat* 13:5 C–F, Neusner, *Tosefta,* 405)

Moore's reasoning is that not until the rabbinic sages began to declare that Christian books were not sacred—and thereby rejected them—did they begin the delimitation process that led to their fixed list of sacred books. His views have not gone uncontested, especially in the Jewish community,[91] but his observations nonetheless deserve some consideration, since it is difficult to otherwise find a time when rabbis deliberated which books "defile the hands" and which do not.

The process of canonization for the Jews *may* have been largely finished before 180 C.E., when Melito of Sardis traveled to the East and

---

[88] Moore, "Definition of the Jewish Canon," 122–23.

[89] Ibid., 125.

[90] The term in question is *hagilyonim,* which G. Moore, "Definition of the Jewish Canon," 122–23; Leiman, *Canonization of the Hebrew Scripture,* 190–91 n. 511; and Lewis, "Problems of Inclusion," 201 n. 179, agree is a reference to the Christian Gospels.

[91] See, for example, Leiman, *Canonization of the Hebrew Scripture,* 190–91 n. 511; and Childs, *Biblical Theology of the Old and New Testaments,* 61.

brought back the list of twenty-two books in the OT, although there is no evidence of a formal decision being made within Judaism about the matter at this time or even later. In spite of Melito's letter, however, it is not clear what the boundaries of the OT canon were in Judaism. And how normative was his list for the majority of Jews in the second century, especially since it does not contain Esther? This *Jewish* canon, as Sundberg shows, had an impact upon the Christian church after the third century, especially when Jerome wrongly considered it to be the canon of Jesus and of the apostles.[92] It appears that only at the end of the second century did the question of fixing the limits of the OT canon in Christian communities *begin* to emerge, and this development probably came about primarily as a result of the Marcionite and gnostic rejection of the OT as sacred Scripture.[93] Jerome's preference for the Jewish biblical canon was a *minority* position in the church in his time that did not prevail until later in the Protestant OT canon.[94]

The Apostolic Fathers, the closest Christian writings to the time of the NT, quote, refer, or allude to 2 Maccabees, Judith, Tobit, Sirach, Wisdom of Solomon, 2 Esdras, and *1 Enoch*—but not to the canonical books of Ruth, Ezra, Nehemiah, Lamentations, Obadiah, Micah, or Haggai.[95] This is important information for those who argue that Jesus' canon could not have included the Apocrypha since he does not cite this literature. Does this argument also extend to the flip side and claim that Jesus did not accept Judges, Ezra, Nehemiah, Lamentations, Obadiah, Micah, or Haggai since he did not cite or quote them? Since the second-century churches were informed by more than the current Protestant OT canonical literature, this raises the question whether today's church should reconsider what literature informs its faith and witness.

Ancient Christian sources, both Eastern and Western, that list the OT books and their order have this in common: they are broader than the Jewish OT canon, and no two lists are identical.[96] This evidence also points to the broad diversity of opinion about such matters in the early Christian communities. If there was a precise list of authoritative and inspired OT books handed on by the apostles stemming from Jesus, then the early church lost it. Rather than the Jewish biblical canon having been settled at the council of Jamnia and the canon of the early church thus

---

[92] Sundberg, *Old Testament of the Early Church,* 154.

[93] Grant, "New Testament Canon," 300, believes that this development probably led the orthodox church to evaluate the NT literature as well.

[94] Athanasius's *Thirty-ninth Festal Letter* lists for the first time the twenty-seven books of our NT and also gives a *larger* OT canon than Protestants accept, i.e., he adds Baruch and the Epistle of Jeremiah. One wonders why Protestants generally ignore his OT canon but assume the validity his NT canon!

[95] This observation is from Jeffery, "Canon of the Old Testament," 40.

[96] See appendixes B–C and Sundberg, *Old Testament of the Early Church,* 58–59.

being essentially that of pre-70 C.E. Judaism in Palestine, the evidence shows that no restrictive Jewish biblical canon obtained in the first century C.E. The very presence of noncanonical literature in the early Christian community and later leads to the conclusion that canonical issues were simply not settled by the time of the separation of Christianity from Judaism.

If such canons did exist in the first century, no surviving evidence confirms their presence in either Christianity or Judaism before the second century C.E. Lightstone perceptively argues that several traditional assumptions about the formation of the Hebrew biblical canon are untenable, interfere with an advance in our understanding of canon formation, and are incapable of proof: (1) the equation of the Law of Moses with the Pentateuch;[97] (2) the linear model of the growth of the canon in three separate phases; (3) a universal normative Judaism in late antiquity that essentially paralleled Pharisaic Judaism of the pre-70 C.E. days in the land of Israel; (4) a normative first-century C.E. biblical canon similar to the canon of late antiquity; and (5) the so-called Council of Jamnia as similar to later church councils in which bishops supposedly decided the contents of a biblical canon.[98] I am in complete agreement with Lightstone's conclusion that only when these traditional assumptions have been shattered can there be an open avenue for a needed reassessment of the canon issue.[99]

Dulles rightly concludes that "if the apostles ever certified a list of biblical books (a most unlikely hypothesis), their testimony was not appealed to or apparently not remembered during the disputes about the canon in subsequent centuries."[100] On this basis, it is easier to believe that such a tradition was not passed on in the church than to believe that it was lost. There is no trace in the first century C.E. of any list of sacred books similar to the list that Melito secured in the East in the late second century. What appears indisputable in regard to the Christian OT canon is that a variety of competing opinions existed in the early Christian community over the scope of its sacred literature. When Christians began to make lists of this literature, very few of the early lists were identical, and many of them contained some of the books now considered apocryphal. (Whether there was a secondary category of inspiration and authority for these writings is not clear.) In short, no fixed biblical canon was handed over to the Christians by Jesus or the apostles. Those who claim otherwise must first provide ancient evidence for such a canon and then account for how the church could lose such a sacred collection.

---

[97] Lightstone here follows the conclusions of J. A. Sanders in *Torah and Canon*.

[98] Lightstone, "Formation of the Biblical Canon."

[99] Ibid., 142–43.

[100] Dulles, "Authority of Scripture," 35.

IX. Summary and Conclusion

The difficulty in speaking about ancient biblical canons, that is, fixed collections of Scriptures, becomes more obvious when we apply the term *canon* in those times. For example, the writings of the Prophets were authoritative for both Jews and Christians long before they were placed into the biblical canon. It is not certain when a fixed number of prophets formed the category Prophets, but the category was open and flexible in the time of Jesus. In other words, the category Prophets existed long before it was fixed. All sacred writings not in the Pentateuch were, for a considerable time, placed among the Prophets, including those (e.g., Psalms, Job, and Daniel) that were later placed in the Writings.

The Jews were probably influenced to adopt a more conservative collection of sacred Scriptures by Hillel, who came from Babylon and accepted only those writings that dated from roughly the time of Ezra and Nehemiah and earlier. Hillel was possibly unaware of other sacred literature until he came to Israel in the first century B.C.E., but by then he had likely already formulated his criteria for what was sacred and what was not. The Qumran literature is thus more reflective of what was widely welcomed among the Jews in the time of Jesus. This is confirmed by the early Christians who adopted the apocryphal literature as a part of their sacred Scripture collection, along with several books now classified as pseudepigraphal.

It cannot be irrelevant that the earliest list of sacred books among the Jews (i.e., *b. Bava Batra* 14b–15a), which was subsequently adopted by the rabbis, comes from Babylon. This tradition dates from the middle of the second century C.E. at the earliest, but there is no indication that it received universal recognition among Jews at that time. If it had, it would have been more widely circulated and known among Jews of the Diaspora as well as in the land of Israel. As a result, the current canon of the HB and the Protestant OT reflects a Babylonian flavor that was not current or popular in the time of Jesus in the land of Israel.

E X C U R S U S

The Use of the Septuagint in the New Testament*

R. Timothy McLay, St. Stephen's University

PAUL'S USE OF SCRIPTURE PROVIDES AN INTERESTING TOPIC FOR CANON STUDIES. For example, what is one to do with his citation in 1 Cor 2:16: *tis gar egnō noun kuriou* ("for who has known the mind of the Lord?"). Paul's citation of Isa 40:13 clearly depends on the earliest recoverable form of the Greek version (the Old Greek) of Isaiah rather than on the Hebrew MT in his choice of "mind" (*nous*) rather than "spirit" (*pneuma*). Moreover, in the context of Paul's argument, the way in which Isa 40:13 is applied is more illuminating for a discussion of the influence of the Old Greek on the theology of the NT than is the actual reference to this verse. The significance of Paul's use of *nous* is that it is also found in the next line of the verse, where Paul concludes his address with *hēmeis de noun christou echomen* ("but we have the mind of Christ"). Given that Paul previously speaks of humanity's inability to know the thoughts of God without the "spirit" (*pneuma*) of God (2:11–12), the use of *nous* in 2:16 adds something to Paul's argument,[1] particularly when the apostle concludes that "we have the *mind* of Christ."

Like the other NT writers, Paul uses Scripture to present a complex of problems that make for fascinating investigation and analysis. For example, the citation of OG Jonah 2:1 in Matt 12:40 (*ēn iōnas en tē koilia tou kētous treis hēmeras kai treis nyktas:* "Jonah was three days and three nights in the

*This essay is based on a paper delivered to the Institute for Biblical Research in San Antonio on Saturday, November 20, 2004. I thank Lee McDonald and Hendrickson Publishers for including it in this volume.

[1]That *nous* and *pneuma* are not synonymous in Paul's usage in 1 Cor 2 (cf. also the distinction that Paul makes between these two words in 14:14–19) argues for the theological significance of the use of the Old Greek. See discussion in my *Use of the Septuagint,* 150–53; and Silva, "Old Testament in Paul," 633–34.

belly of the sea monster") demonstrates Matthew's dependence upon the Old Greek of Jonah and shows its influence on Matthew's theology. Again, it is not so much the citation of the Greek text that is novel, but the theological themes of descending and emerging from hades and the language employed in the Greek form of Jonah's prayer form the matrix for Matthew's theology. After the citation of Jonah 1:17, Matthew adds, "So for three days and three nights the Son of Man will be in the heart of the earth." Matthew's reference to Jesus' being in hades can be understood more clearly against the Old Greek of Jonah, and the passage forms part of a larger theological framework in which Matthew connects Jesus' promise that the gates of hades will not be able to restrain the church in 16:18 with the puzzling reference to the resurrection of the saints in 27:52–53.[2]

In my view, much research remains to be done with respect to the influence of the Greek Jewish Scriptures (commonly called the Septuagint [LXX]) on the theology of the NT writers.[3] Among the various aspects that one must consider for an analysis of the theological influence of the Greek Jewish Scriptures on the NT are two central concerns: what text(s) may or may not have been employed; and what was the guiding methodology of the writer when a text was cited or otherwise employed? The relationship between Septuagint research and the use of Scripture in the early church, however, requires that we turn our attention to other significant critical problems. Specifically, many scholars and students are not able to appreciate the use of the Greek Jewish Scriptures by the NT writers due to their presuppositions. For example, if one does not allow for the possibility that the Greek Jewish Scriptures made an impact on the NT writers that can be isolated and distinguished from the impact of the Hebrew Scriptures in the first place, then what argument could prove otherwise? Thus, the guiding principles for research into the use of Scripture in the early church demand careful analysis, especially the use of textual witnesses.

I. The Understanding of Scripture Presupposed by the New Testament Writers

The fundamental barrier to attaining a greater appreciation of the use of the Greek Jewish Scriptures in the NT is related to underlying presuppositions about the Hebrew Scriptures as constituting the original and only true text for the OT or Hebrew Bible. For Septuagint scholars, this is patently obvious with regard to how the Greek Jewish Scriptures continue to be treated as textual witnesses in Bible translations and textual criticism.

---

[2] See McLay, *Use of the Septuagint,* 159–69.

[3] On the distinctive impact of the Greek Jewish Scriptures on the NT, see Wagner, *Heralds of the Good News;* and Steyn, *Septuagint Quotations.*

However, in the light of the discovery of ancient manuscripts in the Judean Desert in 1947, it is important to evaluate the implications of such a discovery. This data presents scholars with an opportunity to learn far more about the Scriptures than what was previously imagined just over fifty years ago. Do these discoveries alter our understanding of the origins and transmission of the Scriptures? How is the discovery of the Dead Sea Scrolls related to the texts of the Bible preserved in the Greek Jewish Scriptures? Although there are different ways that this problem could be approached, the bias for the Hebrew text is based on three presuppositions.

A. PRESUPPOSITION 1: A HEBREW BIBLICAL CANON IN THE FIRST CENTURY C.E.

It was once commonplace in the scholarly literature to note that the Jewish canon was established at the so-called Council of Jamnia around 100 C.E., but this has proved to be a scholarly fiction. There is no firm evidence for the fixing of the Jewish canon.[4] Despite the convincing demonstration that no such decision was ever made at a Council of Jamnia, one still encounters it occasionally in the scholarly literature.[5] The argument for the first-century date of the canon does not, however, depend solely on the putative Council of Jamnia. In particular, the research of Beckwith is frequently cited as a definitive discussion of the evidence for an early dating of the canon.[6] I direct my criticisms at Beckwith primarily for the sake of convenience. That many scholars cite him as an authority for their position means that they share the same basic point of view.[7]

Several Jewish witnesses testify in some way to the status of their authoritative books or Scriptures. For example, Jesus ben Sira refers to "the study of the law" and "the wisdom of all the ancients" (Sir 39:1), Philo speaks of "laws and oracles delivered through the mouths of the prophets, and psalms and anything else" (*Contempl. Life* 25, LCL), and Josephus, the most important witness to the Hebrew canon, states (*Ag. Ap.* 1.38–40):

> There are . . . twenty-two volumes containing the record of all time, which are rightly trusted.

---

[4] For a history of the development of the idea that the canon had been fixed, how it has been overturned, and an examination of the evidence, see Lewis, "Jamnia Revisited."

[5] Though he does not refer to the canon being fixed at Jamnia, Hengel repeats the date of 100 and makes other references to the Pharisees and Jamnia in his *Septuagint as Christian Scripture,* 105, 126. Robert Hanhart, who provides an introductory essay for Hengel's volume, advocates an even earlier dating for the canon "in the second century BC" (2). See my review of Hengel.

[6] Beckwith, *Old Testament Canon.* See McLay, *Use of the Septuagint,* 138–44, for fuller discussion.

[7] For example, Hengel, *Septuagint as Christian Scripture;* and Dempster, *Dominion and Dynasty,* 31–35.

> Now of these, five are those of Moses, which comprise both the laws and the tradition from human origins until his passing. . . . From Moses' passing until the Artaxerxes who was king of the Persians after Xerxes, the prophets after Moses wrote up what happened in their times [or, as they saw things] in thirteen volumes. The remaining four (volumes) comprise hymns toward God and advice for living among humanity. (Mason, "Josephus and His Twenty-two Book Canon," 113)

In addition, 4QMMT refers to "the book of Moses, the books of the prophets, and of David."[8] The major problem with determining the value of these testimonies for historical construction is that these witnesses either do not specifically name the books to which they refer or do so only in part. In the case of Josephus, for example, scholars are driven to fanciful reconstructions of what Josephus meant. Thus, Beckwith suggests that Josephus's "five" books of Moses refer to the Pentateuch; that "thirteen volumes" of the prophets are Joshua, Judges, Samuel, Kings, Isaiah, Jeremiah-Lamentations, Ezekiel, Minor Prophets, Daniel, Esther, Ezra-Nehemiah, Job, and Chronicles; and that the final "four" are Psalms, Proverbs, Song of Songs, and Ecclesiastes.[9] This reconstruction could be criticized at a number of points. For example, why count Jeremiah-Lamentations as one book? How does this supposed reconstruction—which includes Esther, Ezra-Nehemiah, Job, Daniel, and Chronicles with the prophets—relate to what is known in the Hebrew canon? Beckwith's reconstruction also betrays his concern to somehow equate the *twenty-two* books referred to by Josephus with the current *twenty-four* books of the Jewish Tanak, which is broken down into the three divisions: Law, Prophets, and Writings. Contrary to Beckwith's wishes, the evidence is ambiguous and presents a problem with his harmonization, because Josephus refers to the "prophets after Moses" as having written thirteen books. In other words, Josephus's terminology reflects his view that all of the Jewish Scriptures were written by prophets.[10] Thus, his reference to thirteen prophets after Moses cannot be identified with thirteen books that are part of the prophetic section of the canon. A similar point may be made regarding Jesus ben Sira's reference to "Prophets and the other books" in his prologue. Though his reference to prophetic writings may well have included scrolls of prophets that are recognized as the writing prophets in the prophetic corpus, there is no evidence to determine exactly what he meant, nor should it be naively

---

[8] For a more complete discussion of these statements by Jewish writers and the NT references to the Scriptures, see C. A. Evans, "Scriptures of Jesus."

[9] Beckwith, "Formation of the Hebrew Bible," 50–51; idem, *Old Testament Canon,* 79–80. For a different configuration, see VanderKam, "Questions of Canon Viewed"; and ; Hengel, *Septuagint as Christian Scripture,* 101, though Hengel suggests that Josephus may not have included Song of Songs and Ecclesiastes.

[10] See Barton, *Oracles of God,* 35–48, for a discussion of the NT evidence and the use of the term *prophets.*

concluded that the form of the books he knew was equivalent to the text that eventually developed into the MT.

Beckwith's conclusions appear to be completely subordinated to his presuppositions. His argument is not really based on proving the existence of the present-day twenty-four books of the Hebrew canon. It could be more accurately characterized as a negation of the evidence that depends upon a presupposition. His presupposition is that the twenty-four-book Hebrew canon could have existed in the first century. The Jewish testimony and citations from the NT[11] confirm that there were authoritative books, but they do not give direct evidence about whether there were limits to a canon or even about all of the books that were regarded as Scripture. Beckwith depends upon the confessional stance of the reader who accepts his presupposition. That is, there is no real evidence that the canon existed in this form, only a willingness to believe that it could have existed, particularly since the canon is Holy Scripture. Indeed, for many believers, it *must* have existed in this form. Once this presupposition is accepted, then the remainder of Beckwith's argument consists of explaining how the evidence fits his particular view and excluding what does not. Thus, according to Beckwith all of these witnesses support the existence of a canon, despite his statement that "one cannot, it is true, just assume that all these writers accepted all these canonical books, when *none of them actually mentions more than a proportion*."[12] Even though Beckwith does not show in these sources any list that is equivalent to the present-day Hebrew canon, he assumes that the various parts are all referring to the same whole.[13] His most important Jewish witness, Josephus, explicitly refers to only five books of Moses.

That Beckwith does not distinguish between Scripture and canon leads him to treat any reference to Scripture(s) or oracle(s) as equivalent to canon, as long as it supports his view. Beckwith admits that none of these sources mention all of the books that he assumes to be canonical, yet, based on references to books or the names of biblical characters in the sources, he concludes that "it is very striking that . . . so many writers, of so many classes (Semitic, Hellenistic, Pharisaic, Essene, Christian), show such agreement about the canon—agreement both with each other and with *the present Hebrew Bible*."[14] Beckwith also argues that these various sources "do not speak simply for themselves but at least for their own school of thought among the Jews" and that "many of the books in all three sections

---

[11] Variations on the formula *the law and the prophets* are the most common designation for the Scriptures in the NT. Luke 24:44 is unique in its reference to "the law of Moses, the prophets, and the psalms."

[12] Beckwith, *Old Testament Canon,* 76 (emphasis added).

[13] For example, on p. 274, Beckwith refers to what he earlier established in chapter 2 regarding which books were undisputed in the second century B.C.E.

[14] Ibid., 76–77 (emphasis added).

of the Hebrew canon . . . were accepted as canonical."[15] I find it incredible that Beckwith can include the Septuagint with Philo as "speaking for Hellenistic Judaism" when the only reference he makes to the Septuagint in this discussion is that it "refers to passages in Job with the formula 'it is written' " and "it also attributes Lamentations, in a head-note, to the prophet Jeremiah."[16] What about the different versions of books and the additional books in the Septuagint? How does he account for their witness? Do they not offer counterevidence to his position?

As far as the evidence from the Essenes (Qumran) is concerned, Beckwith's presuppositions are obvious:

> If one excludes the few references to the Book of Meditation, which very likely means nothing other than Holy Scripture, there are only the reference to the Aramaic Testament of Levi in Damascus Document 4.15–19 and the reference to the "Book of the Divisions of the Times into their Jubilees and Weeks" in Damascus Document 16.2–4. Though these were doubtless works which the Essenes greatly esteemed, in neither case is a formula for quoting Scripture used or any clear indication given that the work was of prophetic authority.[17]

One may wonder what counts as evidence when Beckwith is quite willing to accept that a reference in Sirach to Job confirms that Job was regarded as canonical.[18] In addition to the references to Scripture among the Dead Sea Scrolls that Beckwith excludes, one also has to consider what other light the Qumran sect may shed on this subject. The Dead Sea Scrolls highlight the textual diversity that existed in the biblical scrolls at the beginning of the common era. Even if one accepts Tov's original estimate that around 60 percent of the scrolls could be termed proto-MT,[19] it would still be necessary to account for the other 40 percent. Some of the scrolls exhibit distinctive agreements with the Greek Jewish Scriptures, others are aligned with the Samaritan Pentateuch, and still others are described by Tov as nonaligned. While some of these texts may fit into a textual group or family, many texts exhibit a mixture of readings, variously agreeing with the MT, the Greek Jewish Scriptures, or the Samaritan Pentateuch. Therefore, the evidence from Qumran argues that a variety of textual witnesses existed in the first century, which hardly supports the existence of a fixed canon.

A major problem with Beckwith's argument is that he assumes that any reference to Scripture is equivalent to support for the notion of a Hebrew canon. However, the idea of a canon presupposes the existence of

---

[15] Ibid., 77.
[16] Ibid., 75.
[17] Ibid.
[18] Ibid., 73.
[19] Tov, *Textual Criticism of the Hebrew Bible,* 115. In the second edition (2001) of this book, Tov revised this estimate to 35 percent.

Scripture(s), which is how these terms should be understood historically. Initially, a faith community similar to the Jewish communities at the beginning of the common era in Jerusalem, Alexandria, Qumran, and Antioch deemed some particular writings to be Scripture, which basically affirms that these writings were recognized to be authoritative for the faith and practice of their respective communities. The concept of a canon that defines a particular list of books that constitute sacred Scripture for a believing community cannot be dated prior to the fourth century C.E.[20] The concept of a canon does not require the particular terminology, but it is quite evident that the origin of the term also coincides with more extensive discussions regarding what books ought to be categorized as Scripture. Throughout his volume Beckwith constantly assumes that any reference to the Scriptures implies the Hebrew canon, but he does not offer any grounds for this connection.

The references to Scriptures found in the literature of the first century are completely explicable when they are not overlaid with a notion of canon. The Dead Sea Scrolls demonstrate that the Scriptures were characterized by a diversity of textual forms, and the community that produced this literature also offers important evidence about what they viewed as authoritative Scripture. For example, *Jubilees,* which is classified as rewritten Scripture because of the amount of Scripture it includes from the Pentateuch, claims to be an account of what God told Moses on Mount Sinai (1:5) and what he was commanded to write down (1:26) for the instruction of the people. The assumption of *Jubilees* is that it has divine authority and is binding on the people. That approximately fifteen copies of *Jubilees* were found in five different caves at Qumran[21] suggests that the sect at Qumran may have accepted it as Scripture. Likewise, parts of *1 Enoch* (but nothing from the *Similitudes of Enoch,* that is, 37–71) were preserved on twelve scrolls,[22] and it is quite likely that it too was regarded as Scripture at Qumran—particularly since it is regarded as such by Tertullian, it is cited by Jude, and it is included in the canon of the Ethiopian church. Given the contents of other texts like the *Temple Scroll* (another example of rewritten Scripture) and their community texts, it is probable that the Qumran sect had a broader view of what constituted authoritative Scripture than what eventually emerged in the MT. The self-identification of the Qumran community as the true remnant means that it is highly likely that they regarded some of their own compositions as authoritative writings for their community, which by definition is Scripture.

Though Beckwith's position that there was a Hebrew canon may be comforting to some, it hardly gives adequate consideration to the available

---

[20] For an excellent discussion and definition of terms, see Ulrich, "Notion and Definition of Canon."

[21] VanderKam and Flint, *Meaning of the Dead Sea Scrolls,* 197.

[22] Ibid., 195.

evidence. The same methodology that guides his assessment of the Jewish witnesses is evident in his treatment of other evidence as well. So, for example, though Beckwith is not alone in this claim,[23] he argues that the NT writers never cite a book that is not included in the Hebrew Bible. The way that Beckwith disposes of the citation of *1 En.* 1:9 in Jude 14–15 is worth quoting:

> In the case of 1 Enoch he says that "Enoch the seventh from Adam prophesied." . . . However, that Enoch did prophesy in these words is something which 1 Enoch certainly implies . . . by putting the prediction on his lips; and though, if 1 Enoch were a canonical book, one would be inclined to regard this as an endorsement of its canonicity, since it is not, the statement may just be a repetition of what 1 Enoch says happened. . . . Jude need not be doing the same as the Epistle of Barnabas, . . . which calls 1 Enoch "Scripture." . . . For what Gentile Christians from Gentile countries might do in the fourth decade of the second century is not always a guide to what a Jewish Christian from Palestine, like Jude, would do in the first century.[24]

Jude merely "borrows" from *1 Enoch* and the *Assumption of Moses* "because they happen to be edifying and meet his present need."[25] It is difficult to escape the impression that Beckwith will argue anything to support his agenda, particularly when he states "if 1 Enoch were a canonical book, one would be inclined to regard this as an endorsement of its canonicity, [but] since it is not. . . ." Beckwith has already decided what the canon is and what counts as evidence.

In addition to the citation of *1 Enoch* in Jude, that some of the Pseudepigrapha were read as sacred Scripture in the early church is demonstrated by the use of the Greek Scriptures in the NT writings, the inclusion of some of these books in the Greek biblical codices, allusions throughout the NT corpus (see appendix A), and the continuing inclusion of some of these books in the lists of Scripture by the church fathers (see appendixes B–C and appendix E §I.A).

I realize that I have belabored this point, but all of these factors are evidence that has to be accounted for in any historical reconstruction of what was considered to be Scripture and whether there was an established Hebrew canon in the first century C.E. Imagine living in the first century in Alexandria. Given the time needed for travel and communication in those days, plus the errors that occurred in the copying of texts and the expense involved in copying them, how likely it is that all the Jews in the various communities had equal access to the same scrolls of Scripture? Is it probable that everybody had the same access to Scriptures and shared exactly the same notion of Scripture? Did all individuals even within a given

---

[23] As one example, see D. M. Smith, "Pauline Literature," 266.
[24] Beckwith, *Old Testament Canon,* 402.
[25] Ibid., 403.

community hold a common understanding of Scripture? Why should one individual, such as Josephus, be considered the spokesperson for all Jews? Given the evidence of alternative views of Scripture at Qumran, the texts preserved in the LXX, and the historical context, does not the hypothesis that all Jews shared a common canon—the one referred to by Josephus—strike one as a little too neat and tidy? Not only does this hypothesis seem untenable given the historical data, it does not reflect human nature. Is there any one individual upon whom all could agree to represent a doctrinal consensus today? Which canon is the appropriate one today, and who is the authoritative body that establishes it? That the evidence does not support the existence of a Hebrew canon in the first century should allow for a more open assessment of what the NT writers and early church understood to be Scripture.

B. PRESUPPOSITION 2: THE PRIORITY OF THE HEBREW TEXT

A close corollary that emerges from the presupposition of a Hebrew canon in the first century C.E. is the priority that is given to the Hebrew text in matters of textual criticism. Until recent years this bias was reserved primarily for the MT, but with the broadening implications of the discovery of the Dead Sea Scrolls this bias is beginning to encompass the Hebrew Scriptures more generally.[26] For my present purposes, it is not necessary to differentiate between these biases.

Somewhat ironically, over the years the sanctity of the Hebrew text has been encouraged in no small part by Septuagint scholars! Wevers, whom most regard as the foremost living authority on the Greek Pentateuch, constantly stresses his reluctance to emend the Hebrew text. The presupposition for this approach is his conviction that the translators of the Pentateuch regarded their Hebrew text as authoritative, even canonical,[27] and that the Hebrew text from which they translated must have closely resembled the current MT.[28] While this may be generally true for some books of the Hebrew Bible, it certainly is not the case for every book, nor can it be assumed in any particular reading. I am not suggesting that Wevers makes this assumption, but the application of the principle of the priority of the Hebrew text leads many scholars, teachers, and students to an unwarranted bias for the Hebrew text, more specifically the MT.

An excellent example of how bias toward the Hebrew text may emerge is provided in the introduction to the LXX by Jobes and Silva.[29] In

---

[26] See my discussion of Heb 1:6 and Deut 32:43 in "Biblical Texts and the Scriptures for the New Testament Church."

[27] Wevers, "Study in the Narrative Portions of the Greek Exodus."

[28] See the introductions to Wever's volumes on the Greek Pentateuch, *Notes on the Greek Text of Exodus*, xiv.

[29] Jobes and Silva, *Invitation to the Septuagint*.

his review of their book, Barr rightly notes that in not one single case did Jobes and Silva find the LXX reading to be superior to the Masoretic Text: "It was truly amazing to find . . . that there was hardly a single verse in the whole book for which in the end any confident assurance was offered that the Greek text should be preferred to the MT."[30] In their response to Barr, Jobes and Silva take issue with him, but in so doing they fail to address a crucial aspect of his point.[31] Their reply consists primarily of a defense of their position that they have made many positive remarks about the Septuagint. However, one of Barr's fundamental criticisms is that offering no clear examples where the Septuagint is superior to the MT "is not a good way to commend interest in the LXX."[32] Surely, their positive evaluation of the LXX would have been more effectively communicated to students and scholars by selecting examples that clearly illustrate the superiority of some variants in the LXX compared to the MT. Thus, that Barr agrees with some of their decisions is irrelevant to his main criticism that they favor the MT.

In the course of their response to Barr, Jobes and Silva also state, "We do believe (along with many other scholars with differing traditions) that, for most books of the Bible, the textual form preserved in the MT is *generally* more reliable than that found in competing witnesses."[33] Thus, the bias of these Septuagint scholars toward the MT is clear and may have influenced their decisions more than they care to admit. Even more to the point for the present discussion is the following question: on what basis should the MT be granted preference? Given the discovery of more than two hundred biblical scrolls at Qumran and the light that they shed on the transmission of the biblical text, it seems that the only possible justification for ignoring differences between the various textual witnesses in the Greek Jewish Scriptures, Samaritan Pentateuch, MT, and Dead Sea Scrolls is based in either ignorance or confessional/doctrinal bias.[34] (For the record, it does not strike me that Jobes and Silva are ignorant of the implications of these matters.)

The practical result of the discovery of the Dead Sea Scrolls is that they are a double-edged sword for the purposes of textual criticism. On the one hand, that a significant percentage of texts is similar to the MT demonstrates the antiquity of the Masoretic tradition. On the other hand, the presence of text forms that agree with other important textual witnesses (like the Greek Jewish Scriptures) undermines any claim for the authority of the MT and

---

[30] Barr, review of Jobes and Silva, *Invitation to the Septuagint,* 3.

[31] Jobes and Silva, "Response to J. Barr's Review of *Invitation to the Septuagint.*"

[32] Barr, review of Jobes and Silva, *Invitation to the Septuagint,* 27.

[33] Jobes and Silva, "Response to J. Barr's Review," 44 (emphasis original), quoted from the reprint.

[34] On the origin and transmission of the biblical text, see F. M. Cross, "Evolution of a Theory of Local Texts"; Tov, *Textual Criticism of the Hebrew Bible;* and Ulrich, *Dead Sea Scrolls.*

underlines the credibility of these other texts as witnesses to the Hebrew Scriptures. Though the witnesses to the developing MT (or proto-MT) at Qumran support the antiquity and preservation of this form of the Hebrew text, they cannot establish a claim that the (proto-)MT is the best witness to the original text. This point is absolutely crucial for any discussion regarding the textual criticism of the Hebrew Bible and any methodology that is employed to establish the original text. Though one can be grateful for the discovery of the Dead Sea Scrolls, how much more diversity in the texts of Scripture would exist if another cache of scrolls were discovered? The antiquity of the text that became the MT is not equivalent to its being the original text. Therefore, a decision to ratify the textual tradition preserved in the MT is completely arbitrary.

Tov's scholarly position on the historical investigation of the textual witnesses to the OT/HB well illustrates this dilemma. At one time, Tov advocated that "textual criticism aims at that literary composition which has been accepted as binding (authoritative) by Jewish tradition. . . . This implies that the textual criticism of the Hebrew Bible aims at the literary compositions as contained in [the MT], to the exclusion of later (midrashic) compilations . . . and earlier and possibly parallel compositions."[35] In other words, the aim of textual criticism, which should be understood as emerging from Tov's position as a Jewish scholar, was to restore the MT. Later, however, Tov reversed his opinion in this matter and argued that the MT should no longer hold this position since it is only one textual witness: "We suggest that we should single out no stage as the presumed *Urtext*. . . . All these early stages were equally authoritative."[36] This is an amazing admission, given Tov's scholarly position over the years. The point is that the later dominance of the text form in the MT, regardless of its antiquity, should not mislead us when examining the relationship of the texts and what was considered to be Scripture prior to the end of the first century. The consolidation of the proto-MT was a later development.[37] Though it has been common in biblical scholarship to give priority to the MT as the main witness to the Hebrew Bible, this position is no longer historically tenable.

In their discussion of the text-critical issues involved in the relationship between the MT and the LXX, Jobes and Silva correctly note the inherent problems in producing an eclectic text of the Hebrew Bible.[38] For example, the textual differences in Jeremiah seem to be based on different literary

---

[35]Tov, *Textual Criticism of the Hebrew Bible* (1992), 164–80, quotation from 177.

[36]Tov, "Status of the Masoretic Text," 248.

[37]The diversity and the variety of forms (pluriformity) of texts for books of the Hebrew Bible raises questions about the goals of textual criticism for the OT. Is it possible to reconstruct an original text of books such as Jeremiah, Job, and Daniel that have multiple literary editions? See Ulrich, *Dead Sea Scrolls*.

[38]Jobes and Silva, *Invitation to the Septuagint*, 151–53.

editions of the book. Using the Greek Jewish Scriptures also presents problems, because these texts are translations and one has to reconstruct a hypothetical Hebrew source and then determine whether the difference in the Greek is based on an error in scribal transmission or a real variant in the source text.[39] The large divergences between the different literary editions of some books make an eclectic text unfeasible in some cases. This is a main reason why Jobes and Silva, and many other scholars, basically chose a default position. That is, because of the "serious difficulties involved in producing an eclectic edition," they advocate the use of the MT as a starting point.[40] The problem with this principle is that it inevitably leads to other witnesses becoming servants to the MT, which was the methodology formerly proposed by Tov. In spite of the MT having no logical claim to being the original text, it becomes the best witness to the original text by default, which leads to statements like the following by Jobes and Silva: "What needs to be appreciated, in any case, is the unique value of the LXX as a source of Hebrew textual variants."[41] In this view, the LXX is regarded, for the most part, as a mine for textual variants to the MT. It can be used for textual criticism when it seems to have been based on a source text similar to the MT to help create a better MT. Reconstructing a better MT, however, should not be confused with reconstructing the original text.

The evidence from the Dead Sea Scrolls, Samaritan Pentateuch, Greek Jewish Scriptures, and MT reveal that all were used as Scripture during the Second Temple period and that all witness to the Jewish Scriptures, but none may stake a historical claim for being the best witness to the original Jewish Scriptures or the Christian OT. Though this admission may cause some discomfort and lead to questions about how to present the OT in modern Bibles, it is not justification for a unilateral decision to proclaim one text as original. In fact, perhaps the academic community should use the abbreviation MT to stand for *Majority Text;* in much the same way that NT textual critics recognize that the Byzantine Text represents the later consolidation of an ecclesiastical text, so similar forces within Judaism produced its Majority Text.

C. PRESUPPOSITION 3: THE MEANING OF THE HEBREW BEHIND THE GREEK

The reader may be wondering why I am spending so much time building a case against the priority of the Majority Text, especially since the evidence from the NT indicates that the early church employed the Greek Jewish Scriptures with equal authority. The reason is that the presupposition

---

[39] See Tov, *Text-Critical Use of the Septuagint.*

[40] Jobes and Silva, *Invitation to the Septuagint,* 151–52.

[41] Ibid., 151; see also a similar reference to the "unique importance" of the Septuagint on p. 148, which is cited in their "Response to J. Barr's Review," 44.

of a Hebrew canon and the priority of the Hebrew text lead many to conclude that the Hebrew Scriptures form the matrix from which the NT writers developed their theological thinking and informed their citations. Together these presuppositions render it very difficult for an individual who holds these views to appreciate the use of the Greek Jewish Scriptures by the NT authors. Unfortunately, it is more difficult to provide examples of how the Majority Text is favored even when the Greek is cited. So, for example, in his discussion of the sources of Paul's thought, Ladd argues that "the Old Testament was the first Christian Bible,"[42] but he never explicitly addresses the problem that Paul cites passages from the Greek Jewish Scriptures that differ from the Majority Text. One is more likely to encounter a statement similar to that of Bauckham that the NT writers "developed their fresh understanding of the christological identity of God *through* creative exegesis of the Hebrew Scriptures."[43] But then Bauckham also states, "In my view, most early Christian exegesis was done with reference to the Hebrew text, even when the Greek text was also employed."[44] I do not wish to sound too harsh with respect to this comment, but what is the basis for this claim? When the NT writers cite a passage from the Greek Jewish Scriptures that is distinct from the Majority Text, on what logical basis can it be justified that they did so with reference to the Hebrew text? It is impossible to refute such a position, because Bauckham has already pronounced that this is what they must have done. Whether performing textual criticism on the OT passage or reading its citation in a NT passage, these presuppositions collectively serve to elevate the Hebrew Majority Text and marginalize the Greek Jewish Scriptures. The way in which this process excludes the Greek Jewish Scriptures from consideration may differ depending upon the presuppositions of the individual, but the result is the same. Bauckham articulates in print what many do in practice.

Considering the historical evidence regarding the status of the Scriptures during the first century and the indisputable proof that the NT writers relied on the Greek Jewish Scriptures in order to make some of their arguments and claims,[45] a question begs to be asked: why is it that many, even most, evangelical scholars give undue weight and preference to the Majority Text? This position is not, of course, exclusive to evangelical scholars, but it is characteristic of scholars who identify themselves as evangelical. The answer to this question resides in some aspect of confessional/doctrinal bias, which is rooted in one's view of inspiration.[46]

---

[42] Ladd, *Theology of the New Testament,* 394.

[43] Bauckham, *God Crucified,* 72 (emphasis original).

[44] Ibid., 50.

[45] In addition to works already cited, see Gheorghita, *Role of the Septuagint in Hebrews.*

[46] For discussion of inspiration and inerrancy in this regard, see Michaels, "Inerrancy or Verbal Inspiration?"

II. The Use of Scripture and the Inspiration of the Original Text

Several well-known evangelical seminaries emphasize their understanding of Scripture and inspiration by placing this doctrine first in their statements of faith:

> *Gordon-Conwell Theological Seminary:* "The sixty-six canonical books of the Bible as originally written were inspired of God, hence free from error. They constitute the only infallible guide in faith and practice."[47]
>
> *Trinity Evangelical Divinity School:* "We believe the Scriptures, both Old and New Testaments, to be the inspired Word of God, without error in the original writings, the complete revelation of His will for the salvation of men and the Divine and final authority for all Christian faith and life."[48]
>
> *Dallas Theological Seminary:* " . . . We believe that this divine inspiration extends equally and fully to all parts of the writings—historical, poetical, doctrinal, and prophetical—as appeared in the original manuscripts. We believe that the whole Bible in the originals is therefore without error."[49]

Though the formulations differ slightly, in each case these statements connect the notion of scriptural inspiration with the "original writings." Presumably, the preference for the Majority Text is grounded in the original writings of the OT being in the Hebrew and Aramaic languages. The historical basis for this view of Scripture can probably be traced to Luther, who insisted, like Jerome before him, that the OT Scriptures for the Christian should be based on the Hebrew Scriptures accepted by the Jews. Regardless of the origin of the idea, a great deal of evangelical scholarship retains a preference for the Majority Text because scholars presuppose a link between the inspiration of the original manuscripts and the form of the Scriptures preserved in the Majority Text.

The discovery of the Dead Sea Scrolls, however, exposed the link between the original writings and the Majority Text for what it really was: an assumption that completely contradicts the historical evidence! Not only do the early textual witnesses indicate the pluriformity of the texts and a loose collection of writings deemed to be Scripture in the Judaism of the first century, but the evidence from the NT itself clearly demonstrates dependence in many cases on the Greek Jewish Scriptures. Furthermore, within Judaism and the early church, the recognition and use of Scriptures

---

[47] See http://www.gordonconwell.edu/about/basis_faith.php (accessed Nov. 19, 2004).

[48] See http://www.teds.edu/trinity/about/doctrine.htm (accessed Nov. 19, 2004).

[49] See http://www.dts.edu/aboutdts/fulldoctrinalstatement.aspx (accessed Nov. 19, 2004).

extends beyond the original composition or translation of the Scriptures and the texts that descended from them[50]

The lowest common denominator for a solution to this dilemma is to acknowledge that the Majority Text is not equivalent to the original text of the Hebrew Scriptures. It is, for lack of better words, a synagogue text. It is a text that witnesses to the text form adopted by the dominant rabbinic party in Judaism sometime in the late second to third century C.E. Other editions and versions of a number of books existed at this time or had previously existed, but the ruling Jews made decisions to adopt particular books and particular forms of the books as the official Scriptures, and this decision eventually prevailed in the form of the Majority Text because they were the "winners" in the struggle for Jewish orthodoxy. Presumably, the second-century debates with Christians over the meaning of the Scriptures had a significant influence within Judaism on this process.[51] Two results follow from this conclusion: (1) as Tov acknowledges, the Majority Text is only one witness to the hypothetical original text; and (2) given the present evidence it is impossible to reconstruct by means of textual criticism anything close to an original text for books like Exodus, Judges, Samuel, Kings, Esther, Job, Isaiah, Jeremiah, Daniel, Psalms, and Proverbs. The types and number of differences between the textual witnesses to these books vary so considerably that insufficient means are available to reconstruct an original text for any of them as required and assumed by the definitions of the inspiration of Scripture quoted above.

Given that the Majority Text is not equivalent to the original text and that for many books we cannot reconstruct an original text, one could adopt an alternative position. That is, one might say (and perhaps there are those who already do), "I believe in the inspiration of the Scriptures in their original writings, but I really do not know what the original might have said." In the end, this agnostic position may be comforting to some, but it ultimately fails to address the problem raised by the NT writers' use of Scripture.

In many instances the NT writers' citation or allusion to Scripture is equivalent to the Greek Jewish Scriptures.[52] The pervasive agreement between NT citations and the Greek Jewish Scriptures is a formidable argument that by and large the NT writers were working primarily from Greek versions of the Scriptures. In instances where we see a distinct and marked

---

[50] For example, the text that Paul cites in 1 Cor 15:54 is identified with Theodotion's early Christian recension. See my *Use of the Septuagint,* 106. Theodotion is identified as a Christian who revised the Old Greek text in the second century C.E., but it is difficult to determine the date and extent of this work. How, for example, could Paul writing in the first century cite a text identified with Theodotion in the second century?

[51] Useful summaries of the apologetics of the early church fathers with the Jews are found in Hengel, *Septuagint as Christian Scripture,* 26–47; and Müller, *First Bible of the Church,* 67–82.

[52] Swete, *Introduction to the Old Testament in Greek,* 392.

difference between the Greek and Hebrew witnesses, the citation of the Greek Jewish Scriptures by the NT writers (e.g., the citation of Isa 40:13 in 1 Cor 2:16) cannot be explained on the basis of a Hebrew original, nor is it reasonable to assert that the writer could have been thinking about the Hebrew. As Silva argues, the differences between the Greek versions and the available Hebrew texts employed by Paul (and this observation applies to the other NT authors) are normally based in the exegetical practices and methods of the translators and not on a differing Hebrew source text.[53] Therefore, the NT authors' views and uses of Scripture cannot be restricted to a notion regarding the original writing, as required by the evangelical definitions of the inspiration of Scripture quoted above. While one may plead that in some way all Greek citations based on the Greek Jewish Scriptures ultimately rest on the intended meaning of the Hebrew or are based on a lost Hebrew manuscript, such an approach fails to account for the inevitable human element present in the process of translating the Scriptures into Greek and to account for the ways that the NT authors employed the Scriptures. In addition, a position that seeks to explain all deviations from the known Hebrew texts as deviations from unknown Hebrew texts still has to account for (a) the diversity of the textual witnesses in Hebrew and Greek, (b) the citations and use of noncanonical books in the NT and the early church fathers, and (c) the inclusion of noncanonical books in the early codices of the church.

Therefore, whatever else one may choose to regard as nonnegotiable in interpreting the NT and analyzing the use of the Scriptures by the NT writers, it seems to me that the historical evidence requires acknowledgement that the NT writers read and cited the Greek Jewish Scriptures as authoritative Scripture *in the same way* as Scriptures written in Hebrew. It is on this basis alone that one can constructively evaluate the texts and methods that the NT writers employed when they referred to Scripture. It logically follows from this conclusion—that is, the NT writers recognized Scriptures without regard to the original languages in which they were composed—that doctrinal affirmations about the original languages are not supported by the practice of the NT writers. Linking inspiration of Scripture with the original languages is rooted in a theological belief that is driven by the need to protect the inerrancy of Scripture, but it does not reflect the practice of the NT writers or the early church fathers.[54] In fact, some early church fathers argued that the Greek Jewish Scriptures were themselves inspired[55] (which has precedence in *Letter of Aristeas* 307–311, which emphasizes the divine origin of the Greek translation).

---

[53] Silva, "Old Testament in Paul," 632.

[54] Barr correctly points out that the doctrine of the inerrancy of Scripture lies at the heart of fundamentalism in his *Fundamentalism*.

[55] See Hengel, *Septuagint as Christian Scripture*, 25–56; and Müller, *First Bible of the Church*, 68–78.

This viewpoint may lead to two possible misconceptions: (1) acknowledging that the NT writers recognized Scriptures without regard to the original language in which they were composed is not intended to mean that Scripture was not important; and (2) arguing that the historical evidence does not support the priority of the proto-MT is not intended to devalue the necessity of textual criticism, for textual criticism of the texts retains, in my view, preeminent importance in biblical studies.

What then is to be done with a doctrinal statement that aligns the inspiration of Scriptures with the original languages? One could affirm that the NT writers' use of Scripture was not limited to the original languages or to the canon that emerged later, which left the writers free to grapple with the texts. This may also lead to the conviction that the doctrine of the inspiration and authority of the Scriptures does not necessarily have to be linked to their original language. However, one could still choose to affirm the inspiration of the Scriptures in the original languages on the basis of contemporary evangelical, ecclesiastical practice. The authority of the doctrine would then lie in the decree of the church, which would correctly reflect the theological emphasis on the doctrine in evangelical circles and give primacy to the original languages in which the Scriptures were written. In this way, one could still preserve the emphasis on the Majority Text for the OT, not on the basis of any inherent claim it has as the best historical witness to the original writings, but on the basis that it is the best witness to an ancient version of the Hebrew Scriptures/Old Testament in the original language (as advocated by Jobes and Silva). Scholarly integrity, however, would still compel one to acknowledge that the resources do not exist to reconstruct anything close to the original text for some books.

On the basis of this discussion, I suggest that the guiding presupposition for examining the NT authors' use of the Scriptures is to affirm that a multiplicity of texts witnessed to the Scriptures in the first century and that the authors were influenced by and may have drawn upon *any* of them without distinction. This presupposition is the basic step for understanding the ways in which they cited and alluded to Scripture and the possible ways that the Scriptures may have informed their theology. The application of this presupposition will inform the principles of interpretation and will lead to new possibilities as scholars continue in the quest to understand and apply the written word of God.

Part Three

New Testament Canon

CHAPTER NINE

From Story to Scripture: Emergence of the New Testament Writings as Scripture

THE NT CANON BEGAN WITH THE EARLY FOLLOWERS OF JESUS EXPERIENCING HIM as the risen Lord. No part of the NT was written on the basis of a pre-Easter Jesus; indeed, all of the Gospels were written from the perspective of persons who knew the end of the story before they began telling it. Jesus as risen Lord is, therefore, the essential presupposition of all NT writings. While some scholars seek to substantiate the origins of Christian faith in the historical Jesus, that is, a Jesus devoid of miracles and without the supernatural trappings attached to him, nothing in the NT supports this. Because Jesus was acknowledged as Lord on the basis of his resurrection from the dead, he was at the heart of religious faith and experience in the early church.[1] Therefore, his life, ministry, teachings, and fate (death and resurrection) were critical factors in the emergence and development of the early church. Early Christianity began in response to what its adherents believed had happened to them through Jesus of Nazareth. Their experience with the risen Lord is the presupposition for their continuing existence as a community of faith and their acknowledgement of their own writings as sacred Scripture.[2] This is true not only for the organization of the church, but also for the emergence of the literature that was eventually recognized as Scripture and canon in the church.

According to Sundberg, there were three stages in the history of the NT canon: (1) the rise of the NT writings to the status of Scripture; (2) the conscious groupings of such literature into closed collections (e.g., the four

---

[1] McDonald and Porter, *Early Christianity and Its Sacred Literature,* 13–18, 178–83.

[2] For discussions on the presence, centrality, and value of religious experience in the NT, see Johnson, *Religious Experience in Earliest Christianity;* and Berger, *Identity and Experience in the New Testament.*

Gospels and the Epistles of Paul); and (3) the formation of a closed list of authoritative literature.[3] These transitions and the various processes that led to the recognition of Christian writings as Scripture and eventually as canon are the subjects of this and the following chapters. Because the early church left no record of how its biblical canon was either born or developed—and much of the information that we do possess is therefore inferential—scholars disagree on these topics.

The earliest Christian community did not possess a fixed canon of *Christian* Scriptures, even though it freely and naturally adopted from Judaism the OT Scriptures as its Bible. The selective use of the OT Scriptures, however, shows that the interpretation of the OT was not the driving force behind the early church, but rather the church's interpretation of the significance of the Christ event—the life and teachings of Jesus of Nazareth, and especially his death and resurrection. The early Christian message focused on Jesus, who as the promised Messiah who called their community of faith into existence through his teachings, death, and resurrection.

The core of the OT Scriptures was the Mosaic Law. The Law, however, appears to be at variance with much of the NT focus on grace, especially the teaching of Jesus (e.g., Matt 5:21–22, 27–28, 31–32, 33–34, 38–39, 43–44), Paul (e.g., Gal 3–4; Rom 3–4), and Hellenistic Jewish Christianity (e.g., Heb. 8:8–11). Recognition of this change helps to explain why the early Christians' use of the OT is quite narrow, even though citations and quotations in the NT come from most of the Hebrew Scriptures. The most frequently cited OT texts in the NT are from the Psalms and the Prophets—not the Law.[4]

The problem of how to live free in Christ and yet be subject to the legal codes of the Law was a critical issue for the early Gentile Christian

---

[3] Sundberg, "Making of the New Testament Canon," 1217. A careful description of the canonical process may be found in J. A. Sanders, *Canon and Community,* 21–45. Sanders's *From Sacred Story,* 127–47, 175–90, contains an excellent discussion of the process of recognition of the authority and the stabilization of the OT biblical text, which is also applicable to the NT. See also idem, "Text and Canon: Old Testament and New."

[4] According to Andrew E. Hill, *Baker's Handbook of Bible Lists* (Grand Rapids: Baker, 1981), 102–3, the Old Testament books most frequently cited (or quoted or alluded to) in the New Testament are the following (number of references in parentheses):

Isaiah (419)
Psalms (414)
Exodus (240)
Genesis (238)
Deuteronomy (196)
Ezekiel (141)
Daniel (133)
Jeremiah (125)
Leviticus (107)
Numbers (73)

community, and it dealt with this problem in several contrasting ways: (1) by ignoring vast portions of the Law and adopting something of a "canon within the canon" approach to the Scriptures; (2) by allegorizing legal portions of the OT to bring them into harmony with the teachings of Jesus; (3) by emphasizing the faith principle that preceded the Law (as Paul did in Gal 3–4 and Rom 3–4), which in effect created a "canon with the canon"; (4) by rejecting the whole of the OT as Marcion did; or (5) by redefining the meaning of the Law as did Justin and others after him. However one chose to deal with the issue, it did not appear possible to have complete loyalty to a literal understanding of the OT Scriptures and at the same time give loyalty to the essentials of the Christian faith. Some interpretive or hermeneutical steps were taken in order to make the OT a *Christian* book and to allow the OT texts to be more relevant to the needs of the church and at one with the essentials of the Christian faith. This hermeneutical activity attests to the church's strong desire to have continuity with the faith of its Jewish ancestors.

The earliest *regula* (canon) for the Christian community was Jesus himself, whose words, deeds, and fate were interpreted afresh in numerous sociological contexts where the early Christians lived. The prophetic voice, which some Jews believed had ceased in Israel, was still very much alive in the early Christian community. In their early preaching, it is clear that the followers of Jesus believed that the age of prophecy—that is, the age of the Spirit and prophet expected to be manifested at the end of the age (Mal 4:5–6; cf. Joel 2:28–29; Ezek 36:27; 37:14)—was now alive in the power of the church's preaching (Acts 2:16–47; cf. Luke 4:14–19). The early Christians believed that the power of God was first manifested in Jesus and then in the church's witness to the risen Lord (Acts 1:8).[5]

The most frequently cited individual Old Testament texts in the New Testament are the following (number of times in parentheses):

Ps 110:1 (18)
Dan 12:1 (13)
Isa 6:1 (12)
Ezek 1:26–28 (12)
2 Chr 18:18/Ps 47:8/1 Kgs 22:19 (11)
Ps 2:7 (10)
Isa 53:7 (10)
Amos 3:13 (10)
Amos 4:13 (10)
Lev 19:18 (10)

[5] Although a critical interpretation of the book of Acts is plagued with difficulties because of the numerous historical and theological problems in the book, I believe that its depiction of the life and faith of the early church in its initial simplistic organization and beliefs—especially with the emphasis on the presence and power of the Spirit among them—is a fair representation of the actual state of affairs. The presence of charismatic preachers called prophets in the early church (e.g., 1 Cor 12:28; Eph 2:20; 4:11) is evidence of the widespread belief that the presence of the Spirit and the age of fulfillment had begun in the event of Jesus.

I. From Oral Tradition to Written Documents

Jesus himself never wrote a book, and, with the exception of the command of the risen Lord to the angels of the seven churches of Asia Minor (Rev 2:1, 8, 12, 18; 3:1, 7, 14), neither did he tell any of his followers to write a book. Written Christian documents were produced in the last half of the first century C.E., but only in the last decades of the first century did they begin to have a significant role in the life of the churches of Asia Minor. For example, the author of the book of Revelation claims an inspired status for his own writing (22:18–19), and by implication one can also see this in John 20:30–31.[6] Paul himself may have made a claim to inspiration for his letter to the Corinthians (1 Cor 7:40), or at least for advice that he gave to the church in writing. It is clear, however, that what Jesus said or did, whether it existed in oral or written form, was authoritative for the church.[7]

From the beginning, however, the proclamation about the death and resurrection of Jesus, as well as his life and teaching, circulated among the Christian churches in oral form. While some of this tradition was written down quite early (ca. 50–65),[8] much of it was transmitted orally for a considerable time. As late as the second century, for example, Papias[9] could still say that he preferred oral communications about Jesus to the written messages of books: "For I did not suppose that information from books would help me so much as the word of a living and surviving voice" (Eusebius, *Hist. eccl.* 3.39.4, LCL).[10] Although he did not reject written traditions about Jesus, it is clear that he preferred oral tradition. According to F. C. Baur, Papias appears to have wanted "to keep the immediacy of the

---

[6] See also 1 John 1:4; 2:1, 7, 12–14, 26; and 5:13, which point to the value of a *written* message.

[7] See, e.g., 1 Cor 7:10, 17; 9:14; 11:23; John 2:22; 6:63; 12:48–50; and 2 Pet 3:2. Notice also that the role of the Paraclete in John 14:26 is to bring to mind what Jesus *said*. In Rev 3:8–11, the risen Christ praised the Christians in Philadelphia because they "have kept my word and have not denied my name."

[8] Many scholars agree that prior to the writings of the NT, some early writings that are no longer extant were produced for the church, such as Q, the earliest form of Mark 16:9–20, some of the sayings in the *Gospel of Thomas,* and possibly an earlier form of Mark ("UrMark"). Luke 1:1–4 indicates that Luke was aware of others who had written on the story of Jesus.

[9] Von Campenhausen believes that it is possible to date Papias as early as the end of the first century, but it is more likely that he said these words while leader of the church in Hieropolis in the third or fourth decade of the second century. Von Campenhausen also believes that it is unlikely that Papias knew of more Gospels than Matthew and Mark; *Formation of the Christian Bible,* 129–30, 133.

[10] Papias's statement is evidence of the growing use and significance of the Gospels (at least Matthew and Mark) in the church, as well as their not yet equal status with the OT Scriptures. There is at this time no reliable witness that the Gospels were read liturgically or scripturally in the church.

original revelation as a present reality by clinging to the living word, not to the dead, transient written text."[11]

Barr makes the interesting observation that both Plato and the Pharisees had a "cultural presupposition" that the writing down of a profound truth was "an *unworthy* mode of transmission."[12] Plato, telling the words of Socrates to Phaedrus, shows concern that the mere writing of something will adversely affect the superior ability of the mind to memorize:

> For this invention [writing] will produce forgetfulness in the minds of those who learn to use it, because they will not practice their memory. Their trust in writing, produced by external characters which are no part of themselves, will discourage the use of their own memory within them. . . .
>
> He who thinks, then, that he has left behind him any art in writing, and he who receives it in the belief that anything in writing will be clear and certain, would be an utterly simple person, and in truth ignorant of the prophecy of Ammon, if he thinks written words are of any use except to remind him who knows the matter about which they are written. (Plato, *Phaedrus* 275AC, LCL)

The rabbis had several sayings that suggested that the "oral Torah" ought not to be put into writing (*b. Gittin* 60b; *b. Temura* 14b).[13] Because Jesus neither wrote nor commanded his disciples to write anything down, Barr concludes that the "idea of a Christian faith governed by Christian written holy Scriptures was not an essential part of the foundation plan of Christianity."[14] The church passed on this "living witness" of Jesus the Christ first through the apostles and subsequently through prophets and teachers, who continued to have a significant role in the Christian community well into the second century. Even in the late second century, the Christians had a great deal of appreciation for the oral tradition of the church.[15]

Perkins argues that orthodox and gnostic Christians of the second century preserved their link with the past largely through oral tradition.[16] Following von Campenhausen's lead,[17] Perkins maintains that the only authoritative text for Christians, both orthodox and gnostic, in this period was the OT writings, which were perceived as witnesses to the tradition

---

[11] F. C. Baur, as quoted by von Campenhausen, *Formation of the Christian Bible,* 135. It is also quite likely that the author of the *Didache* used Matthew, or a tradition shared with Matthew, as well as oral traditions circulating about Jesus at the end of the first century; see Grant, "New Testament Canon," 290.

[12] Barr, *Holy Scripture,* 12 (emphasis original), who also suggests that this perspective may lie behind 2 Cor 3:6. Barr follows Gerhardsson, *Memory and Manuscript,* 157–59, who cites an ancient rabbinic saying that "the Torah is transmitted on the lips" and must be transmitted orally.

[13] Gerhardsson, *Memory and Manuscript,* 159.

[14] Barr, *Holy Scripture,* 12.

[15] Grant, "New Testament Canon," 297.

[16] Perkins, *Gnostic Dialogue,* 196–201.

[17] Von Campenhausen, *Formation of the Christian Bible,* 103–21.

embodied in the community at large. Irenaeus, though strongly committed to a fixed written tradition, believed that the Christian community would have preserved its message accurately even if there had been no written Gospels:[18]

> Since therefore we have such proofs [of the truth], which is easily obtained from the Church, it is not necessary to seek the truth among others [heretics]. [This is so] because, the apostles, like a rich man who [deposited his money] in a bank, placed in her [the Church's] hands most copiously an abundance of all things pertaining to the truth: so that every man, whosoever will, can draw from her the water of life. For she is the entrance to life and all others are thieves and robbers. Because of this are we are obligated to avoid them [the heretics], and to choose of the things pertaining to the Church with the utmost diligence laying hold of the tradition of the truth. Now how do we decide the issue? Suppose there arose a dispute relative to some important question among us. Should we not be obliged to turn to the most ancient Churches with which the apostles had dialogue and learn from them what is certain and clear in regard to the present question? And what should we do if the apostles themselves had not left us writings? Would it not be necessary, [in that case,] to follow the course of the tradition that they handed down to those to whom they entrusted the leadership of the Churches? (*Haer.* 3.4.1, *ANF*)

Generally speaking, there were no authoritative Christian texts in the early second century, and the only texts reckoned to be binding on the Christian community were the OT Scriptures. Hermeneutical reflection was thus largely on OT writings and *not* on the NT. The second century saw a growing awareness of the value of Christian writings,[19] and largely with Justin and Irenaeus the center of authority moved away from oral traditions to a fixed normative text, even though the prompting for such a move in the orthodox community *may* have started earlier with Marcion.

At this point, one must ask why the literature of the NT was written down at all, since we know that the church's message existed for a considerable period of time in oral form. Why was the written tradition preserved and given priority in the church? Many motives are possible, but the first, of course, is that over time memory fails. Poorly kept (i.e., poorly remembered) oral tradition would result in flawed theology and polity.[20]

Second, even though the fairly reliable means of communicating significant amounts of information through Jewish oral traditions was, as form-

---

[18] Perkins, *Gnostic Dialogue,* 197.

[19] The primary focus of the NT Gospels is the words and deeds of Jesus; and in the Apostolic Fathers, with the exception of *1 Clement,* NT texts are referred to more frequently than are OT texts (but most of these refer to the words of Jesus and not the texts themselves). See Aland, *Problem of the New Testament Canon,* 3.

[20] For examples from the early church fathers that illustrate the difficulty of certifying oral tradition, see Grant, "Creation of the Christian Tradition," 14–15, who also argues that as Christianity spread into the big cities the only tradition that could have survived was preserved in books.

critical scholars reasonably show, used by the early Christians,[21] the deaths of some of the first witnesses to the Christ event (the apostles) and the delay of the Parousia (the second coming of Jesus) must have influenced to some degree the writing down and preservation of those oral traditions.

Third, apologetic motives likely stand behind the writing of several of the NT documents. For example, the Acts may have been written *in part* to emphasize certain catholicizing tendencies in both Jewish Christianity (represented by Peter) and Hellenistic Christianity (represented especially by Paul) to come together as one unified church (Acts 15). The Pastoral Epistles may have been written in the name of Paul to meet both the practical and organizational needs of the church as well as the doctrinal needs of a post-Marcionite Christian community.[22]

Fourth, although most of the literature of the NT was written prior to the end of the first century, the need for such literature for community worship, instruction, and apologetic purposes became more apparent to the church in the second century. And to some extent the NT authors themselves saw the value of Christian writing (e.g., Rom 15:15; the whole of Galatians; 2 Cor 1:13; John 20:30–31; 1 John 2:1, 7–8).

Finally, the Epistles especially, but possibly also the Gospels, were written in part as matters of policy for an expanding church when it became more difficult to communicate in person. Paul's Letters often indicate that they were sent in lieu of a visit or to prepare the community for his visits (e.g., Rom 1:9–15; 15:24; 2 Cor 1:13–16; Col 4:15–16; 1 Thess 3:5; cf. 2 John 12 and 3 John 13).[23]

Perhaps all of these reasons, and others as well, encouraged the writers of the NT to produce Christian literature, but, with the exception of the author of the book of Revelation, no conscious or clear effort was made by these authors to produce *Christian* Scriptures. It is only at a later stage in the second century, when the literature they produced began to function authoritatively within the Christian community, that its status as Scripture began to be acknowledged. Two closed collections of NT writings gained widespread recognition and acceptance (canon 1) in the early church: the Gospels and the Letters of Paul.

---

[21] See especially Gerhardsson, *Memory and Manuscript,* 324–35; and Cranfield, "Gospel of Mark," 271.

[22] The teaching that the resurrection was already past or that it was a spiritual event (2 Tim 2:18), the teaching that persons should abstain from marriage (1 Tim 2:15; 4:3; 5:14) as well as from certain foods (1 Tim 4:3; 5:23; Titus 1:15), and the references to myths and genealogies (1 Tim 1:4; Titus 3:9) all suggest some form of gnosticizing tendencies in the church, but because of the focus on the Law (1 Tim 1:7–11), perhaps some form of a Jewish-flavored heresy in the community was addressed in the letter. The need to clarify the function of various offices and ministries in the church (1 Tim 3–5) probably suggests a developed Christian community that was most likely postapostolic.

[23] Brown in Turro and Brown, "Canonicity," 525, maintains that the geographical distance separating the churches was overcome through the circulation of letters.

II. Gospels

A. AUTHORITY OF THE GOSPELS IN THE EARLY CHURCH

It is not surprising that the early Christians made frequent use of and eventually cited by name the writings that we now call the canonical Gospels. Given that Jesus was the final authority for the church, it would be strange, indeed, if the early Christians had ignored the various witnesses to his life, ministry, death, and resurrection that were in circulation in the first two centuries of the church's life. The literature that focused on Jesus' words and deeds was welcomed in the churches probably from the time of its production. The authority of this tradition—canonical or noncanonical gospels—was widely acknowledged in the churches. The sources used to produce the canonical Gospels were primarily oral traditions that were eventually written down and perhaps edited over a period of time to produce what the church later called Gospels. These Gospels were utilized in the church's worship and catechetical instruction, in its defense in the pagan world, and in its response to the heretical challenges it faced by the end of the first century and beyond. Smith rightly concludes that those who wrote the Gospels initially did so with the idea of producing an authoritative guide to the Christian faith for the churches and also with the idea of continuing the biblical story. He adds that the continuation of the biblical story is a further distinguishing feature of the NT writings in general and that they presuppose the biblical story of salvation history for the people of God as they interpret history.[24] Von Campenhausen agrees and says the Evangelists intended from the beginning that what they wrote would be read in the churches.[25]

Scholars have long been aware that the way the Gospels were crafted displays the church's long use of these materials in their oral transmission prior to being written down. Christians were not devoid of teaching materials before the Gospels were produced in the churches.[26] Early Christians employed the skills developed by Jews to transmit and teach orally their story about Jesus and religious traditions. Gerhardsson supports this view with several examples of how these traditions were passed on in the churches.[27] Some scholars contend that the early followers of Jesus were not sophisticated enough to utilize such methods or were simply unaware of them. Gerhardsson calls into question three common erroneous assumptions that scholars of Christian origins often hold: (1) that there was no positive relationship between Pharisaic teachers on the one side and

---

[24] D. M. Smith, "When Did the Gospels Become Scripture?" 8–9.

[25] Von Campenhausen, *Formation of the Christian Bible,* 122–23.

[26] Teaching was an important ingredient in the churches from the beginning (Acts 2:42; 6:2–4; 28:31; 1 Cor 12:28; Rom 12:7; Eph 4:11; etc.).

[27] Gerhardsson, *Memory and Manuscript,* 324–35.

Jesus and the early church on the other; (2) that Jesus, his disciples, and other leaders of the early church were, and remained, simple and unlearned; and (3) that the "spontaneous charismatic aspect of Jesus and early Christianity ruled out acceptance of traditional forms, conscious technique and reasoned behaviour."[28]

This does not mean, of course, that the Gospels were understood as sacred Scripture either in their oral transmission or when those traditions were put into written form. Because of their subject matter, however, namely, the words and activity of Jesus, it was clear early on that these writings would be taken seriously by the churches for which they were produced—and they were! The widespread appeal of this tradition in the church, even in its oral stage of development, can be seen in the NT writings themselves.[29] There is considerable evidence for the widespread acceptance of this tradition in both its oral transmission stage (e.g., in Paul's Letters, Acts, 1 Peter, and James) and the writings of the church fathers, who depended on both the oral and written transmission of that tradition about Jesus.[30]

How and when did the church adopt the canonical Gospels as Scripture, and when did it say "these four and no more" and put them in the place of priority that they have in all of the surviving manuscripts and catalogues of NT Scriptures? When and why were they (usually) placed in their current order in the NT? The whole church did not immediately or unanimously accept all of the canonical Gospels, for other writings competed for a place among them. Many Christians in the fourth century and later continued to prefer noncanonical writings such as Tatian's *Diatessaron* and the *Infancy Gospel of James*. The Syrian churches especially gave priority to Tatian's harmonization of the canonical Gospels over the individual canonical Gospels. Tatian's use of the canonical Gospels to produce his harmony underscores, of course, the value that he attributed to them, but nevertheless his *Diatessaron* shows that other gospels were used in churches for several centuries more.

The churches of the first and second centuries welcomed and utilized the traditions that had been handed down to them in both oral and written form, and this time is foundational for their future in the church. While the available sources are scanty, we can trace some of the developing influence and acceptance of the Gospel tradition and how this tradition was put into writing and then accepted in the churches as Scripture at the earliest

---

[28] Ibid., 23.

[29] For a useful discussion of the influence of the sayings of Jesus in their oral or prewritten stage of development in the writings of Paul, see the older but still valuable contribution by Dungan, *Sayings of Jesus in the Churches of Paul*.

[30] For examples of the early church's use of the canonical Gospels and other Christian literature, see Koester, *Ancient Christian Gospels;* idem, *Synoptischen Überlieferung;* Massaux, *Influence of the Gospel of Saint Matthew;* and Metzger, *Canon of the New Testament*.

by the end of the second century. Initially the Gospel traditions were received as reliable reports of the sayings and deeds of Jesus, and the second-century references or allusions to them are not to the Gospels themselves but rather to the sayings and deeds of Jesus.

Generally speaking, there are few references to the books themselves or to their authors throughout the first two-thirds of the second century. Eusebius (ca. 320–30) indicates that Papias (ca. 130–40) knew of the traditions of Jesus in Mark and Matthew and that he made use of 1 John, 1 Peter, and the *Gospel of Hebrews* (*Hist. eccl.* 3.39.14–17). The names of the writers of the Gospels were relatively unimportant, however, until later in the second century, beginning with Irenaeus. These names became more important in the fourth century when matters of canon were discussed in the various churches and it was assumed that if an *apostle* wrote a document, then the churches would accept it as Scripture. Gregory describes this state of affairs: "There was then no formation of the canon in the sense that a general council took up the question. The number of books in the NT simply grew. When anyone had the question as to the sacred character of a book to decide, he was very likely to ask whether it was from an apostle or not."[31]

From the time when the Gospels were written until the middle of the second century at the earliest, apostolic authorship was not yet viewed as one of the significant features of the new Christian writings.[32] The canonical Gospels were produced anonymously, but in the middle to late second century names of apostles (Matthew and John) and those who assisted them (Mark and Luke) began to be attached to these writings to lend credibility to their reports. What led the church to add apostolic names to the NT literature (the Gospels, but perhaps also 1 John and Hebrews) is not clear, but it probably *started* when both the eyewitnesses and those who heard them had died and issues of credibility were raised in the churches. At roughly the same time, pseudonymous writings in the names of the apostolic community began to appear throughout the second century. The name of an apostle was apparently intended to validate the reliability of a pseudonymous writing.

The early dating and reliability of Mark and Luke have in part been supported precisely because their work was *not* attributed to an apostle. Could these nonapostolic works have survived antiquity had they been produced in the second century when apostolic names were the order of the day and were attached to pseudonymous writings? The widespread acceptance and use of the canonical Gospels, especially Matthew, reflects the churches' awareness of the Synoptic tradition in the churches. Eventually the Gospels of Matthew and John were acknowledged by the churches to

[31] Gregory, *Canon and Text of New Testament,* 293.

[32] For example, Clement of Rome shows an awareness of the language of 1 Cor 15:23 and 12:21 (*1 Clem.* 37.3–4), but makes no mention of Paul as the author, even though he knew it (*1 Clem.* 47.1–3). Because Paul's name appears on all of his writings, his name is more frequently mentioned in the second century, but not always.

be apostolic in origin, but this was long after their use in the churches. The long list of references to these works in the Apostolic Fathers shows that the focus of the citations was on the sayings of Jesus rather than on the documents themselves. The interpreting, presuming, and continuing of the biblical story, and especially the story and significance of Jesus, appears to be an important ingredient in the NT Gospels and in many of the Epistles.[33]

The Bible is not a collection of writings that simply deposits the revelation of God into loosely connected texts, but rather it sets forth a story in which the revelation of God unfolds historically and is proclaimed and explained. While extracanonical gospels produced by anonymous and pseudonymous writers probably contain some authentic sayings of Jesus (e.g., *Gospel of Thomas, Dialogue of the Saviour, Apocryphon of John,* and *Sophia of Jesus Christ*), they are generally without a context or narrative for understanding them, which is not the case in the canonical Gospels.

The value of the Gospels as reliable reports of the church's sacred traditions about Jesus was soon recognized in the churches, and several books were probably circulating among the churches within at least a few decades of their production. By the end of the second century, the canonical Gospels were also beginning to be received by many Christians as their authoritative Scriptures.

B. CITATIONS OF THE GOSPEL TRADITION IN THE EARLY CHURCH

The authority initially attributed to the canonical Gospels in the early churches was doubtless because they told the story of Jesus, the Lord of the church. This is why the early church writings appealed to the sayings of Jesus themselves rather than to the apostles or to the books they reportedly produced. The widespread and early reception of the canonical Gospels in the churches was due to their continuing a popular tradition that had long been circulating in these churches. The tradition (written or oral) that lies behind the Synoptic Gospels was widely received in the churches years before the actual production of these Gospels. The information in them was compatible with the basic outlines and teachings of the Gospel of John and with much of the rest of the NT writings.

---

[33] D. M. Smith, "When Did the Gospels Become Scripture?" 17–18, makes this point. Along with the Gospels, several of Paul's Letters were also read publicly in various churches (Col 4:16), and this suggests that they too were received as authoritative writings of some sort early on, perhaps from Paul himself. Notice, for example, Paul's authoritative tone in many passages in his letters that suggests that he viewed his writings as authoritative if not prophetic (1 Cor 5:3–5; 6:1–6; 7:10–11, 17–20, 40; 11:23–34; Gal 5:1–4). The author of 2 Pet 3:15–16 (perhaps ca. 90–100 or as late as ca. 150–80) also acknowledged Paul's writings as Scripture, and his comments may be reflective of what many churches believed about the Letters of Paul by the end of the second century.

Dungan suggests that Paul was significantly interested in the sayings and traditions about Jesus. He claims that even when Paul does not specifically refer to the words and deeds of Jesus, he nevertheless assumes their familiarity among his readers (e.g., 1 Cor 7:1–7; 9:4–18). Dungan concludes that "the alleged contrast between Pauline Christianity and that branch of the early Church which preserved the Palestinian Jesus-tradition that finally ended up in the Synoptic gospels is a figment of the imagination. In fact, they were one and the same branch."[34]

While Dungan suggests many similarities between the Synoptic tradition and Paul, especially with Matthew, he asserts that there are no parallels in that tradition to support Paul's stand on the law: "The reason Paul did not appeal to any sayings of Jesus in support of his stand on the Torah was because there weren't any"![35] He also shows that Paul "stands squarely within the tradition that led to the Synoptic gospels, and is of one mind with the editors of those gospels, not only in the way he understands what Jesus (the Lord) was actually commanding in the sayings themselves but also in the way he prefigures the Synoptic editors' use of them."[36]

Koester agrees with Dungan and shows that, even though Paul's references to sayings of Jesus are rare, he nonetheless makes several allusions to the Synoptic sayings of Jesus (cf. e.g., 1 Cor 7:10–11 and Mark 10:11–12; 1 Cor 9:14 and Luke 10:7 [Q]; and 1 Cor 11:23–26 and Mark 14:22–25; cf. 1 Cor 7:25, where Paul has "no command of the Lord"). Other Pauline parallels to the Synoptic tradition fit a particular pattern related to church life and order and are concentrated in Rom 12–14; 1 Cor 7–14; and 1 Thess 5.[37] Koester concludes that the Synoptic parallels are either church-order materials from the Gospel of Mark or sayings from Luke's Sermon on the Plain (Luke 6:17–49). Only in the case of 1 Cor 9:14 is the Synoptic parallel from a different context.[38] Paul's familiarity with the largely oral tradition that was later preserved in the Synoptic Gospels indicates that this oral tradition was commonly circulating in the first-century churches. The Synoptic tradition also has significant parallels in 1–2 Peter and James.[39]

---

[34] Dungan, *Sayings of Jesus in the Churches of Paul,* 150.

[35] Ibid.

[36] Ibid., 139.

[37] Other Pauline-Synoptic parallels include the following:
Rom 12:14 and Luke 6:27 (Q)
Rom 12:17 and Luke 6:29 (Q)
Rom 12:18 and Mark 9:50 (possibly)
Rom 13:7 and Mark 12:13–17
Rom 14:10 and Luke 6:37 (Q)
Rom 14:13 and Mark 9:42
Rom 14:14 and Mark 7:15
1 Thess 5:2 and Luke 12:39 (Q)
1 Thess 5:13 and Mark 9:50
1 Thess 5:15 and Luke 6:29 (Q)

[38] Koester, *Ancient Christian Gospels,* 52–54.

[39] Koester, *Ancient Christian Gospels,* 64–65, 71–73, lists the following parallels between the Synoptic tradition and 1–2 Peter and James:

Numerous Synoptic parallels and citations may be found in the writings of the second-century church fathers.[40] The sayings of Jesus, whether oral or written, were considered canonical, that is, they were authoritative in the early church (canon 1), even though their location in the written Gospels produced by apostles was of little consequence until around the middle of the second century. The available second-century evidence allows us to infer that dependence on the Synoptic Gospels is likely when the word selection and word order in the church fathers closely matches that found in the Synoptic traditions. In other cases, however, the words are similar but not exact, which suggests that the writers were either borrowing loosely from the Synoptic tradition and/or that a common oral or written tradition about Jesus circulating in the early church was known to both the Evangelists and the second-century church fathers. Matthew is by far the most popular gospel in the second century, having more parallels in the second-century writings than do Mark, Luke or John.[41]

Jas 1:5 and Luke 11:9/Matt 7:7
Jas 2:5 and Luke 6:20/Matt 5:3
Jas 4:2–3 and Matt 7:7, 11
Jas 4:9 and Luke 6:21/Matt 5:4
Jas 4:10 and Luke 14:11/Matt 23:12
Jas 5:1 and Luke 6:24–25
Jas 5:2–3 and Matt 6:20/Luke 12:33
Jas 5:12 and Matt 5:34–37
1 Pet 2:12 and Matt 5:16
1 Pet 2:19–20 and Luke 6:32–33
1 Pet 3:9, 16 and Luke 6:28
1 Pet 3:14 and Matt 5:10
1 Pet 4:14 and Luke 6:22
2 Pet 1:16–18 and Mark 9:2–8/Matt 17:1–8/Luke 9:28–36

[40] See Massaux, *Influence of the Gospel of Saint Matthew,* 1:166–72; 2:351–66; and 3:250–58, for useful lists of parallels and citations of the canonical Gospel literature. See Oxford Society of Historical Theology, *New Testament in the Apostolic Fathers,* a helpful guide to many of these references. Koester's *Synoptische Überlieferung* is still one of the best discussions of the significance of these references, though his work is limited to the Gospels.

[41] Second-century parallels with the Synoptic Gospels are too numerous to list here; for a full list, see Massaux, *Influence of the Gospel of Saint Matthew,* 1.166–72; 2.351–66; and 3.250–58 (see also the useful addenda in 1.58, 83, 121; 2.25, 52, 164, 242, 262, 293; 3.9, 102, 115, 119, 132, 143, 181); and Metzger, *Canon of the New Testament,* 39–73. Some of the more obvious Matthean parallels are the following:

1 Clem. 16.17 and Matt 11:29
1 Clem. 24.5 and Matt 13:3–9
1 Clem. 46.8 and Matt 26:24; 18:6
2 Clem. 3.2 and Matt 10:32
2 Clem. 4.2 and Matt 7:21
2 Clem. 6.2 and Matt 16:26
Ign. *Phld.* 3.1 and Matt 15:13
Ign. *Smyrn.* 1.1 and Matt 3:15
Pol. *Phil.* 2.3 and Matt 5:3, 10
Pol. *Phil.* 12.3 and Matt 5:16, 44, 48

Clement of Rome (ca. 95), for example, cites mostly the OT Scriptures, but shows an awareness of Matthew and several other NT writings, especially Paul's Letters. He generally does not cite them by name or author, except in one case where he clearly states that Paul is the author of 1 Corinthians and then calls Paul's letter a "gospel": "Take up the epistle of the blessed Paul the Apostle. What did he first write to you at the beginning of the gospel [*tou euangeliou*]? With true inspiration [*ep' alētheias pneumatikōs*] he charged you concerning himself and Cephas and Apollos, because even then you had made yourselves partisans" (*1 Clem.* 47.1–3, adapted from LCL).[42] The Pseudo-Clementine letter (ca. 130–40) known as *2 Clement* was written three or four decades after *1 Clement* and shows varying degrees of dependence on the Synoptic Gospels.[43]

My point is that Christian writers in the early part of the second century show many parallels with the Synoptic tradition, whether oral or written,

---

Mart. Pol. 4 and Matt 10:23
Mart. Pol. 6.2 and Matt 10:36; 27:5
Mart. Pol. 7.1 and Matt 26:55; 6:10
Mart. Pol. 8.1 and Matt 21:7
Mart. Pol. 11.2 and Matt 25:46
Mart. Pol. 14.2 and Matt 20:22–23
Barn. 4.14 and Matt 22:14
Barn. 5.8–9 and Matt 9:13
Barn. 7.9 and Matt 27:28

[42] It may seem odd that Clement appealed to Paul's writings more than to the Synoptic tradition—and even stranger that Paul is later ignored by Justin in favor of the Synoptic tradition. There are no clear references to Paul in Justin's writings, but Clement of Rome acknowledges the inspiration of Paul's writings (*1 Clem.* 47.1–2). The reason for this change is that Marcion appealed almost exclusively to Paul to justify his rejection of the Jewish Scriptures and traditions. Marcion's contemporary, Justin, was conversely anxious to root Christian faith squarely within the tradition of Israel and its Scriptures. Since Paul was used by Marcion to support his anti-Jewish bias, it is not surprising that Justin ignored Paul and appealed to the tradition that Marcion apparently rejected.

[43] Close similarities between *2 Clement* and the Synoptic Gospels indicate strong dependence:

2 Clem. 13 and Matt 5:7; 6:14; 7:1–2
2 Clem. 46 and Matt 26:24; 18:6; Mark 14:21; 9:42; Luke 22:22; 17:1–2
Some parallels between these two writings are not as sharp:
2 Clem. 2.4 and Matt 9:13; Mark 2:17
2 Clem. 3.2 and Matt 10:32
2 Clem. 6.1 and Matt 6:24; Luke 16:13
2 Clem. 6.2 and Matt 16:26; Mark 8:36
Finally, other texts are close in subject matter, but do not use parallel words:
2 Clem. 2.7 and Luke 19:10
2 Clem. 4.2 and Matt 7:21
2 Clem. 8.5 and Luke 16:10–12
2 Clem. 9.11 and Matt 12:50; Mark 3:35; Luke 8:21
2 Clem. 13.4 and Luke 6:32, 35

and that the Synoptic tradition was well known in the second-century Christian communities. Even though the NT writers are generally not mentioned by name *as writers* during this time (except for Paul in *1 Clem.* 47 and the NT writers named by Papias in Eusebius, *Hist. eccl.* 3.39.14–17), the many allusions to and direct citations of the Synoptic Gospels in the second century testify to their widespread acceptance in the early churches. In sum, all of this detail indicates that the sources from which the church fathers obtained their traditions about Jesus were either widely known or perhaps unimportant to them.[44]

C. EMERGENCE OF AUTHORSHIP: ORAL TRADITION TO MEMOIRS

Given the place of priority that the apostles had in the NT and in the early church fathers, it often seems strange to students that several important books of the NT were produced anonymously, namely, the Gospels, Acts, Hebrews, and 1 John. In the mid-second century, when both the eyewitnesses and those who heard them were gone, apostolic authorship became an important matter in the church. At that time, numerous pseudonymous gospels, acts, and letters were produced in an apostle's name.[45] Many scholars contend that some of the early church's pseudonymous literature actually made it into the NT canon precisely because it was attributed to an apostle, namely, the Pastoral Epistles, 2 Thessalonians, perhaps Ephesians and Colossians, 2 Peter, and the canonical Gospels. Such literature, they claim, was produced when the practice of attaching apostolic names to literature had grown in significance in the churches (ca. 130–50 C.E.).

When the canonical Gospels were written, apostolic authorship had not yet emerged within the church as a significant feature of Christian writings, and this probably accounts for their anonymity.[46] When the notion emerged that apostolic authorship added credibility to the various traditions that were circulating about Jesus in the churches, *then* the names of apostles, who *remembered* the words and deeds of Jesus, were commonly

[44] The early church fathers cite the *sayings* of Jesus more accurately than they do the various *narrative* materials in the Gospels. This could mean that the sayings circulated at first, and for a longer period of time, without the narratives in which they are currently located, or that the second-century church fathers saw the sayings of Jesus as more valuable and handed them on more carefully in the churches.

[45] For a comprehensive collection of these pseudonymous writings, along with significant comment, see Schneemelcher, *New Testament Apocrypha.*

[46] When Papias speaks of the Gospels (Eusebius, *Hist. eccl.* 3.39.15–16), he discusses Mark's Gospel first and then Matthew's even though he considered Matthew to be the author of "oracles" of Jesus. Also, in neither instance does he call these productions gospels, and authorship is apparently not a factor in his preference for the oral tradition.

noted and appealed to for guidance in church life and its witness.[47] This development also lies behind, and gave rise to, Irenaeus's notion of apostolic succession (*Haer.* 3.3.3). His point was that those closest to Jesus would likely tell a more accurate story about who he was, what he said and did, and what was done to him than would those who were not eyewitnesses. Those eyewitnesses would most likely also pass on that sacred tradition to their successors. While Irenaeus preferred the use of the apostolic writings in his argument, he also acknowledged the importance of the apostolic tradition handed on in the churches: "For how should it be if the apostles themselves had not left us writings? Would it not be necessary in that case to follow the course of the tradition that they handed down to those to whom they handed over the leadership of the churches?" (*Haer.* 3.4.1, adapted from *ANF*).

Until Irenaeus, apostolic authority in the churches was generally focused on the apostles *as a group* and not on individual apostles who reportedly produced the Gospels. This growth in the importance of apostolic authority was accompanied in the churches by references to the "memoirs" or "remembrances" of the apostles. In Justin, for instance, it is not clear which writings he had in mind since he cites or alludes to more traditions than the canonical Gospels. In the middle of the second century, priority began to be given to certain writings precisely because of their supposed apostolic origin. Evidence for the widespread approval of "apostolic" literature in the churches by the latter half of the second century can be seen in the use and citation not only of canonical literature but also of extracanonical literature that was produced under apostolic names: *Gospel of Thomas, Infancy Gospel of James, Acts of Paul, Gospel of Peter, Acts of Andrew,* and many others.

The gnostic community also appealed to "remembered" knowledge from the apostles. The remembrances of the apostles was the source of a secret knowledge that the gnostics claimed was passed on by the apostles to certain individuals in the church. In turn, those individuals remembered these words and committed them to writing. The implication of this was, of course, that the writings that contained the remembered words of the apostles became recognized as authoritative teachings in their churches. Koester shows that the word *remember* was a decisive term for the trustworthiness of oral tradition and that it played an important role in establishing the credibility of other literature. For example, in the *Apocryphon of James* (ca. 130–150), the author claims that "the twelve disciples [were] all sitting together at the same time and remembering what the Savior had said to each one of them, whether in secret or openly, and [putting it]

[47] The authority of the apostles was clearly acknowledged in the church's earliest traditions (1 Cor 12:28; Gal 1:15–17; 2:9; Eph 4:11; Acts 2:42; 6:2, 6; 8:1), but attaching their names to the story of Jesus to show the reliability of the reports was a later development.

in books."[48] This emphasis on the apostles is also found in the gnostic *Letter of Peter to Philip,* where what the apostles said by way of instruction from Jesus is repeated frequently to clarify its significance for faith (e.g., §§133, 136, 138–140).

Justin, writing from Rome (ca. 160), refers to the apostolic tradition: "For the apostles in the memoirs composed by them, which are called Gospels, have thus delivered to us what was enjoined upon them; 'that Jesus took bread, and when He had given thanks,' said, 'This do you in remembrance of me, this is my body'; and, 'after the same manner . . .' " (*1 Apol.* 66.3, adapted from *ANF*). For Justin, the memoirs were writings of the apostles that gradually became known as Gospels. In other words, they were reliable written reports of the good news about Jesus, and written documents were considered more reliable than the oral traditions circulating in the churches. Justin shows that the Gospels or the "memoirs of the apostles" (*apomnēmoneuata tōn apostolōn*) as he calls them, were used to establish doctrine (*Dial.* 100.1) and to relate the story of Jesus' passion. For instance, when introducing quotations from Luke 22:42, 44, he writes, "For in the memoirs which I say were drawn up by His apostles and those who followed them, [it is recorded that] His sweat fell down like drops of blood" (*Dial.* 103.8, *ANF*). He also appeals to the canonical Gospels (Mark 14:22–24, which is similar to 1 Cor 11:23–25) when explaining the apostolic testimony regarding the Eucharist: "The Apostles commanded them: that Jesus, taking bread and having given thanks, he said . . ." (*1 Apol.* 66.3, Richardson, *Early Christian Fathers,* 286). In his account of a typical worship service in the Christian community, he describes the use of the Gospels as reading materials in Christian worship, either alongside of or used alternatively with the OT writings: "On the day called Sunday there is a meeting in one place of those who live in cities or the country, and the memoirs of the apostles or the writings of the prophets are read as long as time permits" (*1 Apol.* 67.3, Richardson, *Early Christian Fathers,* 287).

Koester claims that Justin does not use any previously established philosophical memorabilia to try to make the gospels more acceptable to others, but rather he uses *apomnēmoneuō,* a compound of the common verb "to remember," to say that what was remembered and passed on was also reliable. This word and its cognates, Koester explains, were "often used in the quotation formulae for orally transmitted sayings of Jesus."[49] While Justin uses this term only twice in his *1 Apology,* he uses it thirteen times in his *Dialogue with Trypho.*[50] Apparently Justin employs the term

---

[48] Koester, *Ancient Christian Gospels,* 34, quoting Nag Hammadi Codex I.2, 7–15.

[49] Koester, *Ancient Christian Gospels,* 33–34, 38–39. The Papias tradition in Eusebius, *Hist. eccl.* 3.39.3–16, uses the word *mnēmoneuō* several times.

[50] See *Dial.* 100.4; 101.3; 102.5; 103.6, 8; 104.1; 105.1, 5, 6; 106.1, 3, 4; 107.1. Justin also refers (*Dial.* 106.3) to Papias's statement about Mark's "remembering" Peter's words (see Eusebius, *Hist. eccl.* 3.39.3–4, 15) and calls them "Memoirs of Peter" when he is referring to Mark 3:16–17.

memoirs to lend credibility to the Gospels when he uses them to support his arguments against Trypho.

All of this presupposes that Justin himself accepted the Gospels as reliable history, but did he accept them as sacred Scripture? While the memoirs were read in worship along with the Prophets—a short step to recognizing their scriptural status—Justin nevertheless does not call them Scripture nor explicitly place them on an equal footing with the Prophets. Koester maintains that even though Justin uses the formula *it is written* in reference to Gospel quotations, this does not mean "it is written in Holy Scripture," but rather "it is recorded in a written document that Jesus said" (as in *Dial.* 100.1).[51] He supports this argument by showing that quotations from the Gospels are sometimes referred to as "acts" (*aktōn*) (*1 Apol.* 35.9; 48.3; cf. 38.7), in which cases the Gospels are referred to as reliable witnesses to what Jesus did or said. Justin valued the Gospels for their reliability, believed that they faithfully documented the historical fulfillment of prophecy and therefore also the truth of the Christian faith, and he drew frequently on the Gospels of Matthew and Luke in his summary of the life of Jesus (e.g., *1 Apol.* 31.7). But again, he does not generally cite the Gospels by their authors' names. That comes later with Irenaeus.

At the beginning of the third century, the focus on apostolic authorship clearly shifts to individual apostolic authors. This can be seen in Tertullian giving priority to John and Matthew over Luke and Mark (notice the order) because the latter were not written by apostles: "Of the apostles, therefore, John and Matthew first instill faith into us; whilst of apostolic men, Luke and Mark renew it afterward" (*Marc.* 4.2.2, *ANF*). He likewise criticized Marcion for using only the Gospel of Luke instead of one by an apostle: "Luke, however, was not an apostle, but only an apostolic man; not a master, but a disciple, and so inferior to a master—at least as far subsequent to him as the apostle whom he followed was subsequent to the others" (*Marc.* 4.2.5, *ANF*). Tertullian received Luke and Mark, but he did not place them on the same level as Matthew and John. He held the apostolic witness to be more important in the church than nonapostolic writings. In a short time, the acceptance of the reliability and authority of apostolic documents in telling the story of Jesus no doubt contributed to the churches acknowledging their scriptural status as well.

D. AUTHORSHIP AND AUTHORITY: MEMOIRS TO GOSPELS

For centuries the church has referred to those writings in the NT that describe the ministry, passion, and resurrection of Jesus as Gospels, and it is easy to forget that these literary compositions were not so designated when they were first produced. Initially the term referred to "good news," but in the second century it was used of a genre of literature.

[51] Koester, *Ancient Christian Gospels,* 41.

The term *gospel* (*euangelion*) is common in the Greek OT. In Luke 4:18–19, Jesus cites Isa 61:1–2 to speak of the "good news" that God is about to bring to his people through his ministry. In Rom 10:15, Paul cites Isa 52:7 to tell of the blessings of those who bring the "good news" to others, which is similar to how the term was used in the Greco-Roman world.[52] When the gospel is proclaimed by Paul, he is normally preaching that the grace of God comes to the believer through the activity of God in Jesus. For Paul, the term *gospel* had first of all to do with the substance of the proclamation about God's saving work in Jesus Christ (e.g., Rom 1:1–4, 15–16; 1 Cor 15:1–5; 1 Thess 1:5–9; 2:8–10).

In the Gospels and Acts, however, the term is used for the good news of the announced kingdom of God that takes place in the ministry, passion, and resurrection of Jesus. For example, in the early church proclamation summarized in Acts 10:34–43, Peter preaches the gospel by telling the story of Jesus: "You know the message he sent to the people of Israel, preaching [*euangelizomenos*] peace by Jesus Christ—he is Lord of all." This proclamation in Acts is generally accompanied by a call for faith and repentance (8:12, 25, 40; 10:36; 11:20; 13:32; 14:7, 15, 21; 15:7; 16:10; 17:18; 20:24; cf. 28:31).[53] The term is not found in John's Gospel, but the basic contours of what John had to say are certainly compatible with the Synoptic Gospels, even if his particular gospel shares only a few stories in common with the Synoptics.

Eventually, the term *gospel* came to refer to a particular genre of literature that focused on the story and significance of Jesus at roughly the same time that memoirs or remembrances of the apostles were circulating in the churches. Given the scarcity of available witnesses, we cannot be certain when the term began to refer to a literary production, but it likely happened sometime around the middle of the second century. A few vague references in the early part of the second century to the word *gospel* may well suggest a written document. In the *Didache*,[54] for instance, the writer

---

[52] A well-known inscription at Priene speaks of the birth of Roman Emperor Caesar Augustus (Octavian): "And since Caesar through his appearance has exceeded the hopes of all former good messages [*euangelia*], surpassing not only the benefactors who came before him, but also leaving no hope that anyone in the future would surpass him, and since for the world the birthday of the god was the beginning of his good messages [*euangeliōn*] [may it therefore be decided that . . .]" (Koester, *Ancient Christian Gospels*, 3–4). See also Gerhard Friedrich, "εὐαγγελίζομαι," *TDNT* 2.707–37.

[53] Surprisingly, Acts 20:35 passes on a saying of Jesus not found in the canonical Gospels. Koester, *Ancient Christian Gospels*, 58–59, also notes that Paul, using the formula *as it is written*, quotes a text in 1 Cor 2:9 that only roughly approximates Isa 64:4. The *Gospel of Thomas* 17 cites the same saying but attributes it to Jesus!

[54] While it is impossible to date the *Didache* with precision, it was likely written between 70 and 120. It shows both early conflicts between local church leaders and wandering charismatic prophets in the church (*Did.* 11–13) and an early structure and worship order (*Did.* 14–15). Some scholars believe that the *Didache*

admonishes his readers: "And reprove one another not in wrath but in peace as you find in the Gospel, and let none speak with any who has done a wrong to his neighbour, nor let him hear a word from you until he repents. But your prayers and alms and all your acts perform as ye find in the Gospel of our Lord" (*Did.* 15.3–4, LCL). The pseudonymous *2 Clement* (ca. 140–150) introduces a saying of Jesus from Luke 16:10–12 with the words, "For the Lord says in the Gospel" (*2 Clem.* 8.5, LCL). Speaking of those who deny their faith under threat of persecution, the *Martyrdom of Polycarp* (ca. 160–170) apparently refers to a written document: "For this reason, therefore, brethren, we do not commend those who give themselves up, since the Gospel does not give this teaching" (*Mart. Pol.* 4.1, LCL).

The notion of a written Gospel may be traced to the opening comments of Mark's story of Jesus: "The beginning of the good news of Jesus Christ, the Son of God" (Mark 1:1). With this opening, Mark proceeds to tell the story of Jesus' activities, beginning with his fulfillment of the Scriptures (Mal 3:1; Isa 40:3), and continuing with his healing ministry, his exorcisms, his teachings, and finally his death and resurrection.[55] While Mark may have initiated or perpetuated in written form the gospel genre, Luke did not restrict himself to this pattern. Luke continued the story about how God advanced the work that he began with Jesus through the influence and spread of the gospel (the Christian proclamation) in the nonbelieving communities, beginning in Jerusalem and eventually arriving in Rome.[56] While all four canonical Gospels tell the story of Jesus and his significance for faith, only Mark begins his story of Jesus using the term *gospel.* The other canonical Gospels did not follow his example. When the author of the *Gospel of Thomas* ends his work with the words "The Gospel according to Thomas," this is probably the oldest document actually claiming to be a gospel.

Although there are some notable similarities between ancient biographies and the canonical Gospels, there are no exact parallels because an-

---

depends on *Barnabas* (ca. 140 C.E.) because of the considerable similarity in their use of the "two ways" tradition (*Did.* 1–6; *Barn.* 18–20), which may, however, simply be an appeal by both writers to a common oral or written tradition (the wording is not close enough to betray dependence). While it may be that it was written as late as the middle of the second century (Massaux, *Influence of the Gospel of Saint Matthew,* 3.1), this seems unlikely given the status of church worship and order in it. For more on the date and provenance of the *Didache,* see van de Sandt and Flusser, *Didache;* Niederwimmer, *Didache;* and Milavec, *Didache.*

[55] Stanton, *Gospels and Jesus,* 30–33, makes this point.

[56] Acts, the second part of a two-part work, does not fit neatly within the traditional gospel genre (or *Gattung*). No evidence is available on when the two volumes were separated, except that Acts was not a part of Marcion's collection of NT writings (ca. 140–50). Acts did not serve Marcion's purposes well (it is not clear that he was even aware of its existence), and so either he separated it from Luke, or, more likely, the two volumes were already separated when he made use of the Gospel of Luke.

cient biographies were not produced anonymously and generally did not focus on one short moment in the person's life, as in the case of the Gospels, which focus primarily on Jesus' ministry, passion, and resurrection. More important, unlike other ancient biographies, the canonical Gospels circulated in an oral tradition for a considerable period of time prior to being produced in written form. Contrary to some scholarly opinion, Philostratus's *Life of Apollonius of Tyana,* Xenophon's *Memorabilia,* and Suetonius's *Lives of the Caesars* are not comparable parallels. Stanton agrees that these ancient sources "all contain a memorable beginning and ending with climactic moments, dramatic scenes and vividly drawn characters," but the canonical Gospels still have no parallels elsewhere in antiquity.[57]

By roughly 120–130, the term *gospel* began to be used in the churches in reference to the written stories about Jesus and his teaching, but without changing its earlier meaning as a reference to the content or substance of the message of God's salvation in Jesus the Christ. While this change may have its roots in early Christian preaching and the Gospel of Mark (1:1) and in the writing down of the early Christian proclamation (Acts 10:34–43), who was responsible for this change in the greater church? Since Justin, the earliest writer to make an explicit reference to Gospels as literary productions, did not use the word *gospel* to describe the kerygma of the church or show an awareness of the kerygmatic structure of the gospel writings, it is not likely that this notion began with him.

Koester argues that Marcion understood the tradition of Paul's gospel (Rom 2:16; 16:25; 2 Cor 4:3; Gal 1:11; 1 Thess 1:5; 2 Thess 1:8; 2:14) to be the substance of the Gospel of Luke. As a result, Koester suggests, Marcion equated the two.[58] Justin wrote a treatise against Marcion called "Stigma against All Heresies" (referred to in *1 Apol.* 26.8) and was therefore likely to know about Marcion's equating Paul's "gospel" with Luke's written Gospel.[59] Among the Gospels, Marcion accepted only the Gospel of Luke and excised what did not please him, namely, the Jewish element. He accepted the writings of Paul (without the Pastorals), but denied that the apostles faithfully told the story of Jesus and therefore rejected the traditions about Jesus passed on in their names (Matthew, Mark, and John?). Marcion accepted Paul's thesis that Jesus Christ was the end of the law, but unlike Paul he believed that this meant a rejection of the Scriptures of Israel.

The notion of Paul's gospel being conveyed in Luke's Gospel appears for the first time in Irenaeus, who shows both understandings of the word

---

[57] Stanton, *Gospels and Jesus,* 28, but also 15–33. This conclusion is challenged by Burridge, *What Are the Gospels?* For further discussion, see Talbert, *What Is a Gospel?* Shuler, *Genre for the Gospels;* Aune, *New Testament in Its Literary Environment,* 17–76; and Cox, *Biography in Late Antiquity.*

[58] Koester, *Synoptische Überlieferung,* 6–8; idem, *Ancient Christian Gospels,* 35–36.

[59] Koester, *Ancient Christian Gospels,* 35–36.

gospel: the proclamation of the early church ("for the Lord of all gave to His apostles the power of the Gospel through whom also we have known the truth, that is, the doctrine of the Son of God" [*Haer.* preface, *ANF*]; "we have learned from none others the plan of our salvation, than from those through whom the Gospel has come down to us" [*Haer.* 3.1, *ANF*]) and a written document ("Luke also, the companion of Paul, recorded in a book the Gospel preached by him" [*Haer.* 3.1, *ANF*]). Eusebius likewise passes on this tradition and indicates that the gospel proclaimed by the early church was also put in writing:

> Luke . . . had careful conversation with the other Apostles [besides Paul], and in two books left us examples of the medicine for souls which he gained from them—the Gospel, which he testifies that he had planned according to the tradition . . . , and the Acts of the Apostles which he composed no longer on the evidence of hearing but of his own eyes. And they say that Paul was actually accustomed to quote from Luke's Gospel since when writing of some Gospel as his own he used to say, "According to my Gospel." (*Hist. eccl.* 3.4.6–7, LCL)

Did the story about Luke's recording Paul's gospel originate *before* the time of Marcion and consequently influence him, or did Marcion's practice influence this tradition? Regardless of which came first, the tradition was passed on in the churches and repeated by Irenaeus and Eusebius. This view may have roots in *1 Clem.* 47.1–2, but the difficulty of dating the Apostolic Fathers makes this uncertain. Since these writings, at least the *Didache,* probably precede Marcion, and since they suggest the notion of a *written* gospel as well, the tradition may antedate Marcion. Perhaps as a result of Marcion's misunderstanding, he produced a list of books to read in his churches that included the Gospel of Luke and ten letters of Paul.[60] While Marcion may have rejected all Christian literature except the Pauline corpus, his followers seem to have been more open to reading additional Christian writings in their churches.[61] In the second century, at least up to

---

[60]He omitted the Pastoral Epistles from his collection, but added the Letter to the Laodiceans, which may be the same as the Letter to the Ephesians in the canonical NT.

[61]Remarkably, after Marcion, some of his churches appear to have made use of Matthew's Gospel. Origen quotes a Marcionite interpretation of Matt 19:12 in his *Commentary on Matthew* 15.3. It is not certain that this comment came from Marcion, but it is instructive that the community he left behind was aware of Matthew's Gospel. Hahneman suggests that Marcion, contrary to popular scholarly opinion, may not have rejected the other canonical Gospels (Matthew, Mark, and John). For example, Ephraem Syrus (ca. 306–73) claims that the followers of Marcion did not reject Matt 23:8 (see Ephraem, *Song* 24.1), and Marcus, a Marcionite, directly quotes John 13:34 and 15:19 in Adamantius's *Dialogue* 2.16, 20. Rather, as Hahneman claims, the Marcionites did not reject Christian writings so much as they edited them for use in their churches. His followers include a collection of psalms and even admit verses from the other canonical Gospels into their Scriptures; see Hahneman, *Muratorian Fragment,* 90–92, who cites as evidence Adamantius's *Dialogue* 2.18 and Tertullian's *Marc.* 4.5. It is likely that the later

the last quarter of that century, the Gospels were used in the churches primarily as reliable witnesses to the sayings of Jesus and were not generally called Scripture or made equal to the Prophets—even if they were placed alongside of them and read in the churches. By this act they were on their way to becoming the new Scriptures of the church.[62]

Justin (150–160) speaks of "the apostles in the memoirs which are called gospels" (*1 Apol.* 63.3) and cites rather freely or loosely from Matthew and Mark.[63] He probably knew all four canonical Gospels,[64] but he largely made use of the Synoptic Gospels. It is not, however, always clear what writings Justin had in mind when he spoke of the "memoirs of the apostles" or the "Gospels." For example, when he refers to Jesus being born in a cave he is alluding to *Protevangelium of James* 18–19; he shows awareness of the *Arabic Gospel of the Infancy* and *Gospel of Thomas* 13 in his *Dial.* 88–89; and he cites the apocryphal *Acts of Pilate* 6–8 in *1 Apol.* 48. Although Justin used the word *gospel* to refer to written stories about Jesus, it is not certain that he had only the canonical Gospels in mind when he did so.

III. Paul's Writings

In addition to his prominence in the book of Acts, which reports his remarkable missionary journeys, Paul is well known as the author of the letters that bear his name. These letters were nonliterary correspondences mainly

---

Marcionites also accepted the reading of Tatian's *Diatessaron* in their churches; see Casey, "Armenian Marcionites." This all suggests, of course, that the contours of Marcion's canon may not have been so firmly fixed as was once thought and that he may not have produced the earliest *fixed* biblical canon, as von Campenhausen, *Formation of the Christian Bible,* 152–53, and others after him argue. For further discussion, see chapter 11 §I.

[62] See Barton, *How the Bible Came to Be,* 53–72, for a useful summary of this process.

[63] Quotations of Matthew and Mark in *1 Apology* include the following:
Matt 22:14 in *1 Apol.* 4
Matt 9:18 in *1 Apol.* 5
Matt 20:16 in *1 Apol.* 6
Matt 22:45 in *1 Apol.* 12
Mark 10:23–24 in *1 Apol.* 20

[64] It is likely that Justin knew the Gospel of John, but this is widely disputed. The most significant parallel is *1 Apol.* 61.4–5, which is an almost word-for-word quotation of John 3:3–5. Other parallels are close but not exact (see Massaux, *Influence of the Gospel of Saint Matthew,* 3.46–47):
1 Apol. 6.2 and John 4:24
1 Apol. 32.9–11 and John 1:13–14
1 Apol. 33.2 and John 14:29
1 Apol. 35.8 and John 19:23–24
1 Apol. 52.12 and John 19:37
1 Apol. 63.15 and John 1:1
2 Apol. 6.3 and John 1:3

with churches that he either founded or was about to visit and a few to individuals. While there is some literary character to these letters, they were sent as a substitute for a face-to-face visit. Such letters are well known in the ancient world, and many were published after the death of the writer (e.g., Cicero, Pliny, Seneca, Alciphron, Aelian, and Philostratus). Seneca (4 B.C.E.–65 C.E.), for instance, tells readers who complained about the nonliterary style of his letters that this is the way he wanted his letters to be:

> You have been complaining that my letters to you are rather carelessly written. Now who talks carefully unless he also desires to talk affectedly? I prefer that my letters should be just what my conversation would be if you and I were sitting in one another's company or taking walks together—spontaneous and easy; for my letters have nothing strained or artificial about them. (*Epistles* 75.1–2, LCL)

The nonliterary aspect of such correspondence, even when written well, lent itself to their production in codices or tablets, rather than on the more literary scrolls or rolls. The value of Paul presenting his theology through letters allows it to be much more personal and direct and also allows him to respond theologically to specific situations in his churches. In some cases, Paul intended that his letters be shared with or read in other churches (Col 4:16), but sometimes the issues addressed were much more localized, as in the case of 1–2 Corinthians and Galatians. In time, other churches saw great value in reading his letters in their congregations as well.

This practice of sharing letters in various churches probably took place near the end of the first century. Scholars generally conclude that several of Paul's letters were circulating together in the churches no later than the end of the first century, at least in Asia Minor and probably also elsewhere. Clement of Rome (ca. 95) is the first of the Apostolic Fathers to refer to Paul's writings, namely, 1 Corinthians, Ephesians, and possibly Titus.

Somewhat later, some of Paul's letters were used or cited in the letters of Ignatius (ca. 115), and they were used or cited thereafter with growing frequency in the early church writings. Goodspeed argues that nine of Paul's writings were collected and circulated together near the end of the first century under the cover of the Letter to the Ephesians.[65] Perhaps Onesimus, the runaway slave who worked with Paul and later became bishop in Ephesus after the death of Paul, produced this collection. Since no extant biblical manuscript introduces Paul's writings with Ephesians, Goodspeed's theory is largely rejected today.

Trobisch oddly proposes that Paul himself was responsible for the initial collection of his writings and that he even edited four of them (Romans–

[65] E. J. Goodspeed, *The Key to Ephesians* (Chicago: University of Chicago, 1956); idem, *The Meaning of Ephesians* (Chicago: University of Chicago, 1933); and idem, *An Introduction to the New Testament,* 191–211. (Chicago: University of Chicago, 1937).

Galatians) and circulated them in Ephesus.[66] According to this theory, Rom 16 served as an introduction to that collection, and Ephesians and other letters were added to Paul's collection after his death in three stages: the collection of letters sent to churches (Ephesians–2 Thessalonians), personal letters (1 Timothy–Philemon), and Hebrews. The occasion for the base set of letters was the collection of money for the Jerusalem church, which was discussed significantly in one of the four letters (2 Cor 9–13) and in a limited way in the other three, and one of Paul's purposes for collecting these funds was his attempt to resolve his conflict with the Jerusalem church (Gal 2:11–14). Trobisch rightly concludes that the seriousness of this conflict gave little chance for immediate resolution, but he probably overestimates the role that the collection played in Romans, 1 Corinthians, and Galatians. In any case, according to Trobisch, in the process of collecting and sending these letters to Ephesus and subsequently elsewhere, Paul unconsciously initiated the birth of the NT canon.

Trobisch ably informs the reader of the processes by which the Letters of Paul were produced, ordered, and transmitted by the early church, and he shows how $\mathfrak{P}^{46}$ (the oldest known collection of Paul's Letters, ca. 200 C.E.) arranged the letters according to length but placed Hebrews *after* Romans and *before* 1 Corinthians (which is slightly longer than Hebrews), in order to keep the Corinthian letters from being separated in the corpus.[67] Trobisch rightly observes the absence of the Pastorals and Philemon from $\mathfrak{P}^{46}$, but he apparently does not see the implications of this for the formation of the NT canon. Since $\mathfrak{P}^{46}$ is the earliest surviving manuscript of Paul's Letters, the omission of the Pastorals and Philemon in this document strongly suggests that they had not yet been added to the recognized collection of Paul's Letters by the end of the first century. (This could be an important factor in determining the date of the Muratorian Fragment, which does include the Pastorals (see chapter 13 §I.D).

Trobisch makes a good case that Paul's Letters were arranged into three groups within the Pauline corpus, each of which began with the largest book in that group. This explains why Ephesians is some nine hundred characters longer than Galatians but strangely stands *after* Galatians: Galatians is the smallest letter in the first group, and Ephesians is the largest in the second. He correctly observes that chronology was not a factor in the sequence of each group.

Trobisch also rejects the popular view that 1–2 Corinthians is made up of four earlier writings of Paul, but he claims instead that they contain some seven letters that Paul himself later edited and sent out in their current form.[68]

---

[66] Trobisch, *Paul's Letter Collection,* 50–54.

[67] Ibid., 16–17.

[68] Ibid., 72–73. Trobisch discerns individual letters in (1) 1 Cor 1:10–4:21; (2) 1 Cor 5:1–6:11; (3) 1 Cor 6:12–16:24; (4) 2 Cor 1:3–2:11; (5) 2 Cor 2:14–7:3; (6) 2 Cor

Several arguments go against Trobisch's primary thesis. First, it is widely acknowledged that the style of writing in Galatians is hurried, choppy, and not presented in a manner that reflects careful editing, as in Romans. The contrast between Romans and Galatians is difficult to explain if Paul had taken the time to edit Galatians at a later time. In other words, if Trobisch is correct, we should expect to see more uniformity in style and presentation in these letters. Second, Trobisch concludes from the examples of Marcus Tullius Cicero (died ca. 44 B.C.E.) and Cyprian (died 258 C.E.)—who produced, edited, and circulated their own letters—that Paul must have done the same. This kind of argument, however, falls short of demonstration. Third, it is strange that 1 Thessalonians, one of the earliest of Paul's writings, receives little attention in Trobisch's work. In fact, he has no significant discussion of 1 Thessalonians, Philippians, or Philemon, all of which are undisputed letters of Paul. Although Trobisch claims to trace the origins of Paul's letter collection, these letters and their place in the Pauline corpus deserve more attention than what he has given to them. Finally, no biblical manuscripts show that Romans through Galatians ever circulated as a collection or that they were ever introduced by Rom 16.

Little information is available on what was taking place with Paul's Letters from the time of his death until the end of the first century. Clement of Rome and Ignatius of Antioch both knew and referred to Paul's Letters, and so did Marcion, who circulated a collection of ten of Paul's Letters in his churches, but their earlier history still remains a mystery.

Ephesians was most likely intended to be an encyclical letter to all the faithful in Asia Minor since nothing in it ties it to any one particular community: *en ephesō* ("in Ephesus") in Eph 1:1 has limited manuscript evidence, and Eph 4:20–22 indicates that the writer had not yet met the church. Since Paul had already visited Ephesus, it is doubtful that the letter as it now stands was intended for this congregation alone. The letter itself *may* reflect a post-Pauline era and (per Goodspeed) *may* have been attached as an introduction to the Letters of Paul, although no textual evidence substantiates this. It is also possible that several of Paul's Letters, whether or not in a collection led by Ephesians, may have circulated in Asia Minor (the birthplace of Marcion) and probably even to a wider audi-

---

7:4–9:15; and (7) 2 Cor 10:1–13:13. Most scholars agree that there are natural breaks between these sections, but Trobisch has not sufficiently demonstrated his case for seven separate letters. He argues quite cogently, however, that Rom 16 was only later added to Romans and that its original destination was not the church at Rome, but rather the church at Ephesus. His discussion of the redactional inserts that Paul added to his own correspondence (1 Cor 9; 13) is helpful and gives the reader a feeling that we are looking over Paul's shoulder as he composed the letters.

On the other hand, Trobisch's discussion of personal names in Paul's Letters (59–62) is not convincing. He asserts that Paul did not mention specific individuals in later correspondence, whom he had named in his earlier correspondence, because these individuals had ceased being friends with Paul in the intervening time. This is speculative, of course, and does not contribute to his primary thesis.

ence by the end of the first century. Similarities between the Pauline corpus and the *Didache*,[69] Clement of Rome (who gives the earliest reference to Paul's death in *1 Clem.* 5:5–7),[70] and Ignatius of Antioch[71] suggest that

---

[69] Pauline-*Didache* parallels include the following:
Did. 5.1 and Rom 1:29–30
Did. 5.2 and Rom 12:9
Did. 10.6 and 1 Cor 16:22
Did. 13.1 and 1 Cor 9:13–14; 1 Tim 5:17–18
Did. 16.4 and 2 Thess 2:9
Did. 16.6–7 and 1 Cor 15:22; 1 Thess 4:16

[70] Pauline-Clement parallels include the following:
1 Clem. 13.1 and 1 Cor 1:31; 2 Cor 10:17
1 Clem. 24.1 and 1 Cor 15:20
1 Clem. 24.5 and 1 Cor 15:36–41
1 Clem. 32.2 and Rom 9:3
1 Clem. 33.1 and Rom 6:1
1 Clem. 34.8 and 1 Cor 2:9
1 Clem. 35.5 and Rom 1:29–32
1 Clem. 35.7 and Rom 1:32
1 Clem. 37.5 and 1 Cor 12:21
1 Clem. 46.6–7 and Eph 4:4–6
1 Clem. 47.1–2 and 1 Cor 1:10–17
1 Clem. 48.5 and 1 Cor 12:8–9
1 Clem. 49.5 and 1 Cor 13:4–7
1 Clem. 50.6 and Rom 4:7–9
1 Clem. 59.3 and Eph 1:18
1 Clem. 61.2 and 1 Tim 5:17

[71] Pauline-Ignatius parallels include the following:
Eph. 8.2 and Rom 8:5, 8
Eph. 10.1 and 1 Thess 5:17
Eph. 10.2–3 and Col 1:23; Rom 4:20; 1 Cor 16:13
Eph. 14.1–2 and 1 Tim 1:5
Eph. 15.3 and 1 Cor 3:16
Eph. 16.1 and 1 Cor 6:9–10; Eph 5:5
Eph. 18.1 and Gal 5:11 and 1 Cor 1:20
Eph. 18.2 and Rom 1:3 and 2 Tim 2:8
Eph. 19.3 and Rom 6:4
Eph. 20.2 and Rom 1:3
Magn. 10.2 and 1 Cor 5:7
Trall. 5.2 and Col 1:16
Trall. 9.2 and 1 Cor 15:12–19
Trall. 12.3 and 1 Cor 9:27
Rom. 2.1 and 1 Thess 2:4
Rom. 4.3 and 1 Cor 7:22
Rom. 6.1 and 1 Cor 9:15
Rom. 7.2–3 and Rom 1:3 and 2 Tim 2:3
Rom. 9.2 and 1 Cor 15:8–9
Rom. 10.3 and 2 Thess 3:5
Phld. 3.3 and 1 Cor 6:9–10
Phld. 4.1 and 1 Cor 10:16–17
Phld. 7.1 and 1 Cor 2:10

several of Paul's Letters were known and highly esteemed in the late first and early second centuries in the churches. None of these sources say that Paul wrote Scripture, but they are indicative of the circulation of his letters in the late first and early second centuries.

Justin Martyr does not refer to Paul's writings or ministry, and this neglect, some scholars suggest, may have been a response to Marcion's sole use of Paul's Letters to the exclusion of other NT writings (save Luke), and a response to the gnostics' frequent appeal to Paul.[72] It certainly does not indicate Justin's ignorance of either Paul or his letters. Despite this neglect, Paul's writings were highly esteemed in most churches both before and after Justin, even though there is little direct appeal to Paul in the apologetic writings of this period.

It is safe to say that several of Paul's writings were circulating in Asia Minor at the end of the first century. Marcion probably took over an existing collection of Paul's writings.[73] Clement of Rome refers to four of Paul's Letters. And the early editorial work on the Corinthian letters, Romans, and Philippians suggests an early interest in Paul's writings. It is generally agreed that in the early second century, collections of some seven to ten of Paul's Letters circulated in various parts of the Roman Empire, for example, in Rome, Ephesus, and Alexandria. Bishop Polycarp of Smyrna, for example, spoke of Paul's Letters and encouraged his readers at Philippi to examine them carefully:

> For neither am I, nor is any other like me, able to follow the wisdom of the blessed and glorious Paul, who when he was among you in the presence of the men of that time taught accurately and stedfastly the word of truth, and also when he was absent wrote letters to you, from the study of which you will be able to build yourselves up into the faith given you. (Pol. *Phil.* 3.2, LCL)

Polycarp assumes, of course, that those in Philippi were aware of Paul's Letters (plural) just as he was at Smyrna.

These examples are sufficient to show that Paul's writings, along with the Gospels, significantly influenced the early churches and were among the earliest writings to be read as Scripture.[74]

Smyrn. intro. and 1 Cor 1:7
Smyrn. 1.1 and Rom 1:3
Smyrn. 1.2 and Eph 2:16
Smyrn. 4.2 and Phil 4:13
Smyrn. 10.2 and 2 Tim 1:16
Smyrn. 11.3 and Phil 3:15
Pol. 1.2 and Eph 4:2
Pol. 4.3 and 1 Tim 6:2
Pol. 5.1 and Eph 5:25, 29
Pol. 6.2 and 2 Tim 2:4

[72] Gamble, *New Testament Canon,* 43–46.

[73] Ibid., 41.

[74] See Patzia, "Canon," 87–89.

IV. From Authoritative Documents to Scripture

The early use of and references to the Gospels and Paul's Letters does not mean that these writings were received *initially* as sacred Scripture on par with the writings of the OT, but rather that they were useful in the life and ministry of the early churches. This is the first step in a process that moves from the recognition of authority of Christian writings to their scriptural status and eventually to their placement in a fixed collection or catalogue of Christian Scriptures.

A. NEW TESTAMENT WRITINGS FUNCTIONING AS SCRIPTURE

When the NT writings were placed alongside the Scriptures of the OT and appealed to authoritatively in the life and worship of the early church, they functioned as Scripture in the church even if they were not yet called Scripture.[75] This function occurred, as one would expect, earlier than the time when the term Scripture was actually employed to designate those writings. Do the numerous references, citations, quotations, and allusions to the NT writings in the Apostolic Fathers of the second century necessarily mean that the NT writings were considered Scripture? More specifically, when were they actually called "Scripture" (*hē graphē*) and introduced with "the Scripture says" (*hē graphē legei*), "it is written" (*gegraptai*), "that which is written" (*to gegrammenon*), or any comparable formulas regularly used in reference to the OT?[76] Scholars of the second century do not agree on the answer, but the words of Jesus apparently had a Scripture-like status from the very beginning of the church (e.g., 1 Cor 7:10, 12, 17, 25; 1 Thess 4:15; Matt 28:18). It is not overstating the case to say for the church that "if Jesus said it, that settled the matter." He was, after all, the Lord of the church, and his words from the beginning of the church would have had significant authority attached to them.

Clement of Rome acknowledges the authority of the teaching of Jesus for the church:

> Let us, therefore, be humble-minded, brethren, putting aside all arrogance and conceit and foolishness and wrath, and let us do that which is written (for the Holy Spirit says, "Let not the wise man boast himself in his wisdom, nor the strong man in his strength, nor the rich man in his riches, but he that boasteth

---

[75] Metzger, *Canon of the New Testament,* 6–7, notes that when the apostolic writings began to be translated into Syriac, Latin, and Coptic in the second and third centuries, this was done for the purpose of using them in public worship. As Christian writings began to be used in worship in the Christian communities, they also began to take on Scripture-like status, even if they were not yet so acknowledged.

[76] For a helpful listing and discussion of these formulas, see Metzger, "Formulas Introducing Quotations."

> let him boast in the Lord, to seek him out and to do judgment and righteousness"), especially *remembering the words of the Lord Jesus* which he spoke when he was teaching gentleness and longsuffering. For he spoke thus: "Be merciful, that ye may obtain mercy. Forgive, that ye may be forgiven. As ye do, so shall it be done unto you. As ye give, so shall it be given unto you. As ye judge, so shall ye be judged. As ye are kind, so shall kindness be shown you. With what measure ye mete, it shall be measured to you." *With this commandment and with these injunctions* let us strengthen ourselves to walk in obedience to *his hallowed words* and let us be humble-minded, for the holy word says, "On whom shall I look, but on the meek and gentle and him who trembles at my oracles." (*1 Clem.* 13.1–4, LCL, emphasis added)

> Why do we divide and tear asunder the members of Christ, and raise up strife against our own body, and reach such a pitch of madness as to forget that we are members one of another? *Remember the words of the Lord Jesus;* for he said, "Woe unto that man: it were good for him if he had not been born, than that he should offend one of my elect." (*1 Clem.* 46.7–8, LCL, emphasis added)

Clement's appeals for order are based on the warning of Jesus, which he emphasizes and introduces with "remember[ing] the words of the Lord Jesus." Metzger notes, however, that these are the only two direct references to the words of Jesus in *1 Clement,* compared with over one hundred references to the OT Scriptures.[77] Clement was aware of Paul's Epistles and Hebrews, and he refers to them throughout his letter, but does not call them Scripture.[78]

In his well-known *Letter to Flora,* gnostic teacher Ptolemy (ca. 160) frequently referred to the "words of the Savior" (e.g., 3.5, 8; 4.1, 4; cf. 7.5, 10) as the authority for his instruction. Ptolemy's devotion to the teaching of Jesus may be seen in his explanation of the proper way to understand the Law of Moses and Ptolemy's reference to those who have misunderstood it:

> That is what happens to people who do not see what follows from *the words of the Saviour.* For a house or city divided against itself cannot stand, our Saviour declared. Furthermore the apostle says that the creation of the world was peculiar to Him and that all things were made through him, and apart from him nothing was made, refuting the flimsy wisdom of these liars; not the creation of a god who corrupts, but of a just God who hates evil. That is the opinion of heedless men who do not understand the cause of the providence of the Demiurge, who are blind not only in the eye of the soul but also in that of the body.

> How they have strayed from the truth is clear to you from what has been said. Two groups have gone astray each in their peculiar fashion, the one through ignorance of the God of justice, the other through ignorance of the Father of All, whom only he who alone knew him revealed at his coming. Now it remains for us who have been granted the knowledge of both of these, to ex-

[77] Metzger, *Canon of the New Testament,* 41–42.
[78] Ibid.

> plain the Law to you with accuracy, what its nature is and the one by whom it has been given, the Lawgiver, proving our demonstrations from *the words of our Saviour*, through which alone it is possible without error to travel toward the comprehension of reality.
>
> First one must learn that the whole Law which is contained in the Pentateuch of Moses has not been decreed by some one person, I mean by God alone; but there are also some commandments in it given by men; and that it is tripartite *the words of the Saviour* teach us. For one part is ascribed to God himself and his legislation; another is ascribed to Moses, not meaning that God gave the law through him, but that Moses legislated starting from his own understanding; and the third is ascribed to the elders of the people, who are themselves found from the beginning introducing ordinances of their own. How this came about you may learn from *the words of the Saviour*. When the Saviour was talking somewhere to those arguing with him about divorce, which was allowed by the Law, he said to them, Moses because of the hardness of your hearts permitted a man to put away his wife; from the beginning it was not so. For God joined them together, and what God has joined, let not a man, he said, put asunder. Here he shows that the law of God is one thing—it forbids a woman to be divorced by her husband—and the law of Moses is another—it permits this bond to be sundered because of hardness of heart. So in this way Moses ordains a law contrary to God, for divorce is contrary to no divorce. (Stevenson, *New Eusebius*, 92–93, emphasis added)

For both Clement of Rome and Ptolemy, the words of Jesus undoubtedly functioned as sacred Scripture even though the specific scriptural formulas are not used in these passages.

In terms of the NT literature itself, citations of or allusions to the Gospels (mostly Matthew) and to a lesser extent the NT Epistles were commonplace in the second century. This practice indicates recognition—sometimes explicit, sometimes veiled—of the esteem and authority of this literature in the Christian community, though not necessarily its scriptural status. Von Campenhausen adds an important qualification to these references by drawing a distinction between the authoritative words or commands of Jesus and the Gospels that contained them: the words of Jesus were given prominence and recognition in the written and oral tradition and had a Scripture-like status in the church, but this did not extend to the whole Gospel itself.[79] In the first one and a half centuries of church history no prominence was given to a Gospel writer or to a Gospel as a *written* document.[80] Although the Gospels may have been intended at the outset to be used (or read) in the churches alongside the OT Scriptures, they did not claim exclusive authority, "nor did they acquire it,"[81] at least not at first, as seen in the history of their redaction.

---

[79] Von Campenhausen, *Formation of the Christian Bible,* 118–21.
[80] Ibid., 121.
[81] Ibid., 123.

B. SCRIPTURE-LIKE REFERENCES TO NEW TESTAMENT WRITINGS

The following list provides examples of positive attitudes toward the NT writings in the second century.

1. 2 Clement (ca. 120–140, but no later than 170)

The unknown author of *2 Clement* acknowledges as the authority for his comments the "Scripture" (no doubt the Jewish Scriptures) and "the books and the Apostles":

> Now I imagine that you are not ignorant that the living "Church is the body of Christ." For the scripture says, "God made man male and female"; the male is Christ, the female is the church. And moreover *the books and the Apostles* declare that the Church belongs not to the present, but has existed from the beginning; for she was spiritual, as was also our Jesus, but he was made manifest in the last days that he might save us. (*2 Clem.* 14.2, LCL, emphasis added)

It is almost certain that "the Books" (*ta biblia*) is a reference to the OT Scriptures (cf. 2 Tim 4:13), and "the apostles" (*hoi apostoloi*) is probably a reference to the NT tradition common in the churches in both oral and written form.[82] If so, then this text is an early indication that the NT tradition was placed in a parallel relationship to the OT Scriptures in that both are appealed to in an authoritative manner for support of the author's teaching about the preexistent church. The apostles appear at this early date to function as the "guarantors" of the NT tradition.[83]

The author of *2 Clement* quotes Mark 2:17 (or Matt 9:13) as Scripture: "And another Scripture [*graphē*] also says, 'I came not to call righteous, but sinners'; He means that those who are perishing must be saved, for it is great and wonderful to give strength, not to the things which are standing, but to those which are falling" (*2 Clem.* 2.4–6, LCL). Here, as in 14.2, the words of Jesus, which had not yet found a universally acknowledged fixed form, were apparently recognized as being on a par with or closely related to the authority of the OT Scriptures in support of theological arguments and moral behavior in the early church.[84]

2. Barnabas (ca. 90–130)

The pseudonymous theological treatise known as the *Epistle of Barnabas,* produced by a Gentile Christian concerned about the death of Jesus as

---

[82] Von Campenhausen, *Formation of the Christian Bible,* 62; Farmer and Farkasfalvy, *Formation of the New Testament Canon,* 173 n. 97. It is possible but doubtful that *ta biblia* refers to the Gospels; see Koester, *Synoptische Überlieferung,* 76–78.

[83] So Koester, *Synoptische Überlieferung,* 68. "The Apostles" may be a reference to the "commandment of the Lord" handed down to the apostles (2 Pet 3:2).

[84] Kümmel, *Introduction to the New Testament,* 340.

a sacrifice in the OT sense, introduces one of its two Gospel quotations (Matt 22:14) in a Scripture-like manner: "Let us take heed lest *as it is written* [*hōs gegraptai*] we be found 'many called but few chosen'" (*Barn.* 4:14, LCL, emphasis added). This suggests that the words of Jesus were equal in authority to the OT—that is, the words of Jesus, when written down, became Scripture. Kümmel goes a step further and says that this text is evidence that an individual Gospel writing—the whole text itself—was beginning to be valued as equal in authority to the OT Scriptures.[85] More proof from antiquity is necessary, however, before accepting such a claim.

3. Ignatius (ca. 100–107)

In an often-quoted passage from his *Letter to the Philadelphians,* Ignatius showed his preference for the gospel, which is probably the kerygma or preaching about Jesus that was current in the oral traditions of the church. Remarkably, he appears to prefer its authority over the OT Scriptures:

> But I beseech you to do nothing in factiousness, but after the teaching of Christ. For I heard some men saying, "If I find it not in the charters,[86] I do not believe in the gospel." And when I said to them that it is in the Scripture, they answered me, "That is exactly the question." But to me the charters are Jesus Christ, the inviolable charter is his cross, and death, and resurrection, and the faith which is through him—in these I desire to be justified by your prayers. (Ign. *Phld.* 8.2, adapted from LCL)

This text strongly indicates that Ignatius gave priority to the proclamation about Jesus over the OT Scriptures. For Ignatius, the primary locus of authority for Christian faith was in Jesus Christ, more specifically in the early Christian kerygma about "his cross, and death, and resurrection." The full extent of this is not clear, but it appears that the oral and/or written traditions about Jesus the Christ were more important to Ignatius than were the OT Scriptures.[87] In Ignatius's threefold locus of authority (Jesus, the apostles, and the prophets), he gave priority to Jesus:

> Brethren, I am overflowing with love to you, and exceedingly joyful in watching over your safety. Yet not I, but Jesus Christ, whose bonds I bear, but am the more fearful in that I am not yet perfected; but your prayer will make me perfect

---

[85] Ibid.

[86] "Charters" (*archeiois*) is generally considered to be a reference to the OT Scriptures. Metzger, *Canon of the New Testament,* 48, translates this term "archives." Ehrman, on the other hand, translates it "ancient records" (LCL 1.291).

[87] See Metzger, *Canon of the New Testament,* 43–49, for a helpful summary of Ignatius's familiarity with some of the NT literature, probably the Gospels of Matthew and John and several letters of Paul. Although Ignatius did not call this literature Scripture, the obvious parallels noted by Metzger (and listed above) show Ignatius's knowledge and acceptance of them as documents that express for him the proper Christian attitudes and conduct.

> for God, that I may attain the lot wherein I found mercy, making *the Gospel* my refuge as the flesh of Jesus, and *the Apostles* as the presbytery of the Church. And *the prophets* also do we love, because they also have announced the Gospel, and are hoping in him and waiting for him, by faith in whom they also obtain salvation, being united with Jesus Christ, for they are worthy of love and saints worthy of admiration, approved by Jesus Christ, and numbered together in the Gospel of the common hope. (Ign. *Phld.* 5.1–2, LCL, emphasis added)

4. Polycarp (ca. 140–155)

In his *Letter to the Philippians,* Polycarp cites Ps 4:4 and Eph 4:26 and calls them both Scriptures:[88]

> For I am confident that you are well versed *in the Scriptures* [*in sacris literis*], and from you nothing is hid; but to me this is not granted. Only, *as it is said in these Scriptures* [*modo, ut his scripturis dictum est*], "Be ye angry and sin not," and "Let not the sun go down upon your wrath." Blessed is the man who remembers this, and I believe that it is so with you. (Pol. *Phil.* 12:1, LCL, emphasis added)

Polycarp appears to have consciously placed an OT Scripture and a Christian writing on an equal authoritative footing. The least one could say about this conjunction is that an authoritative appeal to these texts promises that persons following their advice will be blessed—and this is certainly close to a description of inspired literature in any religious community.

Polycarp also recognizes the authority of Jesus' teaching in the Sermon on the Mount and admonishes his hearers to obey and imitate Jesus' examples.

> Now "he who raised him" from the dead "will also raise us up" if we do his will, and *walk in his commandments* and love the things which he loved, refraining from all unrighteousness, covetousness, love of money, evil speaking, false witness, "rendering not evil for evil, or railing for railing," or blow for blow, or curse for curse, *but remembering what the Lord taught* when he said, "Judge not that ye be not judged, forgive and it shall be forgiven unto you, be merciful that ye may obtain mercy, with what measure ye mete, it shall be measured to you again," and, "Blessed are the poor, and they who are persecuted for righteousness' sake, for theirs is the Kingdom of God." (Pol. *Phil.* 2.2–3, LCL, emphasis added)

The words of Jesus had authority in the early Christian communities where Polycarp was ministering, and he warned his readers not to tamper with them (cf. Rev. 22:18–19 and Deut. 4:2):

> For everyone who does not confess that Jesus Christ has come in the flesh is an anti-Christ [compare I John 4:2]; and whosoever does not confess the testi-

---

[88] Since the original Greek text for this passage is missing and is supplied in Latin, an argument could be made for a late dating of this reference, though that is generally considered unlikely.

> mony of the Cross is of the devil: and whosoever *perverts the oracles of the Lord* for his own lusts, and says that there is neither resurrection nor judgment—this man is the first-born of Satan. Wherefore, leaving the foolishness of the crowd, and their false teaching, let us turn back to the word which was delivered to us in the beginning, "watching unto prayer" and persevering in fasting, beseeching the all-seeing God in our supplications "to lead us not into temptation," even as the Lord said, "The spirit is willing, but the flesh is weak." (Pol. *Phil.* 7.1–2, LCL, emphasis added)

For Polycarp, Jesus serves as a rule or guide to the Christian community: "Let us then be imitators of his endurance, and if we suffer for his name's sake let us glorify him. For this is the example which he gave us in himself, and this is what we have believed" (Pol. *Phil.* 8.2, LCL).

Like Ignatius, Polycarp gives evidence of a threefold locus of authority in the church: "So then 'let us serve *him* with fear and all reverence,' as he himself commanded us, and as did the *Apostles,* who brought us the Gospel, and the *Prophets* who foretold the coming of our Lord" (Pol. *Phil.* 6.3, LCL, emphasis added). What is abundantly clear from these examples is that *Jesus himself was the authoritative canon* of the church for Polycarp. The words of Jesus, when written down, take on the function of Scripture, even if they were not specifically called Scripture.

5. 2 Peter (ca. 150, but possibly as late as ca. 180)

The author of 2 Peter, a pseudonymous NT writing,[89] refers to Paul's writings being twisted by "ignorant and unstable" people "as they do the other scriptures" (*hōs kai tas loipas graphas*) (3:15–16). This author apparently places Paul's Epistles on an equal footing with the OT Scriptures or, less likely, with other Christian writings that were recognized as authoritative or normative at that time. He is also aware of the heretical use of Paul's Letters, possibly a veiled reference to Marcion or the gnostics.

6. Ptolemy (ca. 160)

In his *Letter to Flora,* Ptolemy seeks to define the integrity of the Jewish Scriptures (3.6) and establish their correct interpretation. The author appeals throughout to the words (3.5, 8; 4.1, 4), command of the Savior (5.10), and teachings (7.9) of Jesus as his primary authority. He also cites John 1:3 with the words "the apostle says" (3:6), much as one would quote

---

[89] The dating of 2 Peter is quite difficult because there are no certain references to it in the church fathers in the first two centuries. It is common for scholars to date all NT writings to the end of the first century if they cannot otherwise link them to the lives of the persons in whose names they were published. Most standard NT introductions, however, place this writing somewhere in the second century. It betrays a time well into the second century and likely condemns the gnostic interpretation of the Scriptures (2:4–10). See Pearson, "James, 1–2 Peter, Jude," 382–85; and Koester, *Introduction to the New Testament,* 2.298–300.

Scripture. Along with a properly interpreted OT, Ptolemy completes his threefold authority with the words of the Savior and the apostles (at least John and probably Matthew), giving priority to the words of the Savior:

> First one must learn that the whole Law which is contained in the Pentateuch of Moses has not been decreed by some one person, I mean by God alone; but there are also some commandments in it given by men; and that it is tripartite *the words of the Saviour* teach us. For one part is ascribed to God himself and his legislation; another is ascribed to Moses, not meaning that God gave the law through him, but that Moses legislated starting from his own understanding; and the third is ascribed to the elders of the people, who are themselves found from the beginning introducing ordinances of their own. How this came about you may learn from *the words of the Saviour*. (Stevenson, *New Eusebius*, 92, emphasis added)

Although Jesus is clearly his primary authority, Ptolemy cites the apostle Paul as one would cite Scripture:

> *The disciples of the Savior and the apostle Paul* showed that this theory is true, speaking of the part dealing with images, as we have already said, in mentioning "the Passover for us" and the "unleavened bread"; of the law interwoven with injustice when he says that "the law of commandments in ordinances was destroyed" [Eph 2:15]; and of that not mixed with anything inferior when he says that "the law is holy, and the commandment is holy and just and good" [Rom 7:12]. (Barnstone, *Other Bible*, 624, emphasis added)

These references are especially meaningful since Ptolemy comes from outside mainstream orthodox Christianity.

7. Martyrs of Lyons and Vienne (ca. 175–177)

A letter preserved in Eusebius's *Hist. eccl.* 5.1 contains many references, allusions, and quotations from the NT literature and noncanonical literature. One of the most interesting is a reference to Rev 22:11, which is preceded by "that the Scripture might be fulfilled" (*Hist. eccl.* 5.1.58, LCL). Not only does this show the high regard for the book of Revelation in the Western churches, but it is one of the earliest references to the book as "Scripture." (It is possible, however, that the reference to "Scripture" was provided by Eusebius to clarify what he thought was intended by the writing he was quoting, which is a common practice by Eusebius.)

8. Tatian (ca. 160–170)

Interestingly, Tatian did not consider the four canonical Gospels as inviolable Scripture, even though he saw great value for the church in these documents. His creation of the church's first harmony of the four Evangelists (with other gospel traditions) into one account known as the *Diatessaron*, was used in the Syrian church up to the fifth century:

> Their former leader Tatian composed in some way a combination and collection of the gospels, and gave this the name of *The Diatessaron,* and this is still extant in some places. And they say that he ventured to paraphrase some words of the apostle, *as though correcting their style*. He has left a great number of writings, of which the most famous, quoted by many, is his discourse *Against the Greeks*. In it he deals with primitive history, and shows that Moses and the prophets of the Hebrews preceded all those who are celebrated among the Greeks. This seems to be the best and most helpful of all his writings. Such are the facts of this period. (*Hist. eccl.* 4.29.6–7, LCL, emphasis added)

Tatian's willingness to change or correct the four canonical Gospels is important to us in many regards, not the least of which is his perception about their inspired status. Although he valued them sufficiently that they served as his primary sources for compiling his *Diatessaron,* he was not afraid to change them in order to produce a unified text. Eusebius indicates that Tatian also "paraphrased some words of the apostle," probably a reference to the Apostle Paul.

9. Athenagoras (ca. 180)

Second-century church teacher Athenagorus made use of Paul's writings alongside the Gospels in a manner that shows that he accepted them as normative Christian literature:

> The result of all of this is very plain to everyone—namely, that, in the language of the apostle [*kata ton apostolon*], "This corruptible (and dissoluble) must put on incorruption [1 Cor 15:54], in order that those who were dead . . . may, in accordance with justice, receive what he has done by the body, whether it be good or bad." (*Resurrection of the Dead* 18, *ANF*)

10. Theophilus of Antioch (ca. 190–200)

Late second-century orthodox teacher Theophilus of Antioch shows heavy dependence upon the writings of Paul and calls Rom 2:7–9 and 1 Cor 2:9 "prophetic Scriptures":

> But you also, please give reverential attention to the prophetic Scriptures, for they will make it plain to you how to escape the eternal punishments and obtain the eternal prizes of God. For He who gave the mouth for speech, and formed the ear to hear and made the eye to see will examine all things and will judge [with] righteous judgment. [He will also] render merited awards for those who seek immortality, and He will give life everlasting, joy, peace, rest, and abundance of good things, which neither has the eye seen nor ear heard nor has it entered into the heart of man to conceive. But to the unbelieving and despisers, who do not obey the truth but are obedient to adulteries and fornications, and filthiness, and covetousness, and unlawful idolatries, there shall be anger and wrath, tribulation and anguish, and at the last an everlasting fire shall possess them. (*Autol.* 1.14, adapted from *ANF*)

11. Summary

The significance of these selected references is that they show a growing tendency on the part of the second-century church to transfer the recognized authority of the teaching of Jesus *found in the Gospels* to *the documents themselves,* including the Letters of Paul. This transfer of authority is seen most clearly in the writings of Justin, and after him with increasing frequency and clarity in the writings of Irenaeus, Theophilus of Antioch, and Athenagoras.

By 200, an imprecise collection of Christian writings, which had as its core the one or more canonical Gospels and the writings of Paul, had achieved the status of Scripture in many churches. This was by no means a closed canon of NT writings, even though, for Irenaeus, only the four canonical Gospels among the literature of that genre had obtained widely recognized scriptural status in the church. He was aware that some Christians used the four canonical Gospels and other writings as well, for example, the *Gospel of Truth,* and he refers to them with biting criticism (*Haer.* 3.11.9). The authority of Jesus was nevertheless the most important authority in the church at the end of the second century, even though his surviving teachings were located almost exclusively in the written canonical Gospels, with a few notable exceptions. The authoritative writings for the church now included the OT Scriptures, the teachings of Jesus—located primarily in the canonical Gospels—and the Epistles of Paul. However, other NT writings were circulating in the churches and gaining appreciation and, in the case of some books (i.e., the book of Revelation), a Scripture-like status.

One is tempted to venture guesses as to why literature that had possessed no scriptural status in the first-century church took on that distinction in the churches by the end of the second century. Indeed, it is strange that the Christian writings, which were generally not even acknowledged as Scripture in the second century, were cited more frequently than the OT Scriptures. This is somewhat parallel to the growth of the OT canon in Judaism. During the reforms of Josiah, only the core of the law had scriptural importance for the Jews. After the time of Ezra, the whole Pentateuch and possibly the Former Prophets became important in Jewish faith communities. By no later than 200 B.C.E., the Latter Prophets also obtained an important position in the community of Israel. When many of the religious leaders believed that the prophetic presence had ceased in Israel, there was a tendency to "inscripturate" the writings from an earlier time when the prophetic presence of the Lord was believed to have resided in Israel.

In the case of the second-century church, however, there are no clear examples of a time when the church believed that the age of the Spirit and prophecy had ceased, even though the office of prophet had already begun to diminish in favor of teachers and a more stable local bishop-presbyter. Chronological distance from the primary events that called the church into existence no doubt played some role in the recognition of the value of the testimony of the first generation of Christians. The further removed the church was from the eyewitnesses of the events primary to the church's confession of faith, so it seems, the more venerated those early documents became.

The conclusion that the second-century sources cited above demonstrate the seeds of the NT's later recognition as Scripture calls for three important cautions. First, acknowledgment of the authority of one part of the NT at this time does not imply that all parts were so recognized. Second, although the NT writings (especially the Gospels and Paul) are frequently used in worship and catechetical teaching, they are not generally called Scripture in the second-century church. Finally, even if some of the NT writings were recognized as having the status of Scripture in the second century, this is not the same as a closed canon of Scriptures. What is clear is that, with the recognition of the authority of certain Christian writings, the canonical process was in motion.

V. Conclusion

In the first century, the Synoptic tradition about Jesus was widely accepted and circulated in the churches first in oral transmission and subsequently in the written canonical Gospels. Throughout the second century, the church fathers made regular use of the canonical Gospels in worship, teaching, and apologetic writings; in addition they often cited several other sources, including some of the noncanonical gospels that were later excluded from the churches' sacred collections. Long ago, Gould noted that the second-century church fathers cited extra-canonical sources "freely and without apology." Regardless of this practice, the picture of Jesus was not remarkably changed, and in fact, Gould concluded, "the historicity [of the story of Jesus] is more triumphantly established by the corroborative testimony than by the absence of other witnesses."[90] The first and second centuries were foundational in the acceptance of the canonical Gospels and writings of Paul as authoritative writings in the church. These writings reached the status of Scripture for many Christians late in the second century and eventually became the bedrock authority in the churches. Even so, some early churches also received in a Scripture-like manner other testimonies that were eventually excluded from the NT canon.[91]

Even in the fourth century, when the four canonical Gospels were widely acknowledged in the majority of churches, we cannot say that *only* the four canonical Gospels and no others received recognition and

---

[90] Gould, *Mark,* xxxiii–xxxiv, who cites examples of the use of the noncanonical sources in the early church fathers (xxxiv–xl).

[91] Ibid., xxxiv–xlii.

acceptance in the churches, for some noncanonical gospels, acts, and letters continued to be read in several churches. For example, the *Infancy Gospel of James* had considerable influence in the fourth and fifth centuries and significantly affected the results of the Council of Ephesus in 431, which found support in this apocryphal gospel for its conclusion that Mary was the "mother of God," the *Theotokos* ("God-bearer"). Following this, the *Infancy Gospel of James* exerted considerable influence on Christian art and piety, and, as Mary was venerated, groups within the church turned to it for inspiration and guidance.[92]

Other noncanonical gospels filled various voids in the NT texts, such as details about Jesus' birth, childhood, and family members and even additional information about his resurrection and ascension. In other genres, the *Letter to the Laodiceans* was produced under Paul's name (see Col 4:16), and the *Acts of Paul and Thecla* describes Paul's appearance and his ministry in Iconium, although its focus is on a young woman named Thecla. The early church seemed anxious to leave nothing to the imagination, and in the second and third centuries the Christians produced many pseudonymous or apocryphal writings to fill the voids in the NT literature. Attaching an apostle's name to that literature helped it gain acceptance in the churches and lets us know that apostolic authorship added credibility to the churches' emerging *Christian* Scriptures.

Many sayings of Jesus circulating in the early churches were not included in any of the canonical Gospels. Popularly called agrapha, these sayings clearly functioned in an authoritative manner in the churches that received them and passed them on to other Christians. Found in noncanonical literature (*Gospel of Thomas, Gospel of Peter*), in writings of the early church fathers, and in NT manuscripts, this collection now includes some 266 sayings of Jesus.[93] Jeremias believes that only eighteen of the Jesus sayings are authentic, while Hofius claims that only nine of the agrapha need be taken seriously, and of these only four are probably authentic to Jesus.[94] Here is the list of Hofius' nine probable sayings (the four most likely authentic agrapha are marked by an asterisk):

1. "As you are found, so will you be led away [to judgment]." (*Syriac Liber Graduum, Sermon* 3.3; 15.4)

2. "Ask for the great things, and God will add to you what is small." (Clement of Alexandria, *Strom.* 1.24.158)

---

[92] See Hock, "Favored One"; and Limberis, "Battle over Mary."

[93] For details, see Stroker, *Extracanonical Sayings of Jesus;* Hofius, "Unknown Sayings of Jesus"; idem, "Isolated Sayings of Jesus"; Theron, *Evidence of Tradition,* 96–99; Charlesworth and Evans, "Jesus in the Agrapha and Apocryphal Gospels"; Morrice, *Hidden Sayings of Jesus;* and Jeremias, *Unknown Sayings of Jesus.*

[94] Jeremias, *Unknown Sayings of Jesus,* 42–43; Hofius, "Unknown Sayings of Jesus."

3. "Be competent [approved] money-changers!" (*Pseudo-Clementine Homilies* 2.51.1; 3.50.2; 18.20.4)

*4. "On the same day he [Jesus] saw a man working on the sabbath. He said to him: 'Man, if you know what you are doing, you are blessed; but if you do not know, you are accursed and a transgressor of the law' " (Luke 6:5 Codex Bezae [D])

*5. "He who is near me is near the fire; he who is far from me is far from the kingdom." (*Gospel of Thomas* 82; Origen, *Homilies on Jeremiah* (Latin) 3.3; Didymus, *Commentary on Psalms* 88.8)

*6. "(He who today) stands far off will tomorrow be (near to you)." (Papyrus Oxyrhynchus 1224)

*7. "And only then shall you be glad, when you look on your brother with love." (*Gospel of the Hebrews* 5, preserved in Jerome, *Commentary on Ephesians* 5.4 [on Eph 5:4])

8. "The kingdom is like a wise fisherman who cast his net into the sea; he drew it up from the sea full of small fish; among them he found a large (and) good fish; that wise fisherman threw all the small fish down into the sea; he chose the large fish without regret." (*Gospel of Thomas* 8)

9. "How is it then with you? For you are here in the temple. Are you then clean? . . . Woe to you blind who see not! You have washed yourself in water that is poured forth, in which dogs and swine lie night and day, and washed and scoured your outer skin, which harlots and flute girls also anoint, bathe, scour, and beautify to arouse desire in men, but inwardly they are filled with scorpions and with [all manner of ev]il. But I and [my disciples], of whom you say that we have not [bathed, have bath]ed ourselves in the liv[ing and clean] water, which comes down from [the father in heaven]." (Papyrus Oxyrhynchus 840.2)

These extracanonical sayings of Jesus no doubt functioned as canon 1, that is as authority, in the communities in which they were discovered and circulated, even though they never became a part of a fixed canonical collection (canon 2) in the developing Christian communities.

The question today is not so much whether authentic sayings of Jesus may be found here or there in noncanonical sources, but rather what to do with them. More specifically, should they be added to the canonical Scriptures of the Christian community if it can be reasonably demonstrated that they are authentic sayings of Jesus? Should they inform the theology of the church or be read in churches today, as was true of them in ancient times? Should they form a part of the authoritative base for constructing the church's teachings? Do they provide an independent tradition or source for scholars to reconstruct the life and teaching of Jesus? There is no agreement among scholars on these questions, but they do acknowledge that some authentic sayings of Jesus exist in the noncanonical sources. While there is no consensus on which agrapha are authentic, a growing number of scholars agree that they are arguably an important resource for historical-Jesus research. If this is so, they also raise important questions for the study of the biblical canon.

This discovery brings us back to our starting point, namely, that all writings of the NT and early Christianity derive their authority from the church's one true Lord, Jesus the Christ. All writings that were believed to convey faithfully the story of Jesus and his significance for faith were welcomed in the early church and utilized in its life and mission. When there was doubt whether a writing faithfully told the story and significance of Jesus the Christ, various criteria were employed to discern the matter. The first criterion employed by the early churches was the coherence of the writing with what was already commonly received in the churches (orthodoxy). Soon after that, apostolic authorship became the standard norm for determining the credibility and authority of a written document. By the fourth century, other criteria (e.g., antiquity and use) were also employed by the church to decide the question (see chapter 14). In the transition of Christian writings from acknowledged authorities to sacred Scriptures, Justin, Irenaeus, and other key church leaders filled pivotal roles.

CHAPTER TEN

From Scripture to Canon: Tracing the Origins of the New Testament Canon

THE CORRIDORS OF CANON RESEARCH ARE DIMLY LIT AND THE KIND OF EVIDENCE that one would hope to find is strangely missing, namely, a credible ancient document that tells what led the church to acknowledge a NT canon of Scriptures. Fortunately, some key individuals played important roles in the process from the recognition of Christian writings as Scripture to the end of the canonization process.

I. Justin and the Roots of Christian Scripture

Justin Martyr (writing ca. 150–160) offers two strands of evidence for the recognition of the scriptural status of the canonical Gospels.[1] First, he refers to Jesus' words in Matt 11:27 with the following Scripture-like designation: "In the Gospel *it is written* [*gegraptai*] that He said: 'All things are delivered unto me by My Father'; and, 'no man knoweth the Father but the Son; nor the Son but the Father, and they to whom the Son will reveal Him' " (*Dial.* 100:1–2, cf. 101.3, *ANF,* emphasis added).

Second, Justin shows that the Gospels, or the "memoirs of the apostles" (*apomnēmoneuata tōn apostolōn*) as he calls them, were used to establish doctrine (*Dial.* 100.1) and to relate the story of Jesus' passion.

[1]Justin did not make use of Paul's Epistles in his writings and placed little emphasis on the major themes of Paul's theology. He was likely aware of these letters, due to their popularity in the early church, but he may have wished to avoid Marcion's primary sources, or perhaps he was unimpressed with Paul's focus on the cross, atonement, and Spirit and Paul's lack of interest in philosophy and his apparent attacks on it (1 Cor 1:18–31; Col 2:8). Irenaeus overcame Justin's hesitation to use Paul and introduced Paul's Epistles as an important part of his NT.

For instance, when introducing quotations from Luke 22:44, Justin writes, "For *in the memoirs* which I say were drawn up by His apostles and those who followed them, [it is recorded] His sweat fell down like drops of blood" (*Dial.* 103.8, *ANF,* emphasis added). He appeals to the canonical Gospels (Mark 14:22–24; cf. 1 Cor 11:23–25) when explaining the apostolic testimony regarding the Eucharist: "The Apostles commanded them: that Jesus, taking bread and having given thanks he said" (*1 Apol.* 66.3, Richardson, *Early Christian Fathers,* 286). He also describes the use of the Gospels as reading materials in church worship, either alongside of or used alternatively with the OT writings, in his account of a typical worship service in the Christian community: "On the day called Sunday there is a meeting in one place of those who live in cities or the country, and *the memoirs of the apostles or the writings of the prophets are read as long as time permits* (*1 Apol.* 67.3, Richardson, *Early Christian Fathers,* 287, emphasis added).

For Justin, the canonical Gospels functioned authoritatively equal to the OT Scriptures. Strangely, however, he makes no clear reference to Paul's writings, which were surely known in Rome well before Justin's time. On the other hand, Justin does refer to the book of Revelation with favor (*Dial.* 81.4), giving one of the earliest expositions of a text from that document, which was welcomed in the Western churches and in the East up to the end of the fourth century. He calls Revelation one of "our writings" (*hēmetera sungrammata*) (*1 Apol.* 28.1).[2]

The years following Marcion were mixed and troubled as a result of the impact of his challenge to the emerging orthodox church, especially with regard to the church's use of the OT (see chapter 11 §I). Justin Martyr, who appears to have given implicit scriptural status to Christian writings, tried to make it clear that, in spite of Marcion's objections, the OT was a *Christian* book. In his defense of the OT, Justin became the first orthodox writer to set forth a doctrine of Holy Scripture. He specifically answered the question of how Christians could reject the normative status of the law (a common practice by that time) and yet still accept the OT as Scripture. This problem was first addressed by Paul in Gal 3:15–22, who showed that historically faith preceded the law and that the law had only a temporary purpose in the economy of God.[3] Although some scholars suggest that law in Paul was basically halakah (the legal prescriptive laws and regulations), Sanders stresses that it was also haggadah ("story" or *mythos*). Haggadah answers who we are, and halakah answers what we are to do. Sanders ar-

---

[2]See Schneemelcher, "General Introduction," 31–32.

[3]J. A. Sanders offers a helpful survey of the suggested solutions to the problem of understanding Paul's view of the law in his *From Sacred Story,* 115–23. For a discussion of the problem that the OT posed for Christian faith and Paul's solution to the problem—reading the Scriptures correctly through faith in Jesus Christ—see von Campenhausen's helpful discussion in *Formation of the Christian Bible,* 21–61.

gues that Paul maintained a high regard for the Torah as haggadah, but that the legal regulations of the Torah did not apply. For Paul, Jesus had become the "new Torah" and superseded the Torah era, but he did not eradicate the Torah, which was "caught up in Christ in a new age."[4]

Later, and in more detail, Justin tries to rescue the OT as a Christian book in two important ways. First, he appeals to a historical scheme of prophecy and fulfillment, namely, that the truthfulness of *all* Scripture is proved by the OT prophecies that were fulfilled in Jesus. His unwillingness to subject the OT to careful assessment and his blind appeal to its infallibility, even when he could not respond to critical questions related to it, however, are not his best defense:

> If you spoke these words, Trypho, and then kept silence in simplicity and with no ill intent, neither repeating what goes before nor adding what comes after, you must be forgiven; but if you have done so because you imagined that you could throw doubt on the passage, in order that I might say the Scriptures contradicted one another, you have erred. But I shall not venture to suppose or to say such a thing, and if a Scripture that appears to be of such a kind be brought forward, and if there be a pretext for saying that it is contrary to some other, since I am entirely convinced that no Scripture contradicts another, I shall admit rather that I do not understand what is recorded, and shall strive to persuade those who imagine that the Scriptures are contradictory to be rather of the same opinion as myself. (*Dial.* 65.2, *ANF*)

More important, in defending the Christian use of the OT, Justin makes little use of the readily available allegorical or typological exegesis of the law, which at any rate would have been understandable only to Christians and would not have satisfied the Marcionite Christians, who rejected this kind of exegesis.[5]

Second, Justin uniquely interprets the law as *divine ordinances* given by God because of Israelite disobedience. He argues that the law, that is, its various prescriptions and proscriptions, was intended solely for the Jews as punishment for their sins. Although Justin accepts that circumcision preceded Moses' giving of the law, he adds that the other ordinances came as a result of Israel's failure. Trypho apparently agrees with some of his argument:

> Then I answered, "you [Trypho] perceive that God by Moses laid all such ordinances upon you on account of the hardness of your people's hearts, so that, by the large number of them, you might obey God continually in every action, before your eyes and never begin to act unjustly or impiously." (*Dial.* 46.5, *ANF;* see also 27.2–4)[6]

---

[4] J. A. Sanders, *From Sacred Story,* 120.

[5] Von Campenhausen, *Formation of the Christian Bible,* 93–94.

[6] Most scholars reject the reliability of most of the ancient dialogues with the Jews, which became a genre for promoting Christian propaganda at the expense of

Even the Sabbath, circumcision, temple sacrifices, dietary laws, and ritual washings, Justin claims, were God's punishments for a disobedient people. In a clear reference to the recent edict of Roman Emperor Hadrian (135 C.E.) to expel the Jews from Jerusalem (Aelia Capitolina), Justin argues that God gave circumcision to the Jews as a sign of identification so they could be punished:

> For the circumcision according to the flesh, which is from Abraham, was given for a sign; that you may be separated from other nations, and from us; and that you alone may suffer and your land be made desolate and your cities burned with fire, and so that strangers may eat your fruit in your presence, and not one of you may go up to Jerusalem. (*Dial.* 16.2, *ANF* 202)[7]

Justin concludes that the OT laws were not in themselves harmful and that it would not be wrong to keep them, even though they would not be beneficial to those who do (see *Dial.* 27.2–4 and 46.5). His attempt to rescue the OT for Christian use in this way appears to have been both successful and influential since the same argument was picked up later by both Irenaeus (*Haer.* 4.15; 16.3, 5; 2.1, 28) and Tertullian (*Marc.* 2.18–22). Justin does not specifically call for a new collection of Christian Scriptures, even though he unquestionably recognizes the authority of the "memoirs of the apostles" for Christian faith and claims that they were used in Rome in liturgical readings along with the OT Scriptures (*1 Apol.* 66–67).[8] The memoirs were an authoritative guide to the teaching of Jesus on church matters, for example, on the Eucharist (*1 Apol.* 67), and they appear to have been restricted to the Synoptic Gospels.[9]

Justin, in the earliest description of Christian worship, indicates that these memoirs were read along with the Prophets and even had priority over them because they were read first:

---

the Jews. In most cases the Jew in the dialogue is a "fall guy" who succumbs to the superior wisdom of the Christian and eventually becomes a Christian. These dialogues may reflect the great desire of the church to see the Jewish people respond favorably to the Christian gospel as well as the Christians' frustration because they had not. In this case, however, Trypho not only does not become a Christian, something highly unusual in this genre, but he also asks some questions that are not easy for Justin to answer. For these reasons, the *Dialogue with Trypho* is given more credibility than other dialogues in this genre.

[7] For further examples of this kind of meaning given to the OT laws, see *Dial.* 19.2, 5–6; 20.1, 4; 21.1; 22.1, 11; 23.5; 92.3. Von Campenhausen, *Formation of the Christian Bible,* 93–95, has a helpful discussion of this issue.

[8] Metzger, *Canon of the New Testament,* 145–46, cites several examples from Justin that show conclusively that the memoirists were the Gospel writers. See also Patterson, "Irenaeus and the Valentinians," 8–11; and Metzger, "Canon of the New Testament," 124. These memoirs are elsewhere described as "memoirs of all things concerning our Savior Jesus Christ" (*1 Apol.* 33, 66, Richardson, *Early Christian Fathers,* 263, 286).

[9] On Justin's neglect of John, see R. Collins, *Introduction to the New Testament,* 20–21. See also Metzger, *Canon of the New Testament,* 145–46, for another perspective.

> After these [services] we constantly remind each other of these things. Those who have more come to the aid of those who lack, and we are constantly together. Over all that we receive we bless the Maker of all things through his Son Jesus Christ and through the Holy Spirit. And on the day called Sunday there is a meeting in one place of those who live in cities or the country, and *the memoirs of the apostles* or the writings of the prophets are read as long as time permits. When the reader has finished, the president in a discourse urges and invites [us] to *the imitation of these noble things*. Then we all stand up together and offer prayers. And, as said before, when we have finished the prayer, bread is brought, and wine and water, and the president similarly sends up prayers and thanksgivings to the best of his ability, and the congregation assents, saying the Amen; the distribution, and reception of the consecrated [elements] by each one, takes place and they are sent to the absent by the deacons. Those who prosper, and who so wish, contribute, each one as much as he chooses to. What is collected is deposited with the president, and he takes care of orphans and widows, and those who are in bonds, and the strangers who are sojourners among [us], and, briefly, he is the protector of all those in need. We all hold this common gathering on Sunday, since it is the first day, on which God transforming darkness and matter made the universe, and Jesus Christ our Savior rose from the dead on the same day. For they crucified him on the day before Saturday, and on the day after Saturday, he appeared to his apostles and disciples and taught them these things which I have passed on to you also for your serious consideration. (*1 Apol.* 67, Richardson, *Early Christian Fathers,* 287–88, emphasis added)

"Imitation of these noble things" is a call for recognition of their value in the life of the Christian community. This practice eventually led Christians to recognize the gospel literature as Scripture; because this literature served the cultic needs of the community of faith and was viewed as normative, it was shortly thereafter called Scripture in the church. Justin's practice, as well as that of the church that he attended in Rome, of placing Christian literature alongside the OT for reading during Christian worship services helped pave the way for Irenaeus's later recognition of the Christian writings as Scripture and his designation of those two bodies of sacred literature as the OT and NT.

II. Irenaeus and the Principle of Scripture

A. THE PRINCIPLE OF SCRIPTURE

Irenaeus of Lyons (writing ca. 170–180) is the first to promote a fixed four-gospel canon, and he also signals an important transition in the church when he refers to the NT writings as *Scriptures*. While not the first to call Christian writings Scriptures, from the time of Irenaeus onward, this becomes common practice in the churches. After him, the practice of accepting Christian writings as Scripture is widespread, though it is not clear whether he is the primary influence on this practice, which became universal in the churches by the fourth century, even if they often disagreed on which writings were Scripture. Irenaeus may have been the first church teacher to designate the Christians writings as "New Testament" (Melito appears to have done so at roughly the same time) and the earlier Scriptures of the church as "Old Testament." What he includes in these collections is not clear from his extant writings, but Eusebius later supplies a list.[10]

When the term *canon* came to mean a fairly precise collection of sacred writings in the latter part of the fourth century C.E., the canonical Gospels were already in the place of priority in all such collections and were often placed in the same order that they are found in the Bible today. Along with Irenaeus, the church's teachers toward the end of the second century exhibit a growing tendency to recognize Christian writings as Scripture. It is difficult to pinpoint precisely when this occurs, but the earliest writings to receive this designation were predominantly the canonical Gospels and some letters of Paul.

Irenaeus argued that the four canonical Gospels and other unspecified NT literature, along with an unspecified collection of OT writings, were the normative Scriptures for the churches, and he unambiguously called these writings "Scripture" (see *Haer.* 1.9.4; 2.26.1–2; 3.1.1). Although Irenaeus promotes the necessity and authority of the four canonical Evangelists, "these four and no more," he also argues for something that no one before him claimed: the Christian message was somehow incomplete if less than four Gospels were used to articulate the Christian faith.

Luke made use of Mark and appears to have had the other "accounts" before him, but tried to improve them, at least in the case of Mark, apparently wanting to correct them with a "[more] orderly account" (Luke 1:1–4).[11] Luke, Matthew, and even John must surely have known of Mark, even if John offers a different picture of Jesus' life, message, death, and resurrection. John does not suggest that his Gospel needs the other Gospels to support his claims or even that he supplements them.[12] Although Irenaeus may have seen the need for four "pillars" (i.e., Gospels) for the church, it is difficult to establish that the Evangelists themselves or anyone before Irenaeus saw such a need. Indeed, ample evidence shows that, even after Irenaeus, there was considerable variety of acceptance of

[10] In the fourth century, Eusebius (*Hist. eccl.* 5.8.2–8) analyzed Irenaeus's writings and claimed that Irenaeus accepted as Scripture Matthew, Mark, Luke, John, Revelation, 1 John, 1 Peter, *Shepherd of Hermas,* and Wisdom of Solomon. Paul is listed, but his individual writings are not identified.

[11] Gamble, *New Testament Canon,* 24–25, makes this argument and adds that Matthew and Luke must not have had a very high view of their sources (especially Mark), since they took liberties in adding to and altering the sources they used.

[12] This is not the intent of his concluding remarks in John 20:30, though the hyperbole in the later Johannine appendix in 21:25 may warrant this speculation.

the canonical Gospels in the churches at the end of the second century and even later.

In defense of his view that the church should only use the four canonical Gospels, Irenaeus employs arguments that by today's standards are considered strange, and even in the ancient world his reasoning for limiting the Gospels to four was not the most convincing line of argument:

> It is not possible that the Gospels can be either more or fewer in number than they are. For, since there are four zones of the world in which we live, and four principal winds, while the Church is scattered throughout all the world and while the "pillar and ground" of the Church is the Gospel and the spirit of life, it is fitting, therefore, that she [the Church] should have four pillars, breathing out immortality on every side, and vivifying men afresh. From this fact, it is evident that the Word, the Artificer of all, who sits upon the cherubim and who contains all things and was manifested to men, has given us the Gospel under four aspects, but bound together by one Spirit. . . .
>
> But that these [four canonical] Gospels alone are true and reliable and admit neither an increase nor diminution of the aforesaid number, I have proved by so many such arguments. (*Haer.* 3.11.8–9, *ANF;* cf. 3.1.1)

We should not conclude from this, however, that all four canonical Gospels—and only these Gospels—were widely received as Scriptures everywhere in the last part of the second century. This common assumption is simply not supported by the evidence. For example, Clement of Alexandria (ca. 180) cites other noncanonical gospel sources in his *Stromata: Gospel of the Egyptians* (eight times), *Gospel of the Hebrews* (three times), and *Traditions of Matthias* (three times). He also introduces a reference to the *Gospel of the Hebrews* with the formula, "It is written" (*gegraptai*). During a debate with a gnostic, Clement quotes from the *Gospel according to the Egyptians:* "When Salome inquired how long death should have power, the Lord (not meaning that life is evil, and the creation bad) said: 'As long as you women give birth to children' " (*Strom.* 3.6.45). He even concedes: "We do not have this saying [of Jesus to Salome] in the four traditional Gospels, but in the *Gospel according to the Egyptians.*"[13] He accepts *Barnabas* as apostolic and quotes *Barn.* 1.5 and 2.3 in an authoritative manner (*Strom.* 2.6 and 2.15.67). Clement also cites *1 Clement, Shepherd of Hermas,* Sirach, Tatian's *Against the Greeks, Preaching of Peter, Apocalypse of Peter,* and even *Sibylline Oracles.* Irenaeus's view of "these four and no more" was not widely accepted in his day as we have seen. In fact, we cannot find any other source in his day that makes this same unqualified claim.

When asked by Christians in Rhossus for permission to read the *Gospel of Peter* in the church, Bishop Serapion of Antioch (ca. 200) at first agreed.

---

[13] Ancient references to these sources are supplied by Metzger, *Canon of the New Testament,* 132, and 171.

Would he reasonably have done so if he had previously accepted Irenaeus's notion of a closed four-gospel canon? Only after reading for himself the *Gospel of Peter* did Serapion see that it denied the humanity of Jesus, and so he reversed his earlier decision to allow it to be read in the churches. He did so, not on the basis of a widely accepted closed-gospel canon, but on the basis of a *canon of truth* that was circulating in the churches. Eusebius preserves Serapion's letter of reversal:

> For our part, brethren, we receive both Peter and the other apostles as Christ, but the writings which falsely bear their names we reject, as men of experience, knowing that such were not handed down to us. For I myself, when I came among you, imagined that all of you clung to the true faith; and, without going through the Gospel put forward by them in the name of Peter, I said, If this is the only thing that seemingly causes captious feelings among you, let it be read. But since I have now learnt, from what has been told me, that their mind was lurking in some hole of heresy, I shall give diligence to come again to you; wherefore, brethren, expect me quickly. But we, brethren, gathering [an understanding] to what kind of heresy Marcianus [perhaps Marcion] belonged (who used to contradict himself, not knowing what he was saying, as ye will learn from what has been written to you), were enabled [to understand] by others who studied this very Gospel, that is, by the successors of those who began it, whom we call Docetae [Docetics] (for most of the ideas belong to their teaching)—using [the material supplied] by them, [we] were enabled to go through it and discover that [the Gospel of Peter for] the most part indeed was in accordance with the true teaching of the Saviour, but that some things were added, which also we place below for your benefit. (*Hist. eccl.* 6.12.3–6, LCL)

This widespread concern for the truth—that is, the correct understanding of the story of Jesus—was significant in the church's decision about what literature to read in its worship. What did not conform to this tradition was eventually considered heresy and rejected.[14]

Finally, Justin's pupil, Tatian, compiled a harmony of the Gospels—his famous *Diatessaron* (a Greek word meaning "according to four")—using the four canonical Gospels and traditions from noncanonical gospels.[15]

---

[14] A heretical group roughly contemporary with Irenaeus, the so-called Alogi in Asia Minor, opposed the use of the Gospel of John, Acts, Hebrews, Revelation, and probably 1 John in their churches (see Epiphanius, *Pan.* 51; Irenaeus, *Haer.* 3.11.12). Likewise, the Ebionite Christians "use[d] the Gospel according to Matthew only, and repudiate[d] the Apostle Paul, maintaining that he was an apostate from the Law" (Irenaeus, *Haer.* 1.26.2, *ANF*). Eusebius's report that the Ebionites used the *Gospel of the Hebrews* (*Hist. eccl.* 3.27.4) seems to be confirmed by Epiphanius (*Pan.* 30), who claims that the Ebionites received the Gospel of Matthew, but called it the *Gospel of the Hebrews.*

[15] Because Tatian founded a rigorous ascetic movement that rejected marriage and the use of wine, it is not surprising that he incorporated other writings into the *Diatessaron* to support those views. In his commentary on the *Diatessaron,* Ephraem Syrus (died ca. 373) claims that Tatian used noncanonical gospels.

Originally known as "The Gospel of the Mixed" according to Ephraem Syrus, the *Diatessaron* was likely composed around 173–175 probably at Syria, but possibly at Rome.[16] Tatian not only smoothed out some differences between the canonical Gospels, but he also eliminated the genealogies of Jesus and Luke's ascension story.[17] The only extant piece of Tatian's *Diatessaron* is a small, badly damaged fragment that nevertheless shows the nature and extent of Tatian's harmonizing work:[18]

> . . . the mother of the sons of Zebed]ee (Matt. xxvii.56) and Salome (Mark xv.40) and the wives [of those who] had followed him from [Galile]e to see the crucified (Luke xxiii.49b–c). And [the da]y was Preparation; the sabbath was daw[ning] (Luke xxiii.54). And when it was evening (Matt. xxvii.57), on the Prep[aration], that is, the day before the sabbath (Mark xv.42), [there came] up a man (Matt. xxvii.57), a c[i]ty of [Jude]a (Luke xxiii.51b), by name Jo[seph] (Matt. xxvii.57), be[ing] a member of the council (Luke xxiii.50), from Arimathea (Matt. xxvii.57), g[o]od and ri[ghteous] (Luke xxiii.50), being a disciple of Jesus, but se[cret]ly, for fear of the [Jew]s (John xix.38). And he (Matt. xxvii.57) was looking for [the] k[ingdom] of God (Luke xxiii.51c). This man [had] not [con]sented to [their] p[urpose] (Luke xxiii.51a).[19]

Tatian's *Diatessaron* was known as far east as China and as far west as England and was cited authoritatively as recently as the fourteenth century! Although probably originally produced in Syriac in Syria, the same location where Ephraem wrote a commentary on it, the *Diatessaron* was translated into Greek, Latin, Old High German, Georgian, Armenian, and others, and its influence was widely felt. Eusebius speaks of the continuing use of the

---

Petersen, "Tatian's Diatessaron," 430, suggests that Tatian's other sources included the Jewish-Christian *Gospel of the Hebrews* and possibly the *Gospel of the Egyptians*. Metzger, *Canon of the New Testament,* 115, correctly argues that Tatian regarded the four canonical Gospels as authoritative, "otherwise it is unlikely that Tatian would have dared to combine them into one gospel account." There is no evidence, however, that Tatian regarded *only* the four canonical Gospels as authoritative. Tatian's views, of course, were unlike those of the later church, when changing, eliminating, or adding Gospels texts would have been unthinkable.

[16] Justin's harmony of the Gospels, which focused mostly on Matthew and Luke with some parallels to Mark and fewer still to the Gospel of John, may have influenced Tatian. See Koester, *Ancient Christian Gospels,* 365–402.

[17] If the four canonical Gospels had been considered by Tatian and his community to be inviolable Scripture, why did he exclude some sections? Petersen ("Tatian's Diatessaron," 430) cites important early witnesses (e.g., Theodoret of Cyrrhus, *History of Heresies* 1.20) to document that these pericopes were not included in the *Diatessaron.*

[18] Although the original is lost (except for the fragment reproduced above), scholars have been able to piece together the *Diatessaron* from various translations and writings from antiquity. A reconstructed text is available on the Internet at http://www.earlychristianwritings.com/text/diatessaron.html.

[19] Quotation from Metzger, *Canon of the New Testament,* 115, who supplies the bracketed words and the Scripture references.

Diatessaron in the fourth century in the West (*Hist. eccl.* 4.29.6), and it was widely used in the Syrian churches well into the sixth century. It continued to influence churches long after this, but eventually yielded ground to the later Syriac Peshitta translation of the NT, which included all four canonical Gospels. The *Diatessaron* was eventually suppressed by the Roman Catholic and Eastern Orthodox churches because its author was viewed as a heretic. This document continues to be valuable as a resource for textual criticism because it is one of the earliest witnesses to the text of the Gospels.[20]

The point that I am trying to establish here is that in Irenaeus's day few Christians limited the number of Gospels to be read in their churches to the same four that he did. In fact, Irenaeus is the only witness in his generation who acknowledges only the four canonical Gospels in his NT Scripture collection. Unlike Tertullian who followed him, he does not distinguish between Matthew and John as apostolic authors and Luke and Mark who are not. At the end of the second century, a canonical Gospel might likely be read alongside one or more noncanonical gospels. Although many scholars argue that Irenaeus's position on a fixed four-gospel canon reflected the status or opinion on the matter in a majority of churches in his day, this argument does not square with the available evidence.

Widespread acceptance of the four canonical Gospels took time, and limiting the Gospels to four took even longer. It is likely that Irenaeus's aim was to defend the use of John's Gospel, which was under attack in his time. The thrust of his argument for four Gospels was to gain acceptance for the Gospel of John, rather than to limit their number to four. It is noteworthy that the Muratorian Fragment, a fourth-century document, simply lists the four canonical Gospels with no defense (see chapter 13 §I.D). Earlier in the century, Eusebius listed the four canonical Gospels as a closed unit, giving them priority in a "recognized" (*homolegoumena*) sacred collection. He describes them collectively as "the holy tetrad of the Gospels" (*Hist. eccl.* 3.25.1, LCL), but the four Gospels had not yet achieved this prominence at the end of the second century, which is likely why Irenaeus defended them so vigorously.

B. IRENAEUS AND THE NOTION OF CANON

Irenaeus succinctly expresses the triptych of the early church, the threefold source of authority in the church: "The Lord doth testify, as the apostles confess, and as the prophets announce" (*Haer.* 3.17.4, *ANF*). His ordering of these three, with the prophets last, is still very much like that found elsewhere in second-century writers (e.g., Ign. *Phld.* 5.1–2).

---

[20] For an extended discussion of the *Diatessaron,* see the works by Petersen: *Tatian's Diatessaron;* "Diatessaron of Tatian"; and "Tatian's Diatessaron."

According to von Campenhausen, Irenaeus marked "the transition from the earlier period of belief in tradition [primitive Christianity] to the new age of deliberate canonical standardization."[21] Unlike Justin, he did not defend the OT Scriptures alone, but he also explicitly named and defended the scriptural authority of Christian writings. His point, however, was not so much to establish a biblical canon, or a closed collection of sacred writings, as it was to defend the truth of the Christian message.[22] Outside of the four canonical Gospels, he does not list his own fixed list of Christian Scriptures. In fact, the "canon" of Irenaeus was not a list of inspired books, but rather the faith of and about Jesus the Christ, which he believed had been passed on in the church by the apostles—that is, the apostolic tradition (*Haer.* 3.2.2). Irenaeus's summary of the faith on which the church depended for its life and witness is set forth in a major text that merits close attention since the tenets of faith expressed in this passage became the foundation pillars of orthodoxy in the church and were a major part of most significant ancient creedal formulations. This canon, or *regula fidei* (lit., "rule of faith"), was also a distinguishing feature in later canonical decisions that incorporated or excluded certain Christian writings from the biblical canon:

> The Church, though dispersed throughout the whole world, even to the ends of the earth, has received from the apostles and their disciples this faith: It believes in one God, the Father Almighty, Maker of heaven, and earth and the sea and all things that are in them and in one Christ Jesus, the Son of God, who became incarnate for our salvation and in the Holy Spirit, who proclaimed through the prophets the dispensations of God, the advents, the birth from a virgin, the passion, the resurrection from the dead, and the ascension into heaven in the flesh of the beloved Christ Jesus, our Lord. He also proclaimed through the prophets his future manifestation from heaven in the glory of the Father "to gather all things in one," and to raise up anew all flesh of the whole human race. [This will take place] in order that to Christ Jesus, our Lord, God, Saviour, and King, according to the will of the invisible Father, [so that] "every knee should bow, of things in heaven, and things in earth, and things under the earth, and that every tongue should confess" him. And he will execute just judgment towards all sending into everlasting fire "spiritual wickednesses," and the angels who transgressed and became apostates, together with the ungodly, and unrighteous, and wicked, and profane among men. But he will, in the exercise of his grace, confer immortality on the righteous and holy, and those who have kept his commandments, and have persevered in his love, some from the beginning of their Christian course, and others from the time of their repentance. He will surround them with everlasting glory. (*Haer.* 1.10.1, *ANF;* cf. 3.4.2)

---

[21] Von Campenhausen, *Formation of the Christian Bible,* 182.

[22] See also Goodspeed, *History of Early Christian Literature,* 120; and Patterson, "Irenaeus and the Valentinians," 189–220.

Irenaeus began to use both the OT Scriptures and selected Christian Scriptures as a basis for demonstrating the authenticity of Christian teaching. He was the first, so far as our present knowledge shows, to use the terms *Old Testament* and *New Testament,*[23] and he accepted that both Testaments were Scripture and, consequently, authoritative books for Christian faith. For example, Irenaeus introduces a premise for his line of argument with these words: "Inasmuch, then, as in both testaments there is the same righteousness of God [displayed] . . ." (*Haer.* 4.28.1, *ANF*). Elsewhere he illustrates his view of authority in the church this way:

> The preaching of the apostles, the authoritative teaching of the Lord, the announcements of the prophets, the dictated utterances of the apostles, and the ministration of the law—all of which praise one and the same Being, the God and Father of all, and not many diverse beings . . . are all in harmony with our statements. (*Haer.* 2.35.4, *ANF*)

> If, therefore, even in the New Testament the apostles are found granting certain precepts in consideration of human infirmity, . . . it ought not to be wondered at, if also in the Old Testament the same God permitted similar indulgences for the benefit of His people . . . so that they might obtain the gift of salvation through them. (*Haer.* 4.15.2 *ANF*)

Von Campenhausen, referring to Irenaeus's larger list of authoritative writings, explains that he was "the first catholic theologian who dared to adopt the Marcionite principle of a new 'Scripture' in order to use it in his turn against Marcion and all heretics."[24] The establishing of a closed canon of inspired Scriptures, however, was not Irenaeus's primary concern, but rather to defend the Christian message with all the tools at his disposal. He sought to root his teaching in the apostolic teaching and tradition that, he argued, was passed on in the church through the succession of bishops as well as by the authority of both the OT and NT.

Irenaeus's strongest argument that the rule of faith, or the tradition that he proclaimed, was rooted in his belief in "apostolic succession." He emphasized this again and again, but nowhere more clearly than in the following well-known text:

> The blessed apostles, then, having founded and built up the Church, committed into the hands of Linus the office of episcopate. Paul makes mention of this Linus in the Epistles to Timothy. Anacletus succeeded him, and Clement was allotted the bishopric. Clement, since he had seen the blessed apostles and had been conversant with them, might be said to have the preaching of the apostles still echoing in his ears, and their traditions before his eyes. . . . Evaristus succeeded Clement, and he was succeeded by Sixtus, the sixth from

[23] This does not necessarily mean that he coined the terms, but he is the first *known* writer to use them.

[24] Von Campenhausen, *Formation of the Christian Bible,* 186.

> the apostles. After him came Telephorus, who was gloriously martyred, then Hyginus, after him Pius, and then after him Anicetus was appointed. Anicetus was succeeded by Soter and Eleutherius, who is the twelfth from the apostles and now holds the inheritance of the episcopate. *In this order, and by this succession, the ecclesiastical tradition from the apostles and the preaching of the truth have come down to us.* And this is the most abundant proof that there is one and the same vivifying faith, which has been preserved in the Church from the apostles until now, and handed down in truth. (*Haer.* 3.3.3, adapted from *ANF,* emphasis added)[25]

If questions were not clearly dealt with in this "apostolic deposit," or if no deposit had been left, where would one turn for the answer? For Irenaeus, the obvious answer lies with those to whom the apostolic deposit was given: the bishops of the churches: "For how should it be if the apostles themselves had not left us writings? Would it not be necessary in that case to follow the course of the tradition that they handed down to those to whom they handed over the leadership of the churches?" (*Haer.* 3.4.1, adapted from *ANF*).

The effect of Irenaeus's concern to preserve the truth of the gospel was that the church began to recognize a collection of authoritative NT writings (the Gospels especially, but also Paul), which, as Koester notes, was later followed—though not uniformly—by the churches in Asia Minor, Greece, Antioch, Carthage, and Rome.[26] This collection was not yet closed in Irenaeus's day, even though he acknowledged only the four canonical Gospels.

With Irenaeus, the boundaries of the Christian faith became more precise than before, relative to the catholic dimensions of the church. For him the church was broader in scope than Marcion would allow, though not yet broad enough to include Marcion or the gnostic Christians. Nonetheless, recognition of the normative status of the Christian writings emerged during a period when the definition of what it meant to be a Christian was being framed and even challenged by heretical elements in the church. What grew out of the polemic against heresy was a church that was clarifying its identity and its Bible within a broad and often conflicting tradition that was partially oral in form. Again, Irenaeus's *primary* concern was to defend the Christian message, which was his "canon," and he limited this message to the apostolic tradition resident in the church, which in turn was limited to (i.e., found in only) the primary literature of the second-century church (i.e., four NT Gospels and an imprecise collection of Paul's Letters).

---

[25] For Irenaeus, the apostolic witness was the primary determining principle for the recognition of the authority of NT Scriptures (*Haer.* 3.2.2). He did not limit the succession of the apostolic witness, however, to the bishops at Rome alone (*Haer.* 3.3.2).

[26] Koester, *Introduction to the New Testament,* 2.11.

C. IRENAEUS'S INFLUENCE

Irenaeus claims that his canon of faith (*regula fidei*) did not originate with him, but that he received it through the succession of church bishops from the apostles. Although some scholars question whether Irenaeus's canon originated with the apostles, most agree that it reflects beliefs of longer standing in the church. Not only were there earlier creedal formulations (some quite well known) in the first and early second centuries of the church (1 Cor 15:3–4; Phil 2:5–11; Rom 10:9–10; 1 Tim 3:16),[27] there was also a high regard for the canonical Gospels (especially Matthew in Syria and the West, John in Asia Minor) and for Paul.[28] Such precedents were not new in the time of Irenaeus, but the recognition and actual referral of such literature as Scripture was rather recent, even though it appears that the church had been moving in that direction for some time.

The literature that became normative in the second-century churches no doubt included what was most relevant to their own needs. (This is a logical inference evidenced by the many differing collections of Christian Scriptures in the fourth-century churches.) Most Christian churches at the end of the second century appear to have been in basic agreement with the core of Irenaeus's collection of NT Scriptures (the canonical Gospels and some of Paul's Letters), even though no precise limitations were imposed on the collection at this time. What becomes apparent is that this wide (but not exclusive) agreement emerged from the local churches themselves and not from any church council. There were, in fact, no council decisions regarding the scope of the NT Scriptures before the last half of the fourth century.

What this suggests, of course, is the wide popularity of creedal beliefs similar to those advanced by Irenaeus. In this sense, the literature that found wide acceptance was in basic agreement with this tradition of faith. Objections of the orthodox against the gnostic heresies were not based on some new or developing notion of what was true, but on what had earlier roots within the church itself. Among all of the diversity that existed in the early church, the broad parameters of the Christian message were not in serious doubt. For example, though it continued to be difficult for Christians to agree on the human/divine nature of Jesus, the Trinitarian formulations of this issue were, for the most part, developed later in the church's tradition, especially in the fourth century.[29] Nevertheless, by the end of the

---

[27] Kelly, *Early Christian Doctrines,* 82–83, lists two other creeds roughly contemporary with the last half of the second century.

[28] Clement of Rome speaks of Paul as inspired (*1 Clem.* 47.3) and refers or alludes to his letters several times (e.g., 13.1; 24.1; 33.1; 34.8, 37.3, 5; and especially 46.1–3).

[29] Athenagoras, of course, is an exception, but his conclusions are not representative of most Christologies in the second century. His Trinitarian-type of formulation is, however, anticipatory of the fourth century, when God and Jesus Christ are described in Greek philosophical categories, especially Platonic categories.

first century the true humanity of Jesus was a widely accepted in Christian faith (1 John 4:1–3), and all four Gospels evidence this (e.g., Jesus was tempted, he was tired, he was hungry, he ate, slept, and died). On the other hand, some churches continued to debate whether Jesus should be identified as a spirit, as *the* Spirit, as an angel, or as a divinely empowered man. The range of perspectives on this topic in the second and third centuries appears to have been quite broad. Eschatological perspectives also varied in the earliest Christian literature, but all theologies had a hope in the future blessing of God for those who put their faith in Jesus the Christ, the Savior of the world and the Son of God. Within this diversity, therefore, some longstanding elements of Christian faith must have played a role in the churches' decisions as to what literature was useful in their life, faith, and worship.

Orthodox Christian opposition to Marcion's limited collection of Christian writings and his rejection of the OT and opposition to the many sacred writings of the gnostics came from local churches, based on an understanding of the Christian faith that was believed to be normative in the majority of the churches. In other words, opposition to the so-called heresies of the second centuries did not come from organized church councils, but from local church leaders.

Early creedal statements, just like all subsequent creedal formulations of any era, were forged in particular contexts in the churches and often were formed in a controversial setting (e.g., the author of 1 John 4:1–3, 6, 13–16 opposed the Docetic controversy of the late first century). The result was that the theology of the ancient Christian churches always developed in different directions, being heavily influenced by diverse social contexts.[30] This, in part, is why ancient Christian theology was neither monolithic nor arrived at, even when many churches agreed on its substance, at the same time and in all of the churches. Amid some very basic general agreements, the theology, teaching, and worship of local churches often varied.

At the end of the second century, when the Christian community was interacting with what some considered to be extreme diversity (i.e.,

---

Athenagoras comes close to the later position of the church: "We speak of God, of his Son, his Word, and of the Holy Spirit; and we say that the Father, the Son, and the Spirit are united in power. For the Son is the intelligence, reason, and wisdom of the Father, and the Spirit is an effluence, as light from fire" (Athenagoras, *A Plea for the Christians* 24, Richardson, *Early Christian Fathers,* 326). At any rate, it is debatable whether Athenagoras's view of the Spirit was representative of the views of the Ante-Nicene or Nicene fathers.

[30] Understanding the social context in which early Christianity emerged and how it affected the early church is quite useful. The canonization of Scripture did not take place in a vacuum, but has parallels in the use and canonization of Greco-Roman literature. See Rutgers et al., *Use of Sacred Books,* for the published results of an international conference on the social context that gave rise to the Christian understanding of sacred literature.

heresy), there was a growing sense of need for uniformity in the Christian community, especially in the churches of the West, where the Romans themselves were calling for uniformity in social and religious matters. In January 250, the emperor Decius (died June 251) began the first empire-wide persecution of Christians with the execution of Bishop Fabian of Rome. In large measure the result of the Romans' demand for uniformity and their fear of nonconformity, the short-lived Decian persecution had the unintended consequence of influencing the development of orthodoxy by bringing to the fore the issue of the Christians' lack of uniformity with regard to their sacred writings.[31]

Whatever his original source or motivation, Irenaeus's influence on his and subsequent generations regarding the recognition of Christian Scriptures was strong—but not strong enough to solidify which Christian writings were recognized as Scripture. Von Campenhausen argues that Irenaeus's influence spread rapidly and that the move toward the recognition of new Scriptures in this era could not be checked.[32] Although there was broad agreement on the Gospels and Paul—even among many of the heretical groups—the collection of sacred Christian writings was not thereby closed, as von Campenhausen explains:

> Attempts were made to secure as comprehensive and solid a collection as possible; and in the process people from various churches naturally liked to adopt such books as confirmed their own points of view. There was thus a danger that even recent, tendentious works would find their way into the canon, as, for example, 2 Peter or the Shepherd of Hermas.[33]

D. IRENAEUS'S LIST OF SCRIPTURES

Irenaeus did not make a complete list of authoritative Christian writings. He listed the four canonical Gospels and often referred to many NT passages for support of his positions against heresy. This practice was not presented as something new, but was for him a reflection of a long-standing tradition in the church (see, e.g., *Haer.* 3.3.3; 3.11.8; 3.12.15; 3.14.1–15.1; 3.21.3–4). Irenaeus considered the NT literature as Scripture on a par with the OT, even though he did not clearly define the parameters of the NT Scriptures.[34] If his few references to and citations of Hebrews are any indication of what Irenaeus considered authoritative and inspired of

---

[31] In the fourth century, another Roman emperor, Constantine, also tried to achieve harmony in Roman society. Using a vastly different methodology, he continually involved himself in church councils with the clear intention of bringing about harmony in the church—not simply as a means of purifying Christian doctrine (see §VIII below).

[32] Von Campenhausen, *Formation of the Christian Bible,* 210.

[33] Ibid., 211.

[34] Goodspeed, "Canon of the New Testament," 64–65.

God, he may not have considered this book equal in authority to the other NT writings, nor does he mention James, Jude, or 2 Peter. On the other hand, he appears to have acknowledged the authority of the *Shepherd of Hermas* and *1 Clement*. This may prove nothing, however, since he was writing to address specific issues (heresy), and he would naturally utilize the writings that best suited his argument.

The Scriptures, for Irenaeus, were evidently made up of the still fluid collection of OT writings (still fluid, that is, in the churches) and *at least* the four Gospels and Paul's writings, but we cannot demonstrate this from his extant writings. In an overly optimistic statement about the interpretation of Scripture, he enthuses: "the entire Scriptures, the prophets and the Gospels, can be clearly, unambiguously understood by all" (*Haer.* 2.27.2, *ANF*). Later, however, he seems to reverse himself and says that if we fail to understand some parts of Scriptures we should leave these matters to God because the Scriptures "are indeed perfect since they were spoken by the Word of God and His Spirit" (2.28.2, *ANF*).

Failure to mention an ancient source does not necessarily mean this source was either unknown or not viewed as authoritative by Irenaeus. The ad hoc nature of his writings must surely have had a considerable effect on the literature that he cited to support his positions. For example, *Against Heresies* is directed to the church and against gnostics, Marcion, and Marcionites. The sources that Irenaeus would have found helpful in *this* apologetic defense of orthodoxy do not necessarily include all that he thought was either scriptural or authoritative in the churches. Even though he makes fewer references to the OT literature than to the NT literature, we cannot draw the conclusion that he did not accept the books he did not cite. Therefore, contrary to the arguments of some scholars, we are unable to find *in Irenaeus* a canon of NT Scriptures (the description in *Hist. eccl.* 5.8.2–8 is a likely invention by Eusebius). True, Irenaeus recognizes the "apostles" as a collection of writings, but he nowhere clarifies what writings were in this group (see *Haer.* 1.3.6). Apart from his four-gospel canon, then, nothing in his writings suggests that he carried out any canonizing procedure on the rest of the NT literature. This became the task of later Christian writers, who now had in hand the principle of recognizing a new set of Christian writings.

III. Clement of Alexandria and a Broad Scripture Collection

Titus Flavius Clemens (ca. 150–215), more commonly known as Clement of Alexandria, was probably born in Athens of pagan parents, converted to the Christian faith, and came eventually to study under Pantaenus, the director of the catechetical school in Alexandria, the first school of its kind in the church. He succeeded Pantaenus as director of the school (ca. 190–200) and expanded the original catechetical aim of the school (to educate new converts) to make it a training center "for the cultivation of theologians."[35] During the persecutions of Septimus Severus (emperor 193–211), Clement fled Egypt and finally settled in Cappadocia.[36]

Like others before him, Clement refers to or cites as Scripture many of the writings of the NT: the four canonical Gospels, Acts, fourteen Letters of Paul (the Pastorals and Hebrews were attributed to Paul), 1–2 John, 1 Peter, Jude, and Revelation. He makes no mention of James, 2 Peter, or 3 John. He also quotes from *Barnabas, 1 Clement, Shepherd of Hermas, Preaching of Peter, Sibylline Oracles,* and the *Didache* for support of his ideas. Eusebius describes the writings that informed Clement's theology:

> Now in the *Stromateis* he [Clement] has composed a patchwork, not only of the divine Scripture, but of the writings of the Greeks as well, if he thought that they also had said anything useful, and he mentions opinions from many sources, explaining Greek and barbarian alike, and moreover sifts the false opinions of the heresiarchs; and unfolding much history he gives us a work of great erudition. With all these he mingles also the opinions of philosophers, and so he has suitably made the title of the Stromateis to correspond to the work itself. And in them he has also made use of testimonies from the disputed writings, the book known as the Wisdom of Solomon, and the Wisdom of Jesus the Son of Sirach, and the Epistle to the Hebrews, and those of Barnabas, and Clement, and Jude; and he mentions Tatian's book *Against the Greeks,* and Cassian, since he also had composed a chronography, and moreover Philo and Aristobulus and Josephus and Demetrius and Eupolemus, Jewish writers, in that they would show, all of them, in writing, that Moses and the Jewish race went back further in their origins than the Greeks. And the books of Clement, of which we are speaking, are full of much other useful learning. In the first of these he shows with reference to himself that he came very near to the successors of the Apostles; and he promises in them also to write a commentary on Genesis. . . .
>
> And in the *Hypotyposeis,* to speak briefly, he has given concise explanations of all the Canonical [*endiathēkē;* lit., "testamented"] Scriptures, not passing over even the disputed writings, I mean the Epistle of Jude and the remaining Catholic Epistles, and the Epistle of Barnabas, and the Apocalypse known as Peter's. And as for the Epistle to the Hebrews, he says indeed that it is Paul's, but that it was written for Hebrews in the Hebrew tongue, and that Luke, having carefully translated it, published it for the Greeks; hence, as a result of this translation, the same complexion of style is found in this Epistle and in the Acts: but that the [words] "Paul an apostle" were naturally not prefixed. For, says he, "in writing to Hebrews who had conceived a prejudice against him

---

[35] Ellens, "Ancient Library of Alexandria," 33, 39.

[36] See Crossan, *Four Other Gospels,* 94–98, for a helpful summary of Clement's life.

and were suspicious of him, he very wisely did not repel them at the beginning by putting his name." . . .

And again in the same books Clement has inserted a tradition of the primitive elders with regard to the order of the Gospels, as follows. He said that those Gospels were first written which include the genealogies, but that the Gospel according to Mark came into being in this manner: When Peter had publicly preached the word at Rome, and by the Spirit had proclaimed the Gospel, that those present, who were many, exhorted Mark, as one who had followed him for a long time and remembered what had been spoken, to make a record of what was said; and that he did this, and distributed the Gospel among those that asked him. And that when the matter came to Peter's knowledge he neither strongly forbade it nor urged it forward. But that John, last of all, conscious that the outward facts had been set forth in the Gospels, was urged on by his disciples, and, divinely moved by the Spirit, composed a spiritual Gospel. This is Clement's account. (*Hist. eccl.* 6.13.4–8; 6.14.1–3, 5–7; LCL)

Clement's scope of sacred Scriptures appears to have been much broader than that of Irenaeus. Metzger appropriately observes that Clement "delighted to welcome truth in unexpected places!"[37] Clement also knew of the *Gospel of the Hebrews, Gospel of the Egyptians,* and *Tradition of Matthias* and did not condemn them as heretical documents, though he apparently did not acknowledge them as Scripture (i.e., normative).[38]

What is most surprising about Clement is his high regard for Greek philosophy as a means of preparing one to receive the Christian message:

Even if Greek philosophy does not comprehend the truth in its entirety and, in addition, lacks the strength to fulfill the Lord's command, yet at least it prepares the way for the teaching which is royal in the highest sense of the word, by making a man self-controlled, by molding his character, and by making him ready to receive the truth. (*Strom.* 7.20, *ANF*)[39]

If Clement of Alexandria had a closed biblical canon, it is nowhere apparent. In his pursuit of the knowledge of God, he was informed by a broad selection of literature.

IV. Tertullian and Levels of Scriptural Authority

A well-educated native of Carthage in Africa and often called the "father of Latin theology" in the church, Tertullian (ca. 160–225), like

[37] Metzger, "Canon of the New Testament," 124. See also Goodspeed, "Canon of the New Testament," 65.

[38] Metzger, "Canon of the New Testament," 124.

[39] Oulton and Chadwick, *Alexandrian Christianity,* 21, note the parallel here with what Paul says about the law of Moses being a *paidagōgos* (Gal 3:24) to bring one to Christ.

Irenaeus before him, acknowledges all four canonical Gospels, but adds that they were written by the apostles or those whose masters were apostles: "Of the apostles, therefore, John and Matthew first instill faith into us; whilst of apostolic men, Luke and Mark renew it afterwards. These all start with the same principles of faith" (Tertullian, *Marc.* 4.2.2, *ANF*). Both here and elsewhere Tertullian acknowledges that Mark and Luke were not apostles, and he places them in a lower category than Matthew and John. For example, he criticizes Marcion for selecting Luke instead of an "apostolic" gospel:

> Now of the authors whom we possess, Marcion seems to have singled out Luke for his mutilating process. Luke, however, was not an apostle, but only an apostolic man; *not a master, but a disciple, and so inferior to a master*—at least as far subsequent to him as the apostle whom he followed . . . was subsequent to the others. (*Marc.* 4.2.5, *ANF,* emphasis added)

For Tertullian, apostolicity was the chief criterion for recognizing the authority of the Gospels. For him, this same apostolic authority, which was passed on by them through the succession of bishops, guaranteed the truthfulness of the gospel. The apostolic writings formed for him the NT:

> If I fail in resolving this article (of our faith) by passages which may admit of dispute out of the Old Testament, I will take out of the New Testament a confirmation of our view, that you may not straightway attribute to the Father every possible (relation and condition) which I ascribe to the Son. Behold, then, I find both in the Gospels and in the (writings of the) apostles [i.e., the epistles] a visible and an invisible God (revealed to us), under a manifest and personal distinction in the condition of both. (*Prax.* 15, *ANF*)

Tertullian cites or quotes the four canonical Gospels, thirteen Letters of Paul, Acts, 1 John, 1 Peter, Jude, and Revelation; however, he did not produce a closed or fixed list of NT Scriptures, even though he cites these and other writings in an authoritative manner and on one occasion refers to them as an "entire volume" (*Praescr.* 32). He also adds that Rome "mingles the Law and the prophets in one volume" (*Praescr.* 36). Beare notes that before Tertullian became a Montanist he included in his collection of Scriptures the *Shepherd of Hermas,* but later dismissed it with scorn. Surprisingly, Tertullian also treats Hebrews as marginal because he believes that it was written by Barnabas.[40] Like other scholars, however, Beare overstates the case that Tertullian had a closed canon of Old and NT Scriptures (Beare cites as support *Prax.* 15, quoted above).[41] Nowhere in his extant writings, however, do we find any specific listing or identification of precisely what was in Tertullian's OT or NT. None of the NT books that Tertullian appears to

[40] Beare, "Canon of the NT," 528–29.
[41] Ibid., 528.

have accepted as authoritative was later rejected by the church at large, except, of course, the Montanist prophecies (see chapter 11 §III).

V. Origen and the Use of Written Traditions

Sundberg concludes that the transition from the authority of *oral* tradition to the authority of *written* traditions, which began with Irenaeus, was completed with Origen (ca. 184–254).[42] Like Clement of Alexandria, Origen drew from the four canonical Gospels, fourteen Letters of Paul (including Hebrews), 1 Peter, 1 John, and Revelation. As in the case of Clement of Alexandria, once again Eusebius is our primary witness to what Origen considered to be scriptural:

> In the first of his [*Commentaries*] *on the Gospel according to Matthew*, defending the canon [*kanona*] of the Church, he [Origen] gives his testimony that he knows only four Gospels, writing somewhat as follows: " . . . having learnt by tradition concerning the four Gospels, which alone are unquestionable in the Church of God under heaven, that first was written that according to Matthew, who was once a tax-collector but afterwards an apostle of Jesus Christ, who published it for those who from Judaism came to believe, composed as it was in the Hebrew language. Secondly, that according to Mark, who wrote it in accordance with Peter's instructions, whom also Peter acknowledged as his son in the catholic epistle, speaking in these terms: 'She that is in Babylon, elect together with you, saluteth you; and so doth Mark my son' [1 Peter 5:13]. And thirdly, that according to Luke, who wrote, for those who from the Gentiles [came to believe], the Gospel that was praised by Paul. After them all, that according to John."
>
> And in the fifth of his *Expositions on the Gospel according to John* the same person [Origen] says this with reference to the epistles of the apostles: "But he who was made sufficient to become a minister of the new covenant, not of the letter but of the spirit, even Paul, who fully preached the Gospel from Jerusalem and round about even unto Illyricum, did not so much as write to all the churches that he taught; and even to those to which he wrote he sent but a few lines [*oligous stichous*]. And Peter, on whom the Church of Christ is built, against which the gates of Hades shall not prevail, has left one acknowledged epistle [*mian epistolēn homologoumenēn*], and, it may be [*estō*], a second also; for it is doubted. Why need I speak of him who leaned back on Jesus' breast, John, who has left behind one Gospel, confessing that he could write so many [books about Jesus] that even the world itself could not contain them; and wrote also the Apocalypse, being ordered to keep silence and not to write the voices of seven thunders? He has left also an epistle of a very few lines, and, it may be, a second and a third; for not all say that these are genuine. Only, the two of them together are not a hundred lines long."

---

[42] Sundberg, "Making of the New Testament Canon," 1222–23.

> Furthermore, he thus discusses the Epistle to the Hebrews, in his *Homilies* upon it: "That the character of the diction of the epistle entitled To the Hebrews has not the apostle's [Paul's] rudeness in speech, who confessed himself rude in speech [2 Cor 11:6], that is, in style, but the epistle is better Greek in the framing of its diction, will be admitted by everyone who is able to discern differences of style. But again, on the other hand, that the thoughts of the epistle are admirable, and not inferior to the acknowledged writings [*homologoumenōn grammatōn*] of the apostle, to this also everyone will consent as true who has given attention to reading the apostle."
>
> Further on, he adds the following remarks: "But as for myself, if I were to state my own opinion, I should say that the thoughts are the apostle's, but that the style and composition belong to one who called to mind the apostle's teachings and, as it were, made short notes of what his master said. If any church, therefore, holds this epistle as Paul's, let it be commended for this also. For not without reason have the men of old time handed it down as Paul's. But who wrote the epistle, in truth God knows. Yet the account which has reached us [is twofold], some saying that Clement, who was bishop of the Romans, wrote the epistle, others, that it was Luke, he who wrote the Gospel and the Acts." (Eusebius, *Hist. eccl.* 6.25.3–14, LCL)[43]

Origen's NT canonical list is very likely a creation of Eusebius and Rufinus in the fourth century, a hundred years after the death of Origen.[44] Eusebius's source for Origen's canon may well have been his own collection of references or citations to the NT literature in Origen's writings. Rufinus's translations of Origen's works are clearly inferior and unreliable (e.g., whenever he found difficult passages in Origen, he simply left them out of his translation, believing that they were interpolations by heretics). This practice calls into question the NT canon that Rufinus attributes to Origen:[45]

> But when our Lord Jesus Christ comes, whose arrival that prior son of Nun designated, he sends priests, his apostles, bearing "trumpets hammered thin," the magnificent and heavenly instruction of proclamation. Matthew first

[43] B. J. Bruce, *Origen,* 75 n. 5, notes that Origen credits Peter with a second epistle and attributes Hebrews to Paul (*Homilies on Leviticus* 4.4; 9.9), which contradicts Eusebius's opposing claims (*Hist. eccl.* 6.25.8, 13).

[44] Hanson, *Origen's Doctrine of Tradition,* 133–45, argues convincingly that Origen's classification system was an invention of Eusebius and that Origen had neither a NT list of books nor any notion of a NT canon. See also Sundberg, "Canon Muratori," 36–37; Kalin, "Re-examining New Testament Canon History," 277–79; and Schneemelcher, "History of the New Testament Canon," 31.

[45] Kalin, "Re-examining New Testament Canon History," 281, claims that Rufinus's Latin translation of Origen's *Homilies on Joshua* 7.1 is inaccurate, and he doubts seriously whether the list in its present form is from Origen. Kalin cites numerous problems in the translation by Rufinus and concludes that he "does not believe that *Homilies on Joshua* 7.1 presents us with Origen's NT canon any more than Eusebius's *Ecclesiastical History* 6.25 does."

sounded the priestly trumpet in his gospel; Mark also; Luke and John each played their own priestly trumpets. Even Peter cries out with trumpets in two of his epistles; also James[46] and Jude. In addition, John also sounds the trumpet through his epistles, and Luke, as he describes the Acts of the Apostles. And now that last one comes, the one who said, "I think God displays us apostles last," and in fourteen of his epistles, thundering with trumpets, he casts down the walls of Jericho and all the devices of idolatry and dogmas of philosophers, all the way to the foundations. (*Homilies on Joshua* 7.1, B. J. Bruce, *Origen,* 74–75)

Kalin believes that all such canonical lists were produced in the fourth century or later and correctly argues (with Harnack) that the second-century heresies in the church were not addressed with a canon of *Scripture,* but rather with "the canon of truth, the canon of faith (*regula fidei* or *kanon tes pisteos*), those confessional statements about God and about Jesus Christ in which the church centered its faith and life."[47]

In addition to writings "recognized" (*homologoumena*) as Scripture and a few doubtful writings (e.g., Hebrews, 2 Peter, 2–3 John, James, and Jude), Origen also refers to *Barnabas, Shepherd of Hermas,* and *Didache,* apparently acknowledging them as Scripture. Kalin observes that in *Against Celsus,* Origen introduces *Barn.* 1.63 with the words, "It is written in the catholic epistle of Barnabas." Likewise, in his *First Principles* 2.1.5, Origen establishes his argument on the basis of Scripture texts, among which he cites the *Shepherd of Hermas.*[48] If one claims that Origen acknowledged James and Jude as canon because he made use of them, then the same could also be said for *Barnabas, Shepherd of Hermas,* and *Didache.* Metzger, evidently seeking to support the notion of Origen's acceptance of the NT literature alone as his NT canon, observes that Origen never wrote a commentary on a book *not* found in the later NT.[49] Metzger does not point out, however, that so far as our present information goes, Origen did not write a commentary on every book of the NT. And if we carry Metzger's argument further, Origen's canon would be rather limited to the books that he both cited and on which he prepared commentaries!

The main problem with a supposed canon of Origen is that we have no solid evidence *from him* as to what his biblical canon might be. The supposed lists of canonical books presented in both Rufinus and Eusebius are likely inventions by these authors. The evidence from Origen is not strong enough to conclude that he accepted all of the writings that make up our current NT canon—especially 2 Peter, 2 John, and 3 John—nor do

---

[46] Beare, "Canon of NT," 529, claims that Origen is the first writer to refer to James.

[47] Kalin, "Re-examining New Testament Canon History," 277–79, quotation at 282.

[48] Ibid., 281.

[49] Metzger, "Canon of the New Testament," 125.

we have sufficient evidence to argue that Origen excluded *Barnabas* or the *Shepherd of Hermas* from his collection of sacred writings. The scholarly consensus is that Origen never had a closed canon of NT Scriptures.[50]

VI. Eusebius and the Emergence of a Fixed Biblical Canon

Bishop Eusebius of Caesarea (writing around 320–342) set forth the first clearly identifiable listing or catalogue of NT Scriptures. This so-called canon is not, however, as precise as many subsequent theologians would have hoped, and it demonstrates the existing confusion in churches over their sacred Scriptures at the *initial* stages of closed biblical canonical lists:

> At this point it seems reasonable to summarize the writings of the New Testament which have been quoted. In the first place should be put the holy tetrad of the Gospels. To them follows the writing of the Acts of the Apostles. After this should be reckoned the Epistles of Paul. Following them the Epistle of John called the first, and in the same way should be recognized the Epistle of Peter. In addition to these should be put, if it seem desirable, the Revelation of John, the arguments concerning which we will expound at the proper time. These belong to the *Recognized Books* [*homologoumenois*]. Of the *Disputed Books* [*tōn d' antilegoumenōn*] which are nevertheless known to most are the Epistle called of James, that of Jude, the second Epistle of Peter, and the so-called second and third Epistles of John which may be the work of the evangelist or of some other with the same name. Among the *books which are not genuine* [*en tois nothois*] must be reckoned the Acts of Paul, the work entitled the Shepherd, the Apocalypse of Peter, and in addition to them the letter called of Barnabas and the so-called Teachings of the Apostles [*Didache*]. And in addition, as I said, the Revelation of John, if this view prevail. For, as I said, some reject it, but others count it among the Recognized Books. Some have also counted the Gospel according to the Hebrews in which those of the Hebrews who have accepted Christ take a special pleasure. These would all belong to the disputed books, but we have nevertheless been obliged to make a list of them, distinguishing between those writings which, according to the tradition of the Church [lit., ecclesiastical tradition], are true, genuine, and recognized [scriptures] [*alētheis kai aplastous kai anōmologēmenas graphas*], and those which differ from them in that they are not canonical [*ouk endiathēkous*] but disputed, yet nevertheless are known to most of the writers of the Church, in order that we might know them and the writings which are put forward by heretics under the name of the apostles containing gospels such as those of Peter, and Thomas, and Matthias, and some others besides, or Acts such as those of Andrew and John and the other apostles. To none of these has any who belonged to the succession of the orthodox ever thought it right to refer

[50] In addition to the works by Kalin and Sundberg cited in the previous notes, see also Hahneman, *Muratorian Fragment,* 133, 136.

in his writings. Moreover, the type of phraseology differs from apostolic style, and the opinion and tendency of their contents is widely dissonant from true orthodoxy and clearly shows that they are the forgeries of heretics. They ought, therefore, to be reckoned not even among spurious [*en nothois*] books but shunned as altogether wicked and impious. (*Hist. eccl.* 3.25.1–7, LCL, emphasis added)

Eusebius's list reflects the uncertainty and lack of unanimity in the church about which writings were authoritative Scriptures. His threefold classification is similar to that attributed to Origen in *Hist. eccl.* 6.24–25:

1. Books recognized as authoritative Scripture:[51] the four Gospels, Acts, fourteen epistles of Paul,[52] 1 John, 1 Peter, and possibly Revelation.
2. Disputed books (*antilegomenos*) known to most churches: James, Jude, 2 Peter,[53] 2 John, and 3 John.
3. Spurious books (*nothos*) that are not genuine: *Acts of Paul, Shepherd of Hermas, Apocalypse of Peter, Barnabas, Didache,* and possibly Revelation.

One cannot argue clearly that Eusebius himself accepted as canonical any more than the twenty books that he lists as "recognized" Scriptures (i.e., the books in the first category except for Hebrews and Revelation).[54] He had doubts about some of the others and especially strong negative feelings about the final category. From this Metzger concludes that Eusebius saw that "it is not always possible to give a definite affirmative or negative answer to the question whether a book should be in the Canon."[55] Eusebius's view, however, that some books could be held in

---

[51] Eusebius's uses various terminology for this type of writing:
homologoumenos ("recognized") (3.3.3; 3.25.3)
anomologeō ("admitted") (3.3.1; 3.25.6)
endiathēkos ("testamented") (3.3.1; 3.25.6)
anamphilektos ("undisputed") (3.3.1, 5)
paradosis graphē ("handed down scripture") (3.25.6; 5.8.1)

[52] Elsewhere Eusebius attributes Hebrews to Paul (*Hist. eccl.* 3.3.5), but not without question. See also 6.25.11–14.

[53] Elsewhere Eusebius lists 2 Peter among the noncanonical writings: "Of Peter, one epistle, that which is called his first, is admitted, and the ancient presbyters used this in their own writings as unquestioned, but the so-called second Epistle we have not received as canonical [*ouk endiathēkon*], but nevertheless it has appeared useful to many, and has been studied with other Scriptures" (*Hist. eccl.* 3.3.1, LCL).

[54] On two occasions Eusebius calls *1 Clement* "recognized": "There is one recognized [*homologoumenē*] epistle of Clement" (*Hist. eccl.* 3.16.1); "the recognized writing [*homologoumenē graphē*] of Clement is well known" (*Hist. eccl.* 3.39.1). He does not, however, call it *endiathekos* ("testamented"), his favored word for Scripture.

[55] Metzger, "Canon of the New Testament," 125.

question, did not prevail, and the church preferred certainty over ambiguity, even though historically it was never able to agree on which books should receive the normative status of Scripture.

Up to this point we can detect in the greater church in the early fourth century widespread agreement on the authoritative status (canon 2) of most of our NT writings, and this agreement was accomplished without any council decisions by gathered leaders in the church. This collection of twenty NT writings was widely recognized at the grass roots level of the church, but the church hierarchy debated the remaining seven books and others in its various councils after the time of Eusebius. The broad support for and use of the NT writings is undoubtedly the reason that later church councils eventually recognized their authenticity and canonicity.

This does not mean that all other Christian writings were excluded by all the churches, as we see in the various lists and catalogues published after Eusebius (see chapter 13). On the other hand, up to and including the time of Eusebius, no hierarchical council had been involved in any decision regarding the status of Christian writings, and very few lists, if any, of NT Scriptures were produced. After Eusebius, numerous lists of authoritative NT writings began circulating in the churches, and it is probable that Eusebius was the leader in a move toward the stabilization of the biblical canon in the Eastern churches. This may have come as a result of his being asked by Constantine to produce fifty copies of the church's Scriptures, which involved the consequent need to identify precisely what those Scriptures were (see §IX below).

Eusebius was the most influential person of the fourth century in regard to the emergence of a NT biblical canon. He was the first to provide a catalogue of books that were approved, not approved, or disputed. Eventually, the church accepted the books in Eusebius's disputed list and rejected those in his spurious category, which validates his decision to suspend judgment until the books proved themselves. By classifying books in these three categories, Eusebius thereby provided a basis for genuine dialogue within churches about the sacredness of these books—a necessary step in the process of fixing a canon of NT Scriptures (canon 2).[56]

VII. Burning Sacred Books

On February 23, 303, Emperor Diocletian launched the last empire-wide persecution of Christians. The reasons for this attack are not alto-

[56] Kalin, "New Testament Canon of Eusebius," contends that Eusebius is pivotal in our understanding the canonization process that began in the first century and was largely completed by the end of the fourth century. In some matters, such as a final fixed text, that process had barely begun in the time of Eusebius, but this does not take away from his pivotal role in the canonization processes.

gether clear, but its acts of hostility against the Christians are well known. Problems of loyalty to the emperor and threats of the disintegration of the empire loomed large in the empire, especially in Britain, Persia, and North Africa. Diocletian, in an almost paranoid state of mind, significantly increased the size of the military and initiated many large rebuilding programs, hoping to return the empire to its former glory. More significant for our purposes, however, were Diocletian's actions aimed at restoring the Roman virtues, whose religious roots lay in earlier acts of devotion to the Roman deities. His edict (ca. 295) *Concerning Marriages (De nuptiis)* focuses on the theme of a need to return to religious uniformity.[57]

Diocletian insisted that no blood be shed, but demanded that all Christian churches be destroyed and that their sacred Scriptures be burned. Christians in public office were removed, and those in the upper classes had their privileges taken away. Finally, he declared that Christian slaves could no longer be freed. Unlike the earlier Decian persecution (250–251), which required Christians to sacrifice to the emperor, the Diocletian persecution sought to destroy the organization and life of the church by eliminating the books, buildings, and offices of the Christians. Contrary to Diocletian's original plan, however, many Christians died when they refused to turn over their sacred Scriptures, and some Christians were forced to offer pagan sacrifices as well.[58]

In May 303, the Roman authorities attempted to destroy the Christian Scriptures in Alexandria, Egypt:

> In the eighth and seventh consulships of Diocletian and Maximian, 19th May, from the records of Munatius Felix, high priest of the province for life, mayor of the colony of Cirta, arrived at the house where the Christians used to meet, the mayor said to Paul the bishop: "Bring out the writings of the law and anything else you have here, according to the order, so that you may obey the command."
>
> *The Bishop:* "The readers have the scriptures, but we will give what we have here."
>
> *The Mayor:* "Point out the readers or send for them."
>
> *The Bishop:* "You all know them."
>
> *The Mayor:* "We do not know them."
>
> *The Bishop:* "The municipal office knows them, that is, the clerks Edusius and Junius."
>
> *The Mayor:* "Leaving over the matter of the readers, whom the office will point out, produce what you have."

---

[57] Frend, *Rise of Christianity,* 452–61, has a helpful discussion of this matter.
[58] Ibid., 457–58.

Then follows an inventory of the church plate and other property, including large stores of male and female clothes and shoes, produced in the presence of the clergy, who include three priests, two deacons, and four subdeacons, all named, and a number of "diggers."

The Mayor: "Bring out what you have."

Silvanus and Carosus (two of the subdeacons): "We have thrown out everything that was here."

The Mayor: "Your answer is entered on the record."

After some empty cupboards have been found in the library, Silvanus then produced a silver box and a silver lamp, which he said he had found behind a barrel.

Victor (the mayor's clerk): "You would have been a dead man if you hadn't found them."

The Mayor: "Look more carefully, in case there is anything left here."

Silvanus: "There is nothing left. We have thrown everything out."

And when the dining-room was opened, there were found there four bins and six barrels.

The Mayor: "Bring out the scriptures that you have so that we can obey the orders and command of the emperors."

Catullinus (another subdeacon) produced one very large volume.

The Mayor: "Why have you given one volume only? Produce the scriptures that you have."

Marcuclius and Catullinus (two subdeacons): "We haven't any more, because we are subdeacons; the readers have the books."

The Mayor: "Show me the readers."

Marcuclius and Catullinus: "We don't know where they live."

The Mayor: "If you don't know where they live, tell me their names."

Marcuclius and Catullinus: "We are not traitors: here we are, order us to be killed."

The Mayor: "Put them under arrest."

They apparently weakened so far as to reveal one reader, for the Mayor now moved on to the house of Eugenius, who produced four books.

The Mayor now turned on the other two subdeacons, Silvanus and Carosus:

The Mayor: "Show me the other readers."

> *Silvanus and Carosus:* "The bishop has already said that Edusius and Junius the clerks know them all: they will show you the way to their houses."
>
> *Edusius and Junius:* "We will show them, sir."
>
> The Mayor went on to visit the six remaining readers. Four produced their books without demur. One declared he had none, and the Mayor was content with entering his statement of the record. The last was out, but his wife produced his books; the Mayor had the house searched by the public slave to make sure that none had been overlooked. This task over, he addressed the subdeacons: "If there has been any omission, the responsibility is yours." (*Gesta apud Zenophilum,* Stevenson, *New Eusebius,* 287–89)

Eusebius describes this persecution in significant detail, emphasizing especially the martyrs at Nicomedia (*Hist. eccl.* 8.5–6). His introduction to the Diocletian persecution specifically mentions the burning of the sacred Scriptures:

> All things in truth were fulfilled in our day, when we saw with our very eyes the houses of prayer cast down to their foundations from top to bottom, and the inspired and sacred Scriptures committed to the flames in the midst of the market-places, and the pastors of the churches, some shamefully hiding themselves here and there, while others were ignominiously captured and made a mockery by their enemies; when also, according to another prophetic word, He poureth contempt upon princes, and causeth them to wander in the waste, where there is no way. . . .
>
> It was the nineteenth year of the reign of Diocletian, and the month Dystrus, or March, as the Romans would call it, in which, as the festival of the Saviour's Passion was coming on, an imperial letter was everywhere promulgated, ordering the razing of the churches to the ground and the destruction by fire of the Scriptures, and proclaiming that those who held high positions would lose all civil rights, while those in households, if they persisted in their profession of Christianity, would be deprived of their liberty. Such was the first document against us. But not long afterwards we were further visited with other letters, and in them the order was given that the presidents of the churches should all, in every place, be first committed to prison, and then afterwards compelled by every kind of device to sacrifice. (*Hist. eccl.* 8.2.1, 4–5, LCL)

During this persecution, Christians who yielded and handed over their Scriptures to the Roman authorities were called *traditores* ("traitors"). They were despised by the Christians, especially the Donatists, who were not at all forgiving of those who betrayed their sacred Scriptures. These Donatists condemned all *traditor* clergy as those who had committed a sacrilegious act worthy of damnation in an everlasting fire because they sought "to destroy the testaments and divine commands of Almighty God and our Lord Jesus Christ" (*Acta Saturnini* 18.701, Frend, *Rise of Christianity,* 462). Christians who did not give into the persecutions and tortures and survived were called *confessors* (*homologētai*), and those who suffered abuse and died were called *martyrs* (*martyres*). A problem emerged in the fourth-century church about how to deal with the *traditores* or *lapsi,* and the controversy eventually involved Constantine himself.[59]

At any rate, the matter of knowing which books could be handed over to the authorities without receiving the charge of *traditor* became a very important issue and was evidently settled in *individual* churches, but not yet in regional or empire-wide church councils. The handing over of Christian writings to Roman authorities presupposes knowledge on the part of Christians about what books were considered Scriptures, but complete agreement in all churches was not present. Even though wide agreement on the majority of the NT Scriptures was present at that time, later on in the fourth and fifth centuries, church councils met to deliberate the matter of which literature would serve the church as its Scriptures.

VIII. Constantine and the Call to Uniformity

Diocletian's actions against the church to force loyalty to the emperor through emperor worship, sacrifices to the emperor, religious unity, and conformity to pagan Roman worship were all in keeping with a characteristic trait of Roman society that sought conformity and peace (*Pax Romana*). Remarkably, this same tendency toward unity and conformity during the reign of Constantine (306–337) had several important consequences for the church and may have played a role in the churches' establishment of a biblical canon. Thereafter many moves toward canon conformity or stabilization were initiated, and it is not by accident that the emergence of lists of authoritative Christian Scriptures are products of this period of history.

It is indisputable that the reign of Constantine marked the highly significant transition of the church from a community persecuted by a pagan government to a community favored by the state. At first, it was an especially beneficial relationship for the church because the severe hostilities toward it ceased and reparations began. Later this union made even more profound and lasting changes in the makeup and mission of the church that were not as positive.

The so-called conversion of Constantine came as a result of his most famous vision (Eusebius, *Life of Constantine* 1.27–30; 3.2–3) and led to many significant benefits for the church, the most important of which was, of course, freedom for Christians to worship without fear of persecution (2.24). This was accomplished especially through the Edict of Milan in 313, which gave religious freedom to all Roman subjects, not just to the Christians, even though the Christians were clearly favored by the emperor. Benefits for the Christians increased later when Constantine ordered, at

---

[59] Kelly, *Early Christian Doctrines,* 410–12.

Rome's expense, the repair of old church buildings that were damaged or destroyed in the severe persecutions of 303 and following. He also ordered, again at Rome's expense, the bestowal of extravagant gifts upon the church (2.46; 3.1) and its leaders (3.16). He requested the production of extra copies of the church's "inspired records" that had been destroyed (3.1). Finally, he "took vengeance" upon those who had persecuted the Christians (3.1).

Constantine's decisions had a significant influence on the life of the churches. Indeed, as we can see in the euphoric manner in which he describes these events, Eusebius and the whole church were understandably delighted to see the end of hostilities against them and the new honors and blessings bestowed upon them. They had only praise for Constantine: "like a powerful herald of God" (2.61), "pious emperor" (2.73), "the divinely favored emperor" (3.1), and one who "thus made it his constant aim to glorify his Saviour God" (3.54).

Although Eusebius mentions no fault or weakness in Constantine, church historians are not in agreement on Constantine's conversion to Christianity.[60] Constantine appears to have been only fond of Christianity at first and later grew into a more complete acceptance of its teachings. He was not baptized until shortly before his death. Following his conversion, he still revered the god of his father and tended toward a syncretistic Christianity in which he identified the Christian God with the sun. He made the first day of the week (the Lord's Day) a holiday and called it "the venerable day of the sun" (Sunday). Eusebius seems to have ignored many of Constantine's faults, even passing over his breaking of his pledge not to murder Caesar Licinius, his wife, and his son.

The impact of Constantine's conversion upon the church was nonetheless an important historical event and brought the church into an altogether new age. Eusebius proudly claims that with Constantine, "a new and fresh era of existence had begun to appear, and a light heretofore unknown suddenly [brought the church] to the dawn from the midst of darkness on the human race" (3.1).

Constantine's involvement in the affairs of the church was extensive. Although he was initially invited by the Christians to become involved in settling church controversies, almost from the beginning he saw it as his duty to become involved in the decisions of the church. This involved the calling (in effect, the ordering) together of bishops and other church leaders to attend various church councils (3.6; 4.41–43), the resolving of theological disputes (e.g., concerning Arius; 2.61), where to send bishops (e.g., Eusebius to Antioch; 3.59–61), settling the time for the celebration of Easter

---

[60] See, for example, MacMullen, *Christianizing the Roman Empire,* 43–58, who raises valid questions about the extent of Constantine's conversion by highlighting his brutality toward non-Christians and his coercion of the church.

(3.6–18), whether and how to punish heretics (3.20, 64–65), and when, where, and how to build churches (3.29–43).

Constantine not only arbitrated in such matters, but he also reconvened a council when its decision went contrary to his own wishes, as in the case of the Donatist controversy in North Africa. Constantine threatened bishops under penalty of banishment if they did not obey his orders to convene at Tyre (4.41–42), and he even sent his representative of "consular rank" (Dionysus) to insure order at the church council and to remind the bishops of their duty (4.42). Finally, he ordered the same church leaders to come to Jerusalem to help him celebrate the dedication of the new church building there!

It is ironic that on one occasion he wrote that, while the bishops were overseers of the internal affairs of the church, he himself was a "bishop, ordained by God to overlook whatever is external to the church" (4.24). One is hard pressed, however, to find an internal issue in which he did *not* involve himself!

No one would deny Constantine's interest in all matters related to the church, but it is clear from Eusebius that he would tolerate no threats to the rule of peace and harmony either in his empire or in the churches. Although he was not as cruel as his predecessors toward the church, he nonetheless wanted harmony (uniformity) *at all costs*. Those whose doctrines were not in keeping with the orthodoxy of the day were banished into exile, their writings burned, and their meeting places confiscated (3.66).

Unity and peace were more important to Constantine than what he called the "trifling" matter of the dispute over the person of Christ. In his letter to Bishop of Alexandria, Alexander, and to Arius the Presbyter, he states clearly his purpose for writing:

> Victor Constantinus, Maximus Augustus, to Alexander and Arius.
>
> "I call that God to witness, as well I may, who is the helper of my endeavors, and the Preserver of all men, that I had a twofold reason for undertaking that duty which I have now performed.
>
> "My design then was, first, to bring the diverse judgments formed by all nations respecting the Deity to a condition, as it were, of settled uniformity; and, secondly, to restore to health the system of the world, then suffering under the malignant power of a grievous distemper. Keeping these objects in view, I sought to accomplish the one by the secret eye of thought, while the other I tried to rectify by the power of military authority. For I was aware that, if I should succeed in establishing, according to my hopes, a common harmony of sentiment among all the servants of God, the general course of affairs would also experience a change correspondent to the pious desires of them all.
>
> "And yet, having made a careful enquiry into the origin and foundation of these differences, I find *the cause to be of a truly insignificant character,* and

> quite unworthy of such fierce contention. Feeling myself, therefore, compelled to address you in this letter, and to appeal at the same time to your unanimity and sagacity, I call on Divine Providence to assist me in the task, while I interrupt your dissension in the character of a minister of peace. And with reason: for if I might expect, with the help of a higher Power, to be able without difficulty, by a judicious appeal to the pious feelings of those who heard me, to recall them to a better spirit, even though the occasion of the disagreement were a greater one, how can I refrain from promising myself a far easier and more speedy adjustment of this difference, *when the cause which hinders general harmony of sentiment is intrinsically trifling and of little moment?"* (*Life of Constantine,* 2.64–65, 68, *NPNF,* emphasis added)

One is led to believe that peace and harmony were Constantine's major doctrines. The majority of churches affirmed the doctrines he favored, and he expected all others to conform to them.

At times Constantine was gracious, generous, and even humble, but he did not easily or long tolerate differences of opinion or challenges to his authority in church matters (4.42). His understanding of harmony was not so much peaceful coexistence, as it was uniform thinking—that is, to bring about a consensus from the people. On the one hand he destroyed several pagan temples and banned the practices of sacrificing and idol worship (2.44; 3.54–58), and on the other he intimidated the dissident bishops into conformity to his wishes or with those of the majority of the bishops (3.13).

As with earlier emperors, Constantine seems to have viewed anything out of step as a threat to be dealt with. Several previous Roman rulers considered any opposition to or rejection of Roman deities as a threat to the empire. Constantine, at times, appears to have changed only the favored deity and religion, not the example of his predecessors. His overriding concern does not appear to be the moral and inner transformation of the Christian faith so much as "peace at any price" in its outward social manifestation. Following the suppression of heresy, Eusebius wrote with pleasure. "Thus the members of the entire body became united, and compacted in one harmonious whole . . . while no heretical or schismatic body anywhere continued to exist" (3.66, *NPNF*).

Constantine's pressure to unify the church under the all-powerful state, which had the right to convene councils of bishops and to discipline dissident church members, appears to have established the authoritative pattern for later popes to follow in dealing with ecclesiastical activities, heresy, and with the appointment of bishops in the church. Constantine's title *Pontifex Maximus* ("chief priest")—a title used by the Roman emperors before him, starting with Augustus (31 B.C.E.–12 C.E.), which Constantine kept throughout his rule and perhaps influenced his decision to become actively involved in church decisions—is not a distant example of the kind of power that was ultimately vested in the popes. His granting of the power of the bishop's council over decisions of local magistrates (3.20) was also followed later, and that act helped to politicize the clergy.

The major consequence of Constantine's conversion for the church was the Christianizing of the Roman Empire, which not only included the cessation of the persecution of the Christians, but also guaranteed the triumph of orthodoxy (primarily Western orthodoxy) over the whole church. Major dissidents within the church were all but silenced during this time. The theological stance that later became identified with orthodoxy became the leading position of the church during this time. Consequently, in terms of the formation of the Christian biblical canon, the theological views adopted by the churches—or were imposed on them—played an important role in the process of adopting the Christian Scriptures that received priority and gained canonicity in the churches. In this sense, Constantine's actions toward the church surely must have had an important, if not easily measurable, impact on the formation of the Christian biblical canon.

IX. Production of Fifty Sacred Books

When Constantine relocated the capitol of his empire from Rome to Byzantium and named it "New Rome" (later Constantinople and subsequently Istanbul), he requested that Eusebius produce fifty copies of the church's Scriptures for the churches in the city. Eusebius prepared them in accordance with the best literary production of the day. Constantine's call for the careful, and indeed exquisite, production of these Christian Scriptures shows that at least Eusebius, who was charged with the duty of making the copies, was aware or soon became aware of the parameters of this collection of Scriptures. His own choices in this matter may be reflected in the fifty copies he produced.

Not all Christians in the fourth century agreed on the books that belonged in the canon of Christian Scriptures. In fact, differences of opinion on what is sacred Scripture in the church have never been completely silenced, in spite of the decisions of the later church councils. The decisions reached in this period with the assistance of Constantine were highly influential in decisions made by churches in subsequent generations.

The role of Constantine in the delimiting process of the Christian biblical canon may be considerable if we acknowledge his role in the selection process and copying of the fifty copies. For example, Eusebius himself did not acknowledge the scriptural status of the book of Revelation (*Hist. eccl.* 3.25.4), but because of Constantine's preference for the book, it was added. Remarkably, this book was included in fourth-century lists and manuscripts from the Eastern region of the empire, where its popular reception was often cold! If the matter of which books belonged in the Christian Bible was not finalized before then (325–330), as one surmises from Eusebius's comments in *Hist. eccl.* 3.25.1–7, then it probably was settled at least for Eusebius by the time he produced the fifty copies of the Christian

Scriptures. In Eusebius's own words, the production of these copies of sacred Scriptures went as follows:

> Ever careful for the welfare of the churches of God, the emperor addressed me personally in a letter on the means of providing copies of the inspired oracles. . . .
>
> "Victor Constantinus, Maximus Augustus, to Eusebius.
>
> "It happens, through the favoring providence of God our Saviour, that great numbers have united themselves to the most holy church in the city which is called by my name [Constantinople]. It seems, therefore, highly requisite, since that city is rapidly advancing in prosperity in all other respects, that the number of churches should also be increased. Do you, therefore, receive with all readiness my determination on this behalf. I have thought it expedient to instruct your Prudence to order fifty copies of the sacred Scriptures, the provision and use of which you know to be most needful for the instruction of the Church, to be written on prepared parchment in a legible manner, and in a convenient, portable form, by professional transcribers thoroughly practiced in their art. The catholicus of the diocese has also received instructions by letter from our Clemency to be careful to furnish all things necessary for the preparation of such copies; and it will be for you to take special care that they be completed with as little delay as possible. You have authority also, in virtue of this letter, to use two of the public carriages for their conveyance, by which arrangement the copies when fairly written will most easily be forwarded for my personal inspection; and one of the deacons of your church may be intrusted with this service, who, on his arrival here, shall experience my liberality. God preserve you, beloved brother!"
>
> Such were the emperor's commands, which were followed by the immediate execution of the work itself, which we sent him in magnificent and elaborately bound volumes of a threefold and fourfold form (*trissa kai tetrassa*).[61] This fact is attested by another letter, which the emperor wrote in acknowledgment, in which, having heard that the city Constantia in our country, the inhabitants of which had been more than commonly devoted to superstition, had been impelled by a sense of religion to abandon their past idolatry, he testified his joy, and approval of their conduct. (*Life of Constantine* 4.34, 36–37, *NPNF*)

By the time of Constantine's request of Eusebius (perhaps ca. 334–336), one can presume that there was a fairly well-defined collection of both OT and NT Scriptures, even though several books of the NT, as well as some books that did not eventually make it into the NT canon, continued to be debated in later councils of the church. Eusebius's copies of the church's Scriptures may well have become the standard for the expertly copied codices of

---

[61] The important words *trissa kai tetrassa* are perplexing. They may refer to making three or four copies at a time or to three or four columns per page. For discussion, see Robbins, "Fifty Copies of the Sacred Writings," 93–94.

the fourth and fifth centuries. In fact, some scholars suggest that either Codex Vaticanus, or Codex Sinaiticus, or Washington Codex may be among the fifty copies produced by Eusebius. Codex Vaticanus (B) may be a defective copy rejected by Eusebius, or a descendent of one of the fifty copies.[62] More likely, the kind of text employed in the fifty copies is a forerunner of the Byzantine (majority) text.[63] If Constantine's fifty copies included the current twenty-seven books of the NT,[64] this in itself would have had a powerful impact on the eventual acceptance of a twenty-seven book NT canon.[65] Whatever the case, Eusebius's account is pivotal in the history of the formation of the Christian biblical canon, and Constantine himself most likely influenced the current form of our NT canon.[66]

X. Summary

A brief summary of the historical development of the Christian canon up to this point is in order before looking at how heretics influenced the process:

1. The primary authority of the earliest Christian community was Jesus himself. Not only was the early church's faith linked to his death and resurrection, but it also focused on the sayings of Jesus. These sayings were at first, and for some time, passed on in oral form in the church, but many of them were written down quite early and circulated among the Christians, even though the books in which they were found (the Gospels) were not yet viewed as Scripture. The Scriptures of the first-century Christians included the OT Scriptures, which were not yet well defined by either Christians or Jews.

2. In the second century, Christian writings, especially the Gospels, began to be referred to with greater frequency in the life of the church. At first, the words of Jesus, when written down, *functioned* as Scripture, but the focus was not on books or their authors/editors, but rather on the words of Jesus. In the second century, many (but not all) churches used the Letters of Paul in their worship and teaching, and some of them were even acknowledged as Scriptures by the middle to late second century and were used in admonitions to Christians. The many allusions to the Pauline literature in the Apostolic

[62] Lake, "Sinaitic and Vatican Manuscripts"; and Skeat, "Use of Dictation."

[63] F. F. Bruce, *Canon of Scripture,* 204.

[64] Robbins, "Fifty Copies of Sacred Writings," 97–98, argues that only the Gospels—not the entire Bible—were copied.

[65] F. F. Bruce, *Canon of Scripture,* 205.

[66] Farmer, *Jesus and the Gospel,* 273–75, argues that Constantine's call for fifty copies of the Scriptures influenced the form and status of the NT.

Fathers at least shows deep respect for Paul and a willingness to hear his advice on church matters (*1 Clem.* 47). By the end of the first century C.E., collections of Paul's writings circulated freely among many churches, along with one or more of the canonical Gospels.

3. Justin defended the OT as *Christian* Scripture and also indicated that the church regularly used the Gospels ("memoirs of the apostles") in its worship alongside (or on occasion instead of) the OT Scriptures.

4. With Irenaeus came the first clear designation of Christian writings as Scripture and the first NT collection of Scriptures separate from the OT Scriptures. Irenaeus had a closed-gospel canon, but he was not precise on the boundaries of the rest of the Christian Scriptures. So far as can be determined *from his writings,* apart from the four canonical Gospels, he did not clarify what was NT Scripture and what was not.

5. Diocletian's edict to force the Christians to hand over their sacred Scriptures for burning must have influenced many churches to come to grips with the question of which of their books were sacred Scripture and could not be turned over. Many Christians were willing to hand over nonscriptural writings in an attempt to satisfy the authorities, but this act, of course, presumes a knowledge of what was and what was not Scripture.

6. Eusebius was instrumental in setting forth catalogues or lists of sacred collections in the church and is the first, so far as can presently be determined, to produce such lists. His focus on the stabilization of the Scriptures of the church eventually became a dominant concern of the church in the fourth century when the word *canon* came to mean a fairly precise collection of sacred writings.

7. Constantine played an important role in the churches' agreement on the broad outlines of the biblical canon through his many actions promoting unity and uniformity in the church and asking Eusebius to produce fifty copies of the Scriptures. Whatever Eusebius produced undoubtedly had an important impact on the churches in the region of New Rome, if not throughout the empire, even though there was as yet no consensus on the matter among the leaders of the church of the fourth century.

We are not well served by those who insist on the inclusion and exclusion stages of canon development, as if the church was initially open to everything and then by the fourth century it began delimiting or excluding books. Inclusion and exclusion in the canonical processes were in a constant dynamic relationship almost from the beginning. The church in the fourth century was open to new words from the Lord just as Christians in the first and second centuries were. Likewise, some Christians in the second century were just as opposed to some Christian writings as those in the fourth century were. Opposition to writings that did not conform to the *regula fidei* was just as present earlier as it was later in the church.[67] At least half of the current NT writings, if not more, were *functioning* as Scripture by the end of the second century, if not sooner. The fixing of the precise boundaries of the sacred collection(s), however, was a later decision for the church. The boundaries of the Christian biblical canon were in a state of flux for a considerable time in the church at large. Indeed, what was fixed in one segment of the church could still be under debate in another, and the church never agreed fully on the scope of its Bible.

[67] Barton, *Holy Writings, Sacred Text,* 35–36, makes this point and underscores both the flux and stability in early Christianity

CHAPTER ELEVEN

Influence of "Heretics"

WHILE THE WORD *HERESY* IS RATHER COMMON TODAY, ITS MEANING WAS FAR from clear in antiquity. Normally the term refers to individuals or groups within the Christian tradition who stray from orthodoxy, generally in reference to the nature of God or Jesus.[1] The difficulty in defining heresy in antiquity is that normative Christianity (orthodoxy) had not yet been universally defined and that those later identified as heretics did not have a fixed Bible by which to determine such matters. Initially many voices were heard in the church, before orthodoxy became fully established, as various theological stances were adopted and subsequently accepted or rejected by teachers in the church. For example, Paul rejects the strange teaching of the antinomians in the church (Rom 6:1) and there were those at the end of the first century who denied the humanity of Jesus (1 John 4:2–3) or other aspects of accepted Christian teaching (Col 2:8; 1 Cor 15:12–19).

These so-called heretical groups were not insignificant in number, and indeed if combined they may have outnumbered those in the so-called orthodox churches through most of the second century.[2] For our purposes, the question is whether the so-called heretical groups had a significant influence on the selection of literature that was included in the Christian Bible. Several scholars argue strongly that the church was moved to identify its Christian sacred Scriptures, the NT, because of second-century heresies that promoted more or less sacred literature than the church was willing to accept. As a result, the church came to grips with the scope of its

---

[1]The term *heresy* usually refers to a conscious or willful rejection of beliefs that are considered normative by a church, a group of churches, or theologians within the greater church. Roman Catholics, for instance define a heretic as a member of the church who denies the truth of any revealed teaching of the church. Protestants usually define a heretic as one who rejects any truth taught in the Bible. The term is not used of non-Christian groups, such as Buddhists, but only of those who claim to be Christian, and even scriptural, and have been rejected by the church as holding non-Christian views or those contrary to Scripture.

[2]This view is reasonably argued by Bauer, *Orthodoxy and Heresy in Earliest Christianity;* and Robinson and Koester, *Trajectories through Early Christianity*.

own sacred literature in response to heretical movements in the church in the second century, namely, Marcion and his followers, gnostics, and Montanists.

By the mid-second century C.E., the church was gradually recognizing the usefulness of a body of *Christian* literature for its life and worship, but there were as yet no fixed normative collections to which one could appeal. While Christians acknowledged as Scripture most of the literature that currently makes up the HB and several other books as well, their Scripture canon was not yet closed, and specifically Christian writings were not yet called Scripture. Christians were more identified by the word *gospel* than by a collection of Christian Scriptures, even if several NT writings (the Gospels) were functioning that way in the churches. Christians at that time were a community drawn into existence by a collection of beliefs and teachings that were generally summarized under the caption *gospel,* a term initially used to identify what had happened to Jesus and the relevance of this event for the salvation of humanity. There was also a significant appreciation for the apostles, the first leaders of the church who, the early Christians believed, faithfully passed on to their successors this gospel about God's activity in Jesus. The *written* Gospels were welcomed as reliable witnesses of what God had accomplished in Jesus, and they were believed to convey faithfully in written form what had been circulating within the Christian communities for some time, namely, the proclamation of the early church. By the mid-second century, the words *gospel-apostle* (sometimes *Lord-apostle*), representing the words of Jesus and the letters of the apostles, began to be placed alongside the Prophets (i.e., OT Scriptures) as authorities in the early church. This triptych of authority is also represented in the so-called heretical groups in the church. We will now examine the most prominent heresies of the second century and their influence, if any, on the formation of the NT canon.

I. Marcion and Marcionites

Marcion (active ca. 140–160), a wealthy shipowner and native of Sinope in Pontus, like many of his contemporaries, recognized the importance of a collection of authoritative Christian writings for worship and teaching in his community of churches.[3] He even recognized the familiar gospel-apostle tradition that was circulating in the churches,[4] but Marcion is best known for three important positions related to the Scriptures and

---

[3]For a useful summary of Marcion's career and accomplishments, see Clabeaux, "Marcion"; idem, "Marcionite Prologues to Paul"; and idem, *Lost Edition of the Letters of Paul.*

[4]Von Campenhausen, *Formation of the Christian Bible,* 153, believes that Marcion created the gospel-apostle form that was later followed by the church, but

God: (1) he rejected the OT Scriptures of the Jews, believing that they could be made relevant to the church only by allegorizing them; (2) he did not believe that the God of the Jews was the same as the loving and unknown God of Jesus; and (3) he limited the collection of Christian writings to an edited version of the Gospel of Luke and ten letters of Paul.[5]

Marcion's primary aim was separating the Christian tradition from the influence of Judaism, and therefore he selected writings that reflected this goal: Luke and Paul.[6] In addition, he freely deleted from his truncated canon any references to the Jewish Scriptures (e.g., Luke's Gospel lacked the story of Jesus' birth and began with Luke 3:1).[7] Bishop Epiphanius of Salamis (315–403) identifies the specific books in Marcion's collection:

Such is Marcion's spurious composition, which contains the text and wording of Luke's gospel and the incomplete writings of the apostle Paul, meaning not all of his letters, but only Romans, Ephesians, Colossians, Laodiceans, Galatians, First and Second Corinthians, First and Second Thessalonians, Philemon, and Philippians. But he includes none of First and Second Timothy, Titus, and Hebrews [and even?] those he includes [are mutilated?], so that they are not complete, but are as though corrupted. (*Pan.* 11.9–11, quoted from Hultgren and Haggmark, *Earliest Christian Heretics,* 115)

Many consider it strange that Marcion did not include the Pastoral Epistles or Hebrews, but perhaps he simply did not know about these letters. Whether Marcion was aware of the other canonical Gospels is debated, though he likely was familiar with the Gospel of Matthew, the most often quoted Gospel in the second-century churches. His followers certainly knew this Gospel and quoted it.

Marcion acknowledged that the Jewish Scriptures accurately told the story of the creation of the world, but he taught that a god (or Demiurge) who was both vengeful and evil created the world. He also taught that it was necessary for his followers to read the Jewish Scriptures so they would know their incompatibility with Christian teaching. Unlike widespread Christian practice in the second century, he rejected the spiritualizing of the Jewish Scriptures to make them relevant to the Christian community.

---

this conclusion is neither required nor even likely. Rather, this order grew out of the church's recognition of its threefold canon of authority—law, gospel, apostle—well before the time of Marcion.

[5]Marcion may have been one of the first persons to call one of the canonical Gospels a "gospel." R. Collins, *Introduction to the New Testament,* 22, suggests the possibility that Marcion assumed that when Paul spoke of "his gospel" he was referring to the Gospel of Luke. Marcion, Collins claims, evidently presumed that Paul had in mind a written source, so he set out to restore it.

[6]We have no evidence that Marcion specifically called his collection of writings Scripture or canon, though it clearly functioned as Scripture later in his churches.

[7]This is the only known version of Luke's Gospel without the birth narrative.

He rejected all Jewish influences on the early Christian proclamation. This rejection of Jewish teachings may have stemmed from the current anti-Jewish sentiment that was widespread in the Roman Empire following the second Jewish rebellion in Palestine against Rome (132–135 C.E.).

According to Harnack, after Marcion established the first biblical canon, the church responded to this challenge by first excommunicating Marcion and then establishing a larger *Christian* collection and reemphasizing its acceptance of the Jewish Scriptures.[8] This view was popular in academic circles throughout most of the last century, but several scholars now acknowledge that Marcion's purpose was not so much an insight into the value of a limited number of NT writings or even the establishing of a fixed biblical canon.[9] Rather, Marcion believed that the Christian gospel was absolute love and contrary to the legalistic and oppressive law of the Jewish Scriptures that was taught by the early church's leaders in Jerusalem, especially Peter and James. He also rejected the allegorical or spiritualizing hermeneutic for interpreting the law in order to make it relevant in Christian communities. He instead focused on the literal interpretation of the biblical text.

Marcion wrote a collection of *Antitheses* that supported his rejection of the OT and his restriction of the NT to Luke and ten letters of Paul.[10] *Antitheses* was essentially a doctrinal handbook arguing for the incompatibility of law and gospel and an understanding of his gospel. Marcion believed that Judaism heavily influenced Peter and James and that only Paul adequately separated himself from it.

Along with his rejection of Judaistic influences on Christianity, Marcion also rejected the typological and allegorical hermeneutical approaches to the OT that Christian writers of his day commonly employed to make it relevant for Christian faith. In the ancient world, allegorizing ancient texts was a signal of recognizing their sacredness in a religious community. Indeed, as Barton observes, it was "the characteristic mark of a holy text in the ancient world."[11] This rejection of the OT as a holy book supported Marcion's belief that Christianity was something completely new. He stressed that the God of the law was a Demiurge,[12] a creator-god similar to

---

[8] See Harnack, *Marcion;* and idem, *Origin of the New Testament.*

[9] Barton, *Holy Writings, Sacred Text,* 34–62; and idem, "Marcion Revisited."

[10] The *Antitheses* is now lost but it is discussed in ancient orthodox writings and, as a result, has been reconstructed to some degree.

[11] Barton, *Holy Writings, Sacred Text,* 61. In his defense of the church's apparent lack of sophistication, Origen once mentioned "intelligent people who readily interpret allegorically" (*Contra Celsus* 1.23, Barton, "Marcion Revisited," 349).

[12] "Demiurge" or "craftsman" (Gk. *dēmiourgos*) is Plato's term for the creator of the universe. In the second and third centuries C.E., the creator-god was also referred to by some gnostics as "Ialdabaoth," a nonspiritual being (Layton, *Gnostic Scriptures,* 12–16). Ptolemy, head of the Valentinian gnostic school in the second century, claimed that the Demiurge was an angel, the parent of all animate things, who was the God of Israel and *ordinary* Christians (ibid., 279).

the one found in Gnosticism.[13] He argued that the God of the OT was not the same as the unknown God of the gospel and of Jesus; therefore, he turned his efforts toward a total separation of Christianity from its Jewish roots and influences.

Earlier scholars accused Marcion of being a gnostic Christian, or at least heavily influenced by them, and it appears that he borrowed the name of the evil god of creation from the gnostic community, but he himself was not a gnostic. Irenaeus, however, identifies Marcion as a gnostic, claiming that the gnostic Cerdo took his system of philosophy from the followers of Simon Magus (Acts 8:9–24) and that "Marcion of Pontus succeeded him [Cerdo], and developed his doctrine" (*Haer.* 1.27.1). Unlike the gnostics, however, Marcion rejected all of the Jewish Scriptures and the allegorical interpretations of these Scriptures. He avoided any focus on secret knowledge and had little sympathy with the mythological speculations that were characteristic of the gnostic Christian movement. He apparently was also something of an ascetic and taught sexual abstinence: "The so-called Encratites proceeding from Saturninus and Marcion preached against marriage, annulling the original creation of God, and tacitly condemning him who made male and female" (Eusebius, *Hist. eccl.* 4.29.1–2, LCL).

Some scholars speculate that Marcion's churches outnumbered, or at least equaled, those of the orthodox in the mid-second century. His influence is seen in the large number of important church teachers between the end of the second century and the fifth century who attacked his views: Justin, Irenaeus, Hippolytus of Rome, Clement of Alexandria, Tertullian, Origen, Eusebius, and Epiphanius. Since all of Marcion's works have been lost (or destroyed), we are dependent on the early church fathers to reconstruct his views and activities. Fortunately, they appear to be consistent in describing many important details about him and his followers, but, as in all antiheresy literature of ancient times, they also tend to make many *ad hominem* attacks as well.

Tertullian's criticisms of Marcion included five lengthy books against him and his followers called *The Five Books against Marcion* (ca. 190–200). These books show not only the difficulty that the church had in answering Marcion's teachings, but they also indicate his significant influence in the greater church for a considerable period of time. What did Marcion believe that led to his excommunication from the churches in Rome and elsewhere and resulted in the strong criticisms against him by the great teachers of the church long after his death? Reflecting on Marcion's two most significant teachings, Tertullian writes in a passage that is difficult to translate:

> Marcion's special and principal work is the separation of the law and the gospel; and his disciples will not deny that in this point they have their very best pretext for initiating and confirming themselves in his heresy. These are

[13] Cross and Livingstone, *Oxford Dictionary of the Christian Church,* 1034.

> Marcion's *Antitheses,* or contradictory propositions, which aim at distinguishing the gospel from the law in order that from the diversity of the two documents[14] that contain them, they may contend for a diversity of gods also. Since, therefore, it is this very contrast between the law and the gospel that has suggested [to the Marcionites] that the God of the gospel is different from the God of the law, it is clear that, before the said separation [i.e., before the gospel came], that God [of the Christians] could not have been known who became known from the argument of the separation itself. He therefore could not have been revealed by Christ, who came before the separation, but must have been devised by Marcion who is the author of the breach of peace between the gospel and the law. Now this peace, which had remained unhurt and unshaken from Christ's appearance to the time of Marcion's audacious doctrine, was no doubt maintained by that way of thinking which firmly held that the God of both law and gospel was none other than the Creator, against whom after so long a time a separation has been introduced by the heretic of Pontus [i.e., Marcion]. (*Marc.* 1.19, adapted from *ANF*).

In the fifth century, Cyril of Jerusalem warned his parishioners to avoid Marcionite churches,[15] and he attacked Marcion as "that mouthpiece of ungodliness" and the "second inventor of more mischief" (Simon Magus of Acts 8 being the first):

> Being confuted by the testimonies from the Old Testament which are quoted in the New, he was the first who dared to cut those testimonies out, and leave the preaching of the word of faith without witness, thus effacing the true God: and sought to undermine the Church's faith, as if there were no heralds of it. (*Catechetical Lectures* 6.16, *NPNF)*

Marcion recognized perhaps more clearly than others of his day the difficulty of interpreting the OT for the early church. Paul himself spoke of the inability of the legal aspects of the law to bring persons into a right relationship with God and denied works righteousness as a means of attaining salvation (Gal 3–4; Rom 4:5). This stands behind Marcion's rejection of the law. Further, the God of the OT seemed to him to be quite harsh, even cruel at times, and especially vengeful and changeable. The moral standard of an "eye for an eye" was hard for him to reconcile with the call of Jesus to "turn the other cheek" and to love one's enemies (Matt 5:38–48). It became impossible for Marcion to ascribe a normative value to the OT, which he saw as no longer binding upon the Christian. This was especially true of the legal and moral codes and traditions associated with keeping the law. Taking his cue from Paul, he argued that Christians are free from the law and, therefore, have no reason to give allegiance to that which has been rendered obsolete by faith in Jesus Christ.

Barton concludes that Marcion was important for two reasons: he rejected the OT, viewing it as the document of an alien religion, and he saw

---

[14] "Two documents" is perhaps a reference to the OT and NT.

[15] Clabeaux, "Marcion," 515.

the role of Jesus as one who would deliver those in bondage to the evil creator-god of the OT.[16] Marcion concluded that only by arbitrary means of interpreting (i.e., allegory or typology or *pesher* exegesis) could the OT have the slightest camouflaged meaning at all.[17] Marcion's rejection of the OT writings, together with his use of a more literal hermeneutical approach for interpreting it, stripped the church not only of its first Scriptures, but also of its prized claim to the heritage of Israel's antiquity and to being the religion of historical fulfillment.[18]

Like Harnack before him, von Campenhausen argues that Marcion was the originator of both a *Christian* Scriptures and the first Christian biblical canon and claims that both ideas came from Marcion. After surveying the literature of the second century, he unambiguously concludes, "From every side we converge on the same result: the idea and reality of a Christian Bible were the work of Marcion, and the Church which rejected his point of view simply followed his example."[19] This is an overstatement, however, and flies in the face of several realities, namely, that other writers before Marcion appealed to the gospel-apostle model and that we do not have anything that survives directly from Marcion to show how he understood the word *Scripture*. If he had produced a biblical canon, it is odd that his own followers apparently never followed it.

By using these writings (Luke and Paul) in the church, Marcion was doing nothing unlike what other Christians before him had done, namely, adopting a particular gospel and welcoming several letters from Paul. It is difficult to argue that any first-century church had more than one gospel, and most had only a few of the letters of Paul and perhaps one or more of the Catholic Epistles. Marcion evidently acknowledged the value of gospel and apostle traditions in the church, but that is not why he was criticized.[20] His primary uniqueness was in his rejection of the Jewish Scriptures and the allegorical hermeneutics used to interpret them in the church. Barton is correct when he contends that Marcion's primary aim was to *exclude* books with a Jewish bias that were in use in the church, not to collect them into a fixed tradition: "Marcion was not responsible for Christians' adopting a New Testament; he was responsible 'for their retaining the Old Testament.'" Barton concludes that "Marcion was not a major influence on the formation of the New Testament; he was simply a Marcionite."[21] Marcion's apparent rejection of some of the NT writings and all of the Jewish Scriptures acknowledges that those writings were already functioning authoritatively in some

---

[16] Barton, "Marcion Revisited," 354.

[17] Von Campenhausen, *Formation of the Christian Bible,* 148–174.

[18] Ibid., 151.

[19] Ibid., 148.

[20] See Bovon's "Canonical Structure of Gospel and Apostle" for evidence of the prevalence of this structure in the early church.

[21] Barton, "Marcion Revisited," 350, 354.

churches (canon 1), so the notion that he invented Christian Scriptures is not a careful reflection on Marcion's contributions or activities in antiquity. In fact, none of his second-century critics accused him of seeking to establish a fixed biblical canon or of inventing Christian Scriptures. Although Marcion restricted the use of some Christian writings in his churches, that is not the same as inventing the notion of Christian Scriptures or establishing a biblical canon. Had he intended the latter, it is amazing that not even his followers followed his example since they cited and interpreted Christian literature other than Luke's Gospel and the Letters of Paul. For example, Hahneman shows how later Marcionites welcomed verses from the other Gospels: Ephraem Syrus claimed that Marcionites had not rejected Matt 23:8, Adamantius said that Marcionites quoted John 13:34 and 15:19 and corrupted Matt 5:17, and Origen quoted a Marcionite interpretation of Matt 19:12.[22] Hahneman further adds that the Armenian Marcionites appear to have received Tatian's *Diatessaron*. He concludes that since we have no direct evidence from Marcion or his followers that they formed a fixed Scripture canon, it is inappropriate to argue that he created a NT biblical canon.[23]

Tertullian notes that "Marcion expressly and openly used the knife, not the pen, since he made such an excision of the Scriptures as suited his own subject matter" (*Praescr.* 38.7, *ANF*). More specifically, Tertullian mentions Marcion's process of excising the Jewish elements from Luke: "Now, of the authors whom we posses, Marcion seems to have singled out Luke for his mutilating process" (*Marc.* 4.2, *ANF*). Tertullian also comments on Marcion's editorial work on Paul's Epistles: "As our heretic is so fond of his pruning knife, I do not wonder when syllables are expunged by his hand, seeing that entire pages are usually the matter on which he practices his effacing process" (*Marc.* 5.18.1, *ANF*). Tertullian offers five examples of this "effacing process" in Ephesians, which Tertullian (and evidently Marcion) believed was written by Paul (*Marc.* 5.16–18). It is difficult to conclude that later notions of inviolable Scripture were present when Marcion was active. His rejecting the OT Scriptures and cutting what he did not like from Luke's and Paul's writings are incompatible with later more developed notions of Scripture or canon. Marcion apparently added nothing new to these documents except perhaps his introductions, or prologues.[24]

---

[22] Details are given in Hahneman, *Muratorian Fragment,* 91.

[23] Ibid., 92–93. See also Casey, "Armenian Marcionites."

[24] The Marcionite prologues are listed in Theron's *Evidence of Tradition,* 78–83, and discussed in Clabeaux, "Marcionite Prologues to Paul." See also Dahl, "Origin of the Earliest Prologues." Whether Marcion produced these prologues is debated, but they were friendly to his positions and probably came from the second or third century. The church responded to these prologues by later producing their own "Anti-Marcionite prologues" to Christian writings; for a brief summary, see McDonald, "Anti-Marcionite (Gospel) Prologues"; and Grant, "Oldest Gospel Prologues." Perhaps influenced by Marcion's prologues, Jerome produced his own Gospel prologues in his commentary on Matthew (see Theron, *Evidence of Tradition,* 51–55).

Although Marcion's personal knowledge of all four canonical Gospels is uncertain at this early date (Papias, a contemporary of Marcion, refers to only Matthew and Mark), it is probable that he was at least aware of the Gospel of Matthew because of its widespread popularity in the second century and perhaps also the Gospel of John because it was popular in Asia Minor in the second century. It is doubtful, however, that his collection was the first collection of Pauline Epistles. In fact, it makes more sense to assume that his collection was possible only because churches before him had made use of Paul's writings and had circulated them to other churches (see Col 4:16, which should not be considered an isolated case). Dahl argues that a ten-letter Pauline corpus was available before the time of Marcion and that he simply made use of it and edited it.[25]

Marcion's rejection of Judaism can be seen in his (or his followers') prologues to the Epistles of Paul, which survive only in medieval Latin Vulgate manuscripts. It is not clear how they managed to be included in these Scriptures of the orthodox community, but they are indicative of what is known of Marcion's or his followers' feelings toward those with Judaizing tendencies in the church. The following prologues to Paul's letters to Romans, 1 Corinthians, and Titus are representative of this line of thought.

> The Romans "live" in the regions of Italy. *They had been reached beforehand by false apostles, and under the name of our Lord Jesus Christ they were misled into the Law and the Prophets.* The Apostle [Paul], writing to them from Corinth, calls them back to the true evangelical faith.
>
> The Corinthians are Achaeans. And they similarly heard the word of truth from the Apostles, but *they were subverted in many ways by false apostles—some were misled by verbose eloquence of philosophy, others by a sect of the Jewish law.* [Paul], writing to them from Ephesus by Timothy, calls them back to the truth and evangelical wisdom.
>
> He [Paul] reminds and instructs Titus concerning the constitution of a presbytery and concerning spiritual walk and *heretics who believe in Jewish books,* and who must be avoided.[26]

For the sake of canonical studies, Marcion undoubtedly was an important catalyst who may well have spurred the greater church into coming to grips with the question of which literature best conveyed its true identity. He may also have been a contributing factor in forcing the church to identify what literature would eventually be called Scripture, but the evidence here is slim and only inferential. Heretics, it seems, have always had this

---

[25] Dahl, "Origin of the Earliest Prologues."

[26] Quoted from Theron, *Evidence of Tradition,* 79–83 (emphasis added), who translated them from Erwin Preuschen's *Analecta.*

kind of positive effect upon the church![27] Both Irenaeus (*Haer.* 4.29–34) and Tertullian (*Marc.* 4.2) reacted against Marcion's rejection of the OT and most of the Gospel literature, but it is only with Marcion that we find the first clear references to Luke and to a collection of the writings of Paul. More complete collections of NT writings began to appear only later in the time of Irenaeus, whose four-gospel canon may have come in part as a response to the teachings of Marcion.[28] Marcion's rejection of all Judaistic influences on the gospel and his exclusive opting for an edited Luke has an interesting counter part in the Ebionites, who, according to Irenaeus, also had a one-gospel canon (Matthew) but rejected Paul: "Those who are called Ebionites . . . use the Gospel according to Matthew only, and repudiate the Apostle Paul, maintaining that he was an apostate from the Law" (*Haer.* 1.26.2, *ANF*).

It is too strong to suggest, as Harnack and von Campenhausen do, that Marcion was the "creator of the Christian holy Scripture"[29] since there were tendencies in that direction before Marcion, but it is generally acknowledged that he was the first known individual to set forth a well-defined but evidently not yet fixed collection of Christian writings. Regardless of his motive to separate Christianity from the influences of Judaism,[30] Marcion had the effect of spurring the church into rethinking its understanding of its Scriptures. The setting forth of a collection, however, is considerably different from setting forth a closed biblical canon. Later Marcionite communities did not limit themselves to Marcion's so-called canon, and Marcion himself may not have rejected other Christian Scriptures so much as edited them. It is not clear how many of the early Christian writings were familiar to Marcion, but those who followed Marcion felt free to edit his work and apparently welcomed into their writings verses from the canonical Gospels. If the Marcionites added *verses* to their collection, they could also have added *sources*. It was not an inviolable fixed catalogue of Scriptures to which nothing could be added or taken away.[31] Since the followers of Marcion also used a collection of psalms that was rejected by the author of the Muratorian Fragment, it seems clear that in Marcion we are not yet talking about a closed biblical canon or even a biblical canon at all, but rather a

---

[27] J. A. Sanders, *Canon and Community,* 37, maintains that the church, in opposition to Marcion, insisted upon multiple voices from the OT and other Christian literature rather than limiting its voice to Paul and Luke. If this is the case, then Marcion may be responsible for spurring the church into making a conscious and deliberate decision in this matter, but more proof is needed before drawing this conclusion.

[28] Von Campenhausen, *Formation of the Christian Bible,* 171, makes this suggestion.

[29] Ibid., 163.

[30] Frend, *Rise of Christianity,* 212–17; calls this an "acute Hellenization of the Church."

[31] Hahneman, *Muratorian Fragment,* 92.

bias against Judaism. The writings in Marcion's collection no doubt functioned as Scripture in his communities (canon 1), but there was no firmly fixed collection of Scriptures at this time (canon 2).

Even though the church eventually recognized the need for a canon of Christian Scriptures without the aid of Marcion,[32] he may have been one of the influences that caused the church to consider more carefully the scope of its authoritative literature, but this has yet to be demonstrated. The notion of canonicity—that is, a clearly defined and fixed catalogue of Scriptures—is not found in Marcion, even though such notions were beginning to circulate in second-century Judaism. It cannot be shown that establishing a biblical canon was either his intention when setting forth his collection or the effect of this selective activity. The only known goal in his setting forth a collection of Luke and Paul was to rid the church of its Judaistic influences. It is mere speculation to go beyond that, given the scarcity of evidence today.

The initial impetus for Marcion's anti-Judaism may have been the events surrounding and following the Bar Kokhba rebellion in Palestine in 132–35 C.E., but this is not clear in the limited sources that survive. It may be that he saw as a part of his mission the need to radicalize what he believed was the logical implications of Paul's message for his day, namely, the salvation of humanity apart from the works of the law. Marcion's prologues to the Epistles of Paul—if they were in fact written by him—suggest that he intended Paul's writings to function as Scripture for his congregations, but he does not clearly state this.

II. Gnostics and Gnosticism

One of the most influential heresies of the second century is popularly known as gnostic Christianity. What the adherents of this group (or groups) of heretical Christians taught or espoused is commonly called Gnosticism. The term *gnostic* comes from the Greek word *gnōstikos,* a term with ancient roots that stems from the word *gnōsis* ("knowledge"). Meaning something like "capable of attaining knowledge," *gnōstikos* was rare among the Greeks. It referred to disciplines of study and inferred something along the lines of that which "leads to knowledge." The Greeks themselves did not speak of those who pursued a particular form of knowledge for religious purposes as gnostics. The term *gnostic* appears to have become a later designation attached to gnostic adherents by their opponents and was interchangeable with the word *heresy*. Although the term eventually became associated with the ancient and highly diverse systems of thought in early Christianity in the second century, we do not know the precise dating

[32] Blackman, *Marcion and His Influence,* 32.

of this or the circumstances that gave rise to it. It was common to say that the heretic named Simon Magus (Acts 8:9–24) was the father of this community, but this is ancient rhetoric rather than factually based information (e.g., in the fifth century, Cyril of Jerusalem states that "the inventor of all heresy was Simon Magus: that Simon, who in the Acts of the Apostles thought to purchase with money the unsaleable grace of the Spirit"; *Catechetical Lectures* 6.14, *NPNF*). Those drawn to this group were generally better educated than most, had no hope for the world improving (much like the Jewish apocalyptic writers), and produced a considerable amount of esoteric literature that generally denigrated the created world and focused on self-awareness.[33]

In the second century, a significantly large element of gnostic Christians emerged with a system (or several systems) of thought that challenged the basic underlying beliefs of traditional Christianity. Adherents of this new philosophy were labeled "gnostics" in subsequent generations (especially in the modern era), and what they taught or believed is called "Gnosticism." They thrived throughout the second and third centuries and continued much longer than that in some areas (e.g., the Mandeans in the East).[34] They produced a vast amount of literature, but apparently were not interested in a biblical canon as such. Since much of their literature is their allegorical or spiritual interpretation of the OT and NT Scriptures, it may be that they drew selectively from an undeclared collection of Jewish and Christian Scriptures, with their own writings viewed as supplements for the sake of dialogue.

With the discovery of nearly fifty gnostic documents at Nag Hammadi, Egypt, in 1945, for the first time scholars were able to see direct information about the gnostic community based on their own writings and perspectives.[35] Before then, scholarship was solely dependent upon the opponents of Gnosticism—namely, orthodox Christians in antiquity—for their understanding of gnostics. This polemical context always defined them as heretics, especially Irenaeus, who levels severe attacks against them in book 1 of his *Against Heresies*. These gnostic documents, which originally came from outside of Egypt and were later translated into Coptic, have for the first time permitted us to view gnostic Christianity from the *gnostic* perspective and from the mid-fourth century and before.

It is difficult to date the origins of gnostic belief and even more difficult to define or identify its adherents with a scheme of beliefs and practices. It is also a challenge to identify all of the characteristics attributed to them in each of their writings. There was apparently a considerable variety of views and practices among the gnostic sects. Irenaeus, for example, criti-

---

[33] Layton, *Gnostic Scriptures,* 5–9.

[34] See Lupieri, *Mandaeans.*

[35] See Robinson, *Nag Hammadi Library;* and Layton, *Gnostic Scriptures,* for English translations.

cizes the heretical teachings of Marcion, Tatian, Saturninus, and Valentinus: they formed "one set of doctrines out of totally different systems of opinions, and then again others from others, they insist upon teaching something new, declaring themselves the inventors of any sort of opinion which they may have been able to call into existence" (*Haer.* 1.28.1, *ANF*). After criticizing these individuals, he goes on to say that "besides those, however, among these heretics who are Simonians, and of whom we have already spoken, *a multitude of Gnostics have sprung up,* and have been manifested like mushrooms growing out of the ground" (*Haer.* 1.29.1, *ANF,* emphasis added).

The gnostic Christians apparently included in their systems of thought an amalgamation of several theological and philosophical perspectives in antiquity, including those of Iranian Zoroastrian theology, Jewish apocalypticism, Platonism, Hellenistic philosophy, and various elements of early Christianity, especially the notion of Jesus as redeemer. They saw themselves as Christians, that is, members of the greater church. They tended to have an elitist perspective of themselves, however, believing that while other Christians had a place in the family of God, they themselves had a higher standing because of their greater knowledge. They rejected all political and religious institutions, including their values, authorities, and most moral codes. Some gnostic Christians became ascetics, and others antinomian. Some rejected marriage and the pursuit of physical pleasure, while others entertained numerous spouses and sexual partners. Their adherents stretched from western Persia (now Iraq) in the east to Lyon, France, in the west, and from Egypt in the south to Ancyra (now Ankara) and Satala (in Asia Minor) in the north. Although we now have a good deal of their literature, we are not yet certain about the date of their origins or the provenance of this literature (the most likely dates range between the time of Philo around 10 B.C.E. to the death of Plotinus the Neoplatonist in 270 C.E.).

Wink argues that the key to understanding the diversity among this large community of gnostics is their understanding of the "powers," that is, "the social structures of reality, political systems, human institutions such as the family or religion."[36] Gnostics demonized all of these powers, or institutions, and none of them will be saved from final destruction. Wink observes that in gnostic thought salvation is not deliverance from personal sin, since that is based on imposed moral codes that the gnostics rejected, but rather deliverance from the powers of the social and religious institutions that enslave. A "waking up" is needed (cf. 1 Thess 5:5–7) to find deliverance from such evils. The gnostic *Gospel of Philip* appeals to its readers to recognize the root of evil (i.e., the powers), so they can be destroyed and have no power over them:

---

[36] Wink, *Cracking the Gnostic Code,* vii, 17.

> Let each of us dig down after the root of evil that is within us, and let us pluck it out of our hearts from the root. It will be plucked out if we recognize it. But if we are ignorant of it, it takes root in us and produces its fruit in our heart. It masters us. We are its slaves. It takes us captive, to make us do what we do not want; and what we do want we do not do. It is powerful because we have not recognized it. While it exists it is active. (*Gospel of Philip* 83.18–30, adapted from Wink, *Cracking the Gnostic Code,* 37)

Wink shows how the gnostic enterprise is both similar and contrary to what the NT teaches: "Gnosticism taught escape from a world imprisoned under tyranny of evil powers. The New Testament teaches liberation from the tyranny of evil powers in order to recover a lost unity with the created world. This world is not only the sphere of alienated existence, but also the object of God's redemptive love. Therefore we are not to flee the world, but to recall it to its Source."[37]

Gnostic Christians generally believed that there was a divine spark (spirit) from God in humanity and that it was their goal through special knowledge to be restored to God through the work of a redeemer, Jesus, who removed ignorance and restored self-knowledge to those who were spiritual.[38] Despite this common belief, scholars of this ancient phenomenon are generally agreed that they have yet to find a satisfactory definition that fits all traces of this community in antiquity—or even find a convenient term for this literature.[39] Although there is little agreement on a meaningful and accurate definition of Gnosticism, scholars continue to use the designation since there is little else to put in its place.

By way of summary, generally speaking, (1) gnostic Christians denied that the Christian God was also the creator of the world. For them, matter was evil and was created by a Demiurge, an evil and distant emanation from the *plērōma* ("fullness") of the divine. In this they were similar to the Marcionites. (2) They often rejected the OT, but not uniformly; unlike Marcion, they often allegorized it to find meaning for Christian faith (Ptolemy's *Letter to Flora* is an important example of this). (3) They distinguished the heavenly Savior/Redeemer from the human Jesus of Nazareth, a teaching not unlike various positions of Docetism that claimed that Jesus only "seemed" human. (4) They believed that full salvation was only for the pneumatics or spiritually elite (i.e., themselves), but that a lesser degree of salvation could be obtained by those who have only faith without this

---

[37] Ibid., 52.

[38] Grant, *Gnosticism,* 16.

[39] I am indebted to Karen King for her criticisms of my previous discussion of gnosticism. King's own work on this subject is superb, and she provides a careful and critical evaluation of this religious movement in her *Gospel of Mary,* her *Revelation of the Unknowable God,* and her more recent work, *What is Gnosticism?* 5–19. See also Rudolph, "'Gnosis' and 'Gnosticism'"; Grant, *Gnosticism,* 13–18; Layton, *Gnostic Scriptures,* 8–9; and Perkins, "Gnosticism and the Christian Bible," 355.

special *gnōsis*. Those completely involved in the world, however, had no hope of salvation. (5) They claimed that they had received secret gospels from the apostles themselves. The oldest gospel that purports to be of apostolic authorship (no canonical Gospel makes such a claim for itself) is the apocryphal *Gospel of Thomas,* a gnostic document.[40]

The esoteric writings of the gnostics, along with their claims to secret revelations from the apostles, were rejected by Irenaeus, who argued instead for the legitimacy of the Christian truth or rule of faith (*regula fidei*), which he contends was passed on in the church by apostolic succession through the bishops: "For if the apostles had known hidden mysteries, which they were in the habit of imparting to 'the perfect' apart and privately from the rest, they would have delivered them especially to those to whom they were also committing the leadership of the churches themselves" (*Haer.* 3.3.1, adapted from *ANF*). One can scarcely deny Irenaeus's logic here.

The question for us is whether such writings prompted the Christians to decide which Christian writings were sacred and which were not? Did the gnostics consider what they wrote as sacred Scripture and binding upon their readers? We have no evidence that they did. Perkins observes that the gnostics "never set up individuals as heroes of the divine" and did not observe the ecclesiastical structures that began to develop in the second and third centuries of the church.[41] To the contrary, Irenaeus accused the gnostic Christians of saying that the Scriptures were incorrect, that they were not authoritative, that they were ambiguous, and that the truth cannot be discovered by someone who is ignorant of the truth (*Haer.* 3.2.1).[42] Perkins further challenges the tendency among scholars to assume that the gnostic Christians simply "followed the orthodox canon with one of their own": "It should be apparent by now that nothing could be farther from the truth. These Gnostic writings reflect the liturgy, teaching, preaching and polemic of their respective communities. But they never claim to do more than to embody true tradition." Perkins concludes that the gnostics did not have a normative text that gave them the limits of their theological reflection,[43] that "gnostic exegetes were only interested in elaborating their mythic and theological speculations concerning the origins of the universe,

---

[40]Because gnostic belief is highly complex, the student is advised to consult the following works: Jonas, *Gnostic Religion;* Rudolph, *Gnosis;* Layton, *Gnostic Scriptures,* xv–xxvii, 5–22; van Baaren, "Towards a Definition of Gnosticism"; MacRae, "Why the Church Rejected Gnosticism"; Filoramo, *History of Gnosticism;* Pearson, *Gnosticism, Judaism, and Egyptian Christianity;* Perkins, *Gnosticism and the New Testament;* King, *What Is Gnosticism?;* Walker, *Gnosticism;* Goehring et al., *Gnosticism and the Early Christian World;* Hedrick and Hodgson, *Nag Hammadi, Gnosticism, and Early Christianity;* Logan, *Gnostic Truth and Christian Heresy.*

[41]Perkins, *Gnostic Dialogue,* 192–96.

[42]Ibid., 199–200.

[43]Ibid., 201–2.

not in appropriating a received canonical tradition," and that "hermeneutics, not canon formation, is the central point at issue between Irenaeus and his Valentinian opponents."[44]

Did the gnostics' production of esoteric literature force the Christians to come to grips with the scope their own Scriptures? Since gnostics did not claim that they had produced sacred inspired literature that was binding on all, arguments against them were not based on establishing Christian Scriptures that were binding on all. Rather, Irenaeus and others who argued against the gnostics in the second and third centuries did not combat heresy with a canon of Scripture, but with a canon of faith (*regula fidei*) that had been passed on from the apostles to their successors in the churches.

III. Montanists

Around 170, a man (possibly a priest of Cybele)[45] named Montanus and two women, Priscilla and Maximilla, came to Phrygia in Asia Minor claiming to be inspired by the Paraclete (Holy Spirit) and having an announcement of the Parousia (the second coming of the Lord). They had a major impact upon the people of Phrygia and were received with enthusiasm by many Christians through the Greco-Roman world. Their message was apocalyptic in focus, strongly advocating their interpretation of the message of the book of Revelation. They emphasized prophecy, rigid asceticism, martyrdom, and the presence and power of the Holy Spirit. Frend points to the long history of prophetic movements in this region and indicates that the orthodox were not well prepared to deal with the situation.[46] Unlike in many religions, both men and women became prophets in Montanism.[47] By 200 they had expanded their influence to Rome and North Africa, though their primary influence was among rural communities.[48]

What is most surprising about the Montanists, however, is that Tertullian became their best-known convert. Numerous suggestions try to explain this, but perhaps their strong emphasis on a rigorous ascetic lifestyle enticed him, who was already a highly disciplined man with little toleration for weak and undisciplined souls. His hesitation to baptize converts or children too early is well known and illustrates his call for a careful and consistent behavior:

---

[44] Perkins, "Gnosticism and the Christian Bible," 371.

[45] Frend, *Rise of Christianity,* 253, makes this suggestion.

[46] Ibid., 254–55.

[47] In his discussion of Montanism, which he calls the "Cataphrygian heresy," Eusebius mentions several times that women were a significant part of the movement (*Hist. eccl.* 5.14–19).

[48] Frend, *Rise of Christianity,* 256.

According to circumstance and disposition and even age of the individual person, it may be better to delay baptism; and especially so in the case of little children. Why, indeed, is it necessary—if it be not a case of necessity—that the sponsors too be thrust into danger, when they themselves may fail to fulfill their promises by reason of death, or when they may be disappointed by growth of an evil disposition? . . .

For no less cause should the unmarried also be deferred, in whom there is an aptness to temptation—in virgins on account of their ripeness as also in the widowed on account of their freedom—until either they are married or are better strengthened for continence. Anyone who understands the seriousness of Baptism will fear its reception more than its deferral. Sound faith is secure of salvation! (Tertullian, *Baptism* 18.4, Jurgens, *Faith of the Early Fathers,* 128–29)

Tertullian may have been impressed with the charismatic focus of the Montanists, which was always acknowledged in the greater church as a legitimate and authentic expression of Christian faith, but which had declined rapidly in the second-century church.

The most vigorous opponents of the Montanists in Asia Minor were the so-called Alogi, a heretical group that looked askance at both the Gospel of John and the book of Revelation because of their supposed gnostic origins. The Alogi even called the book of Hebrews into question because of its view of the hopeless condition of the apostate Christian, which coincided with the Montanists' harsh penitential practice.[49] The response of the church at large was a rejection of the Montanist movement and a reserve toward the Gospel of John because of its focus on the Paraclete and a similar reserve toward the book of Revelation (especially in the Eastern churches in the second and third centuries) because of its apocalyptic emphasis.

Von Campenhausen contends that the emergence of Montanism was a significant factor in prompting orthodox Christians to determine the scope of the Christian Scriptures. Based on the observation of Hippolytus of Rome that the Montanists produced "innumerable books" (*Elenchus* 8.19.1), von Campenhausen concludes that the church was forced to make a decision about its canon:

It is obvious that such an attitude can no longer be content with recognizing a rough list of sacred writings and with rejecting others as heretical forgeries; it now has to be clearly decided which books are to belong to the "New Testament" and which are not. At this point the final stage of the formation of the Canon has begun. It did not at once reach its goal; but the necessity of a "closed" canon had been grasped in principle.[50]

---

[49] So argue R. Collins, *Introduction to the New Testament,* 26; and von Campenhausen, *Formation of the Christian Bible,* 232.

[50] Von Campenhausen, *Formation of the Christian Bible,* 231–32.

In other words, according to von Campenhausen, the Montanists generated numerous books that they believed were divinely inspired, and the greater church therefore saw the need to identify more precisely which literature was divinely inspired by God and, therefore, authoritative in the church.[51] On the other hand, Schneemelcher challenges whether the Montanists produced *any* literature.[52] Hippolytus's well-known criticism of the Montanists and their books has bearing on this debate:

> But there are others who themselves are even more heretical in nature [than the foregoing], and are Phrygians by birth. These have been rendered victims of error from being previously captivated by [two] wretched women, called a certain Priscilla and Maximilla, whom they supposed [to be] prophetesses. And they assert that into these the Paraclete Spirit had departed; and antecedently to them, they in like manner consider Montanus as a prophet. And being in possession of an infinite number of their books, [the Phrygians] are overrun with delusion; and they do not judge whatever statements are made by them, according to [the criterion of] reason; nor do they give heed unto those who are competent to decide; but they are heedlessly swept onward, by the reliance which they place on these [imposters]. And they allege that they have learned something more through these, than from law, and prophets, and the Gospels. (*Refutation of All Heresies* 8.12, *ANF*)

On the other hand, Tertullian defends the Montanist focus on recent revelation:

> It is, he says, mere prejudice to heed and value only past demonstrations of power and grace. "Those people who condemn the one power of the one Holy Spirit in accordance with chronological eras should beware." It is the recent instances to which far higher respect ought to be paid; for they already belong to the time of the End, and are to be prized as a superabundant increase of grace, "which God, in accordance with the testimony of scripture, has destined for precisely this period of time." ("Introduction" to *Passio perpetuae* 1.1–2. Von Campenhausen, *Formation of the Christian Bible,* 229)

According to von Campenhausen, the mainstream churches rejected the Montanist prophecies essentially on the grounds that their prophecies were contrary to the earlier Christian writings (now called Scriptures).[53] In one polemic against the Montanists, recorded by Eusebius, a certain Apolinarius wrote:

> For a long and protracted time, my dear Abercius Marcellus, I have been urged by you to compose a treatise against the sect of those called after Miltiades, but until now I was somewhat reluctant, not from any lack of ability to refute the lie and testify to the truth, but from timidity and scruples lest

---

[51] Ibid., 227–32.

[52] Schneemelcher, *New Testament Apocrypha,* 685 n. 2.

[53] Von Campenhausen, *Formation of the Christian Bible,* 231.

> I might seem to some to be adding to the writings or injunctions of the word of the new covenant of the gospel, to which no one who has chosen to live according to the gospel itself can add and from which he cannot take away. But when I had just come to Ancyra in Galatia and perceived that the church in that place was torn in two by this new movement [the Montanists] which is not, as they call it, prophecy but much rather, as will be shown, false prophecy, I disputed concerning these people themselves and their propositions so far as I could, with the Lord's help, for many days continuously in the church. Thus the church rejoiced and was strengthened in the truth, but our opponents were crushed for the moment and our adversaries were distressed. (*Hist. eccl.* 5.16.3–4, LCL)

From this and other criticisms against the Montanists, von Campenhausen concludes that the church could no longer have a roughly defined canon of Scriptures and it could no longer be content with rejecting heretical forgeries as they appeared. Consequently, he argues, the Montanists and their production of books were the primary factors that led the churches to define more precisely which books belonged in their NT and which books did not.[54] It was at this point, von Campenhausen claims, that the last phase of the canonical process began[55] (though it will become clear that this phase was by no means completed as a result of the polemic against the Montanists). If the church at large was interested in closing the NT canon at this time, one might expect to find numerous lists of canonical literature in this period. Instead, the only possibility of such a list of NT books is the Muratorian Fragment, which does not come from the second century (see chapter 13 §I.D).

Schneemelcher concludes that the sayings of Montanus and his prophetesses were collected and handed down as authoritative literature (possibly something like canon 1), and even used and defended as such by Tertullian, but this does not mean that they became Scripture in those communities.[56] Schneemelcher calls von Campenhausen's view that the Montanists influenced the church to establish its own biblical canon a

---

[54] Ibid., 231. Metzger, *Canon of the New Testament,* 106, also makes this observation, adding that with Marcion the church saw the need to expand its written corpus of authoritative writings and with the Montanists it saw the need to limit the corpus. This process of limitation, he claims, was "the first step [taken by the church] toward the adoption of a closed canon of Scripture."

[55] Von Campenhausen, *Formation of the Christian Bible,* 232. See 232–42 for a discussion of the rather troubled history in the church of the literature that the Montanists appealed to most: the various apocalypses, the Gospel of John, and Hebrews.

[56] Schneemelcher, *New Testament Apocrypha,* 688–89. He also questions how much the movement was influenced by apocalyptic thoughts, which do not appear to be in the forefront of the authentic sayings of Montanus and the prophetesses (listed on 686–87). Since the cutting edge of the movement was its focus on ethical renewal, Schneemelcher concludes that on the whole Montanism was a prophetic—not an apocalyptic—movement.

hypothesis that must be distinguished from "demonstratable facts" and says that the available evidence does not allow such conclusions.[57]

IV. Conclusion

There is no convincing evidence that Marcion, the gnostics, or the Montanists were interested in producing a biblical canon, and likewise, no evidence suggests that the early church responded to their threats by establishing a sacred collection of books. Rather the response of the second-century church was to produce a canon of faith (*regula fidei*), but not a canon of sacred books.

Marcion, whose primary concern was to eliminate all Judaistic influences—including the OT itself—from the Christian message, created a limited collection of writings in order to more clearly define his gospel. But the emergence of multiple writings from the gnostic Christians and the Montanists did not lead the church to consider the scope of its own scriptural traditions. The major sections of the NT Scriptures—especially the Gospels and Letters of Paul—were generally (though not completely) acknowledged at the end of the second century.

V. Excursus: New Testament Apocrypha

In addition to the books that were later included in the NT, many other Christian writings also battled for the heart of the ancient church.[58] In the fourth century, Eusebius identified and challenged the inclusion of literature that was falsely produced under the name of an apostle in the Christians' Scripture collections. He distinguished genuine writings from those produced pseudonymously:

> Among the books which are not genuine must be reckoned the Acts of Paul, the work entitled the Shepherd, the Apocalypse of Peter, and in addition to them the letter called of Barnabas and the so-called Teachings of the Apostles [i.e., the *Didache*]. And in addition, as I said, the Revelation of John, if this view prevail. For as I said, some reject it, but others count it among the Recognized Books. Some have also counted the Gospel according to the Hebrews in which those of the Hebrews who have accepted Christ take a special pleasure. These would all belong to the disputed books, but we have nevertheless been obliged to make a list of them, distinguishing between those writings which, according to the tradition of the Church, are true, genuine, and recognized, and those which differ from them in that they are not canonical but disputed,

[57] Schneemelcher, "General Introduction," 24.

[58] See Ehrman's *Lost Christianities* and *Lost Scriptures*.

> yet nevertheless are known to most of the writers of the Church, in order that we might know them and the writings that are put forward by heretics under the name of the apostles containing gospels such as those of Peter, and Thomas, and Matthias, and some others besides, or Acts such as those of Andrew and John and the other apostles. To none of these has any who belonged to the succession of the orthodox ever thought it right to refer in his writings. . . . They ought, therefore, to be reckoned not even among spurious books but shunned as altogether wicked and impious. (*Hist. eccl.* 3.25.4–7, LCL)

The many Christian pseudepigraphal writings, many of which are now lost in antiquity, include gospels, acts, epistles, and apocalypses. This literature is generally sectarian and mostly appeals to an apostle's name in order to find acceptance in various segments of the Christian community. The following writings, some of which currently exist only in fragments, are representatives of this body of literature:[59]

1. Gospels[60]
   - *Protevangelium of James*
   - *Infancy Gospel of Thomas*
   - *Gospel of Peter*
   - *Gospel of Nicodemus*
   - *Gospel of the Nazoreans*
   - *Gospel of the Ebionites*
   - *Gospel of the Hebrews*
   - *Gospel of the Egyptians*
   - *Gospel of Thomas*
   - *Gospel of Philip*
   - *Gospel of Mary*
2. Acts[61]
   - *Acts of John*
   - *Acts of Peter*
   - *Acts of Paul*
   - *Acts of Andrew*
   - *Acts of Thomas*
   - *Acts of Andrew and Matthias*
   - *Acts of Philip*
   - *Acts of Thaddaeus*
   - *Acts of Peter and Paul*

---

[59] Adapted from MacDonald, "Apocryphal New Testament."

[60] For an excellent discussion of apocryphal gospels, see Koester, *Ancient Christian Gospels*.

[61] The first five works are called the "Leucian Acts" and circulated together. A useful source on apocryphal acts is Bovon, Brock, and Matthews, *Apocryphal Acts of the Apostles*.

Acts of Peter and Andrew
Martyrdom of Matthew
Slavonic Act of Peter
Acts of Peter and the Twelve Apostles

3. Epistles[62]
Third Corinthians
Epistle to the Laodiceans
Letters of Paul and Seneca
Letters of Jesus and Abgar
Letter of Lentulus
Epistle of Titus

4. Apocalypses[63]
Apocalypse of Peter
Coptic Apocalypse of Paul
Apocalypse of Paul
First Apocalypse of James
Second Apocalypse of James
Apocryphon of John
Sophia of Jesus Christ
Letter of Peter to Philip
Apocalypse of Mary

Numerous examples of pseudepigraphy from antiquity fall outside that produced within Judaism and early Christianity. For example, well-known classical writers like Plato, Pythagoras, Socrates, Xenophon, Apollonius, and Galen had writings attributed to them by their students or others who came after them.[64]

A pseudonym is generally understood as a fictitious or assumed name used by authors who, for whatever reasons, may want to conceal their actual identity. The practice of writing under an assumed name was common during the intertestamental period, when writers frequently made use of well-known names from the OT (Solomon, Enoch, Moses, etc.). The ethics of producing pseudonymous literature in the ancient Jewish

---

[62]Some include the canonical Pastoral Epistles and 2 Peter in this category.

[63]The term *apocalypse* is a transliteration of the Greek *apokalypsis* ("revelation, disclosure"). Aune, *Prophecy in Early Christianity,* 108, defines this literary genre as a form of revelatory literature in which the author narrates both the visions he or she has purportedly experienced and their meaning, usually elicited through a dialogue between the seer and an interpreting angel. The substance of these revelatory visions is the imminent intervention of God into human affairs to bring the present evil world system to an end and to replace it with an ideal one. This transformation is accompanied by the punishment of the wicked and the reward of the righteous.

[64]Charlesworth, "Pseudepigraphy," 776. See also Ehrman, *Lost Scriptures.*

and Christian communities is debated among scholars. As yet there is no agreement on why it emerged, though there is growing awareness that distinctions should be made in the kinds of literature that fall into this category. For some Christians, however, the main issue has to do with how forged documents can or ever could serve as inspired and sacred literature for the church.

Aune notes three explanations for the practice of writing pseudonymously: (1) it arose at a time when the biblical canon was already closed and well-known names were used to secure acceptance, (2) it was used to protect the identity of the writer who might be in danger if his or her true identity were known, and (3) apocalyptic visionaries may have had visions from the figures to whom they attributed their work.[65] Aune believes that the first of these options is the more likely, but not without several qualifications. As a legitimating device intended to accord to the writing in question the esteem and prestige given to the earlier well-known figure, "pseudonymity is functional only if readers accept the false attribution."[66] It is probably best, however, not to conclude that all writers of pseudepigraphy wrote for purposes of deception. Aune notes seven categories of pseudepigraphy in early Christian literature, including some in the biblical canon:

> (1) works not by an author but probably containing some of his own thoughts (Ephesians and Colossians); (2) documents by someone who was influenced by another person to whom the work is ascribed (1 Peter and maybe James); (3) compositions influenced by earlier works of an author to whom they are assigned (1 Timothy, 2 Timothy, Titus); (4) Gospels (eventually) attributed to an apostle but deriving from later circles or schools of learned individuals (Matthew and John); (5) Christian writings attributed by their authors to an Old Testament personality (*Testament of Adam, Odes of Solomon, Apocalypse of Elijah, Ascension of Isaiah*); (6) once-anonymous works now correctly (perhaps Mark, Luke, and Acts) or incorrectly credited to someone (some manuscripts attribute Hebrews to Paul); (7) compositions that intentionally try to deceive the reader into thinking that the author is someone famous (2 Peter).[67]

While some pseudonymous literature may well have been produced with a view toward deception, some books were likely written in the sincere belief that the writing represented that for which the earlier hero—often a prophetic figure or an apostle—was known. Many biblical scholars agree that pseudepigraphy is found in the biblical canon. For example, most scholars hold that the OT book of Daniel is pseudonymous, but a few argue that the earliest form of the book derives from the Hebrew prophet and that only its latest or final form stems from the mid-second century

---

[65] Aune, *Prophecy in Early Christianity,* 109.
[66] Ibid., 110.
[67] Ibid.

B.C.E. Some scholars question whether the Gospels of Matthew and John were written by these apostles, and many also dismiss Markan and Lukan authorship of the Gospels that have their name attached. In the strictest sense of the term, however, the canonical Gospels are not pseudepigraphal in that the original Gospels did not have apostolic names attached to them. Perhaps they could be more appropriately designated as "anonymous" literature. The earliest writer to claim apostolic authorship for his gospel is the writer of the *Gospel of Thomas* (roughly 90 or as late as 170)[68]. Further, most NT scholars agree that Paul did not write all of the literature that was later attributed to him, especially the Pastoral Epistles (1–2 Timothy and Titus), Hebrews, and possibly Ephesians, Colossians, and 2 Thessalonians.

Many other writings not in our NT canon are also generally acknowledged as pseudonymous works: *Didache, 2 Clement, Apostolic Constitutions, Gospel of Thomas, Barnabas,* and others. The practice of writing under an assumed name or category of office, as in the case of the *Didache* or the *Apostolic Constitutions,* was quite common in the early church until the mid-second century, when it was called into question. Serapion of Antioch, for example, questions the *Gospel of Peter,* in this account by Eusebius:

> [Serapion] has written refuting the false statements in it [*Gospel of Peter*], because of certain in the community of Rhossus, who on the ground of the said writing turned aside into heterodox teachings (*heterodoxous didaskalias*). It will not be unreasonable to quote a short passage from this work [Serapion's refutation], in which he puts forward the view he held about the book, writing as follows: "For our part, brethren, we receive both Peter and the other apostles as Christ, but the writings which falsely bear their names [*ta de onomati autōn pseudepigrapha*] we reject, as men of experience, knowing that such were not handed down to us." (*Hist. eccl.* 6.12.2–3, LCL)

Interestingly, the *Apostolic Constitutions* (ca. 350–400), which itself may be called a pseudepigraphal work, warns Christians against reading pseudepigraphal literature! After first claiming to be apostles, the author(s) of this work then go on to warn about *other* pseudonymous writings:

> On whose account also we, who are now assembled in one place—Peter and Andrew; James and John, sons of Zebedee; Philip and Bartholomew; Thomas and Matthew; James the son of Alphaeus; and Lebbaeus who is surnamed Thaddaeus; and Simon the Canaanite, and Matthias, who instead of Judas was numbered with us; and James the brother of the Lord and bishop of Jerusalem, and Paul the teacher of the Gentiles, the chosen vessel, having all met together, have written to you this Catholic doctrine for the confirmation of you, to whom the oversight of the universal church is committed. . . .

---

[68] See Perrin, *Thomas and Tation,* 1–47.

> We have sent all things to you, that you may know our opinion, what it is; and that ye may not receive those books which obtain in our name, but are written by the ungodly. For you are not to attend to the names of the apostles, but to the nature of the things, and their settled opinions. For we know that Simon and Cleobius, and their followers, have compiled poisonous books under the name of Christ and of His disciples, and do carry them about in order to deceive you who love Christ, and us his servants. And among the ancients also some have written apocryphal books of Moses, and Enoch, and Adam, and Isaiah, and David, and Elijah, and of the three patriarchs, pernicious and repugnant to the truth. The same things even now have the wicked heretics done, reproaching the creation, marriage, providence, the begetting of children, the law, and the prophets; inscribing certain barbarous names, and as they think, of angels, but to speak the truth, of demons, which suggest things to them; whose doctrine eschew, that ye may not be partakers of the punishment due to those that write such things for the seduction and perdition of the faithful and unblameable disciples of the Lord Jesus. (*Apostolic Constitutions* 6.14, 16, *ANF*)

This implies that the standard applied to pseudepigraphy was orthodoxy. If a particular writing fit theologically with what was acceptable to a particular Christian community, then the writing itself it was acceptable, even though someone other than the author listed may have written it.[69]

Koch observes that particular names were able to attract entire genres of literature. For example, all divine law came from Moses, wisdom from Solomon, and church regulations from apostles, as in the case of the *Didache* and the *Apostolic Constitutions*.[70] Pseudonymous writings thus imply on the part of the writer a consciousness that "association with a tradition confers legitimacy." Koch explains: "In many cases the authors to whom the writings are ascribed are considered as alive in heaven and therefore still effective in the present. To this extent attribution of authorship to men of God is similar to ascribing it to God, Jesus, or angels. Since what is involved is not the conscious use of an inaccurate name, the designation 'pseudonymous' should be used only with reservations."[71] Charlesworth agrees and warns against calling all such literature forgeries. Not all pseudepigraphal writings intended to deceive the readers, he maintains, but rather, the authors considered it acceptable to attribute a writing to one who had inspired them.[72]

Disbelief and disappointment are the almost universal responses of Christians who hear for the first time that the ascribed author of one of the biblical books may not have actually written the work to which the supposed author's name is attached. This is understandable, and some of this

---

[69] For further discussion, see Jenkins, *Hidden Gospels*.
[70] Koch, "Pseudonymous Writing."
[71] Ibid., 713.
[72] Charlesworth, "Pseudepigraphy," 766.

concern undoubtedly comes from our living in an age when both plagiarism and writing in another person's name are looked upon as unethical. It is therefore easy to assume unethical motivations on the part of those who produced such literature in the ancient religious communities. Although deception may be the motive in some cases, still in other instances writings were written in honor of a particular hero in the prophetic or apostolic tradition. It is not always easy to determine if the reason was to gain acceptance for a particular perspective that may not have been otherwise well received, or to give honor to an earlier hero of the faith, or simply to deceive.

Whether the author of the Pastoral Epistles simply wanted apostolic sanction for his views on church organization and discipline and therefore attached Paul's name to his own writings cannot be determined, especially since authentic Pauline traditions are probably carried in this collection, for example, the rejection of Paul in Asia Minor, the manner of the apostle's death, and many of the closing comments to colleagues in 2 Tim 4:14–22. A satisfactory explanation for the presence of these traditions within these otherwise pseudonymous writings has not yet been made. The tendency among scholars is either to accept or reject them *totally* as the work of Paul. Since, however, not all pseudonymous literature in the ancient world was cut from the same cloth, care should be taken in each instance to determine not only authorship (whenever possible), but also the motive and procedure in producing the writing.

Another question often comes from the more conservative student of Scripture: how can the writing be maintained in our canon if the work was not written by the one to whom it was ascribed? In other words, how can its inspiration be legitimate if it is a forgery? Along the same line, does divine inspiration depend on apostolic authorship? Is the writing inspired *because* a particular writer wrote it or because the writing inherently has a recognized divine message that addressed the needs and circumstances of the church to whom it was written and continues to have relevance for the church today? Nothing in antiquity suggests that *only* the apostolic witness was inspired and that all other voices were not. On the contrary, the early church did not believe that the role of inspiration was limited to the apostles or even to writings per se, but rather that inspiration was given to the whole church in perpetuity.

Acts 2 clearly shows that the early followers of Jesus believed they were in the last days when the presence of and empowerment by the Holy Spirit were unleashed upon the church, and there is no definite time when this age was perceived to have stopped. They also believed that the role of inspiration was not restricted to writing, but also included the ministry of proclamation. Thus, in the first five centuries of the church, everything that was true was also considered inspired of God. Only if it was untrue was it considered uninspired. The reason why a book like Hebrews was retained in our biblical canon, even though many early church fathers did not believe that Paul wrote it, was because of its useful message to Christians facing uncertain futures. Although some church fathers accepted it because they thought Paul wrote it, still many others had serious questions about its authorship and placed it in their canons at the *end* of Paul's Letters, generally after the smallest of Paul's Letters, Philemon, and not next to 2 Corinthians where, according to its size, it would have been placed if there had been strong arguments for attributing it to Paul. In other words, its place in our current biblical canon reflects the early church's uncertainty over its authorship.

But again, what about questioning the canonical status of a writing because of its apostolic authorship? If a writing made it into the biblical canon only because it was reputed to have been written by an apostle, should that writing be taken out of the canon today if it can be reasonably argued that an apostle never wrote it? This would be a logical response *only if apostolic authorship were the sole criterion* for canonicity and if inspiration and authorship were inseparable. It is better to see how a writing speaks to the needs and mission of the church and then determine its inspiration based on that, as well as on its faithfulness to the authentic witness of Jesus preserved in the early Christian literature. It is important to remember that even our present biblical canon is consciously not limited to apostolic authorship (e.g., Mark and Luke-Acts), but the church found these writings particularly helpful for their use in worship and catechetical instruction. Cannot, then, a similar case be made for literature earlier attributed to an apostle but subsequently determined to be otherwise?[73]

The value of pseudonymous literature for the study of early Christianity cannot be overestimated. Along with the canonical literature, the apocryphal and pseudepigraphal literature presents at times what Barnstone calls "a lucid picture of the life and ideals of the early Christendom."[74] Without it we have an incomplete and sometimes vague understanding of the emergence and growth of Christianity. This literature also reflects the great diversity in the formative years of the Christian community, something that was not tolerated later on. This body of literature is invaluable in bringing some clarity to our understanding of many commonly used terms and ideas in the NT literature, for example, Son of Man, angels, eschatology, kingdom, messianic expectations, and the NT use of the OT. Most interpreters of Scripture today see the immense value of this literature for informing our understanding of the context and aiding the interpretation of the significant theological focus of the NT literature, as well as aiding our understanding of the origins, growth, and stabilization of the Bible.

---

[73] For further study of this topic, see Metzger, "Literary Forgeries and Canonical Pseudepigrapha"; and Meade, *Pseudonymity and Canon.*

[74] Barnstone, *Other Bible,* 19

CHAPTER TWELVE

Books, Texts, and Translations

SOME IMPORTANT, YET PRACTICAL, MATTERS ARE OFTEN IGNORED WHEN CONSIDering canon formation: Which text of the NT is canon for the church? How carefully and completely was the biblical canon transmitted until the invention of the printing press in the sixteenth century? Which modern translation best reflects the biblical canon? What effect, if any, did the *means* of transmitting the Scriptures in the early centuries have on the books included in the biblical canon? For example, did concerns over available space in a manuscript or codex have any bearing on what was included? If space had been no problem, how many more books might have been included in the Christian Bible? When discussions of the biblical canon took place in antiquity, they centered on the *books* that comprised the sacred collection and not so much on the question of the particular text of Scripture or the translations. No ancient discussions of such issues resolved them for the church.

None of the earliest transmission vehicles, such as scrolls and codices, contained all of the books of the NT, and none of them has the same text. Initially (i.e., for the first hundred years or so), only a few books could reasonably fit in a codex or scroll. Did this initial limitation affect the contours or shape of the Bible? It was quite common in the second and third centuries for biblical manuscripts to contain only portions of our current NT canon, and often these manuscripts contained only one gospel and a few letters. The technological development of the codex took several centuries before all of the current books of our Bible could be included in one volume, but even when that happened in the fourth century, no manuscripts contained the same books that are currently included in Christian Bibles.

Does the authority of the biblical text relate only to the *original* language(s), or does it transcend the Hebrew, Aramaic, and Greek texts and emerge in the vast variety of languages present today? The Bible of the early Christians was not the HB, but the Greek translation of the Hebrew Scriptures. The notion that the authority of the Scriptures did not transfer to the LXX does not, however, appear in early Christianity—even though there are considerable differences between the Hebrew text and the LXX (and later translations). What bearing does the concept of translation have on inspiration? Does inspiration apply only to the original manuscripts of the Bible (which we no longer have)? Does inspiration apply to nonoriginal manuscripts, all of which contain mistakes of one sort or another? And what about our modern English Bibles, which are based on these faulty manuscripts?

Historically, the church has not spoken with a single voice on matters such as these, even though from the beginning of the church the writings of the NT were translated into different languages. The church as a whole has never decided on one translation of the Bible, though there were moves in this direction (i.e., the several Greek versions and Jerome's Latin Vulgate). While many Christians still argue for the sacredness of the King James Bible, what does that say to those who speak German, Chinese, Arabic, or French or those who use any other English translation? Are those translations any less inspired? These issues—books, text, transmission, and translation—have a direct bearing on issues of authority and canon for the church today.

I. Books and the Biblical Canon

A. THE ART OF WRITING

In the ancient world, the act of writing something down often carried with it the implication of authority and sometimes even divine authority. Because initially writing materials were expensive and often inaccessible to many, most of what was written was considered significant. Important communications were sometimes etched in stone or other permanent media and put on public display.

At first ancient writings were inscribed on stone, wood, beaten metal, or clay tablets (ca. 3100 B.C.E. and following). Eventually, around the turn of the common era, wooden blocks were bound together to make tablets (*codices*) to contain nonliterary documents such as bills of sale and personal correspondence, while more important writings in a literary format remained on scrolls of papyrus or animal skins. Some important writings were etched in stone (Exod 31:18) or painted on walls (Dan 5:5–9) or even placed on flattened metal (chiefly copper and silver sheets hammered to a smooth surface) and potsherds. By far, however, papyrus (plural papyri; cf. paper) was the most common writing material employed during the life of Jesus and even later.

The papyrus plant grew in abundance along the banks of the Nile River in Egypt and was harvested and made into writing materials rather easily and cheaply. It was commonly called *byblos,* because large quantities of this material were shipped out of the Syrian harbor city of Byblos.

Byblos (or *bibles*) is the root of our word *Bible,* which means "book." Papyrus sheets were often pasted together to form a lengthy roll.

Eventually scrolls made of animal skins became the standard writing vehicle for conveying the OT Scriptures (cf. 2 Tim 4:13). Parchment was first developed in ancient Pergamum and spread from there to the whole empire. The value of parchment was that it was easier to write on and easier to erase when mistakes were made or when a writer wanted to reuse the writing material for a different purpose. Because of the considerable expense of these materials, it was not uncommon to erase them entirely and use them again.

Before the collection and transmission of the books of the Bible began, many ancient peoples of the Middle East had already produced several important literary documents.[1] Long before the existence of the Jewish people, writing was a part of life in the ancient world. Mesopotamia, Egypt, and Anatolia all had distinctive scripts from around 3000 B.C.E., and these states had professional secretaries or scribes who, in special cases, functioned something like a secretary of state: they kept records, produced official state documents, and performed many other functions. The scribes often wore distinctive clothing to set them apart, and the custom of wearing a white tunic and carrying a bag containing writing equipment—ink, pens, brushes, writing material, and a cloth or rag for washing off errors—led to the scribal profession being identified as the "white kilt" profession (see Ezek 9:2–3, 11). Priestly scribal schools existed in Israel following the Babylonian exile (ca. 530–500 B.C.E.), but not much before then.

When the NT writings began to appear, the roll was used for all literary documents in the Greco-Roman world, while informal writings were put in notebooks (tablets) or handbooks and had more informality and abbreviations in them. The Jews regularly used scrolls to copy their sacred Scriptures. At first single books, and then major sections of the OT, were placed on one scroll. But even when technology improved sufficiently so that the whole OT could be placed on a single scroll (fourth century C.E.), the Jews continued to separate the Pentateuch from the rest of the Jewish Scriptures and write it on its own scroll, thirty or more feet in length. This practice meant that each of the three groupings of the OT writings were generally transmitted together on separate scrolls devoted to Law, Prophets, or Writings. By the fourth century, Christians began putting all of their sacred writings in one book (or codex), and several examples that have survived antiquity, for example, Codex Vaticanus and Codex Sinaiticus, contain the OT and NT.

The first copies of the NT Scriptures were written entirely in capital (uncial) letters with no spaces between the words in order to conserve expen-

---

[1] On the art and practice of writing in ancient Israel, see Demsky, "Writing in Ancient Israel and Early Judaism"; and Bar-Ilan, "Writing in Ancient Israel and Early Judaism."

sive writing materials. By the middle to late fourth century, Christian professional scribes began producing manuscripts of higher quality, yet still, perhaps because of custom, manuscripts had no spaces between words for several centuries to come.

Beginning in the eighth century, scribes began to insert spaces between words and to write in lowercase letters (minuscule). These manuscripts are commonly called "cursive" (from Latin, *cursivus*, "to run") because of the practice of writing all of the letters of a word without lifting the pen from the page (i.e., a running hand). Up until Gutenberg invented the printing press (1454) and published the whole Bible (1456), all biblical texts were produced by hand in lowercase lettering, often with colorful imagery (i.e., decorative letters and illustrations), especially at the beginning of books and chapters.

B. THE CODEX AND THE BIBLICAL CANON

One of the peculiarities of the early Christian community is its preference for the codex by no later than 100. The codex undoubtedly appealed to Christians because of its portability and convenience (see chapter 8 §VII). Later improvements in the making of the codex allowed all of the sacred books to be published in a single volume, and this converged at roughly the same time with the emergence of a fixed biblical canon in the church. The technology of producing books may thus have played a minor role in the selection of which books were included or excluded from the Christian canon.

If it is true that the biblical canon reflects what the early church accepted as sacred—and not what church councils dictated—then it follows that various lists or catalogues of sacred books may not be as important as actual manuscripts in letting us know what the real situation was in the churches. In other words, what do the contents of the surviving biblical manuscripts tell us about the books that the church believed were sacred?

Unfortunately, Greek New Testaments on the market today do not tell us what is in the manuscripts used to produce them. At best, the reader is given only a general category—Gospels, Acts, Pauline Letters, Catholic Epistles, or Revelation—followed by a Roman numeral indicating the century in which the manuscript was produced. This is quite misleading since one is then led to believe that *all* of the gospels or *all* of the Letters of Paul are found in the manuscript in question, which is only rarely true. And no critical edition of the Greek NT indicates that noncanonical writings may also be included in the same manuscript, as in the case of Codex Sinaiticus and Codex Vaticanus. Sadly, there are few places to turn to in order to discover the actual contents of the ancient biblical manuscripts.

Whatever the ancient lists may show (see appendixes B–D), one could make a strong case for including noncanonical writings in the church's Bible because they appeared in biblical manuscripts that were used by early churches. For example, Codex Vaticanus is one of the oldest surviving

Greek manuscripts containing both the OT and NT. It also includes several OT apocryphal books (Judith, Tobit, 2 Esdras, Baruch, and Epistle of Jeremiah) among the canonical OT books and not in a separate location. The manuscript probably accidentally omits 1–2 Maccabees, but apparently intentionally omits the Pastoral Letters. The Nestle-Aland Greek NT simply indicates that this uncial manuscript contains the Gospels, Acts, and Paul's Letters. The editors do not tell us that Hebrews is only partially included, that it is not currently where it was originally intended (the page numbers are out of sequence), or that a later scribe added both the conclusion of Hebrews and all of Revelation. In addition, the present form of Vaticanus contains all of the Catholic Epistles, but places them between Acts and the Epistles of Paul, a common sequence in many NT manuscripts in antiquity. Unfortunately, none of this information can be learned from the brief notations in the United Bible Society Greek NT (fourth edition) or the Nestle-Aland Greek NT (twenty-seventh edition) despite what this says about the scope of the church's biblical canon for the producers and readers of Codex Vaticanus.

Schmidt and Epp provide a very valuable service for canon inquiry by calling our attention to many of these omissions and by asking what this all means for canon formation.[2] They rightly see that the manuscripts themselves served in a canonical fashion in the communities where they were found (or produced), and they contain not merely *books* but also *words*. Before the invention of the printing press, no two copies of the biblical writings were alike. Many errors, whether intentional or unintentional, entered into the various manuscripts, and these served in a canonical manner in the churches that received them and read them. Epp correctly concludes:

Most if not all such competing variants were held to be canonical, wittingly or not, at various times and places in real-life Christian contexts, requiring the disquieting conclusion that canonicity of readings has virtually the same degree of multiformity as do the meaningful competing variants in a variation unit. That is, in many, many instances the term "canonical" can no longer be applied only to one variant reading; hence, no longer only to a single form of a New Testament writing.[3]

Although speaking about textual variation in the book of Psalms, Sanders is in substantial agreement with Epp: "There were probably as many canons as there were communities." He explains that the problem of fluidity of these texts in the various communities brings "attention to the question of literature considered authoritative—that is, functionally canonical—by one Jewish or Christian community but not by another."[4]

---

[2] Schmidt, "Greek New Testament as a Codex"; and Epp, "Issues in the Interrelation"; see also idem, "Multivalence of the Term 'Original Text' "; and idem, "Textual Criticism in the Exegesis of the New Testament."

[3] Epp, "Issues in the Interrelation," 515.

[4] J. A. Sanders, "Scripture as Canon for Post-Modern Times," 58.

Schmidt shows that manuscripts containing all of the books of the NT—and only these books—are relatively late in the history of the church and few in number. While he correctly observes that some earlier manuscripts do contain all of the writings of the NT, the oldest uncial manuscripts contain writings of both Testaments and noncanonical writings that are not found in today's Christian biblical canon.[5]

Many assume that the stabilization or fixation of the biblical canon took place in 367 when Athanasius sent out his famous *Thirty-ninth Festal Letter* listing the books in both Testaments. After systematically going through many of the surviving manuscripts, both uncial and minuscule, however, Schmidt can find no exact parallel to Athanasius's specific books *and their order* until 1116 in a minuscule manuscript discovered in a monastery at Mount Athos in Greece.[6]

Epp shows that whatever else the lists from the fourth and fifth centuries may indicate, what in fact represents the various canons of the Christian communities up to and beyond that time is the manuscripts that were actually used in the various churches. They reflect more accurately the actual situation in the churches. Moreover, there is less uniformity in them than what one might expect given the listing of books in the church fathers and church councils.[7]

Epp makes the point that textual and biblical scholars tend to discuss only the biblical manuscripts found at Oxyrhynchus and not the noncanonical material also discovered there:[8]

seven copies of the *Shepherd of Hermas*
three copies of the *Gospel of Thomas*
two copies of the *Gospel of Mary*
one copy of the *Acts of Peter*
one copy of the *Acts of John*
one copy of the *Acts of Paul*
one copy of the *Didache*
one copy of the *Sophia of Jesus Christ*
two copies of the *Gospel of Peter*
single copies of three unknown gospels/sayings of Jesus
one copy of the *Acts of Paul and Thecla*
one copy of the *Protevangelium of James*
one copy of the *Letter of Abgar to Jesus*

---

[5] Schmidt, "Greek New Testament as Codex" 469.

[6] Ibid., 476–77.

[7] Epp, "Issues in the Interrelation," 495–96. For example, the Pastoral Epistles are not in P^{46} or Vaticanus, although at least one scholar holds that the Pastorals were originally in P^{46}; see Duff, "P^{46} and the Pastorals."

[8] Epp, "Oxyrhynchus New Testament Papyri," 14–17.

While many early NT manuscripts were found at Oxyrhynchus, we must not overlook the nine apocryphal books and the unknown gospel-like writings also found there.[9]

While we cannot repeat all of Epp's and Schmidt's arguments here, their conclusions are well supported, and they rightly raise questions about which books of the NT, including those not in the NT, functioned as canon for the early church. It is likely that all of the biblical and noncanonical writings discovered in the ancient world functioned as Scripture *and* canon for Christians in the communities where they were found. That being the case, a more careful examination of the contents of the ancient biblical manuscripts is in order.

II. Textual Criticism

Textual criticism is sometimes referred to as "lower criticism" because it is the foundational work on which all other biblical studies are based. Unless there is some agreement on the original wording of a biblical passage, it is difficult if not impossible to find its meaning. This is not to suggest that careful evaluation of the various biblical texts that survived antiquity will in the end yield exact information for every passage of the Bible. Many passages are still unclear to textual critics and biblical scholars alike, even after long and difficult work spent examining a variety of witnesses to ancient biblical texts. The process of evaluating textual variants is known as textual criticism. This discipline has often been overlooked or misunderstood in terms of its importance both for interpreting the biblical text and for understanding the processes of canonization.

The first responsibility of any interpreter of the Bible is to determine precisely what the author wrote. The primary goal of textual criticism is to establish the original wording of a text insofar as that is possible. Since none of the original manuscripts, or autographs, has survived antiquity, text-critical scholars evaluate a myriad of ancient manuscripts that often are remarkably different from each other, in order to determine the earliest or most original reading possible. This lofty goal is often not possible to achieve, as recent textual critics readily acknowledge.

Epp observes that scholars are finding that the original text is more and more elusive as new manuscripts are discovered and other factors such as deliberate changes are acknowledged and factored into the equation.[10] When we understand how freely the early copiers altered the texts of the NT, we begin to see the difficulty in trying to recover the original text. Most

---

[9] Ibid., 18. Epp further notes (18–20) the discovery at Oxyrhynchus of one Old Latin and twenty-three Greek manuscripts of the LXX that included portions of Wisdom of Solomon, Tobit, *Apocalypse of Baruch,* and *1 Enoch.*

[10] Epp, "Issues in New Testament Textual Criticism," 71–72.

NT scholars today teach that Matthew and Luke made use of Mark's Gospel and often have word-for-word parallels with Mark, but Matthew and Luke often differ in wording and sequence in the materials that they have in common with each other, which is commonly referred to as Q. For example, the Sermon on the Mount (Matt 5–7) is in large measure the Sermon on the Plain in Luke 6, but some of Matthew's Sermon on the Mount is not found in Luke 6, but rather scattered throughout Luke's Gospel. Textual criticism also shows that John 21:15–17 (the basis for many sermons on the two Greek words for love: *agapē* and *philia*) and Mark 16:9–20 (the source of sermons on mission) were not originally a part of the Gospels in which they now appear. Modern translations typically put Mark 16:9–20 in a footnote to indicate its lack of good textual support, and the last chapter of John seems, on the basis of internal evidence, to suggest that it was an addition to the Gospel, which had earlier concluded in 20:31.[11]

Which text and translation of Scripture, then, should be read in the pulpits on Sunday mornings—King James Version, New Revised Standard Version, New International Version, or New Jerusalem Bible? While all of these translations are reasonably good and a great deal of work went into producing them, none of them is exactly the same, and this is not just because of the variety of ways to translate a Greek or Hebrew sentence. Frequently the translators preferred one set of manuscripts to support a reading instead of another.

The question naturally arises: did textual variants arise because early copiers and transmitters of the biblical books felt free to change the text, or because they received a different form of the biblical books that were circulating in Christian churches when they produced their copies? For example, Matthew and Luke may not have had the same version of Mark before them. Aland and Aland acknowledge that some variants in the biblical text may not be due to scribal error but "may be explained by its [the biblical text's] character as a 'living text.'"[12] While there are many examples of scribal error in copying the biblical books, some changes and editions were made on the basis of theological perspective, as Ehrman shows.[13] Initially, the NT writings were not treated as Scripture in the same

---

[11] For example, in John 20, Jesus appeared to the disciples, imparted to them the Holy Spirit, and commissioned them for ministry. In John 21, they are back in Galilee fishing and do not recognize Jesus when he comes to them. Jesus' confrontation with Peter about his love for him clearly seems designed to reverse Peter's threefold denial rather than focus on the differences in the words for love. The oldest translations of this passage (Syriac Peshitta and Old Latin) do not have two different words for love here. Be that as it may, 21:24 suggests that others were involved in this passage.

[12] Aland and Aland, *Text of the New Testament*, 69.

[13] In *Orthodox Corruption of Scripture*, Ehrman argues convincingly that because the books of the emerging Christian Scriptures were circulating in manuscript form in the fourth century and were copied by hand, one would expect some

way that the OT books were, and many transcribers freely made changes to their texts for practical or theological reasons. This, of course, complicates the task of textual criticism to recover the original text. Epp focuses on the problem when he asks, "If it is plausible that the Gospel of Mark used by Matthew differed from the Mark used by Luke, then which is the original Mark? And if it is plausible that our present Mark differed from Matthew's Mark, and Luke's Mark, then do we not have three possible originals?"[14] Given what we know of the fluidity of the text in its initial stages, the task of textual critics is formidable indeed. How does one distinguish between the autograph and the interpretive changes to the text? In many cases it is possible to determine that a text was changed for theological reasons,[15] but often it is difficult to determine. Could a corrector of a text actually have returned it to its original (or to a better) state?[16]

Epp suggests that rather than seeking an original text, textual scholars are now more likely to be looking for "several layers, levels, or meanings" of the text, though he prefers to call them "*dimensions* of originality."[17] The most recent principles of textual criticism are incorporated into modern critical editions of the Bible (both Hebrew and Greek) and also in newer translations of the Bible such as New Revised Standard Version, Revised English Bible, New International Version, and New Jerusalem Bible.

---

changes, both intentional and unintentional: "The texts of these books were by no means inviolable; to the contrary, they were altered with relative ease and alarming frequency. Most of the changes were accidental, the result of scribal ineptitude, carelessness, or fatigue. Others were intentional, and reflect the controversial milieux within which they were produced" (275). He points to many examples where the Christology of the church led many copiers to make changes to bring out the clarity of their particular christological views as they were copying and transmitting the church's Scriptures (274–75). He also shows that the scribes "occasionally altered the words of the text by putting them 'in other words.' To this extent, they were textual interpreters. At the same time, by *physically* altering the words, they did something quite different from other exegetes, and this difference is by no means to be minimized" (280, emphasis original). While some of Ehrman's arguments may be contested, his main point is no doubt correct that the fluidity of the text of NT manuscripts continued well into the third century. Aland and Aland, *Text of the New Testament,* 70, estimate that only ten to twenty percent of the Greek manuscripts of the NT preserved the text types of their exemplars.

[14]Epp, "Issues in New Testament Textual Criticism," 73–74.

[15]For example, a later addition was made for theological reasons to 1 John 5:7–8, and that addition was used by the translators of the King James Bible: "There are three that bear record in heaven, the Father, the Word, and the Holy Ghost: and these three are one."

[16]Silva, "Response," 147–49, suggests that intentional alterations of the biblical text—whether for theological, historical, stylistic, or other reasons—stand behind Epp's use of the phrase *multivalence of the term "original text."* See Epp's essay by this title and idem, "Issues in New Testament Textual Criticism," 74–75.

[17]Epp, "Issues in New Testament Textual Criticism," 75.

When the books of the NT were first written, preserved, and circulated in the churches, they were all hand copied. In time many wore out and were discarded or stored in a variety of ways. Over the last century, thousands of Greek manuscripts and fragments of manuscripts of the NT writings have been found and continue to be investigated. Roughly only eight percent of these cover most of the NT, while the vast majority contain only small portions of the NT writings and often exist in fragmentary form. In 1994 the official registry of biblical manuscripts, the Institute for New Testament Textual Research at Münster, Germany, listed over five thousand Greek manuscripts of the NT: 115 papyri, 306 uncial manuscripts, 2,812 minuscule manuscripts, and 2,281 lectionaries.[18] Now there are some 5,668 known manuscripts.

While copyists of the NT manuscripts were generally quite careful in their transmission of the biblical text, they still made mistakes by adding or omitting letters, words, or lines of Scripture text.[19] By and large, however, at first they were not consciously preparing either sacred or literary documents, and because of the considerable costs involved in producing quality literary copies, many mistakes in the manuscripts were made and subsequently transmitted in the churches.[20] This suggests that these documents were not generally recognized as Scripture until the end of the second century C.E. Scribal attempts at improvements in the texts occurred regularly, and apparently no attempts were made to stop this activity until the fourth century, when more stability in the text of the NT began to take place. Thus, inadvertent and deliberate mistakes made in the first two centuries were passed on for centuries in subsequent copies. In time some copyists saw that older manuscripts differed from the ones they were familiar with, and they made what they thought were corrective changes in order to get back to what they believed was the original text of Scripture. Not all such errors were caught, however, and numerous questions about the original text of the Bible still persist among scholars.

Many, if not most, textual variants in the NT manuscripts occurred before 200. That there were so many variants initially strongly suggests that later views of inspiration and inviolability of the text were not yet in place.[21] This coincides well with our knowledge that the NT writings were

---

[18] This information is supplied by Schnabel, "Textual Criticism." The figures change almost annually as more manuscripts are found or placed in the public domain.

[19] Good discussion of the types of scribal errors may be found in Aland and Aland, *Text of the New Testament,* 282–316; and Metzger, *Text of the New Testament,* 186–206.

[20] Scribes in the ancient world were paid well: approximately two to three times the average worker's wages; Metzger, *Text of the New Testament,* 15. The church did not regularly employ scribes of careful skill until the fourth century and following, and the lack of good literary skill in transmission is often seen in the earlier papyrus manuscripts.

[21] Koester, "Text of the Synoptic Gospels," 37.

read and cited in the early churches of the second century more frequently than the OT texts, but not generally called Scripture until the third century and later. But because no original manuscripts remain from either the OT or the NT, modern scholars must rely on textual criticism to make informed decisions about the original or earliest biblical text available. There are more than two hundred thousand variants in the surviving NT manuscripts.

For purposes of canonical inquiry, this investigation raises many questions about which text of the Bible is authoritative for the church or believing communities. The wide diversity among texts is evidence that for centuries the church's interest in canon related primarily to the books that were included, but recent scholars of the church see the necessity of seeking a more reliable and stable text of its sacred Scriptures. That Greek text is sometimes referred to as an eclectic, or selective, text, represented by the UBS^4 and Nestle-Aland^{27} texts. Despite this diversity, one must remember that the vast majority, if not all, of the thousands of extant biblical manuscripts were considered canonical and were used in local church worship and instruction for Christian living. What brought these texts—and their variety of changes and interpretations—into a manageable collection? Undoubtedly the church's view of orthodoxy had a major part in the process, for diversity was held in check by the *regula fidei,* a collection of widely accepted beliefs that were operative in the greater church during this period. There was surely acceptable diversity, but boundaries were imposed on such diversity. The church's vigorous challenge against heresy in the second through the fourth centuries testifies to limits that were acceptable.

III. Translations

The Bible has been translated into more languages than any other piece of literature in the history of the world: of the more than 6,800 living languages and dialects in the world today, the Bible has been fully translated into only 371 of them, and portions of the Bible have been translated into another 1,862 languages and dialects.[22] By the early seventh century, the Scriptures of the church existed in Greek, Latin, Gothic, Syriac, Coptic, Armenian, Georgian, Ethiopic, and Sogdian in the East. By 1454–1456, when the Gutenberg printing press and moveable type were invented, only about thirty-three languages had portions of the Bible. What bearing do these translations have on canon studies? Which of these translations are inspired and therefore authoritative for the church? Which ones best convey the original meaning? When almost all Christians read the Bible in translation, is there a standard authoritative translation of Scripture for the church?

---

[22] Metzger, *Bible in Translation,* 8–9.

A. EARLY TRANSLATIONS

Many early Christian translations are an excellent resource on what the translators thought was important, if not sacred, literature. Because of the Christians' universal focus on their mission, they freely translated the Christian Scriptures and the OT into several languages. The earliest translations of the NT were Old Latin, Syriac (especially the Peshitta), and Armenian, which date mostly from the third century and later. It is probably fair to say that when the Christian writings were translated, they had already achieved sacred status (canon 1) among those who translated them and probably among those who received them. It is also fair to say that the end product (i.e., the new translation) formed something of a canon (canon 2) for the community for which it was translated. The following early translations are the most important for understanding the development of the Christian biblical canon:

1. Old Syriac: Although only the four canonical Gospels are preserved in two fragmented manuscripts that date from the fourth or fifth century, the Old Syriac translation probably dates to the end of the second or beginning of the third century. The Eastern church fathers also refer to Acts and the Letters of Paul, but Old Syriac manuscripts of these writings have not survived.

2. Peshitta (or Syriac Vulgate): The Syriac Peshitta likely comes from the beginning of the fifth century and contains twenty-two of the NT books (it omits 2 Peter, 2 John, 3 John, Jude, and Revelation).

3. Philoxenian: Perhaps produced in the early sixth century, the Philoxenian version in Syriac is also known as the Harclean version because of a later revision by Thomas of Harkel in the early seventh century. With this translation, for the first time the minor Catholic Epistles and Revelation were added to Syrian churches' Scriptures.

4. Palestinian Syriac: Only a few fragments of the fifth-century Palestinian Syriac translation exist, and they contain the Gospels, Acts, and some of the Letters of Paul.

5. Old Latin: Many Old Latin manuscripts were produced during the third and later centuries, and they fall generally into two categories: African and European versions. The surviving manuscripts contain portions of the four canonical Gospels, Acts, some of Paul's Letters, and a few fragments of Revelation.

6. Latin Vulgate : Produced by Jerome in the last quarter of the fourth century, the Latin Vulgate survives in many manuscripts containing the whole Bible. Two manuscripts (Codex Dublinensis [ca. eighth century] and Codex Fuldensis [ca. sixth century]) also contain the apocryphal letter of Paul to the Laodiceans.

7. Coptic: Produced around the beginning of the third century), the Sahidic and Bohairic are the most important Coptic versions. The various manuscripts that have survived contain the four Gospels, Acts, and the Pauline Letters.

8. Gothic: The surviving Gothic manuscripts (ca. middle to end of fourth century) contain the four Gospels and some Pauline Letters, along with a portion of Neh 5–7.

9. Armenian: First produced in the late fourth and early fifth centuries, the Armenian version now survives in more than fifteen hundred copies from the eighth century and later. Some have all, others only part of the current NT.

10. Georgian: The Georgian version possibly goes back to the fourth or fifth century, but the oldest manuscripts date from the ninth century. The Georgian text contains the four Gospels, Acts, and the Catholic Epistles. By the tenth century, Revelation was added.

11. Ethiopic: First produced as early as the fourth or as late as the seventh century, most of the surviving manuscripts of the Ethiopic version date after the thirteenth century. The Ethiopic canon of the NT contains the twenty-seven NT books plus *Sinodos, 1 Clement, Book of the Covenant,* and *Didascalia*.

Examination of these translations shows that none from the fourth century or earlier contain all of the writings that we now have in our current NT, and few after that time do. While some of them expanded in time to include other canonical books, none of the early manuscripts of these versions contain all of the books of the NT. Whatever else these translations may tell us, they also indicate what books were received as authoritative in the churches that translated and used them.

B. MODERN TRANSLATIONS

Most translations made between 1380 (Wycliffe) and the first part of the twentieth century were based on late minuscule (lowercase) manuscripts copied between the tenth and fourteenth centuries. Even though it was the best English translation of its kind ever made, the King James Bible was based on inferior manuscripts (i.e., they contain many mistakes and corruptions of the text) that are considerably later in origin than those now available.

Because of the work of textual critics, many recent translations are on the whole much more accurate than the King James Version and other translations made before 1950. Important ancient manuscripts found over the last century and a half take us much closer to the original texts, in some cases as much as one thousand years closer to the original biblical texts. Analysis of these texts leads to several conclusions:

1. Three and possibly four major textual families survived antiquity: Alexandrian, Western, Byzantine, and possibly Caesarean. Some textual families were more accurate (Alexandrian) than others (Byzantine), and some reflect an earlier form of the original writings of the NT.
2. Extensive comparison of the manuscripts shows that numerous corruptions of the text crept into *all* NT manuscripts over the centuries and that the more reliable earlier texts better reflect what the original writers wrote.
3. All translations produced before the middle of the twentieth century are essentially out of date and do not accurately reflect the text of the earliest biblical manuscripts. I hasten to add, however, that no manuscripts take us back to the first century when the NT authors wrote, and some ambiguity and uncertainty therefore still remains in all Bible translations.

IV. Conclusion

Lists of sacred books in ancient writers and references to these books in the early church fathers are important in our understanding of the origins of the biblical canon, but equally important are the earliest texts and translations of the Scriptures. The extent to which the production of books also affected the scope of the biblical canon has not been clearly determined, but several scholars today agree that the limits of space may well have been a factor initially. When space no longer seemed to be a problem, the sheer cost of producing manuscripts of all of the books that were deemed sacred in the Christian communities was staggering. What the manuscript evidence shows is that few churches and fewer individuals had a complete copy of the NT Scriptures before the fourth century, and even after that the Bible of one community did not match that of another.

Historically, the church debated only about which books to include in the Christian Bibles; they did not debate the specific text of the Bible, even though no two handwritten texts were identical. The implications of this are obviously quite significant for understanding the development of the biblical canon. Likewise, the relative lack of comment on which translation of the Bible Christians should use is also strange. It seems to have mattered little if Christians read their Scriptures in Greek, Hebrew, Latin, or Syriac. Strictly speaking, canon *then* (fourth to sixth centuries) had to do with the books that made up the sacred collections, not the text or translations that were involved. Today these questions are far more important than they were in antiquity, since scholars are more familiar with the variety of texts that survived. Which books, therefore, should be canonized in the church? The textual critic, the canonical scholar, and the translator are all very much interested in those matters today.

CHAPTER THIRTEEN

Collections and Citations of Christian Scriptures

I. Ancient Lists of Scripture

A. INTRODUCTION

Most ancient collections or lists of Christian Scriptures date after the first half of the fourth century.[1] The existence of a list of sacred writings does not, however, mean that its author(s) had a canon or closed collection of Christian Scriptures.[2] Often it is simply a list of allusions, citations, or quotations from the NT and other ancient literature used by some of the church fathers. Merely collecting and tabulating these references does not constitute a biblical canon; it says no more than that the theology of the early church fathers was *informed* by these earlier writings. And until we come to the fourth century, such references for the most part do not prove that the literature was even acknowledged to be Scripture.[3] Although the study of such references can be extremely valuable, especially as one examines the context in which each of these allusions or citations is found, a

[1] For the lists, see Alexander, *Canon of the Old and New Testaments;* F. F. Bruce, *Canon of Scripture,* 205–51; Farmer and Farkasfalvy, *Formation of the New Testament Canon,* 9–22; Grant, *Formation of the New Testament,* 148–80; Grosheide, *Some Early Lists;* Hahneman, *Muratorian Fragment,* 132–82; Koester, *Synoptische Überlieferung;* Kümmel, *Introduction to the New Testament,* 340–55; Metzger, *Canon of the New Testament,* 209–47, 305–15; Souter, *Text and Canon,* 205–37; and Stuart, *Critical History and Defense;* McDonald and Sanders, *Canon Debate,* 591–97.

[2] The term *list* is not the best term to describe these collections since it suggests that their patristic authors drew up a closed list of Christian Scriptures. Irenaeus, Clement, and Origen, for example, made no such lists. See Sundberg, "Bible Canon," 364–65.

[3] This inference is prevalent in the works of Souter, Kümmel, and Farmer and Farkasfalvy.

common error in the study of the biblical canon is to view all these references as citations of Scripture.

Because of this common practice it is important to add a few cautionary comments. First, the presence of citations or references to the NT literature in the writings of the church fathers does not in itself necessarily prove that the documents referred to were viewed as sacred Scripture.[4] Second, the absence of a particular Christian document from the writings of a church father does not necessarily mean that he was either unaware of it or did not believe that it was Scripture. Quite often the writings that survived from antiquity were produced in response to a problem in the church, and the writer would seldom have occasion in such ad hoc writings to cite all of the works he considered to be inspired Scriptures. Third, the writings quoted or referred to by one church father in one area are not necessarily representative of all Christians in the same area and even less representative of Christians in other areas. Finally, only a small portion of the total number of ancient written documents is known today. Many were destroyed by the enemies of the church, and some were destroyed by Christians themselves in heresy hunts. Some of these writings were simply lost (e.g., a part of Paul's Corinthian correspondence—see 1 Cor 5:9), and still others were at some point deemed no longer relevant to the needs of the local church and were either discarded or stored in undiscovered locations. The possibility still exits that additional discoveries, such as those at Qumran and Nag Hammadi, will reveal documents that will give us even greater insight into the perplexing questions about the Christian canon. The recent discovery of numerous biblical and nonbiblical manuscripts at a monastery at Mount Athos in Greece holds great promise for biblical, canonical, and textual scholars.

Although no part of the NT was consciously written as a part of an already existing collection of sacred documents, many of these writings began to appear together in the second century. It is not unreasonable to think that a collection of Paul's Epistles circulated in many churches by the end of the first century,[5] and in the last half of the second century at least three of the canonical Gospels were grouped together by Justin and all four by Irenaeus. Grant believes that the first collection of Christian Scriptures arose in Alexandria, Egypt, no later than the early second century. He contends that Basilides, who wrote during the reign of Hadrian (ca. 117–138), made explicit what other Christians already believed in that region—namely, that the writings of Paul and the Gospels (Matthew, Luke,

---

[4] Brown argues (in Turro and Brown, "Canonicity," 530) that the patristic citations do, however, give evidence of the acceptance of this literature as authoritative in the life of the church and indicate the beginnings of a Christian canon of Scripture. The specific context of each citation, however, is important before a judgment can be made in this regard.

[5] Kümmel, *Introduction to the New Testament,* 338.

John) were considered to be Scriptures on a par with the OT.[6] Even though Grant depends heavily on Hippolytus's attack against Basilides in his *Refutations of All Heresies* (ca. 220–230), a source that not all scholars consider reliable, no precise collection of NT writings and no closed biblical canon are attributed to Basilides by Hippolytus. The clearest second-century example of a limited collection of Christian Scriptures is Marcion's, but his list of Christian writings was far from what came to be known as a canon of Christian Scriptures.

What becomes obvious in all such listings or collections of NT documents from the time of Marcion until the beginning of the fourth century is the absence of any agreement on what such a grouping means and whether these collections should be considered lists of sacred Scriptures. With the fourth-century catalogues, we can begin to speak of *"canonical* lists," but before then it is not clear what the *precise* boundaries of the Christian Scriptures were. And not until the end of the fourth century was a general consensus reached on *most* of the twenty-seven books that make up our present NT. Aland correctly observes that it took centuries longer for a consensus to be reached on our present twenty-seven books.[7]

The first undisputed closed collections of Christian Scriptures begin with Eusebius, probably the creator of such lists, in the fourth century. Hahneman and Kalin contend that Eusebius *created* his lists from reading the writings of Irenaeus (*Hist. eccl.* 5.8.1), Clement of Alexandria (*Hist. eccl.* 6.14.1–7), and Origen (*Hist. eccl.* 6.25.3–14).[8] Hahneman claims that "Eusebius simply wove together various texts from their [the purported authors'] works in order to create the impression that each of these Church Fathers had a 'canon.' It was Eusebius who created the 'canon' from their comments, not the writers themselves, so that none of these lists are original catalogues."[9] Hahneman identifies fifteen undisputed catalogues of canonical Scriptures from the fourth and early fifth centuries, to which I have added four manuscripts (#16–#20):[10]

Source	**Date**	**Provenance**
1. Eusebius, *Hist. eccl.* 3.25.1–7	303–325	Palestine/Western Syria
2. Codex Claromontanus, D^P	Sixth century	Alexandria, Egypt
3. Cyril of Jerusalem, *Catechetical Lectures* 4.33	ca. 350	Palestine
4. Athanasius, *Thirty-ninth Festal Letter*	ca. 367	Alexandria, Egypt

[6] Grant, *Formation of the New Testament,* 121–24.

[7] Aland, *Problem of the New Testament Canon,* 12.

[8] Hahneman, *Muratorian Fragment,* 133, 136; and Kalin, "Re-examining New Testament Canon History."

[9] Hahneman, *Muratorian Fragment,* 136.

[10] Ibid., 133, 171, 172. See Appendix C-2 and C-4 for the books in each of these canons.

5. Mommsen Catalogue	ca. 365–390	Northern Africa
6. Epiphanius, *Refutation of All Heresies* 76.5	ca. 374–377	Palestine/Western Syria
7. Apostolic Canon 85	ca. 380	Palestine/Western Syria
8. Gregory of Nazianzus, *Carmina* 12.31	ca. 383–390	Asia Minor
9. African Canons	ca. 393–419	Northern Africa
10. Jerome, *Letter* 53	ca. 394	Palestine
11. Augustine, *Christian Doctrine* 2.8.12	ca. 396–397	Northern Africa
12. Amphilochius, *Iambics for Seleucus* 289–319	ca. 396	Asia Minor
13. Rufinus, *Commentary on the Apostles' Creed* 36	ca. 400	Rome
14. Innocent I, *Letter to Exuperius of Toulouse*	ca. 405	Rome
15. Syrian catalogue of St. Catherine's Monastery	ca. 400	Eastern Syria
16. Codex Vaticanus	mid-fourth century	Alexandria, Egypt
17. Codex Sinaiticus	mid-fourth century	Alexandria, Egypt
18. Codex Alexandrinus	fifth century	Asia Minor
19. Syriac Peshitta	ca. 400	Eastern Syria
20. Muratorian Fragment	ca. 350–360	Eastern Mediterranean

These and other lists indicate the variety of views on what literature informed the beliefs and thought of the earliest Christian communities and what was considered authoritative in those communities for faith and practice. Although not all of the literature in these lists was specifically called Scripture, for the most part, it seemed to function in that way in the churches. These lists indicate to some extent the broad acceptance in the early churches of the majority of the books that constitute our present NT canon—and also the fair amount of diversity that existed in the church well into the fifth century.

A. MARCION

Marcion (died ca. 160) produced the first known collection of Christian Scriptures[11] around the mid-second century, but since no independent Marcionite sources or documents survive from antiquity, we depend completely on his orthodox critics, especially Irenaeus and Tertullian, for information. Fortunately, their reports are extensive and generally considered reliable.

[11] Marcion does not call what he has collected a set of Christian Scriptures. Since the Christian writings of the first century are not generally called Scripture until the end of the second century, it is also unlikely that Marcion used this designation for the writings used in his churches for catechetical purposes.

Marcion rejected the whole of the OT and accepted only an edited form of the Gospel of Luke and ten of Paul's Epistles. Marcion's collection did not include the Pastoral Epistles, and it is not likely that he knew of them.[12] Tertullian, on the other hand, claims that Marcion both knew and *rejected* the Pastoral Letters: "I wonder, however, when he received this letter [Philemon] which was written but to one man, that he rejected the two epistles to Timothy and the one to Titus, which all treat of ecclesiastical discipline. His aim, was, I suppose, to carry out his interpolating process even to the number of epistles [of Paul]" (*Marc.* 5.21, *ANF*).

Marcion may have been aware of the other canonical Gospels (see chapter 11 §I). It is fairly certain, however, that Marcion initially adopted only Luke and Paul. Whether he specifically rejected other Christian writings is not clear, and it is impossible with our current knowledge to say that Marcion had a closed biblical canon. In any case, the community of churches that followed him demonstrated that their canon was not closed.

C. VALENTINUS

Some awareness of a collection of writings may have been known earlier than the time of Marcion. Tertullian states that Valentinus (ca. 135–160), in contrast to Marcion, used all the Scriptures and perverted them:.

> One man perverts the Scriptures with his hand, another their meaning by his exposition. For although Valentinus seems to use the entire volume, he has none the less laid violent hands on the truth only with a more cunning mind and skill than Marcion. Marcion expressly and openly used the knife, not the pen, since he made such an excision of the Scriptures[13] as suited his own subject-matter. Valentinus, however, abstained from such excision, because he did not invent Scriptures to square with his own subject-matter, but adapted his matter to the Scriptures; and yet he took away more, and added more, by removing the proper meaning of every particular word, and adding fantastic arrangements of things which had no real existence. (*Praescr.* 38.4–6, *ANF*)

The phrase *entire volume* (Latin *integro instrumento*) appears to refer to a collection of Scriptures, probably the NT writings, but possibly the OT Scriptures as well. The context favors the former since Tertullian asks both Marcion and Valentinus what right they have to use the Scripture received from the Apostles (*Praescr.* 32), which could not, of course, refer to the OT writings. While Tertullian uses the term in reference to the OT as one volume (*Praescr.* 36), the context here seems to favor a NT collection. Tertullian evidently believed that Valentinus used a collection of NT writ-

[12] Koester, *Introduction to the New Testament,* 2.297–305, suggests that they may have been written after the time of Marcion and in response to him (see 1 Tim 6:20).

[13] The term *Scripture* for the NT writings is probably anachronistic on Tertullian's part.

ings similar to his own. Metzger notes that the discovery of the *Gospel of Truth,* believed by some scholars to have been written by Valentinus, shows acquaintance with the four Gospels, several of Paul's Epistles, Hebrews, and Revelation.[14] If an early dating of this work is accepted, it becomes the most complete collection list of the OT and NT writings from a decidedly Western orientation. It is possible, however, that Tertullian's judgment of Valentinus was in part based on an understanding of the NT Scriptures from his own time (ca. 200 C.E.) and not necessarily from Valentinus's time, when the status of canonical literature was vaguer and still in a state of imprecise definition.

D. MURATORIAN FRAGMENT

In 1738–1740 Lodovico Antonio Muratori discovered in Milan and edited what many canonical scholars believe is one of the most important documents for establishing a late-second-century date for the formation of a NT canon. Commonly called the Muratorian Canon or Muratorian Fragment, the document that Muratori found is a seventh-century or eighth-century fragment of a Latin document usually dated around 180–200 and thought to have been written in Rome or its vicinity.[15] Optimistically, it is hailed as "the oldest extant list of sacred books of the New Testament."[16] Consisting of some eighty-five lines, the Muratorian Fragment is missing the opening lines and probably also the conclusion.[17] It is generally agreed that it was originally written in Greek and later translated into very poor Latin.[18] Because of the significant amount of scholarly attention that the Muratorian Fragment has received and its importance for canonical research in the late-second-century NT canon, it is worth quoting in full:[19]

> . . . at which nevertheless he was present, and so he placed [them in his narrative]. (2) The third book of the Gospel is that according to Luke. (3) Luke, the well-known physician, after the ascension of Christ, (4–5) when Paul had

---

[14] Metzger, "Canon of the New Testament," 124.

[15] Metzger, *Canon of the New Testament,* 193.

[16] Farmer and Farkasfalvy, *Formation of the New Testament Canon,* 161 n. 1.

[17] Hahneman, *Muratorian Fragment,* 5, makes a good case that the end of the Muratorian Fragment was truncated and was longer in its original form.

[18] Hahneman, ibid., 8, discusses the many "clerical blunders" in the Muratorian Fragment and concludes that the "carelessness of this particular scribe is probably responsible for a significant portion of the barbarous transcription of the Fragment." Metzger, *Canon of the New Testament,* 192, also notes "the carelessness of the scribe" of the Muratorian Fragment.

[19] Quoted from Metzger, *Canon of the New Testament,* 305–7, who added clarifying material in square brackets and alternative translations in parentheses. Numbers in parentheses are line numbers. I added the paragraph breaks and the missing numbers for lines 19, 61, and 69. For the Latin text, both original and restored, see Theron, *Evidence of Tradition,* 106–12.

taken him with him as one zealous for the law, (6) composed it in his own name, according to [the general] belief. Yet he himself had not (7) seen the Lord in the flesh; and therefore, as he was able to ascertain events, (8) so indeed he begins to tell the story from the birth of John.

(9) The fourth of the Gospels is that of John, [one] of the disciples. (10) To his fellow disciples and bishops, who had been urging him [to write], (11) he said, "Fast with me from today for three days, and what (12) will be revealed to each one (13) let us tell it to one another." In the same night it was revealed (14) to Andrew, [one] of the apostles, (15–16) that John should write down all things in his own name while all of them should review it. And so, though various (17) elements may be taught in the individual books of the Gospels, (18) nevertheless this makes no difference to the faith (19) of believers, since by the one sovereign Spirit all things (20) have been declared in all [the Gospels]: concerning the (21) nativity, concerning the passion, concerning the resurrection, (22) concerning life with his disciples, (23) and concerning his twofold coming; (24) the first in lowliness when he was despised, which has taken place, (25) the second glorious in royal power, (26) which is still in the future. What (27) marvel is it, then if John so consistently (28) mentions these particular points also in his Epistles, (29) saying about himself: "What we have seen with our eyes (30) and heard with our ears and our hands (31) have handled, these things we have written to you"? (32) For in this way he professes [himself] to be not only an eye-witness and hearer, (33) but also a writer of all the marvelous deeds of the Lord, in their order.

(34) Moreover, the acts of all the apostles (35) were written in one book. For "most excellent Theophilus" Luke compiled (36) the individual events that took place in his presence—(37) as he plainly shows by omitting the martyrdom of Peter (38) as well as the departure of Paul from the city [of Rome] (39) when he journeyed to Spain. As for the Epistles of (40–41) Paul, they themselves make clear to those desiring to understand, which ones [they are], from what place, or for what reason they were sent. (42) First of all, to the Corinthians, prohibiting their heretical schisms; (43) next, to the Galatians, against circumcision; (44–46) then to the Romans he wrote at length, explaining the order (or, plan) of the Scriptures, and also that Christ is their principle (or, main theme).

It is necessary (47) for us to discuss these one by one, since the blessed (48) apostle Paul himself, following the example of his predecessor (49–50) John, writes by name to only seven churches in the following sequence: to the Corinthians (51) first, to the Ephesians second, to the Philippians third, (52) to the Colossians fourth, to the Galatians fifth, (53) to the Thessalonians sixth, to the Romans (54–55) seventh. It is true that he writes once more to the Corinthians and to the Thessalonians for the sake of admonition, (56–57), yet it is clearly recognizable that there is one Church spread throughout the whole extent of the earth. For John also in the (58) Apocalypse, though he writes to seven churches, (59–60) nevertheless speaks to all. [Paul also wrote] out of affection and love one to Philemon, one to Titus, and two to Timothy; (61) and these are held sacred (62–63) in the esteem of the Church catholic for the regulation of ecclesiastical discipline.

There is current also [an epistle] to (64) the Laodiceans, [and] another to the Alexandrians, [both] forged in Paul's (65) name to [further] the heresy of Marcion, and several others (66) which cannot be received into the catholic church (67)—for it is not fitting that gall be mixed with honey. (68) Moreover, the Epistle of Jude and two of the above-mentioned (or, bearing the name of) (69) John are counted (or, used) in the catholic [Church]; and [the book of] Wisdom, (70) written by the friends of Solomon in his honour. (71) We receive only the apocalypses of John and Peter, (72) though some of us are not willing that the latter be read in church.

(73) But Hermas wrote the *Shepherd* (74) very recently, in our times, in the city of Rome, (75) while bishop Pius, his brother, was occupying the [episcopal] chair (76) of the church of the city of Rome. (77) And therefore it ought indeed to be read; but (78) it cannot be read publicly to the people in church either among (79) the prophets, whose number is complete, or among (80) the apostles, for it is after [their] time.

(81) But we accept nothing whatever of Arsinous or Valentinus or Miltiades, (82) who also composed (83) a new book of psalms for Marcion, (84–85) together with Basilides, the Asian founder of the Cataphrygians. . . .

Some scholars date the original text of the Muratorian Fragment near or before the end of the late second century and claim that it was written from the vicinity of Rome on the basis of internal evidence:[20] (1) The *Shepherd of Hermas* was rejected because "Hermas wrote the *Shepherd* very recently, in our times [*vero nuperrime temporibus nostris*]" (lines 73–74). Hermas lived around 100–145 and was not considered to be part of the apostolic era since the author of the Muratorian Fragment evidently separated apostolic times from all other times. The statement that the brother of Hermas, Pius, was currently the bishop of Rome (lines 75–76) suggests that "our times" is a reference to the second century and no later than 200.[21] (2) In lines 38 and 76, the Muratorian Fragment mentions *urbs* and *urbs Roma,* which demonstrates a Roman origin.[22] (3) The absence of James and Hebrews from the list suggests that the document originated in the West, since Hebrews and James were excluded from the canons in the East. (4) The presence of the book of Revelation in the list suggests that the document originated in the West since Revelation was not held in high esteem in the Eastern churches. (5) Von Campenhausen claims a Western origin of the

[20] See Grant, *Formation of the New Testament,* 301; Metzger, "Canon of the New Testament," 124; Beare, "Canon of the NT," 527; Goodspeed, *History of Early Christian Literature,* 31; Schneemelcher, "General Introduction," 42; and von Campenhausen, *Formation of the Christian Bible,* 242–262.

[21] Metzger, *Canon of the New Testament,* 193–94.

[22] Ibid.

fragment because it lists the *Apocalypse of John* and *Apocalypse of Peter* as acceptable books. The Eastern churches, he contends, routinely rejected these apocalypses.[23] Von Campenhausen also argues that the Muratorian Fragment could not have been written later than the end of the second century:

> At a later period it is hardly conceivable that the Catholic Epistles would be limited to three or four, with no mention of those attributed to Peter, or, on the other hand, that the Apocalypse of Peter and the Wisdom of Solomon would have been acknowledged as part of the NT Canon. Furthermore, the heretics and heresies named by the *Muratorianum* all still belong to the second century.[24]

On the other hand, several important objections to the traditional view of the date and provenance of the Muratorian Fragment are proposed by Sundberg, who concludes that the fragment was written around 350–400 in the East.[25] (1) Permission was granted to read the *Shepherd of Hermas* in the Muratorian Fragment even though it was considered outside the canon. In the time of Irenaeus and Tertullian, the *Shepherd of Hermas* was considered an authoritative book and not an outside book. Only later and in the West was the *Shepherd of Hermas* excluded. (2) The *Apocalypse of John* and *Apocalypse of Peter* are in equivocal positions (lines 71–72), which Sundberg argues is more characteristic of Eastern than Western churches in the third and fourth centuries. (3) The closest parallel to this list is the one produced by Eusebius (ca. 325) in the East. (4) There are no similar lists in the second century anywhere. Sundberg contends that even if the Muratorian Fragment were written in the second century, it has no parallels until the fourth century and could not have played the significant role in the development of the Christian canon of Scriptures that is ascribed to it.[26] (5) The argument that the *Shepherd of Hermas* was written "very recently, in our times" is simply a reference to how the ancient churches distinguished the apostolic times from their own; "our times" is a reference to a *postapostolic* era as opposed to the times of the apostles. Sundberg gives several examples of this practice, including one from Irenaeus who uses "our times" (*temporibus nostris*) of an event one hundred years before him![27]

---

[23] Von Campenhausen, *Formation of the Christian Bible,* 244–45 n. 192.

[24] Ibid.

[25] Sundberg, "Canon Muratori." Farmer and Farkasfalvy, *Formation of the New Testament Canon,* 161, dismiss Sundberg's article in a footnote without seriously considering his major arguments.

[26] Sundberg, "Bible Canon," 362, makes a strong point that if neither Irenaeus nor Origen had lists of canonical NT Scriptures, then the Muratorian Fragment has no parallels until the fourth century. The document appears to have come from the middle to late fourth century, when the ambiguity about accepting several disputed books in Eusebius's three groups disappeared.

[27] Sundberg, "Canon Muratori," 8–11.

Ferguson wrote a carefully balanced response to Sundberg's proposal on the date and location for the writing of the Muratorian Fragment that, according to Metzger, "demolished" Sundberg's thesis.[28] Ferguson grants the possibility that "in our times" could refer to anytime after the apostolic times, but holds that it is compatible with a second-century dating of the document and was not the usual way of distinguishing those times.[29] He is not bothered by the lack of parallels with the Muratorian Fragment until the fourth century.

If the reasons for placing the Muratorian Fragment in the late second century are valid—and I question whether they are—the date and provenance of the document remain problematic since no one today seriously dates the *Shepherd of Hermas* as late as 180–200 (the date most commonly assigned to the Muratorian Fragment). At least two bishops (Anicetus and Soter) come between Pius and Eleutherius, who was the bishop of Rome in the time of Irenaeus (*Haer.* 3.3.3). If the Muratorian Fragment must be dated in the second century, why not stress the most logical time around 140–150, which would place it in the time of the *Shepherd of Hermas*? This date is more in keeping with a strict interpretation of the words "very recently in our times" than a late-second-century dating of the manuscript suggests. The reason most scholars do not date the document any earlier than the last quarter of the second century is because of its references to the followers of Marcion.

Objections to the traditional dating (end of the second century) and provenance (Rome) of the Muratorian Fragment include the following:

1. If the Muratorian Fragment were a second-century document from the West, one would expect to see other parallels to it from that general time and location, but none exists. The Muratorian Fragment most probably originated in the middle to late fourth century in the East, since all of the closest parallels are from that time and location. The strength of Sundberg's observation that there are no clear parallels to the Muratorian Fragment until the fourth century is conceded by Ferguson. He acknowledges that this is the weakest part of his argument, but concludes nevertheless that "we once more confront the matter of a list as the only thing which distinguishes the *Canon Muratori* from the situation at the beginning of the third century. Each person must decide how much of a novelty a list was and how

---

[28] Metzger, *Canon of the New Testament,* 193. Rather than dealing with Sundberg's arguments, Metzger appears to have simply dismissed them. At the time he was preparing his volume, however, most biblical scholars accepted the second-century dating and the Western provenance of the Muratorian Fragment. Recently there has been a considerable shift in scholarly opinion on the matter, and now a growing number of biblical scholars place the Muratorian Fragment in the mid- to late fourth century in the East.

[29] Ferguson, "Canon Muratori," 677–78.

much weight to put on the absence of lists before the fourth century."[30] He claims that the argument based on parallels is "so tenuous as to fail to carry conviction."[31] I agree that somebody had to be first to make a list, but it stretches credibility to say that the Muratorian Fragment did it 150 years before anyone else!

2. The Muratorian Fragment's listing of the four canonical Gospels without any defense, such as we find in Irenaeus, is evidence of their fixed status in the church and is an argument against a second--century dating of the fragment. The closest contemporary writing from the West in the last quarter of the second century is Irenaeus. His strange way of arguing for these four—and only these four—Gospels suggests that not everyone in the second century was as convinced about their canonicity as he was. Tatian's use of *more* than the four canonical Gospels in his *Diatessaron* and the preference for the Gospel of John in Asia seems to show that not all of Irenaeus's contemporaries agreed that the Gospels should be limited to the four canonical Gospels, at least not as rigidly as Irenaeus proposed. Even if some of Tatian's followers later inserted clauses from the *Gospel of Hebrews* and the *Protevangelium of James* into the *Diatessaron,* as seems likely, one still cannot find in Tatian the loyalty to the inspired text that one finds in Rev 22:18–19 or in Irenaeus's defense of the four-gospel canon. In regard to the four canonical Gospels, Irenaeus stands alone in the second century. The fragment of the *Diatessaron* that has survived clearly shows that much of the context, especially from the Synoptic Gospels, is omitted. Does this mean that the canonical and inspired status of the four Gospels was not yet fully recognized by Tatian and many of his other contemporaries? No doubt he saw them as responsible and faithful documents, but not as inviolable texts.[32] Although it can be argued that Irenaeus's canon was not universally accepted in his day, hence Irenaeus's need to provide a defense of the four Gospels, the same cannot be said about the Muratorian Fragment, in which the acceptance of four canonical Gospels is assumed without debate. The only question for the writer of the Muratorian Fragment is what besides these four is to be added. This document is more similar to Eusebius's "holy tetrad" in the fourth century than to any writer of the second century.

3. The Muratorian Fragment (lines 69–70) includes the Wisdom of Solomon, an OT pseudepigraphal writing, in a *New Testament* collection! This is highly unusual and has its only parallels in the fourth-century writings of Eusebius (*Hist. eccl.* 5.8.1–8; ca. 325–330) and Epiphanius

[30] Ibid., 681.
[31] Ibid.
[32] Metzger, *Canon of the New Testament,* 115–16.

(*Pan*. 76.5; ca. 375–400). Metzger is aware of the anomaly here and admits that "why this intertestamental book should be included in a list of Christian gospels and epistles is a puzzle that has never been satisfactorily resolved."[33] The obvious conclusion is that the Muratorian Fragment is a fourth-century document.[34] Ferguson acknowledges that the Wisdom of Solomon had more popularity in the East than in the West, but also claims that the document was referred to by Western theologians as well, and he cites several texts as evidence (Heb 1:3; *1 Clem*. 3.4; 7.5; 27.5; and Tertullian, *Praescr*. 7 and *Against the Valentinians* 2).[35] This OT apocryphal book in a NT list only has parallels in the fourth century and later.

4. Most of the other writings in Codex Muratori are assigned to the fourth century.[36] The others (*De Abraam* and *Expositio fidei chatolice*) are probably later than the Muratorian Fragment, but not by much.

5. The language of the Muratorian Fragment is decidedly fourth-century Latin and probably a translation from a Greek original from the East. Although the transition from Greek to Latin in the West began around the middle of the second century, the Latin used in the Muratorian Fragment has some peculiarities that come from the fourth century:[37] spelling and pronunciation that derives from Latin in the third and fourth centuries, several terms that first appear elsewhere only from the end of the fourth century,[38] and several confusing passages in the Latin text that are probably mistranslations of the Greek. If a Greek original is presumed and the early dating of the Muratorian Fragment is not maintained, then it is likely that the document originated in the East, where the transition to the Latin in the Christian communities began in the fourth century.[39]

6. The reference to *urbs Roma* in line 76 does not favor a Western (Roman) community, as Ferguson argues, but rather the East. Hahneman

---

[33] Ibid., 197–98.

[34] Hahneman, *Muratorian Fragment,* 200–205, also makes this point. F. F. Bruce, *Canon of Scripture,* 81 n. 52, is aware of the parallels to Epiphanius, but does not draw the same inference from it. He appears to have missed the reference in Eusebius.

[35] Ferguson, "*Canon Muratori,*" 681–83.

[36] Hahneman, *Muratorian Fragment,* 20–22.

[37] Ibid., 183–214.

[38] Ibid., 12–13, citing J. Compos, who shows, for example, that *intimans* (line 45) is first found in *Historica Augusta* (ca. 400), *visor* (line 32) in Augustine's *Against the Academics* 2.7, 19 (ca. 386), and *per ordinem* (lines 33–34) in Jerome's OT Vulgate. In fact, Hahneman claims (*Muratorian Fragment,* 13) that the Latin text of the Muratorian Fragment shows enough similarity to the Vulgate to argue that it was not composed in Latin until the fifth century.

[39] Ibid., 12–13.

shows that the more normal phrase employed for Rome in the West was *hic in urbe Roma*.[40]

7. The argument for the Western provenance of the Muratorian Fragment based on the absence of James and Hebrews from the list and the inclusion of the book of Revelation and the *Apocalypse of Peter* does not hold up under closer scrutiny. Revelation, for example, was cited frequently in the East and was accepted as Scripture in the East as much as in the West in the second and third centuries:

   a. Papias referred to Revelation (Andreas Caesariensis, *Revelation* 34, Sermon 12; Oecumenius and Arethas, *Commentary on Revelation* 12.7).[41]

   b. Melito of Sardis wrote a book on Revelation (Eusebius, *Hist. eccl.* 4.26.2; Jerome, *Illustrious Men* 24).

   c. Theophilus of Antioch alluded to Revelation (*Autol.* 2.28) and used its testimonies in a lost work against Hermogenes (Eusebius, *Hist. eccl.* 4.24.1).

   d. Apollonius of Hierapolis used the testimonies of Revelation (Eusebius, *Hist. eccl.* 5.18.13).

   e. Clement of Alexandria quoted Revelation approvingly (*Christ the Educator* 1.6; 2.11; *Strom.* 6.13, 25).

   f. Origen frequently cited Revelation (*First Principles* 1.2.10; 4.1.25; *Commentary on John* 1.1, 2, 14, 23, 42). Significant rejection of Revelation in the East did not occur until the end of the fourth century, and Cyril of Jerusalem was the first to exclude Revelation without comment (*Catechetical Lectures* 4.36). On the other hand, Epiphanius of Salamis still included it at the end of the fourth century (*Pan.* 76.5) as did Jerome (*Letter* 53) and Codex Alexandrinus (ca. 425).[42]

8. For Hahneman, the absence of James and Hebrews from the Muratorian Fragment is not as surprising as the omission of 1 Peter, since the list included the *Apocalypse of Peter.* He agrees with Westcott, who earlier concluded that the striking omissions from the Muratorian Fragment made little sense. Westcott claims that 1 Peter, Hebrews, and James "could scarcely have been altogether passed over in an enumeration of books in which the Epistle of St. Jude, and even Apocryphal writings of heretics, found a place."[43] Hahneman

---

[40] Ibid., 22–23.
[41] Ibid., 23, drawing on A. H. Charteris.
[42] Ibid., 23–25.
[43] Ibid., 25; Westcott, *General Survey,* 219.

concludes with Tregelles that the Muratorian Fragment may have contained other works that have been lost in the transmission and translation of the text and that as a result the absence of James and Hebrews from the list is inconclusive.[44]

9. Hahneman and Sundberg state that the plainest meaning of the phrase *nuperrim e(t) temporibus nostris* ("very recently, in our times") (lines 74–75) is that the *Shepherd of Hermas* was written during Pius's episcopacy around 140–54, with the writing of the Muratorian Fragment shortly after that.[45] The problem with this view is the difficulty of dating the Muratorian Fragment this early. Hahneman adds that the best evidence points to the writing of the *Shepherd of Hermas* around 100 and not the middle of the second century. Part of his argument for this date is the widespread support for and use of the *Shepherd of Hermas* in the second through fourth centuries. Irenaeus, for example calls it Scripture (*hē graphē*) in *Haer.* 4.20.2. Eusebius knew this and acknowledged Irenaeus's reception of the *Shepherd of Hermas:* "And he [Irenaeus] not only knew but also received the writing of the Shepherd, saying, 'Well did the Scripture say [*kalōs oun hē graphē hē legousa*] "first of all believe that God is one who created and fitted together all things," and so on.' He also made some quotations all but verbally from the Wisdom of Solomon" (*Hist. eccl.* 5.8.7, LCL). Recognition of the *Shepherd of Hermas* also came from Clement of Alexandria (*Strom.* 1.1.1; 1.85.4; *Ecoligae propheticae* 45), who frequently quoted the *Shepherd of Hermas* in the same manner that he quoted other Scriptures from both the Old and New Testament writings. Tertullian also refers to the work before his conversion to Montanism. The *Shepherd of Hermas* is also included in Codex Sinaiticus and Codex Claromontanus (even though in a secondary position). Eusebius appears to be the first to place the *Shepherd of Hermas* in a disputed category (*Hist. eccl.* 3.3.6), but still recognized that many held it in high esteem (*Hist. eccl.* 5.8.7). Eusebius himself placed it among the "spurious" (*nothos*) books (3.25.1–5). Athanasius called the book "most edifying" (*ōphelimōtatēs*) in his earlier *De incarnatione verbi dei*

---

[44] Hahneman, *Muratorian Fragment,* 25–26; Tregelles, *Canon Muratorianus,* 98.

[45] Hahneman, *Muratorian Fragment,* 71–72; and Sundberg, "Canon Muratori." Verheyden, "Canon Muratori," 512–17, strongly criticizes Sundberg's and Hahneman's arguments, even though he agrees that there is no foolproof way to date the Muratorian Fragment. Verheyden opts for what he calls "circumstantial evidence" to date the Muratorian Fragment to the second century, but he fails to show that it had any parallels in the second century or had any influence on any thinkers of the church for another 150 years. While Verheyden advances our understanding of this difficult text, he has yet to resolve all of the issues related to it, especially why the Wisdom of Solomon shows up in a New Testament catalogue and why the Muratorian Fragment has no parallels until the fourth and fifth centuries.

(ca. 318) but changed his mind by the time of his famous *Thirty-ninth Festal Letter* (339).[46] Both Jerome (*Prologue to Kings [Prologus Galestus]; Illustrious Men* 10) and Rufinus (*Commentary on the Apostolic Creed* 38) spoke respectfully of the book, even though they placed it in a secondary position, that is, not as a part of the NT canon.[47] The relegation of the *Shepherd of Hermas* to a secondary position, or its outright rejection as sacred literature, as we see in the Muratorian Fragment lines 73–78, is most likely a fourth-century development and not a second-century position.

On the whole, Sundberg's and especially Hahneman's arguments carry the day. Since there are no parallels to the Muratorian Fragment until after Eusebius, the document should probably be dated some time after the mid-fourth century in the East—though we cannot insist on that.[48] Although von Campenhausen's, Ferguson's, and Metzger's arguments are significant, and their discussion of the Muratorian Fragment very important, it is not as clear, as they assume, that the Catholic Epistles listed in the Muratorian Fragment were accepted by the majority of churches at the end of the second century or that the *Shepherd of Hermas* was rejected at that time. Conversely, there is no widespread support for the scriptural status and authority of the Pastoral Epistles—which are mentioned in the Muratorian Fragment—in the churches at the end of the second century. Likewise the inclusion of 2 and 3 John and Jude, which are *disputed* in Eusebius in the early fourth century (*Hist. eccl.* 3.25), is strange if the Muratorian Fragment is second century. They are fully accepted only in the last half of the fourth century.

The Muratorian Fragment is an important document for understanding the growth and development of the NT canon of the early Christian church, but it is not as pivotal a document as many scholars once thought. If von Campenhausen and others are correct about the early dating of this document, it had no effect on the rest of the church for almost 150 years and is not referred to anywhere in the ancient church. As a late-second-century document, the Muratorian Fragment's impact on the churches of that time is completely negligible and therefore cannot be of any consequence in piecing together the rather complicated puzzle of the formation of the Christian Bible. As a fourth-century document, however, its existence is far more understandable and allows us to see the concerns and criteria of the church of that era in establishing its canon of Scriptures.

---

[46] Hahneman, *Muratorian Fragment,* 61–69.

[47] Ibid., 68–69.

[48] The discovery of the Muratorian Fragment in the West, despite its Greek origins, and the lateness of its translation into Latin, suggests the possibility of a Western origin, but again, the nature of the list itself appears to be Eastern, as well as many of the peculiarities within it. For a recent statement of this argument, see Hahneman, "Muratorian Fragment."

E. ATHANASIUS OF ALEXANDRIA (CA. 296–373)

The most famous of the lists of NT canonical Scriptures that eventually carried the day is Athanasius's *Thirty-ninth Festal Letter* from Alexandria, which corresponds to the twenty-seven books of the NT acknowledged in the church today. The Council of Nicea (325) settled the issue of when to celebrate Easter and appointed Athanasius to announce to his fellow bishops each year the date of the following Easter, which he did regularly from 328 to 373 in the form of a *Festal Letter* in which he would also include remarks about important matters. In his *Thirty-ninth Festal Letter* he dealt with the canons of the Old and New Testament:[49]

> Since, however, I have spoken of the heretics as dead but of ourselves as possessors of the divine writings unto salvation, I am actually afraid lest in any way, as Paul said in writing to the Corinthians, a few of the undefiled may be led astray from the simplicity and purity by the craftiness of certain men and thereafter begin to pay attention to other books, the so-called sacred (books). Therefore, because of fear of you being deceived by these books possessing the same names as the genuine books, and because of the present stress of the Church, I exhort you to bear with me for your own benefit as I actually make mention of these heretical writings, which you already know about.
>
> As I am about to mention these matters, I will back up my venturesomeness by following the example of the evangelist Luke. And I will also will say that since certain men have attempted to arrange for themselves the so-called secret writings and to mingle them with the God-inspired Scripture, concerning which we have been fully informed even as they were handed down to our fathers by those who were eyewitnesses and servants of the word from the beginning, having been encouraged by true brethren and learning all from the beginning, I also resolved to set forth in order the writings that are in the list and handed down and believed to be divine. I have done this so that each person, if he has been deceived, may condemn those who led him astray, and that he who has remained stainless may rejoice, being again reminded of the truth.
>
> There are then of the Old Testament books . . . [omitted here]
>
> Those of the New Testament I must not shrink from mentioning in their turn. They are these: Four Gospels, according to Matthew, according to Mark, according to Luke, and according to John.
>
> Then after these are Acts of the Apostles and the seven letters of the Apostles called the "Catholic" letters, which are as follows: one from James, two from Peter, three from John, and after these one from Jude.
>
> In addition, there are fourteen letters of Paul the apostle, written in the following order: the first to the Romans, then two to the Corinthians, and thereafter

---

[49] This background information from F. F. Bruce, *Canon of Scripture,* 77–78.

one to the Galatians, one to the Ephesians, one to the Philippians, one to the Colossians, two to the Thessalonians, one to the Hebrews, and, without a break, two letters to Timothy, one to Titus, and one written to Philemon. Last, from John again comes the Revelation.

These are springs of salvation, so that he that is thirsty may be filled with the (divine) responses in them; in these alone is the good news of the teaching of true religion proclaimed; let no one add to them or take away aught of them. It was in regard to these that the Lord was ashamed of the Sadducees, saying: "You are being led astray, since you do not know the scripture," and he exhorted the Jews, saying, "Search the scriptures, for they are the very writings that witness concerning me."

But for the sake of being more exact in detail, I also add this admonition, writing out of necessity, that there are also other books apart from these that are not indeed in the above list, but were produced by our ancestors to be read by those who are just coming forward to receive oral instruction in the word of true religion. These include the Wisdom of Solomon, the Wisdom of Sirach, Esther, Judith, Tobias, the so-called Teaching of the Apostles, and the Shepherd.

And nevertheless, beloved, though the former writings be in the list [or "are listed," *kanonizomenōn*] and the latter are read, nowhere is there mention of the secret writings (the Apocrypha). They are, rather, a device of heretics, who write them when they will be furnishing them with dates and adding them, in order that by bringing them forth as ancient books they may thus have an excuse for deceiving the undefiled. (Adapted from Schneemelcher, "General Introduction," 59–60, and Souter, *Text and Canon,* 196–200)

Athanasius was probably the first to use the term *canon* (*kanōn*) in reference to a closed body of sacred literature, and he also appears to be the first to list the twenty-seven books of our current NT canon.[50] One should not conclude from the use of the verb *kanonizomenōn* ("canonized" or "listed") in Athanasius's letter that all subsequent church leaders agreed fully with Athanasius's canon. He unhesitatingly accepted the book of Revelation as a part of his biblical canon, but several other churches in the East did not follow his example. Cyril of Jerusalem and Gregory of Nazianzus left it out,[51] and even today the Greek Orthodox lectionary does not include readings

[50]Kümmel, *Introduction to the New Testament,* 350, agrees with this claim. This conclusion depends, however, on how early one dates Amphilochius's writing (see §1G below). Some scholars claim that Eusebius was the first to use the term in relation to sacred literature in his discussion of Clement of Alexandria: "In the first of his [Commentaries] on the Gospel according to Matthew, defending the canon [*kanona*] of the Church, he gives his testimony that he knows only four Gospels" (*Hist. eccl.* 6.25.3, LCL). It is not certain, however, that Eusebius's use of the term *kanona* has to do with a collection of writings; it may refer to the faith of the church.

[51]F. F. Bruce, *Canon of Scripture,* 213.

from Revelation.[52] While the canon set forth by Athanasius ultimately prevailed in the majority of the churches in succeeding centuries, there is no evidence that it had much impact on all of the churches of his day or even on those of his own region of Egypt. Not until almost seven hundred years later was the book of Revelation universally accepted into the canon.

F. CYRIL OF JERUSALEM (CA. 315–386)

Cyril gave a list of Scriptures similar to that of Athanasius, only he excluded Revelation:

> But the four Gospels alone belong to the New Testament; the rest happens to be pseudepigrapha and harmful. The Manicheans also wrote [the] Gospel according to Thomas, which indeed, having been camouflaged by the sweetness of its title derived from an evangelist, corrupts the souls of the simpler ones. But accept also the Acts of the twelve Apostles. In addition to these [accept] the seven Catholic Epistles: [the one] of James and [the two] of Peter and [the three] of John and [the one] of Jude; and accept lastly as the seal of all, even of the disciples, the fourteen Epistles of Paul. Let all the rest, however, be placed in secondary [rank]. And those which are not read in the Church, do not even read them privately as you have heard, "So much" then about these. (Cyrillus, *Catechetical Lectures* 4.36, Theron, *Evidence of Tradition,* 177)

G. OTHER RELATED LISTS

Bishop Amphilochius of Iconium (after 394) appears to have accepted all of the books in Athanasius's canon except Revelation (which he called spurious), though he also raised doubt about Hebrews and the Catholic Epistles, questioning whether there should be seven or three letters in this grouping.[53] He appears to be the second person to use the term *canon* (*kanon*) in reference to a list of Christian Scriptures.[54] Further examples of differences of opinion about what comprised the NT canon are Chrysostom (407) who never alluded to Revelation or to the last four Catholic Epistles, and the *Apostolic Constitutions* (no earlier than the fourth century), which added to Athanasius's list *1–2 Clement* and the eight books of the *Constitutions* themselves, but omitted Revelation.[55] In the late fourth and early fifth centuries, some Eastern churches rejected Revelation, even though they appear to have been in substantial agreement regarding most of the other

---

[52] Ibid., 215.

[53] See Theron, *Evidence of Tradition,* 117.

[54] After listing his books, Amphilochius concludes, "This is perhaps the most faithful [lit., "unfalsified"] canon [*kanōn*] of the divinely inspired scriptures." The use of the optative with the particle *an* suggests both an element of doubt and a statement of what he hopes will obtain in the churches. See Grosheide, *Some Early Lists,* 20.

[55] Metzger, *Canon of the New Testament,* 214–15.

Christian literature in Athanasius's canon. Dionysius of Alexandria (ca. 230) accepted Revelation as authoritative Scripture, but did not believe that the Apostle John had written it. He made one of the earliest critical assessments of the text, noting that the vocabulary and style of Revelation were not John's:

> In a word, it is obvious that those who observe their character throughout will see at a glance that the Gospel [John] and Epistle [1 John] have one and the same complexion. But the Apocalypse is utterly different from, and foreign to, these writings; it has no connexion, no affinity, in any way with them; it scarcely, so to speak, has even a syllable in common with them. Nay more, neither does the Epistle (not to speak of the Gospel) contain any mention or thought of the Apocalypse, nor the Apocalypse of the Epistle, whereas Paul in his epistles gave us a little light also on his revelations, which he did not record separately.
>
> And further, by means of the style one can estimate the difference between the Gospel and Epistle and the Apocalypse. For the former are not only written in faultless Greek, but also show the greatest literary skill in their diction, their reasonings, and the constructions in which they are expressed. There is a complete absence of any barbarous word, or solecism, or any vulgarism whatever. For their author had, as it seems, both kinds of word, by the free gift of the Lord, the word of knowledge and the word of speech. But I will not deny that the other writer had seen revelations and received knowledge and prophecy; nevertheless I observe his style and that his use of the Greek language is not accurate, but that he employs barbarous idioms, in some places committing downright solecisms. These there is no necessity to single out now. For I have not said these things in mockery (let no one think it), but merely to establish the dissimilarity of these writings. (*Hist. eccl.* 7.25.22–27, LCL)

Koester observes that Revelation is absent from many of the Greek manuscripts of the NT literature.[56] This may well have had to do as much with the uncertainty over who wrote the book, as Dionysius shows, as with the actual contents of the book.

Still further, several ancient biblical manuscripts include early noncanonical Christian writings.[57] For example, Codex Claramontanus, a bilingual Greek-Latin manuscript dating to the fifth-sixth century, includes *Shepherd of Hermas, Acts of Paul,* and *Revelation of Peter.* Codex Alexandrinus (fifth century) contains *1–2 Clement.* Codex Constantinopolitanus (eleventh century) includes *1–2 Clement, Barnabas, Didache,* and an interpolated text of the letters of Ignatius. *Barnabas* and *Shepherd of Hermas* are also included in the fourth-century Codex Sinaiticus. In fact, *Barnabas* became canonical literature in some circles, was quoted by Clement of Alexandria as Scripture, and was even called a "Catholic Epistle" by Origen.[58]

---

[56] Koester, *Introduction to the New Testament,* 2:256.

[57] See discussion of these ancient manuscripts in ibid., 2:11.

[58] See Lake, *Apostolic Fathers,* 1.339.

H. SUMMARY OF LISTS

Other ancient canonical lists could be mentioned, but enough has been shown to argue reasonably that the notion of a closed NT canon was not a second-century development in the early church and that there were still considerable differences of opinion about what should comprise that canon even in the fourth and fifth centuries. There was never a time in the fourth or fifth centuries, however, when the *whole* church adopted as Scripture all of the twenty-seven books of the NT and those books alone. The four canonical Gospels, for example, were set aside in the Syrian churches in favor of Tatian's *Diatessaron* until after approximately 400. Many Christians continued to reject *in practice* parts of the greater church's canon long after there was a general recognition of it.[59]

Only during the Reformation did the Catholics achieve unity on the NT canon with the decree by the Council of Trent, but by that time Luther had already denied full canonical status to James, Hebrews, Jude, and Revelation, not to mention the deuterocanonical books (the Apocrypha). The Protestants have affirmed, with Luther, the shorter OT canon, while the Eastern Orthodox has a larger canon than the Roman Catholics. Quite apart from these traditional church communions, the Ethiopian church, which traces its roots to the fourth-century church, claims a canon of some eighty-one books.[60] At no time in history has the whole church agreed completely on what literature should make up its canon of Scriptures. There has been, however, general agreement—but not unanimity—since the third century regarding the authoritative, or scriptural, status of the four Gospels, Acts, Paul's Epistles, 1 Peter, and 1 John. The rest of the NT canon appears to have been decided in various councils based perhaps on wide church use,

---

[59] Aland, *Problem of the New Testament Canon,* 12, gives the example of Cassiodorus (ca. 550), who could not obtain a Western commentary on Hebrews and therefore had the one by Chrysostom translated from Greek. Aland also cites the case of the Spanish synods around 600, which were still fighting against those who rejected Revelation.

[60] Kealy, "Canon," 17–19, notes that the Ethiopian canon contains forty-six OT books and thirty-five NT books and claims that this canon of Scriptures was carried by Christian missionaries to Ethiopia in 330. Metzger, *Canon of the New Testament,* 227, lists the Ethiopian NT collection as follows: the four Gospels, Acts, the seven Catholic Epistles, fourteen Epistles of Paul (Hebrews included), Revelation, *Sinodos* (four sections), Ethiopian *Clement* (which is different from *1 Clement*). *Book of the Covenant* (two sections), and *Didascalia.* When the canon was subsequently settled in other parts of the church, the Ethiopian community of Christians was isolated from the rest of the Christian world because of the Islamic conquests especially in the seventh century and for nine centuries did not know of the canonical decisions by the rest of the churches. Hence, they have a much larger canon, which may represent a much older tradition than does the present biblical canon. See also Cowley, "Biblical Canon."

but within individual churches, reservations continued to linger about "doubted" books in the NT canon.

One result of this examination of lists and their many variations must be to raise the question of whether the church was correct in perceiving the need of a closed canon since historically it has never completely agreed on what must go into the canon of Scriptures. Even the criteria that the church used to define its Scripture and canon are somewhat vague and imprecise (see chapter 14). If the earliest Christians intended for the church that followed them to have a closed canon of Scriptures, no clear tradition from them makes that clear.

The historical context of the fourth and fifth centuries, however, may be the major key in understanding why the church began to try to close its canon of Scriptures. The theological controversies (Marcionism, Gnosticism, Montanism) of the second and third centuries no doubt gave an initial impetus to the church to define more precisely what was believed to be Christian. At the very moment when the church began to reject some writings, the final stages of canonization started. The era of conformity that characterized the reign of Constantine and the Roman world probably gave the church a major push toward the conformity and unity that it also desired. The subsequent development of a closed biblical canon of authoritative Scriptures and the exclusion (and in some cases destruction) of all other Christian writings surely helped to secure this unity.

II. Early Citations, Parallels, and Allusions to New Testament Writings

Without question, the NT books most widely quoted or cited by the church fathers are the canonical Gospels and the Letters of Paul. In time, other literature began to be cited by the church fathers and to find their way into the surviving manuscripts of the NT literature. The following survey demonstrates the use of the twenty-seven NT books by the church fathers.

A. GOSPELS

1. Matthew

Matthew was by far the most quoted gospel in the early church (except in Asia Minor). Apparent similarities between the language found in Matthew and other early Christian writings may, however, reflect a common oral tradition rather than dependency upon Matthew's Gospel itself.

The earliest parallels to sayings found in Matthew's Gospel come from Ignatius in the early second century (e.g., Ign. *Smyrn.* 1.1 and Matt 3:15;

Ign. *Eph.* 19.1–3 and Matt 2:1–12; Ign. *Pol.* 2.2 and Matt 10:16). These are not attributed to Matthew, but essentially refer to words found in Matthew. While some scholars believe that there is clear dependence, others suggest a common oral tradition behind both. It is likely that when Ignatius speaks of "the gospel" (Ign. *Phld.* 5.1–2; 8.2) he has in mind the Gospel of Matthew. The assumption here is that since Ignatius cites Matthew's Jesus as authoritative, then Matthew itself was viewed as a reliable source for the teaching of Jesus.

Polycarp refers to the words of Jesus in Matthew (Pol. *Phil.* 2.3 and Matt 7:1–2 and 5:3, 10; Pol. *Phil.* 7.2 and Matt 26:41; Pol. *Phil.* 12.3 and Matt 5.44).

Similar or common language and subject matter is found in *1 Clement* (*1 Clem.* 7.7 and Matt 12:41; *1 Clem.* 13.2 and Matt 5:7 and 6:14–15; *1 Clem.* 46.7–9 and Matt 26:24 and 18:6) and *2 Clement* (*2 Clem.* 2.4 and Matt 9:13; *2 Clem.* 3.2 and Matt 10:32; *2 Clem.* 3.5 and Matt 15:8; *2 Clem.* 4.1 and Matt 7:21; *2 Clem.* 6.1 and Matt 6:24 and 16:26).

Papias (ca. 130) refers to Matthew as the author of a collection of "oracles" or sayings (Eusebius, *Hist. eccl.* 3.39.16).

The *Didache* (late first century) has some language parallels with Matthew (*Did.* 1.2–3 and Matt 7:12 and 5:44–47; *Did.* 3.7 and Matt 5:5; *Did.* 8.1–3 and Matt 6:5–16).

Barnabas (ca. 130–140) has parallels in wording with Matthew (*Barn.* 4.14 and Matt 22:14; *Barn.* 7.3–5 and Matt 27:34, 48).

2. Mark

Mark was known by name from the time of Papias but was not used as much as Matthew and Luke. Justin Martyr (*Dial.* 106.2–3) points to a passage in Mark and refers to it as "Memoirs" from Peter. Clement of Alexandria has the first clear quotations from Mark in his *Paedagogus* 1.2 and *Strom.* 6.14 (citing Mark 8:36). Irenaeus (*Haer.* 3.14.3) cites Mark by name and quotes Mark 1:1. Papias is the first known person to refer to the Gospel of Mark by name, and he refers to it before he speaks of Matthew, which may indicate Papias's view of which gospel was produced first (Eusebius, *Hist. eccl.* 3.39.14–16). The Apostolic Fathers also refer to Mark (*1 Clem.* 24.5 and Mark 4:3; *1 Clem.* 46.7–9 and Mark 14:21 and 9:42; *Barn.* 5.9 and Mark 2:17).

3. Luke

Marcion (ca. 140) edited the Gospel of Luke for his own purposes, as attested in the late-second-century *Anti-Marcionite Gospel Prologues.* Language from Luke is similar to that found in the Apostolic Fathers, though the gospel itself is not cited by name (e.g., *1 Clem.* 46.7–9 and Luke 17.2; *1 Clem.* 48.4 and Luke 1:75; *2 Clem.* 6.1 and Luke 6:24; *2 Clem.* 8.5 and Luke 16:10–12; *2 Clem.* 13.4 and Luke 6:32, 35; *Did.* 1.4 and Luke 6:29; *Barn.* 14.9 and Luke 4:17–19). The evidence of Luke as a separate writing is first discussed by Irenaeus (ca. 170–80, as reported in Eusebius, *Hist. eccl.* 5.8.3).

4. John

As with the other Gospels, there are some parallels between the language of John and the Apostolic Fathers. There are some similarities between John 3:5 and the *Herm. Sim.* 9.15.2 and 9.16.2. Both *Gospel of Philip* and *Testimony of Truth* in the Nag Hammadi gnostic collection make use of John. John was used by Tatian in his *Diatessaron* (ca. 170). Irenaeus, originally from Asia, where John was the most popular gospel, argued for a four-gospel canon, probably to insure the continued use of John in the churches (*Haer.* 3.1.1).[61]

B. ACTS

References to the book of Acts are rather vague until the time of Justin Martyr (155–60). Some argue that the Pastoral Epistles made use of Acts, but this is highly unlikely. The similar topics found in Acts and the Pastorals—ordination, the laying on of hands, the institution of elders by Paul, Timothy's family (Acts 16:1–3; 2 Tim 1:5), and Paul's ministry in Lystra, Iconium, and Derbe (Acts 14:1–20; 16:1; 2 Tim 3:11)—do not necessarily involve dependence. The similarities could easily be the result of tradition held in common, and since there are no exact word parallels the strength of the case for dependence is not convincing. Parallels in content between Acts and other late-first-century and second-century documents probably demonstrate a common oral or written tradition:

1 Clem. 2.1 and Acts 20:35
1 Clem. 2.2 and Acts 2:17
1 Clem. 18.1 and Acts 13:22
1 Clem. 59.2 and Acts 26:18
2 Clem. 4.4 and Acts 5:29
2 Clem. 20.5 and Acts 3:15 and 5:31
Pol. *Phil.* 1.2 and Acts 2:24
Pol. *Phil.* 2.3 and Acts 20:35
Pol. *Phil.* 6.3 and Acts 7:52
Pol. *Phil.* 12.2 and Acts 2:5; 4:12; 8:31; and 20:32
Did. 1.5 and Acts 20:35
Did. 4.8 and Acts 4:32
Barn. 7.2 and Acts 10:42
Barn. 19.8 and Acts 4:32
Herm. *Sim.* 9.28.2 and Acts 5:41; 9:16; and 15:26

There are other parallels with Acts 20:17–38 with Ign. *Eph.* 12.1–2, *Diogn.* 3.4, and *Epistula Apostolorum,* but we have no clear evidence of

[61] See also Eusebius, *Hist. eccl.* 5.8.2–4 and the witness of Clement of Alexandria and Origen preserved in Eusebius, *Hist. eccl.* 6.14.5–7 and 6.25.3–6.

dependence. Justin shows awareness of Luke as a written source (e.g., *1 Apol.* 50.12), but he does not refer to Acts as either Scripture or an authoritative source (cf. *1 Apol.* 39.3 and Acts 4:13; *1 Apol.* 49.5 and Acts 13:48; *2 Apol.* 10.6 and Acts 17:23), even though Justin's argument regarding unclean foods (*Dial.* 20.3–4) could have been enhanced by an appeal to Acts 10:14 or 15:29.

While the *Martyrs of Lyons and Vienne* (preserved in *Hist. eccl.* 5.2.5) has impressive word parallels with Acts that strongly suggests dependence, Irenaeus is the first clear source to appeal to Acts in an authoritative manner (e.g., *Haer.* 1.26.3 and Acts 6:1–6; *Haer.* 3.12.1 and Acts 1:16–17; *Haer.* 4.23.2 and Acts 8). In his many cases of clear dependence, Irenaeus views Acts as an authoritative source for substantiating his arguments against heresy in the church. In other words, he uses Acts in a Scripture-like manner. In the second century, Acts is not yet cited as Scripture or found in any collections of sacred literature. Appeals to the book, however, continued on in the third century and even increased.

Tertullian makes considerable use of Acts in his arguments against what he considered heresy (*Marc.* 5.1–2 and *Praescr.* 22). The author of the *Acts of Paul* (ca. 197) also refers to Acts, and there are word parallels in the *Anti-Marcionite Gospel Prologues* (ca. late second century). In the fourth century, Eusebius has no hesitation in placing the book in the collection of "recognized" (*homologoumena*) books (*Hist. eccl.* 3.25.1; cf. 3.4.1, where he acknowledges that Luke is the author of the Acts). Elsewhere Eusebius cites Acts as a historical source (*Hist. eccl.* 2.22.1, 6–7, etc.), and he is the earliest writer to include it in a list of Scriptures (*Hist. eccl.* 3.4.6).

In several lists of canonical Scriptures, Acts does *not* serve as a bridge to the Epistles (Mommsen or Cheltenham Catalogue of ca. 360; Clermont ca. 303); and in Cyril of Jerusalem (*Catechetical Lectures* 4.33) and Athanasius (*Thirty-ninth Festal Letter*) Acts is placed between the Gospels and the Catholic Epistles, which is then followed by the Pauline collection. In Epiphanius (*Pan.* 76.5), Acts comes between the Pauline Epistles and the Catholic Epistles. Pope Innocent placed Acts after all the Epistles and before Revelation. In the Mommsen Catalogue, Luke stands last in the collection, which may be evidence of an earlier time when Luke and Acts were not separated. Rather than use Acts, Marcion may have substituted his own *Antitheses*. At any rate, it is clear that Luke and Acts were separated by the time of Marcion (ca. 140). There was apparently no time in the second-century church when the two volumes circulated together, and it must be concluded that they circulated separately before the end of the first century.

C. PAUL'S WRITINGS

The writings of Paul have early attestation in the Christian community and were very influential in many churches during the second century. Romans and 1 Corinthians are clearly known to Clement of Rome, who wrote *1 Clement* (ca. 95), and as churches circulated letters of Paul to each other, other letters attributed to Paul became attached to them. Initially the Pastorals and Philemon were not included in the collection, but eventually thirteen letters plus Hebrews were all attributed to Paul. The following lists are illustrative of the parallels between Paul's Letters and the writings of the early church fathers.[62] Some of the parallels show obvious dependence, but others may simply be a shared common tradition in the church. The following evidence shows that Romans, 1 Corinthians, and Ephesians are cited more frequently in the early church than Paul's other letters, and this does not change significantly in the rest of the second century.

1. Romans

One of the oldest and most influential commentaries on Paul's Letter to the Romans was written by Origen (185–254). This extensive commentary (i.e., fifteen volumes) was translated into Latin around 400 by Rufinus, who abbreviated the work into ten volumes. Early references to the book of Romans include the following:

Rom 1:3–4 has parallels in word and thought with Ign. *Smyrn.* 1.1.
Rom 1:21 has parallels in thought with *1 Clem.* 36.2.
Rom 1:29–32 has such close parallels with *1 Clem.* 35.5–6 that it is certain that Clement was familiar with Paul's letter.
Rom 3:21–26 appears to be behind *Diogn.* 9.1.
Rom 4:3, 10, 17–18 has parallels in *Barn.* 13.7.
Rom 4:7–9 is similar to *1 Clem.* 50.6–7 in terms of the blessing mentioned at the beginning of the quotation from Ps 32:1–2.
Rom 6:1 is similar in word and thought to *1 Clem.* 33.1.
Rom 6:4 is similar to Ign. *Eph.* 19.3.
Rom 8:5, 8 is similar to Ign. *Eph.* 8.2.
Rom 8:32 has parallel language in *Diogn.* 9.2.
Rom 9:5 is very similar to *1 Clem.* 32.2.
Rom 9:7–13 has parallels in *Barn.* 13.2–3, even if the latter uses it differently than does Paul.
Rom 12:4 has parallel words and thought with *1 Clem.* 38.1.
Rom 12:10 is similar in thought to Pol. *Phil.* 10.1.
Rom 14:10, 12 has several verbal parallels with Pol. *Phil.* 6.2.

2. 1 Corinthians

1 Cor 1:11–13 is the same in thought as *1 Clem.* 47.1–3, and dependence seems obvious.

---

[62] Much of what follows was gleaned from Oxford Society of Historical Theology's *New Testament in the Apostolic Fathers,* supplemented by more recent materials.

1 Cor 1:18, 20 is similar in word and thought to Ign. *Eph.* 18.1.
1 Cor 2:9 is similar in word and thought to *1 Clem.* 34.8.
1 Cor 2:10 is close to *1 Clem.* 40.1 and Ign. *Phld.* 7.1.
1 Cor 3:1, 16, 18–20 has several parallels in word and notion with *Barn.* 4.11.
1 Cor 4:1 has some word parallels with Ign. *Trall.* 2.3, but dependence is difficult to prove.
1 Cor 4:4 has close word and thought parallels with Ign. *Rom.* 5.1.
1 Cor 4:12 may be quoted in *Diogn.* 5.15.
1 Cor 5:7 is close in word to Ign. *Magn.* 10.2.
1 Cor 6:2 has word parallels with Pol. *Phil.* 11.2.
1 Cor 6:9–10 has very close word parallels with Pol. *Phil.* 5.3 and Ign. *Eph.* 16.1.
1 Cor 6:15 is similar in thought to *1 Clem.* 46.7.
1 Cor 7:22 is similar in word to Ign. *Rom.* 4.3 (cf. 1 Cor 9:1).
1 Cor 7:39–40 has several close word and thought parallels with *Herm. Mand.* 4.4.1–2.
1 Cor 8:1 is clearly cited in *Diogn.* 12.5.
1 Cor 9:15 is close to Ign. *Rom.* 6.1.
1 Cor 9:17 has word parallels in *Diogn.* 7.1.
1 Cor 9:24 and *1 Clem.* 5.1, 5 may be parallel.
1 Cor 10:16–17 is similar to Ign. *Phld.* 4.1.
1 Cor 10:24, 33 is similar to *1 Clem.* 48.6.
1 Cor 12:8–9 is similar to *1 Clem.* 48.5, perhaps suggesting dependence
1 Cor 12:12–26 has clear parallels with *1 Clem.* 37.5 and 38.1, and dependence seems obvious.
1 Cor 12:26 is similar to Pol. *Phil.* 11.4.
1 Cor 13:4–7 has parallels in *1 Clem.* 49.5, and dependence seems clear.
1 Cor 15:20 and *1 Clem.* 24.1 both speak of firstfruits.
1 Cor 15:23 has an exact correspondence with *1 Clem.* 37.3.
1 Cor 15:28 is similar to Pol. *Phil.* 2.1.
1 Cor 15:36–37 has several parallels in thought and word with *1 Clem.* 24.4–5.
1 Cor 16:17 is similar in thought to *1 Clem.* 38.2.

3. 2 Corinthians

2 Cor 3:18 is similar to *1 Clem.* 36.2.
2 Cor 4:14 has verbal parallels with Pol. *Phil.* 2.2.
2 Cor 5:10 has parallels in word and substance with *Barn.* 4.11–14 and Pol. *Phil.* 6.2.
2 Cor 6:9–10 appears to be cited in *Diogn.* 5.12–16.
2 Cor 6:16 has a close parallel with Ign. *Eph.* 15.3.
2 Cor 10:3 has word parallels in *Diogn.* 5.8.

4. *Galatians*

Galatians is alluded to or cited several times in both the Apostolic Fathers and in several other second and third century church fathers.

Gal 1:1 is very similar to Ign. *Phld.* 1.1.
Gal 2:9 is similar to *1 Clem.* 5.2.
Gal 2:21 has clear word parallels with Ign. *Trall.* 10.1.
Gal 3:1 is similar to *1 Clem.* 2.1, but the coincidence is not certain.
Gal 4:26 and Pol. *Phil.* 3.3 share a metaphor.
Gal 5:11 has clear word parallels with Ign. *Eph.* 18.1.
Gal 5:17 is similar in wording and thought to Pol. *Phil.* 5.3 and *Diogn.* 6.5.
Gal 5:21 has clear word parallels with Ign. *Eph.* 16.1.
Gal 6:2 has a parallel thought in *Diogn.* 10.6.
Gal 6:7 has verbal and thought parallels with Pol. *Phil.* 5.1.
Gal 6:14 has clear word parallels with Ign. *Rom.* 7.2.

5. *Ephesians*

Ephesians was included in Marcion's collection of ten Pauline Letters, possibly as the Letter to the Laodiceans, and was widely believed to have been addressed to the Ephesian church. It was cited by Irenaeus (e.g., *Haer.* 1.3.1, 4; 1.8.4; 5.2.36), Clement of Alexandria (*Strom.* 4.65), and Origen (*Against Celsus* 3.20). It was cited frequently in the Apostolic Fathers and in subsequent church fathers.

Eph 1:4–6 has parallels with *Barn.* 3.6, especially the notion of what is found and possessed "in the beloved."
Eph 1:18 has word parallels with *1 Clem.* 59.3 (cf. *1 Clem.* 36.2).
Eph 2:8–9 has several verbal parallels with Pol. *Phil.* 1.3.
Eph 2:10 has parallels in *Barn.* 6.11.
Eph 2:16 has exact word parallels with Ign. *Smyrn.* 1.1.
Eph 2:20–22 has similar words and thoughts with Ign. *Eph.* 9.1 and *Barn.* 6.11.
Eph 3:17 has parallels in *Barn.* 6.11.
Eph 4:3–6 is close in word and thought to *Herm. Sim.* 9.13.5 and *1 Clem.* 46.6–7, but because of the popularity of these words in the first and second centuries, it is not possible to tell dependence.
Eph 4:18 is similar to *1 Clem.* 36.2 and 51.5.
Eph 4:22–24 has parallels in *Barn.* 6.11.
Eph 4:25–30 has several parallels in word and thought with *Herm. Mand.* 10.2.1–6, although the *Shepherd of Hermas* develops the thought in his own way.

Eph 4:26 is quite similar to Pol. *Phil.* 12.1.
Eph 5:1 is similar to Ign. *Eph.* 1.1.
Eph 5:5 is quite similar to Pol. *Phil.* 11.2.
Eph 5:16 has word parallels with *Barn.* 2.1 that are close enough to suggest dependence.
Eph 5:25 has several parallels in word and thought with Ign. *Pol.* 5.1.
Eph 6:18 is similar in thought to Pol. *Phil.* 12.3.

6. Philippians

Philippians was influential in the early church among the orthodox and heretics alike. It was in the collection of Marcion (see Hippolytus, *Refutation of all Heresies* 5.143; 10.318), and Phil 2:6–7 was cited by the Sethians, an Orphite sect of the second century. Philippians is referred to by *1 Clement,* Ignatius, and *Diognetus.* At the close of the second century, it was used by Irenaeus (*Haer.* 4.18.4), Clement of Alexandria (*Christ the Educator* 1.524; *Strom.* 4.12, 19, 94), and Tertullian (*Resurrection of the Flesh* 23; *Against Marcion* 5.20; *Praescr.* 26). Eusebius says that the *Martyrs of Lyons and Vienne* also cited Phil 2:6–7 (*Hist. eccl.* 5.2.2). References or allusions in the Apostolic Fathers include the following:

Phil 1:27 is close in thought and word to *1 Clem.* 3.4, but no clear dependence can be shown.
Phil 2:10 is similar in both word and thought to Pol. *Phil.* 2.1 (cf. Phil 3:21).
Phil 2:17 has several verbal parallels with Pol. *Phil.* 1.1, but they are not strong enough to demonstrate dependence.
Phil 3:15 has several important words and thoughts that are parallel with Ign. *Smyrn.* 11.3.
Phil 3:18 has similar thoughts as Pol. *Phil.* 12.3.
Phil 4:13 has close word parallels with Ign. *Smyrn.* 4.2.

7. Colossians

Colossians has early attestation among the second-century church fathers, including Justin (*Dial.* 85.2; 138.2), Irenaeus (*Haer.* 3.14.1), Tertullian (*Praescr.* 7), and Clement of Alexandria (*Strom.* 1.1). In other words, there was not much doubt about receiving this book in the early church as a letter from Paul. Marcion also accepted it as a part of his collection of writings. References or allusions in the Apostolic Fathers are as follows:

Col 1:16–20 is similar to *Barn.* 12.7.
Col 1:23 has verbal parallels with Pol. *Phil.* 10.1.

There are several other word parallels between Ignatius's writings and Colossians, but none suggest direct dependence:

Col 1:7 and Ign. *Eph.* 2.1
Col 1:16 and Ign. *Trall.* 5.2
Col 1:18 and Ign. *Smyrn.* 1.2
Col 1:23 and Ign. *Eph.* 10.2
Col 2:2 and Ign. *Eph.* 17.2
Col 2:14 and Ign. *Smyrn.* 1.2
Col 4:7 and Ign. *Eph.* 2.1

8. 1–2 Thessalonians

There is little solid evidence that Ignatius knew 1 Thessalonians. The parallels may have been simply shared oral tradition circulating in the churches. Throughout the rest of the second century there are a few allusions and slight references to these letters. The following are a few parallels in the Apostolic Fathers.

1 Thess 2:4 has word and thought parallels with Ign. *Rom.* 2.1.
1 Thess 5:17 has exact word parallels with Ign. *Eph.* 10.1.
2 Thess 1:4 is similar to Pol. *Phil.* 11.3, which mentions Paul by name.
2 Thess 3:5 has word parallels with Ign. *Rom.* 10.3.
2 Thess 3:15 is quite similar in thought to Pol. *Phil.* 11.4, and dependence is likely.

9. The Pastoral Epistles

The Pastoral Epistles (1–2 Timothy and Titus) are not clearly cited in the church until the late second and early third centuries—and then mostly by Irenaeus.[63] The *Shepherd of Hermas* has some parallel language, but no clear citation of these letters. Some scholars believe that they were written in response to Marcion by someone in the Pauline tradition, that is, in a church founded by Paul that continued as a Christian community largely in ways set out by Paul in his letters. The Pastoral Epistles have parallels in some of the Apostolic Fathers, but clear dependence is difficult to establish. Often some of the same thoughts or words were circulating in the broader church and may simply reflect the use of widely known views in the early church. The Pastoral Epistles were not, according to Tertullian (*Marc.* 5.21), a part of Marcion's collection of Paul's Letters.[64] Marshall

[63] For a useful introduction, see Wall, "Function of the Pastoral Epistles."

[64] "To this epistle [Philemon] alone did its brevity avail to protect it against the falsifying hands of Marcion. I wonder, however, when he received (into his *Apostolicon*) this letter which was written but to one man, that he rejected the two epistles to Timothy and the one to Titus, which all treat of ecclesiastical discipline. His aim, was, I suppose, to carry out his interpolating process even to the number of (St. Paul's) letters" (*Marc.* 3.473–475, *ANF*).

claims that the Pastoral Epistles are cited in Theophilus's *Letter to Autolycum* 3.14,[65] but this passage makes a single allusion to the Pastorals when Theophilus calls upon his readers to lead a life of submission to leaders and to pray for them so that "we may lead a quiet and peaceable life" (2 Tim 2:2). This may be nothing more than a shared oral tradition that has its roots in Paul or others. Similarly, Marshall claims that Athenagoras's *Plea for the Christians* 37.2 "echoes" 1 Tim 2:2 and Titus 3:1, but once again these texts may simply reflect what Paul said in Rom 13:1–7 or elsewhere.[66] Justin (*Dial.* 47.15) uses language similar to Titus 3:4 ("the goodness and loving kindness of God"), but again this may be only a vague echo of something from the *lingua franca* of the day. Marshall also puts forward Irenaeus's *Haer.* preface 1 as evidence of Irenaeus's acceptance of the Pastoral Epistles.[67] Irenaeus's reference to "vain genealogies," however, is only vaguely parallel to "myths and endless genealogies" in 1 Tim 1:4. On the other hand, a clear case can be made for Irenaeus's citing Titus 3:10 in *Haer.* 1.16.3, where he mentions Paul by name (other clear examples of Irenaeus's acceptance and citation of the Pastoral Epistles are *Haer.* 2.14.7 citing 1 Tim 6:20; *Haer.* 3.3.3 referring to 2 Tim 4:21; and *Haer.* 3.14.1 citing 2 Tim 4:10–11). The following examples from the Apostolic Fathers are generally parallel rather than a clear citation.

a. 1 Timothy

1 Tim 1:3–5 has strong thought and word parallels with Ign. *Eph.* 14.1 and 20.1 and Ign. *Magn.* 8.1.

1 Tim 1:15–16 is similar in word and idea to *Barn.* 5.9.

1 Tim 1:17 has several similar words as *2 Clem.* 20.5, but the words are also common Jewish liturgical expressions.

1 Tim 3:8 has similar words and thought parallels with Pol. *Phil.* 5.2.

1 Tim 3:16 has exact wording parallels with *Barn.* 5.6, though the notion may have been a common theme in the oral tradition behind both writings. This same text, which is creedal in formulation, also has a parallel in *Diogn.* 11.3.

1 Tim 5:5 has several word and thought parallels with Pol. *Phil.* 4.3, and dependence is likely.

1 Tim 6:7 (see also 6:10) has several word and thought parallels with Pol. *Phil.* 4.1, and dependence is likely.

b. 2 Timothy

2 Tim 1:10 is quite similar to *Barn.* 5.6.

2 Tim 1:16 has several words that overlap with Ign. *Eph.* 21 and Ign. *Smyrn.* 10.2.

2 Tim 2:3 is similar to Ign. *Pol.* 6.2.

---

[65] Marshall, *Pastoral Epistles,* 5–6.

[66] Ibid., 6.

[67] Ibid., 6.

2 Tim 2:25 has clear word parallels with Pol. *Phil.* 5.2, and dependence is likely, but it is not clear which writer is depending on the other.
2 Tim 4:1 is similar to *Barn.* 7.2; this may reflect a common Christian perspective of faith that was transmitted orally in the second century.
2 Tim 4:10 is similar in word and thought to Pol. *Phil.* 9.2.

c. Titus

Titus 1:2 is similar to *Barn.* 1.3–4, 6 in both word and thought.
Titus 1:14 (cf. 3:9) has parallel thoughts with Ign. *Magn.* 8.1.
Titus 2:4–5 has several corresponding phrases in *1 Clem.* 1.3.
Titus 3:1 is similar to *1 Clem.* 2.7 and 34.4.
Titus 3:5–8 is similar to *Barn* 1.3–4, 6 in both word and thought.

10. Philemon

Philemon 20 has some word parallel with Ign. *Eph.* 2.2, but it is remote that Ignatius knew of Philemon. The apostolic church fathers and the rest of the second-century writers seem to have ignored this little letter.

D. HEBREWS

The canonical status of Hebrews was insured when a second-century editor (possibly Pantaenus, the director of a theological school in Alexandria around 170) incorporated this writing into the Pauline corpus of letters. The book's scriptural status was never questioned after that in Alexandria. Eventually the Syrian churches also agreed that Hebrews was written by Paul, and they received it into their Scripture canon. The book was both known and quoted in the East and West, but that did not mean that the Western churches accepted it as Scripture. Clement of Rome, for example, made obvious use of Hebrews and incorporated its words into his letter without referring to it as Scripture or making any direct reference to the letter or its author (see *1 Clem.* 9.3 and Heb 11:5; *1 Clem.* 10.7 and Heb 11:17; *1 Clem.* 17.1 and Heb 11:37; *1 Clem.* 19.2 and Heb 12:1; and especially *1 Clem.* 36.1–5 and Heb 2:18; 3:1; 1:3–4, 7, 13). Other parallels appear in Justin Martyr (ca. 160) who, like Heb 3:1, strangely refers to Christ as an "apostle" (*1 Apol.* 1.12, 63; see also *Dial.* 34 and Heb 8:7; *Dial.* 13 and Heb 9:13–14; and *Dial.* 67 and Heb 12:18–19).

When Eusebius accepted Hebrews as one of fourteen "obvious and plain" letters by Paul, he conceded that others disputed its authorship and that the church in Rome even denied that Paul had written it (*Hist. eccl.* 3.3.4–5). The authorship of the book was central to its acceptance in the churches.

Clement of Alexandria was the first, according to Eusebius, to say that Paul had written Hebrews, but he claimed that it was originally written in Hebrew and that Luke translated it into Greek and omitted Paul's name so as not to offend the Jewish-Christians who were prejudiced against him (*Hist.*

eccl. 6.14.2–4). Although Origen acknowledged that some accepted Hebrews as Paul's letter, while others attributed it to Clement of Rome or Luke (*Hist. eccl.* 6.25.11–14), he himself held an agnostic position on the authorship of Hebrews. Tertullian later claimed that Barnabas wrote it (*Modesty* 20).

Hebrews had a questionable position in the Peshitta and was placed after the Epistles of Paul, not unlike in the current biblical canon, where its position is somewhat equivocal. Augustine and Jerome had doubts about the authorship of Hebrews, but they nevertheless accepted it as Paul's to insure its inclusion in the biblical canon. Jerome observed that the churches to the West (the "Latins") "do not receive it among the canonical scriptures as St. Paul's" (*Letter to Dardanus* 129). The book was eventually included in many of the Scripture canons of the West at the Synod of Hippo in 393 and at the Third and Sixth Synods of Carthage in 397 and 419.

E. GENERAL EPISTLES

Except for James, 1 Peter, and 1 John, the General Epistles were not widely known in the churches throughout the second century, and they were variously disputed even in the fourth and fifth centuries.[68]

1. James

James had a mixed reception in early Christianity, probably as a result of its apparent contradiction of Paul's teaching on works (cf. Rom 4 and Jas 2). Eusebius classifies the book as one of the disputed writings (*antilegomena*) (*Hist. eccl.* 3.25.1–5), and it is missing from several fourth-century lists of NT books. Clement of Rome apparently knew of the writing in the late first century and balanced the teaching of Paul with that of James on the issue of works and the law. So also *Didache,* Ignatius, *Barnabas,* Polycarp, *Shepherd of Hermas, Diognetus,* and Justin cite or allude to James. Eusebius (*Hist. eccl.* 5.11.5) says that Clement of Alexandria taught directly "from Peter and James and John and Paul" (i.e. their writings). The first person to clearly refer to James as Scripture and claim that it was written by James the brother of Jesus is Origen (*Commentary on John* 19.6; compare *Homilies on Exodus* 15.25). The same views emerge later in Dionysius of Alexandria (ca. 250–265) and in Gregory the Thaumaturge (ca. 250–265).

2. 1 Peter

Although there are several parallel phrases in *Barnabas* and 1 Peter (*Barn.* 5.6 and 1 Pet 1:20), it is only with Polycarp that clear use of 1 Peter is found (e.g., Pol. *Phil.* 1.3 and 1 Pet 1:8; Pol. *Phil.* 10.2 and 1 Pet 2:12). The author of 2 Pet 3:1 (ca. 100–125, or possibly as late as 180) refers to the

[68] For a useful introduction to the canonical inclusion of the Catholic Epistles, see Wall, "Unifying Theology of the Catholic Epistles."

existence of an earlier letter by the Apostle Peter. Eusebius claimed that Papias (ca. 100–150) knew and used 1 Peter (*Hist. eccl.* 3.39.17), and he includes it in the list of the recognized books (3.25.2 and 3.3.1). Irenaeus was the first to use 1 Peter by name (*Haer.* 4.9.2; 4.16.5; 5.7.2), and thereafter many references are made to the book by the early church fathers. Early witnesses validate the use of the book in the church, and it does not appear to have been seriously questioned in the fourth century, even though it is missing in the Muratorian Fragment.

3. 2 Peter

Essentially, 2 Peter was under suspicion in the church until the time of Athanasius's *Thirty-ninth Festal Letter* in 367. Eusebius rejected it (*Hist. eccl.* 3.25.3) and was aware of the widespread doubts about its authenticity (*Hist. eccl.* 3.3.1–4). The Syrian churches appear to have held it in question until the sixth century. It is absent from the recension of Lucian of Antioch, and the most prominent church father from Antioch, John Chrysostom, never referred to it. The same is true of Theodore of Mopsuestia. Athanasius of Alexandria apparently set the stage for the acceptance of 2 Peter in the churches, but it was questioned as late as the Reformation, when Martin Luther concluded that the Christian message did not shine well through it.

4. 1 John

First John was one of the earliest books besides the Gospels and Epistles of Paul to be acknowledged as Scripture and subsequently as a part of the Christian canon. Both Eusebius (*Hist. eccl.* 3.24.17) and Origen (Eusebius, *Hist. eccl.* 6.25.10) accepted it as a part of their sacred collection of Christian Scriptures. It is cited by Irenaeus (*Haer.* 3.17.5, 8), Clement of Alexandria (*Fragmente in Adumbrationes*), and Tertullian (*Prax.* 15; *Marc.* 5.16; *Antidote for the Scorpion's Sting* 12). Apart from the Alogi from Asia Minor in the last third of the second century, who rejected the Gospel of John, Acts, Revelation (see Irenaeus's report in *Haer.* 3.11.12), and probably 1 John as well, few were opposed to the authenticity of this letter, and most writers of antiquity agreed that the Apostle John had written it. Eusebius in the fourth century states that very few leaders of the church ever questioned its authenticity. It was accepted into the Syriac Peshitta no later than the fifth century, but was not included in the early stages of its formation. The earliest obvious citations of the letter appear in Pol. *Phil.* 7; Justin, *Dial.* 123.9; and probably also Ign. *Eph.* 7.2; *Diogn.* 10.3; and *Gospel of Truth* 27.24 and 31.4–5.

5. 2 and 3 John

Very little attestation for 2–3 John is found prior to the fourth century, and both Eusebius (*Hist. eccl.* 3.25.3) and Origen (Eusebius, *Hist. eccl.*

6.25.10, which may be a Eusebius invention) have doubts about their authenticity. Before then, precious little ancient testimony speaks to their authenticity or authority. A few possible parallels in the Apostolic Fathers are not conclusive (e.g., Pol. *Phil.* 7.1 and 2 John 7 [cf. also Tertullian, *Flesh of Christ* 24]; Ign. *Smyrn.* 4.1 and 2 John 10–11). Better information is available on the use of these two letters from the time of Clement of Alexandria (*Strom.* 2.15.66). Irenaeus quotes 2 John 11 and 7 in *Haer.* 3.17.8. According to Eusebius, Dionysius of Alexandria knew all three letters of John (*Hist. eccl.* 7.25.11). Eusebius also claims that Papias wrote a commentary on them (*Hist. eccl.* 3.39.1–3). Irenaeus and Tertullian do not mention 3 John, and even the fourth-century Muratorian Fragment (lines 68–69) knew only two letters of John. Elsewhere in the fourth century the three letters are known, but are not yet generally accepted among the churches as Scripture. They are included in Anthanasius's *Thirty-ninth Festal Letter,* Cyril of Jerusalem (*Catechetical Lectures* 4.36), and the Mommsen or Cheltenham Catalogue (ca. 360 in North Africa), but doubts were still expressed about their inspiration and canonicity by Jerome (ca. 420) in *Illustrious Men* 9.18. Cyprian cites 2 John 10–11 in his *Sententiae episcoporum* 81. They are also included in the Muratorian Fragment (lines 68–69).

There appears to have been a time when only two letters of John were accepted in the West and in Alexandria. There is no certain reference to 3 John until the time of Jerome and Augustine. Although some scholars argue that 2 John and 3 John circulated at first as one letter—hence their common designation under one name and frequent references to only two letters of John—the evidence for this is not convincing. Both 2 John and 3 John have a slim history of use in the church and are seldom referred to until the fourth and fifth centuries, when they both appear in lists of Scriptures and subsequently in theological treatises, where their authority and reception are both questioned and accepted.

6. Jude

The Epistle of Jude is used in several early Christian writings: Pol. *Phil.* 3.2 and Jude 3, 20; Pol. *Phil.* 11.4 and Jude 20, 23; *Barn.* 2.10 and Jude 3–4; Athenagoras, *Supplication for Christians* 24–25; Theophilus of Antioch 2.15; Clement of Alexandria, *Christ the Educator* 3.8.44 (quoting Jude 5–6 by name); 3.8.45 (quoting Jude 11); *Strom.* 3.2.11 (quoting Jude 8–16 by name). Eusebius notes Clement's acceptance of Jude (*Hist. eccl.* 6.13.6; 6.14.1). Tertullian implies that Jude was known in Latin translation (*Apparel of Women* 1.3). The book was fully accepted by Athanasius in his *Thirty-ninth Festal Letter* of 367. The Muratorian Fragment (lines 68–69) mentions Jude in an awkward manner, possibly showing some element of doubt about its acceptance. This is consistent with the questions raised about Jude in the fourth century.

Origen knew of questions about Jude, but this does not deter him from citing the book (e.g., *Commentary on Matthew* 17.30 and Jude 6; *Commentary on Matthew* 10.17, where Jude is called a servant of "our Lord Jesus Christ and a brother of James"; *Commentary on John* 13.37 and Jude 6; *Homily on Ezekiel* 4.1 and Jude 8–9; and *First Principles* 3.2.1, which shows awareness of the book). He was apparently attracted to Jude because of its views on angelology. The widely acknowledged use of Jude in 2 Peter gives further witness to the widespread use of Jude in the second century.

In the fourth and fifth centuries Jude was called into question primarily as a result of its use of *1 En.* 1:9 in Jude 14–15. Throughout the first two centuries of the church, *1 Enoch* was accepted as inspired and sacred in many Christian communities. For example, *1 Enoch* was used by *Assumption of Moses, Jubilees, Apocalypse of Baruch* (ca. 70 C.E.), and *Testaments of the Twelve Patriarchs.* In the Christian era, the author of *Barnabas* cites *1 Enoch* three times, twice referring to it as Scripture: "It has been written, just as Enoch says" (*Barn.* 4.3, referring to *1 En.* 89:61–64; 90:17) and "For the Scripture says" (*Barn.* 16.5, citing *1 En.* 89:55, 66–67). The appeal of Jude to *1 Enoch,* therefore, was not a problem in the Christian communities. Only in the third century and later do we find doubts expressed about the canonicity of *1 Enoch,* mostly because of its attributing carnal lust to heavenly beings. Consequently, in the fourth century and later Jude's use of *1 Enoch* led to questions about the place of Jude itself in the Scripture canon.

Eusebius lists Jude among the "doubted" (*antilegomena*) writings in the church (*Hist. eccl.* 3.25.3; cf. 2.23.25), and Jerome (*Illustrious Men* 4) felt obligated to deal with the issue of Jude's use of *1 Enoch*. Didymus of Alexandria (ca. 395) defended Jude against those who attacked its use of *1 Enoch* (see Migne, *Patrologia graeca* 39.1811–18). Jude's offense was not that he made use of *1 Enoch,* as other Christian writers had, but that he referred to the writing *by name.* Jude used Jewish apocalypses in much the same manner as did 1–2 Peter. Although Jude cites *1 Enoch* by name, he is nonetheless still within the bounds of what was acceptable in his day.

F. REVELATION

There are no certain traces of Revelation in the Apostolic Fathers. The closest parallels, of course, come from the *Visions* section of the *Shepherd of Hermas:*

Herm. Vis. 1.1.3 and Rev 17:3
Herm. Vis. 2.2.7; 4.2.5; 4.3.6 and Rev 3:10 and 7:14
Herm. Vis. 2.4 and Rev 12:1
Herm. Vis. 4.1.6 and Rev 9:3
Herm. Sim. 8.2.1, 3 and Rev 2:10; 3:11; and 6:11
Barn. 7.9 and Rev 1:7, 13
Barn. 21.3 and Rev 22:10–12

Charles claims that Revelation was all but universally accepted (and consequently used in an authoritative manner) in Asia Minor, western Syria, Africa, Rome, and south Gaul in the second century.[69] Justin appears to have been the first to say that the book of Revelation was written by John the Apostle (*Dial.* 81.15; cf. also *1 Apol.* 28, which refers to Rev 12:9). According to Eusebius, Apollonius used Revelation in the second century to write against the Montanists (*Hist. eccl.* 5.18.14). Clement of Alexandria (*Christ the Educator* 2.119) cites Revelation as Scripture and as the work of John the Apostle (*Salvation of the Rich* 42 and *Strom.* 6.106–107). Charles further notes that, according to Tertullian, Marcion rejected the traditional authorship of John and the Alogi of the second century rejected the writing altogether.

According to Eusebius, Dionysius the Great of Alexandria (ca. 260–64) wrote a critical appraisal of the authorship of the book (*Hist. eccl.* 7.24–25) and concluded that it was not written by John the Apostle. Eusebius placed Revelation among the doubtful books in his own collection of Christian writings (*Hist. eccl.* 3.24.18; 3.25.4). Cyril of Jerusalem rejected the book altogether and forbade its use in public or private (*Catechetical Lectures* 4.36). Around 360, Revelation did not get included in the canon list of the Council of Laodicea or in the canon 85 of the *Apostolic Constitutions.* Most scholars contend, as Charles shows[70] that Revelation was ignored or rejected in many Eastern churches in the fourth century. On the other hand, some Eastern writers did accept and refer to Revelation: Melito of Sardis, Jerome, Theophilus of Antioch, Apollonius of Hierapolis, Clement of Alexandria, and Origen (see details in §I.D item #7 above).

Significant rejection of Revelation in the East did not occur until the end of the fourth century, when Cyril of Jerusalem excluded Revelation without comment (*Catechetical Lectures* 4.36). On the other hand, Epiphanius of Salamis still included it at the end of the fourth century (*Pan.* 76.5), as did Jerome (*Letter to Paul* 53) and Codex Alexandrinus (425).

III. Summary

The recognition of Christian literature as authoritative and useful in the life and worship of the church came sooner than its formal recognition as Scripture. In general, such writings were not called Scripture in the second century, even though they no doubt functioned that way for many Christians. By the end of the second century, the principle of *Christian* Scriptures had already been recognized by vast segments of the Christian community. This conclusion, however, calls for three important cautions

[69] Charles, *Revelation of St. John,* 1.xcvii–ciii.

[70] Ibid., ci–ciii

that are also reminders of how we began this chapter. First, acknowledgment of the authority of *one* part of the NT literature at this time does not imply that *all* of it was so recognized everywhere. Second, because *one* writer may refer to a part of the NT as Scripture does not mean that *all* Christians of the same era came to the same conclusion. Finally, even if some of the NT writings were recognized as having the status of Scripture in the second century, this is not the same as a closed canon of Scriptures, even though it is clear that with the recognition of the authority of certain Christian writings canonical processes were in motion.

CHAPTER FOURTEEN

The Criteria Question

HAVING EXAMINED A VARIETY OF ISSUES RELATED TO THE FORMATION OF THE NT biblical canon, we have yet to ask why the early church settled on the books that make up the NT canon, and why it did not include other books that had been used widely and cited frequently in the early church.[1] Biblical scholars generally agree that the writings of the NT addressed the needs of specific communities and that the writers had these needs in mind when telling their story (Gospels) or admonishing specific churches (Letters). Since the letters were ad hoc letters, that is, they were addressed to specific congregations in specific circumstances, it is remarkable that early on these writings were accepted as having significant value for the wider Christian community. What is it about these writings that led the churches to preserve them as sacred literature? Smith has argued well that a distinguishing feature of the NT writings is that they generally continue or presuppose the biblical story of salvation history for the people of God and interpret history.[2] Those who wrote the gospels initially did so with the idea of producing an authoritative guide to the Christian faith for the church and with the idea of continuing the biblical story.

Some works that were selected for inclusion in the Christian Bible, especially the Gospels and Paul's Letters, were recognized by the end of the first century and the early second century to have considerable value for church life and ministry. These writings may have been produced consciously as sacred story (Scripture) with a scriptural quality inherent in them, as Smith suggests, because they continued the story and the hope of the earlier Scriptures that the church had inherited, the OT or First Testament. The value of these and other writings was soon recognized. Several NT books, as well as some noncanonical books, were functioning like Scripture (i.e., authoritatively) in many churches in the early second century and were probably circulating among the churches a few decades

[1]Portions of this chapter are adaptated from McDonald, "Identifying Scripture and Canon."

[2]D. M. Smith, "When Did the Gospels Become Scripture?" 8–9.

earlier. In some cases, the NT writings were first recognized as authoritative by their writers (Rev 22:18–19; 1 Cor 7:39–40). They were beginning to be called Scripture by the end of the second century.

I. Identifying Christian Scriptures

Several factors indicate that Christians viewed certain writings as sacred Scripture. First, of course, is the manner in which the NT writings are cited in the various communities of faith. When these citations or allusions recognize the authority of the writing to settle issues of faith, mission, and disciplinary matters, or when they are used in worship in a liturgical setting, we can be assured that they carried a sacred authority not found in other writings of the time. For example, around the middle of the second century, Justin Martyr describes how the prophets and the "memoirs of the apostles" were read as the community gathered together for worship on the first day of the week (*1 Apol.* 67). Most scholars agree that the "memoirs of the apostles" are probably only the Synoptic Gospels (*1 Apol.* 66). Justin does not say, however, that the Gospels were read in worship services *alongside* the "Prophets" (a common reference for the OT Scriptures in the churches of his day), but rather that they were sometimes read *instead* of the Prophets: "On the day called Sunday there is a meeting in one place of those who live in cities or the country, and the memoirs of the apostles or the writings of the prophets are read as long as time permits" (*1 Apol.* 67, *ANF*). This, of course, indicates the stature that these writings had attained by that time and may refer to a long-standing practice in the church of giving special attention "to the apostles' teaching" (Acts 2:42).

A second indicator is holiness. When a church perceived a writing's holiness, it became Scripture for that community of faith. Barton cites Origen's arguement that if the reader did not understand what was read in the Scriptures, nevertheless "those powers which are present with us do understand, and they delight to be with us as though summoned by the words of a charm, and to lend us their aid."[3] Barton shows several ways in which Scripture was perceived as holy in the churches and treated as sacred. He points to (a) the non-triviality of the text. For instance, in 1 Cor 9:9 Paul quotes Deut 25:4, a relatively unimportant OT text regarding the treatment of an ox treading out grain, as a very important text for the life of the Christian community.[4] The text appears trivial, but because it is Scripture, Paul defends its relevance.

Barton claims that the sacredness of a writing is seen in its (b) non-ephemerality. In other words, a text is sacred if it is relevant to all ages, not

[3] Barton, *Holy Writings, Sacred Text,* 129.
[4] Ibid., 134–36.

merely to a particular time in history. Scripture was always read as relevant to one's own day and situation. Early Christian writers, he says, "seem to take it for granted that what Jesus said will always have a bearing on present problems, aspirations, conflicts, and hopes: these sayings are canonical."[5]

Barton maintains that if a writing was believed to be Scripture, it was also believed to be (c) internally self-consistent and not self-contradictory. For example, in Justin's famous *Dialogue with Trypho,* he admonishes that if Trypho had spoken ill of the Scriptures in error or without ill intent, he would be forgiven, but

> if you have done so because you imagined that you could throw doubt on the passage, in order that I might say the scriptures contradicted one another, you have erred. But I shall not venture to suppose or to say such a thing, and if a scripture that appears to be of such a kind be brought forward, and if there be a pretext for saying that it is contrary to some other, since I am entirely convinced that no scripture contradicts another, I shall admit rather that I do not understand what is recorded, and shall strive to persuade those who imagine that the scriptures are contradictory to be rather of the same opinion as myself. (*Dial.* 65.2, adapted from *ANF*)

The concern to maintain the inward consistency of a text is a clear signal of its perceived scriptural status. Speaking about the canonical process of the OT, Ulrich draws attention to the creative work of scribes to harmonize Scriptures:[6] "Sometimes the presupposition behind harmonization is that this text can be juxtaposed to that text because God is the author of both. That presupposition is clearly behind some of the Qumran, NT, and rabbinic texts."[7] The harmonizing activity of scribes assumes the sacredness of both of the traditions that they are trying to reconcile.

Barton further contends that the early church believed scriptural texts had (d) an excess of meaning. He cites as an example Gal 3:15–18, where Paul emphasizes the special meaning of the singular "seed" of Abraham in Gen 12:7, rather than plural "seeds," indicating that the promises to Abraham would find fulfillment in one man, Jesus. The multilayered meanings of a biblical text, often discovered through allegorical exegesis, emphasized that the text had fluidity and adaptability to ever-changing circumstances. Writings that were searched for deeper meanings by means of the various hermeneutical methodologies, especially allegorical exegesis, were generally acknowledged as sacred texts.[8] Multiple interpretations of texts were often followed by extended interpretations or commentaries, such as

---

[5] Ibid., 137–39.

[6] For example, Isa 2:2–4 //Mic 4:1–4; and Obad 1–10 // Jer 49:7–22. In a personal communication, J. A. Sanders reminds me that the Masoretes protected the differences and discrepancies in the Masorah; they appear to have abhorred harmonization.

[7] Ulrich, *Dead Sea Scrolls,* 77 n. 75.

[8] Barton, *Holy Writings, Sacred Text,* 142–43, 160.

those produced by Origen on biblical books. Along with this, and roughly at the same time, many translations of texts were produced, an activity that also suggests that what was translated was viewed as sacred.

Finally, Barton observes that when (e) *nomina sacra* appear in ancient manuscripts, those manuscripts were considered sacred. That early Christian scribes contracted special words from both the OT and the NT suggests that they viewed both collections as sacred in the same sense.[9]

When a text was actually called Scripture is a different matter than when or whether it became part of a fixed collection of sacred Scriptures. Scriptural identity could and often did change over time before the final fixing of the NT canon. For example, the *Shepherd of Hermas* called the ancient writing *Eldad and Modad* Scripture: "The Lord is near those that turn to him, as it is written [*hōs gegraptai*] in the Book of Eldad and Modat, who prophesied to the people in the wilderness" (*Herm. Vis.* 2.3.4, LCL).[10]

Although we may see specific writings recognized or identified as Scripture by individual churches or ancient writers, it does not follow that all churches of the same time or even in the same location acknowledged the same writings as Scripture. To the contrary, there was considerable variety in what the early churches considered authoritative or sacred writings, especially in the second century. For example, most churches did not accept *Eldad and Modad* as Scripture; *1 Enoch* is recognized as inspired by Jude; and the Alogi rejected John's Gospel, Revelation, and the book of Hebrews. Other writings that were earlier regarded as sacred Scripture by a large segment of the Christian community were later excluded from that category. For example, *1 Clement,* the letters of Ignatius, the *Shepherd of Hermas,* and *Barnabas* were all called Scripture by certain writers and were even placed in various collections of Scripture through the fourth and fifth centuries, but eventually these writings were dropped from the sacred collections.

After determining that certain Christian writings were sacred and functioned as Scripture alongside the OT Scriptures (and at times in their place), the final step of the canonization process was delimitation or deselection. In other words, the process was complete when a clearly defined collection of Christian literature existed from which some writings were excluded and nothing else accepted as canon for the Christian community.

At this stage, roughly the fourth and fifth centuries, the recognized adaptability of this literature to various contexts further recommended its selection and placement in the NT canon. But recognition of the sacredness of the book did not mean that the text was automatically fixed. The canonical process extended only to the books as such, not to the individual words in them, and the various Christian communities took considerable

---

[9]Ibid., 122–23. Barton shows examples of this practice.

[10]This apocalypse is possibly also alluded to in *2 Clem.* 11.2. The two names are mentioned in Num 11:26.

liberty with the texts over the centuries.[11] There was as yet no invariable biblical *text,* even if such a list of *books* had already emerged.

Finally, it appears that Christian writers of the second century did not cite the OT as much as the NT. Barton tabulates the frequency of citations in the late-first-century and early-second-century church fathers: *Shepherd of Hermas, 2 Clement,* Ignatius, *Didache,* Polycarp. He shows that the Christian Scriptures were cited many times more often in this period than were the OT Scriptures and that this was a common practice until the third century, when the citations began to balance out. Barton concludes that this practice probably reflects a scarcity of OT texts and a relative abundance of Christian texts in the churches. His findings lead him to question the appropriateness of appealing to citations in ancient literature to determine what was considered sacred in the early churches.[12]

II. What Criteria Did the Churches Employ?

What criteria were employed by the early church to identify those writings that would eventually make up its biblical canon? It is generally acknowledged that the church used several criteria in order to determine the contents of its NT. No surviving evidence, however, suggests that all churches used the same criteria in selecting their sacred collections. Likewise, no evidence suggests that each separate criterion weighed equally with others in deliberations about canon. In fact, the variety of Scripture canons from the fourth to the sixth centuries suggests otherwise (see appendixes B–E). The most common criteria employed in the canonical process include apostolicity, orthodoxy, antiquity, and use. Two other features of ancient Scripture, namely, its adaptability and inspiration, also figure in the process.[13]

---

[11] Ulrich, *Dead Sea Scrolls,* 57–58, and Metzger, *Canon of the New Testament,* 269–70, make this argument for the OT writings and the NT writings, respectively. Metzger illustrates this point with Eusebius and Jerome, both of whom saw textual differences in various manuscripts and wondered which to follow, but neither chose a particular text. Metzger notes that in antiquity "the question of canonicity pertains to the document *qua* document, and not to one particular form or version of that document" (270).

[12] Barton, *Holy Writings, Sacred Text,* 18–19 and 64–65, following Franz Stuhlhofer.

[13] To avoid confusion, it is best to follow the advice of Sundberg and Ulrich, who employ the term *canon* to refer to a delimited collection of Christian literature that makes up our current biblical canon. The term is reserved for selected literature in only the postbiblical era, when such notions of a closed biblical canon were discussed. Sundberg distinguishes between the terms *Scripture* and *canon,* in that the latter presumes the former, but not the other way around. Scripture was perceived long before the notion of a closed biblical canon emerged. See his "Toward a Revised History." Ulrich concurs with Sundberg and notes three aspects of canon: (1) canon represents a reflexive judgment on the part of a religious community, (2) canon denotes a

The NT itself contains exhortations to discern prophets who claim to speak in the power of the Spirit (1 Cor 12:10; 1 John 4:2). The author(s) of the *Didache* gave similar advice concerning both the doctrine and conduct of a prophet or apostle. Similarly, guidelines were needed to determine which books should be included in their Scripture collections and which should not.

Some writings were produced in the name of an apostle in order to secure wider acceptance of a position or stance that otherwise would probably not have received much of a hearing. In this sense, apostolicity insured acceptance. Early in the church's history the inappropriate use of well-known names to secure acceptance of a writing was common. Paul himself needed to affix his own peculiar signature to his letters to ensure that other writings circulating in his name would not be taken as genuine (1 Cor 16:21; Gal 6:11; Col 4:18; 2 Thess 3:17; and Phlm 19).[14]

A. APOSTOLICITY

If a writing was believed to have been produced by an apostle, it was eventually accepted as sacred Scripture and included in the NT canon. Eusebius's argument against the apostolic authorship of the pseudepigraphal literature reflects the universally acknowledged authority of apostolic writings and the rejection of writings believed to have not come from an apostle. After listing the writings that were widely accepted (*homologoumenon*) or "canonical" (lit., "encovenanted"; *endiathēkē*), he spoke of those writings that were disputed (*antilegomenon*) and yet were known to most writers of the church: "In order that we might know them and the writings which are put forward by heretics under the name of the apostles containing gospels such as those of Peter, and Thomas, and Matthias, and some others besides, or Acts such as those of Andrew and John and the other apostles" (*Hist. eccl.* 3.25.6, LCL).

From early times the church's most important weapon against gnostics and other heretics was its claim to apostolicity, which guaranteed that its oral and written traditions were genuine. "Apostolic succession" represented a claim that the faith received by the apostles from the Lord was passed on by successive leaders in the church. After listing the succession of leaders in the church, Irenaeus explains the implications of apostolic succession:

> The blessed apostles, then, having founded and built up the church committed into the hands of Linus the office of episcopate [he then lists twelve successive

---

closed list of biblical books, and (3) canon concerns biblical books rather than the specific text of those books. See his *Dead Sea Scrolls,* 53–61.

[14] From the large list of pseudonymous literature in antiquity, we see that this problem was already widespread in the second century and that care was needed in the church. Considerable doubt persists regarding the authorship of Colossians and 2 Thessalonians.

> leaders]. . . . In this order, and by this succession, the ecclesiastical tradition from the apostles and the preaching of the truth have come down to us. And this is the most abundant proof that there is one and the same vivifying faith, which has been preserved in the Church from the apostles until now, and handed down in truth. (*Haer.* 3.3.3, *ANF*)

Later he writes: "How should it be if the apostles themselves had not left us writings? Would it not be necessary in that case to follow the course of the tradition which they handed down to those to whom they handed over the leadership of the churches?" (*Haer.* 3.4.1, adapted from *ANF*) The authoritative NT literature reflected the "apostolic deposit." The church upheld the apostolic witness in its sacred literature as a way of grounding its faith in Jesus, represented by the apostles' teaching, and insuring that the church's tradition was not severed from its historical roots and proximity to Jesus, the primary authority of the early church. All NT literature was believed to be written by apostles or those connected to an apostle. Scholars differ, of course, on how successful this was.[15]

Tertullian (ca. 200) indicated that the Gospels were written either by the apostles or by "apostolic men" and gave the former priority over the latter: "John and Matthew first instill faith in us, but Luke and Mark, who are apostolic men, renew it afterward" (*Marc.* 4.2.2, *ANF*). Later he criticizes Marcion for choosing Luke over the other Gospels because Luke "was not an apostle, but only an apostolic man; not a master, but a disciple, and so inferior to a master" (*Marc.* 4.2.5, *ANF*). Clearly, for Tertullian, apostolicity was so significant that Scriptures written by an apostle were superior to those written by "apostolic men." In contrast, apostolicity did not seem to be an important factor in the initial production of Christian literature, as apostolic names were not placed on the Gospels until the end of the second century.

The criterion of apostolicity poses several problems today. Many scholars question how much of the NT was actually written by apostles. For example, it is difficult to establish that John and Matthew wrote the Gospels that bear their names. While some scholars argue strongly for the apostolicity of 1 Peter and 1 John, the arguments are not conclusive. And there are lingering doubts about Paul's authorship of Ephesians, Colossians, 2 Thessalonians, and especially the Pastoral Epistles, even if they may contain some authentic Pauline traditions (e.g., 2 Tim 1:15; 4:16–17).[16] Best rightly observes that the ancient church's judgments about the apostolic authorship of the NT writings will be evaluated very differently today.[17]

---

[15] Funk, *Parables and Presence,* 182–86, discusses the success of the church's attempt to ground its faith (traditions) in Jesus through a closed apostolic canon. He acknowledges that the early churches' appeal to their apostolic roots aimed at supporting their traditions, but he questions the outcome of their efforts.

[16] Several important recent works discuss the problems of Pauline authorship of the Pastorals: Quinn and Wacker, *First and Second Letters to Timothy;* Marshall, *The Pastoral Epistles;* and J. D. Miller, *Pastoral Letters as Composite Documents.*

[17] Best, "Scripture, Tradition, and the Canon," 279.

How was the criterion of apostolicity applied in antiquity? Eusebius's doubts about accepting 2 Peter focused on the issue of its apostolicity. He accepted 1 Peter because it was widely regarded as genuine, but 2 Peter was not: "Of Peter, one epistle, that which is called his first, is admitted, and the ancient presbyters used this in their own writings as unquestioned, but the so-called second Epistle we have not received as canonical, but nevertheless it has appeared useful to many, and has been studied with other Scriptures" (*Hist. eccl.* 3.3.1, LCL). Eusebius probably accepted as canonical ("recognized") only twenty or twenty-one of the books of our current NT canon. Besides 2 Peter, he questioned the legitimacy of James, 2 John, 3 John, Jude, Revelation, and may not have included Hebrews with the Letters of Paul.

The gnostic Christians of the second century and the Donatists of the fourth century also claimed apostolic support for their teachings.[18] The gnostic *Gospel of Thomas* is the first gospel that specifically claims apostolic authorship, and while most reject this claim, some scholars today acknowledge that some twenty or more of the sayings of Jesus in it may be authentic.[19]

After lengthy debate, the early church concluded that Paul wrote the book of Hebrews, something that modern scholarship, for a variety of reasons (style, theology, vocabulary, etc.), universally rejects. Attributing it to Paul may have stemmed from the desire to get a cherished writing into the canon rather than from the sincere belief that Paul actually wrote it. Origen, like many others in the ancient church, had serious doubts about who wrote the letter. Observing that the thoughts were Paul's but that the style and composition belonged to someone else, he concludes that "who wrote the epistle, in truth God knows" (Eusebius, *Hist. eccl.* 6.25.14). Attributing the work to Paul, however, secured its place in the Christian canon. This leads us to conclude that other criteria may have been operating, probably subconsciously. At times apostolic authorship may have been attributed to a writing that was cherished and considered useful in segments of the Christian community in order to justify its use in the churches.

In the early church, the concern for apostolicity essentially had to do with the proximity of the apostles to Jesus and their presumed firsthand knowledge of him and his ministry. Since Jesus was the ultimate "canon" of the church, in the sense that he was the primary authority figure of the

---

[18]See the many gnostic documents in Robinson, *Nag Hammadi Library,* that claim either implicitly or explicitly the apostolic tradition, for example, *Acts of Peter* 1 (289) and *Apocryphon of John* 2 and 32 (105–6, 123).

[19]See especially the important collection of noncanonical sayings of Jesus in Crossan, *Sayings Parallels.* Although Crossan has a reputation for finding what he thinks are authentic sayings of Jesus in the most unusual places (e.g., *Gospel of Peter* and Egerton Papyri), and probably more than exist, he raises important questions about the application of the apostolic criterion in early Christianity.

church, the opportunity to glean information from those closest to him was highly valued. This is why Tertullian relegated John and Matthew to higher positions of authority than Mark and Luke. When the apostolic authorship of ancient writings was doubted, typically their canonical status was also questioned.[20]

Another factor that points to the importance of apostolic authorship is the presence of pseudonymous literature circulating in the early church. Many writings attributed to apostles nonetheless failed to be included in the canon, largely because they were considered pseudonymous. Representatives of all the genres present in the NT (gospel, acts, epistle, and apocalypse) are attributed to well-known apostles. This mostly sectarian literature was written in an apostle's name in order to find acceptance in the church.[21] In several instances the apostolic authorship of some writings was questioned in antiquity, but some churches nevertheless received them and were reserved in their comments about their origins. From early on, it appears that the question of pseudepigraphy was a controversial issue in the church. Discussing the literature that was considered sacred in the fourth-century church, Eusebius describes those who falsely publish their own writings in the name of an apostle:

> Some have also counted [as canonical or recognized] the Gospel according to the Hebrews in which those of the Hebrews who have accepted Christ take a special pleasure. These would all belong to the disputed books, but we have nevertheless been obliged to make a list of them, distinguishing between those writings which, according to the tradition of the Church, are true, genuine, and recognized, and those which differ from them in that they are not canonical but disputed, yet nevertheless are known to most of the writers of the Church, in order that we might know them and the writings which are put forward by heretics under the name of the apostles containing gospels such as those of Peter, and Thomas, and Matthias, and some others besides, or Acts such as those of Andrew and John and the other apostles. To none of these has any who belonged to the succession of the orthodox ever thought it right to refer in his writings. Moreover, the type and phraseology differs from apostolic style, and the opinion and tendency of their contents is widely dissonant from true orthodoxy and clearly shows that they are the forgeries of heretics. They ought, therefore, to be reckoned not even among spurious books but shunned as altogether wicked and impious. (*Hist. eccl.* 3.25.6–7, LCL)

In sum, if it was believed that an apostle wrote a particular book, that writing was accepted and treated as Scripture. There is no doubt that several books of the NT were placed in the canon because the majority believed that they were written by apostles or members of the apostolic community.

---

[20] F. F. Bruce, *Canon of Scripture,* 259, makes this point.

[21] See the list in chapter 11 §V and Schneemelcher, *New Testament Apocrypha,* for detailed descriptions and translations.

B. ORTHODOXY

Theological issues were a significant concern to the early church and played an important role in its development. Simonetti offers a fair assessment of the role of Scripture in the church's theological inquiry:

> We might say that the whole life of the community was conditioned by the interpretation of Scripture. It has been said that the history of doctrine is the history of exegesis, in that the whole development of catholic doctrine is based on the interpretation of a certain number of passages in Scripture in the light of particular needs; but the same could be said of any other aspect of the Church's life: organization, discipline, worship, and so on. For this reason, the study of Holy Scripture was the real foundation of Christian culture in the Church of the earliest centuries.[22]

This theological concern led the early church to employ the "rule of faith" as the criterion of orthodoxy to determine which writings could be used in the church. Bishop Serapion (ca. 200) rejected the reading of the *Gospel of Peter* in church because of this criterion of truth. When asked by the church at Rhossus, under his jurisdiction, whether the *Gospel of Peter* could be read in their services, he at first agreed because it had an apostle's name attached. But later he reversed his decision: "Since I have now learnt, from what has been told me, that their mind was lurking in some hole of heresy, I shall give diligence to come again to you; wherefore, brethren expect me quickly" (Eusebius, *Hist. eccl.* 6.12.4, LCL). His rejection was based upon the book's divergence from what was generally accepted as true in the churches of his day. It was not because of its questionable authorship, though that may have played a small role, but because the theology was considered out of step with the "rule of faith" operating in the church. Serapion's initial willingness to accept the reading of the *Gospel of Peter* in his churches is also instructive. Had there been a widely recognized closed four-gospel canon at that time (ca. 200), he might well have rejected the *Gospel of Peter* on such grounds. In this example, apostolicity and antiquity evidently took a back seat to the criterion of truth. If a writing was too far away from what was believed to be the core or central teaching that had been handed on in the churches, it was rejected (see also Eusebius, *Hist. eccl.* 3.25.7).

Several scholars argue that one of the distinguishing features of the NT literature is the truth, or canon of faith, that it presents.[23] However, as one

---

[22] Simonetti, *Biblical Interpretation in the Early Church*, 1–2.

[23] See, for example, Ewert, *From Ancient Tablets to Modern Translations*, 131; Barker, Lane, and Michaels, *The New Testament Speaks*, 30–31 (who ask, "was that which was written a genuine witness to Christ and from Christ? . . . The church was confident that if a document were genuinely inspired it would conform to the truth which God had revealed through tested witnesses"); and E. Harrison, *Introduction to the New Testament*, 11–12.

examines the NT literature more carefully, it is difficult to reconcile many of its theological positions and practical guidelines for living.[24] Käsemann argues that such theological variety in the early church is "so wide even in the NT that we are compelled to admit the existence not merely of significant tensions, but, not infrequently, of irreconcilable theological contradictions."[25] Stendahl agrees that such differences cannot and should not be resolved through clever exegesis because "when they are overcome by harmonization, the very points intended by the writers are dulled an distorted."[26]

In the midst of the diversity in the NT, is there also a common core of beliefs typical of early Christianity and essential to the church? Dunn contends that if the NT has a theological core everywhere acknowledged or reasonably assumed, it is simply this, "Jesus-the-man-now-exalted."[27] Perhaps we should add to this that Jesus is also worthy of faithful obedience and that the promise of the blessing of God awaits all who follow him. This confession, however, is not confined to the NT literature, but is affirmed in numerous noncanonical Christian writings as well.[28] Nevertheless the church unquestionably *believed* that the NT writings reliably conveyed the essential message of and about Jesus the Christ. Apostolicity witnessed to this, but apostolicity was not a substitute for content.[29]

While it may be somewhat in vogue to claim that all theologies of the Bible and all theologies outside of the Bible equally represent the proclamation of the earliest Christian community, and that there was no theological core, but rather considerable confusion, this is simply not the case. One scholar, for instance, contends that there were justifiable reasons why the

---

[24] For example, the Synoptic Gospels declare the arrival of the kingdom of God in the near future (Mark 1:15; 13:3–37) as well as its presence in the ministry of Jesus (Luke 11:20; 17:21; 7:18–23), while John emphasizes the present nature of eternal life (John 3:16; 10:10; 20:30–31). Does Paul's view of the death of Jesus "for our sins" (1 Cor 15:3; Rom 3:23–25; Gal 2:21) square with Luke's lack of interest in that matter (Acts 2:14–39; 3:11–26)? Paul's argument in Rom 13:1–3 that Christians ought to be subject to and not resist the governing authorities because they were appointed by God is difficult to square with Acts 4:19 and 5:28–29, which reject the authority of governing officials in favor of obedience to God. The baptismal formulas in the book of Acts (2:38; 10:48; 19:5) differ from that in Matt 28:19 (see Hartman, *Into the Name of the Lord Jesus*). And what about the organizational structure of the early church in Acts, compared to that in Paul, John, the Pastorals, and Matt 16:18–19? For other examples of problems of harmonization in the NT literature, see Best, "Scripture, Tradition, and the Canon," 272–280.

[25] Käsemann, "Canon of the New Testament," 100.

[26] Stendahl, *Meanings,* 63.

[27] Dunn, *Unity and Diversity in the New Testament,* 377.

[28] All of the Apostolic Fathers—Clement of Rome, Ignatius, Polycarp, the Shepherd of Hermas, Barnabas, and the Didachist—could or did agree to this. So also could Marcion and the Montanists for that matter.

[29] Von Campenhausen, *Formation of the Christian Bible,* 330, makes this point. See also Bauer, *Orthodoxy and Heresy in Earliest Christianity.*

ancient church rejected the gnostic esoteric and ahistorical interpretation of Christian faith.[30] Although the Christian proclamation of the first century is broader than the late-second-century orthodoxy of Rome that eventually obtained prominence in the churches, all ancient theologies were *not* equally representative of the faith. There was a typical understanding of God, Christ, Scripture, and hope in the majority of the churches coming out of the second century. This understanding became more pronounced in subsequent generations. Theissen asserts that most Christian communities shared certain beliefs and that these beliefs had a role in determining which writings were welcomed into the biblical canon. Other writings and groups that did not measure up to this theological core, such as the *Gospel of Peter* and the other gnostic texts, were excluded. He adds that "primitive Christianity is governed by two basic axioms, monotheism and belief in the redeemer. In addition there are eleven [*sic*] basic motifs: the motifs of creation, wisdom and miracle; of renewal, representation and indwelling; of faith, agape and a change of position; and finally the motif of judgment."[31] To this we should add the belief in the activity of God in the life, death, and resurrection of the "redeemer" Jesus.

C. ANTIQUITY

The traditional understanding of canon formation is that the church at first recognized only the OT writings as Scripture. Later, as the Gospels and Epistles (at first only Paul's) began to circulate among the churches, they too were accorded scriptural status. Barton, however, challenges this traditional view, noting that in the first two centuries Christians generally referred to their own writings more than to the OT. They did not cite the OT equally until it was becoming finalized for the church. He also notes that during the second century "all but a very few OT books (such as Isaiah or the Psalms) already play second fiddle to the Christians' own writings."[32] Nevertheless, he acknowledges that antiquity played a significant role in the ancient world; a religion's antiquity enhanced its credibility. A high value was placed upon the past, and what was old was generally considered more reliable and acceptable than what was new. This attitude continued in the church until the time of the Enlightenment. Nevertheless, the early Christians believed that with the advent of Jesus something new and important had arrived, surpassing everything that had gone before it.[33] For the church, the ministry of Jesus had become the defining moment in his-

---

[30] MacRae, "Why the Church Rejected Gnosticism."

[31] Theissen, *A Theory of Primitive Christian Religion,* 282. Farmer, "Reflections on Jesus," emphasizes the importance of the *regula fidei* for the life of the early church and the formation of its canon.

[32] Barton, *Holy Writings, Sacred Text,* 64.

[33] Ibid., 64–65.

tory. Consequently, the church's most important authorities were those closest to this defining moment.[34] The early Christians believed that the books and writings that gave them their best access to the story of Jesus, and thus defined their identity and mission, were those that came from the apostolic era. Barton further makes the astonishing claim that these books, the Gospels and Epistles, were so important to the early church that they "were more important than 'Scripture,' and to cite them as *graphē* [Scripture] might have diminished rather than enhanced them."[35] With time, as prophecy declined, the church appealed more to antiquity and its roots in the OT. But the church continued to give priority to the period of Jesus' ministry as the defining moment for the church and to the apostles as those who were closest to him and were the best representatives and communicators of this crucial period.

The church excluded from the biblical canon any writings that it believed were written *after* the period of apostolic ministry. The tradition that came from the time of Jesus' ministry took priority over all other periods. That is certainly the perspective of the author of the Muratorian Fragment (ca. 350), who spoke against accepting the *Shepherd of Hermas* as Scripture because it was not written in the apostolic age:[36]

> But Hermas wrote the *Shepherd* very recently, in our times, in the city of Rome, while bishop Pius, his brother, was occupying the [episcopal] chair of the church of the city of Rome. And therefore it ought indeed to be read; but it cannot be read publicly to the people in church either among the prophets, whose number is complete, or among the apostles, for it is after [their] time. (*Muratorian Fragment* lines 73–80, Metzger, *Canon of the New Testament,* 307)

While antiquity appears to have been an important criterion for canonicity for some of the churches, it is not, however, easy to determine which Christian writings were the earliest in the church. Many biblical scholars argue convincingly that some of the literature of the NT—especially 2 Peter and probably the Pastorals—was written later than noncanonical Christian books such as the *Didache, 1 Clement,* letters of Ignatius, *Barnabas, Shepherd of Hermas,* the *Martyrdom of Polycarp,* and *2 Clement.* A few scholars also argue that even some of the apocryphal gospels may make similar claims.[37] This should be enough to show that the criterion of antiquity was not applied with unfailing success in the patristic church. If antiquity alone were the chief criterion for canonicity, some rethinking regarding the present biblical canon would be in order. In any

---

[34] Ibid., 64–67.

[35] Ibid., 68.

[36] For discussion, see chapter 13 §I.D and Hahneman, *Muratorian Fragment,* 34–72.

[37] See Koester, "Apocryphal and Canonical Gospels."

case, it is unwise to place too much emphasis on such a changing and imprecise criterion, given the variety of opinion among NT scholars on the dating of the NT writings. Earlier writings cannot be considered ipso facto more reliable. However, the Christian church has always been concerned to recover the earliest and most reliable traditions about Jesus, and the attempt to do so cannot be an ill-informed quest. The grounding of Christian faith and doctrine in the life, teachings, death, and resurrection of Jesus has been a constant since the beginning of the church, and the appropriately cautious use of the criterion of antiquity—along with apostolicity—continues to be an appropriate means of getting closer to the defining and fundamental moment of the Christian faith.

D. USE

The regular use of writings in the ancient churches was also an important factor in their selection for the NT canon. This is what Eusebius had in mind (*Hist. eccl.* 3.25.1–7) when he mentioned that certain writings were "recognized" (*homolegoumenon*) among the churches and became "encovenanted" (*endiathēkē,* lit., "testamented" or "canonical"). The widespread use of the NT writings in the churches may have been the most determinative factor in the canonical process. That the authorship of Hebrews was strongly questioned, yet it made it into the NT canon, suggests that churches were reluctant to dismiss a useful and cherished document. An important factor was who favored the acceptance of a particular document. Athanasius and Epiphanius, for instance, had a greater influence on the church than many lesser-known figures. Also, larger churches in the metropolitan centers such as Antioch, Alexandria, Rome, Ephesus, and Constantinople were more likely to have a greater influence on which books were included than were the smaller churches in rural areas. While most NT writings were known and used by most of the churches in Eusebius's day, doubt lingered over others. These "disputed" (*antilegomenon*) writings included James, 2 Peter, 2 John, 3 John, Jude, probably Revelation, and possibly Hebrews. Eusebius, for example, acknowledges wide acceptance of 1 John, but is reluctant to accept 2 John, 3 John, and Revelation. For him, the Gospel of John and 1 John have been "accepted without controversy by ancients and moderns alike but the other two are disputed, and as to the Revelation there have been many advocates of either opinion up to the present. This, too, shall be similarly illustrated by quotations from the ancients at the proper time" (*Hist. eccl.* 3.24.18, LCL). This shows his considerable interest in what the majority of churches concluded about the matter of canon.

The writings eventually incorporated into the NT apparently met the worship and instructional needs of the churches, while the others did not. The writings that did not remain in the church's sacred collections were those that did not meet the needs of the greater church and had more difficulty being adapted to the churches' changing needs. Ulrich states that "the use of Scripture—whether homiletical or liturgical, whether ancient or contemporary—involves a tripolar dynamic of interaction between the traditional text, the contemporary cultural situation, and the experience of the minister within the community. This tripolar dynamic is a reflection of, and is in faithful continuity with, the process by which the Scriptures were composed."[38]

Not all of the NT writings were used extensively in worship and church life. For example, Philemon, 2 Peter, Jude, 2 John, and 3 John were not cited or used as often as noncanonical sources such as as *1 Clement,* the *Shepherd of Hermas, Didache, Barnabas,* the letters of Ignatius, and *Martyrdom of Polycarp.* If frequency of citation is a guide, there is considerable room for doubt. Realizing this, Collins concludes that not all of the NT teachings and writings are of equal value for Christian faith and ministry, nor are they necessarily more important or closer to the canon of truth than certain noncanonical Christian writings. While acknowledging the strong influence of the present NT canon on Christian thought, he states that "a concern for the truth of history calls for the admission that some books within the canon have had a more influential function in shaping the expression of the church's faith than have others within the canon" and that "some books outside of the canon have had a more striking impact on the formulation of the church's faith than have some individual books among the canonical twenty-seven."[39]

Another side of the criterion of use is what Bruce calls the criterion of "catholicity," by which he means the unwillingness of a church to be out of step with other churches in regard to which documents were recognized as authoritative.[40] Without question, the classic case for the relationship between church use and canonicity comes from Augustine who admonishes the reader of Scripture to

> prefer those [writings] that are received by all Catholic Churches to those which some of them do not receive. Among those, again, which are not received by all, let him prefer those which the more numerous and the weightier churches receive to those which fewer and less authoritative churches hold. But if, however, he finds some held by the more numerous, and some held by the churches of more authority (though this is not very likely to happen), I think that in such a case they ought to be regarded as of equal authority. (*Christian Instruction* 2.12, Metzger, *Canon of the New Testament,* 237)

The variety in the canonical lists of Scriptures of the fourth century shows that the catholicity criterion was far from absolute. Probably other historical circumstances besides utilization by large numbers and influential

---

[38] Ulrich, *Dead Sea Scrolls,* 74.

[39] R. Collins, *Introduction to the New Testament,* 39.

[40] F. F. Bruce, "Tradition and the Canon of Scripture," 74.

churches helped determine which books were included in the church's authoritative list. The reaction against Montanism prompted a broad suspicion of prophetic literature, leading to its neglect in succeeding generations of the church, especially in the East. The *Apocalypse of Peter* was not cited as frequently after the Montanist controversies as before, and the book of Revelation also had a stormy reception, especially through the fourth century.

E. ADAPTABILITY

Scriptures were also adaptable to the changing circumstances of the church's life. Some writings that functioned as Scripture earlier in the church's history, such as *Barnabas, 1 Clement,* the letters of Ignatius, *Shepherd of Hermas,* and *Eldad and Modad,* did not survive the criterion of adaptability. They fell into disuse and dropped from the Scripture collections. This happened mostly while the notion of canon was still fluid in the churches, namely, before the fourth century. Some noncanonical writings, however, occasionally appear in NT codices into the fourth and fifth centuries. For instance, *Barnabas* and the *Shepherd of Hermas* are in Codex Alexandrinus, and *1–2 Clement* are in Codex Vaticanus.

Sanders focuses considerable attention on the adaptability of the OT and NT Scriptures to the continually changing circumstances of the communities of faith. The sacred writings that brought hope in a hopeless situation for the people of Israel told a story that could be applied to new circumstances. This story, significantly enhanced through the creative hermeneutics that were employed by the church, offered hope and life to the new people of faith.[41] This is, of course, the story of God's activity in Jesus, the proclaimed Christ. This story continues to be adaptable to the changing circumstances of life of a variety of persons in a variety of cultures. Through it, persons of faith perceive that God continues to release from bondage, to bring healing, and to offer hope to the hopeless. This story is adaptable and continues to inspire persons in every generation—and this is what the church canonized.

F. INSPIRATION

To what extent did inspiration play a role in the canonization process? Traditionally, many have argued that the biblical canon resulted from the church's recognition of the inspired status of certain writings. However, it is more accurate to say that inspiration was a corollary, rather than a crite-

[41]J. A. Sanders, *From Sacred Story,* 9–39, deals with the adaptability issue in detail. He makes the case that what holds true for ancient Israel in this regard is also true for the church, namely, that the story that had sufficient adaptability to meet the ever-changing needs of the church was preserved and canonized.

rion, of canonicity. That is, acceptance of a writing as Scripture and its inclusion in the biblical canon demonstrated that the writing was inspired by God. The problem with adding inspiration to the above criteria is twofold. First is the difficulty of determining what is or is not inspired. This difficulty stems from the term's fluidity of meaning in ancient Christianity. In fact, the church has never presented a comprehensive and clear definition of inspiration. The resultant ambiguity is seen in the variety of ways the term has been used throughout the ages, including our own. Second, and more important, the early church never limited the concept of inspiration to its sacred writings, but rather extended it to everything considered theologically true, whether it was written, taught, or preached.

The ancient church fathers believed that their Scriptures were inspired, but inspiration alone was not the basis for including those works in the NT canon. Several writers of sacred truth believed that they were inspired as they wrote. The author of the book of Revelation, for example, claims prophetic inspiration: "I warn everyone who hears the words of the prophecy of this book: if anyone adds to them, God will add to that person the plagues described in this book; if anyone takes away from the words of the book of this prophecy, God will take away that person's share in the tree of life and in the holy city, which are described in this book" (Rev 22:18–19). Clearly the author of these words believed that he had the voice of prophecy and was inspired when he wrote.

The ancient churches assumed the inspiration of their Scriptures, but to what extent did inspiration play a part in the canonizing process? Irenaeus makes it clear that the Scriptures, even when they are not clearly understood, "were spoken by the Word of God and by His Spirit" (*Haer.* 2.28.2, *ANF*). Similarly, Origen maintained that "the Scriptures were written by the Spirit of God, and have a meaning, not such only as is apparent at first sight, but also another which escapes the notice of most" (*First Principles* preface 8, *ANF*).[42] Seeking to discredit the *Doctrine of Peter,* he says that he can show that it was not written by Peter "or by any other person inspired by the Spirit of God" (*First Principles* preface 8, *ANF*). The operating assumption here, of course, is that Scripture is inspired, but heresy and falsehood are not.

Theophilus of Antioch (ca. 180) reflects the belief that the Scriptures were inspired when he asserts that "the holy writings teach us, and all the spirit-bearing [inspired] men . . . that at first God was alone, and the Word in Him" (*Autol.* 2.22, *ANF*). Inspiration involved "men of God carrying in them a holy spirit [*pneumatophoroi*] and becoming prophets, being inspired and made wise by God, became God-taught, and holy and

[42]F. F. Bruce, *Canon of Scripture,* 267–68, notes that Irenaeus was the first Christian writer to allegorize the NT writings because he was among the first to treat NT writings as unreservedly inspired. Thereafter, Origen and others felt free to allegorize the Scriptures *because* they were considered inspired of God.

righteous" (*Autol.* 2.9).[43] The author of *2 Clement* believed that *1 Clement* was an inspired document and cites *1 Clem.* 23.3–4 with the words "for the prophetic word also says [*legei gar kai ho prophētikos logos*] (*2 Clem.* 11.2), the usual words to designate inspired writings. *Barnabas* 16.5 introduces a passage from *2 Enoch* with the words "for the Scripture says [*legei gar hē graphē*]." In a somewhat different light, Clement of Rome (ca. 95) told his readers that Paul's letter, 1 Corinthians, was written "with true inspiration [*ep' alētheias pneumatikōs*]" (*1 Clem.* 47.3) and he later claimed the same inspiration for himself, saying that his own letter was written "through the Holy Spirit [*gegrammenois dia tou hagiou pneumatos*]" (*1 Clem.* 63.2). Ignatius likewise expressed awareness of his own inspiration: "I spoke with a great voice—with God's own voice. . . . But some suspected me of saying this because I had previous knowledge of the division of some persons: but he in whom I am bound is my witness that I had no knowledge of this from any human being, but the Spirit was preaching and saying this [*to de pneuma ekēryssen legon tade*]" (Ign. *Phld.* 7.1b–2, LCL).

There are in fact many examples of noncanonical authors who claimed, or were acknowledged by others, to have been filled or inspired by the Spirit in their speaking or writing.[44] The point is that the Scriptures were not the *only* ancient writings that were believed to be inspired by God. Generally speaking, in the early church the common word for "inspiration" (*theopneustos;* see 2 Tim 3:16) was used not only in reference to the Scriptures (OT or NT), but also of individuals who spoke or wrote the truth of God. For example, Gregory of Nyssa (ca. 330–95) describes Basil's (330–79) commentary on the creation story and claims that the work was inspired and that his words even surpassed those of Moses in terms of beauty, complexity, and form: it was an "exposition given by inspiration of God . . . [admired] no less than the words composed by Moses himself."[45] Kalin notes that the famous epitaph of Abercius from about the fourth century was called an "inspired inscription [*theopneuston epigramma*]" and that a synodical letter of the Council of Ephesus (ca. 433) describing the council's condemnation of Nestorius was termed "their inspired judgment [or decision] [*tēs auton theopneustou kriseōs*]."[46]

---

[43]This passage clarifies what Theophilus means by inspiration and perhaps how it was understood by his and other communities.

[44]Other examples are listed in Sundberg, "Bible Canon," 365–71; and Kalin, "Inspired Community."

[45]Gregory of Nyssa, *Apologia hexaemeron,* quoted from Metzger, *Canon of the New Testament,* 256; see also Kalin, "Argument from Inspiration," 170.

[46]*Vita Abercii* 76. The writing was apparently penned by Abercius Marcellus himself, who was bishop of Hieropolis in Phrygia of Asia Minor in the late second century. He died ca. 200 C.E. Kalin gives several other examples of the ancient use of the term "inspired" (*theopneustos*) to show that it was not exclusively used of Scriptures. See Kalin, "The Inspired Community," 169–73.

From these and many other examples, we see that the ancient church did not limit inspiration to the Scriptures or even to literature alone. In his *Dialogue with Trypho,* Justin Martyr argues that "the prophetical gifts remain with us even to the present time. And hence you ought to understand that [the gifts] formerly among your nation [Israel] have been transferred to us" (*Dial.* 82, *ANF;* see also *Dial.* 87–88). Even in writings that dealt with the Montanist controversy (see Eusebius, *Hist. eccl.* 5.14–19) in the latter third of the second century, Kalin finds no evidence that the early church confined inspiration to an already past apostolic age or even to a collection of sacred writings.[47] The traditional assumption that the early Christians believed that *only* the canonical writings were inspired is highly questionable. The rabbinic notion that "when the latter prophets died, that is, Haggai, Zechariah, and Malachi, then the Holy Spirit came to an end in Israel" (*t. Sotah* 13:2, Neusner, *Tosefta,* 885) was simply not shared by the church.[48] From his investigation of the church fathers up to 400, Kalin failed to turn up one example where an orthodox but noncanonical writing was ever called uninspired; such a designation was reserved for heretical authors. He concludes: "If the Scriptures were the *only* writings the church fathers considered inspired, one would expect them to say so, at least once in a while."[49] He adds that in the early church inspiration applied not only to all Scripture, but also to the Christian community, as it bore "living witness of Jesus Christ." Only heresy was considered to be noninspired, because it was contrary to this witness.[50] Von Campenhausen agrees but adds that the presence of prophetic literature among the Montanists—literature believed by the Montanists to be born of or prompted by the Holy Spirit but by others to be misguided—shows that at the end of the second century belief in inspiration was beginning to be confined to first-century literature.[51]

Inspiration played no discernible role in the later discussion of the formation of the biblical canon. Barr summarizes the traditional understanding of the role of inspiration and canon formation as follows: "If we take a really strict old-fashioned view of inspiration, all books within the

---

[47] Kalin, "Inspired Community," 543, who concludes from his study of Irenaeus, Origen, Eusebius, and other ancient fathers that only the work of the false prophets mentioned in the OT, the heathen oracles, and philosophy were noninspired. See also Kalin, "Argument from Inspiration," 163, 168.

[48] See Blenkinsopp, "Formation of the Hebrew Bible Canon," 54 n. 3: "The Holy Spirit (meaning the spirit of prophecy) departed from Israel after the destruction of Solomon's temple (*b. B. Bat.* 12a; *b. Yoma* 21b; *b. Soṭah* 48a) or after the death of the last biblical prophets (*b. Yoma* 9b; *b. Sanh.* 11a)." See also idem, "Prophecy and Priesthood in Josephus"; and J. A. Sanders, "Spinning the Bible," for a similar perspective.

[49] Kalin, "Inspired Community," 544–45.

[50] Ibid., 547.

[51] Von Campenhausen, *Formation of the Christian Bible,* 234–35.

canon are fully inspired by the Holy Spirit, and no books outside it, however good in other respects, are inspired."[52] He later stresses that one of the difficulties in the whole notion of canon in the early church is the difficulty of distinguishing inspired and noninspired writings.[53] The problem the early church had in deciding what literature was inspired demonstrates a lack of agreement on the meaning of inspiration.[54] The ongoing prophetic ministry of the Spirit, which called individuals through the proclamation of the good news to faith in Jesus Christ, was believed by the church to be resident in *their* community of faith and in *their* ministry, just as it was in the first century. The Christian community believed that God continued to inspire individuals in their proclamation, just as God inspired the writers of the NT literature. They believed that the Spirit was the gift of God to the whole church, not just to writers of sacred literature.

Does this conclusion pose an affront to the uniqueness and authority of the biblical literature? That would be the case if its only unique characteristic were its inspiration. But inspiration was not the distinguishing factor that separated either the apostles from subsequent Christians or the Christian Scriptures from all other Christian literature. Stendahl summarizes the role that inspiration played in early Christianity and biblical tradition: "Inspiration, to be sure, is the divine presupposition for the NT, but the twenty-seven books were never chosen because they, and only they, were recognized as inspired. Strange as it may sound, inspiration was not enough. Other standards had to be applied."[55] Bruce agrees, adding that "inspiration is no longer a criterion of canonicity: it is a corollary of canonicity."[56] Similarly, Metzger notes that the focus of inspiration was on the truth claims of what was written, not inspiration itself: "While it is true that the Biblical authors were inspired by God, this does not mean that inspiration is a criterion of canonicity. A writing is not canonical because the author was inspired, but rather an author is considered to be inspired because what he has written is recognized as canonical, that is, is recognized as authoritative."[57] Inspiration was not a *criterion* by which a NT book was given the status of Scripture and later placed into a fixed biblical canon, but rather a *corollary* to its recognized status.

---

[52] Barr, *Holy Scripture,* 49. Similarly, Achtemeier, *Inspiration of Scripture,* 119, says that the prevailing view is that "God inspired the canonical books with no exception, and no noncanonical books are inspired, with no exception."

[53] Barr, *Holy Scripture,* 57.

[54] For example, Clement of Alexandria cited the *Didache* as Scripture (*Strom.* 1.100.4) and believed that *1 Clement, Barnabas, Shepherd of Hermas, Preaching of Peter,* and the *Apocalypse of Peter* were inspired literature. See Grant, "New Testament Canon," 302.

[55] Stendahl, "Apocalypse of John," 245.

[56] F. F. Bruce, *Canon of Scripture,* 268.

[57] Metzger, *Canon of the New Testament,* 257.

III. Summary

The historical circumstances that led to the canonization of the NT literature are not completely clear today, since no surviving literature identifies the canonical process. But it seems likely that all of the above criteria played some role in shaping the NT canon. Ultimately, it appears that the writings that were accorded scriptural status were the ones that best conveyed the earliest Christian proclamation and that also best met the growing needs of local churches in the third and fourth centuries. Conversely, literature that was deemed no longer relevant to the church's needs, even though it may have been considered pertinent at an earlier time, was eliminated from consideration. If this is true, it is not the only time that the church focused on literature that was most relevant to its own historical situation; NT scholars have long recognized that the social circumstances of the life of the church played a significant role in the selection, organization, and editing of the materials that form the NT Gospels. The relevance of NT writings to the churches in subsequent generations must have played some role in their preservation, while other contenders that ceased to be useful to the church gradually disappeared. This explanation best accounts for the variety of books in the surviving OT and NT collections in the ancient church. Although the leaders of the church in the fourth century and later pushed for unity in the recognition of which books were inspired, authoritative, and therefore canonical, unanimity proved unattainable due to diverse circumstances in the churches. Nevertheless, the key to understanding the preservation and canonization of the books that make up our current NT is probably usage, especially usage in the larger churches during the third through the fifth centuries.

In summary, it was important to the church that apostles, or those close to them, produced its writings. It was also important to the church, especially in the second through fourth centuries, that these writings conform to the church's broad core of beliefs. The significance of the NT writings to the churches is shown by their widespread use in the life, teaching, and worship of those churches, and such use also contributed to their canonization. The end product of the long and complex canonization process was an authoritative and inspired instrument that continued to be useful in and adaptible to the ministry and worship of a changing church. That instrument clarified the church's essential identity and mission as a community of Christ.

CHAPTER FIFTEEN

Final Reflections

THE EARLIEST CHRISTIANS RECOGNIZED ABOVE ALL OTHERS THE AUTHORITY OF Jesus as the living witness in the apostolic community.[1] If Jesus said it, that settled the matter. He was the unassailable authority for the church; he was its Lord. From the beginning, the Christians also accepted the not-yet-stabilized OT collection of Scriptures—especially its predictive witness to the Christ event as an apologetic for Christian preaching. There were few occasions in the first century when the followers of Jesus saw a need for anything more than the oral traditions about Jesus circulating among the Christians and the Scriptures of the Jews, what later was called the OT. While the memory of the apostolic witness was still fresh in the minds of the Christians and conveyed by eyewitnesses to the events of Jesus' life and fate, there was little need in the church for attention to be given to written records. To the degree that the early Christians believed that they could find adequate witness to Jesus the Christ and the kerygma about him in the OT Scriptures, there was no need to focus on the priority of "apostolic" documents, let alone *Christian* Scriptures.[2] Quite early, however, the ancient church circulated and often referred to Christian documents, as well as the oral tradition behind them, as a resource for Christian identity and guidance in the ongoing life of their churches, even though this literature was not yet on a par with the OT Scriptures.

In the middle to late second century, however, and largely as a result of the challenges to what was believed at that time to be the norm for Christian faith and practice, many of the leaders of the church began to defend the legitimacy and truthfulness of their message by appealing to the succession of the apostolic preaching, that is, the "apostolic deposit" that was believed by the church to have originated with eyewitness authority.[3]

---

[1] For a helpful discussion, see Koester, "*Gnomai Diaphoroi,*" 117–18.

[2] Shelley, *By What Authority?* 57.

[3] The importance of the apostolic tradition in the early church, or the apostolic eyewitness account of the words and event of Jesus, was established quite soon after the death of Jesus (1 Cor 15:3–8; Acts 1:21–22) and after the death of the

The church also believed that this deposit was conveyed faithfully in succeeding generations through the church's bishops. It was affirmed not only that the bishops carefully handed on this canon of faith in the churches, but also that some early Christian literature was believed to have faithfully conveyed that same apostolic message. Throughout the last half of the second century, no closed orthodox canon of authoritative Christian writings was universally acknowledged,[4] but the literature that was believed to have faithfully transmitted the message of Jesus Christ began to be widely recognized and played a useful role in the life and worship of the church.

Some of this literature was acknowledged early on as Scripture—possibly in the early decades of the second century—though that would have been an exception rather than the rule in the churches at that time. In the last quarter of the second century some core documents (mainly the four Gospels and *some* Letters of Paul) emerged as authoritative Scriptures in the life and worship of the church equal in authority, at least functionally, with the OT. These writings were not, however, a closed biblical canon at that stage; closed canons began to emerge in the fourth and fifth centuries. The practice of drawing up closed lists of authoritative NT Scriptures appears to have started with Eusebius, and within a short time such lists began to appear frequently in both the East and the West. With the possible exceptions of Melito and Origen, Christian OT canons also began to appear in the fourth century. These two earlier exceptions, however, are found only in Eusebius's *Ecclesiastical History,* a fourth-century document. Prior to this time, one searches in vain for such canonical lists of sacred Scriptures. At first, these lists were products of individuals and subsequently (especially in the fifth century) began to grow out of council decisions.

To what extent were these developments a result of the church's response to heresy, that is, its response to a proliferation of inspired writings thrust upon the Christian community by gnostic and charismatic communities, or to the conscious decisions at grassroots levels of the churches regarding which books could be handed over to be burned? To what extent were these natural developments in the church in view of or in response to the Roman cultural influence, which called for conformity and consensus? In what way was the biblical canon affected by contemporary and parallel notions in the ancient world? Why did a need for such a precisely defined

---

apostles. It was taken up into the church's witness both for inward community concern (*1 Clem.* 42.1; 2 Pet 3:2) and polemical argument against heresy (Justin, *1 Apol.* 42.4; 50.12; Irenaeus, *Haer.* 3.3.1–3; Tertullian, *Praescr.* 6). In the examples from Irenaeus and Tertullian the guarantee of the accuracy of the church's canon of faith was secured by apostolic succession wherein the truthfulness of their understanding of the gospel was passed on through the church's bishops from the apostles.

[4]Orthodoxy itself was only in its early formative stages at this time.

collection of sacred Scriptures arise in the churches? What are the roots of the notion of a canon of Scripture? Why does such an idea come forth (first of all in Judaism) only after Alexander the Great and during a time when other canons were widely employed in the Hellenistic world? To what extent was the biblical canon strongly influenced by the idea of a perfect guide (from the divine, as in Plato) in the Hellenistic world or of peace and harmony in the Roman world? Was that a legitimate influence on a church that has always claimed to be free in Jesus Christ and alive in the power of the Spirit? In other words, are fixed scriptural canons Christian? There can be little doubt that scriptural canons had the effect of legitimizing only one branch of Christianity.

Whatever our response to these and other related questions, a careful survey of the literature that makes up the present Christian canon of both OT and NT Scriptures shows clearly that the church was not of one mind in this matter or in many others (a fixed biblical text, an approved translation, etc.). As our historical survey shows, *final* agreement on the scope of the biblical canon was not reached through a general recognition or consensus in the churches. Rather, attempts were made to arrive at a consensus by council decisions of the church hierarchy, whose decisions were not always followed by the churches themselves. Also, the precise boundaries of the Christian faith (i.e., beliefs that defined the nature of Christianity) were never fully agreed upon either, even though there was finally some agreement by the orthodox churches (those of a "Roman bent") that the church was not broad enough to allow for the presence of Docetics, gnostics, Marcionites, Ebionites, and Montanists.

The primary criterion by which the ancient church established its canon of authoritative Scriptures was clearly a modified form of apostolicity, but the task of determining what was apostolic was not easy since even the heretical Christians claimed to have an apostolic heritage. Eventually the view that carried the day was that the apostolic deposit—genuine witness to and from Jesus Christ (the church's true *canon*)—was transmitted faithfully from the apostles to the church through its succession of bishops. What does not appear to have been given serious consideration in the late-second-century church is that the earliest apostolic community may not have been so monolithic in its passing on of a single orthodox tradition as the later church apparently supposed. This is so, in spite of Irenaeus's overly optimistic and somewhat naive assertion that "the churches which have been planted in Germany do not believe or hand down anything different, nor do those in Spain, nor those in Gaul, nor those in the East, nor those in Egypt, nor those in Libya, nor those which have been established in the central regions of the world. . . . The Catholic church possesses one and the same faith throughout the whole world, as we have already said" (*Haer.* 3.10.2–3, *ANF*). What the church eventually recognized as apostolic was in no way monolithic or uniform throughout the churches in Irenaeus's day. This lack of theological and historical agreement, however, may not have been a fault if one sees from the NT itself that the church thereby canonized breadth and diversity.[5]

Nevertheless, did the church *need* a fixed catalogue of Scriptures for its continuing existence and for dealing with the various heresies in the community of faith? There can be no doubt about the advantages of possessing an early written reflection of the Christ event that called the church into existence. What else could have reminded the church of its true identity when the oral tradition of and about Jesus began to fade in the church's memory in the second century? Since Christianity is a historical religion—its faith is directed toward a historical character who lived, died, and rose from the dead in Palestine around 30—how could it fail to have an interest in the documents that were believed to be closest to these events, purporting not only to report them, but also to express their significance? A fixed collection of Christian writings, like the collection of Gospels put forth by Irenaeus, was not as important to the church in earlier times, for example, before Marcion,[6] because the continuing circulation of oral tradition was still fresh in the early second century and was deemed sufficient for the church's needs.

It is perhaps also likely that the heretical threats to the church by the Judaizers and Docetics were such that they could be identified and dealt with easier by the oral tradition of the church than at a later time when the church faced Marcionite, gnostic, and Montanist heresies.[7] Shelley suggests that the earlier Judaizing and Docetic heresies were not the type to call for a theory of apostolic authority as were the later Marcionite and gnostic heresies. The heretical groups of the middle to late second century and later appealed to an apostolic tradition as foundation for their teachings. The church, therefore, understandably appealed to an apostolic tradition that it claimed was passed on in the churches by the apostles through the bishops, who, it was believed, inherited the leadership of the churches from the apostles.

The obvious difficulty that the church had in defining the precise limits of its canon, as well as the problem that closed canons began to emerge late in the church (the fourth century)—not to mention the problem that

---

[5] So argues Dunn, *Unity and Diversity in the New Testament,* 377.

[6] Although a Pauline corpus of writings was probably in circulation by the end of the first century, and most assuredly collections of the sayings of Jesus (e.g., Q, Matthew, Luke, *Gospel of Thomas*) were in existence well before that time, there appeared to be no need at that time for a fixed or closed list of such writings. This is evidence of a church whose oral traditions were still serving it quite well some one hundred years after its beginnings. Apart from Irenaeus's gospel canon, probably no other *closed* canon of Christian literature existed before Eusebius. Origen's list was probably an invention by Eusebius, although he does have a fixed four-gospel canon.

[7] Shelley, *By What Authority?* 57–58.

this canon had in defining the nature of Christian faith adequately[8]—raises several important questions.

First and most important, of course, is the church right in perceiving the need for a closed canon of Scriptures? If the term *Christian* is best defined by the examples and beliefs passed on by earliest followers of Jesus, then we must at least ponder the question of whether the notion of a biblical canon is necessarily Christian. The best available information about the earliest followers of Jesus shows that they did not have such canons as the church presently possesses today, nor did they indicate that their successors should draw them up. Even the church's collection of OT Scriptures was considerably broader in scope than those presently found in either the Catholic or Protestant canons and with much more flexibility than our present collections allow. To the extent that this is true, one is forced to ask the question of whether biblical canons are in fact Christian?

Second, has the present biblical canon legitimized the practice of slavery (Eph 6:5–8; Col 3:22–25)[9] or the subjugation of half of the human race, which has an equal claim to having been created in the image of God (Eph 5:22–23; Col 3:18; 1 Tim 2:11–15; and 1 Pet 3:1–6)? In other words, does the biblical canon as the word of God ever become a "letter of the law," thereby missing the true liberating gospel? Stendahl, observing how the Bible has been used throughout the history of the church to justify the unjustifiable, comments that "there never has been an evil cause in the world that has not become more evil if it has been possible to argue it on biblical grounds."[10] More specifically, Stendahl argues that slavery in the Western world would have vanished more quickly were it not that slavery is neither condemned nor discouraged in the Bible.

Third, did such a move toward a closed canon of Scriptures ultimately (and unconsciously) limit the presence and power of the Holy Spirit in the church? More precisely, does the recognition of absoluteness of the biblical canon minimize the presence and activity of God in the church today? Does God act in the church today and by the same Spirit? On what biblical or historical basis has the inspiration of God been limited to written documents that the church now calls its Bible?

Fourth, should the church be limited to an OT canon to which Jesus and his first disciples were clearly not limited? Writings from a much broader perspective informed the theology and practice of the early Christian community. The final limits of the OT canon used by the Protestants

---

[8]Why else would so many creeds crop up in the church after the relative acceptance of a canon unless the message of that canon was somewhat blurred or imprecise?

[9]It is well established that the church as a whole had very little conscience about this matter for the first six centuries of its history.

[10]Stendahl, "Ancient Scripture in the Modern World," 205.

were in part defined by Jewish polemic against the church. What obligation does the church have to limit itself today to a canon of OT Scriptures that was not the precise canon of the earliest Christians?

Fifth, if apostolicity is a still a legitimate criterion for canonicity of the NT literature as it was for the churches that first began to draw up biblical canons, should the church today continue to recognize the authority of 2 Peter, the Pastorals, and other nonapostolic literature of the NT? If the Spirit was not limited to apostolic documents alone, can we and should we not make other arguments for their inclusion in the biblical canon? For example, should our attention be on the authorship of a document or on the substance of the document itself to determine its inspiration and authority in the church? Although there was considerable doubt about the authorship of Hebrews among the church fathers, the book nevertheless was included in the biblical canon because its message was both relevant and important to the Christian communities that preserved and adopted it as Scripture.

Sixth, is it appropriate to tie the modern church to a canon that emerged out of the historical circumstances in the second to fifth centuries? Are we necessarily supposed to make absolute the experience of that church for all time, even though its historical context is not that of the earliest Christian community or that of the present church? Those who argue for the infallibility or the inerrancy of Scripture logically should also claim the same infallibility for the churches in the fourth and fifth centuries, whose decisions and historical circumstances have left us with our present Bible. This is apparently what would be required if we were to acknowledge only the twenty-seven NT books that were set forth by the church in that context. Did the church in the Nicene and post-Nicene eras make an infallible decision?[11]

Finally, if the Spirit inspired only the *written* documents of the first century, does that mean that the same Spirit does not speak today in the church about matters that are of *more* significant concern now than then, for example, the use of contraceptives, abortion, liberation, ecological irresponsibility, equal rights, pulling the plug on a comatose patient, nuclear proliferation, global genocide, economic and social justice, and so on?

In an age when biblical scholarship has advanced our understanding of the historical context of the early church and the background and interpretation of its biblical literature beyond the critical skills of the ancient church that first dealt with the notion of a canon of Christian Scriptures, it may be that the time has come for the church to examine anew this series of questions related to its biblical canon. To do so, of course, would be to open up Pandora's Box, and it is doubtful whether we could ever hope to arrive at a consensus in the church on precisely what books should make

[11] Best, "Scripture, Tradition, and the Canon," 271–77, also raises this question.

up any new canon. Although some scholars are ready to open this issue,[12] advising that some books be jettisoned from the NT and others be included, it is not likely that the gain from such an enterprise would be worth the pain in the long or short run. It is not clear that the inclusion of some noncanonical gospels, acts, or letters would necessarily enhance or accurately improve the picture of Jesus provided in the NT writings.

New inquiry into the origins of the biblical canon might permit the church to feel freer to allow other ancient (or modern) voices to inform its understanding of God today. I say this even though I am *not* in favor of rejecting the present biblical canon in order to create a new closed canon of Scriptures. The church would trade in its present Bible for another only at its own peril. The documents we possess sufficiently inform the church of the core of the gospel—the good news of God in Jesus Christ. More important, they inform us that Jesus Christ alone is the true and final canon for the child of God (Matt 28:18). There should be no fear, however, of allowing other ancient literature to inform our faith since some of that extrabiblical literature (the Apocrypha, Pseudepigrapha, and other early Christian literature) informed the faith of the earliest Christians and even later ones. And some of the noncanonical gospels may indeed contain a few authentic strands of the teachings and sayings of Jesus. If that is the case, why should Christians avoid listening to them, at least in a careful and critical manner?

If some of the agrapha, or the isolated sayings of Jesus, found in the early church fathers, in ancient manuscripts, and in some apocryphal sources are indeed the authentic sayings of Jesus, should we not allow those sayings to inform the picture of Jesus established through biblical research? In spite of what is believed to be a reasonable and important call to listen to other ancient voices, it must be stressed in closing that no other ancient documents are *on the whole* more reliable in informing the church's faith than our present biblical canon. Nevertheless, it must also be stressed that the *final* authority of the church is not its Bible, but its Lord (Matt 28:18), who preceded the origins of the Bible and continues to lay claim to humanity's loyalty and devotion.

My aim in this study has been to bring some light to the often dimly lit corridors that led to the formation of our Bible and, in that process, to re-

---

[12]Robert Funk and several scholars from the controversial Jesus Seminar have initiated the discussion that may try to gain a scholarly consensus in the matter. In an interview Funk claimed that "the Christian movement hasn't seriously examined the question of canon since the 15th century" and added that "it's time for academic scholars to raise the issue." See Sheler, "Cutting Loose the Holy Canon," 75. The group has also created a Canon Seminar to create what they call a "Scholars' Canon," which may include the *Gospel of Thomas* and exclude the book of Revelation. The Canon Seminar participants backed away from calling the results of their work a new "Bible" since many are employed by "mainline denomination-owned universities and colleges." See Perkes, "Scripture Revision Won't Be a Bible."

mind the reader of the true canon of faith for the church: our Lord Jesus Christ. The Bible is still the church's book, without which the Christian faith would be a blur. Without it, Christians would have difficulty in articulating their identity and mission. Without it, there could be little basis for renewal of the believing communities around the world. Careful study of the biblical message in its historical environment and in the community of faith in which it was first acknowledged as Scripture and canon will prove invaluable to the church. Lessons learned from this approach will not only free the church from inappropriate loyalties, but will also help the church to focus more clearly on the true object and final authority of its faith.

APPENDIX A

An Outline of Canon Research: Primary Sources and Questions

I. The Old Testament Canon

A. PRIMARY SOURCES FOR THE STUDY OF THE FORMATION OF THE OLD TESTAMENT CANON

1. Ezra 9–10 and Neh 8–9: the reading of the law of Moses and what writings were authoritative in the fifth century B.C.E.
2. Sirach 49:8–10: Ezekiel, Job, and the Twelve Prophets. See also the broader context of Sir 44:1–50:25, which focuses on the "Praise of Famous Men."
3. Prologue to Sirach: three groupings of sacred literature. The third group is indistinct, and none of the literature is specifically identified within the groupings.
4. 1 Macc 1:54–57: the destruction of the Jewish sacred writings during the Seleucid tyranny against Israel.
5. 2 Macc 2:13–15: Judas Maccabeus's recovery and collection of unidentified Jewish sacred writings.
6. 4QMMT (perhaps ca. 150 B.C.E.): a very difficult text to interpret because of its corruption, but it does describe three or four vague groupings of sacred writings.
7. *Letter of Aristeas* 308–311 (ca. 110–100 B.C.E.): the origins of the LXX, which included only the law of Moses.
8. Philo, *Contempl. Life* 25–29 and *Moses* 2.37–40: three or four categories of sacred writings of the Therapeutae (Essenes) in Egypt roughly just before the ministry of Jesus.

9. Luke 11:48–51: Jesus' reference to the martyrs in the OT beginning with the first (Abel) and concluding with the last (Zechariah), perhaps indicating that 2 Chronicles was the last book in Jesus' OT canon.

10. Luke 24:44: Jesus' mention of the law, prophets, and psalms, perhaps a reference to the whole of the Writings, only the book of Psalms, or simply some of the psalms.

11. *Jub.* 2:23–24, as cited by Epiphanius, *On Weights and Measures* 22 (ca. 380 C.E.): a twenty-two-book biblical canon.

12. Josephus, *Ag. Ap.* 1.37–43 (ca. 90 C.E.): a three-part twenty-two-book biblical canon.

13. Josephus, *Ag. Ap.* 1.41; *Ant.* 13.311–13; *J.W.* 6.286; 6.300–309: prophecy ceased at the time of Ezra.

14. *4 Ezra* 14:22–48 (ca. 90–100 C.E.): the divine translation of ninety-four holy books—twenty-four plus seventy others, probably a reference to the sacredness of the apocryphal and pseudepigraphal literature as well as to a twenty-four-book collection of Hebrew Bible Scriptures.

15. Mishnah, completed under the direction of Rabbi Judah the Prince (ca. 200–210 C.E.): *m. Yadayim* 3.2–5 and 4.6 refer to books that "defile the hands."

16. Babylonian Talmud, tractate *Bava Batra* 14b–15a (ca. middle to late second century C.E.): a specific list by name of the twenty-four books of the Hebrew Bible in three distinct categories.

17. Other rabbinic literature debating the place of some books in the sacred collection:
    a. Song of Songs (*m. Yadayim* 3:5; *b. Megillah* 7a)
    b. Ecclesiastes (*m. Yadayim* 3:5; *b. Shabbat* 100a)
    c. Ruth (*b. Megillah* 7a)
    d. Esther (*b. Sanhedrin* 100a; *b. Megillah* 7a)
    e. Proverbs (*b. Shabbat* 30b)
    f. Ezekiel (*b. Shabbat* 13b; *b. Hagigah* 13a; *b. Menahot* 45a)

18. The church fathers' references to the OT Scriptures:
    a. Justin Martyr, *Dial.* 100; *1 Apol.* 28.1; 67.3
    b. Melito (in Eusebius, *Hist. eccl.* 4.26.12–14)
    c. Irenaeus, *Haer.* 2.27.2; 3.3.3; 3.11.8; 3.12.15; 3.14.1–15.1; 3.17.4; 3.21.3–4
    d. Clement of Alexandria, *Strom.* 7.20 (cf. Eusebius, *Hist. eccl.* 6.13.4–8; 6.25.1–2)
    e. Origen, *Letter to Africanus* 13 (cf. Julius Africanus, *History of Susanna*)

f. Tertullian, *Marc.* 4.2.2, 5; *Prax.* 15; *Praescr.* 32 (cf. *Marc.* 1.29; 4.2; 5.18.1; *Praescr.* 38.7)
g. Augustine, *On Christian Learning* 2.13
h. Athanasius, *Thirty-ninth Festal Letter*
i. Cyril of Jerusalem, *Catechetical Lectures* 4.36
j. Rufinus, *On the Creed* 36
k. Epiphanius, *On Weights and Measures* 22–23; *Panarion* 8.6.1

19. Canonical lists of the fourth and fifth centuries from both the East and the West: see appendixes B–C.

20. Cairo Genizah: a cache of recovered documents deemed sacred among the Jews in Cairo in the eighth and ninth centuries C.E., plus nonsacred writings that contained sacred names.

21. Canonical "glue" texts that unite portions of the OT literature: Deut 34:1–12; 2 Chron 36:22–23; Ezra 1:1–4; Mal 4:4–6. See also Prov 25:1.

B. QUESTIONS FOR THE STUDY OF THE FORMATION OF THE OLD TESTAMENT CANON

1. Do Josephus's apologetic comments in *Ag. Ap.* 1.37–43 reflect the actual state of the OT canon for all Jews at the end of the first century C.E.?

2. Did the *Copper Scroll* and the *Damascus Document* function as canon at Qumran? Was the Psalter at Qumran the same as it was for the rest of Judaism (especially in light of the discoveries at Cave 11)? Do the two small fragments of Sirach (the latter identified as Sir 6:20–31) found at Qumran (2Q18) have any bearing on canon? Was the Scripture canon of the Essenes and the Pharisees the same, as some scholars contend?

3. In the first century C.E., did the Sadducees have a smaller biblical canon than that of the Pharisees or the Essenes (see Josephus, *Ant.* 18.16; 13.297; Matt 22:23–33; Acts 23:6–10; Origen, *Against Celsus* 1.49; and Jerome, *Commentary on Matthew* 22.31).

4. Should the Samaritans, because of the nature of their biblical canon and the time of their separation from mainstream Judaism, be factored into the discussion of the Hebrew biblical canon? Did both groups have the same Scripture canon (the Torah) at the time of their separation? Were other biblical canons present in Palestine in the first century C.E., namely, those of the Essenes, Sadducees, and Samaritans?

5. Do the words "you have heard it said . . . but I say unto you" attributed to Jesus (Matt 5:21–22, 27–28, 31–32, 33–34, 38–39, 43–44) suggest for Jesus that not all Scripture was inviolable? Does Matt 5:18

reflect the notion of a fixed OT canon in the time of Jesus? Did it refer to only the Law?

6. Was the OT canon complete or fixed (canon 2) before or by the time of Jesus? What is the evidence? If it was fixed, what comprised this canon? What evidence suggests that there were three well-defined and firmly fixed parts of the OT canon (Law, Prophets, and Writings) before, during, or after the time of Jesus?

7. Why are there so few references to the Hebrew Scriptures in the Mishnah? Does this reflect second-century rabbinic notions of authority or a changing notion of authority within Judaism at that time?

8. Does the second-century *b. Bava Batra* 14b–15a, the first reference in ancient Judaism to specifically identify the twenty-four books in the Jewish Scripture canon, reflect what was believed about the Scripture canon by all Jews of the same time? Why was this *baraita* not included in the Mishnah if it represented widespread second-century views?

9. Why do references in rabbinic literature from the second and third century C.E. indicate a conflict over the placing of some books in Judaism's Scripture canon? Was not the matter settled much earlier?

10. Are the writings of rabbinic Judaism of the second–sixth centuries anachronistic? Do they necessarily tell what happened during an earlier period (first century C.E.) or only what was believed to have happened at that time by the rabbinic sages of the later period?

11. What criteria were employed in selecting OT writings for inclusion in the Hebrew Bible? Did the criteria include whether a book was written in Hebrew, originated in Palestine, or had common use among the Jews?

12. Why were the letters of the Hebrew alphabet used by the writer of Ps 119 and elsewhere to identify sections of the psalm? Why did Josephus use the number twenty-two to identify his collection? Was this practice borrowed from the Greeks? Why did the writer of *4 Ezra* refer to twenty-four books and not to twenty-two if the latter was commonly held, as Josephus asserts?

13. Is D. N. Freedman's emphasis on balance and symmetry valid in canonical formation? Why did it take so long for scholars to discover this symmetry?

14. What do the NT references and allusions to the OT and the noncanonical writings suggest (e.g., *1 En.* 1:9 in Jude 14)? Does the author of Hebrews make use of Wis 7:25 in Heb 1:3 and Wis 7:22–30 in Heb 4:12?

15. Was there a complete Hebrew biblical canon before or shortly after Jamnia (ca. 90 C.E.)? If before, was it formed by Judas Maccabeus (ca. 164 B.C.E.)? If after, was it formed by Judah the Prince (ca. 200 C.E.), or later?

16. What do the variations in the canonical lists from the fourth through sixth centuries suggest about the dating of the finalization of the biblical canon? Do such lists indicate a lack of clarity in the church on the matter at that time? Does any evidence suggest that there was more clarity on the scope of the Bible canon at an earlier date?

II. The New Testament Canon

A. PRIMARY SOURCES FOR THE STUDY OF THE FORMATION OF THE NEW TESTAMENT CANON

1. Apostolic Fathers who cite the NT authoritatively: *1 Clem.* 13.1–3; *Barn.* 4.14; Ign. *Phld.* 5.1–2; 8.2; Pol. *Phil.* 2.2–3; 3.2; 6.3; 7.1–2; 8.2; 12.1; *2 Clem.* 2.4–6; 14.2.

2. Ptolemy, *Letter to Flora* 3.5–8; 4.1, 4; 7.5, 10: Jesus' words in early gnostic teaching.

3. Justin, *Dial.* 28.1; 65.2; 84.4; 100.1–8; *1 Apol.* 66–67: NT writings used to support teaching and worship.

4. Marcion, *Marcionite Gospel Prologues;* Tertullian, *Marc.* 4.2–5; Adamantius, *Dialogue* 2.18; Eusebius, *Hist. eccl.* 6.12.3–6: Marcion's limited collection of NT Scriptures.

5. Irenaeus, *Haer.* 1.26.2; 2.27.2; 2.28.2; 2.35.4; 3.2.2; 3.3.1–3; 3.4.1–2; 3.11.8–9; 3.14.1; 3.15.1; 3.17.4; 4.15.2; 4.29–34: use of Scripture against heretics.

6. Origen, *Commentary on Matthew* 15.3, and *Homily on Joshua* 7: awareness of NT literature.

7. Clement of Alexandria, *Strom.* 1.20: the value of philosophy for understanding God's truth (cf. 7.16).

8. 2 Pet 3:15–16: second-century reference to Paul's writings as Scripture.

9. Athanagoras, *Resurrection of the Dead* 18 (ca. 180): citation of Paul in Scripture-like manner.

10. Theophilus, *Autol.* 1.14: heavy dependence on Paul.

11. Tertullian, *Marc.* 1.29; 4.2; 5.18.1; 5.21; *Praescr.* 32, 36, 38.4–7; *Prax.* 15: Marcion's editing of Luke and Paul.

12. Hippolytus, *Elenchus* 8.19.1 and *Refutation of All Heresies:* earlier collections of Scriptures in the second century.

13. *Gesta apud Zenophilum* 26 and *Acta Saturnini* 18: burning sacred books during the Diocletian persecution (303 C.E.).

14. Eusebius, *Hist. eccl.* discussing Christian writings: (a) his own perspective (3.3.1–5; 3.25.1–7); (b) Papias's preference for oral sources over written sources (3.39.4); (c) Martyrs of Lyons and Vienne (5.1.3–63); (d) Montanists (5.14–19); (e) persecution and burning of sacred books (8.5–6); (f) Irenaeus' NT canon and LXX collection (5.8.1–15); (g) Origen's OT and NT canon (6.24–25); (h) Clement of Alexandria's collection of divine names (6.13.4–8; 6.14.1–24); (i) Serapion's rejection of the *Gospel of Peter* (6.12.1–6); (j) Dionysius's perspective on Scripture (7.25.22–27); (k) Constantine's role in the churches and his ordering of fifty copies of Scriptures (*Life of Constantine* 2.2–4, 34–3, 65, 68).

15. New Testament canonical lists: see appendix C.

B. QUESTIONS FOR THE STUDY OF THE FORMATION OF THE NEW TESTAMENT CANON

1. What is a biblical canon, and when did it become operative in ancient Israel and in the church? Why did the church see the need for a scriptural canon in the first place?

2. If the second-century heresies of the Marcionites, gnostics, and Montanists led the church to develop a sacred collection of NT Scriptures, why were all of the responses to these groups made with a canon of truth (*regula fidei*) and not a canon of Scriptures?

3. Since there are no terms available in the second century to describe a sacred collection of NT Scriptures and none exist until the fourth century, what evidence suggests that the church was even interested in the question of a biblical canon in the second century or before?

4. Does the fact that the terms Old Testament and New Testament begin to appear in the late second century (first in Irenaeus, *Haer.* 4.15.2) suggest that both Testaments were complete by that time? Were the meanings of these two terms clear to the broad Christian community in the third century, when Origen had to clarify them (*Commentary on John* 5.4 and *First Principles* 4.11), or even to the fourth-century readers, when Eusebius also had to explain them (*Hist. eccl.* 3.9.5). Does the appearance of the Wisdom of Solomon (a pre-Christian book) in a NT list in the fourth century show that there was no precision in the identity of the literature that belonged to these collections

for a considerable period after the terms began to appear in the second century?

5. What is the date of the Muratorian Fragment (second or fourth century)? Is this document the Achilles' heel of NT canon studies? Do any second-century or fourth-century sources display style or content similar to that of the Muratorian Fragment?

6. Did Eusebius exclude the *antilegomena* or "disputed" books from his own Scripture canon (see *Hist. eccl.* 3.25.3)?

7. Does the citing of an ancient text always mean that the text was canonical for the one who cited it?

8. What do the differences in the canonical lists in the fourth and fifth centuries suggest about the development of the NT canon?

9. Are the traditional criteria for establishing the biblical canon (apostolicity, antiquity, orthodoxy, usefulness) still valid? Should they be reapplied today in light of new historical research? Can a book continue as a part of the biblical canon if it was accepted for the wrong reasons, for example, on the basis of presumed apostolic authorship?

10. What form of the biblical text is canonical for the church today? Is it the compositional/original form or the developed/final form?

11. What do we do with the authentic agrapha? Should the authentic noncanonical sayings of Jesus be included in the NT canon? On what basis?

12. How final can the current scope of the biblical canon be for the church, when Christians have never fully agreed on its contents?

13. When did the NT literature first function as Scripture and canon? Are these two notions the same?

14. What historical factors gave rise to a NT canon? What role did the burning of Christian books during the Diocletian persecution in the early fourth century have in the formation of the biblical canon?

15. Was Eusebius's production of fifty copies of the Scriptures under the direction of Constantine a critical factor in which books were selected for the biblical canon?

16. Did Constantine play a role in the formation of the biblical canon through his activity in bringing unity to the church?

17. What if another apostolic book were found? Is the canon still open *in principle?* Why? Why not?

18. Is the theological integrity of our current biblical canon affirmed by historical inquiry or by Christian experience, that is, by the church's recognition of the usefulness of these Scriptures for its faith and mission?

III. Conclusions

1. Some scholars urge that there is a conservative or evangelical position on the formation of the OT canon, namely, that it was formed or completed well before the time of Jesus, and that the NT canon was largely completed by the end of the second century C.E., with only minor modifications later. Since the origin of the biblical canon is a historical question, it seems that the only defensible position is one that can be historically coherent and can best account for the surviving traditions in the church.

2. Much work still needs to be done on this subject, but the current evidence points to the fourth century as the primary period of definition in the canonical process. The origins of the OT canonization process probably began in the fifth century B.C.E., but it was not finalized for most of the church until the fifth and sixth centuries C.E.

3. The origins of the NT canonization process began in the second century, first with the recognition of the value of Christian writings for teaching and preaching and subsequently with the recognition of its authority in the life of the church. The process did not enter into its final stages, however, until the work of Eusebius in the early part of the fourth century.

4. The biblical canon is difficult to describe since there is no certain way to speak about the normative value of the NT writings for Christian faith. The literature we have cannot be fully accounted for on the basis of any of the traditional criteria for establishing either the OT or the NT. For whatever reason, therefore, the literature that best suited the needs of the church in the fourth to sixth centuries is the literature that survived in its traditions and became a part of its sacred Scriptures.

APPENDIX B

Lists and Catalogues of Old Testament Collections

Table B-1: Old Testament Lists from the Eastern Churches

Melito[1]	*Origen*[2]	*Athanasius*[3]	*Cyril*[4]
Gen	Gen	Gen	Gen
Exod	Exod	Exod	Exod
Num	Lev	Lev	Lev
Lev	Num	Num	Num
Deut	Deut	Deut	Deut
Josh	Josh	Josh	Josh
Judg	Judg/Ruth	Judg	Judg/Ruth
Ruth	1–2 Kgs	Ruth	1–2 Kgs
1–4 Kgs	3–4 Kgs	1–2 Kgs	3–4 Kgs
1–2 Chr	1–2 Chr	3–4 Kgs	1–2 Chr
Pss	1–2 Esd	1–2 Chr	1–2 Esd
Prov	Pss	1–2 Esd	Esth
Wis	Prov	Pss	Job
Eccl	Eccl	Prov	Pss
Song	Song	Eccl	Prov
Job	Isa	Song	Eccl
Isa	Jer/Lam/Ep Jer	Job	Song
Jer	(Twelve omitted)	Twelve	Twelve
Twelve	Dan	Isa	Isa
Dan	Ezek	Jer/Bar/Lam/Ep Jer	Jer/Lam/Ep Jer/Bar
Ezek	Job	Ezek	Ezek
Esd	Esth	Dan	Dan
(Esth omitted)			

[1] Eusebius, *Hist. eccl.* 4.26.14 (ca. 320–325, Caesarea, Palestine).
[2] Eusebius, *Hist. eccl.* 6.25.2 (ca. 320–325, Caesarea, Palestine).
[3] Athanasius, *Ep. fest.* 39.4 (ca. 367, Alexandria, Egypt).
[4] Cyril of Jerusalem, *Catechetical Lectures* 4.35 (ca. 394, Bethlehem, Palestine).

(Table B-1, continued)

Epiphanius[5]	*Epiphanius*[6]	*Epiphanius*[7]	*Gregory*[8]	*Amphilochius*[9]
Gen	Gen	Gen	Gen	Gen
Exod	Exod	Exod	Exod	Exod
Lev	Lev	Lev	Lev	Lev
Num	Num	Num	Num	Num
Deut	Deut	Deut	Deut	Deut
Josh	Job	Josh	Josh	Josh
Judg	Pss	Job	Judg/Ruth	Judg
Ruth	Prov	Judg	1–4 Kgs	Ruth
Job	Eccl	Ruth	1–2 Chr	1–4 Kgs
Pss	Song	Pss	1–2 Esd	1–2 Chr
Prov	Josh	1 Chr	Job	1–2 Esd
Eccl	Judg/Ruth	2 Chr	Pss	Job
1 Kgs	1–2 Chr	1 Kgs	Eccl	Pss
2 Kgs	1–2 Kgs	2 Kgs	Song	Prov
3 Kgs	3–4 Kgs	3 Kgs	Prov	Eccl
4 Kgs	Twelve	4 Kgs	Twelve	Song
1 Chr	Isa	Prov	Isa	Twelve
2 Chr	Jer	Eccl	Jer	Isa
Twelve	Ezek	Song	Ezek	Jer
Isa	Dan	Twelve	Dan	Ezek
Jer/Lam/Ep Jer/Bar	1–2 Esd	Isa		Dan
Ezek	Esth	Jer		Esth
Dan		Ezek		
1 Esd		Dan		
2 Esd		1 Esd		
		2 Esd		
		Esth		

[5] *Haer.* 1.1.6 (ca. 374–377, Salamis, Western Syria).
[6] *De mensuribus et ponderibus* 4 (ca. 374–377, Salamis, Western Syria).
[7] *De mensuribus et ponderibus* 23 (ca. 374–377, Salamis, Western Syria).
[8] Gregory of Nazianzus, *Carm.* 1.12.5 (ca. 390, Cappadocia, Asia Minor).
[9] Amphilochius, *Iambi ad Seleucum* 2.51–88 (ca. 396, Iconium, Asia Minor).

Table B-2: Old Testament Lists from the Western Churches

Hilary[1]	*Jerome*[2]	*Jerome*[3]	*Rufinus*[4]	*Augustine*[5]	*Carthage*[6]
Moses (5)	Gen	Gen	Gen	Gen	Gen
Josh	Exod	Exod	Exod	Exod	Exod
Jdgs/Ruth	Lev	Lev	Lev	Lev	Lev
1–2 Kgs	Num	Num	Num	Num	Num
3–4 Kgs	Deut	Deut	Deut	Deut	Deut
1–2 Chr	Job	Josh	Josh	Josh	Josh
1–2 Esd	Josh	Judg/Ruth	Judg/Ruth	Judg	Judg
Pss	Judg	1–2 Kgs	1–2 Kgs	Ruth	Ruth
Prov	Ruth	3–4 Kgs	3–4 Kgs	1–4 Kgs	1–4 Kgs
Eccl	Sam	Isa	1–2 Chr	1–2 Chr	1–2 Chr
Song	3–4 Kgs	Jer	1–2 Esd	Job	Job
Twelve	Twelve	Ezek	Esth	Tob	Pss
Isa	Isa	Twelve	Isa	Esth	1–5 Sol[7]
Jer/Lam/Ep Jer	Jer	Job	Jer	Jdt	Twelve
Dan	Ezek	Pss	Ezek	1–2 Macc	Isa
Ezek	Dan	Prov	Dan	1–2 Esd	Jer
Job	Pss	Eccl	Twelve	Pss	Ezek
Esth	Prov?	Song	Job	Prov	Dan
(Tob)	Song	Dan	Pss	Song	Tob
(Jdt)	Esth	1–2 Chr	Prov	Eccl	Jdt
	1–2 Chr	1–2 Esd	Eccl	Wis	Esth
	Ezra-Neh	Esth	Song	Sir	1–2 Esd
				Twelve	1–2 Macc
				Isa	
				Jer	
				Dan	
				Ezek	

[1] Hilary of Poitiers, *Prologue in the Book of Psalms* 15 (ca. 350–365).

[2] Jerome, *Epistle* 53.8 (ca. 394, Bethlehem, Palestine).

[3] Jerome, *Preface to the Books of Samuel and Kings* (ca. 394, Bethlehem, Palestine).

[4] Rufinus, *Commentarius in symbolum apostolorum* 35 (ca. 404, Rome, Italy).

[5] Augustine, *De doctrina christiana* 2.13 (ca. 395, Hippo Regius, North Africa).

[6] Council of Carthage (397 C.E.), canon 26.

[7] It is likely, but not definitely known, that 1–5 Sol is Prov, Eccl, Song, Sir, and Wis.

Table B-3: Old Testament Lists from Important Uncial Manuscripts

Vaticanus (B) *(4th cent.)*	*Sinaiticus* (א) *(4th cent.)*	*Alexandrinus (A)* *(5th cent.)*
Gen	Gen . . .[1]	Gen
Exod	. . .	Exod
Lev	. . .	Lev
Deut	Num . . .	Num
Josh	. . .	Deut
Judg	. . .	Josh
Ruth	. . .	Judg
1–4 Kgs	. . .	Ruth
1–2 Chron	1 Chron . . .	1–4 Kgs
1–2 Esd	. . . 2 Esd	1–2 Chron
Ps . . .	Esth	Hos
Prov	Tob	Amos
Eccl	Jdt . . .	Mic
Song	1+4 Macc	Joel
Job	Isa	Obad
Wis	Jer	Jon
Sir	Lam . . .	Nah
Esth	Joel	Hab
Jdt	Obad	Zeph
Tob	Jon	Hag
Hos	Nah	Zech
Amos	Hab	Mal
Mic	Zeph	Isa
Joel	Hag	Jer
Obad	Zech	Bar
Jon	Mal	Lam
Nah	Ps	Ep Jer
Hab	Prov	Ezek
Zeph	Eccl	Dan
Hag	Song	Esth
Zech	Wis	Tob
Mal	Sir	Jdt
Isa	Job	1–2 Esd
Jer		1–4 Macc
Bar		Ps[2]
Lam		Ps 151[3]
Ep Jer		Job
Ezek		Prov
Dan		Song
		Wis
		Sir

[1] Ellipses (. . .) indicate losses or omissions in the manuscript.

[2] Before the Psalms there is a letter of Athanasius to Marcellinus about the Psalter and a summary of the contents of the Psalms by Eusebius.

[3] After the Psalms, there are a number of canticles (called Odes) extracted from other parts of the Bible.

Table B-4: Current Canons of the Hebrew Bible/Old Testament

Jewish[1]	*Orthodox*[2]	*Roman Catholic*[3]	*Protestant*
Torah:	*Historical Books:*	*Pentateuch:*	*Pentateuch:*
Gen	Gen	Gen	Gen
Exod	Exod	Exod	Exod
Lev	Lev	Lev	Lev
Num	Num	Num	Num
Deut	Deut	Deut	Deut
	Josh		
Prophets:[4]	Judg	*Historical Books:*	*Historical Books:*
Josha	Ruth	Josh	Josh
Judg	1 Kgdms[5]	Judg	Judg
1–2 Sam	2 Kgdms	Ruth	Ruth
1–2 Kgs	3 Kgdms	1 Sam	1 Sam
	4 Kgdms	2 Sam	2 Sam
Isa	1 Chron	1 Kgs	1 Kgs
Jer	2 Chron	2 Kgs	2 Kgs
Ezek	1 Esd[6]	1 Chron	1 Chron
Twelve	2 Esd	2 Chron	2 Chron
Hos	Neh	Ezra	Ezra
Joel	Tob	Neh	Neh
Amos	Jdt	Tob	Esth
Obad	Esth[7]	Jdt	
Jonah	1 Macc	Esth[8]	*Poetic Books:*
Mic	2 Macc	1 Macc	Job
Nah	3 Macc	2 Macc	Pss
Hab			Prov

This table is based on Appendix D of *The SBL Handbook of Style* (Peabody: Hendrickson, 1999), 168–71.

[1]The traditional number of books in the Jewish canon is twenty-four.

[2]"Orthodox" here refers to the Greek and Russian Orthodox churches, the Slavonic Bible being the traditional text of the latter. In Orthodox Bibles, 4 Maccabees and the Prayer of Manasseh—and in Slavonic, 3 Esdras—are in an appendix.

[3]The traditional number of books in the Roman Catholic canon is forty-nine. The order of books in Roman Catholic Bibles varies. This order reflects current editions, such as the Jerusalem Bible and the New American Bible. The appendix of the Latin Vulgate contains 3 Esdras, 4 Esdras, and the Prayer of Manasseh.

[4]The two subgroupings of the Prophets are traditionally known as the Former Prophets and the Latter Prophets. The Book of the Twelve counts as one of the Latter Prophets.

[5]1 and 2 Kingdoms are the books of Samuel; 3 and 4 Kingdoms are the books of Kings.

[6]This 1 Esdras is called 2 Esdras in Slavonic Bibles. The 2 Esdras in this canon is equivalent to the book of Ezra in the NRSV; in some Bibles it also includes Nehemiah.

[7]Includes six additions.

[8]Includes six additions.

(Table B-4, continued)

Zeph	*Poetic and Didactic Books:*	*Wisdom Books:*	Eccl
Hag	Pss[9]	Job	Song
Zech	Job	Pss	
Mal	Prov	Prov	*Prophetic Books:*
	Eccl	Eccl	Isa
Writings:	Song	Song	Jer
Pss	Wis	Wis	Lam
Prov	Sir	Ecclus	Ezek
Job			Dan
Song	*Prophetic Books:*	*Prophetic Books:*	Hos
Ruth	Hos	Isa	Joel
Lam	Amos	Jer	Amos
Eccl	Mic	Lam	Obad
Esth	Joel	Bar[10]	Jonah
Dan	Obad	Ezek	Micah
Neh	Jonah	Dan[11]	Nah
1–2 Chron	Nah	Hos	Hab
	Hab	Joel	Zeph
	Zeph	Amos	Hag
	Hag	Obad	Zech
	Zech	Jonah	Mal
	Mal	Mic	
	Isa	Nah	
	Jer	Hab	
	Bar	Zeph	
	Lam Jer	Hag	
	Ep Jer	Zech	
	Ezek	Mal	
	Dan[12]		

[9] Includes Psalm 151.

[10] Includes Epistle of Jeremiah.

[11] Includes Prayer of Azariah and Song of the Three Young Men, Susanna, and Bel and the Dragon.

[12] Includes Prayer of Azariah and Song of the Three Young Men, Susanna, and Bel and the Dragon.

APPENDIX C

Lists and Catalogues of New Testament Collections

Table C-1: Three Early New Testament Lists Based on Eusebius[1]

Irenaeus[2]	*Clement of Alexandria*[3]	*Origen*[4]
Matt	Jude	Matt
Mark	*Barn.*	Mark
Luke	*Apoc. Pet.*	Luke
John	Heb	John
Rev	Acts	1 Pet
1 John	Paul (nothing listed)	2 Pet (?)
1 Pet		Rev
Herm.	*Gospels:*	1 John
Wis	Matt	2–3 John (?)
Paul (mentioned but epistles not listed)	Luke	Heb
	Mark	Paul (mentioned but epistles not listed)
	John	

[1]The following collections are modified somewhat from the collections found in A. Souter, G. M. Hahneman, B. M. Metzger, and F. F. Bruce (see the Bibliography).

[2]Eusebius, *Hist. eccl.* 5.8.2–8 (ca. 320–330, Caesarea, Palestine). While Eusebius attributes this "canon" *(peri tōn endiathēkon graphōn)* collection to Irenaeus (170–180), it is probably nothing more than Eusebius's listing of the references made by Irenaeus.

[3]Eusebius, *Hist. eccl.* 6.14.1–7 (ca. 320–330, Caesarea, Palestine). While Eusebius attributes this "canon" *(pasēs tēs endiathēkou graphēs)* collection to Clement (170), it is probably nothing more than Eusebius's listing of the references made by Clement.

[4]Eusebius, *Hist. eccl.* 6.25.3–14. As we observed above, it is likely that this list is Eusebius's invention based on a compilation of references to literature that Origen (220–230) cited.

Table C-2: New Testament Lists from the Fourth Century

Eusebius[1]	*Cyril of Jerusalem*[2]	*Athanasius*[3]	*Cheltenham*[4]
Recognized:	Gospels (4)	*Gospels:*	*Gospels:*
Gospels (4)	Acts	Matt	Matt
Acts		Mark	Mark
Paul's epistles (14?)	*Catholic Epistles (7):*	Luke	Luke
1 John	Jas	John	John
1 Pet	1–2 Pet		
Rev (?)	1–3 John	Acts	Paul's epistles (13)
	Jude?		Acts
Doubtful:		*Catholic Epistles:*	Rev
Jas	Paul's epistles (14)	Jas	1–3 John
Jude		1–2 Pet	1–2 Pet
2 Pet	*Pseudepigrapha:*	1–3 John	(no Heb)
2, 3 John	*Gos. Thom.*	Jude	
Rejected:		*Paul's Epistles (14):*	
Acts Paul		Rom	
Herm.		1–2 Cor	
Apoc. Pet.		Gal	
Barn.		Eph	
Did.		Phil	
Rev (?)		Col	
Gos. Heb. (?)		1–2 Thess	
		Heb	
Cited by Heretics:		1–2 Tim	
Gos. Pet.		Titus	
Gos. Thom.		Phlm	
Gos. Matt.			
Acts Andr.		Rev	
Acts John			
		Catechetical:	
		Did.	
		Herm.	

[1] Eusebius, *Hist. eccl.* 3.25.1–7 (ca. 320–330, Caesarea, Palestine).

[2] Cyril of Jerusalem, *Catechetical Lectures* 4.33 (ca. 350, Jerusalem).

[3] Athanasius, *Ep. fest.* 39 (ca. 367, Alexandria, Egypt).

[4] The Cheltenham Canon is also known as the Mommsen Catalogue (ca. 360–370, Northern Africa).

(Table C-2, continued)

Epiphanius[5]	*Apostolic Canons*[6]	*Gregory of Nazianzus*[7]	*African Canons*[8]	*Jerome*[9]
Gospels (4)	*Gospels (4):*	Matt	Gospels (4)	*"Lord's Four":*
Paul's epistles (13)	Matt	Mark	Acts	Matt
Acts	Mark	Luke	Paul's epistles (13)	Mark
	Luke	John	Heb	Luke
Catholic Epistles:	John	Acts	1–2 Pet.	John
Jas		Paul's epistles (14)	1–3 John	
Pet	Paul's epistles (14)[10]		Jas	*Paul's Epistles (14):*
1–3 John	Peter's epistles (2)	*Catholic Epistles (7):*	Jude	Rom
Jude	1–3 John	Jas	Rev	1–2 Cor
	Jas	1–2 Pet		Gal
Rev	Jude	1–3 John	*OK to Read:*	Eph
Wis	*1–2 Clem.*	Jude	Acts of martyrs	Phil
Sir	Acts			1–2 Thess
				Col
				1–2 Tim
				Titus
				Phlm
				Heb
				1–2 Pet
				1–3 John
				Jude
				Jas
				Acts
				Rev

[5] Epiphanius, *Pan.* 76.5 (ca. 374–377, Salamis, Western Syria).

[6] *Apostolic Canons* 85 in Apostolic Canons and Constitutions 8.47 (ca. 380, Western Syria).

[7] Gregory of Nazianzus, *Carm.* 12.31 (ca. 390, Cappadocia, Asia Minor) and later ratified by the Trullan Synod in 692.

[8] African Canons (ca. 393–419, Northern Africa).

[9] Jerome, *Epistle* 53, ca. 394 (Bethlehem, Palestine).

[10] The number 14 indicates that Hebrews was included as one of Paul's letters.

(Table C-2, continued)

Augustine[11]	*Amphilochius*[12]	*Rufinus*[13]	*Innocent*[14]	*Syrian Catalogue*[15]
Gospels (4):	*Gospels (4):*	*Gospels (4):*	Gospels (4)	*Gospels (4):*
Matt	Matt	Matt	Paul's epistles (13)[16]	Matt
Mark	Mark	Mark	1–3 John	Mark
Luke	Luke	Luke	1–2 Pet	Luke
John	John	John	Jude	John
			Jas	
Paul's Epistles (14):	Acts	Acts	Acts	Acts
Rom		Paul's epistles (14)	Rev	Gal
1–2 Cor	*Paul's Epistles (14):*	1–2 Pet		Rom
Gal	Rom	Jas	*Repudiated:*	Heb
Eph	1–2 Cor	Jude	Matthias/	Col
Phil	Gal	1,2,3 John	James the less	Eph
1–2 Thess	Eph	Rev	Peter + John =	Phil
Col	Phil		Leucian	1–2 Thess
1–2 Tim	Col	*Ecclesiastical:*	(Andrew =	1–2 Tim
Titus	1–2 Thess	*Herm.*	Xenocharides	Titus
Phlm	1–2 Tim	*Two Ways*	& Leonidas)	Phlm
Heb	Titus	*Pre. Pet.*	*Gos. Thom.*	
	Phlm			
1–2 Pet	Heb (?)			
1–3 John				
Jude	*Catholic Epistles (7?):*			
Jas	Jas			
Acts	Pet			
Rev	John			
	Jude (?)			
	Rev (?)			

[11]Augustine, *Christian Instruction* 2.8–9.12–14 (ca. 395–400, Hippo Regius, North Africa).

[12]Amphilochius, *Iambi ad Seleucum* 289–319 (ca. 396, Iconium, Asia Minor). The list concludes by acknowledging that some have questions about 2 Pet, 2–3 John, Heb, Jude and Rev.

[13]Rufinus, *Commentarius in symbolum apostolorum* 36 (ca. 394, Rome, Italy).

[14]Pope Innocent I, *Ad Exsuperius Toulouse* 2.1–2 (ca. 405, Rome, Italy).

[15]Syrian catalogue of St. Catherine's (ca. 400, Eastern Syria).

[16]Some add Hebrews to this and make it 14. It is uncertain.

(Table C-2, continued)

Muratorian Fragment[17]	*Laodicea Synod*[18]	*Carthage Synod*[19]
Gospels:	*Gospels (4):*	Gospels (4)
. . .	Matt	Acts
. . .	Mark	Paul (13)
Luke ("third book")	Luke	Heb
John ("fourth book)	John	1–2 Pet
		1–3 John
John's epistles	Acts	Jas
Acts		Jude
	Catholic Epistles (7):	Rev (later added)
Paul's Epistles to Churches:	Jas	
Cor	1–2 Pet	
Eph	1,2,3 John	
Phil	Jude	
Col		
Gal	*Paul's Epistles (14):*	
Thess	Rom	
Rom	1–2 Cor	
	Gal	
Epistles to Individuals:	Eph	
Phlm	Phil	
Titus	Col	
1–2 Tim	1–2 Thess	
	Heb	
Jude	1–2 Tim	
1, 2 or 3 Jn (2 Eps.)	Titus	
Wis	Phlm	
Rev		
Apoc. Pet.	(Rev missing)	
Forged (rejected):		
Ep. Lao.		
Ep. Alex.		
Others (? rejected):		
Herm.		
Works of Arsinous		
Valentinus		
Miltiades		
Basilides		
. . .		

[17] The Muratorian Fragment. While many scholars contend that this was a late second-century C.E. fragment originating in or around Rome, a growing number hold that it was produced around the middle of the fourth century (ca. 350–375) and that it originated somewhere in the eastern part of the Roman Empire, possibly in Syria.

[18] Synod of Laodicea, Canon 60 (ca. 363, Asia Minor).

[19] Synod of Carthage, Canon 39 (397, North Africa). Revelation was added later in 419 at the subsequent synod at Carthage.

Table C-3: New Testament Lists from the Fifth and Sixth Centuries

Eucherius[1]	*Gelasius*[2]	*Junilius*[3]	*Cassiodorus*[4]	*Isidore*[5]
Matt	*Gospels:*	*Gospels:*	*Gospels:*	*Gospels:*
Mark	Matt	Matt	Matt	Matt
Luke	Mark	Mark	Mark	Mark
John	Luke	Luke	Luke	Luke
Rom	John	John	John	John
1 Cor				
2 Cor	Acts	Acts	Acts	*Paul's*
				Epistles
				(14):
(Gal missing)		Rev	1 Pet	Rom
Eph	*Paul's Epistles (14):*		Jas	1–2 Cor
1 Thess	Rom	*Paul's Epistles (14):*	1 John	Gal
(2 Thess missing)	1–2 Cor	Rom		Eph
Col	Eph	1–2 Cor	*Paul's Epistles (13):*	Phil
1 Tim	1–2 Thess	Gal	Rom	1–2 Thess
2 Tim	Gal	Eph	1 Cor	Col
(Titus missing)	Phil	Phil	2 Cor	1–2 Tim
(Phlm missing)	Col	1–2 Thess	Gal	Titus
Heb	1–2 Tim	Col	Phil	Phlm
Acts	Titus	1–2 Tim	Col	Heb
Jas	Phlm	Titus	Eph	
1 John	Heb	Phlm	1–2 Thess	1–3 John
(2–3 John missing)		Heb	1–2 Tim	1–2 Pet
(Jude missing)	Rev		Titus	Jude
Rev	1–2 Pet	Jas	Phlm	Jas
	1 John	1–2 Pet	Rev	Acts
	2–3 John	Jude		Rev
	Jude	1–2 John	*Omitted:*	
			(2 Pet)	
			(2–3 John)	
			(Jude)	
			(Heb)	

[1] Eucherius, *Instructiones* (ca. 424–55, Lyons).

[2] *Decretum gelasianum de libris recipiendis et non recipiendis* (ca. sixth cent.). This canon list is attributed to Pope Gelasius I (492–496), but it is more likely from the sixth century.

[3] Junilius, *Instituta regularia divinae legis,* book I (ca. 551, North Africa).

[4] Cassiodorus, *Institutiones divinarum et saecularium litterarum* (ca. 551–562, Rome).

[5] Isidore, bishop of Seville, *In libros Veteris ac Novi Testamenti prooemia* (ca. 600).

Table C-4: New Testament Lists from Biblical Manuscripts of the Fourth and Fifth Centuries

Vaticanus (B)	*Sinaiticus (א)*	*Peshitta (Syr^{P})*	*Alexandrinus (A)*	*Claromantanus (D)*
Matt	Matt	Matt	Matt	Matt
Mark	Mark	Mark	Mark	John
Luke	Luke	Luke	Luke	Mark
John	John	John	John	Luke
Acts	Rom	Acts	Acts	Rom
Jas	1 Cor	Jas	Jas	1–2 Cor
I Pet	2 Cor	1 Pet	I Pet	Gal
2 Pet	Gal	1 John	2 Pet	Eph
1 John	Eph	Rom	1 John	1–2 Tim
2 John	Phil	1 Cor	2 John	Titus
3 John	Col	2 Cor	3 John	Col
Jude	1 Thess	Gal	Jude	Phlm
Rom	2 Thess	Eph	Rom	1–2 Pet
1 Cor	Heb	Phil	1 Cor	Jas
2 Cor	1 Tim	Col	2 Cor	1–3 John
Gal	2 Tim	1 Thess	Gal	Jude
Eph	Titus	2 Thess	Eph	*Barn.*
Phil	Phlm	Heb	Phil	Rev
Col	Acts	1 Tim	Col	Acts
1 Thess	Jas	2 Tim	1 Thess	
2 Thess	1 Pet	Titus	2 Thess	*Others:*
Heb	2 Pet	Phlm	Heb	*Herm.*
	1 John	Heb	1 Tim	*Acts Paul*
Omitted:	2 John		2 Tim	*Apoc. Pet.*
(1 Tim)	3 John		Titus	
(2 Tim)	Jude		Phlm	*Omitted:*
(Titus)	Rev		Rev	(Phil)
(Phlm)	*Barn.*		*1 Clem.*	(1–2 Thess)
(Rev)	*Herm.*		*2 Clem.*	(Heb)
	. . .		*Pss. Sol.*	

APPENDIX D

New Testament Citations of and Allusions to Apocryphal and Pseudepigraphal Writings[1]

Matthew	4:4	Wisdom of Solomon	16:26
	4:15	1 Maccabees	5:15
	5:2–12	Sirach	25:7–12
	5:4	Sirach	48:24
	5:5	*1 Enoch*	5:7
	5:11	4 Esdras	7:14
	5:18	Baruch	4:1
	5:28	Sirach	9:8
	6:7	Sirach	7:14
	6:9	Sirach	23:1
	6:9	Sirach	23:4
	6:10	1 Maccabees	3:60
	6:12	Sirach	28:2
	6:13	Sirach	33:1
	6:20	4 Esdras	7:77
	6:20	Sirach	29:10–11
	6:23	Sirach	14:10
	6:26	*Psalms of Solomon*	5:9–19
	6:29	3 Esdras	1:4
	6:33	Wisdom of Solomon	7:11
	7:12	Tobit	4:15
	7:12	Sirach	31:15
	7:13	4 Esdras	7:6–14

[1] Source: Adapted from *Novum Testamentum Graece* (27th ed.; ed. B. Aland, K. Aland, J. Karavidopoulos, C. M. Martini, and B. M. Metzger; Stuttgart: Deutsche Bibelgesellschaft, 1993), 800–806. A more complete listing is in C. A. Evans, *Ancient Texts for New Testament Studies,* Appendix Two, 342–409.

7:16	Sirach	27:6
8:11	4 Maccabees	13:17
8:11	Baruch	4:37
8:21	Tobit	4:3
9:36	Judith	11:19
9:38	1 Maccabees	12:17
10:16	Sirach	13:17
10:22	4 Esdras	6:25
10:28	4 Maccabees	13:14
11:14	Sirach	48:10
11:22	Judith	16:17
11:23	*Psalms of Solomon*	1:5
11:25	Tobit	7:17
11:25	Sirach	51:1
11:28	Sirach	24:19
11:28	Sirach	51:23
11:29	Sirach	6:24–25
11:29	Sirach	6:28–29
11:29	Sirach	51:26–27
12:4	2 Maccabees	10:3
13:3	4 Esdras	8:41
13:3	4 Esdras	9:31–37
13:5	Sirach	40:15
13:6	*Psalms of Solomon*	18:6–7
13:39	3 Esdras	7:113
13:39	*1 Enoch*	16:1
13:44	Sirach	20:30–31
16:18	Wisdom of Solomon	16:13
16:22	1 Maccabees	2:21
16:27	Sirach	35:22
17:11	Sirach	48:10
18:10	Tobit	12:15
19:28	*Psalms of Solomon*	17:26
19:28	*Psalms of Solomon*	17:29
20:2	Tobit	5:15
21:12	*Psalms of Solomon*	17:30
22:13	Wisdom of Solomon	17:2
22:14	4 Esdras	8:3
22:14	4 Esdras	8:41
22:32	4 Maccabees	7:19
22:32	4 Maccabees	16:25
23:38	Tobit	14:4
24:15	1 Maccabees	1:54
24:15	2 Maccabees	8:17
24:16	1 Maccabees	2:28

	25:31	*1 Enoch*	61:8
	25:31	*1 Enoch*	62:2–3
	25:31	*1 Enoch*	69:27
	25:35	Tobit	4:17
	25:36	Sirach	7:32–35
	26:13	*1 Enoch*	103:4
	26:24	*1 Enoch*	38:2
	26:38	Sirach	37:2
	26:64	*1 Enoch*	69:27
	27:24	Susanna	46
	27:43	Wisdom of Solomon	2:13
	27:43	Wisdom of Solomon	2:18–20
Mark	1:15	Tobit	14:5
	3:27	*Psalms of Solomon*	5:3
	4:5	Sirach	40:15
	4:11	Wisdom of Solomon	2:22
	4:14	4 Esdras	8:41
	4:14	4 Esdras	9:31–37
	5:34	Judith	8:35
	6:49	Wisdom of Solomon	17:15
	8:29	*1 Enoch*	48:10
	8:37	Sirach	26:14
	9:31	Sirach	2:18
	9:48	Judith	16:17
	10:19	Sirach	4:1
	12:25	*1 Enoch*	15:6–7
	12:25	*1 Enoch*	51:4
	13:8	4 Esdras	13:30–32
	13:13	4 Esdras	6:25
	14:34	Sirach	37:2
	15:29	Wisdom of Solomon	2:17–18
Luke	1:17	Sirach	48:10
	1:19	Tobit	12:15
	1:42	Judith	13:18
	1:42	2 Baruch	54:10
	1:52	Sirach	10:14
	2:11	*Psalms of Solomon*	17:32
	2:14	*Psalms of Solomon*	18:10
	2:29	Tobit	11:9
	2:37	Judith	8:6
	6:12	4 Maccabees	3:13–19
	6:24	*1 Enoch*	94:8
	6:35	Wisdom of Solomon	15:1
	7:22	Sirach	48:5
	9:8	Sirach	48:10

	10:17	Tobit	7:17
	10:19	Sirach	11:19
	10:21	Sirach	51:1
	12:19	Tobit	7:10
	12:19	*1 Enoch*	97:8–10
	12:20	Wisdom of Solomon	15:8
	13:27	1 Maccabees	3:6
	13:29	Baruch	4:37
	13:35	Tobit	14:4
	14:13	Tobit	2:2
	15:12	1 Maccabees	10:29[30]
	15:12	Tobit	3:17
	16:23	4 Maccabees	13:15
	16:9	*1 Enoch*	39:4
	16:9	*1 Enoch*	63:10
	16:26	4 Esdras	7:36
	16:26	*1 Enoch*	22:9–14
	18:7	Sirach	35:22
	19:44	Wisdom of Solomon	3:7
	20:37	4 Maccabees	7:19
	20:37	4 Maccabees	16:25
	21:24	Tobit	14:5
	21:24	Sirach	28:18
	21:24	*Psalms of Solomon*	17:25
	21:25	Wisdom of Solomon	5:22
	21:28	*1 Enoch*	51:2
	22:37	*Psalms of Solomon*	16:5
	24:4	2 Maccabees	3:26
	24:31	2 Maccabees	3:34
	24:50	Sirach	50:20–21
	24:53	Sirach	50:22
John	1:3	Wisdom of Solomon	9:1
	1:14	*Psalms of Solomon*	7:6
	3:8	Sirach	16:21
	3:12	Wisdom of Solomon	9:16
	3:12	Wisdom of Solomon	18:15–16
	3:13	4 Esdras	4:8
	3:13	Baruch	3:29
	3:21	Tobit	4:6
	3:27	*Psalms of Solomon*	5:3–4
	3:29	1 Maccabees	9:39
	4:9	Sirach	50:25–26
	4:48	Wisdom of Solomon	8:8
	5:18	Wisdom of Solomon	2:16
	5:22	*1 Enoch*	69:27

	6:35	Sirach	24:21
	7:38	Sirach	24:30–31
	7:42	*Psalms of Solomon*	11:21
	8:44	Wisdom of Solomon	2:24
	8:53	Sirach	44:19
	10:20	Wisdom of Solomon	5:4
	10:22	1 Maccabees	4:59
	12:26	4 Maccabees	17:20
	14:15	Wisdom of Solomon	6:18
	15:9–10	Wisdom of Solomon	3:9
	15:25	*Psalms of Solomon*	7:1
	17:3	Wisdom of Solomon	15:3
	20:22	Wisdom of Solomon	15:11
Acts	1:8	*Psalms of Solomon*	8:15
	1:10	2 Maccabees	3:26
	1:18	Wisdom of Solomon	4:19
	2:4	Sirach	48:12
	2:11	Sirach	36:7
	2:39	Sirach	24:32
	4:24	Judith	9:12
	5:2	2 Maccabees	4:32
	5:7	3 Maccabees	4:17
	5:21	1 Maccabees	12:6
	5:21	2 Maccabees	1:10
	5:39	2 Maccabees	7:19
	7:36	*Assumption of Moses*	3:11
	9:1–29	2 Maccabees	3:24–40
	9:1–29	4 Maccabees	4:1–14
	9:2	1 Maccabees	15:21
	9:7	Wisdom of Solomon	18:1
	10:2	Tobit	12:8
	10:22	1 Maccabees	10:25
	10:22	1 Maccabees	11:30
	10:22	1 Maccabees	11:33, etc.
	10:26	Wisdom of Solomon	7:1
	10:30	2 Maccabees	11:8
	10:34	Sirach	35:12–13
	10:36	Wisdom of Solomon	6:7
	10:36	Wisdom of Solomon	8:3, etc.
	11:18	Wisdom of Solomon	12:19
	12:5	Judith	4:9
	12:10	Sirach	19:26
	12:23	1 Maccabees	7:41
	12:23	2 Maccabees	9:9
	12:23	Judith	16:17

	12:23	Sirach	48:21
	13:10	Sirach	1:30
	13:17	Wisdom of Solomon	19:10
	14:14	Judith	14:16–17
	14:15	4 Maccabees	12:13
	14:15	Wisdom of Solomon	7:3
	15:4	Judith	8:26
	15:29	4 Maccabees	5:2
	16:14	2 Maccabees	1:4
	16:23	*Testament of Joseph*	8:5
	16:25	*Testament of Joseph*	8:5
	17:23	Wisdom of Solomon	14:20
	17:23	Wisdom of Solomon	15:17
	17:24	Tobit	7:17
	17:24	Wisdom of Solomon	9:9
	17:24–25	Wisdom of Solomon	9:1
	17:26	Wisdom of Solomon	7:18
	17:27	Wisdom of Solomon	13:6
	17:29	Wisdom of Solomon	13:10
	17:30	Sirach	28:7
	19:27	Wisdom of Solomon	3:17
	19:28	Bel and the Dragon	18
	19:28	Bel and the Dragon	41
	20:26	Susanna	46
	20:32	Wisdom of Solomon	5:5
	20:35	Sirach	4:31
	21:26	1 Maccabees	3:49
	22:9	Wisdom of Solomon	18:1
	24:2	2 Maccabees	4:6
	24:14	4 Maccabees	12:17
	26:18	Wisdom of Solomon	5:5
	26:25	Judith	10:13
Romans	1:4	*Testament of Levi*	18:7
	1:18	*1 Enoch*	91:7
	1:19	2 Baruch	54:17–18
	1:19–32	Wisdom of Solomon	13–15
	1:21	4 Esdras	8:60
	1:21	Wisdom of Solomon	13:1
	1:21	*1 Enoch*	99:8
	1:23	Wisdom of Solomon	11:15
	1:23	Wisdom of Solomon	12:24
	1:25	*Assumption of Moses*	5:4
	1:26	*Testament of Joseph*	7:8
	1:28	2 Maccabees	6:4
	1:28	3 Maccabees	4:16

1:29–31	4 Maccabees	1:26
1:29–31	4 Maccabees	2:15
2:3	*Psalms of Solomon*	15:8
2:4	Wisdom of Solomon	11:23
2:5	*Psalms of Solomon*	9:5
2:5	*Testament of Levi*	3:2
2:11	Sirach	35:12–13
2:15	Wisdom of Solomon	17:11
2:15	2 Baruch	57:2
2:15	*Testament of Reuben*	4:3
2:17	*Psalms of Solomon*	17:1
2:17	2 Baruch	48:22
2:22	*Testament of Levi*	14:4
2:29	*Jubilees*	1:23
3:3	*Psalms of Solomon*	8:28
4:13	Sirach	44:21
4:13	*Jubilees*	19:21, etc.
4:13	2 Baruch	14:13
4:13	2 Baruch	51:3
4:17	Sirach	44:19
4:17	2 Baruch	48:8
5:3	*Testament of Joseph*	10:1
5:5	Sirach	18:11
5:12	4 Esdras	3:21–22
5:12	4 Esdras	3:26
5:12	Wisdom of Solomon	2:24
5:12	2 Baruch	23:4
5:12	2 Baruch	54:15
5:16	4 Esdras	7:118–19
7:7	4 Maccabees	2:5–6
7:10	*Psalms of Solomon*	14:1
7:12	4 Esdras	9:37
7:23	4 Esdras	7:72
8:18	2 Baruch	15:8
8:18	2 Baruch	32:6
8:19	4 Esdras	7:11
8:19	4 Esdras	7:75
8:22	4 Esdras	10:9
8:28	*Psalms of Solomon*	4:25, etc.
9:4	2 Maccabees	6:23
9:4	Sirach	44:12
9:4	Sirach	44:18, etc.
9:16	*Assumption of Moses*	12:7
9:19	Wisdom of Solomon	12:12
9:21	Wisdom of Solomon	15:7

	9:22	2 Baruch	59:6
	9:24	*Jubilees*	2:19
	9:31	Sirach	27:8
	9:31	Wisdom of Solomon	2:11
	10:6	4 Esdras	4:8
	10:6	Baruch	3:29
	10:7	Wisdom of Solomon	16:13
	11:4	2 Maccabees	2:4
	11:15	Sirach	10:20–21
	11:25	4 Esdras	4:35–36
	11:25	*Testament of Zebulun*	9–10
	11:33	Wisdom of Solomon	17:1
	11:33	2 Baruch	14:8–9
	12:1	*Testament of Levi*	3:6
	12:15	Sirach	7:34
	12:21	*Testament of Benjamin*	4:3–4
	13:1	Sirach	4:27
	13:1	Wisdom of Solomon	6:3–4
	13:9	4 Maccabees	2:6
	13:10	Wisdom of Solomon	6:18
	15:4	1 Maccabees	12:9
	15:8	Sirach	36:20
	15:16	4 Maccabees	7:8 variant
	15:33	*Testament of Dan*	5:2
	16:27	4 Maccabees	18:24
1 Corinthians	1:24	Wisdom of Solomon	7:24–25
	2:9	Sirach	1:10
	2:16	Wisdom of Solomon	9:13
	4:13	Tobit	5:19
	4:14	Wisdom of Solomon	11:10
	4:17	*1 Enoch*	104:13
	6:2	Wisdom of Solomon	3:8
	6:12	Sirach	37:28
	6:13	Sirach	36:18
	6:18	Sirach	23:17
	6:18	*Testament of Reuben*	5:5
	7:19	Sirach	32:23
	9:10	Sirach	6:19
	9:25	Wisdom of Solomon	4:2
	10:1	Wisdom of Solomon	19:7–8
	10:20	Baruch	4:7
	10:23	Sirach	37:28
	11:7	Sirach	17:3
	11:7	Wisdom of Solomon	2:23
	11:24	Wisdom of Solomon	16:6

	12:2	3 Maccabees	4:16
	13:13	3 Esdras	4:38
	15:19	*Apocalypse of Baruch*	21:13
	15:29	2 Maccabees	12:43–44
	15:32	Wisdom of Solomon	2:5–6
	15:34	Wisdom of Solomon	13:1
2 Corinthians	5:1	Wisdom of Solomon	9:15
	5:4	Wisdom of Solomon	9:15
	11:14	*Life of Adam and Eve*	9
	12:2	*Testament of Levi*	2
	12:12	Wisdom of Solomon	10:16
Galatians	1:5	4 Maccabees	18:24
	2:6	Sirach	35:13
	4:4	Tobit	14:5
	4:10	*1 Enoch*	72–82
	6:1	Wisdom of Solomon	17:17
	6:17	3 Maccabees	2:29
Ephesians	1:6	Sirach	45:1
	1:6	Sirach	46:13
	1:17	Wisdom of Solomon	7:7
	3:9	3 Maccabees	2:3
	4:14	Sirach	5:9
	4:24	Wisdom of Solomon	9:3
	6:13	Wisdom of Solomon	5:17
	6:14	Wisdom of Solomon	5:18
	6:16	Wisdom of Solomon	5:19
	6:16	Wisdom of Solomon	5:21
	6:24	*Psalms of Solomon*	4:25, etc.
Philippians	4:5	Wisdom of Solomon	2:19
	4:13	Wisdom of Solomon	7:23
	4:18	Sirach	35:6
Colossians	1:22	*1 Enoch*	102:5
	2:3	Sirach	1:24–25
	2:3	*1 Enoch*	46:3
1 Thessalonians	1:3	4 Maccabees	17:4
	1:8	4 Maccabees	16:12
	3:11	Judith	12:8
	4:6	Sirach	5:3
	4:13	Wisdom of Solomon	3:18
	5:1	Wisdom of Solomon	8:8
	5:2	Wisdom of Solomon	18:14–15
	5:3	Wisdom of Solomon	17:14
	5:3	*1 Enoch*	62:4
	5:8	Wisdom of Solomon	5:18
2 Thessalonians	2:1	2 Maccabees	2:7

1 Timothy	1:17	Tobit	13:7
	1:17	Tobit	13:11
	2:2	2 Maccabees	3:11
	2:2	Baruch	1:11–12
	3:16	4 Maccabees	6:31
	3:16	4 Maccabees	7:16
	3:16	4 Maccabees	16:1
	6:15	2 Maccabees	12:15
	6:15	2 Maccabees	13:4
	6:15	3 Maccabees	5:35
	6:15	Sirach	46:5
2 Timothy	2:19	Sirach	17:26
	2:19	Sirach	23:10 variant
	2:19	Sirach	35:3
	3:11	*Psalms of Solomon*	4:23
	4:8	Wisdom of Solomon	5:16
	4:17	1 Maccabees	2:60
Titus	2:11	2 Maccabees	3:30
	2:11	3 Maccabees	6:9
	3:4	Wisdom of Solomon	1:6
Hebrews	1:3	Wisdom of Solomon	7:25–26
	2:5	Sirach	17:17
	4:12	Wisdom of Solomon	7:22–30
	4:12	Wisdom of Solomon	18:15–16
	4:13	*1 Enoch*	9:5
	4:15	*Psalms of Solomon*	17:36
	5:6	1 Maccabees	14:41
	6:12	*Psalms of Solomon*	12:6
	7:22	Sirach	29:14–20
	9:26	*Testament of Levi*	18:9
	11:5	Sirach	44:16
	11:5	Wisdom of Solomon	4:10
	11:6	Wisdom of Solomon	10:17
	11:10	2 Maccabees	4:1
	11:10	Wisdom of Solomon	13:1
	11:17	Sirach	2:52
	11:17	1 Maccabees	44:20
	11:25	4 Maccabees	15:2
	11:25	4 Maccabees	15:8
	11:27	Sirach	2:2
	11:28	Wisdom of Solomon	18:25
	11:35	2 Maccabees	6:18–7:42
	11:37	*Martyrdom and Ascension of Isaiah*	5:11–14
	12:1	4 Maccabees	16:16

	12:1	4 Maccabees	17:10–15
	12:4	2 Maccabees	13:14
	12:7	*Psalms of Solomon*	10:2
	12:7	*Psalms of Solomon*	14:1
	12:9	2 Maccabees	3:24
	12:12	Sirach	25:23
	12:17	Wisdom of Solomon	12:10
	12:21	1 Maccabees	13:2
	12:23	*1 Enoch*	22:9
	13:7	Sirach	33:19
	13:7	Wisdom of Solomon	2:17
	13:15	*Psalms of Solomon*	15:2–3
James	1:1	2 Maccabees	1:27
	1:2	Sirach	2:1
	1:2	Wisdom of Solomon	3:4–5
	1:3	4 Maccabees	1:11
	1:3	*Testament of Joseph*	10:1
	1:4	4 Maccabees	15:7
	1:13	Sirach	15:11–20
	1:14	*1 Enoch*	98:4
	1:19	Sirach	5:11
	1:21	Sirach	3:17
	2:13	Tobit	4:10
	2:23	Wisdom of Solomon	7:27
	3:2	Sirach	14:1
	3:6	Sirach	5:13
	3:6	*1 Enoch*	48:7
	3:9	Sirach	23:1
	3:9	Sirach	23:4
	3:10	Sirach	5:13
	3:10	Sirach	28:12
	3:13	Sirach	3:17
	4:2	1 Maccabees	8:16
	4:7	*Testament of Naphtali*	8:4
	4:8	*Testament of Dan*	6:2
	4:11	Wisdom of Solomon	1:11
	4:13	*1 Enoch*	97:8–10
	5:1	*1 Enoch*	94:8
	5:3	Judith	16:17
	5:3	Sirach	29:10
	5:4	Tobit	4:14
	5:6	Wisdom of Solomon	2:10
	5:6	Wisdom of Solomon	2:12
	5:6	Wisdom of Solomon	2:19
	5:10	4 Maccabees	9:8

1 Peter	1:3	Sirach	16:12
	1:7	Sirach	2:5
	1:12	*1 Enoch*	1:2
	1:12	*1 Enoch*	16:3
	2:25	Wisdom of Solomon	1:6
	3:19	*1 Enoch*	9:10
	3:19	*1 Enoch*	10:11–15
	4:19	2 Maccabees	1:24, etc.
	5:7	Wisdom of Solomon	12:13
2 Peter	1:19	4 Esdras	12:42
	2:2	Wisdom of Solomon	5:6
	2:4	*1 Enoch*	10:4–5
	2:4	*1 Enoch*	10:11–14
	2:4	*1 Enoch*	91:15
	2:7	3 Maccabees	2:13
	2:7	Wisdom of Solomon	10:6
	3:6	*1 Enoch*	83:3–5
	3:9	Sirach	35:19
	3:18	Sirach	18:10
1 John	4:6	*Psalms of Solomon*	8:14
	5:21	Epistle of Jeremiah	72
Jude	4	*1 Enoch*	48:10
	6	*1 Enoch*	10:6
	6	*1 Enoch*	12:4
	6	*1 Enoch*	22:11
	13	Wisdom of Solomon	14:1
	13	*1 Enoch*	18:15–16
	13	*1 Enoch*	21:5–6
	14	*1 Enoch*	1:9
	14	*1 Enoch*	60:8
	14	*1 Enoch*	93:3
	16	*1 Enoch*	5:4
Revelation	1:18	Sirach	18:1
	2:10	2 Maccabees	13:14
	2:12	Wisdom of Solomon	18:15–16
	2:17	2 Maccabees	2:4–8
	2:27	*Psalms of Solomon*	17:23–24
	3:18	*Psalms of Solomon*	17:43
	4:11	3 Maccabees	2:3
	4:11	Sirach	18:1
	4:11	Wisdom of Solomon	1:14
	5:7	Sirach	1:8
	5:11	*1 Enoch*	14:22
	5:11	*1 Enoch*	40:1
	7:9	2 Maccabees	10:7

8:1	Wisdom of Solomon	18:14
8:2	Tobit	12:15
8:3	Tobit	12:12
8:7	Sirach	39:29
8:7	Wisdom of Solomon	16:22
8:8	*1 Enoch*	18:13
8:8	*1 Enoch*	21:3
8:10	*1 Enoch*	86:1
9:3	Wisdom of Solomon	16:9
11:19	2 Maccabees	2:4–8
13:14	*1 Enoch*	54:6
15:3	*1 Enoch*	9:4
16:5	*1 Enoch*	66:2
17:9	*1 Enoch*	21:3
17:14	2 Maccabees	13:4
17:14	3 Maccabees	5:35
17:14	*1 Enoch*	9:4
18:2	Baruch	4:35
19:1	Tobit	13:18
19:1	*Psalms of Solomon*	8:2
19:11	2 Maccabees	3:25
19:11	2 Maccabees	11:8
19:16	2 Maccabees	13:4
19:20	*1 Enoch*	10:6
20:3	*1 Enoch*	18:16
20:3	*1 Enoch*	21:6
20:12–13	Sirach	16:12
20:13	*1 Enoch*	51:1
20:13	*1 Enoch*	61:5
21:19–20	Tobit	13:17
22:1	*1 Enoch*	14:19
22:2	*Psalms of Solomon*	14:3

APPENDIX E

Brevard Childs's Canonical Approach

MANY OF US WHO SERVE IN PASTORAL POSITIONS STRUGGLE WITH THE HISTORICAL-critical training we received in seminary as we prepare to preach and teach laypeople. What do we do when our training does not correspond with the beliefs of our congregants? For example, Jesus probably did not say the last line of the traditional Lord's prayer in Matt 6:13: "For thine is the kingdom, and the power, and the glory for ever. Amen" (King James Version). Paul probably did not write the Pastoral Epistles or the book of Hebrews. And 1 John 5:7b–8a—"there are three that testify in heaven, the Father, the Word, and the Holy Spirit, and these three are one. And there are three that testify on earth" (NRSV margin)—was also not written by John but by a zealous scribe who was anxious at a later date to clarify his understanding of Christology.

Most of us have been trained to lean heavily on texts that report what Jesus actually said and less on those about which there is some doubt. In the last two centuries the historical-critical disciplines developed in the post-Enlightenment era have peeled back several layers of tradition that became attached to the original writings of the OT and NT, and as a result we have been able to get closer to the original biblical texts than was possible before. The idea behind this endeavor was, of course, that we should base our doctrine, worship, and ministry not on what later voices added to the biblical text but on what the original authors themselves said.

Now, after years of exposure to critical scholarship through pastors and educators in the church, many nonprofessional persons in the church are becoming familiar with how the Bible was written and transmitted within the Christian community. Some are also becoming aware of the many changes (whether intentional or unintentional) to the biblical text that occurred in its transmission. On the other hand, the average layperson and pastor are ill equipped to make critical judgments about the authenticity of various biblical texts.

Laypersons and pastors who make use of the Bible regularly in their church life and worship may well wonder if Bible scholars will ever agree on the meaning of the biblical text or on what constitutes the most reliable or authoritative biblical text for the church. This apparent indecision on the part of the scholarly community raises questions for those practicing ministry on a daily basis. Are clergy and laity to wait for final decisions about the Bible from the church's theologians before they utilize it in their ministries? How can we decide what Jesus said when scholars differ so radically about the matter? What text should we use for preaching and teaching the Bible in the church? Whose interpretation of the Bible do we adopt for our message on Sunday morning?

Years ago it seemed that the meaning of the Bible was confined to the past and had relevance only for the biblical scholar with the adequate technical expertise to understand it. Once the Bible had been decanonized[1] or relativized in this process and appeared to be without canonical authority for the church, its marginalization and disuse in the church was all but assured. In response to the growing lack of confidence in the Bible and in the understanding of the Bible, the last two generations of clergy began to draw away from its use, especially in mainline churches. Their lack of confidence in the Bible and consequent minimal use of it in their ministries prompted Smart to challenge the neglect of the Bible in the churches.[2] His criticism was especially appropriate for many of the mainline denominational churches. It seemed that for many in the church the Bible had become the possession of the Bible scholars and less the source of strength, encouragement, and enlightenment for the people in the churches.

In the mid-1960s Brevard Childs responded to this problem and gave his attention to unlocking the Bible from its historical-critical past and to removing the chains that had bound the Bible to the biblical specialist's desk far too long and had undermined the authoritative role it once held in the church.[3] Sanders also, and initially for different reasons, believed that there was need for a reevaluation of the formation and function of the biblical canon.[4] Both Childs and Sanders agreed that the Bible had become a catalogue of isolated texts for the specialist, leading to the fragmentation—what Childs calls the "atomization"—of the biblical text.

Childs stresses that the historical-critical practice of dividing biblical passages into their various historical stages (a "diachronic approach") and developments often destroyed the "synchronic" dimension of viewing the

---

[1] J. A. Sanders, "Canonical Context and Canonical Criticism," 176, cites G. T. Sheppard, who concludes that it is "little wonder that once the biblical text had been securely anchored in the historical past by 'decanonizing' it, the interpreter has difficulty applying it to the modern religious context."

[2] Smart, *Strange Silence of the Bible.*

[3] Childs, "Interpretation in Faith."

[4] J. A. Sanders, "Cave 11 Surprises," 284–98.

text as a whole. He rejects the fragmentation of the biblical text and instead calls for a synchronic approach that views the Bible as a whole in its final form rather than in its various literary stages of development. In order for the church to see the Bible as the word of God, it must, he claims, be viewed as a whole and not as a collection of isolated texts.[5] For him, the Bible comes to us not just from individuals, but primarily from ancient communities of faith. He and Sanders agree that "the Bible, the sum as well as all of its parts, comes to us out of the liturgical and instructional life of early believing communities."[6]

But for Childs, the canon of the Bible, or its continuing authority in the churches, includes the contributions of the later editors of its texts, the superscriptions that were later added by the communities of faith, and "all the redactional seams." The shift here is from what scholars call the quest for an *Urtext*—that is, the earliest form of a text—to its final form that was frozen by the church and passed on in its communities of faith. Childs specifically rejects the use of the term *canonical criticism* as a description of his work. Sanders embraces the term, but defines it differently than does Childs.[7] Childs and Sanders are in agreement, however, that the focus on how a document functioned as canon in the religious community is an essential feature of theological inquiry.

This relatively new approach to the biblical literature was launched chiefly through the writings of Sanders and Childs, but it is also carried on by other capable scholars who agree with their goal in a canonical understanding of the Bible.[8] The canonical focus has developed into an important new approach to the biblical literature, which asks *in part* what form of the biblical text is authoritative for the church today. Does the church choose as its authoritative base the earliest form of a biblical writing, the various stages of development of the text in which it functioned variously for differing communities, or the latest redacted form of the writing that we presently possess and that the church has traditionally accepted as its inspired and authoritative literature? Sanders views the biblical text from a

[5] Childs, *Biblical Theology in Crisis,* 149–219.

[6] J. A. Sanders, "Canonical Context and Canonical Criticism," 182.

[7] J. A. Sanders, ibid., 187, describes canonical criticism as a subdiscipline of biblical criticism that is a means of "unlocking the Bible from the past into which criticism has tended to seal it" but observes that because of the often negative value that biblical criticism has for the believing communities, Childs rejects the use of the term *criticism* altogether.

[8] See, for instance, Wall and Lemcio, *New Testament as Canon;* Wall, "Acts of the Apostles in Canonical Context"; and Wall, "Reading the New Testament in Canonical Context." Rendtorff is right, however, to observe that Childs has brought few followers into his fold; see *Canon and Theology,* 47–51. This is because Childs focuses almost exclusively on the conclusion of the canonical process, and the majority of the biblical scholars believe, as Rendtorff correctly observes, that the earlier stages of the biblical text "are also worth independent interpretation" (51).

number of contexts in which sacred Scripture is ever renewing itself as canon within the communities of faith, Childs shows interest in only the latest stage of that development, though he is not uninformed about the earlier stages. Sanders rightly asks the difficult question of whether we recognize as canonical and inspired the author or the biblical documents.[9] Both he and Childs focus on the documents, but in clearly differing ways. Sanders emphasizes that the Bible is a product of history and examines how it functions as canon—that is, as an authoritative book in the life of the church.

Sanders's most important disagreements with Childs have to do with Childs's apparent divorcing of the development and growth of the literature of the Bible from its historical context. Childs focuses on the final form of the text exclusively and opts for the MT for the OT and apparently the Textus Receptus for the NT. Sanders is critical of Childs at this point because his selected, frozen text leaves out the LXX, which is appealed to in more than 90 percent of the NT references to the OT. Are we certain that the MT is a more faithful witness to the OT than is the LXX? Sanders claims that "canon, by its very nature, is adaptable, not just stable," and that "one must keep in mind all the texts and all the canons and all the communities."[10] He objects to Childs's focus on only one form of a stabilized Scripture text and claims that Childs completely dissociates the Scriptures from history "as though that final canonical redaction had a timeless theology in mind for all generations and centuries to come."[11] Sanders contends that the cure for the fragmentation of the Scriptures that came from inappropriate application of the historical-critical methodologies is not an escape from the historical context of the Scriptures and their development, but rather a reemphasis on the notion of the Scriptures as canon for the church. Hence, canonical criticism, for Sanders, "focuses on the function of Scripture in the believing communities."[12]

Childs agrees with Sanders on this last point and stresses that "the whole point of focusing on Scripture as canon in opposition to the anthropocentric tradition of liberal Protestantism is to emphasize that the biblical text and its theological function as authoritative form belong inextricably together."[13] He is correct in saying that the very notion of canon is a theological function in the believing community and not simply a description of the canonical process of a text becoming acknowledged as holy Scripture

---

[9] J. A. Sanders, *Canon and Community,* 17; idem, *Torah and Canon;* and idem, *From Sacred Story,* 155–72, where he contrasts his own view of the canonical text that the church receives with the view of Childs. Also important is his emphasis on the value of history and historical criticism, which Childs tends to deemphasize in his work.

[10] J. A. Sanders, "Canonical Context and Canonical Criticism," 187.

[11] Ibid., 190.

[12] Ibid., 193.

[13] Childs, *Biblical Theology of the Old and New Testaments,* 72.

in the church. I agree with Childs that a proper focus on the biblical canon in the church, which is the basis of biblical theology, cannot be reduced simply to a *descriptive* process, but must also include a *prescriptive* responsibility if the text is to be truly understood as Scripture for the church. I also agree with Childs that the Bible's message is not fully grasped through the descriptive work of biblical exegesis alone, but rather in an encounter with the living God.[14] This encounter with God, however—and happily so—need not be separated from a careful interpretation of the biblical text, employing the various critical disciplines to explicate its meaning. This is what I believe Childs is saying about the role of faith and surrender to God as a means of appropriating the full meaning of the biblical text. This is certainly nothing new to biblical theology. Both Barth and Bultmann made similar claims. They agreed that biblical faith could not be understood apart from the obligation of faith to surrender to the call of God that comes in the preaching of the Christian message.

Also connected to Childs's focus on the meaning of the biblical text within the household of faith is his emphasis on the canonical understanding of the various texts within the Scriptures. Is it not true that a different message is gleaned from the Gospel of John as the Fourth Gospel rather than simply as the Gospel of John unattached to the rest of the NT literature? Matthew's Gospel is different in its meaning when we see it as one of four witnesses to the Christ event rather than when we see it as the only gospel known to the first community of Christians, who read it for the first time without its association with the other gospels. Does John presuppose the virgin birth in Matthew's Gospel, and Matthew the preexistence of Jesus in John's Gospel? Is the composite picture of Jesus that we gain from looking at all four gospels different from the picture that we get from reading only one? Smith argues cogently that the character of the final canon, including its final order, "projects a kind of intention that can scarcely be ignored."[15] He explains that the Fourth Gospel stands last in the gospel canon as if it were to be read after the Synoptics.[16] The Gospel of John is here because it is a part of the biblical canon and needs to be understood in that way, but we should ask whether the original meaning of a text intended by its author can be different from the meaning it acquired as preserved in the canon of Scriptures. Can, for instance, the picture of Jesus be distorted in the canon rather than communicated as each Evangelist intended? Luke intended his two-volume work to be circulated together, but in the biblical canon they are separate, with Acts functioning as an introduction to the epistles of Paul.[17]

---

[14] Ibid., 719–26.
[15] D. M. Smith, "John, the Synoptics, and the Canonical Approach," 171.
[16] Ibid., 176.
[17] For more discussion, see Wall, "Acts of the Apostles in Canonical Context."

With reference to the OT, for example, Childs opts for the final canonical form of Second Isaiah, which its final redactor places in the eighth century B.C.E., rather than in its actual historical setting in the sixth century B.C.E., as the church's normative text.[18] I suggest, however, that Second Isaiah is most meaningful to the community of faith today precisely when the sixth-century setting of Isa 40–55 is understood and clarified. As a pastor who has taught the book of Isaiah both ways, I can testify that the message of its original historical context, namely, Second Isaiah from the sixth century B.C.E., is readily understood and appreciated by the congregation.[19]

The same can be said with regard to the Pastoral Epistles, which, when compared to the genuine Pauline Epistles, are clearly different in focus and style from what we have learned to expect from Paul. If it can be explained to the congregation that Paul did not write these books in their present form, even though they do reflect some genuine reflections of the end of Paul's career, then the astute layperson will not be so confused by the seeming contradictions between the Pastorals and Paul's genuine writings, especially in terms of eschatology, pneumatology, church organizational structure, and even vocabulary. Once it is shown that Paul did not write this literature, does it necessarily mean that the documents have no meaning for the church today? By no means! If rightly understood, this literature shows how the church of a later generation recognized a new application of the teaching of the Apostle Paul in a new context. This is what Dunn means when he writes: "The Pastorals made their first impact and took the first step towards formal authentic reexpression of the Pauline heritage and tradition and not as the products of Paul's pen as such."[20] As the church struggled to meet the theological challenges of a later historical context with the same determination and sense of the presence of God as did those Christians of the first century, they found a reinterpretation of the message of Paul for their own age (the Pastorals) quite useful in fulfilling their mission, and they incorporated this new interpretation into their canon.

The biggest problem with Childs's enterprise has to do with the form of the text that he selects as canon or authority for the church. Where is the evidence that the early church intended to read the Scriptures in the canonical context of the MT or Textus Receptus as opposed to the earliest

---

[18] Childs, *Old Testament as Scripture,* 311–38.

[19] Fowl's criticism of Childs in "Canonical Approach of Brevard Childs" is significant. He shares J. A. Sanders's concern about Childs's seeming lack of concern for the original historical context of a writing or event in favor of the final interpretation of the writing or event. J. A. Sanders, *From Sacred Story,* 165–70, also criticizes Childs's seeming lack of appreciation for the historical development of a given biblical text (a diachronic approach) in favor of a leveling of the tradition by seeing it as a whole without any development (a synchronic approach). See also his frustration with Childs's acceptance of the biblical text at a single "frozen point" in idem, "Canonical Context and Canonical Criticism," 173–97.

[20] Dunn, *Living Word,* 83.

form of the writing or the meaning intended by its original author? Surely, one must condemn those who write in the name of a NT personality in order to pass their literature along with credibility in the Christian community. The rejection of that literature, as in Eusebius' *Hist. eccl.* 3.25, is based in part on a standard that was accepted by the so-called canonical community—the community that established the current biblical canon that we use in our churches—namely, that it had to be apostolic and ancient. Books were received into the biblical canon precisely because they were deemed apostolic and did not originate at a later period. Should the criteria adopted by the earliest church be supplanted by the received text that allows other voices to speak with the authority formerly reserved for those who lived and walked with Jesus? Those people are the ones who the church believed best preserved the witness and implications for living that came from Jesus himself, the church's first and most important canon.

If Jesus truly was the canon or final rule for the early church and presumably for the contemporary church, then what should we do with sayings or deeds attributed to Jesus that he did not say or do, for example, John 3:13b, 1 John 5:7b–8a, and so on? Since these texts came into existence long after the writing of the NT documents, should they have equal authority as the earlier or original sayings of Jesus? If they should, we have a major shift in the canonical base of the church, and I question whether we could call the new focus on the final text form *Christian,* since it replaces the oldest established canonical base of the Christian community—Jesus and the apostles—with a later and different authority. These are issues that demand clarification from Childs.

The biggest problem that emerges in the application of Childs's canonical emphasis is finding the final acceptable form of the canonical text of Scripture.[21] What and where is that text? Childs's focus on the biblical text at the end of the canonical process, which includes the redactional material added to the writer's original message and intentions, is at variance with the perspective of the very canonical community that he is anxious to preserve. Why should the second-century through fourth-century additions to the biblical text be included in the canon base of the church or be given equal weight to those of the apostolic community? Has the authoritative base of the church shifted from Jesus and those who first knew him to include equally the redactors of later generations? Does that not fly in the face of all that the earliest Christian community believed they were recognizing in the first place? What else does the criterion of apostolicity suggest if not that? Why should the text of a later generation of Christians, which is admittedly corrupted by mistakes, glosses, and deliberate changes, be given priority over the earliest recoverable text? Childs does not answer

---

[21] See Childs's *New Testament as Canon, Old Testament Theology,* and *Biblical Theology of the Old and New Testaments.*

this question satisfactorily. His work, in practice if not in principle, denies the valuable work of textual critics and historical critics who have made great strides in recovering the historical context, date, authorship, and provenance of many of the biblical writings, all of which have aided significantly in our ability to understand the meaning of the text.

Childs also has difficulty in identifying precisely what canonical community he has in mind in his work. Since the biblical canon emerged over a long period of time and since it took the church centuries to recognize our current NT canon, which is still not universally accepted by all Christians, one must ask again which canonical community he has in mind as the authoritative community for the church. Childs's canonical focus on the question of how the biblical text came to be recognized as authoritative Scripture in the community of faith emphasizes the final form of the biblical text that spoke to a community of faith in conjunction with the other parts of the Bible. The Bible canonically is seen as a whole, and each part of this whole is examined to determine how it functioned as authority (canon) in the life of the church. Canonical critics speak in terms of how a particular writing functioned alongside other canonical writings in a particular community of faith. They freely acknowledge that the original meaning of a book, or even its original text, may have been changed by a later community of Christians from that originally intended by the author who wrote it, but they give priority to its later canonical form and significance.

Were not the risen Lord Jesus and those who had contact with him the church's authority? For example, what else is the basis for Paul's claim to be heard in 1 Cor 9:1–5 and Gal 1:1, 12–17 if not his apostleship from the Lord? Does he not claim a personal encounter with the risen Lord as the basis of his authority to preach? Or, what is the basis for the selection of Matthias to replace Judas Iscariot in Acts 1:21–26 if not his claim to be one of the earliest witnesses to the events that formed the basis for early Christian preaching? Even the much later Muratorian Fragment (ca. 350–375) denies equal authority to the *Shepherd of Hermas* specifically because it was not written in the earliest apostolic period (see chapter 13 §I.D). The gnostic Christian communities, who were the first to attribute apostolic authorship to their gospels (for example, the *Gospel of Thomas* was the first gospel to have an apostolic name attributed to it), were also aware of the value of appealing to the earliest witnesses to the Christian faith to substantiate their positions. For the earliest church, certainly the author was who made the text authoritative, not a nameless redacted text or just any author without close ties to the original events that the document describes. What did the patristic church's focus on the apostolic origin of a document mean if it did not at least imply a serious attempt by the Christian communities of the second through sixth centuries to establish Christian faith on the basis of the *earliest* witnesses to the events and proclamation of their faith?

Why should modern exegetes ignore the earliest form of a text if they can with some reasonable assurance recover it? The Christian communities of the second through sixth centuries did not see themselves as the *canonical* community, but instead sought to build their faith upon what was believed to have been the tradition and writings from the earliest or apostolic Christian community. Since the appeal to such witnesses was done by the canonical community that handed down our present text, why should the church not be interested in that same quest today, especially if they can come closer to it than the churches of the fourth and fifth centuries did? Best asks whether the earliest Christian community, had it been equipped with the critical skills available to the church today, especially in determining the date, authorship, and setting of a writing, would have made other choices about the scope of the NT canon.[22]

Ackroyd suggests that balance is needed in seeking an authoritative text of Scripture.[23] He claims that the original text may be impossible to find and that the search for it may become unproductive, but the acceptance of the finally agreed canonical form is also unacceptable. He contends that authority lies between the text and the reader and between the text and the expositor.[24] However, to ignore the original text in favor of a final received text, even though the original text is sometimes capable of being located, comes dangerously close to removing Christianity from its historical moorings. This practice ignores the emphasis of all of early Christianity and favors the imagined Christ born out of the later Christian community over the historic biblical Christ of the NT and the early Christian community. Christian faith, as is true of biblical criticism, is always interested in the primal history of the texts that help define faith.

Biblical criticism plays an important role in helping the church recover the canonical base that is always the ground for the church's reformation. This canonical base is undoubtedly Jesus, the Lord and Christ of the church (Matt 28:19–20), and the apostolic community. Although as one who has served for years as a pastor I am in sympathy with the vision for a new methodology that will do justice to the significant historical-critical finds of the post-Enlightenment age and to the church's confession of faith that the Scriptures provide for us "a true and faithful vehicle for understanding the will of God,"[25] I am not impressed with how well this vision has been realized in Childs's own work. He is more convinced than I am that the fourth-century church, and even later, is the authority for the church today in determining its text and what Christian literature was inspired and canonical. This raises a valid question: at what point(s) do we accept the opinions of the ancient church as normative for the church today, especially if some of those opinions were based on faulty information?

---

[22] See Best, "Scripture, Tradition, and the Canon," 259.

[23] Ackroyd, "Original Text and Canonical Text.

[24] Ibid., 172.

[25] Childs, *New Testament as Canon,* 37.

I agree with Childs's understanding that the role of biblical theology has been too limited to a descriptive role without much focus on the prescriptive nature of the Scriptures as canon, but he is especially difficult to follow because he seems to presuppose the very "canonical intentionality"[26] of the ancient Christian church that he sets out to establish. He simply does not follow that intentionality of the ancient church as carefully as he should.

---

[26] Ibid., 38.

Select Bibliography

Abegg, M. G. "The Hebrew of the Dead Sea Scrolls." Pages 325–58 in vol. 1 of *The Dead Sea Scrolls after Fifty Years: A Comprehensive Assessment*. Edited by P. W. Flint and J. C. VanderKam. Leiden: Brill, 1998.

Abegg, M. G., P. Flint, and E. Ulrich. *The Dead Sea Scrolls Bible: The Oldest Known Bible Translated for the First Time into English*. San Francisco: Harper, 1999.

Abraham, W. J. *Canon and Criterion in Christian Theology: From Fathers to Feminism*. Oxford: Clarendon, 1998.

Achtemeier, P. J. *The Inspiration of Scripture: Problems and Proposals*. Philadelphia: Westminster, 1980.

Ackroyd, P. R. "The Open Canon." Pages 209–24 in *Studies in the Religious Tradition of the Old Testament*. Edited by P. R. Ackroyd. London: SCM, 1987.

———. "Original Text and Canonical Text." *Union Seminary Quarterly Review* 32 (1977): 166–73.

Adler, W. "The Pseudepigrapha in the Early Church." Pages 211–28 in *The Canon Debate*. Edited by L. M. McDonald and J. A. Sanders. Peabody, Mass.: Hendrickson, 2002.

Akenson, D. H. *Surpassing Wonder: The Invention of the Bible and the Talmuds*. New York: Harcourt Brace, 1998.

Aland, K. "Die Entstehung des Corpus Paulinum." Pages 302–50 in *Neutestamenliche Entwurfe*. Edited by Kurt Aland. Theologische Bücherei 63. Munich: Kaiser, 1979.

———. *The Problem of the New Testament Canon*. Oxford: Mowbray, 1962.

———. "The Problem of Anonymity and Pseudonymity in Christian Literature of the First Two Centuries." *Journal of Theological Studies* 12 (1961): 39–49.

Aland, K., and B. Aland. *The Text of the New Testament: An Introduction to the Critical Editions and to the Theory and Practice of Modern Textual Criticism*. Revised and enlarged edition. Translated by E. R. Rhodes. Grand Rapids: Eerdmans, 1989.

Alexander, A. *The Canon of the Old and New Testaments Ascertained.* New York: Princeton Press, 1826.

———. *The Problem of the New Testament Canon.* Oxford: Mowbray, 1962.

Alexander, L. "The Living Voice: Skepticism toward the Written Word in Early Christian and in Graeco-Roman Texts." Pages 221–47 in *The Bible in Three Dimensions.* Edited by D. J. A. Clines. Sheffield: JSOT Press, 1990.

Alexander, P. H., et al. *The SBL Handbook of Style for Ancient Near Eastern, Biblical, and Early Christian Studies.* Peabody, Mass.: Hendrickson, 1999.

Allert, Craig D. "The State of the New Testament Canon in the Second Century: Putting Tatian's *Diatessaron* in Perspective." *Bulletin for Biblical Research* 9 (1999): 1–18.

Anderson, G. W. "Canonical and Non-canonical." Pages 113–58 in *The Cambridge History of the Bible,* vol. 1: *From the Beginnings to Jerome.* Edited by P. R. Ackroyd and C. F. Evans. Cambridge: Cambridge University Press, 1970.

Anderson, R. T. "Samaritan Literature." Pages 1052–56 in *Dictionary of New Testament Background.* Edited by C. A. Evans and S. E. Porter. Downers Grove, Ill.: InterVarsity, 2000.

———. "Samaritans." Pages 940–47 in vol. 5 of *Anchor Bible Dictionary.* Edited by D. N. Freedman et al. 6 vols. New York: Doubleday, 1992.

Arnold, C. E., ed. *Zondervan Illustrated Bible Background Commentary.* 4 vols. Grand Rapids: Zondervan, 2002.

Attridge, H. W. "Christianity from the Destruction of Jerusalem to Constantine's Adoption of the New Religion: 70–312 C.E." Pages 151–94 in *Christianity and Judaism: A Parallel History of Their Origins and Early Development.* Edited by Hershel Shanks. Washington, D.C.: Biblical Archaeology Society, 1992.

Audet, J. P. "A Hebrew-Aramaic List of Books of the Old Testament in Greek Transcription." *Journal of Theological Studies* 1 (1950): 135–54.

Aune, D. E. "Charismatic Exegesis in Early Judaism and Early Christianity." Pages 125–50 in *The Pseudepigrapha and Early Biblical Interpretation.* Edited by J. H. Charlesworth and C. A. Evans. Journal for the Study of the New Testament: Supplement Series 119. Sheffield: JSOT Press, 1993.

———. *The New Testament in Its Literary Environment.* Philadelphia: Westminster, 1987.

———. "On the Origins of the 'Council of Javneh' Myth." *Journal of Biblical Literature* 110 (1991): 491–93.

———. *Prophecy in Early Christianity.* Grand Rapids: Eerdmans, 1983.

———. "Qumran and the Book of Revelation." Pages 622–48 in vol. 2 of *The Dead Sea Scrolls after Fifty Years: A Comprehensive Assessment.* Edited by P. W. Flint and J. C. VanderKam. Leiden: Brill, 1998.

Baaren, T. P. van. "Towards a Definition of Gnosticism." Pages 18–20 in *Le origini dello gnosticismo*. Edited by U. Bianchi. Studies in the History of Religions 12. Leiden: Brill, 1967.

Baehr, P., and M. O'Brien. "Founders, Classics and the Concept of a Canon." *Current Sociology* 42 (1994): 1–149.

Balás, D. L. "Marcion Revisited: A 'Post-Harnack' Perspective." Pages 95–108 in *Texts and Testaments: Critical Essays on the Bible and Early Church Fathers: A Volume in Honor of Stuart Dickson Currie*. Edited by W. Eugene March. San Antonio: Trinity University Press, 1980.

Balch, D. L. "The Canon: Adaptable and Stable, Oral and Written. Critical Questions for Kelber and Riesner." *Forum* 7 (1991): 183–205.

Baldermann, I. "Didaktischer und 'kanonischer' Zugang: Der Unterricht vor dem Problem des biblischen Kanons." *Jahrbuch für biblische Theologie* 3 (1988): 97–111.

Balla, Peter. *Challenges to New Testament Theology*. Wissenschaftliche Untersuchungen zum Neuen Testament 2. Reihe 95. Tübingen: J. C. B. Mohr, 1997.

Balz, H. R. "Anonymität und Pseudepigraphie im Urchristentum. Überlengungen zum literarischen und theologischen Problem der urchristlichen und gemeinantiken Pseudepigraphie." *Zeitschrift für Theologie und Kirche* 66 (1969): 403–36.

Bar-Ilan, M. "Writing in Ancient Israel and Early Judaism: Scribes and Books in the late Second Commonwealth and Rabbinic Period." Pages 21–37 in *Mikra: Text, Translation, Reading, and Interpretation of the Hebrew Bible in Ancient Judaism and Early Christianity*. Edited by M. J. Mulder. Compendia rerum iudaicarum ad Novum Testamentum 2.1. Minneapolis: Fortress, 1990.

Barker, G. W., W. L. Lane, and J. R. Michaels. *The New Testament Speaks*. New York: Harper & Row, 1969.

Barnstone, W., ed. *The Other Bible: Jewish Pseudepigrapha, Christian Apocrypha, Gnostic Scriptures, Kabbalah, Dead Sea Scrolls*. San Francisco: Harper, 1984.

Barr, J. *Fundamentalism*. Philadelphia: Westminster, 1977.

———. *Holy Scripture: Canon, Authority, Criticism*. Philadelphia: Westminster, 1983.

———. Review of K. H. Jobes and M. Silva, *Invitation to the Septuagint*. *Review of Biblical Literature* (2002). Online: http://www.bookreviews.org/pdf/1341_3027.pdf.

Barthélemy, Dominique. "La critique canonique." *Revue de l'Institut Catholique de Paris* 36 (1991): 191–220.

Barton, J. "Canon." Pages 101–5 in *A Dictionary of Biblical Interpretation*. Edited by R. J. Coggins and J. L. Houlden. London: SCM, 1990.

———. *Holy Writings, Sacred Text: The Canon in Early Christianity*. Louisville: Westminster John Knox, 1997.

———. *How the Bible Came to Be*. Louisville: Westminster John Knox, 1997.

———. "Marcion Revisited." Pages 341–54 in *The Canon Debate*. Edited by L. M. McDonald and J. A. Sanders. Peabody, Mass.: Hendrickson, 2002.

———. *Oracles of God*. Oxford: Oxford University Press, 1986.

———. *People of the Book? The Authority of the Bible in Christianity*. Louisville: Westminster John Knox, 1988.

———. "Prophecy (Postexilic Hebrew)." Pages 489–95 in vol. 5 of *Anchor Bible Dictionary*. Edited by D. N. Freedman et al. 6 vols. New York: Doubleday, 1992.

———. "The Significance of a Fixed Canon of the Hebrew Bible." Pages 67–83 in vol. I/1 of *Hebrew Bible / Old Testament: The History of Its Interpretation*. Edited by Magne Saebo. Göttingen: Vandenhoeck & Ruprecht, 1996.

———. *The Spirit and the Letter: Studies in the Biblical Canon*. London: SPCK, 1997.

Bauckham, R. J. *God Crucified*. Grand Rapids: Eerdmans, 1998.

———. "Papias and Polycrates on the Origin of the Fourth Gospel." *Journal of Theological Studies* 44 (1993): 24–69.

Baum, Armin D. "Der neutestamentliche Kanon bei Eusebius: (*Hist. eccl.* 3.25.1–7) im Kontext seiner literaturgeschichtlichen Arbeit." *Ephemerides theologicae lovanienses* 73 (1997): 307–48.

———. "Papias, der Vorzug der *Viva Vox* und die Evangelienschriften." *New Testament Studies* 44 (1998): 144–51.

Bauer, W. *Orthodoxy and Heresy in Earliest Christianity*. Edited by R. Kraft and G. Krodel. Philadelphia: Fortress, 1971.

Beare, G. W. "Canon of the NT." Pages 520–32 in vol. 1 of *Interpreter's Dictionary of the Bible*. Edited by G. A. Buttrick. New York: Abingdon, 1962.

Beckwith, R. T. "Canon of the Hebrew Bible and the Old Testament." Pages 100–102 in *The Oxford Companion to the Bible*. Edited by B. M. Metzger and M. D. Coogan. New York: Oxford University Press, 1993.

———. "Formation of the Hebrew Bible." Pages 39–86 in *Mikra: Text, Translation, Reading, and Interpretation of the Hebrew Bible in Ancient Judaism and Early Christianity*. Edited by M. J. Mulder. Compendia rerum iudaicarum ad Novum Testamentum 2.1. Minneapolis: Fortress, 1990.

———. *The Old Testament Canon of the New Testament Church and Its Background in Early Judaism*. Grand Rapids: Eerdmans, 1985.

Bellinzoni, A. J. *The Sayings of Jesus in the Writings of Justin Martyr*. Novum Testamentum Supplements 17. Leiden: Brill, 1967.

Berger, K. *Identity and Experience in the New Testament*. Translated by C. Muenchow. Minneapolis: Fortress, 2003.

Bernstein, M. J. "The Employment and Interpretation of Scripture." Pages 29–51 in *Reading 4QMMT: New Perspectives on Qumran Law and His-*

tory. Edited by J. Kampen and M. J. Bernstein. Atlanta: Scholars Press, 1996.

Best, E. "Scripture, Tradition, and the Canon of the New Testament." *Bulletin of the John Rylands University Library* 61 (1978–79): 258–89.

Betz, Otto. "Das Problem des 'Kanons' in den Texten von Qumran." Pages 70–101 in *Der Kanon der Bibel*. Edited by G. Maier. Giessen: Brunnen, 1990.

Beyer, Hermann Wolfgang. "κανών." Pages 596–602 in vol. 3 of *Theological Dictionary of the New Testament*. Edited by G. Kittel and G. Friedrich. Translated by G. W. Bromiley. 10 vols. Grand Rapids: Eerdmans, 1964–1976.

Bialik, H. N., and Y. H. Ravnitzky. *The Book of Legends, Sefer Ha-Aggadah: Legends from the Talmud and Midrash*. Translated by W. G. Braude. New York: Schocken, 1992.

Bickerman, Elias J. "Some Notes on the Transmission of the Septuagint." Pages 149–78 in *Alexander Marx: Jubilee Volume on the Occasion of His Seventieth Birthday* (English Section). New York: The Jewish Theological Seminary of America, 1950.

Bienert, W. A. "The Picture of the Apostle in Early Christian Tradition." Pages 5–27 in vol. 2 of *New Testament Apocrypha*. Rev. ed. Edited by W. Schneemelcher. Translated by R. McL. Wilson. Louisville: Westminster John Knox, 1992.

Birch, B. C. "Tradition, Canon and Biblical Theology." *Horizons in Biblical Theology* 2 (1980): 113–25.

Blackman, E. C. *Marcion and His Influence*. London: SPCK, 1948.

Blenkinsopp, J. "The Formation of the Hebrew Bible Canon: Isaiah as a Test Case." Pages 53–67 in *The Canon Debate*. Edited by L. M. McDonald and J. A. Sanders. Peabody, Mass.: Hendrickson, 2002.

———. *Prophecy and Canon: A Contribution to the Study of Jewish Origins*. Notre Dame: University of Notre Dame Press, 1977.

———. "Prophecy and Priesthood in Josephus." *Journal of Jewish Studies* 101 (1974): 245–55.

———. " 'We Pay Heed to Heavenly Voices': The 'End of Prophecy' and the Formation of the Canon." Pages 19–31 in *Biblical and Humane: A Festschrift for John F. Priest*. Edited by Linda Bennett Elder, David L. Barr, and Elizabeth Struthers Malbon. Atlanta: Scholars Press, 1996.

Bloch, J. "Outside Books." Pages 202–23 in *The Canon and Masorah of the Hebrew Bible*. Edited by S. Z. Leiman. New York: Ktav, 1974.

Bloom, Harold. *The Western Canon: The Books and Schools of the Age*. New York: Harcourt Brace, 1994.

Blowers, Paul M., ed. and trans. *The Bible in Greek Christian Antiquity*. Notre Dame: University of Notre Dame Press, 1997.

Boccaccini, G., ed. *Enoch and Qumran Origins: New Light on a Forgotten Connection*. Grand Rapids: Eerdmans, 2005.

Boeft, J. Den, and M. L. Van Poll-van De Lisdonk, eds. *The Impact of Scripture in Early Christianity*. Supplements to Vigiliae Christianae 44. Leiden: Brill, 1999.

Bokedal, T. *The Scriptures and the Lord: Formation and Significance of the Christian Biblical Canon*. Lund: Lund University Press, 2005.

Bossman, D. M. "Canon and Culture: Realistic Possibilities for the Biblical Canon." *Biblical Theology Bulletin* 23 (1993): 4–13.

Bovon F. "The Canonical Structure of Gospel and Apostle." Pages 516–27 in *The Canon Debate*. Edited by L. M. McDonald and J. A. Sanders. Peabody, Mass.: Hendrickson, 2002.

———. "Vers une nouvelle edition de la litterature apocryphe chrétienne." *Augustinianum* 23 (1983): 373–78.

———. "The Synoptic Gospels and the Non-Canonical Acts of the Apostles." *Harvard Theological Review* 81 (1988): 19–36.

Bovon, F., A. G. Brock, and C. R. Matthews, eds. *The Apocryphal Acts of the Apostles*. Cambridge: Harvard University Press, 1999.

Bowman, A. K. "The Vindolanda Tablets and the Development of the Book Form." *Zeitschrift für Papyrologie und Epigraphik* 18 (1975): 237–52.

Brakke, David. "Canon Formation and Social Conflict in Fourth-Century Egypt: Athanasius of Alexandria's Thirty-Ninth *Festal Letter*." *Harvard Theological Review* 87 (1994): 395–419.

Brenton, L. C. L. *The Septuagint Version of the Old Testament, according to the Vatican Text*. London: Bagster, 1844.

Brooke, G. "The Explicit Presentation of Scripture in 4QMMT." Pages 67–88 in *Legal Texts and Legal Issues: Proceedings of the Second Meeting of the International Organization for Qumran Studies, Cambridge 1995: Published in Honour of Joseph M. Baumgarten*. Edited by M. Bernstein, F. García Martínez, and J. Kampen. Studies on the Texts of the Desert of Judah 23. Leiden: Brill, 1997.

Broshi, M. "What Jesus Learned from the Essenes: The Blessing of Poverty and the Bane of Divorce." *Biblical Archaeology Review* 30.1 (January–February 2004): 32–37, 64.

Brown, R. E., and R. F. Collins. "Canonicity." Pages 1034–54 in *The New Jerome Biblical Commentary*. Edited by R. E. Brown, J. A. Fitzmyer, and R. E. Murphy. London: Chapman, 1989.

Broyde, M. J. "Defilement of the Hands, Canonization of the Bible, and the Special Status of Esther, Ecclesiastes, and the Song of Songs." *Judaism* 44 (1995): 65–79.

Bruce, B. J. *Origen: Homilies on Joshua*. Fathers of the Church: A New Translation 105. Washington D.C.: Catholic University of America Press, 2002.

Bruce, F. F. *The Books and the Parchments: How We Got Our English Bible*. 4th edition. Old Tappan, N.J.: Revell, 1984.

———. *The Canon of Scripture*. Downers Grove, Ill.: InterVarsity, 1988.

———. "Tradition and the Canon of Scripture." Pages 59–84 in *The Authoritative Word: Essays on the Nature of Scripture*. Edited by D. K. McKim. Grand Rapids: Eerdmans, 1993.

Buchanan, E. S. "The Codex Muratorianus." *Journal of Theological Studies* 8 (1907): 537–39.

Budde, Karl. *Der Kanon des Alten Testaments: Ein Abriss*. Giessen: J. Ricker (Alfred Töpelmann), 1900.

Buhl, Frants P. W. *Kanon und Text des alten Testaments*. Leipzig: Academische Buchhandlung, 1891.

Burns, G. L. "Canon and Power in the Hebrew Scriptures." *Critical Inquiry* 10 (1984): 259–89. Repr. pages 65–84 in *Canons*. Edited by R. von Hallberg. Chicago: University of Chicago Press, 1984.

Burridge, R. A. *What Are the Gospels? A Comparison with Graeco-Roman Biography*. Society for New Testament Studies Monograph Series 70. Cambridge: Cambridge University Press, 1992.

Callaway, Philip R. "The Temple Scroll and the Canonization of the Old Testament." *Revue biblique* 13 (1988): 239–43.

Campenhausen, H. von. *The Formation of the Christian Bible*. Translated by J. A. Baker. Philadelphia: Fortress, 1972.

Carr, D. "Canonization in the Context of Community: An Outline for the Formation of the Tanakh and the Christian Bible." Pages 22–64 in *A Gift of God in Due Season: Essays on Scripture and Community in Honor of James A. Sanders*. Edited by R. Weis and D. Carr. Sheffield: Sheffield Academic Press, 1996.

Carr, D. M. "The Song of Songs as a Microcosm of the Canonization and Decanonization Process." Pages 173–89 in *Canonization and Decanonization*. Edited by A. van der Kooij and K. van der Toorn. Studies in the History of Religion 82. Leiden: Brill, 1998.

Carson, D. A., and John Woodbridge, eds. *Hermeneutics, Authority, and Canon*. Grand Rapids: Zondervan, 1986.

Carson, D. A., and H. G. M. Williamson, eds. *It Is Written: Scripture Citing Scripture: Essays in Honour of Barnabas Lindars, SSF*. Cambridge: Cambridge University Press, 1988.

Casey, R. "The Armenian Marcionites and the Diatessaron." *Journal of Biblical Literature* 57 (1938): 185–92.

Chadwick, O. "The Significance of the Deuterocanonical Writings in the Anglican Tradition." Pages 116–128 in *The Apocrypha in Ecumenical Perspective: The Place of the Late Writings of the Old Testament among the Biblical Writings and Their Significance in the Eastern and Western Church Traditions*. Edited by S. Meurer. Translated by P. Ellingworth. United Bible Societies Monograph Series 6. New York: United Bible Societies, 1991.

Chapman, S. B. *The Law and the Prophets: A Study in Old Testament Canon Formation*. Forschungen zum Alten Testament 27. Tübingen: Mohr, 2000.

———. "'The Law and the Words' as a Canonical Formula within the Old Testament." Pages 26–74 in *The Interpretation of Scripture in Early Judaism and Christianity: Studies in Language and Traditions*. Edited by Craig A. Evans. Journal for the Study of the Pseudepigraphia: Supplement Series 33. Studies in Scripture in Early Judaism and Christianity 7. Sheffield: Sheffield Academic Press, 2000.

Charles, R. H. *The Book of Jubilees or the Little Genesis*. London: Oxford University Press, 1902.

———. *A Critical and Exegetical Commentary on the Revelation of St. John*. 2 vols. International Critical Commentary. Edinburgh: Clark, 1920.

Charles, R. H., ed. *The Apocrypha and Pseudepigrapha of the Old Testament*. 2 vols. Oxford: Clarendon, 1913.

Charlesworth, J. H. "Pseudepigrapha." Pages 836–40 in *Harper's Bible Dictionary*. Edited by P. J. Achtemeier et al. San Francisco: Harper & Row, 1985.

———. "Pseudepigraphy." Pages 961–64 in *Encyclopedia of Early Christianity*. Edited by E. Ferguson. New York: Garland, 1990.

Charlesworth, J. H., and C. A. Evans. "Jesus in the Agrapha and Apocryphal Gospels." Pages 479–533 in *Studying the Historical Jesus: Evaluations of the State of Current Research*. Edited by B. Chilton and C. A. Evans. New Testament Tools and Studies 19. Leiden: Brill, 1994.

Charteris, A. H. *Canonicity: A Collection of Early Testimonies to the Canonical Books of the New Testament*. Edinburgh: William Blackwood & Sons, 1880.

Childs, B. S. *Biblical Theology in Crisis*. Philadelphia: Westminster, 1970.

———. *Biblical Theology of the Old and New Testaments: Theological Reflection on the Christian Bible*. Minneapolis: Fortress, 1993.

———. "The Canonical Shape of the Prophetic Literature." *Interpretation* 32 (1978): 46–55.

———. "The Exegetical Significance of Canon for the Study of the Old Testament." Pages 66–80 in Vetus Testamentum Supplements 29. Leiden: Brill, 1978.

———. "Interpretation in Faith: The Theological Responsibility of an Old Testament Commentary." *Interpretation* 18 (1964): 432–39.

———. *Introduction to the Old Testament as Scripture*. Philadelphia: Fortress, 1979.

———. *The New Testament as Canon: An Introduction*. Philadelphia: Fortress, 1985.

———. *Old Testament Theology in a Canonical Context*. Philadelphia: Fortress, 1986.

Christensen, D. L. "The Centre of the First Testament within the Canonical Process." *Biblical Theology Bulletin* 23 (1993): 48–53.

———. *Explosion of the Canon: The Greek New Testament in Early Church History*. North Richland Hills, Tex.: BIBAL Press, 2004.

———. "Josephus and the Twenty-Two Book Canon of Sacred Scripture." *Journal of the Evangelical Theological Society* 29 (1986): 37–46.

———. "The Lost Books of the Bible." *Bible Review* 14.5 (Oct. 1998): 24–31.

Clabeaux, J. J. *A Lost Edition of the Letters of Paul: A Reassessment of the Text of the Pauline Corpus Attested by Marcion*. Catholic Biblical Quarterly Monograph Series 21. Washington D.C.: Catholic University of America Press, 1989.

———. "Marcion." Pages 514–16 in vol. 4 of *Anchor Bible Dictionary*. Edited by D. N. Freedman et al. 6 vols. New York: Doubleday, 1992.

———. "Marcionite Prologues to Paul." Pages 520–21 in vol. 4 of *Anchor Bible Dictionary*. Edited by D. N. Freedman et al. 6 vols. New York: Doubleday, 1992.

Clarke, Kent D. "Original Text or Canonical Text? Questioning the Shape of the New Testament We Translate." Pages 281–322 in *Issues in Biblical Translation: Responses to Eugene A. Nida*. Edited by S. E. Porter and R. Hess. Journal for the Study of the New Testament: Supplement Series 173. Sheffield: Sheffield Academic Press, 1998.

Coats, George W., and Burke O. Long. *Canon and Authority: Essays in Old Testament Religion and Authority*. Philadelphia: Fortress, 1977.

Collins, A. Y., ed. *Early Christian Apocalypticism: Genre and Social Setting*. Semeia 36. Decatur, Ga.: Scholars Press, 1986.

Collins, J. J. "Before the Canon: Scriptures in Second Temple Judaism." Pages 225–41 in *Old Testament Interpretation: Past, Present, and Future*. Edited by James Luther Mays, David L. Petersen, and Kent Harold Richards. Nashville: Abingdon, 1995.

Collins, J. J., ed. *The Encyclopedia of Apocalypticism*, vol. 1: *The Origins of Apocalypticism in Judaism and Christianity*. New York: Continuum, 1998.

Collins, N. L. *The Library in Alexandria and the Bible in Greek*. Leiden: Brill, 2000.

Collins, R. F. *Introduction to the New Testament*. Garden City, N.Y.: Doubleday, 1983.

Colson F. H., G. H. Whitaker, and R. Marcus, trans. *Philo*. 12 vols. Loeb Classical Library. Cambridge: Harvard University Press, 1929–62.

Comfort, Philip Wesley, ed. *The Origin of the Bible*. Wheaton, Ill.: Tyndale, 1992.

Conrad, J. "Zur Frage nach der Rolle des Gesetzes bei der Bildung des alttestamentlichen Kanons." *Theologia viatorum* 11 (1979): 11–19.

Cook, J. "Septuagint Proverbs—and Canonization." Pages 79–91 in *Canonization and Decanonization*. Edited by A. van der Kooij and K. van der Toorn. Studies in the History of Religion 82. Leiden: Brill, 1998.

Cosgrove, Charles H. "Justin Martyr and the Emerging Christian Canon: Observations on the Purpose and Destination of the Dialogue with Trypho." *Vigiliae christianae* 36 (1982): 209–32.

Cowley, R. W. "The Biblical Canon of the Ethiopian Orthodox Church Today." *Ostkirchliche Studien* 23 (1974): 318–24.

Cox, P. *Biography in Late Antiquity: A Quest for the Holy Man*. Berkeley: University of California Press, 1983.

Cranfield, C. E. B. "The Gospel of Mark." Pages 267–77 in vol. 3 of *Interpreter's Dictionary of the Bible*. Edited by G. A. Buttrick. New York: Abingdon, 1962.

Crawford, White. "The 'Rewritten' Bible at Qumran." *Frank Moore Cross Volume*. Eretz-Israel 26. Jerusalem: IES and Hebrew Union College—Jewish Institute of Religion, 1999.

Cribiore, Raffaella. *Writing, Teachers, and Students in Greco-Roman Egypt*. Atlanta: Scholars Press, 1996.

Cross, F. L. "History and Fiction in the African Canons." *Journal of Theological Studies* 12 (1961): 227–47.

Cross, F. L., and E. A. Livingstone, eds. *The Oxford Dictionary of the Christian Church*. 3rd edition. Oxford: Oxford University Press, 1997.

Cross, F. M. *The Ancient Library at Qumran*. 3rd edition. Minneapolis: Fortress, 1995.

———. "The Evolution of a Theory of Local Texts." Pages 306–20 in *Qumran and the History of the Biblical Text*. Edited by F. M. Cross and S. Talmon. Cambridge: Harvard University Press, 1975.

———. *From Epic to Canon: History and Literature in Ancient Israel*. Baltimore: Johns Hopkins University Press, 1998.

———. "The History of the Biblical Text in the Light of the Discoveries in the Judean Desert." *Harvard Theological Review* 57 (1964): 281–99.

———. "The Text Behind the Text of the Hebrew Bible." Pages 139–55 in *Understanding the Dead Sea Scrolls*. Edited by Hershel Shanks. New York: Vintage, 1992.

Crossan, J. D. *Four Other Gospels*. Minneapolis: Winston, 1985.

———. *Sayings Parallels: A Workbook for the Jesus Tradition*. Philadelphia: Fortress, 1986.

Croy, N. C. *The Mutilation of Mark's Gospel*. Nashville: Abingdon, 2003.

Cruesemann, F. "Das 'portative Vaterland': Struktur und Genese des alttestamentlichen Kanons." Pages 63–79 in vol. 2 of *Kanon und Zensur: Beiträge zur Archäologie der literarischen Kommunikation*. Edited by A. Assmann and J. Assmann. Munich: Wilhelm Fink, 1987.

Cullmann, O. "The Plurality of the Gospels as a Theological Problem in Antiquity." Pages 39–54 in *The Early Church*. Edited by A. J. B. Higgins. Philadelphia: Westminster, 1956.

Cunningham, Philip J. *Exploring Scripture: How the Bible Came to Be*. New York: Paulist, 1992.

Dahl, N. A. "The Origin of the Earliest Prologues to the Pauline Letters." *Semeia* 12 (1978): 233–77.

———. "The Particularity of the Pauline Epistles as a Problem in the Ancient Church." Pages 261–71 in *Neotestamentica et Patristica: Freund-*

esgabe O. Cullmann. Novum Testamentum Supplement 6. Leiden: Brill, 1962.

Danby, H. *The Mishnah*. Oxford: Oxford University Press, 1933. Repr., 1992.

Danker, F. W. *II Corinthians*. Augsburg Commentaries on the New Testament. Minneapolis: Augsburg, 1989.

Dassmann, E. "Wer schuf den Kanon des Neuen Testaments?: Zum neuesten Buch von Bruce M. Metzger." *Jahrbuch für biblische Theologie* 3 (1988): 275–83.

Davidson, S. *The Canon of the Bible: Its Formation, History, and Fluctuations*. London: Henry S. King, 1877.

Davies, P. R. "The Jewish Scriptural Canon in Cultural Perspective." Pages 36–52 in *The Canon Debate*. Edited by L. M. McDonald and J. A. Sanders. Peabody, Mass.: Hendrickson, 2002.

———. " 'Pen of Iron, Point of Diamond' (Jer 17:1): Prophecy as Writing." Pages 65–81 in *Writings and Speech in Israelite and Ancient Near Eastern Prophecy*. Edited by M. Floyd and E. Ben Zvi. Atlanta: Scholars Press, 2000.

———. *Scribes and Schools: The Canonization of the Hebrew Scriptures*. Library of Ancient Israel. Louisville: Westminster John Knox, 1988.

Davies, W. D. "Canon and Christology." Pages 19–36 in *The Glory of Christ in the New Testament: Studies in Christology in Memory of George Bradford Caird*. Edited by L. D. Hurst and N. T. Wright. Oxford: Clarendon, 1987.

De Boer, E. A. *The Gospel of Mary: Listening to the Beloved Disciple*. London: T&T Clark International, 2004.

Dempster, S. *Dominion and Dynasty: A Theology of the Hebrew Bible*. Downers Grove, Ill.: InterVarsity, 2003.

———. "An 'Extraordinary Fact': Torah and Temple and the Contours of the Hebrew Canon." *Tyndale Bulletin* 48 (1997): 23–56, 191–218.

Demsky, A. "Writing in Ancient Israel and Early Judaism: The Biblical Period." Pages 2–20 in *Mikra: Text, Translation, Reading, and Interpretation of the Hebrew Bible in Ancient Judaism and Early Christianity*. Edited by M. J. Mulder. Compendia rerum iudaicarum ad Novum Testamentum 2.1. Minneapolis: Fortress, 1990.

De Troyer, K. *Rewriting the Sacred Text: What the Old Greek Texts Tell Us about the Literary Growth of the Bible*. Text-Critical Studies 4. Altanta: Society of Biblical Literature, 2003.

Dibelius, M. *From Tradition to Gospel*. Translated by B. L. Woolf. London: Nicholson & Watson, 1934.

Dobschütz, E. von. "The Abandonment of the Canonical Ideal." *American Journal of Theology* 19 (1915): 416–29.

Dohmen, C. "Der biblische Kanon in der Diskussion." *Theologische Revue* 91 (1995): 452–60.

Dombrowski, B. W. W. *An Annotated Translation of Miqsat Ma'aseh ha-Torah (4QMMT)*. Krakow-Weenzen, Poland: Enigma, 1993.

Donelson, L. R. *Pseudepigraphy and Ethical Argument in the Pastoral Epistles*. Hermeneutische Untersuchungen zur Theologie 22. Tübingen: J. C. B. Mohr, 1986.

DuBois, J.-D. "L'exégese gnostique et l'histoire du canon des écritures." Pages 89–97 in *Les règles de l'intepretation*. Edited by M. Tardieu. Paris: Cerf, 1987.

Duff, J. "P[46] and the Pastorals: A Misleading Consensus?" *New Testament Studies* 44 (1998): 581–82.

Dulles, A. "The Authority of Scripture: A Catholic Perspective." Pages 14–40 in *Scripture in the Jewish and Christian Traditions*. Edited by F. E. Greenspahn. Nashville: Abingdon, 1982.

Duncker, P. G. "The Canon of the Old Testament at the Council of Trent." *Catholic Biblical Quarterly* 15 (1953): 277–99.

Dungan, D. L. "The New Testament Canon in Recent Study." *Interpretation* 29 (1975): 339–51.

———. *The Sayings of Jesus in the Churches of Paul: The Use of the Synoptic Tradition in the Regulation of Early Church Life*. Philadelphia: Fortress, 1971.

Dunn, J. D. G. "Levels of Canonical Authority." *Horizons in Biblical Theology* 4 (1982): 13–60.

———. *The Living Word*. Philadelphia: Fortress, 1987.

———. *Unity and Diversity in the New Testament*. 2nd edition. Philadelphia: Westminster, 1992.

Dyck, E. "What Do We Mean By Canon?" *Crux* 25 (1989): 17–22.

Edwards, M. J. "The *Epistle to Rheginus:* Valentinianism in the Fourth Century." *Novum Testamentum* 37 (1995): 76–91.

Ehrman, B. D. *Lost Christianities: The Battles for Scripture and the Faiths We Never Knew*. New York: Oxford University Press, 2003.

———. *Lost Scriptures: Books That Did Not Make It into the New Testament*. New York: Oxford University Press, 2003.

———. *Misquoting Jesus: The Story behind who Changed the Bible and Why*. San Francisco: HarperSanFrancisco, 2005.

———. "The New Testament Canon of Didymus the Blind." *Vigiliae christianae* 37 (1983): 1–21.

———. *The Orthodox Corruption of Scripture: The Effect of Early Christological Controversies on the Text of the New Testament*. Oxford: Oxford University Press, 1993.

———. "The Text as Window: New Testament Manuscripts and the Social History of Early Christianity." Pages 361–79 in *The Text of the New Testament in Contemporary Research: Essays on the Status Quaestionis*. Edited by B. D. Ehrman and M. W. Holmes. Studies and Documents 46. Grand Rapids: Eerdmans, 1995.

———. "The Text of the Gospels at the End of the Second Century." Pages 95–122 in *Codex Bezae: Studies from the Lunel Colloquium, June 1994*. Edited by D. C. Parker and C.-B. Amphoux. New Testament Tools and Studies 22. Leiden: Brill, 1996.

Eisenman, R., and M. Wise. *The Dead Sea Scrolls Uncovered: The First Complete Translation and Interpretation of Fifty Key Documents Withheld for over Thirty-five Years*. Rockport, Mass.: Element, 1992.

Ellege, C. D. *The Bible and the Dead Sea Scrolls*. Archaeology and Biblical Studies 14. Atlanta: Society of Biblical Literature, 2005.

Ellens, J. H. "The Ancient Library of Alexandria and Early Christian Theological Development." *Occasional Papers of the Institute for Antiquity and Christianity* 27 (1993): 1–51.

Elliott, J. K. "Manuscripts, the Codex, and the Canon." *Journal for the Study of the New Testament* 63 (1996): 105–23.

Ellis, E. E. *The Making of the New Testament Documents*. Leiden: Brill, 2002.

———. *The Old Testament in Early Christianity: Canon and Interpretation in the Light of Modern Research*. Grand Rapids: Baker, 1992.

Epp, E. J. "The Codex and Literacy in Early Christianity and at Oxyrhynchus: Issues Raised by Harry Y. Gamble's *Books and Readers in the Early Church*." *Critical Review of Books in Religion* 10 (1997): 15–37.

———. "Issues in New Testament Textual Criticism." Pages 17–76 in *Rethinking New Testament Textual Criticism*. Edited by D. A. Black. Grand Rapids: Baker, 2002.

———. "Issues in the Interrelation of New Testament Textual Criticism and Canon." Pages 485–515 in *The Canon Debate*. Edited by L. M. McDonald and J. A. Sanders. Peabody, Mass.: Hendrickson, 2002.

———. *Junia: The First Woman Apostle*. Minneapolis: Fortress, 2005.

———. "The Multivalence of the Term 'Original Text' in New Testament Textual Criticism." *Harvard Theological Review* 92 (1999): 245–81.

———. "The Oxyrhynchus New Testament Papyri: 'Not without Honor Except in Their Hometown'?" *Journal of Biblical Literature* 123 (2004): 5–55.

_____. *Perspectives on New Testament Textual Criticism: Collected Essays, 1962–2004*. Supplements to Novum Testamentum 116. Leiden: Brill, 2005.

———. "Textual Criticism in the Exegesis of the New Testament, with an Excursus on Canon." Pages 73–91 in *Handbook to Exegesis of the New Testament*. Edited by S. E. Porter. New Testament Tools and Studies 25. Leiden: Brill, 1997.

Ernest, J. D. *The Bible in Athanasius of Alexandria*. Leiden: Brill, 2004.

Evans, C. A. *Ancient Texts for New Testament Studies: A Guide to the Background Literature*. Peabody, Mass.: Hendrickson, 2005.

———. *The Bible Knowledge Background Commentary*. 3 vols. Colorado Springs: Victor/Cook, 2003–2004.

———. "Jesus and the Dead Sea Scrolls." Pages 573–98 in vol. 2 of *The Dead Sea Scrolls after Fifty Years: A Comprehensive Assessment*. Edited by P. W. Flint and J. C. VanderKam. Leiden: Brill, 1998.

———. "Luke and the Rewritten Bible: Aspects of Lukan Hagiography." Pages 170–201 in *The Pseudepigrapha and Early Biblical Interpretation*. Edited by J. H. Charlesworth and C. A. Evans. Journal for the Study of the New Testament: Supplement Series 119. Sheffield: JSOT Press, 1993.

———. "Mishna and Messiah 'in Context': Some Comments on Jacob Neusner's Proposals." *Journal of Biblical Literature* 112 (1993): 267–89.

———. "The Scriptures of Jesus and His Earliest Followers." Pages 185–95 in *The Canon Debate*. Edited by L. M. McDonald and J. A. Sanders. Peabody, Mass.: Hendrickson, 2002.

Evans, C. A., R. L. Webb, and R. A. Wiebe, eds. *Nag Hammadi Texts and the Bible*. New Testament Tools and Studies 18. Leiden: Brill, 1993.

Evans, C. F. *Is Holy Scripture Christian?* London: SCM Press, 1971.

Ewert, D. *From Ancient Tablets to Modern Translations*. Grand Rapids: Zondervan, 1983.

Fallon, Francis T. "The Prophets of the Old Testament and the Gnostics. A Note on Irenaeus, *Adversus Haereses*, 1.30.10–11." *Vigiliae christianae* 32 (1978): 191–94.

Farkasfalvy, Denis. "The Early Development of the New Testament Canon." Pages 97–160 in *The Formation of the New Testament Canon*. Edited by Harold W. Attridge. New York: Paulist, 1983.

———. "The Ecclesial Setting of Pseudepigraphy in Second Peter and Its Role in the Formation of the Canon." *Second Century* 5 (1985–1986): 3–29.

Farley, E. *Ecclesial Reflection*. Philadelphia: Fortress, 1982.

Farmer, W. R. "The Church's Gospel Canon: Why Four and No More." Pages 1246–50 in *The International Bible Commentary*. Edited by W. R. Farmer. Collegeville, Minn.: The Liturgical Press, 1998.

———. "A Dismantling of the Church's Canon." Pages 35–55 in *The Gospel of Jesus: The Pastoral Relevance of the Synoptic Problem*. Edited by W. R. Farmer. Louisville: Westminster John Knox, 1994.

———. "Further Reflections on the Fourfold Gospel Canon." Pages 107–13 in *The Early Church in Its Context: Essays in Honor of Everett Ferguson*. Edited by J. Malherbe, F. W. Norris, and J. W. Thompson. Leiden: Brill, 1998.

———. "Galatians and the Second Century Development of the *Regula Fidei*." *The Second Century: A Journal of Early Christian Studies* 4 (Fall 1984): 143–70.

———. *Jesus and the Gospel: Tradition, Scripture and Canon*. Philadelphia: Fortress, 1982.

———. "Matthew and the Bible: An Essay in Canonical Criticism." *Lexington Theological Quarterly* 11 (April 1976): 57–66.

———. "Reflections on Jesus and the New Testament Canon." Pages 321–40 in *The Canon Debate*. Edited by L. M. McDonald and J. A. Sanders. Peabody, Mass.: Hendrickson, 2002.

———. "The Role of Isaiah in the Development of the Christian Canon." Pages 217–22 in *Uncovering Ancient Stones: Festschrift for H. Neil Richardson*. Winona, Ind.: Eisenbrauns, 1994.

Farmer, W. R., and D. M. Farkasfalvy. *The Formation of the New Testament Canon*. Introduction by A. C. Outler. Edited by H. W. Attridge. New York: Paulist Press, 1983.

Feldman, L. H. "Introduction." Pages 17–49 in *Josephus, the Bible, and History*. Edited by L. H. Feldman and G. Hata. Detroit: Wayne State University Press, 1989.

Fenton, J. C. "Pseudonymity and the New Testament." *Theology* 58 (1955): 51–56.

Ferguson, E. *Backgrounds of Early Christianity*. 3rd edition. Grand Rapids: Eerdmans, 2003.

———. "Canon Muratori: Date and Provenance." *Studia patristica* 17.2 (1982): 677–83.

———. Review of G. M. Hahneman, *The Muratorian Fragment and the Development of the Canon*. *Journal of Theological Studies* 44 (1993): 691–97.

Fernández Marcos, N. *The Septuagint in Context: Introduction to the Greek Versions of the Bible*. Translated by W. G. E. Watson. Leiden: Brill, 2001.

Fiedler, L. A., and H. A. Baker Jr., eds. *English Literature: Opening up the Canon*. Baltimore: Johns Hopkins University Press, 1981.

Filoramo, G. *A History of Gnosticism*. Translated by A. Alcock. Oxford: Blackwell, 1990.

Filson, Floyd V. *Which Books Belong in the Bible? A Study of the Canon*. Philadelphia: Westminster, 1957.

Fitzmyer, J. A. *The Dead Sea Scrolls and Christian Origins*. Studies in the Dead Sea Scrolls and Related Literature. Grand Rapids: Eerdmans, 2000.

———. "Paul and the Dead Sea Scrolls." Pages 599–621 in vol. 2 of *The Dead Sea Scrolls after Fifty Years: A Comprehensive Assessment*. Edited by P. W. Flint and J. C. VanderKam. Leiden: Brill, 1998.

Flint, P. " 'Apocrypha,' Other Previously-known Writings, and 'Pseudepigrapha' in the Dead Sea Scrolls." Pages 24–66 in vol. 2 of *The Dead Sea Scrolls after Fifty Years: A Comprehensive Assessment*. Edited by Peter W. Flint and James C. VanderKam. Leiden: Brill, 1999.

———. *The Dead Sea Psalms Scrolls and the Book of Psalms*. Leiden: Brill, 1997.

———. "Noncanonical Writings in the Dead Sea Scrolls." Pages 80–126 in *The Bible at Qumran: Text, Shape, and Interpretation*. Edited by P. W. Flint. Grand Rapids: Eerdmans, 2001.

Flint, P. W., and J. C. VanderKam, eds. *The Dead Sea Scrolls after Fifty Years: A Comprehensive Assessment.* Leiden: Brill, 1998.

Folkert, K. W. "The 'Canons' of Scripture." Pages 170–79 in *Rethinking Scripture: Essays from a Comparative Perspective.* Edited by M. Levering. Albany: SUNY Press, 1989.

Fowl, S. "The Canonical Approach of Brevard Childs." *Expository Times* 96 (1985): 173–76.

France, R. T. *Jesus and the Old Testament.* London: Tyndale, 1971.

Freedman, D. N. "The Earliest Bible." Pages 29–37 in *Backgrounds for the Bible.* Edited by M. P. O'Connor and D. N. Freedman. Winona Lake, Ind.: Eisenbrauns, 1987.

———. "The Symmetry of the Hebrew Bible." *Studia theologica* 46 (1992): 83–108.

———. *The Unity of the Hebrew Bible.* Ann Arbor: University of Michigan Press, 1991.

Frend, W. H. C. *The Rise of Christianity.* Philadelphia: Fortress, 1984.

Frerichs, E. S. "The Torah Canon of Judaism and the Interpretation of Hebrew Scriptures." *Horizons in Biblical Theology* 9 (1987): 13–25.

Friedman, S. "The Holy Scriptures Defile the Hands: The Transformation of a Biblical Concept in Rabbinic Theology." Pages 115–32 in *Biblical and Other Studies Presented to Nahum M. Sarna in Honor of His 70th Birthday.* Edited by M. Bretler and M. Fishbane. Journal for the Study of the Old Testament Supplement 154. Sheffield: Sheffield Academic Press, 1993.

Friedrich, Gerhard "εὐαγγελιζομαι, κτλ." Pages 707–37 in vol. 2 of *Theological Dictionary of the New Testament.* Edited by G. Kittel and G. Friedrich. Translated by G. W. Bromiley. 10 vols. Grand Rapids: Eerdmans, 1964–1976.

Funk, R. W. *Honest to Jesus.* San Francisco: HarperSanFrancisco, 1996 (see especially pages 77–120).

———. "The Incredible Canon." Pages 24–46 in *Christianity in the 21st Century.* Edited by D. A. Brown. New York: Crossroad, 2000.

———. "The New Testament as Tradition and Canon." Pages 151–86 in *Parables and Presence.* Philadelphia: Fortress, 1982.

———. *Parables and Presence.* Philadelphia: Fortress, 1982.

Fürst, J. *Der Kanon des Alten Testaments nach den Überlieferungen in Talmud und Midrasch.* Leipzig: Dörffling und Franke, 1868.

Gamble, Harry Y. *Books and Readers in the Early Church: A History of Early Christian Texts.* New Haven: Yale University Press, 1995.

———. "Canon. New Testament." Pages 852–61 in vol. 1 of *Anchor Bible Dictionary.* Edited by D. N. Freedman et al. 6 vols. New York: Doubleday, 1992.

———. "The Canon of the New Testament." Pages 201–43 in *The New Testament and Its Modern Interpreters.* Edited by E. J. Epp and G. W.

MacRae. Society of Biblical Literature The Bible and Its Modern Interpreters 3. Philadelphia: Fortress, 1989.

———. "Christianity: Scripture and Canon." Pages 36–62 in *The Holy Book in Comparative Perspective*. Edited by F. M. Denney and R. L. Taylor. Studies in Comparative Religion. Columbia: University of South Carolina Press, 1985.

———. *The New Testament Canon: Its Making and Meaning*. Guides to Biblical Scholarship. Philadelphia: Fortress, 1985.

———. "The Pauline Corpus and the Early Christian Book." Pages 265–80 in *Paul and the Legacies of Paul*. Edited by William S. Babcock. Dallas: SMU Press, 1990.

García Martínez, F. *The Dead Sea Scrolls Translated: The Qumran Texts in English*. Translated by W. G. E. Watson. 2nd edition. Grand Rapids: Eerdmans, 1996.

García Martínez, F., and E. J. C. Tigchelaar. *The Dead Sea Scrolls Study Edition*. Leiden: Brill, 1997–98.

Georgi, D. *The Opponents of Paul in Second Corinthians*. Philadelphia: Fortress, 1986.

Gerhardsson, B. *Memory and Manuscript*. Grand Rapids: Eerdmans, 1998.

Gerstenberger, Erhard S. "Canon Criticism and the Meaning of *Sitz im Leben*." Pages 20–31 in *Canon, Theology, and Old Testament Interpretation: Essays in Honor of Brevard S. Childs*. Edited by Gene M. Tucker, David L. Peterson, and Robert R. Wilson. Philadelphia: Fortress, 1988.

Gese, H. "Die dreifache Gestaltwerdung des Alten Testaments." Pages 299–328 in *Mitte der Schrift? Ein jüdisch-christliches Gespräch: Texte des Berner Symposions vom 6.-12. Januar 1985*. Edited by M. A. Klopfenstein et al. Judiaca et Christiana 11. Bern: Peter Lang, 1987.

Gheorghita, R. *The Role of the Septuagint in Hebrews*. Tübingen: Mohr, 2003.

Gilbert, M. "The Book of Ben Sira: Implications for Jewish and Christian Traditions." Pages 81–91 in *Jewish Civilization in the Hellenistic-Roman Period*. Edited by S. Talmon. Philadelphia: Trinity, 1991.

Gnuse, R. *The Authority of the Bible: Theories of Inspiration, Revelation, and the Canon of Scripture*. New York: Paulist, 1985.

Goehring, J. E., C. W. Hedrick, J. T. Sanders, and H. D. Betz, eds. *Gnosticism and the Early Christian World*. Sonoma, Calif.: Polebridge, 1990.

Golb, Norman. *Who Wrote the Dead Sea Scrolls?* New York: Scribners, 1995.

Gooding, David W. "Aristeas and Septuagint Origins: A Review of Recent Studies." *Vetus Testamentum* 13 (1963): 357–78.

Goodspeed, E. J. "The Canon of the New Testament." Pages 63–71 in vol. 1 of *Interpreter's Bible*. Edited by G. A. Buttrick. New York: Abingdon, 1952.

———. *The Formation of the New Testament*. Chicago: University of Chicago Press, 1926.

———. *A History of Early Christian Literature*. Chicago: University of Chicago Press, 1983.

_____. *An Introduction to the New Testament*. Chicago: University of Chicago Press, 1937.

_____. *The Key to Ephesians*. Chicago: University of Chicago Press, 1956.

_____. *The Meaning of Ephesians*. Chicago: University of Chicago Press, 1933.

Gorak, J. *The Making of the Modern Canon: Genesis and Crisis of a Literary Idea*. London: Athlone, 1991.

Gould, E. P. *A Critical and Exegetical Commentary on the Gospel according to St. Mark*. International Critical Commentary. Edinburgh: Clark, 1896.

Graetz, Heinrich H. *Kohelet: Der alttestamantliche Kanon und sein Abschluss*. Anhang 1, Leipzig: Winter Verlag, 1871.

Graham, W. A. *Beyond the Written Word: Oral Aspects of Scripture in the History of Religion*. Cambridge: Cambridge University Press, 1987.

———. "Scripture." Pages 133–45 in vol. 13 of *Encyclopaedia of Religion*. Edited by Mircea Eliade. New York: Macmillan, 1987.

Grant, R. M. "The Creation of the Christian Tradition: From Tradition to Scripture and Back." Pages 18–36 in *Perspectives on Scripture and Tradition*. Edited by J. F. Kelly. Notre Dame: Fides, 1976.

———. *The Formation of the New Testament*. New York: Harper & Row, 1965.

———. "From Tradition to Scripture and Back." Pages 18–36 in *Scripture and Tradition*. Edited by Joseph F. Kelley. Notre Dame: Fides, 1976.

———. *Heresy and Criticism: The Search for Authenticity in Early Christian Literature*. Louisville: Westminster John Knox, 1993.

———. "The New Testament Canon." Pages 284–307 in *The Cambridge History of the Bible*, vol. 1: *From the Beginnings to Jerome*. Edited by P. R. Ackroyd and C. F. Evans. Cambridge: Cambridge University Press, 1970.

———. "The Oldest Gospel Prologues." *Anglican Theological Review* 23 (1941): 231–45.

———. Review of Geoffrey Mark Hahneman, *The Muratorian Fragment and the Development of the Canon*. *Church History* 64 (1995): 639.

Grant, R. M., ed. *Gnosticism: A Source Book of Heretical Writings from the Early Christian Period*. New York: Harper, 1961.

Greenspoon, L. "The Dead Sea Scrolls and the Greek Bible." Pages 101–27 in vol. 1 of *The Dead Sea Scrolls after Fifty Years: A Comprehensive Assessment*. Edited by P. W. Flint and J. C. VanderKam. Leiden: Brill, 1998.

Gregory, C. R. *Canon and Text of the New Testament*. International Theological Library. Edinburgh: Clark, 1907.

Groh, Dennis E. "Hans von Campenhausen on Canon: Positions and Problems." *Interpretation* 28 (1974): 331–43.

Grosheide, F. W. *Some Early Lists of the Books of the New Testament.* Textus minores 1. Leiden: Brill, 1948.

Guillory, J. “Canon.” Pages 233–49 in *Critical Terms for Literary Study.* Edited by F. Lentricchia and T. McLaughlin. Chicago: University of Chicago Press, 1990.

———. *Cultural Capital: The Problem of Literary Canon Formation.* Chicago: University of Chicago Press, 1993.

Gutwenger, Engelbert. “The Anti-Marcionite Prologues.” *Theological Studies* 7 (1946): 393–408.

Hahn, Ferdinand. “Die Heilige Schrift als älteste christliche Tradition und als Kanon.” *Evangelische Theologie* 40 (1980): 456–66.

Hahneman, G. M. “More on Redating the Muratorian Fragment.” Pages 359–65 in *Studia Patristica* 19. Edited by E. A. Livingstone. Leuven: Peeters, 1988.

———. *The Muratorian Fragment and the Development of the Canon.* Oxford Theological Monographs. Oxford: Clarendon, 1992.

———. “The Muratorian Fragment and the Origins of the New Testament Canon.” Pages 405–15 in *The Canon Debate.* Edited by L. M. McDonald and J. A. Sanders. Peabody, Mass.: Hendrickson, 2002.

Hallberg, R. von, ed. *Canons.* Chicago: University of Chicago Press, 1984.

Hanson, R. P. C. *Origen’s Doctrine of Tradition.* London: SPCK, 1954.

Harnack, A. von. *Marcion: Das Evangelium vom fremden Gott.* 2nd edition. Leipzig: Hinrichs, 1924.

———. *The Origin of the New Testament and the Most Important Consequences of the New Creation.* Translated by J. R. Wilkinson. New York: Macmillan, 1925.

Harrington, D. J. “Introduction to the Canon.” Pages 7–21 in vol. 1 of *The New Interpreter’s Bible.* 12 Vols. Nashville: Abingdon, 1994.

———. “The Old Testament Apocrypha in the Early Church and Today.” Pages 196–210 in *The Canon Debate.* Edited by L. M. McDonald and J. A. Sanders. Peabody, Mass.: Hendrickson, 2002.

Harrington, D. J., and J. Strugnell. “Qumran Cave 4 Texts: A New Publication.” *Journal of Biblical Literature* 112 (1993): 491–99.

Harris, J. Rendel. “Marcion and the Canon.” *Expository Times* 18 (1906–1907): 392–94.

Harris, R. Laird. *Inspiration and Canonicity of the Bible: An Historical and Exegetical Study.* Grand Rapids: Zondervan, 1969.

Harris, William. “Why Did the Codex Supplant the Book-Roll?” Pages 71–85 in *Renaissance Society and Culture: Essays in Honor of Eugene F. Rice, Jr.* Edited by John Monfasani and Ronald G. Musto. New York: Italica, 1991.

Harrison, E. F. *Introduction to the New Testament.* Grand Rapids: Eerdmans, 1977.

Harrison, R. K. *Introduction to the Old Testament.* Grand Rapids: Eerdmans, 1969.

Hartman, L. *"Into the Name of the Lord Jesus": Baptism in the Early Church.* Edinburgh: Clark, 1997.

Hatch, W. H. P. "The Position of Hebrews in the Canon of the New Testament." *Harvard Theological Review* 29 (1936): 133–51.

Heckel, Th. *Vom Evangelium des Markus zum viergestaltigen Evangelium.* Wissenschaftliche Untersuchungen zum Neuen Testament 120. Tübingen: J. C. B. Mohr (Paul Siebeck), 1999.

Hedrick, Charles W. "Kingdom Sayings and Parables of Jesus in *The Apocryphon of James:* Tradition and Redaction." *New Testament Studies* 29 (1983): 1–24.

———. "Thomas and the Synoptics: Aiming at a Consensus." *Second Century* 7 (1989– 1990): 39–56.

Hedrick, C. W., and R. Hodgson Jr., eds. *Nag Hammadi, Gnosticism, and Early Christianity.* Peabody, Mass.: Hendrickson, 1986.

Heine, R. E. "The Role of the Gospel of John in the Montanist Controversy." *Second Century* 6 (1987): 1–19.

Helmer, C., and C. Lanmesser, eds. *One Scripture or Many? Canon from Biblical, Theological and Philosophical Perspectives.* New York: Oxford University Press, 2004.

Hengel, M. *The Four Gospels and the One Gospel of Jesus Christ.* Harrisburg, Pa.: Trinity, 2000.

———. *The Septuagint as Christian Scripture: Its Prehistory and the Problem of Its Canon.* Translated by M. E. Biddle. Edinburgh: Clark, 2002.

———. "The Titles of the Gospels and the Gospel of Mark." Pages 64–84 in *Studies in the Gospel of Mark.* Edited by M. Hengel. Translated by J. Bowden. London: SCM, 1985.

Henne, P. "La datation du Canon de Muratori." *Revue biblique* 100 (1993): 54–75.

Hennecke, E. *New Testament Apocrypha.* Edited by W. Schneemelcher. English translation edited by R. M. Wilson. 2 vols. Philadelphia: Westminster, 1963.

Herklots, H. G. G. *How Our Bible Came to Us.* London: Ernest Benn, 1957.

Hill, A. E. *Baker's Handbook of Bible Lists.* Grand Rapids: Baker, 1981.

Hill, C. E. "Justin and the New Testament Writings." Pages 42–48 in *Studia Patristica* 30. Edited by E. A. Livingstone. Leuven: Peeters, 1997.

———. "What Papias Said about John (and Luke). A 'New' Papian Fragment." *Journal of Theological Studies* 49 (1998): 582–629.

Hillmer, M. R. "The Gospel of John in the Second Century." Ph.D. diss., Harvard, 1966.

Hock, R. F. "The Favored One: How Mary Became the Mother of God." *Bible Review* 17.3 (June 2001): 13–25.

Hofius, O. "Isolated Sayings of Jesus." Pages 88–91 in vol. 1 of *New Testament Apocrypha.* Edited by W. Schneemelcher. Translated by R. M. Wilson. Revised edition. Louisville: Westminster John Knox, 1992.

———. "Unknown Sayings of Jesus." Pages 336–60 in *The Gospel and the Gospels*. Edited by P. Stuhlmacher. Grand Rapids: Eerdmans, 1991.

Hoffman, Thomas A. "Inspiration, Normativeness, Canonicity, and the Unique Sacred Character of the Bible." *Catholic Biblical Quarterly* 44 (1982): 447– 69.

Hoffmann, R. Joseph. *Marcion, On the Restitution of Christianity: An Essay on the Development of Radical Paulinist Theology in the Second Century*. Chico, Calif.: Scholars Press, 1984.

Hoover, R. W. "How the Books of the New Testament Were Chosen." *Bible Review* 9 (1993): 44–47.

Horbury, W. "The Wisdom of Solomon in the Muratorian Fragment." *Journal of Theological Studies* 45 (1994): 149–59.

Howorth, H. H. "The Origin and Authority of the Biblical Canon in the Anglican Church." *Journal of Theological Studies* 8 (1906–1907): 1–40.

Hübner, H. "Vetus Testamentum und Vetus Testamentum in Novo receptum: Die Frage nach dem Kanon des Alten Testaments aus neutestamentlicher Sicht." *Jahrbuch für biblische Theologie* 3 (1988): 147–62.

Hughes, J. *Secrets of the Times: Myth and History in Biblical Chronology*. Journal for the Study of the Old Testament: Supplement Series 66. Sheffield: JSOT Press, 1990.

Hultgren, A. J., and S. A. Haggmark, eds. *The Earliest Christian Heretics: Readings from Their Opponents*. Minneapolis: Fortress, 1996.

Hunt, H. "An Examination of the Current Emphasis on the Canon in Old Testament Studies." *Southwestern Journal of Theology* 23 (1980): 55–70.

Hurtado, L. "The Origins of the *Nomina Sacra:* A Proposal." *Journal of Biblical Literature* 117 (1998): 655–73.

Jacob, E. "Principe canonique et formation de l'Ancien Testament." Pages 101–22 of *Congress Volume: Edinburgh 1974*. Vetus Testamentum Supplement 28 Leiden: Brill, 1975.

Jeffery, A. "The Canon of the Old Testament." Pages 32–45 in vol. 1 of *Interpreter's Bible*. Edited by G. A. Buttrick. New York: Abingdon, 1952.

Jenkins, P. *Hidden Gospels: How the Search for Jesus Lost Its Way*. Oxford: Oxford University Press, 2001.

Jepsen, A. "Kanon und Text des Alten Testaments." *Theologische Literaturzeitung* 74 (1949): 65–74.

———. "Zur Kanongeschichte des Alten Testaments." *Zeitschrift für die alttestamentliche Wissenschaft* 71 (1959): 114–36.

Jeremias, J. *The Unknown Sayings of Jesus*. 2nd edition. London: SPCK, 1964.

Jobes, K. H., and M. Silva. *Invitation to the Septuagint*. Grand Rapids: Baker, 2000.

———. "Response to J. Barr's Review of *Invitation to the Septuagint*." *Review of Biblical Literature* (2002). Online: http://www.bookreviews.org/pdf/1341_3027.pdf. Reprinted in *Bulletin of the International Organization for Septuagint and Cognate Studies* 35 (2002): 43–46.

Johnson, L. T. *Religious Experience in Earliest Christianity*. Minneapolis: Fortress, 1998.

———. *The Writings of the New Testament: An Interpretation*. Revised edition. Philadelphia: Fortress, 1999.

Jonas, H. *The Gnostic Religion*. Boston: Beacon, 1963.

Jones, B. A. *The Formation of the Book of the Twelve: A Study in Text and Canon*. Society of Biblical Literature Dissertation Series 149. Atlanta: Scholars Press, 1995.

Jonge, M. de. "The Old Testament in the Pseudepigrapha." Pages 459–86 in *The Biblical Canons*. Edited by J.-M. Auwers and H. J. de Jonge. Bibliotheca ephemeridum theologicarum lovaniensium 163. Leuven: Louvain University Press, 2003.

Jurgens, W. A. *The Faith of the Early Fathers: A Source-book of Theological and Historical Passages from the Christian Writings of the Pre-Nicene and Nicene Eras*. Collegeville, Minn.: Liturgical Press, 1979.

Kaestli, J.-D. "La place du Fragment de Muratori dans l'histoire du canon." *Cristianesimo nella storia* 15 (1995): 609–34.

Kaestli, J.-D., and Otto Wermelinger, eds. *Canon de l'Ancien Testament: Sa formation et son histoire*. Geneva: Labor et Fides, 1984.

Kahle, P. E. *The Cairo Geniza*. 2nd edition. Oxford: Blackwell, 1959.

Kalin, E. R. "Argument from Inspiration in the Canonization of the New Testament." Th.D. diss., Harvard University, 1967.

———. "A Book Worth Discussing: *Canon and Community: A Guide to Canonical Criticism*." *Concordia Theological Monthly* 12 (1985): 310–12.

———. "Early Traditions about Mark's Gospel: Canonical Status Emerges, the Story Grows." *Concordia Theological Monthly* 2 (1975): 332–41.

———. "The Inspired Community: A Glance at Canon History." *Concordia Theological Monthly* 42 (1971): 541–49.

———. "The New Testament Canon of Eusebius." Pages 386–404 in *The Canon Debate*. Edited by L. M. McDonald and J. A. Sanders. Peabody, Mass.: Hendrickson, 2002.

———. "Re-examining New Testament Canon History, 1: The Canon of Origen." *Currents in Theology and Mission* 17 (1990): 274–82.

Käsemann, E. "The Canon of the New Testament and the Unity of the Church." Pages 95–107 in *Essays on New Testament Themes*. London: SCM, 1968.

———. *Das Neue Testament als Kanon: Dokumentation und kritische Analyse zur gegenwärtgen Discussion*. Göttingen: Vandenhoeck & Ruprecht, 1970.

Katz, Peter. "Justin's Old Testament Quotations and the Greek Dodekapropheten Scroll." Pages 343–53 in *Studia Patristica* 1. Edited by K. Aland and F. L. Cross. Berlin: Akademie-Verlag, 1957.

———. *Philo's Bible: The Aberrant Text of Bible Quotations in Some Philonic Writings and Its Place in the Textual History of the Greek Bible*. Cambridge: Cambridge University Press, 1950.

———. "The Old Testament Canon in Palestine and Alexandria." *Zeitschrift für die neutestamentliche Wissenschaft und die Kunde der älteren Kirche* 47 (1956): 191–217.

Kealy, S. F. "The Canon: An African Contribution." *Biblical Theology Bulletin* 9 (1979): 13–26.

Keck, L. E. "Scripture and Canon." *Quarterly Review* 3 (1983): 8–26.

Kee, H. C., ed. *Cambridge Annotated Study Apocrypha: New Revised Standard Version*. Cambridge: Cambridge University Press, 1994.

Keener, C. *The IVP Bible Background Commentary: New Testament*. Downers Grove, Ill.: InterVarsity, 1993.

Kelly, J. F. *Why Is There a New Testament?* Background Books 5. Wilmington, Del.: Michael Glazier, 1986.

Kelly, J. N. D. *Early Christian Doctrines*. New York: Harper & Row, 1978.

Kelsey, D. H. *The Uses of Scripture in Recent Theology*. Philadelphia: Fortress, 1975.

Kermode, F. "The Argument about Canons." Pages 78–96 in *The Bible and the Narrative Tradition*. Edited by F. McConnell. Oxford: Oxford University Press, 1986.

King, K. *The Gospel of Mary*. Santa Rose, Calif.: Polebridge, 2003.

———. *Revelation of the Unknowable God with Text, Translation, and Notes to NHC IX,3 Allogenes*. Santa Rosa, Calif.: Polebridge, 1995.

———. *What Is Gnosticism?* Cambridge: Harvard University Press, 2003.

Kinzig, W. "*Kainē diathēkē:* The Title of the New Testament in the Second and Third Centuries." *Journal of Theological Studies* 45 (1994): 519–44.

Klein, W. W., C. L. Blomberg, and R. L. Hubbard. *Introduction to Biblical Interpretation*. Dallas: Word, 1993.

Klijn, A. J. N. "Die Entstehungsgeschichte des Neuen Testaments." Pages 64–97 in *Aufstieg und Niedergang der römischen Welt: Geschichte und Kultur Roms im Spiegel der neueren Forschung* 2.26.1. Edited by H. Temporini and W. Hasse. Berlin: Walter de Gruyter, 1992.

Knight, D. A. "Canon and the History of Tradition: A Critique of Brevard Childs' *Introduction to the Old Testament as Scripture*." *Horizons in Biblical Theology* 2 (1980): 127–49.

Knox, John. *Marcion and the New Testament*. Chicago: University of Chicago Press, 1942.

Koch, K. "Pseudonymous Writing." Pages 712–14 in *Interpreter's Dictionary of the Bible: Supplementary Volume*. Edited by K. Crim. Nashville: Abingdon, 1976.

Koester, H. *Ancient Christian Gospels: Their History and Development*. Philadelphia: Trinity, 1990.

———. "Apocryphal and Canonical Gospels." *Harvard Theological Review* 73 (1980): 105–30.

———. "*Gnōmai diaphoroi:* The Origin and Nature of Diversification in the History of Early Christianity." Pages 114–57 in *Trajectories through*

Early Christianity. Edited by James M. Robinson and Helmut Koester. Philadelphia: Fortress, 1971.

———. "The Intention and Scope of Trajectories." Pages 269–79 in *Trajectories through Early Christianity*. Edited by James M. Robinson and Helmut Koester. Philadelphia: Fortress, 1971.

———. *Introduction to the New Testament*. 2 vols. 2nd edition. New York: de Gruyter, 1995–2000.

———. *Synoptische Überlieferung bei den apostolischen Vätern*. Texte und Untersuchungen 65. Berlin: Akademie-Verlag, 1957.

———. "The Text of the Synoptic Gospels in the Second Century." Pages 19–37 in *Gospel Traditions in the Second Century: Origins, Recensions, Text, and Transmission*. Edited by W. L. Petersen. Notre Dame: University of Notre Dame Press, 1989.

———. "Writings and the Spirit: Authority and Politics in Ancient Christianity." *Harvard Theological Review* 84 (1991): 353–72.

Kofoed, J. B. *Text History: Historiography and the Study of the Biblical Text*. Winona Lake, Ind.: Eisenbrauns, 2005.

Kohler, W.-D. *Die Rezeption des Matthäusevangeliums in der Zeit vor Irenaeus*. Wissenschaftliche Untersuchungen zum Neuen Testament. Second series 24. Tübingen: Mohr/Siebeck, 1987.

Kohler, W.-D. *Die Rezeption des Matthäusevangeliums in der Zeit vor Irenaeus*. Wissenschaftliche Untersuchungen zum Neuen Testament. Second series 24. Tübingen: Mohr/Siebeck, 1987.

Kooij, A. van der., and K. van der Toorn, eds. *Canonization and Decanonization*. Studies in the History of Religion 82. Leiden: Brill, 1998.

Kortner, U. H. J. *Papias von Hierapolis: Ein Beitrag zur Geschichte des frühen Christentums*. Forschungen zur Religion und Literatur des Alten und Neuen Testaments 133. Göttingen: Vandenhoeck & Ruprecht, 1983.

Kraemer, D. "The Formation of Rabbinic Canon: Authority and Boundaries." *Journal of Biblical Literature* 110 (1991): 613–30.

Kraus, W. and R. G. Wooden, eds. *Septuagint Research: Issues and Challenges in the Study of the Greek Jewish Scriptures*. SBL Septuagint and Cognate Studies 53. Edited by Melvin Peters. Atlanta: Society of Biblical Literature, 2006.

Kuck, D. W. "The Use and Canonization of Acts in the Early Church." Thesis, Yale University, 1975.

Kugel, J. L., and R. A. Greer. *Early Biblical Interpretation*. Library of Early Christianity 3. Philadelphia: Westminster, 1986.

Kümmel, W. G. *Introduction to the New Testament*. Translated by H. C. Kee. London: SCM, 1975 (pages 475–510: "The Formation of the Canon of the New Testament").

Kurtzinger, J. *Papias von Hierapolis und die Evangelien des Neuen Testaments*. Regensberg: Pustet, 1983.

Ladd, G. E. *A Theology of the New Testament*. Grand Rapids: Eerdmans, 1974.

Lake, K. "The Sinaitic and Vatican Manuscripts and the Copies Sent by Eusebius to Constantine." *Harvard Theological Review* 11 (1918): 32–35.

———, trans. *The Apostolic Fathers.* 2 vols. Loeb Classical Library. Cambridge: Harvard University Press, 1912–13.

LaSor, W. S., D. A. Hubbard, and F. W. Bush. *Old Testament Survey: The Message, Form, and Background of the Old Testament*. Grand Rapids: Eerdmans, 1982.

Lawson, R. P. *The Song of Songs: Commentaries and Homilies*. Westminster, Md.: Newman, 1957.

Layton, B. *The Gnostic Scriptures*. Garden City, NY: Doubleday 1987.

Le Boulluec, Alain. "The Bible in Use among the Marginally Orthodox in the Second and Third Centuries." Pages 197–216 in *The Bible in Greek Christian Antiquity*. Edited by P. M. Blowers. Notre Dame: University of Notre Dame Press, 1997.

Lea, T. D. "The Early Christian View of Pseudepigraphic Writings." *Journal of the Evangelical Theological Society* 27 (1984): 65–75.

Leaney, A. R. C. *The Jewish and Christian World, 200 B.C. to A.D. 200.* Cambridge Commentaries on Writings of the Jewish and Christian World, 200 BC to AD 200, no. 7. Cambridge: Cambridge University Press, 1984.

Leiman, S. Z. *The Canonization of the Hebrew Scripture: The Talmudic and Midrashic Evidence*. Hamden, Conn.: Archon, 1976.

———. "Inspiration and Canonicity: Reflections on the Formation of the Biblical Canon." Pages 56–63 and 315–18 in *Jewish and Christian Self-Definition,* vol. 2: *Aspects of Judaism in the Graeco-Roman Period*. Edited by E. P. Sanders, A. I. Baumgarten, and A. Mendelson. Philadelphia: Fortress, 1981.

———. "Josephus and the Canon of the Bible." Pages 50–58 in *Josephus, the Bible, and History*. Edited by L. H. Feldman and G. Hata. Detroit: Wayne State University Press, 1989.

Leiman, S. Z., ed. *The Canon and Masorah of the Hebrew Bible: An Introductory Reader*. New York: Ktav, 1974.

Lemcio, Eugene. "The Gospels and Canonical Criticism." *Biblical Theology Bulletin* 11 (1981): 114–22.

Lesky, A. *A History of Greek Literature*. New York: Crowell, 1966.

Levine, L. I. *The Ancient Synagogue*. New Haven: Yale University Press, 2000.

Levy, B. B. *Fixing God's Torah: The Accuracy of the Hebrew Bible Text in Jewish Law*. Oxford: Oxford University Press, 2001.

Lewis, J. P. "Jamnia (Jabneh), Council of." Pages 634–37 in vol. 3 of *Anchor Bible Dictionary*. Edited by D. N. Freedman et al. 6 vols. New York: Doubleday, 1992.

———. "Jamnia Revisited." Pages 146–62 in *The Canon Debate*. Edited by L. M. McDonald and J. A. Sanders. Peabody, Mass.: Hendrickson, 2002.

———. "Some Aspects of the Problem of Inclusion of the Apocrypha." Pages 161–207 in *The Apocrypha in Ecumenical Perspective: The Place of the Late Writings of the Old Testament among the Biblical Writings and Their Significance in the Eastern and Western Church Traditions*. Edited by S. Meurer. Translated by P. Ellingworth. United Bible Societies Monograph Series 6. New York: United Bible Societies, 1991.

———. "What Do We Mean by Jabneh?" *Journal of Bible and Religion* 32 (1964): 125–32.

Lienhard, Joseph T. *The Bible, the Church, and Authority: The Canon of the Christian Bible in History and Theology*. Collegeville, Minn.: Liturgical Press/Michael Glazier, 1995.

Lietzmann, H. "Wie wurden die Bucher des Neuen Testaments Heilige Schrift?" Pages 15–98 in *Kleine Schriften,* vol. 2. Edited by K. Aland. Texte und Untersuchungen 68. Berlin: Akademie, 1907.

Lightstone, J. N. "The Formation of the Biblical Canon in Judaism of Late Antiquity: Prolegomenon to a General Reassessment." *Studies in Religion* 8 (1979): 135–42.

———. "Mishnah's Rhetoric, Other Material Artifacts of Late-Roman Galilee, and the Social Formation of the Early Rabbinic Guild." Pages 474–504 in *Text and Artifact in the Religions of Mediterranean Antiquity: Essays in Honour of Peter Richardson*. Edited by S. Wilson and M. Desjardins. Studies in Christianity and Judaism. Waterloo: WLU Press, 2000.

———. *Society, the Sacred, and Scripture in Ancient Judaism: A Sociology of Knowledge*. Studies in Christianity and Judaism 3. Waterloo, Ontario: Wilfrid Laurier University Press, 1988.

Lim, T. H. *Holy Scripture in the Qumran Commentaries and Pauline Letters*. Oxford: Clarendon, 1997.

Limberis, V. "The Battle over Mary." *Bible Review* 17.3 (June 2001): 22–23.

Lindemann, A. *Paulus im ältesten Christentum: Das Bild des Apostels und die Rezeption der paulinischen Theologie in der frühchristlichen Literatur bis Markion*. Beiträge zur historischen Theologie 58. Tübingen: Mohr/Siebeck, 1979.

Link, H.-G. "Der Kanon in ökumenischer Sicht." *Jahrbuch für biblische Theologie* 3 (1988): 83–96.

Logan, A. H. B. *Gnostic Truth and Christian Heresy: A Study in the History of Gnosticism*. Peabody, Mass.: Hendrickson, 1996.

Lohr, W. A. "Kanonsgeschichtliche Beobachtungen zum Verhältnis von mundlicher und schriftlicher Tradition im zweiten Jahrhundert." *Zeitschrift für die neutestamentliche Wissenschaft und die Kunde der älteren Kirche* 85 (1994): 234–58.

Lohse, E. *The New Testament Environment*. Translated by J. E. Steely. Nashville: Abingdon, 1976.

Lovering, E. H. "The Collection, Redaction, and Early Circulation of the Corpus Paulinum." Ph.D. diss., Southern Methodist University, 1988.

Luhrmann, D. "Gal. 2.9 und die katholischen Briefe." *Zeitschrift für die neutestamentliche Wissenschaft und die Kunde der älteren Kirche* 72 (1981): 65–87.

Lupieri, E. *The Mandaeans: The Last Gnostics*. Translated by C. Hindley, Grand Rapids: Eerdmans, 2002.

Luttikhuizen, Gerard P. "The Thought Patterns of Gnostic Mythologizers and Their Use of Biblical Traditions." Pages 89–101 in *The Nag Hammadi Library after Fifty Years: Proceedings of the 1995 Society of Biblical Literature Commemoration*. Edited by J. D. Turner and A. McGuire. Leiden: Brill, 1997.

Maccoby, Hyam. *Early Rabbinic Writings*. Cambridge Commentaries on Writings of the Jewish & Christian World, 200 BC to AD 200. Cambridge: Cambridge University Press, 1988.

MacDonald, D. R. "Apocryphal New Testament." Pages 38–39 in *Harper's Bible Dictionary*. Edited by P. J. Achtemeier et al. San Francisco: Harper & Row, 1985.

MacGregor, Geddes. *The Bible in the Making*. London: John Murray, 1961.

MacMullen, R. *Christianizing the Roman Empire (A.D. 100–400)*. New Haven: Yale University Press, 1984.

MacRae, G. W. "Why the Church Rejected Gnosticism." Pages 126–33 and 236–38 in *Jewish and Christian Self-Definition*, vol. 1: *The Shaping of Christianity in the Second and Third Centuries*. Edited by E. P. Sanders. Philadelphia: Fortress, 1980.

Magness, J. *The Archaeology of Qumran and the Dead Sea Scrolls*. Grand Rapids: Eerdmans, 2002.

———. *Debating Qumran: Collected Essays on Its Archaeology*. Interdisciplinary Students in Ancient Culture and Religion 4. Leuven: Peeters, 2004.

Maier, J. "Zur Frage des biblischen Kanons im Frühjudentum im Licht der Qumranfunde." *Jahrbuch für biblische Theologie* 3 (1988): 135–46.

Malamat, A. "A Forerunner of Biblical Prophecy: The Mari Documents." Pages 33–52 in *Ancient Israelite Religion: Essays in Honor of Frank Moore Cross*. Edited by P. D. Miller, P. D. Hanson, and S. D. McBride. Philadelphia: Westminster, 1987.

Margolis, M. L. *The Hebrew Scriptures in the Making*. Philadelphia: Jewish Publication Society, 1922.

Marshall, I. H. *The Pastoral Epistles*. International Critical Commentary. Edinburgh: Clark, 1999.

Marxsen, Willi. *The New Testament as the Church's Book*. Translated by James E. Mignard. Philadelphia: Fortress, 1972.

Mason, S. "Josephus and His Twenty-two Book Canon." Pages 110–27 in *The Canon Debate*. Edited by L. M. McDonald and J. A. Sanders. Peabody, Mass.: Hendrickson, 2002.

———. *Life of Josephus: Translation and Commentary*. Flavius Josephus Translation and Commentary 9. Leiden: Brill, 2000.

Massaux, E. *The Influence of the Gospel of Saint Matthew on Christian Literature before Saint Irenaeus*. Translated by N. J. Belval and S. Hecht. Edited by A. J. Bellinzoni. New Gospel Studies 5/1–3. Macon, Ga.: Mercer, 1990–1993.

McArthur, H. K. "The Eusebian Sections and Canons." *Catholic Biblical Quarterly* 27 (1965): 250–56.

McDonald, L. M. "Anti-Judaism in the Early Church Fathers." Pages 215–52 in *Anti-Semitism and Early Christianity: Issues of Polemic and Faith*. Edited by C. A. Evans and D. A. Hagner. Minneapolis: Fortress, 1993.

———. "Anti-Marcionite (Gospel) Prologues." Pages 262–63 in vol. 1 of *Anchor Bible Dictionary*. Edited by D. N. Freedman et al. 6 vols. New York: Doubleday, 1992.

———. "Canon." Pages 777–809 in *The Oxford Handbook of Biblical Studies*. Edited by J. W. Rogerson and J. M. Lieu. Oxford: Oxford University Press, 2006.

_____. "Canon of the New Testament," in *The New Interpreter's Dictionary of the Bible*. Edited by K. D. Sakenfeld. Nashville: Abingdon, forthcoming.

———. "Canon (of Scripture)." Pages 169–73 in *Encyclopedia of Early Christianity*. Edited by E. Ferguson. New York: Garland, 1990.

———. "The First Testament: Its Origin, Adaptability, and Stability." Pages 287–326 in *From Tradition to Interpretation: Studies in Biblical Intertextuality in Honor of James A. Sanders*. Edited by C. A. Evans and S. Talmon. Biblical Interpretation Series 18. Leiden: Brill, 1997.

———. *The Formation of the Christian Biblical Canon*. 2d ed. Peabody, Mass.: Hendrickson, 1995.

_____. "The Gospels in Early Christianity: Their Origin, Use, and Authority." Pages 150–78 in *Reading the Gospels Today*. Edited by S. E. Porter. Grand Rapids: Eerdmans, 2004.

———. "Identifying Scripture and Canon in the Early Church: The Criteria Question." Pages 416–39 in *The Canon Debate*. Edited by L. M. McDonald and J. A. Sanders. Peabody, Mass.: Hendrickson, 2002.

McDonald, L. M., and J. A. Sanders, eds. *The Canon Debate*. Peabody, Mass.: Hendrickson, 2002.

McDonald, L. M., and S. E. Porter. *Early Christianity and Its Sacred Literature*. Peabody, Mass.: Hendrickson, 2000.

McGrath, A. *In the Beginning: The Story of the King James Bible and How It Changed a Nation, a Language, and a Culture*. Anchor Books. New York: Random House, 2001.

McLay, R. T. "Biblical Texts and the Scriptures for the New Testament Church." In *Hearing the Old Testament through the New: The Use of the Old Testament in the New Testament*. Edited by S. E. Porter. McMaster New Testament Studies. Grand Rapids: Eerdmans, forthcoming.

———. Review of M. Hengel, *The Septuagint as Christian Scripture*. *Bulletin of the International Organization for Septuagint and Cognate Studies* 36 (2003): 139–43.

———. *The Use of the Septuagint in New Testament Research*. Grand Rapids: Eerdmans, 2003.

Meade, D. G. *Pseudonymity and Canon: An Investigation into the Relationship of Authorship and Authority in Jewish and Earliest Christian Tradition*. Grand Rapids: Eerdmans, 1986.

Meecham, Henry G. *The Letter of Aristeas*. Manchester: Manchester University Press, 1935.

———. *The Oldest Version of the Bible*. London: Holborn, 1932.

Metzger, B. M. *The Bible in Translation: Ancient and English Versions*. Grand Rapids: Baker, 2001.

———. "Canon of the New Testament." Pages 123–27 in *Dictionary of the Bible*. Edited by J. Hastings. 2nd edition edited by F. C. Grant and H. H. Rowley. Edinburgh: Clark, 1963.

———. *The Canon of the New Testament: Its Origin, Development, and Significance*. Oxford: Clarendon, 1987.

———. "The Formulas Introducing Quotations of Scripture in the New Testament and in the Mishnah." Pages 52–63 in *Historical and Literary Studies: Pagan, Jewish, and Christian*. Edited by B. M. Metzger. New Testament Tools and Studies 8. Leiden: Brill, 1968.

———. "Introduction to Apocryphal/Deuterocanonical Books." Pages iii–xv in *The New Oxford Annotated Bible with the Apocryphal/Deuterocanonical Books. NRSV*. Edited by B. M. Metzger and R. E. Murphy. New York: Oxford University Press, 1991.

———. *An Introduction to the Apocrypha*. New York: Oxford University Press, 1957.

———. "Literary Forgeries and Canonical Pseudepigrapha." *Journal of Biblical Literature* 91 (1972): 3–24.

———. *The Text of the New Testament: Its Transmission, Corruption, and Restoration*. 3d edition. New York: Oxford University Press, 1992.

Meuer, S., ed. *The Apocrypha in Ecumenical Perspective*. UBS Monograph Series 6. Translated by P. Ellingworth. New York: United Bible Societies, 1991.

Meyer, R. "προφήτης, κτλ." Pages 812–28 in vol. 6 of *Theological Dictionary of the New Testament*. Edited by G. Kittel and G. Friedrich. Translated by G. W. Bromiley. 10 vols. Grand Rapids: Eerdmans, 1964–1976.

———. "Supplement on the Canon and the Apocrypha." Pages 978–87 in vol. 3 of *Theological Dictionary of the New Testament*. Edited by G. Kittel and G. Friedrich. Translated by G. W. Bromiley. 10 vols. Grand Rapids: Eerdmans, 1964–1976.

Michaels, J. R. "Inerrancy or Verbal Inspiration? An Evangelical Dilemma." Pages 49–70 in *Inerrancy and Common Sense*. Edited by R. R. Nicole and J. R. Michaels. Grand Rapids: Baker, 1980.

Milavec, A. *The Didache: Faith, Hope, and Life of the Earliest Christian Communities, 50–70 C.E.* New York: Newman, 2003.

Milgrom, J. "An Amputated Bible, Peradventure." *Bible Review* 39 (1994): 17, 55.

Milik, J. T. *Ten Years of Discovery in the Wilderness of Judaea.* Translated by J. Strugnell. Studies in Biblical Theology 26. London: SCM, 1959.

Miller, J. D. *The Pastoral Letters as Composite Documents.* Society for New Testament Studies Monograph Series 93. Cambridge: Cambridge University Press, 1997.

Miller, J. W. *How the Bible Came to Be: Exploring the Narrative and Message.* Mahwah, N.J.: Paulist, 2004.

———. *The Origins of the Bible: Rethinking Canon History.* Theological Inquiries. New York: Paulist, 1994.

Miller, P. D. "Der Kanon in der gegenwärtigen amerikanischen Diskussion." *Jahrbuch für biblische Theologie* 3 (1988): 217–39.

Moore, C. F., trans. *Tacitus: The Histories.* 2 vols. Loeb Classical Library. Cambridge: Harvard University Press, 1931–37.

Moore, G. F. "The Definition of the Jewish Canon and the Repudiation of Christian Scriptures." Pages 99–125 in *The Canon and Masorah of the Hebrew Bible.* Edited by S. Z. Leiman. New York: Ktav, 1974.

Morgan, Don F. *Between Text and Community: The "Writings" in Canonical Interpretation.* Minneapolis: Fortress, 1990.

———. "Canon and Criticism: Method or Madness?" *Australasian Theological Review* 68 (1986): 83–94.

Morgan, R. L. "Let's Be Honest about the Canon: A Plea to Reconsider a Question the Reformers Failed to Answer." *Christian Century* 84 (1967): 717–19.

Morrice, W. *Hidden Sayings of Jesus: Words Attributed to Jesus outside the Four Gospels.* Peabody, Mass.: Hendrickson, 1997.

Müller, M. *The First Bible of the Church.* Sheffield: JSOT Press, 1996.

Murphy, R. E. "A Symposium on the Canon of Scripture: 1. The Old Testament Canon in the Catholic Church." *Catholic Biblical Quarterly* 28 (1966): 189–93.

Murray, Robert. "How Did the Church Determine the Canon of the New Testament?" *Heythrop Journal* 11 (1970): 115–26.

Neusner, J. "The Formation of Rabbinic Judaism: Yavneh (Jamnia) from A.D. 70–100." Pages 3–42 in vol. 2 of *Aufsteig und Niedergang der römischen Welt: Geschichte und Kultur Roms im Spiegel der Neueren Forschung, Principat.* Edited by W. Haase. Berlin: de Gruyter, 1979.

———. *Judaism and Christianity in the Age of Constantine: History, Messiah, Israel, and the Initial Confrontation.* Chicago: University of Chicago Press, 1987.

———. *Messiah in Context: Israel's History and Destiny in Formative Judaism.* Philadelphia: Fortress, 1984.

———. *Midrash in Context: Exegesis in Formative Judaism*. Philadelphia: Fortress, 1983.

———. "The Mishna in Philosophical Context and out of Canonical Bounds." *Journal of Biblical Literature* 112 (1993): 291–304.

———. "Rabbinic Judaism in Late Antiquity." Pages 72–84 in *Judaism: A People and Its History*. Edited by R. M. Seltzer. New York: Macmillan, 1989.

———. *Rabbinic Literature and the New Testament: What We Cannot Show, We Do Not Know*. Valley Forge, Pa.: Trinity, 1994.

———. *The Rabbinic Tradition about the Pharisees before 70*. 3 vols. Leiden: Brill, 1971.

———. *The Talmud: A Close Encounter*. Minneapolis: Fortress, 1991.

———. "Targums and the New Testament." Pages 616–617 in vol. 2 of *Dictionary of Judaism in the Biblical Period: 450 B.C.E.–600 C.E.* Edited by J. Neusner. New York: Simon & Schuster, 1996.

———. *The Tosefta*. 2 vols. Peabody, Mass.: Hendrickson, 2002.

Neusner, J., and W. S. Green. *Writing with Scripture: The Authority and Uses of the Hebrew Bible in the Torah of Formative Judaism*. Minneapolis: Fortress, 1989.

Niditch, Susan. *Oral Word and Written Word*. Library of Ancient Israel. Nashville: Westminster John Knox, 1996.

Niederwimmer, K. *The Didache: A Commentary*. Translated by L. M. Maloney. Edited by H. W. Attridge. Hermeneia. Minneapolis: Fortress, 1998.

Nordenfalk, Carl. "The Apostolic Canon Tables." *Gazette des beaux–arts* 62 (1963): 17–34.

Oepke, Alrecht. "κρύπτω, κτλ." Pages 957–1000 in vol. 3 of *Theological Dictionary of the New Testament*. Edited by G. Kittel and G. Friedrich. Translated by G. W. Bromiley. 10 vols. Grand Rapids: Eerdmans, 1964–1976.

Ohlig, K.-H. *Woher nimmt die Bibel ihre Autorität? Zum Verhältnis von Schriftkanon, Kirche und Jesus*. Düsseldorf: Patmos Verlag, 1970.

———. *Die theologische Begründung des neutestamentlichen Kanons in der alten Kirche*. Düsseldorf: Patmos Verlag, 1972.

Oikonomos, E. "The Significance of the Deuterocanonical Writings in the Orthodox Church." Pages 16–32 in *The Apocrypha in Ecumenical Perspective: The Place of the Late Writings of the Old Testament among the Biblical Writings and Their Significance in the Eastern and Western Church Traditions*. Edited by S. Meurer. Translated by P. Ellingworth. United Bible Societies Monograph Series 6. New York: United Bible Societies, 1991.

Oliver, William G. "Origen and the New Testament Canon." *Restoration Quarterly* 31 (1989): 13–26.

O'Neill, J. C. "The Lost Written Records of Jesus' Words and Deeds Behind Our Records." *Journal of Theological Studies* 42 (1991): 483–503.

Orlinsky, Harry M. "Some Terms in the Prologue to Ben Sira and the Hebrew Canon." *Journal of Biblical Literature* 110 (1991): 483–90.

Osiek, C. "The Shepherd of Hermas: An Early Tale That Almost Made It into the New Testament." *Bible Review* 10 (1994): 48–54.

Oulton, J. E. L., and H. Chadwick, eds. *Alexandrian Christianity: Selected Translations of Clement and Origen*. Library of Christian Classics 2. Philadelphia: Westminster, 1954.

Outler, A. C. "The 'Logic' of Canon Making and the Tasks of Canon-Criticism." Pages 263–76 in *Texts and Testaments: Critical Essays on the Bible and the Early Church Fathers*. Edited by W. E. March. San Antonio: Trinity University Press, 1980.

Oxford Society of Historical Theology. *The New Testament in the Apostolic Fathers*. Oxford: Clarendon, 1905.

Paap, A. H. R. E. *Nomina Sacra in the Greek Papyri of the First Five Centuries AD: The Sources and Some Deductions*. Leiden: Brill, 1959.

Pagels, E. "Visions, Appearances and Apostolic Authority: Gnostic and Orthodox Traditions." Pages 415–30 in *Gnosis: Festschrift für Hans Jonas*. Edited by B. Aland. Göttingen: Vandenhoeck & Ruprecht, 1978.

Painchaud, Louis. "The Use of Scripture in Gnostic Literature." *Journal of Early Christian Studies* 4 (1996): 129–47.

Patte, C. M. *Communities of the Last Days: The Dead Sea Scrolls, the New Testament, and the Story of Israel*. Downers Grove, Ill.: InterVarsity, 2000.

Patterson, L. G. "Irenaeus and the Valentinians: The Emergence of the Christian Scriptures." Pages 189–220 in *Studia Patristica* 18.3. Edited by E. A. Livingstone. Leuven: Peeters, 1989.

Patzia, A. G. "Canon." Pages 85–92 in *Dictionary of Paul and His Letters*. Edited G. F. Hawthorne and R. P. Martin. Downers Grove, Ill.: InterVarsity, 1993.

———. *The Making of the New Testament: Origin, Collection, Text and Canon*. Downers Grove, Ill.: InterVarsity, 1995.

Paulsen, Henning. "Die Bedeutung des Montanismus für die Herausbildung des Kanons." *Vigiliae christianae* 32 (1978): 19–52.

Pearson, Birger A. "Gnostic Interpretation of the Old Testament in the *Testimony of Truth* (NHC IX,3)." *Harvard Theological Review* 73 (1980): 311–19.

———. "Use, Authority and Exegesis of Miqra in Gnostic Literature." Pages 635–52 in *Mikra: Text, Translation, Reading and Interpretation of the Hebrew Bible*. Edited by Martin J. Mulder and Harry Sysling. Compendia rerum iudaicarum ad Novum Testamentum 2.1. Philadelphia: Fortress, 1988.

Pearson, B. A. "James, 1–2 Peter, Jude." Pages 371–406 in *The New Testament and Its Modern Interpreters*. Edited by E. J. Epp and G. W. MacRae. Society of Biblical Literature: The Bible and Its Modern Interpreters 3. Philadelphia: Fortress/Atlanta: Scholars Press, 1989.

———. *Gnosticism, Judaism, and Egyptian Christianity*. Minneapolis: Fortress, 1990.

Pelikan, J. *Whose Bible Is It? A History of the Scriptures through the Ages*. New York: Viking Penguin, 2005.

Perkes, K. S. L. "Scripture Revision Won't Be a Bible." *Arizona Republic*, October 24, 1993, B1, B4.

Perkins, P. *The Gnostic Dialogue*. New York: Paulist Press, 1980.

———. "Gnosticism and the Christian Bible." Pages 355–71 in *The Canon Debate*. Edited by L. M. McDonald and J. A. Sanders. Peabody, Mass.: Hendrickson, 2002.

———. *Gnosticism and the New Testament*. Minneapolis: Fortress, 1993.

———. "Spirit and Letter: Poking Holes in the Canon." *Journal of Religion* 76 (1996): 307–27.

Perrin, N. *Thomas and Tatian: The Relationship between* The Gospel of Thomas *and the* Diatessaron. Academia Biblica 5. Leiden: Brill, 2002.

Petersen, W. L. "The Diatessaron of Tatian." Pages 77–96 in *The Text of the New Testament in Contemporary Research: Essays on the Status Quaestionis: A Volume in Honor of Bruce M. Metzger*. Edited by B. D. Ehrman and M. W. Holmes. Studies and Documents 46. Grand Rapids: Eerdmans, 1995.

———. "Tatian's Diatessaron." Pages 403–30 in *Ancient Christian Gospels: Their History and Development*, by H. Koester. Philadelphia: Trinity, 1990.

———. *Tatian's Diatessaron: Its Creation, Dissemination, Significance, and History in Scholarship*. Vigiliae christianae Supplement 25. Leiden: Brill, 1994.

———. "Textual Evidence of Tatian's Dependence upon Justin's 'APOMNEMONEUMATA.' " *New Testament Studies* 36 (1990): 512–34.

Pfeiffer, R. H. "Canon of the OT." Pages 498–520 in vol. 1 of *Interpreter's Dictionary of the Bible*. Edited by G. A. Buttrick. New York: Abingdon, 1962.

Pfeiffer, R. *History of Classical Scholarship: From the Beginnings to the End of the Hellenistic Age*. Oxford: Clarendon, 1968.

Pilhofer, P. "Justin und das Petrusevangelium." *Zeitschrift für die neutestamentliche Wissenschaft und die Kunde der älteren Kirche* 81 (1990): 60–78.

Porter, S. E. "Pauline Authorship and the Pastoral Epistles: Implications for Canon." *Bulletin for Biblical Research* 5 (1995): 105–23.

Porter, S. E., ed. *The Language of the New Testament: Classic Essays*. Sheffield: JSOT Press, 1991.

———, ed. *The Pauline Canon*. Leiden: Brill, 2004.

Porton, G. G. "Sadducees." Pages 892–95 in vol. 5 of *Anchor Bible Dictionary*. Edited by D. N. Freedman et al. 6 vols. New York: Doubleday, 1992.

Price, R. M. "The Evolution of the Pauline Canon." *Hervormde teologiese studies* 53 (1997): 36–67.

Purvis, J. D. *The Samaritan Pentateuch and the Origin of the Samaritan Sect.* Harvard Semitic Monographs 2. Cambridge: Harvard University Press, 1968.

———. "The Samaritans and Judaism." Pages 81–98 in *Early Judaism and Its Modern Interpreters.* Edited by R. A. Kraft and G. W. E. Nickelsburg. Atlanta: Scholars Press, 1986.

Qimron, E., and J. Strugnell. *Qumran Cave 4.V: Miqsat Ma'ase ha-Torah.* Discoveries in the Judaean Desert 10. Oxford: Clarendon, 1994.

Quinn, J. D., and W. Wacker. *The First and Second Letters to Timothy.* Eerdmans Critical Commentary. Grand Rapids: Eerdmans, 2000.

Quispel, G. "Marcion and the Text of the New Testament." *Vigiliae christianae* 52 (1998): 349–60.

Reed, S. A., et al., eds. *The Dead Sea Scrolls Catalogue: Documents, Photographs, and Museum Inventory Numbers.* Atlanta: Scholars Press, 1994.

Rendtorff, R. *Canon and Theology: Overtures to an Old Testament Theology.* Overture to Biblical Theology. Minneapolis: Fortress, 1993.

Resnick, Irven M. "The Codex in Early Jewish and Christian Communities." *Journal of Religious History* 17 (1992): 1–17.

Reuss, E. W. *History of the Canon of the Holy Scriptures in the Christian Church.* Translated by D. Hunter. Edinburgh: Hunter, 1891.

Richards, E. Randolph. "The Codex and the Early Collection of Paul's Letters." *Bulletin for Biblical Research* 8 (1998): 151–66.

———. *The Secretary in the Letters of Paul.* Wissenschaftliche Untersuchungen zum Neuen Testament. Second series 42. Tübingen: Mohr/Siebeck, 1991.

Richardson, C. C., ed. *Early Christian Fathers.* New York: Macmillan, 1970.

Rist, M. "Pseudepigraphy and the Early Christians." Pages 75–91 in *Studies in New Testament and Early Christian Literature: Essays in Honor of Allen P. Wikgren.* Edited by D. E. Aune. Novum Testamentum Supplement 33. Leiden: Brill, 1972.

Ritter, A. M. "Die Entstehung des neutestamentlichen Kanons: Selbstdurchsetzung oder autoritative Entscheidung?" Pages 93–99 in vol. 2 of *Kanon und Zensur: Beiträge zur Archäologie der literarischen Kommunikation.* Edited by A. Assman and J. Assmann. Munich: Fink, 1987.

Robbins, G. A. "Eusebius' Lexicon of 'Canonicity.'" *Studia patristica* 25 (1993): 134–41.

———. "'Fifty Copies of Sacred Writings' (*Vigiliae christianae* 4.36): Entire Bibles or Gospel Books?" *Studia patristica* 19 (1989): 91–98.

———. "Muratorian Fragment." Pages 928–29 in vol. 4 of *Anchor Bible Dictionary.* Edited by D. N. Freedman et al. 6 vols. New York: Doubleday, 1992.

———. "*Peri tōn endiathēkōn graphōn:* Eusebius and the Formation of the Christian Bible." PhD diss., Duke University, 1986.

Roberts, B. J. "The Old Testament Canon: A Suggestion." *Bulletin of the John Rylands University Library of Manchester* 46 (1963–1964): 164–78.

Roberts, C. H. "Books in the Greco-Roman World and in the New Testament." Pages 48–66 in vol. 1 of *Cambridge History of the Bible*. Edited by P. R. Ackroyd and C. F. Evans. Cambridge: Cambridge University Press, 1970.

———. "The Christian Book and the Greek Papyri." *Journal of Theological Studies* 50 (1949): 155–68.

———. *Manuscript, Society, and Belief in Early Christian Egypt*. London: Oxford University Press, 1979.

Roberts, C. H., and T. C. Skeat. *The Birth of the Codex*. London: Oxford University Press for the British Academy, 1987.

Robinson, J. M., ed. *The Nag Hammadi Library in English*. 3rd edition. San Francisco: Harper, 1988.

Robinson, J. M., and H. Koester. *Trajectories through Early Christianity*. Philadelphia: Fortress, 1971.

Rudolph, K "'Gnosis' and 'Gnosticism'—The Problems of Their Definition and Their Relation to the Writings of the New Testament." Pages 21–37 in *The New Testament and Gnosis: Essays in Honour of Robert McL. Wilson*. Edited by A. H. B. Logan and A. J. M. Wedderburn. Edinburgh: Clark, 1983.

———. *Gnosis: The Nature and History of Gnosticism*. Translated and edited by R. M. Wilson. San Francisco: Harper & Row, 1987.

Rutgers, L. V. "The Importance of Scripture in the Conflict between Jews and Christians: The Example of Antioch." Pages 293–98 in *The Use of Sacred Books in the Ancient World*. Edited by L. V. Rutgers, P. W. van der Horst, H. W. Havelaar, and L. Teugels. Leuven: Peeters, 1998.

Rutgers, L.V., P. W. van der Horst, H. W. Havelaar, and L. Teugels, eds. *The Use of Sacred Books in the Ancient World*. BET 22. Leuven: Peeters, 1998.

Ruwet, J. "Clement d'Alexandrie: Canon des écritures et apocryphes." *Biblica* 29 (1948): 77–99, 240–68, 391–408.

Ryle, H. E. *The Canon of the Old Testament: An Essay on the Gradual Growth and Formation of the Hebrew Canon of Scripture*. 2nd edition. London: Macmillan, 1909.

Saebo, Magne. *On the Way to Canon: Creative Tradition History in the OT*. Journal for the Study of the Old Testament: Supplement Series 191. Sheffield: Sheffield Academic Press, 1998.

Saldarini, A. J. *Pharisees, Scribes, and Sadducees in Palestinian Society: A Sociological Approach*. Wilmington, Del.: Glazier, 1988.

———. "Within Context: The Judaism Contemporary with Jesus." Pages 21–40 in *Within Context: Essays on Jews and Judaism in the New Testament*. Edited by D. P. Efroymson, E. J. Fisher, and L. Klenicki. Collegeville, Minn.: Liturgical, 1993.

Sand, A. "κανών." Page 249 in vol. 2 of *Exegetical Dictionary of the New Testament*. Edited by H. Balz and G. Schneider. Grand Rapids: Eerdmans, 1990–1993.

Sanders, E. P. "The Dead Sea Sect and Other Jews: Commonalities, Overlaps, and Differences." Pages 7–44 in *The Dead Sea Scrolls in Their Historical Context*. Edited by T. Lim. Edinburgh: Clark, 2000.

Sanders, J. A. "Adaptable for Life: The Nature and Function of Canon." Pages 531–60 in *Magnalia Dei: The Mighty Acts of God: Essays on the Bible and Archaeology in Memory of G. Ernest Wright*. Edited by F. M. Cross, W. E. Lemke, and P. D. Miller Jr. New York: Doubleday, 1976.

———. "Canon: Hebrew Bible." Pages 837–52 in vol. 1 of *Anchor Bible Dictionary*. Edited by D. N. Freedman et al. 6 vols. New York: Doubleday, 1992.

———. *Canon and Community: A Guide to Canonical Criticism*. Guides to Biblical Studies. Philadelphia: Fortress, 1984.

———. "Canon as Shape and Function." Pages 87–97 in *The Promise and Practice of Biblical Theology*. Edited by J. Reumann. Minneapolis: Fortress, 1991.

———. "Canonical Context and Canonical Criticism." *Horizons in Biblical Theology* 2 (1980): 173–97.

———. "Cave 11 Surprises and the Question of Canon." *McCormick Quarterly* 21 (1968): 284–317.

———. "Deuteronomy." Pages 89–102 in *The Books of the Bible*. Vol. 1 of *The Old Testament/The Hebrew Bible*. Edited by B. W. Anderson. New York: Scribner's, 1989.

———. "From Prophecy to Testament: An Epilogue." Pages 252–58 in *From Prophecy to Testament: The Function of the Old Testament in the New*. Edited by C. A. Evans. Peabody, Mass.: Hendrickson, 2004.

———. *From Sacred Story to Sacred Text*. Philadelphia: Fortress, 1987.

———. "Intertexuality and Canon." Pages 316–33 in *On the Way to Nineveh: Studies in Honor of George M. Landes*. Edited by S. Cook and S. Winter. Atlanta: Scholars Press, 1999.

———. "Palestinian Manuscripts 1947–72." *Journal of Jewish Studies* 24 (1973): 74–83.

———. "Scripture as Canon for Post-Modern Times." *Biblical Theology Bulletin* 25 (1995): 56–63.

———. "Scripture as Canon in the Church." Pages 121–43 in *L'interpretazione della Bibbia nella chiesa: Atti del Simposio promosso dalla Congregazione per la dottrina della fede, Roma, Settembre 1999*. Città del Vaticano: Libreria editrice vaticana, 2001.

———. "The Scrolls and the Canonical Process." Pages 1–23 in vol. 2 of *The Dead Sea Scrolls after Fifty Years: A Comprehensive Assessment*. Edited by P. Flint and J. VanderKam. Leiden: Brill, 1999.

———. "Spinning the Bible." *Bible Review* 14 (June 1998): 22–29, 44–45.

———. "Stability and Fluidity in Text and Canon." Pages 203–17 in *Traditions of the Text: Studies Offered to Dominique Barthélemy in Celebration of His 70th Birthday*. Edited by G. Norton and S. Pisano. Göttingen: Vandenhoech & Ruprecht, 1991.

———. "The Stabilization of the Tanak." Pages 225–53 in *A History of Biblical Interpretation: The Ancient Period*. Edited by A. J. Hauser and D. F. Watson. Grand Rapids: Eerdmans, 2003.

———. "Text and Canon: Old Testament and New." Pages 373–94 in *Mélanges Dominique Barthélemy: Études bibliques*. Edited by P. Casetti, O. Keel, and A. Schenker. Orbis biblicus et orientalis 38. Göttingen: Vandenhoeck & Ruprecht, 1981.

———. *Torah and Canon*. Philadelphia: Fortress, 1972.

Sanders, J. N. "The Literature and Canon of the New Testament." Pages 676–82 in *Peake's Commentary of the Bible*. Edited by M. Black and H. H. Rowley. London: Thomas Nelson and Sons, 1962.

Sandmel, S. *Judaism and Christian Beginnings*. New York: Oxford University Press, 1959.

———. "A Symposium on the Canon of Scripture: 3. On Canon." *Catholic Biblical Quarterly* 28 (1966): 203–7.

Sandt, H. van de, and D. Flusser, *The Didache: Its Jewish Sources and Its Place in Early Judaism and Christianity*. Compendia rerum iudaicarum ad Novum Testamentum 3.5. Minneapolis: Fortress, 2002.

Sarna, N. M. "Canon, Text, and Editions." Pages 816–36 in vol. 1 of *Encyclopaedia Judaica*. Jerusalem: Keter, 1971.

Scanlin, Harold P. "What is the Canonical Shape of the Old Testament Text We Translate?" Pages 207–20 in *Issues in Bible Translation*. Edited by Philip C. Stine. UBS Monograph Series 3. London: United Bible Societies, 1988.

Schiffman, L. "The Place of 4QMMT in the Corpus of Qumran MSS." Pages 81–98 in *Reading 4QMMT: New Perspectives on Qumran Law and History*. Edited by J. Kampen and M. J. Bernstein. Atlanta: Scholars Press, 1996.

———. *Reclaiming the Dead Sea Scrolls: Their True Meaning for Judaism and Christianity*. New York: Doubleday, 1995.

Schlossnikel, R. F. *Bedeutung im Rahmen von Text- und Kanongeschichte. Vetus Latina: Die Reste der altlateinischen Bibel 20*. Edited by E. Beuron. Freiburg: Herder, 1991.

———. *Der Brief an die Hebräer und das Corpus Paulinum: Eine linguistische 'Bruchstelle' im Codex Claromontanus*. Paris: Bibliothèque Nationale grec 107 + 107A + 107B, 1991.

Schmidt, D. D. "The Greek New Testament as a Codex." Pages 469–84 in *The Canon Debate*. Edited by L. M. McDonald and J. A. Sanders. Peabody, Mass.: Hendrickson, 2002.

Schmidt, H.-C. "Das Spätdeuteronomistische Geschichtswerk Genesis I–2. Regum XXV und seine theologische Intention." Pages 261–79 in *Congress*

Volume: Cambridge 1995. Edited by J. A. Emerton. Vetus Testamentum Supplement 66. Leiden: Brill, 1997.

Schnabel, E. J. "History, Theology, and the Biblical Canon: An Introduction to Basic Issues." *Themelios* 20 (1995): 16–24.

———. "Textual Criticism: Recent Developments." Pages 59–75 in *The Face of New Testament Studies: A Survey of Recent Research*. Edited by S. McKnight and G. R. Osborne. Grand Rapids: Baker, 2004.

Schneemelcher, W. "General Introduction." Translated by G. Ogg. Pages 19–68 in vol. 1 of E. Hennecke's *New Testament Apocrypha*. Edited by W. Schneemelcher. English translation edited by R. M. Wilson. Philadelphia: Westminster, 1963.

Schneemelcher, W., ed. *New Testament Apocrypha*. Translated by R. M. Wilson. 2nd edition. 2 vols. Louisville: Westminster John Knox, 1991–92.

Schoedel, William R. "Papias." Pages 235–70 in *Aufstieg und Niedergang der römischen Welt: Geschichte und Kultur Roms im Spiegel der neueren Forschung* 2.27.1. Edited by H. Temporini and W. Haase. Berlin: Walter de Gruyter, 1998.

———. "Scripture and the Seventy-two Heavens of the First Apocalypse of James." *Novum Testamentum* 12 (1970): 118–29.

Schrenk, Gottlob. "γραφή, κτλ." Pages 742–73 in vol. 1 of *Theological Dictionary of the New Testament*. Edited by G. Kittel and G. Friedrich. Translated by G. W. Bromiley. 10 vols. Grand Rapids: Eerdmans, 1964–1976.

Schwartz, B. J. "Bible." Pages 121–25 in *The Oxford Dictionary of the Jewish Religion*. Edited by R. J. Z. Werblowsky and G. Wigoder. New York: Oxford University Press, 1997.

Schweizer, Eduard. "Kanon?" *Evangelische Theologie* 31 (1971): 339–57.

Segal, M. H. *Sefer Ben-Sirah ha-Shalem*. Jerusalem: Bialik, 1953.

Shanks, H. "Contrasting Insights of Biblical Giants." *Biblical Archaeology Review* 30.4 (July/August 2004): 32–33.

Sheler, J. L. "Cutting Loose the Holy Canon: A Controversial Re-examination of the Bible." *U.S. News and World Report* (Nov. 8, 1993): 75.

Shelley, B. L. *By What Authority? The Standards of Truth in the Early Church*. Grand Rapids: Eerdmans, 1965.

Sheppard, G. T. "Canon." Pages 62–69 in vol. 3 of *The Encyclopedia of Religion*. Edited by M. Eliade. New York: Macmillan, 1987.

———. "Canonical Criticism." Pages 861–66 in vol. 1 of *Anchor Bible Dictionary*. Edited by D. N. Freedman et al. 6 vols. New York: Doubleday, 1992.

———. "Canonization: Hearing the Voice of the Same God through Historically Dissimilar Traditions." *Interpretation* 37 (1982): 21–33.

Shinn, H. W. *Textual Criticism and the Synoptic Problem in Historical Jesus Research: The Search for Valid Criteria*. BET 36. Leuven: Peeters, 2004.

Shires, H. M. *Finding the Old Testament in the New*. Philadelphia: Westminster, 1974.

Shuler, P. L. *A Genre for the Gospels: The Biographical Character of Matthew*. Philadelphia: Fortress, 1982.

Silberman, Lou H. "The Making of the Old Testament Canon." Pages 1209–15 in *The Interpreter's One-Volume Commentary on the Bible*. Edited by Charles M. Laymon. New York: Abingdon, 1971.

Silva, M. "Old Testament in Paul." Pages 630–42 in *Dictionary of Paul and His Letters*. Edited G. F. Hawthorne and R. P. Martin. Downers Grove, Ill.: InterVarsity, 1993.

———. "Response." Pages 141–50 in *Rethinking New Testament Textual Criticism*. Edited by D. A. Black. Grand Rapids: Baker, 2002.

Silver, D. J. *The Story of Scripture: From Oral Tradition to the Written Word*. New York: Basic Books, 1990.

Simonetti, M. *Biblical Interpretation in the Early Church: An Historical Introduction to Patristic Exegesis*. Translated by J. A. Hughes. Edited by A. Bergquist and M. Bockmuehl. Edinburgh: Clark, 1994.

Skarsaune, O. *The Proof from Prophecy: A Study in Justin Martyr's Proof-Text Tradition: Text-Type, Provenance, Theological Profile*. Novum Testamentum Supplement 56. Leiden: Brill, 1987.

Skeat, T. C. "The Codex Sinaiticus, The Codex Vaticanus, and Constantine." *Journal of Theological Studies* 50 (1999): 583–625.

———. "A Codicological Analysis of the Chester Beatty Papyrus Codex of Gospels and Acts (P^{45})." *Hermathena* 155 (1993): 27–43.

———. "Irenaeus and the Four-Gospel Canon." *Novum Testamentum* 34 (1992): 194–99.

———. "The Oldest Manuscript of the Four Gospels." *New Testament Studies* 43 (1997): 1–34.

———. "The Origin of the Christian Codex." *Zeitschrift für Papyrologie und Epigraphik* 102 (1994): 263–68.

———. "The Use of Dictation in Ancient Book-Production." *Proceedings of the British Academy* 42 (1956): 195–97.

Smart, J. D. *The Strange Silence of the Bible in the Church: A Study in Hermeneutics*. Philadelphia: Westminster, 1970.

Smend, Rudolf. "Questions about the Importance of Canon in the Old Testament Introduction." *Journal for the Study of the Old Testament* 16 (1980): 45–51.

Smith, C. M. and J. W. Bennett. *How the Bible Was Built*. Grand Rapids: Eerdmans, 2005.

Smith, D. M. "John, the Synoptics, and the Canonical Approach to Exegesis." Pages 166–180 in *Tradition and Interpretation in the New Testament: Essays in Honor of E. Earle Ellis*. Edited by G. F. Hawthorne and O. Betz. Grand Rapids: Eerdmans, 1987.

———. "The Pauline Literature." Pages 265–81 in *It Is Written: Scripture Citing Scripture: Essays in Honour of Barnabas Lindars*. Edited by

D. A. Carson and H. G. M. Williamson. Cambridge: Cambridge University Press, 1988.

———. "When Did the Gospels Become Scripture?" *Journal of Biblical Literature* 119 (2000): 3–20.

———. "Why Approaching the New Testament as Canon Matters." *Interpretation* 40 (1986): 407–11.

Smith, J. Z. "Canons, Catalogues, and Classics." Pages 300–307 in *Canonization and Decanonization*. Edited by A. van der Kooij and K. van der Toorn. Studies in the History of Religion 82. Leiden: Brill, 1998.

Smith, M. *Palestinian Parties and Politics That Shaped the Old Testament*. New York: Columbia University Press, 1971.

Souter, A. *The Text and Canon of the New Testament*. New York: Scribner, 1917.

Sparks, H. F. D. *The Formation of the New Testament*. London: SCM, 1952.

———. "Canon of the Old Testament." Pages 121–23 in *Hastings Dictionary of the Bible*. Edited by F. C. Grant and H. H. Rowley. 2d edition. Edinburgh: T&T Clark, 1963.

Spina, Frank A. "Canonical Criticism: Childs versus Sanders." Pages 165–94 in *Interpreting God's Word for Today: An Inquiry into Hermeneutics from a Biblical Theological Perspective*. Edited by W. McCown and J. E. Massey. Anderson, Ind.: Warner, 1982.

Stanton, G. N. *Gospel Truth? New Light on Jesus and the Gospels*. London: HarperCollins, 1995.

———. *The Gospels and Jesus*. Oxford: Oxford University Press, 1989.

Steck, O. H. *Der Abschluss der Prophetie im Alten Testament: Ein Versuch zur Frage der Vorgeschichte des Kanons*. Biblisch-theologische Studien 17. Neukirchen-Vluyn: Neukirchener, 1991.

———. "Der Kanon des hebräischen Alten Testaments." Pages 231–52 in *Vernunft des Glaubens: Wissenschaftliche Theologie und kirchliche Lehre*. Edited by J. Rohls and G. Wenz. Göttingen: Vandenhoeck & Ruprecht, 1988.

Steinmann, Andrew E. *Oracles of God: The Old Testament Canon*. St. Louis, Mo.: Concordia, 1999.

Stendahl, K. "Ancient Scripture in the Modern World." Pages 201–14 in *Scripture in the Jewish and Christian Traditions*. Edited by F. E. Greenspahn. Nashville: Abingdon, 1982.

———. "The Apocalypse of John and the Epistles of Paul in the Muratorian Fragment." Pages 239–45 in *Current Issues in New Testament Interpretation: Essays in Honor of Otto A. Piper*. Edited by W. Klassen and G. F. Snyder. London: SCM, 1962.

———. "The Formation of the Canon: The Apocalypse of John and the Epistles of Paul in the Muratorian Fragment." Pages 239–45 in *Current Issues in New Testament Interpretation: Essays in Honor of Otto A. Piper*. Edited by W. Klassen and G. F. Snyder. London: SCM, 1962.

———. *Meanings: The Bible as Document and Guide*. Philadelphia: Fortress, 1984.

Stendebach, F. J. "The Old Testament Canon in the Roman Catholic Church." Pages 33–45 in *The Apocrypha in Ecumenical Perspective: The Place of the Late Writings of the Old Testament among the Biblical Writings and Their Significance in the Eastern and Western Church Traditions*. Edited by S. Meurer. Translated by P. Ellingworth. United Bible Societies Monograph Series 6. New York: United Bible Societies, 1991.

Stevenson, J. *A New Eusebius: Documents Illustrative of the History of the Church to A.D. 337*. London: SPCK, 1957.

Steyn, G. F. *Septuagint Quotations in the Context of the Petrine and Pauline Speeches of the Acta Apostolorum*. Kampen: Pharos, 1995.

Stone, M. "Esdras, Second Book of." Pages 611–14 in vol. 2 of *Anchor Bible Dictionary*. Edited by D. N. Freedman et al. 6 vols. New York: Doubleday, 1992.

Streeter, B. H. *The Four Gospels: A Study of Origins Treating of the Manuscript Tradition, Sources, Authorship and Date*. London: MacMillan, 1924.

Stroker, W. D. *Extracanonical Sayings of Jesus*. Society of Biblical Literature Resources for Biblical Study 18. Atlanta: Scholars Press, 1989.

Stuart, M. *A Critical History and Defense of the Old Testament Canon*. Andover, Mass.: Allen, Morrill & Wardwell, 1845.

Stuhlhofer, Franz. *Der Gebrauch der Bibel von Jesus bis Euseb: Eine statistische Untersuchung zur Kanongeschichte*. Wuppertal: R. Brockhaus, 1988.

Stuhlmacher, P. "The Significance of the Old Testament Apocrypha and Pseudepigrapha for the Understanding of Jesus and Christology." Pages 1–15 in *The Apocrypha in Ecumenical Perspective: The Place of the Late Writings of the Old Testament among the Biblical Writings and Their Significance in the Eastern and Western Church Traditions*. Edited by S. Meurer. Translated by P. Ellingworth. United Bible Societies Monograph Series 6. New York: United Bible Societies, 1991.

Sundberg, A. C., Jr. "The Bible Canon and the Christian Doctrine of Inspiration." *Interpretation* 29 (1975): 352–71.

———. "Canon Muratori: A Fourth-Century List." *Harvard Theological Review* 66 (1973): 1–41.

———. "Canon of the NT." Pages 136–40 in *Interpreter's Dictionary of the Bible: Supplementary Volume*. Edited by Keith Crim. Nashville: Abingdon, 1976.

———. "Dependent Canonicity in Irenaeus and Tertullian." Pages 403–9 in *Studia evangelica III*. Texte und Untersuchungen 88. Berlin: Akademie-Verlag, 1964.

———. "The Making of the New Testament Canon." Pages 1216–24 in *The Interpreter's One-Volume Commentary on the Bible*. Edited by Charles M. Laymon. New York: Abingdon, 1971.

———. "The Old Testament: A Christian Canon." *Catholic Biblical Quarterly* 30 (1968): 403–9.

———. "The Old Testament of the Early Church." *Harvard Theological Review* 51 (1958): 205–26.

———. *The Old Testament of the Early Church*. Cambridge: Harvard University Press, 1964.

———. " 'The Old Testament of the Early Church' Revisited." *Festschrift in Honor of Charles Speel*. Edited by T. J. Seinkewicz and J. E. Betts. Monmouth, Ill.: Monmouth College Press, 1996.

———. "A Symposium on the Canon of Scripture: 2. The Protestant Old Testament Canon: Should It Be Re-examined?" *Catholic Biblical Quarterly* 28 (1966): 194–203.

———. "Toward a Revised History of the New Testament Canon." Pages 452–61 in *Studia evangelica IV*. Texte und Untersuchungen 89. Berlin: Akademie-Verlag, 1964.

Suter, D. W. "Apocrypha, Old Testament." Pages 36–38 in *Harper's Bible Dictionary*. Edited by P. J. Achtemeier et al. San Francisco: Harper & Row, 1985.

Swanson, T. N. "The Closing of the Collection of Holy Scripture: A Study in the History of the Canonization of the Old Testament." Ph.D. diss., Vanderbilt University, 1970.

Swarat, U. *Alte Kirche und Neues Testament: Theodor Zahn als Patristiker*. Wuppertal: Brockhaus, 1991.

Swete, H. B. *An Introduction to the Old Testament in Greek*. 2nd edition. Revised by R. R. Ottley. Cambridge: Cambridge University Press, 1914. Repr., Peabody, Mass.: Hendrickson, 1989.

Talbert, C. H. *What Is a Gospel? The Genre of the Canonical Gospels*. Philadelphia: Fortress, 1977.

Talmon, S. "Heiliges Schrifttum und kanonische Bücher aus jüdischer Sicht: Überlegungen zur Ausbildung der Grösse 'Die Schrift' im Judentum." Pages 45–79 in *Mitte der Schrift? Ein jüdisch-christliches Gespräch: Texte des Berner Symposions vom 6.–12. January 1985*. Edited by M. Klopfenstein et al. Judaica et christiana 11. Bern: Peter Lang, 1987.

Theissen, G. *A Theory of Primitive Christian Religion*. London: SCM, 1999.

Theobald, C., ed. *Le canon des Ecritures: Etudes historiques, exégétiques et systématiques*. Lectio divina 140. Paris: Cerf, 1990.

Theron, D. J. *Evidence of Tradition*. Grand Rapids: Baker, 1957.

Toit, Andrie B. du. "Canon: New Testament." Pages 102–4 in *The Oxford Companion to the Bible*. Edited by Bruce M. Metzger and M. D. Coogan. New York: Oxford University Press, 1993.

Topping, R. R. "The Canon and the Truth: Brevard Childs and James Barr on the Canon and the Historical Critical Method." *Toronto Journal of Theology* 8 (1992): 239–60.

Tov, E. *The Greek Minor Prophets Scroll from Nahal Hever (8HevXIIgr)*. Discoveries in the Judean Desert 8. Oxford: Clarendon, 1990.

_____. *The Greek and Hebrew Bible: Collected Essays on the Septuagint.* Supplements to Vetus Testamentum, vol. 72; Leiden: Brill, 1999.

_____. "Groups of Biblical Texts Found at Qumran." Pages 85–102 in *Time to Prepare the Way in the Wilderness: Papers on the Qumran Scrolls by Fellows of the Institute for Advanced Studies of the Hebrew University.* Edited by D. Dimant and L. H. Schiffman. Jerusalem: University, 1989–1990.

_____. "Hebrew Biblical Manuscripts from the Judaean Desert: Their Contribution to Textual Criticism." *Journal of Jewish Studies* 39 (1988): 5–37.

_____. "The History and Significance of a Standard Text of the Hebrew Bible." Pages 49–66 in *Hebrew Bible/Old Testament: The History of Its Interpretation.* Vol. 1: *From the Beginnings to the Middle Ages (until 1300).* Göttingen: Vandenhoeck & Ruprecht, 1996.

_____. "The Nature of the Large-Scale Differences between the LXX and MT STV, Compared with Similar Evidence in Other Sources." Pages 121–44 in *The Earliest Text of the Hebrew Bible: The Relationship between the Masoretic Text and the Hebrew Base of the Septuagint Reconsidered.* Edited by Adrian Schenker. Septuagint and Cognate Studies 52. Atlanta: Society of Biblical Literature, 2003.

———. "Recensional Differences between the Masoretic Text and the Septuagint of Proverbs." Pages 43–56 in *Of Scribes and Scrolls: Studies on the Hebrew Bible, Intertestamental Judaism, and Christian Origins Presented to John Strugnell.* Edited by H. W. Attridge, J. J. Collins, and T. H. Tobin. Lanham, Md.: University Press of America, 1990.

_____. "Scribal Practices and Physical Aspects of the Dead Sea Scrolls." Pages 45–60 in *The Bible as a Book.* Edited by J. L. Sharpe and K. Van Kampen. London: Oak Knoll, 1998.

———. "Scribal Practices Reflected in the Paleo-Hebrew Texts from the Judean Desert." *Scripta Classica Israelica* 15 (1996): 268–73.

———. "Scribal Practices Reflected in the Texts from the Judean Desert." Pages 403–29 in vol. 1 of *The Dead Sea Scrolls after Fifty Years: A Comprehensive Assessment.* Edited by P. W. Flint and J. C. VanderKam. Leiden: Brill, 1998.

———. "The Status of the Masoretic Text in Modern Text Editions of the Hebrew Bible: The Relevance of Canon." Pages 234–51 in *The Canon Debate.* Edited by L. M. McDonald and J. A. Sanders. Peabody, Mass.: Hendrickson, 2002.

———. *The Text-Critical Use of the Septuagint in Biblical Research.* 2d edition. Jerusalem: Simor, 1997.

———. *Textual Criticism of the Hebrew Bible.* Minneapolis: Fortress, 1992.

_____. *Textual Criticism of the Hebrew Bible.* 2d rev. edition. Minneapolis: Fortress, 2001.

Tov, E., and S. A. Pfann, eds. *Companion Volume to the Dead Sea Scrolls Microfiche Edition.* Leiden: Brill, 1995.

Towner, W. Sibley. "Daniel 1 in the Context of Canon." Pages 285–98 in *Canon, Theology, and Old Testament Interpretation: Essays in Honor of Brevard S. Childs*. Edited by Gene M. Tucker, David L. Peterson, and Robert R. Wilson. Philadelphia: Fortress, 1988.

Traube, L. *Nomina Sacra: Versuch einer Geschichte der christlichen Kürzung*. Munich: Beck, 1907.

Trebolle Barrera, J. *The Jewish Bible and the Christian Bible: An Introduction to the History of the Bible*. Translated by W. G. E. Watson. Grand Rapids: Eerdmans, 1998.

Tregelles, S. P. *Canon Muratorianus: The Earliest Catalogue of the Books of the New Testament*. Oxford: Clarendon, 1867.

Trobisch, D. *Paul's Letter Collection: Tracing the Origins*. Philadelphia: Fortress, 1994.

Tucker, Gene M. "Prophetic Superscriptions and the Growth of a Canon." Pages 56–70 in *Canon and Authority: Essays in Old Testament Religion and Theology*. Edited by G. W. Coats and B. O. Long. Philadelphia: Fortress, 1977.

Tuckett, C. M. "Nomina Sacra: Yes or No?" Pages 431–58 in *The Biblical Canons*. Edited by J.-M. Auwers and H. J. de Jonge. Bibliotheca ephemeridum theologicarum lovaniensium 163. Leuven: Louvain University Press, 2003.

Turner, C. H. "Appendix to W. Sanday's Article: 'The Cheltenham List of the Canonical Books, and the Writings of Cyprian.' " *Studia Biblica* 3 (1891): 304–25.

———. "Latin Lists of the Canonical Books: 3. From Pope Innocent's Epistle to Exsuperius of Toulouse (A.D. 405)." *Journal of Theological Studies* 13 (1911–1912): 77–82.

Turro, J. C., and R. E. Brown. "Canonicity." Pages 515–34 in vol. 2 of *The Jerome Biblical Commentary*. Edited by R. E. Brown, J. A. Fitzmyer, and R. E. Murphy. Englewood Cliffs, N.J.: Prentice-Hall, 1968.

Ulrich, Eugene. "The Bible in the Making: The Scriptures at Qumran." Pages 77–93 in *The Community of the Renewed Covenant*. Edited by E. Ulrich and J. VanderKam. Christianity and Judaism in Antiquity 10. Notre Dame: University of Notre Dame Press, 1994.

———. "Canon." Pages 117–20 in vol. 1 of *Encyclopedia of the Dead Sea Scrolls*. Edited by L. H. Schiffman and J. C. VanderKam. Oxford: Oxford University Press, 2000.

———. "The Canonical Process, Textual Criticism, and Latter Stages in the Composition of the Bible." Pages 267–91 in *Sha'arei Talmon: Studies in the Bible, Qumran, and the Ancient Near East Presented to Shemaryahu Talmon*. Edited by M. Fishbane and E. Tov. Winona Lake, Ind.: Eisenbrauns, 1992.

———. "The Community of Israel and the Composition of Scriptures." Pages 327–42 in *Studies in Biblical Intertextuality in Honor of James A.*

Sanders. Edited by C. A. Evans and S. Talmon. Biblical Interpretation Series 18. Leiden: Brill, 1997.

———. "The Dead Sea Scrolls and the Biblical Text." Pages 79–100 in vol. 1 of *The Dead Sea Scrolls after Fifty Years: A Comprehensive Assessment*. Edited by P. Flint and J. VanderKam. Leiden: Brill, 1998.

———. *The Dead Sea Scrolls and the Origins of the Bible*. Studies in the Dead Sea Scrolls and Related Literature. Grand Rapids: Eerdmans, 1999.

———. "The Notion and Definition of Canon." Pages 21–35 in *The Canon Debate*. Edited by L. M. McDonald and J. A. Sanders. Peabody, Mass.: Hendrickson, 2002.

———. "Pluriformity in the Biblical Text, Text Groups, and Questions of Canon." Pages 23–41 in *The Madrid Qumran Congress: Proceedings of the International Congress on the Dead Sea Scrolls Madrid 18–21 March, 1991*. Edited by J. Trebolle Barrera and L. Vegas Montaner. 2 vols. Studies on the Texts of the Desert of Judah 11. Leiden: Brill, 1992.

———. "Qumran and the Canon of the Old Testament." Pages 66–75 in *The Biblical Canons*. Edited by J.-M. Auwers and H. J. de Jonge. Bibliotheca ephemeridum theologicarum lovaniensium 163. Leuven: Louvain University Press, 2003.

———. "The Qumran Biblical Scrolls—The Scriptures of Late Second Temple Judaism." Pages 67–87 in *The Dead Sea Scrolls in Their Historical Context*. Edited by T. Lim. Edinburgh: Clark, 2000.

Unnick, W. C. van. "*Hē kainē diathēkē:* A Problem in the Early History of the Canon." *Studia patavina* 4 (1961): 212–27.

Urbach, E. E. "Torah." Pages 85–100 in *Judaism: A People and Its History*. Edited by Robert M. Seltzer. New York: Macmillan, 1989.

Valantasis, R. *The Beliefnet Guide to Gnosticism and Other Vanished Christianities*. New York: Doubleday, 2006.

VanderKam, J. C. "Authoritative Literature in the Dead Sea Scrolls." *Dead Sea Discoveries* 5 (1998): 382–402.

———. *The Dead Sea Scrolls Today*. Grand Rapids: Eerdmans, 1994.

———. "Ezra-Nehemiah or Ezra and Nehemiah." Pages 55–75 in *Priests, Prophets, and Scribes: Essays on the Formation and Heritage of Second Temple Judaism in Honour of Joseph Blenkinsopp*. Edited by E. Ulrich, J. Wright, R. P. Carroll, and P. R. Davies. Journal for the Study of the Old Testament Supplement 149. Sheffield: JSOT Press, 1992.

———. *From Revelation to Canon: Studies in the Hebrew Bible and Second Temple Literature*. Journal for the Study of Judaism Supplement 62. Leiden: Brill, 2000.

———. "Questions of Canon Viewed through the Dead Sea Scrolls." *Bulletin for Biblical Research* 11 (2001): 269–92.

VanderKam, J. C., and W. Adler, eds. *The Jewish Apocalyptic Heritage in Early Christianity*. Compendia rerum iudaicarum ad Novum Testamentum 3.4. Minneapolis: Fortress, 1966.

VanderKam, J. C., and P. Flint. *The Meaning of the Dead Sea Scrolls: Their Significance for Understanding the Bible, Judaism, Jesus, and Christianity*. San Francisco: Harper, 2002.

Verheyden, J. "The Canon Muratori: A Matter of Dispute." Pages 487–556 in *The Biblical Canons*. Edited by J.-M. Auwers and H. J. de Jonge. Bibliotheca ephemeridum theologicarum lovaniensium 163. Leuven: Louvain University Press, 2003.

Vermes, G. *The Complete Dead Sea Scrolls in English*. London: Penguin, 1995.

———. *The Dead Sea Scrolls: Qumran in Perspective*. Philadelphia: Fortress, 1977.

Vokes, F. E. "The Didache and the Canon of the New Testament." Pages 427–36 of *Studia evangelica III*. Texte und Untersuchungen 88. Berlin: Akademie-Verlag, 1964.

Wagner, J. R. *Heralds of the Good News: Isaiah and Paul in Concert in the Letter to the Romans*. Leiden: Brill, 2003.

Wainwright, Geoffrey. "The New Testament as Canon." *Scottish Journal of Theology* 28 (1975): 551–71.

Walker, B. *Gnosticism: Its History and Influence*. Wellingborough, England: Aquarian, 1989.

Wall, R. W. "The Acts of the Apostles in Canonical Context." *Biblical Theology Bulletin* 18 (1986): 1–31.

———. "The Canon and Christian Preaching." *The Christian Ministry* 17/5 (1986): 13–17.

———. "The Canon of the NT." *New Testament Interpretation Today*. Edited by Joel Green. Grand Rapids: Eerdmans, forthcoming.

———. "The Function of the Pastoral Epistles within the Pauline Canon of the New Testament: A Canonical Approach." Pages 27–44 in *The Pauline Canon*. Edited by S. E. Porter. Leiden: Brill, 2004.

———. "Reading the New Testament in Canonical Context." Pages 370–93 in *Hearing the New Testament: Strategies for Interpretation*. Edited by J. B. Green. Grand Rapids: Eerdmans, 1995.

———. "A Unifying Theology of the Catholic Epistles: A Canonical Approach." In *The Catholic Epistles and the Tradition*. Edited by J. Schlosser. Bibliotheca ephemeridum theologicarum lovaniensium 176. Leuven: Leuven University Press Peeters, 2004.

Wall, R. W., and E. Lemcio. *The New Testament as Canon: A Reader in Canonical Criticism*. Sheffield: Sheffield Academic Press, 1992.

Waltke, B. K. "Samaritan Pentateuch." Pages 932–40 in vol. 5 of *Anchor Bible Dictionary*. Edited by D. N. Freedman et al. 6 vols. New York: Doubleday, 1992.

Westcott, B. F. *A General Survey of the History of the Canon of the New Testament*. 6th edition. Cambridge: Macmillan, 1889. Repr., Grand Rapids: Baker, 1980.

Wevers, J. W. *Notes on the Greek Text of Exodus*. Society of Biblical Literature Septuagint and Cognate Studies 30. Atlanta: Scholars Press, 1990.

———. "Septuagint." Pages 273–78 in vol. 4 of *Interpreter's Dictionary of the Bible*. Edited by G. A. Buttrick. New York: Abingdon, 1962.

———. "A Study in the Narrative Portions of the Greek Exodus." Pages 295–303 in *Scripta, Signa, Vocis*. Edited by H. L. J. Vanstiphout et al. Groningen: Egbert Forsten, 1986.

Wildeboer, G. *The Origin of the Canon of the Old Testament*. Translated by B. W. Bacon. London: Luzac, 1895.

Williams, R. R. *Authority in the Apostolic Age*. London: SCM, 1950.

Wink, W. *Cracking the Gnostic Code: The Powers in Gnosticism*. Society of Biblical Literature Monograph 46. Atlanta: Scholars Press, 1993.

Wise, M. O., M. G. Abegg, and E. M. Cook. *The Dead Sea Scrolls: A New Translation*. San Francisco: HarperCollins, 1996.

Yadin, Y. "The Temple Scroll, the Longest and Most Recently Discovered Dead Sea Scroll," Pages 161–77 in vol. 2 of *Archaeology and the Bible: The Best of BAR: Archaeology in the World of Herod, Jesus, and Paul*. Edited by H. Shanks and D. P. Cole. Washington, D.C.: Biblical Archaeology Society, 1990.

———. *The Temple Scroll*. 3 vols. Jerusalem: Israel Exploration Society, 1983.

Yoder, J. H. "The Authority of the Canon." Pages 265–90 in *Essays on Biblical Interpretation: Anabaptist-Mennonite Perspectives*. Edited by Willard Swartley. Text-Reader Series 1. Elkhart, Ind.: Institute of Mennonite Studies, 1984.

Young, F., L. Ayres, and A. Louth, eds. *The Cambridge History of Early Christian Literature*. New York: Cambridge University Press, 2004.

Zahn, Theodore. *Forschungen zur Geschichte des neutestamentlichen Kanons und der altkirchlichen Literatur*. 10 vols. Leipzig: A. Deichert, 1881–1929.

———. *Geschichte des neutestamentlichen Kanons*. 2 vols. Erlangen: A. Deichert, 1888– 1892.

Zeitlin, Solomon. "An Historical Study of the Canonization of Hebrew Scriptures." Pages 164–201 in *Proceedings of the American Academy for Jewish Research* 3 (1931–1932). Repr. in *The Canon and Masorah of the Hebrew Bible*. Edited by Sid Z. Leiman. New York: KTAV, 1974.

Zenger, E., ed. *Die Tora als Kanon für Juden und Christen*. Herders biblische Studien 10. Freiburg: Herder, 1996.

Zetzel, J. E. G. "Re-creating the Canon: Augustan Poetry and the Alexandrian Past." Pages 107–29 in *Canons*. Edited by R. von Hallberg. University of Chicago Press, 1984.

Zevit, Z. "The Second–Third Century Canonization of the Hebrew Bible and Its Influence on Christian Canonizing." Pages 133–60 in *Canonization and Decanonization*. Edited by A. van der Kooij and K. van der Toorn. Studies in the History of Religion 82. Leiden: Brill, 1998.

Zuntz, G. "Aristeas." Pages 219–21 in vol. 1 of *Interpreter's Dictionary of the Bible*. Edited by G. A. Buttrick. New York: Abingdon, 1962.

———. *The Text of the Epistles: A Disquisition upon the* Corpus Paulinum. Schweich Lectures, 1946. London: British Academy Press, 1953.

Index of Modern Authors

Index of Names and Subjects

Index of Ancient Sources

John

Acts

Romans

1 Corinthians